D1613835

CONNECTED MATHEMATICS® 3

Glenda Lappan, Elizabeth Difanis Phillips,
James T. Fey, Susan N. Friel

PEARSON

Boston, Massachusetts • Chandler, Arizona • Glenview, Illinois • Upper Saddle River, New Jersey

Connected Mathematics® was developed at Michigan State University with financial support from the Michigan State University Office of the Provost, Computing and Technology, and the College of Natural Science.

This material is based upon work supported by the National Science Foundation under Grant No. MDR 9150217 and Grant No. ESI 9986372. Opinions expressed are those of the authors and not necessarily those of the Foundation.

As with prior editions of this work, the authors and administration of Michigan State University preserve a tradition of devoting royalties from this publication to support activities sponsored by the MSU Mathematics Education Enrichment Fund.

All **Acknowledgments** pages constitute an extension of this copyright page.

Acknowledgments for *Prime Time* appear on page 106 of *Prime Time.*
Acknowledgments for *Comparing Bits and Pieces* appear on page 126 of *Comparing Bits and Pieces.*
Acknowledgments for *Let's Be Rational* appear on page 88 of *Let's Be Rational.*
Acknowledgments for *Covering and Surrounding* appear on page 119 of *Covering and Surrounding.*
Acknowledgments for *Decimal Ops* appear on page 108 of *Decimal Ops.*
Acknowledgments for *Variables and Patterns* appear on page 130 of *Variables and Patterns.*
Acknowledgments for *Data About Us* appear on page 132 of *Data About Us.*

13-digit ISBN 978-0-13-327812-5
10-digit ISBN 0-13-327812-3
3 4 5 6 7 8 9 10 V011 17 16 15 14

PEARSON

Authors

A Team of Experts

Glenda Lappan is a University Distinguished Professor in the Program in Mathematics Education (PRIME) and the Department of Mathematics at Michigan State University. Her research and development interests are in the connected areas of students' learning of mathematics and mathematics teachers' professional growth and change related to the development and enactment of K–12 curriculum materials.

Elizabeth Difanis Phillips is a Senior Academic Specialist in the Program in Mathematics Education (PRIME) and the Department of Mathematics at Michigan State University. She is interested in teaching and learning mathematics for both teachers and students. These interests have led to curriculum and professional development projects at the middle school and high school levels, as well as projects related to the teaching and learning of algebra across the grades.

James T. Fey is a Professor Emeritus at the University of Maryland. His consistent professional interest has been development and research focused on curriculum materials that engage middle and high school students in problem-based collaborative investigations of mathematical ideas and their applications.

Susan N. Friel is a Professor of Mathematics Education in the School of Education at the University of North Carolina at Chapel Hill. Her research interests focus on statistics education for middle-grade students and, more broadly, on teachers' professional development and growth in teaching mathematics K–8.

With... Yvonne Grant and Jacqueline Stewart

Yvonne Grant teaches mathematics at Portland Middle School in Portland, Michigan. Jacqueline Stewart is a recently retired high school teacher of mathematics at Okemos High School in Okemos, Michigan. Both Yvonne and Jacqueline have worked on a variety of activities related to the development, implementation, and professional development of the CMP curriculum since its beginning in 1991.

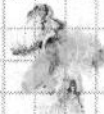

Development Team

CMP3 Authors

Glenda Lappan, University Distinguished Professor, Michigan State University
Elizabeth Difanis Phillips, Senior Academic Specialist, Michigan State University
James T. Fey, Professor Emeritus, University of Maryland
Susan N. Friel, Professor, University of North Carolina – Chapel Hill

With...

Yvonne Grant, Portland Middle School, Michigan
Jacqueline Stewart, Mathematics Consultant, Mason, Michigan

In Memory of... William M. Fitzgerald, Professor (Deceased), Michigan State University, who made substantial contributions to conceptualizing and creating CMP1.

Administrative Assistant

Michigan State University
Judith Martus Miller

Support Staff

Michigan State University
Undergraduate Assistants:
Bradley Robert Corlett, Carly Fleming, Erin Lucian, Scooter Nowak

Development Assistants

Michigan State University
Graduate Research Assistants:
Richard "Abe" Edwards, Nic Gilbertson, Funda Gonulates, Aladar Horvath, Eun Mi Kim, Kevin Lawrence, Jennifer Nimtz, Joanne Philhower, Sasha Wang

Assessment Team

Maine

Falmouth Public Schools
Falmouth Middle School: Shawn Towle

Michigan

Ann Arbor Public Schools
Tappan Middle School
Anne Marie Nicoll-Turner

Portland Public Schools
Portland Middle School
Holly DeRosia, Yvonne Grant

Traverse City Area Public Schools
Traverse City East Middle School
Jane Porath, Mary Beth Schmitt

Traverse City West Middle School
Jennifer Rundio, Karrie Tufts

Ohio

Clark-Shawnee Local Schools
Rockway Middle School: Jim Mamer

Content Consultants

Michigan State University
Peter Lappan, Professor Emeritus, Department of Mathematics

Normandale Community College
Christopher Danielson, Instructor, Department of Mathematics & Statistics

University of North Carolina – Wilmington
Dargan Frierson, Jr., Professor, Department of Mathematics & Statistics

Student Activities

Michigan State University
Brin Keller, Associate Professor, Department of Mathematics

Consultants

Indiana
Purdue University
Mary Bouck, Mathematics Consultant

Michigan
Oakland Schools
Valerie Mills, Mathematics Education Supervisor
Mathematics Education Consultants: Geraldine Devine, Dana Gosen

Ellen Bacon, Independent Mathematics Consultant

New York
University of Rochester
Jeffrey Choppin, Associate Professor

Ohio
University of Toledo
Debra Johanning, Associate Professor

Pennsylvania
University of Pittsburgh
Margaret Smith, Professor

Texas
University of Texas at Austin
Emma Trevino, Supervisor of Mathematics Programs, The Dana Center

Mathematics for All Consulting
Carmen Whitman, Mathematics Consultant

Reviewers

Michigan
Ionia Public Schools
Kathy Dole, Director of Curriculum and Instruction

Grand Valley State University
Lisa Kasmer, Assistant Professor

Portland Public Schools
Teri Keusch, Classroom Teacher

Minnesota
Hopkins School District 270
Michele Luke, Mathematics Coordinator

Field Test Sites for CMP3

Michigan
Ann Arbor Public Schools
Tappan Middle School
Anne Marie Nicoll-Turner*

Portland Public Schools
Portland Middle School: Mark Braun, Angela Buckland, Holly DeRosia, Holly Feldpausch, Angela Foote, Yvonne Grant*, Kristin Roberts, Angie Stump, Tammi Wardwell

Traverse City Area Public Schools
Traverse City East Middle School
Ivanka Baic Berkshire, Brenda Dunscombe, Tracie Herzberg, Deb Larimer, Jan Palkowski, Rebecca Perreault, Jane Porath*, Robert Sagan, Mary Beth Schmitt*

Traverse City West Middle School
Pamela Alfieri, Jennifer Rundio, Maria Taplin, Karrie Tufts*

Maine
Falmouth Public Schools
Falmouth Middle School: Sally Bennett, Chris Driscoll, Sara Jones, Shawn Towle*

Minnesota
Minneapolis Public Schools
Jefferson Community School
Leif Carlson*, Katrina Hayek Munsisoumang*

Ohio
Clark-Shawnee Local Schools
Reid School: Joanne Gilley
Rockway Middle School: Jim Mamer*
Possum School: Tami Thomas

*Indicates a Field Test Site Coordinator

CONNECTED MATHEMATICS® 3

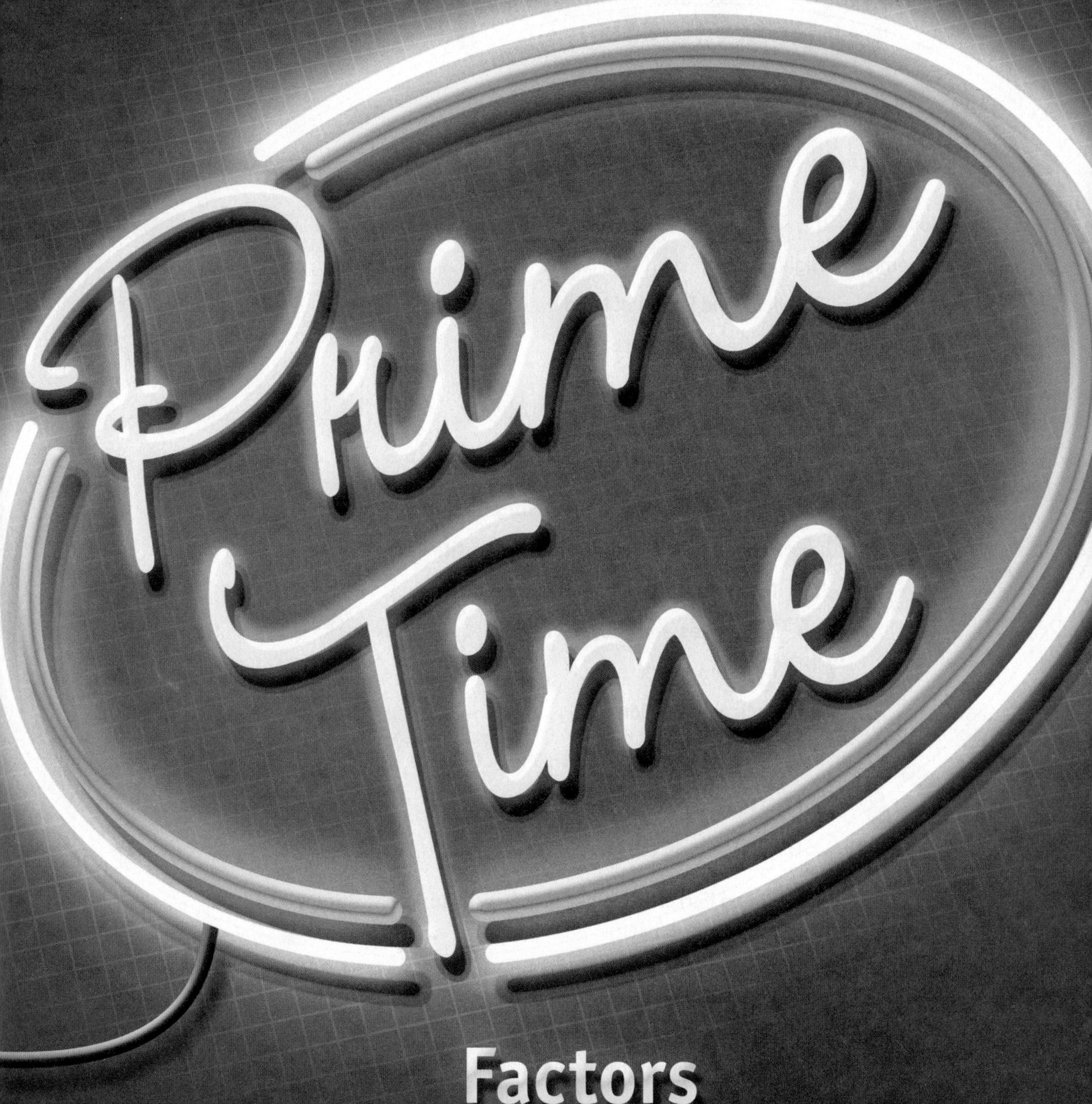

Factors and Multiples

Lappan, Phillips, Fey, Friel

Prime Time

Factors and Multiples

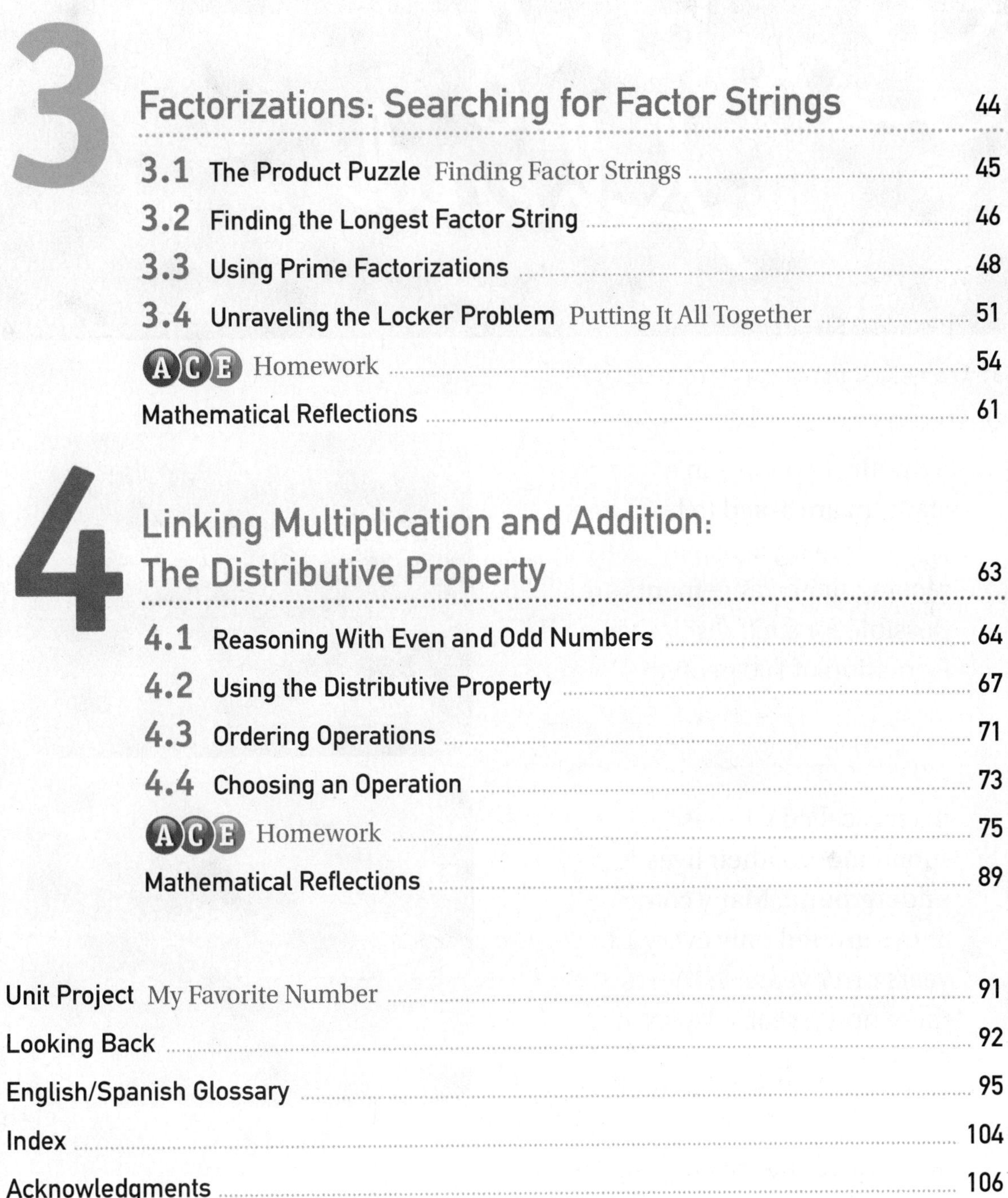

Looking Ahead

Sometimes people in a stadium are asked to hold up cards creating a display. **What** rectangular arrangements are possible for such displays in a formation of 100 people?

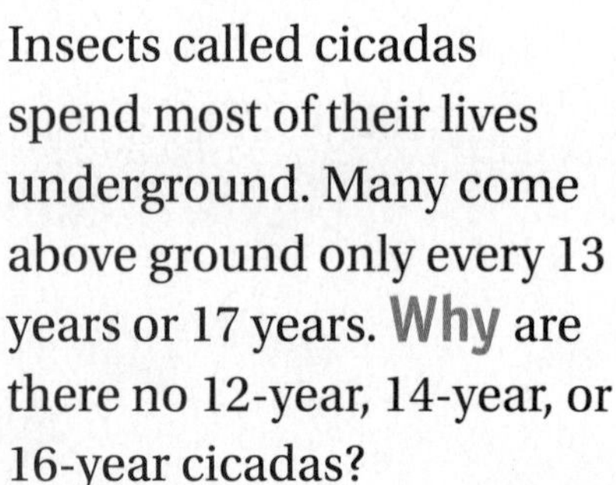

Insects called cicadas spend most of their lives underground. Many come above ground only every 13 years or 17 years. **Why** are there no 12-year, 14-year, or 16-year cicadas?

Why does your birthday fall on a different day of the week from one year to the next? Why is the same pattern also true for New Year's Day and the Fourth of July?

Think about some of the ways you use numbers. You use them to count and to measure. You use numbers to make comparisons and to describe where places are located. Numbers help you communicate and find information. You use numbers to use technology and to make purchases. Numbers can help you think about situations such as those on the previous page.

Whole numbers have interesting properties and structures. Some numbers can be divided by many numbers. Other numbers can be divided by only a few numbers. Some pairs of numbers have lots of factors in common. Some pairs of numbers share only one factor. Some numbers can be written as products or sums of products.

The Investigations in *Prime Time* will help you use ideas about the structure of numbers. You will explain some curious patterns and solve problems. You should think about some interesting questions, including the three on the previous page.

Mathematical Highlights

Factors and Multiples

In *Prime Time,* you will explore important properties of whole numbers. Many of these properties are related to multiplication and division. The Investigations will help you understand relationships among factors, multiples, divisors, and products. You will also learn how the Distributive Property relates multiplication and addition.

The Investigations in this Unit will help you understand the following ideas.

- Classify numbers as prime or composite
- Recognize which situations call for common factors, common multiples, the least common multiple, or the greatest common factor
- Develop strategies for finding factors and multiples, least common multiples, and greatest common factors
- Recognize and use the fact that every whole number can be written in exactly one way as a product of prime numbers
- Use exponential notation to write repeated factors
- Relate the prime factorization of two numbers to the least common multiple and greatest common factor of two numbers
- Recognize that the Distributive Property relates the multiplicative and additive structures of whole numbers
- Use the properties of operations of numbers, including the Distributive Property and the Order of Operations convention, to write equivalent numerical expressions
- Use factors and multiples to solve problems, and explain some numerical facts of everyday life

When you encounter a new problem, it is a good idea to ask yourself questions. In this Unit, you might ask questions such as:

Will breaking a number into factors help me solve the problem?

What common factors and common multiples do the numbers have?

What do the factors and multiples of the numbers tell me about the situation?

When might it be useful to write a number in factored form or as a sum?

Common Core State Standards

Mathematical Practices and Habits of Mind

In the *Connected Mathematics* curriculum you will develop an understanding of important mathematical ideas by solving problems and reflecting on the mathematics involved. Every day, you will use "habits of mind" to make sense of problems and apply what you learn to new situations. Some of these habits are described by the *Common Core State Standards for Mathematical Practices* (MP).

MP1 **Make sense of problems and persevere in solving them.**

When using mathematics to solve a problem, it helps to think carefully about

- data and other facts you are given and what additional information you need to solve the problem;
- strategies you have used to solve similar problems and whether you could solve a related simpler problem first;
- how you could express the problem with equations, diagrams, or graphs;
- whether your answer makes sense.

MP2 **Reason abstractly and quantitatively.**

When you are asked to solve a problem, it often helps to

- focus first on the key mathematical ideas;
- check that your answer makes sense in the problem setting;
- use what you know about the problem setting to guide your mathematical reasoning.

MP3 **Construct viable arguments and critique the reasoning of others.**

When you are asked to explain why a conjecture is correct, you can

- show some examples that fit the claim and explain why they fit;
- show how a new result follows logically from known facts and principles.

When you believe a mathematical claim is incorrect, you can

- show one or more counterexamples—cases that don't fit the claim;
- find steps in the argument that do not follow logically from prior claims.

MP4 Model with mathematics.

When you are asked to solve problems, it often helps to

- think carefully about the numbers or geometric shapes that are the most important factors in the problem, then ask yourself how those factors are related to each other;
- express data and relationships in the problem with tables, graphs, diagrams, or equations, and check your result to see if it makes sense.

MP5 Use appropriate tools strategically.

When working on mathematical questions, you should always

- decide which tools are most helpful for solving the problem and why;
- try a different tool when you get stuck.

MP6 Attend to precision.

In every mathematical exploration or problem-solving task, it is important to

- think carefully about the required accuracy of results; is a number estimate or geometric sketch good enough, or is a precise value or drawing needed?
- report your discoveries with clear and correct mathematical language that can be understood by those to whom you are speaking or writing.

MP7 Look for and make use of structure.

In mathematical explorations and problem solving, it is often helpful to

- look for patterns that show how data points, numbers, or geometric shapes are related to each other;
- use patterns to make predictions.

MP8 Look for and express regularity in repeated reasoning.

When results of a repeated calculation show a pattern, it helps to

- express that pattern as a general rule that can be used in similar cases;
- look for shortcuts that will make the calculation simpler in other cases.

You will use all of the Mathematical Practices in this Unit. Sometimes, when you look at a Problem, it is obvious which practice is most helpful. At other times, you will decide on a practice to use during class explorations and discussions. After completing each Problem, ask yourself:

- What mathematics have I learned by solving this Problem?
- What Mathematical Practices were helpful in learning this mathematics?

Unit Project

My Favorite Number

Many people have a number they think is interesting. Choose a whole number between 10 and 100 that you especially like.

In Your Notebook

- Record your number.
- Explain why you chose that number.
- List three or four mathematical facts about your number.
- List three or four connections you can make between your number and your world.

As you work through the Investigations in *Prime Time,* you will learn about numbers. Think about how these new ideas apply to your favorite number, and add new information about your number to your notebook. Designate one or two "favorite number" pages in your notebook where you can record this information. At the end of the Unit, find an interesting way to report to the class about your favorite number.

Investigation 1 Building on Factors and Multiples

Counting is an important skill in mathematics. You use counting numbers (1, 2, 3, . . .) to answer the questions *How many?* or *How much?* or *When?*

Some counting numbers seem to be used more often than others. For example, there are 12 inches in a foot, 12 eggs in a dozen, and 12 hours on the face of a clock. It's hard to think of places where the numbers 11 and 13 are used.

The difference between the number 12 and the nearby numbers 11 and 13 is that 12 can be separated into equal-sized pieces. You can separate 12 into 1, 2, or 3 equal-sized pieces. You can write this as

$$1 \times 12 = 12$$

$$2 \times 6 = 12$$

$$3 \times 4 = 12$$

The whole-number factors of 12 are 1, 2, 3, 4, 6, and 12. Factors are also called divisors since

$$12 \div 1 = 12 \text{ and } 12 \div 12 = 1$$

$$12 \div 2 = 6 \text{ and } 12 \div 6 = 2$$

$$12 \div 4 = 3 \text{ and } 12 \div 3 = 4$$

All of the whole-number factors of a number less than the number itself are called **proper factors.** The proper factors of 12 are 1, 2, 3, 4, and 6. The numbers 11 and 13 only have 1 as a proper factor. The problems in this Investigation will help you answer this question:

- Why are some counting numbers used more than others?

Common Core State Standards

Essential for 6.NS.B.4 Find the greatest common factor of two whole numbers less than or equal to 100 and the least common multiple of two whole numbers less than or equal to 12. Use the distributive property to express a sum of two whole numbers 1–100 with a common factor as a multiple of a sum of two whole numbers with no common factor.

1.1 Playing the Factor Game: Finding Proper Factors

Playing the Factor Game is a fun way to practice finding factors of whole numbers. You may learn some interesting things about numbers that you didn't know before.

The Factor Game

Directions

1. Player A chooses a number on the game board and circles it.
2. Using a different color, Player B circles all the proper factors of Player A's number.
3. Player B circles a new number, and Player A circles all of the factors of the new number that are not already circled.
4. The players take turns choosing numbers and circling factors.
5. If a player chooses a number with no uncircled factors, that player loses their current turn and scores no points.
6. The game ends when there are no numbers left with uncircled factors.
7. Each player adds the numbers circled with his or her color. The player with the greater total wins.

1	2	3	4	5
6	7	8	9	10
11	12	13	14	15
16	17	18	19	20
21	22	23	24	25
26	27	28	29	30

If you are Player A, what number would you choose as the first move? Why?

Problem 1.1

Play the Factor Game several times with a partner.

A 1. How can you determine whether one number is a factor of another number?

2. If you know a factor of a number, can you find another factor? Explain.

3. Make a list of the factors of 18. Then make a list of the divisors of 18. Are the factors of a number also divisors of the number? Explain your reasoning.

B Give an example of a number that has many factors. Then give an example of a number that has few factors.

C How do you know when you have found all of the factors of a number?

ACE Homework starts on page 17.

1.2 Playing to Win: Prime and Composite Numbers

Did you notice in the Factor Game that some numbers are better first moves than others? If you choose 22, you get 22 points and your opponent only gets $1 + 2 + 11 = 14$ points. However, if you choose 18, you get 18 points and your opponent gets $1 + 2 + 3 + 6 + 9 = 21$ points.

Problem 1.2

A 1. Make a table of all possible first moves (numbers from 1 to 30) in the Factor Game. For each move, list the proper factors of the number. Then record the scores for you and your opponent.

First Move	Proper Factors	My Score	Opponent's Score
1	None	Lose a Turn	0
2	1	2	1
3	1	3	1
4	1, 2	4	3

2. Describe an interesting pattern you see in your table.

B 1. What is the best first move? Why?

2. Which first move makes you lose your turn? Why?

C 1. List all first moves that allow your opponent to score only one point. These numbers are called **prime numbers.** Are all prime numbers good first moves? Explain.

2. List all first moves that allow your opponent to score more than one point. These numbers are called **composite numbers.** Are composite numbers good first moves? Explain.

D Find a number that has exactly

1. two factors. 2. three factors. 3. four factors. 4. six factors.

5. What is special about these numbers? Explain.

E Camila noticed that for some numbers her opponent's score was equal to the number. For example, when her first move was 6, her opponent got 6 points. Are there any other numbers for which this is true?

F 1. For a first move of 24, Anna listed the proper factors as 1, 2, 4, and 6. Was she correct? Explain.

2. How can you be sure that you have listed all of the proper factors of a number?

ACE Homework starts on page 17.

Did You Know?

More than two thousand years ago, there was a Greek mathematician named Euclid. He showed that there are an infinite number of prime numbers. Since then, mathematicians have been searching for formulas that generate prime numbers. So far, they have been unsuccessful. For this reason, large prime numbers are used to encode top-secret information.

In 1999, Nayan Hajratwala found a prime number with more than 2 million digits. The Electronic Frontier Foundation (EFF) awarded him $50,000. In 2008, a group who found a prime number with more than 12 million digits won $100,000 in prize money. You can now win $250,000 for finding a prime number with more than 1,000,000,000 digits.

1.3 The Product Game: Finding Multiples

You used factors of a number to play the Factor Game. In the next game, you will use multiples of numbers. A **multiple** of a number is the product of that number and another whole number. 24 is a multiple of 6 because $6 \times 4 = 24$. Multiples and factors have a back-and-forth relationship.

These sentences use the terms *factor* and *multiple* to describe the relationship $5 \times 3 = 15$.

5 is a factor of 15 because $5 \times 3 = 15$.

3 is a factor of 15 because $3 \times 5 = 15$.

15 is a multiple of 5 because $3 \times 5 = 15$.

15 is a multiple of 3 because $5 \times 3 = 15$.

You can think of other ways to describe this relationship. For example:

15 is divisible by 5 because $15 \div 5 = 3$.

15 is divisible by 3 because $15 \div 3 = 5$.

In the Factor Game, you started with a number and found its factors. In this game, you start with factors and find their product. The Product Game board has a list of factors and a grid of products. The object of the game is to mark four products in a row or diagonally before your opponent does.

The Product Game

Directions

1. Player A puts a paper clip on a number in the factor list. Player A does not mark a square on the product grid because only one factor has been marked. It takes at least two factors to make a product.
2. Player B puts the other paper clip on any number in the factor list. (Player B may select the same number marked by Player A.) Player B then shades or covers the product of the two factors on the product grid.
3. Player A moves *either* of the paper clips to another number. Player A then shades or covers the new product.
4. The players take turns moving one paper clip and marking the product. If a product is already marked, the player does not get a mark for that turn. The winner is the first player to mark four squares in a row. The row can be up and down, across, or diagonal.

1	2	3	4	5	6
7	8	9	10	12	14
15	16	18	20	21	24
25	27	28	30	32	35
36	40	42	45	48	49
54	56	63	64	72	81

Factors:
1 2 3 4 5 6 7 8 9

To play the game, you need a Product Game board, two paper clips, and two colored markers or chips. Each player uses a different color.

Problem 1.3

Play the Product Game several times with a partner. Look for interesting patterns and strategies that help you win. Make notes on your observations.

A 1. Examine the Product Game board. Can you get every number on the product grid by multiplying two numbers on the factor list? Justify your answer.

2. Can you find two numbers in the list of factors whose product is *not* on the product grid?

3. Which numbers on the board can you form by placing both paper clips on the same number?

4. Which squares on the board are the most difficult to mark? Explain why.

B 1. Suppose a game is in progress. One of the paper clips is on 5. What products can you make by moving the other paper clip?

2. The numbers you listed in part (1) are all multiples of 5. List five multiples of 5 that are not on the game board.

C 1. Suppose you want to mark the number 36 on the Product Game board. List all of the ways you can make 36 with the factors and two paper clips.

2. Are the numbers in part (1) all of the factors of 36? Explain.

D How are the Factor Game and the Product Game similar? How are they different?

ACE Homework starts on page 17.

1.4 Rectangles and Factor Pairs

In the Factor Game and the Product Game, you found that factors occur in pairs. Once you know one factor of a number, you can find another factor. For example, 3 is a factor of 12. Since $3 \times 4 = 12$, 4 is also a factor of 12. We call the pair 3, 4 a **factor pair** of 12.

Every year Meridian School has an exhibit of arts and crafts projects done by each class. Every class is given carpet squares to lay out a rectangular exhibit space on the floor of the gym. Each carpet square measures 1 square yard.

- Suppose a class has 12 square yards. What are the possible ways the class can arrange the carpet squares to make a rectangle?
- What are all of the possible arrangements for 6 square yards? For 30 square yards?

Problem 1.4

To help the classes find rectangles for their exhibits, the school made models. The models show possible rectangles formed by carpet squares. The models for the number 15 are shown.

Your teacher will assign your group a few of the numbers from 1 to 30. For each of your numbers, complete the following:

- Write the number at the top of a large sheet of paper.
- Cut out all of the possible models you can make from grid paper for the number.
- Tape all of the models to the paper and label each model with its height by its width.
- List the factors of the number from least to greatest at the bottom of the paper.

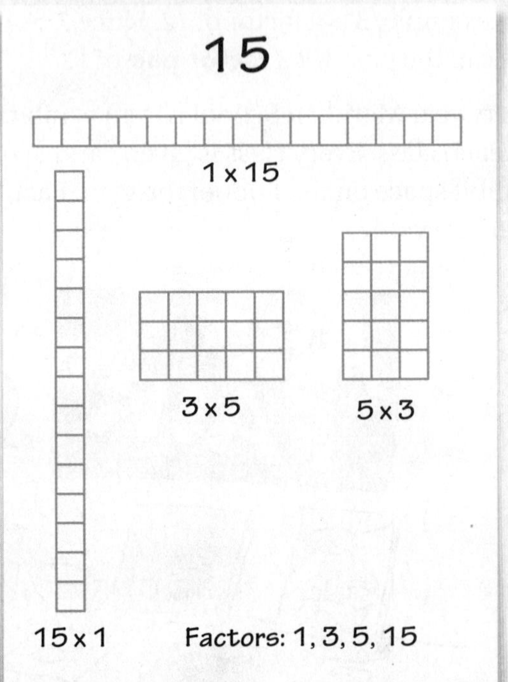

A Look over the set of rectangles that you and your classmates created. What patterns do you notice?

B 1. Which numbers can be represented by the most rectangles? What do these numbers have in common? What kind of numbers are they?

2. Which numbers can be represented by the fewest rectangles? What do these numbers have in common? What kind of numbers are these?

3. A number that can be arranged to form a square with tiles is called a **square number.** Which numbers are square numbers? What do you notice about the factors of a square number?

4. How can you use the rectangle models for a number to list the factors of the number? Use an example to show your thinking.

C Suppose a class has 12 square yards for their exhibit. Which rectangular shape should the class select for their arts and crafts show? What are the advantages and disadvantages of the shape?

Homework starts on page 17.

Applications

1. a. Ben claims that 12 is a factor of 24. How can you check whether he is correct?

   b. How would you test whether 7 is a factor of 291?

2. a. What factor is paired with 6 to give 24?

   b. What factor is paired with 5 to give 45?

   c. What factor is paired with 3 to give 24?

   d. What factor is paired with 6 to give 54?

3. a. Which of the numbers 19, 21, 23, and 25 has the most factors?

   b. Find a number greater than 25 that has more factors than the numbers in part (a).

   c. Find a number smaller than 19 that has more factors than the numbers in part (a).

4. a. The calculator screen below shows the result of dividing 84 by 14.

   What does the answer tell you about 14 and 84?

   b. The calculator screen below shows the result of dividing 84 by 15.

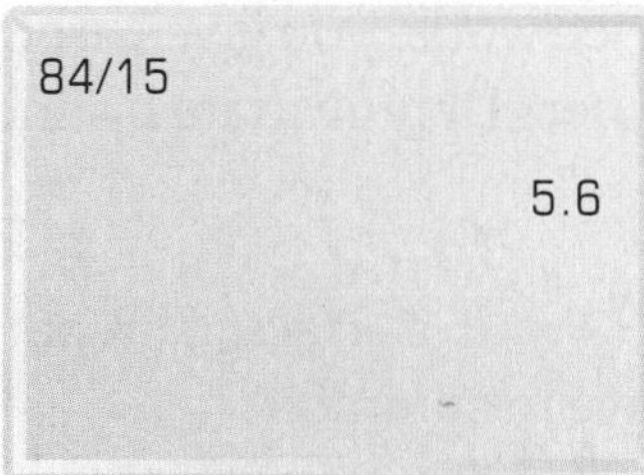

   What does the answer tell you about 15 and 84?

5. a. Is 6 a divisor of 18? Why?

   b. Is 18 a divisor of 6? Why?

6. Which of these numbers are divisors of 64?

   2 6 8 12 16

7. Sam knows that 3 is a factor of 24. This means that $3 \times \blacksquare = 24$. Another way to write this is $3 \times n = 24$. For each statement, find a value of n that makes the statement true.

   a. $3 \times n = 24$

   b. $5 \times n = 60$

   c. $12 \times n = 144$

   d. $160 = 8 \times n$

   e. $2 \times 3 \times n \times n = 54$

8. In the following Factor Game, some of the scores are missing on the tally sheet.

Cathy	Keiko
24	36
21	?
?	9
?	30

   a. In Round 1, Cathy chose 24. Keiko scored 36 points. Make a game board. Mark Cathy's choice and Keiko's factors.

   b. In Round 2, it is Keiko's turn. Cathy scored 21 points. What number did Keiko pick?

   c. In Round 3, it is Cathy's turn. Keiko scored 9 points. What number might Cathy have picked?

   d. In Round 4, it is Keiko's turn. Keiko chose 30. What did Cathy score?

   e. In Round 5, it is Cathy's turn. What is Cathy's best move? Explain your choice.

9. Lareina understands factors. Sometimes she has trouble finding all of the factors of a number. What advice would you give Lareina to help her find all of the factors of a number? Demonstrate by finding all of the factors of 110.

10. a. Find two numbers that have 2, 3, and 5 as factors. What other factors do the two numbers have in common?

   b. Find three numbers that have 2, 4, and 8 as factors. What do these numbers have in common?

11. **a.** Suppose you circle a prime number in the Factor Game. Your opponent receives at most one point. Explain why. Use examples.

b. Suppose you circle a composite number in the Factor Game. Your opponent might receive more points than you. Explain why. Give some examples.

12. The expression $3 \times n$ can be written without the multiplication sign as $3n$. For each expression in parts (a)–(c),

- Use $n = 1, 2, 3, \ldots, 10$ to evaluate the expression.
- Describe the set of ten numbers.
- Suppose the sequence continues for values of n greater than 10. Do the numbers 12, 21, 30, or 210 appear in the sequence?

a. $3n$ **b.** $7n$ **c.** $6n$

13. The Factor Game can be played on a 49 board that includes the whole numbers from 1 to 49.

The Factor Game

1	2	3	4	5	6	7
8	9	10	11	12	13	14
15	16	17	18	19	20	21
22	23	24	25	26	27	28
29	30	31	32	33	34	35
36	37	38	39	40	41	42
43	44	45	46	47	48	49

a. Extend your table for analyzing first moves on a 30 board to include all of the numbers on a 49 board.

b. What new primes can you find?

c. What new square numbers can you find?

d. What is the best first move on a 49 board? Why?

e. What is the worst first move on a 49 board, other than 1? Why?

14. Dewayne and Todd are playing the Product Game. Dewayne's markers are on 16, 18, and 28. Todd's markers are on 14, 21, and 30. The paper clips are on 5 and 6. It is Dewayne's turn to move a paper clip.

The Product Game

a. List the moves Dewayne can make.

b. Which move(s) would give Dewayne three markers in a row?

c. Which move(s) would allow him to block Todd?

d. Which move do you think Dewayne should make? Explain.

15. a. Suppose that one paper clip on the Product Game board is on 3. What products can you make by moving the other paper clip?

b. List five multiples of 3 that are not on the game board.

c. How many multiples of 3 are there on the game board?

16. a. Davis just marked 18 on a Product Game board. On which factors might the paper clips be placed? List all of the possibilities.

b. Are there other factors of 18?

17. Determine whether each number can be made in more than one way in the Product Game. Say whether the number is prime or composite.

a. 36 **b.** 5 **c.** 7 **d.** 9

18. Salvador said that the Product Game could be called the Multiple Game. Do you agree? Why or why not?

19. a. On the Product Game board, which number is both a prime number and an even number?

b. Is there another even prime number? Explain.

20. a. What three factors were used to create this Product Game board?

4	6	9
14	?	49

Factors: ___ ___ ___

b. What product is missing from the grid?

21. a. What four factors were used to create this Product Game board?

9	15	18	
21	?	30	35
	36	42	49

Factors: ___ ___ ___ ___

b. What product is missing from the grid?

For Exercises 22–27, use the dimensions of each rectangle that can be made from the given number of tiles to list all of the factor pairs for each number.

22. 24 **23.** 32 **24.** 48

25. 45 **26.** 60 **27.** 72

28. a. What type of number has exactly two factors? Give examples.

b. What type of number has an odd number of factors? Give examples.

c. Are there any prime numbers that are also square numbers? Give an example or explain why not.

29. How many rectangles can you build with a prime number of square tiles?

30. **Multiple Choice** Which of these numbers is a square number?

A. 128 **B.** 225 **C.** 360 **D.** 399

31. Luke has chosen a mystery number. His number is greater than 12 and less than 40. It has exactly three factors. What might his number be? Use the display of rectangles from Problem 1.4 to find Luke's number. Also, think about what the displays for the numbers 31 to 40 would look like.

32. The Olympic photograph below inspired a school pep club to design card displays for football games. Each display uses 100 square cards. At a game, groups of 100 volunteers will hold up the cards to form complete pictures. They are most effective when the volunteers sit in a rectangular arrangement. What rectangular seating arrangements are possible? Which arrangements would you choose? Why?

33. A school band has 64 members. The band marches in the shape of a rectangle.

a. What rectangles can the band director make by arranging the band members?

b. Which of these arrangements is most appealing to you? Why?

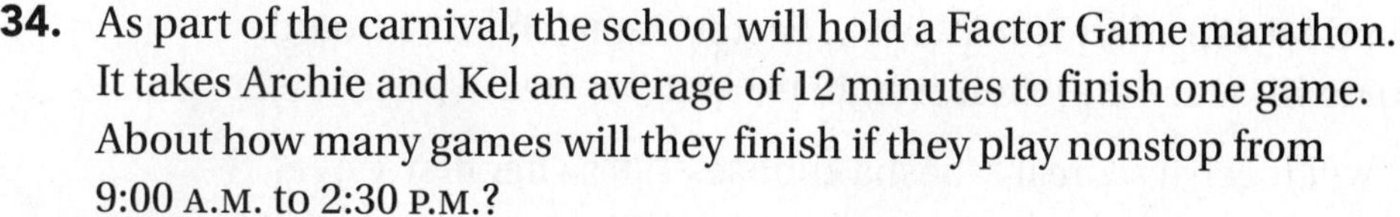

Connections

34. As part of the carnival, the school will hold a Factor Game marathon. It takes Archie and Kel an average of 12 minutes to finish one game. About how many games will they finish if they play nonstop from 9:00 A.M. to 2:30 P.M.?

35. **Multiple Choice** Carlos read a book for language arts class. He finished the book on Friday. On Monday he read 27 pages. On Tuesday he read 31 pages. On Wednesday he read 28 pages. On Thursday and Friday he read the same number of pages each day. The book has 144 pages. How many pages did he read on Thursday?

A. 28 **B.** 29 **C.** 31 **D.** 58

36. The variable n represents a whole number.

a. For what values of n will the sum $n + 3$ be less than 50?

b. For what values of n will the product $3n$ be less than 50?

37. Long ago, people decided to divide the day into units called hours. They chose 24 as the number of hours in one day. Why is 24 a more convenient choice than 23 or 25?

38. In developing the ways of calculating time, astronomers divided an hour into 60 minutes. Why is 60 a better choice than 59 or 61?

39. **a.** Ms. Diaz wants to divide her class of 30 students into 10 groups. The groups do not need to be of equal size. What are some of her choices?

b. Ms. Diaz wants to divide her class of 30 students into equal-sized groups. What are her choices?

c. How is the thinking you did in part (a) different from the thinking you did in part (b)?

40. Allie's aunt has saved \$10,000 in \$20 bills. She spends one \$20 bill every day. How many days will it take her to run out of bills?

Extensions

41. Jocelyn and Moesha decide to play the Factor Game on a 100-board. A 100-board includes the whole numbers from 1 to 100.

a. What will Jocelyn score if Moesha chooses 100 as her first move?

b. What will Jocelyn score if Moesha chooses 99 as her first move?

c. What is the best first move on a 100-board?

42. What number am I?

Clue 1 When you divide me by 5, the remainder is 4.

Clue 2 I have two digits. Both digits are odd.

Clue 3 The sum of my digits is 10.

43. The sum of the proper factors of a number may be *greater than*, *less than*, or *equal to* the number. Mathematicians use this idea to classify numbers as *abundant*, *deficient*, or *perfect*. Each whole number greater than 1 falls into one of these three categories.

a. Draw and label three circles as shown below. The numbers 12, 15, and 6 have been placed in the appropriate circles.

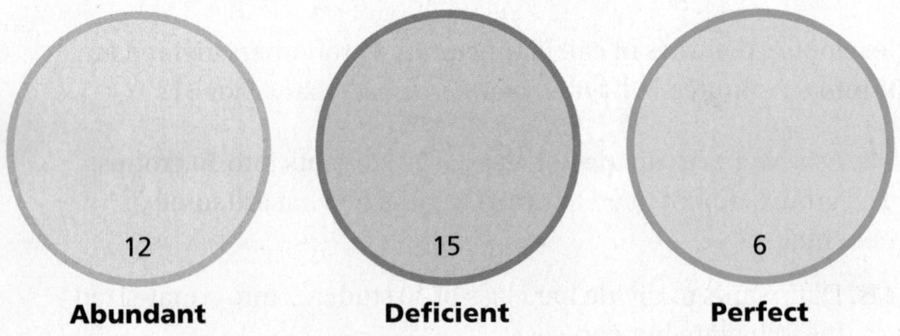

Use your factor list to determine what each label means. Then, write each whole number from 2 to 30 in the correct circle.

b. Are the labels appropriate? Why or why not?

c. In which circle does 36 belong?

d. In which circle does 55 belong?

44. **a.** Suppose you choose 16 as a first move in the 49 Factor Game. How many points does your opponent get? How does your opponent's score for this turn compare to yours?

b. Suppose you choose 4 as a first move. How many points does your opponent get? How does your opponent's score for this turn compare to yours?

c. Find another number on the 49 Factor Game Board that has the same pattern of scoring as 4 and 16. These numbers are called *near-perfect* numbers. Why do you think this name fits?

d. Examine the factor lists for the near-perfect numbers. Use this information to find two more near-perfect numbers.

45. Find three numbers you can multiply together to get 300.

46. **a.** This is the complete list of the proper factors of a certain number.

1, 2, 3, 4, 6, 7, 12, 14, 21, 28, 42, 49, 84, 98, 147, 196, 294

What is the number?

b. List each of the factor pairs for the number.

c. How is the list of factor pairs related to the rectangles that can be made for the factor pairs?

Did You Know?

Is there a largest perfect number? Mathematicians have been trying for hundreds of years to answer this question. After 6 and 28, the next perfect number is 496.

47. Jessica works on many factor problems. She notices that her factor pair list often starts with pairs of numbers such as 1×100, 2×50, and 4×25. Her factor list ends with 25×4, 50×2, and 100×1. At some point, the list begins to repeat the factor pairs in reversed order.

a. Consider the factor pairs of 100. When do the factor pairs reverse order?

b. Consider the factor pairs of 81. When do the factor pairs reverse order?

c. For any square number, when do the factor pairs reverse order?

d. Think about a number that is not a square number. At what point will the factor pairs reverse order? Explain.

e. Is there a point at which a prime number's factor pairs reverse order?

48. Jeff is trying to determine when he can stop looking for more whole number factors of a number. He has collected data about several numbers. For example, 30 has 1×30, 2×15, 3×10, and 5×6 as factor pairs. Then, he can stop looking because the factor pairs repeat. For 36, he can stop looking when he gets to 6×6. For 66, there are no new factor pairs after 6×11. Copy and complete the table below. Is there any pattern that would help Jeff find the point where the factor pairs reverse order?

Place Where There Are No New Factor Pairs

Number	16	30	36	40	50	64	66
Last Factor Pair	■	5×6	6×6	■	■	■	6×11

49. For parts (a)–(c), find composite numbers that can be rewritten as

a. the product of two prime numbers.

b. the product of a prime number and another composite number.

c. the product of two composite numbers.

d. Josh thinks he can find examples of prime numbers that he can write as a product of two primes. Is he correct? Give some examples or explain why not.

Mathematical Reflections 1

In this Investigation, you played and analyzed the Factor Game and the Product Game. You also represented factor pairs as the dimensions of rectangles. The following questions will help you summarize what you have learned.

Think about these questions. Discuss your ideas with other students and your teacher. Then write a summary of your findings in your notebook.

1. a. **Explain** how factors and multiples of a number are related. Use examples.

   b. **Describe** a situation where it is useful to know about factors and multiples.

   c. **Describe** strategies for finding factors or multiples of a number.

2. You can describe a number by both the number of its factors and the kinds of its factors. **Describe** several different kinds of numbers that you studied in this Investigation. Give examples.

Unit Project

Now that you have played the Factor Game and the Product Game, write something new that you learned about your favorite number.

- Would your favorite number be a good first move in either game? Why or why not?
- Is your favorite number abundant, deficient, or perfect?

Common Core Mathematical Practices

As you worked on the Problems in this Investigation, you used prior knowledge to make sense of them. You also applied Mathematical Practices to solve the Problems. Think back over your work, the ways you thought about the Problems, and how you used Mathematical Practices.

Tori described her thoughts in the following way:

We noticed a pattern among the square numbers in Problem 1.4. Square numbers have an odd number of factors. This makes sense since factors come in pairs, but for square numbers, one of the factor pairs must have identical factors. So, you only count this factor once.

Our thinking supports John's thinking. He claims that when checking for all of the factors of a number, you can stop when the factor pairs start to repeat. That happens with the factor pair that is closest to a square number.

Common Core Standards for Mathematical Practice

MP2 Reason abstractly and quantitatively

- What other Mathematical Practices can you identify in Tori's reasoning?
- Describe a Mathematical Practice that you and your classmates used to solve a different Problem in this Investigation.

Common Multiples and Common Factors

Many things happen over and over again in fixed cycles. For example, a morning news program gives a traffic report every 7 minutes. A train arrives at a particular station every 12 minutes. A cuckoo clock sounds every 15 minutes.

- How can you figure out when two events with different cycles will occur at the same time?

You can solve such problems using common multiples or common factors.

Think about the multiples of 20 and 30 greater than 0.

- The multiples of 20 are 20, 40, 60, 80, 100, 120, 140, 160, 180, . . .
- The multiples of 30 are 30, 60, 90, 120, 150, 180, . . .

The numbers 60, 120, 180, . . . , are multiples of both 20 and 30. These numbers are **common multiples** of 20 and 30. The **least common multiple (LCM)** is 60.

Now compare the factors of 20 and 30.

- The factors of 20 are 1, 2, 4, 5, 10, and 20.
- The factors of 30 are 1, 2, 3, 5, 6, 10, 15, and 30.

The numbers 1, 2, 5, and 10 are factors of both 20 and 30. These numbers are **common factors** of 20 and 30. The **greatest common factor (GCF)** is 10.

Common Core State Standards

6.NS.B.4 Find the greatest common factor of two whole numbers less than or equal to 100 and the least common multiple of two whole numbers less than or equal to 12. Use the distributive property to express a sum of two whole numbers 1–100 with a common factor as a multiple of a sum of two whole numbers with no common factor.

2.1 Riding Ferris Wheels: Choosing Common Multiples or Common Factors

One of the more popular rides at a carnival or amusement park is the Ferris wheel. Jeremy and his sister, Deborah, are at a carnival. The carnival has a large and a small Ferris wheel. Jeremy gets on at the bottom of the large Ferris wheel. Deborah gets on at the bottom of the small Ferris wheel. The rides begin at the same time.

For each situation below, how many seconds will pass before Jeremy and Deborah are both at the bottom again?

Problem 2.1

A The large Ferris wheel makes one revolution in 60 seconds. The small Ferris wheel makes one revolution in 20 seconds.

B The large Ferris wheel makes one revolution in 50 seconds. The small Ferris wheel makes one revolution in 30 seconds.

C The large Ferris wheel makes one revolution in 20 seconds. The small Ferris wheel makes one revolution in 11 seconds.

D For Questions A–C, find the number of times each Ferris wheel goes around before Jeremy and his sister are both at the bottom again.

Homework starts on page 34.

2.2 Looking at Cicada Cycles: Choosing Common Multiples or Common Factors

Cicadas (si KAY dahs) spend most of their lives underground. Some populations of cicadas come above ground every 13 years. Other populations come up every 17 years. Cicadas do not cause damage to fruits and vegetables directly. However, the females damage trees when they make slits in them to lay eggs.

Did You Know?

Cicadas are sometimes mistakenly called *locusts*. A locust is a type of grasshopper. It looks nothing like a cicada. The error originated with early European settlers in North America. There, they encountered large outbreaks of cicadas. The swarms of insects reminded the settlers of stories they had heard about swarms of locusts in Egypt.

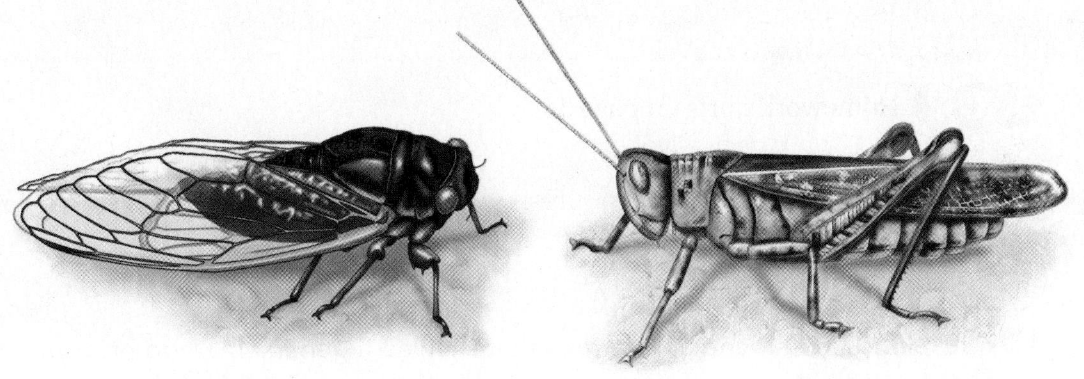

Cicada Locust

Female cicadas lay their eggs in tree branches. When the young cicadas hatch, they drop to the ground and burrow into the soil. They remain underground for 13 or 17 years, feeding off juices from tree roots.

Sometimes 17-year cicadas can overlap with 13-year cicadas. This happened in Missouri in 1998.

When will the 17-year and 13-year cicadas next appear together?

Problem 2.2

Stephan's grandfather told him about how cicadas sometimes damaged his orchard. One year, there were so many cicadas, they wrecked the buds on all of his young trees. Both the 13-year and the 17-year cicadas came up that year.

A Suppose 13-year and 17-year cicadas both appear this year. When will both types of cicadas next appear together? Explain.

B Suppose there are 12-year, 14-year, and 16-year cicadas that all appear this year. After how many years will all three types of cicadas appear together again? Explain.

C Stephan developed a method to determine the next time two types of cicadas will appear together. He says that if you multiply the cycles together, you get the next time that both types will appear together. Does Stephan's method work for any pair of cycles? If so, explain why. If not, provide an example for which Stephan's method does not work.

D For Questions A and B, decide whether the answer is *less than, greater than,* or *equal to* the product of the cicada cycles.

ACE Homework starts on page 34.

Did You Know?

In Question C, you found an example that showed a general method or statement does not always hold true. In mathematics, an example that disproves a statement is called a **counterexample.** If someone claims that a pattern is true for all cases, you only need to find one counterexample to disprove that claim.

2.3 Bagging Snacks: Choosing Common Multiples or Common Factors

You have looked at problems about revolutions of Ferris wheels and life cycles of cicadas. This problem involves packing snacks for a hiking trip.

Problem 2.3

Jane and her friends are going on a hiking trip. Jane wants to make snack packs to take on the trip. She has 24 apples and 36 small bags of trail mix. Each snack pack must have the same number of apples and the same number of bags of trail mix.

A 1. What are the possible numbers of snack packs she can make so that the treats are shared equally? Describe each possibility.

2. What is the greatest number of snack packs Jane can make? Explain.

3. Suppose Jane's pet canary ruins six of the bags of trail mix. Jane wants to share the apples and the remaining bags of trail mix equally. What is the greatest number of snack packs Jane can make?

B Suppose Jane's mother replaces the six bags of trail mix. She also provides the group with 18 cans of juice. Each snack pack has the same number of apples, bags of trail mix, and cans of juice. What is the greatest number of snack packs Jane can make? Explain.

C Compare Problems 2.1, 2.2, and 2.3. For which problems did you use common multiples? For which problems did you use common factors? How did you decide?

ACE Homework starts on page 34.

Applications | Connections | Extensions

Applications

For Exercises 1–8, list the common multiples from 1 to 100 for each pair of numbers. Then find the least common multiple for each pair.

1. 8 and 12 **2.** 3 and 15 **3.** 7 and 11 **4.** 9 and 10

5. 24 and 36 **6.** 20 and 25 **7.** 42 and 14 **8.** 30 and 12

9. **a.** Find three pairs of numbers for which the least common multiple equals the product of the two numbers.

b. Look at the pairs of numbers you found in part (a). What is true about all three pairs of numbers?

For Exercises 10–13, find two pairs of numbers with the given number as their least common multiple.

10. 10 **11.** 36 **12.** 60 **13.** 105

14. **a.** A restaurant is open 24 hours a day. The manager wants to divide the day into work shifts of equal length. The shifts should not overlap. All shift durations should be a whole number of hours. Describe the different ways this can be done.

b. The manager turns on the restaurant's two neon signs at the same time. Both signs blink as they are turned on. One sign blinks every 9 seconds. The other sign blinks every 15 seconds. In how many seconds will they blink together again?

15. The school cafeteria serves pizza every sixth day and applesauce every eighth day. Suppose that pizza and applesauce are both on today's menu. In how many days will they be together on the menu again?

For Exercises 16–23, list the common factors of each pair of numbers. Then find the greatest common factor of each pair.

16. 18 and 30 **17.** 9 and 25 **18.** 60 and 45 **19.** 23 and 29

20. 49 and 14 **21.** 140 and 25 **22.** 142 and 148 **23.** 84 and 105

24. **Multiple Choice** For which pair of numbers is the greatest common factor 8?

A. 2 and 4 **B.** 7 and 15 **C.** 32 and 64 **D.** 56 and 72

25. Multiple Choice For which pair of numbers is the greatest common factor 15?

F. 60 and 75 **G.** 30 and 60 **H.** 10 and 25 **J.** 3 and 5

26. Multiple Choice For which pair of numbers is the greatest common factor 1?

A. 5 and 10 **B.** 8 and 4 **C.** 8 and 10 **D.** 8 and 15

27. a. Mr. Mendoza and his 23 students are planning to have hot dogs at their class picnic. He can buy hot dogs in packages of 12 and hot dog buns in packages of 8.

Mr. Mendoza wants everyone to get the same number of hot dogs and buns with no leftovers. What is the least number of packages of hot dogs and the least number of packages of buns Mr. Mendoza can buy? How many hot dogs and buns will each person get?

b. Suppose that the class invites the principal, the secretary, the bus driver, and three parents to help out at the picnic. Mr. Mendoza still wants everyone to get the same number of hot dogs and buns with no leftovers. How many packages of hot dogs and buns will he need to buy now? How many hot dogs and buns will each person get?

28. The cast of a play had a party. The drama teacher served 20 cookies and 40 carrot sticks as refreshments. Each cast member ate the same number of whole cookies and the same number of whole carrot sticks. Nothing was left over. The drama teacher did not eat. How many cast members might have been at the party? Explain.

29. a. Make up a word problem that you can solve by finding common factors.

b. Make up a different word problem that you can solve by finding common multiples.

c. Solve your problems from parts (a) and (b). Explain how you know that your answers are correct.

30. Mario's watch runs fast. In 1 day, it gains an hour. So in 12 days, it gains 12 hours and is correct again. Julio's watch also runs fast. In 1 day, it gains 20 minutes. Suppose they both set their 12-hour watches correctly at 9:00 A.M. on Monday. When will their watches next show the correct time together?

31. Miriam's uncle donates 120 cans of juice and 90 packs of cheese crackers for a school picnic. Each student must receive the same number of cans of juice and the same number of packs of crackers with no leftovers.

a. What is the greatest number of students who can come to the picnic and share the food equally? How many cans of juice and packs of crackers will each student receive? Explain.

b. Suppose Miriam's uncle eats two packs of crackers before he brings the supplies to school. What is the greatest number of students who can share the food equally? How many cans of juice and packs of crackers will each student receive? Explain.

32. The least common multiple of a number n and 6 is 42. What are all of the possible whole-number values for n?

33. The greatest common factor of a number n and 6 is 3. What are all of the possible whole-number values for n?

34. a. Aaron, Ruth, and Walter created shortcuts for finding the least common multiple of two numbers. Do their methods work for any pair of numbers? Explain why it works or provide a counterexample.

Aaron's Method

- LCM of 3 and 5 is 15
- LCM of 2 and 7 is 14
- LCM of 9 and 4 is 36

Shortcut: Multiply the two numbers.

Ruth's Method

- LCM of 4 and 8 is 8
- LCM of 2 and 12 is 12
- LCM of 5 and 25 is 25

Shortcut: Choose the greater of the two numbers.

Walter's Method

- LCM of 6 and 4 is 12
- LCM of 4 and 10 is 20
- LCM of 14 and 8 is 56

Shortcut: Multiply the two numbers. Then divide by 2.

b. For what types of numbers does Aaron's method work? For what types of numbers does Ruth's method work? For what types of numbers does Walter's method work?

Connections

35. Use the terms *factor, divisor, multiple, product,* and *divisible by* to write as many statements as you can about the number sentence $7 \times 9 = 63$.

For Exercises 36–39, find a number that satisfies the given condition.

36. forms a factor pair with 12 to give 48

37. forms a factor pair with 11 to give 110

38. forms a factor pair with 6 to give 48

39. forms a factor pair with 11 to give 121

40. Use the fact that $135 \times 37 = 4{,}995$ to find the value of $1{,}350 \times 3{,}700$.

41. **a.** Suppose a jet travels 60 kilometers in 5 minutes. How many kilometers will it travel in 2 hours? In 6 hours?

b. How many more kilometers will the jet travel in 6 hours than in 2 hours?

c. If a trip takes 4 hours, how many kilometers does the jet travel?

42. $3 \times 5 \times 7 = 105$. Use this fact to find each product.

a. $9 \times 5 \times 7$

b. $3 \times 5 \times 14$

c. $3 \times 50 \times 7$

d. $3 \times 25 \times 7$

43. Use as many of the words *prime, composite,* and *square* as you can to describe each number.

a. 25

b. 31

c. 51

d. 1

Extensions

44. Ms. Santiago has many pens in her desk drawer. She says that if you divide the total number of pens by 2, 3, 4, 5, or 6, you get a remainder of 1. What is the least number of pens that could be in Ms. Santiago's drawer?

45. What is the mystery number pair?

    Clue 1: The greatest common factor of the mystery pair is 7.

    Clue 2: The least common multiple of the mystery pair is 70.

    Clue 3: Each of the numbers in the mystery pair has two digits.

    Clue 4: One of the numbers in the mystery pair is odd. The other number is even.

For Exercises 46–53, determine whether each statement is *always, sometimes,* or *never* true. Justify your answer.

46. The greatest common factor of two even numbers is 2.

47. The greatest common factor of two different prime numbers is 1.

48. The greatest common factor of any number n and 1 is n.

49. The greatest common factor of any number n and itself is n.

50. The least common multiple of any number n and 1 is n.

51. For any number n greater than 1, the least common multiple of n and itself is $n \times n$.

52. The least common multiple of any number n and 3 is $3n$.

53. The least common multiple of any prime number p and 1 is p.

54. What is another statement you can make about the greatest common factor or least common multiple of two numbers? Determine whether the statement is *always, sometimes,* or *never* true. Justify your answer.

For Exercises 55–58, draw Venn diagrams. A Venn diagram uses circles to group things that belong together. You can use Venn diagrams to explore relationships among whole numbers. For example, the Venn diagram shown sorts the numbers from 1 to 9 according to whether they are prime or multiples of 2.

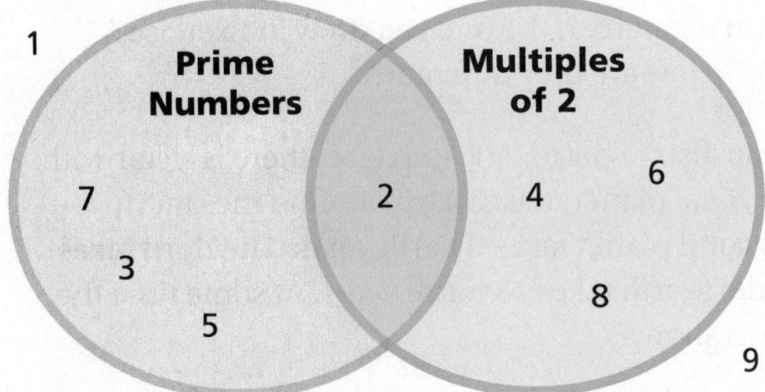

55. List the factors of 30 and the factors of 36.

a. What do the numbers in the intersection (the "overlap") of the circular regions have in common?

b. Explain how you can use your diagram to find the greatest common factor of 30 and 36. What is this greatest common factor?

c. What is the least number that falls in the intersection?

56. List the factors of 20 and the factors of 27.

a. What do the numbers in the intersection of the circular regions have in common?

b. Explain how you can use your diagram to find the greatest common factor of 20 and 27. What is this greatest common factor?

c. Compare this Venn diagram to the one you drew in Exercise 55. How are they alike? How are they different?

57. List the multiples of 5 and the multiples of 4 that are less than or equal to 40.

a. What do the numbers in the intersection have in common?

b. Explain how you can use your diagram to find the least common multiple of 5 and 4. What is this least common multiple?

c. Suppose numbers greater than 40 are allowed. List five more numbers that would be in the intersection. If you could use any number, what would be the greatest possible number in the intersection?

58. List the multiples of 6 and the multiples of 8 that are less than or equal to 48.

a. What do the numbers in the intersection have in common?

b. Explain how you can use your diagram to find the least common multiple of 6 and 8. What is this least common multiple?

c. Compare this Venn diagram to the one you drew in Exercise 57. How are they alike? How are they different?

59. Suppose that, in some distant part of the universe, there is a star with four orbiting planets. One planet makes a trip around the star in 6 Earth years. The second planet takes 9 Earth years. The third takes 15 Earth years, and the fourth takes 18 Earth years. At some time the planets are lined up as shown.

Scientists call this alignment a conjunction. How many Earth years will pass before the planets are lined up again?

60. Eric and his friends practice multiplying by using dominoes. Each half of a domino has dots on it. The number of dots ranges from 0 to 6. The students use the two numbers on a domino as factors. For the domino shown, Eric would say "12."

a. What is the greatest product you can make from numbers on dominoes?

b. What is the least product you can make from numbers on dominoes?

c. Since there are seven different numbers (0–6) that can occur on each half of the domino, Eric reasons that he needs to know 49 different products. This is too many. What did he forget?

61. **a.** Suppose there are 12-year cicadas and that cicadas have predators with 2-year cycles. How often would 12-year cicadas face their predators? Would life be better for 13-year cicadas than for 12-year cicadas? Explain.

b. Suppose that 12-year and 13-year cicadas have predators with both 2-year and 3-year cycles. Suppose that both kinds of cicadas and both kinds of predators came up this year. When would the 12-year cicadas again have to face both kinds of predators at the same time? When would the 13-year cicadas face both? Which type of cicada do you think is better off?

For Exercises 62–69, find a set of numbers that satisfy the conditions.

62. The GCF of two numbers is prime. The LCM of the two numbers is composite.

63. The LCM of two numbers is a square number.

64. The GCF of two numbers is a square number.

65. The GCF and LCM of two numbers are equal.

66. The GCF of two numbers is 12. The LCM of the two numbers is 72.

67. The GCF of three different numbers is 5.

68. The LCM of three different numbers is 24.

69. The GCF of four different numbers is 1.

Mathematical Reflections 2

In this Investigation, you used common factors and common multiples to solve problems. The following questions will help you summarize what you have learned.

Think about these questions. Discuss your ideas with other students and your teacher. Then write a summary of your findings in your notebook.

1. **How** can you decide if finding common multiples or common factors is helpful in solving a problem? Explain.
2. a. **Describe** how you can find the common factors and the greatest common factor of two numbers.
   b. **What** information does the greatest common factor of two numbers provide in a problem?
3. a. **Describe** how you can find the common multiples and the least common multiple of two numbers.
   b. **What** information does the least common multiple of two numbers provide in a problem?

Unit Project

Don't forget to write about your favorite number!

 What new concepts have you learned about your number?

Common Core Mathematical Practices

As you worked on the Problems in this Investigation, you used prior knowledge to make sense of them. You also applied Mathematical Practices to solve the Problems. Think back over your work, the ways you thought about the Problems, and how you used Mathematical Practices.

Hector described his thoughts in the following way:

We noticed in Problem 2.2 that the LCM of two different prime numbers is the product of the two numbers. This is true because any two prime numbers have no common factors other than 1. So the LCM must contain each prime as one of its factors.

Common Core Standards for Mathematical Practice

MP8 Look for and express regularity in repeated reasoning

- What other Mathematical Practices can you identify in Hector's reasoning?
- Describe a Mathematical Practice that you and your classmates used to solve a different Problem in this Investigation.

Factorizations: Searching for Factor Strings

A number may be the product of many different pairs of factors. For example, you can write 100 as 1×100, 2×50, 4×25, 5×20, and 10×10. The number 100 is also the product of three factors, such as $2 \times 2 \times 25$ or $2 \times 5 \times 10$. You can even write 100 as a product of four factors: $2 \times 2 \times 5 \times 5$. Longer factor strings are often useful in solving problems.

You have found the factors of a number by looking at the factor pairs for a number. You also can use factor trees to find factors. Factor trees show how different factor strings are related.

This factor tree represents the factor string $2 \times 50 = 100$. The ends of the branches are the factors.

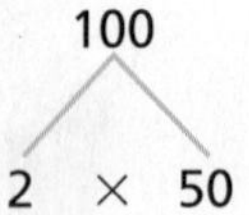

This factor tree represents $2 \times 5 \times 10 = 100$.

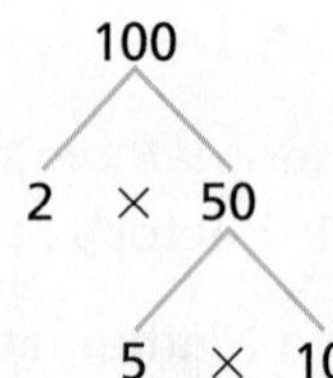

- What factor string does this factor tree represent?

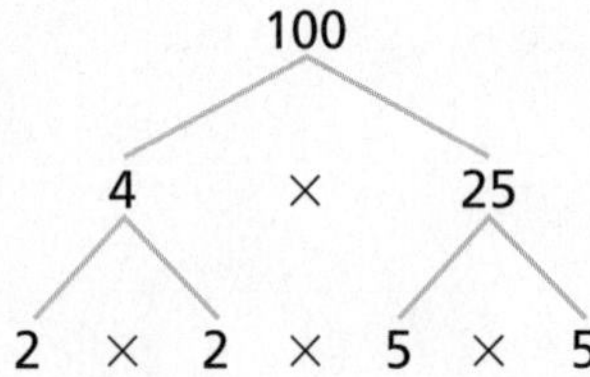

Common Core State Standards

6.NS.B.4 Find the greatest common factor of two whole numbers less than or equal to 100 and the least common multiple of two whole numbers less than or equal to 12 . . .

6.EE.A.1 Write and evaluate numerical expressions involving whole-number exponents.

6.EE.A.2b Identify parts of an expression using mathematical terms (sum, term, product, factor, quotient, coefficient); view one or more parts of an expression as a single entity.

3.1 The Product Puzzle: Finding Factor Strings

In the Product Puzzle, you look for strings of factors with a product of 840. Two factor strings are marked in the puzzle shown.

The Product Puzzle

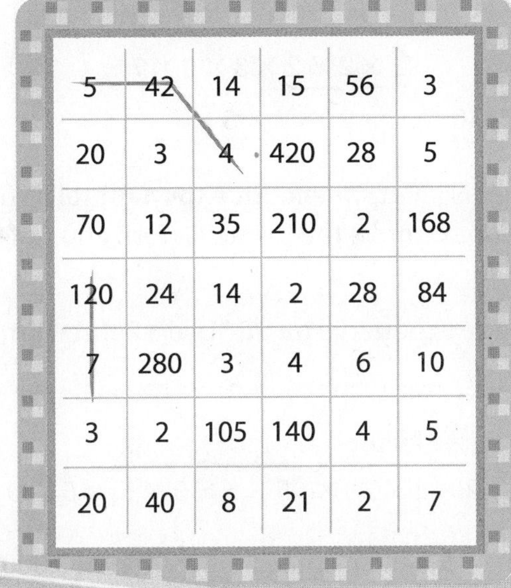

5	42	14	15	56	3
20	3	4	420	28	5
70	12	35	210	2	168
120	24	14	2	28	84
7	280	3	4	6	10
3	2	105	140	4	5
20	40	8	21	2	7

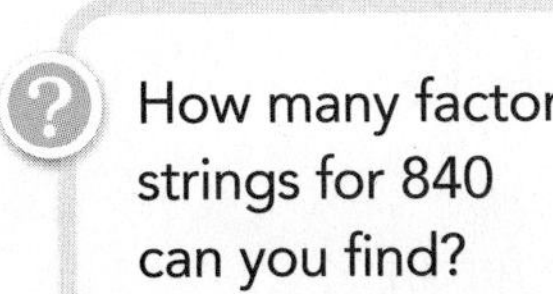

Problem 3.1

A Make a list of the factor strings for 840 in the Product Puzzle. Order the strings by the number of factors.

B Choose a factor string for 840 with two factors. How can you use this string to find a factor string with three factors?

C
1. What is the longest factor string on your list? Is there a longer factor string? Explain.
2. How do you know when you have found the longest string of factors for a number?
3. Strings of factors are different if they differ in a way other than the order of the factors. How many different longest strings of factors are there for 840?

Homework starts on page 54.

3.2 Finding the Longest Factor String

Strings of factors are called **factorizations**. The longest possible factor string for 840 is made up of prime numbers. This string is the **prime factorization** of 840.

You can use a shorthand notation to write prime factorizations. For example,

$$840 = \underbrace{2 \times 2 \times 2}_{2^3} \times 3 \times 5 \times 7$$

$$840 = 2^3 \times 3 \times 5 \times 7$$

The small raised number is an *exponent*. An **exponent** tells you how many times a factor is used. For example, the prime factorization of 840 uses the number 2 three times.

In the product $2^3 \times 5^4$, the exponents mean "Use a 2 three times as a factor and use a 5 four times."

$$2^3 \times 5^4 = \overbrace{2 \times 2 \times 2}^{\text{three factors}} \times \overbrace{5 \times 5 \times 5 \times 5}^{\text{four factors}} = 5{,}000$$

This means that you can write the prime factorization of 5,000 in two ways:

$5{,}000 = 2 \times 2 \times 2 \times 5 \times 5 \times 5 \times 5$	Expanded Form
$= 2^3 \times 5^4$	Exponential Form

You can read some exponents more than one way.

Example	Ways To Read
3^2	"3 to the second power" *or* "3 squared"
5^3	"5 to the third power" *or* "5 cubed"
2^4	"2 to the fourth power" *or* "2 to the power of four"

In this Problem, you will find the prime factorizations of numbers. You will use the factorizations to answer questions about factors and multiples.

Problem 3.2

A 1. Find the prime factorizations of 36. Write the prime factorization using exponents.

2. Choose a factor pair of 36. Show how this factor pair can be found in the prime factorization of 36.

3. How can you use the prime factorization to find the other factor pairs of 36?

4. Use the prime factorization of 36 to find all of its factors.

5. Find a multiple of 36. What does the prime factorization of this multiple have in common with the prime factorization of 36?

B 1. Write the prime factorization of each number below using exponents.

a. 10 b. 100 c. 1,000 d. 10,000

2. The numbers 10; 100; 1,000; and 10,000 can be written as *powers of 10.*

$10 = 10^1$ $100 = 10^2$ $1{,}000 = 10^3$ $10{,}000 = 10^4$

How can you use the prime factorization of the powers of 10 to find the prime factorization of 270,000?

C 1. The prime factorization of a number is $2^4 \times 3^2 \times 5$. What is the number?

2. Is $2^2 \times 3$ a factor of the number? Explain.

3. Mari claims that $2^5 \times 3^2 \times 5$ is a multiple of the number. Is she correct? Explain.

D Which expressions below are equal to each other? Solve without computing the actual product.

$2 \times 5^2 \times 6 \times 11 \times 12$ $3 \times 11 \times 25 \times 44$

$5 \times 12^2 \times 55$ $5 \times 10 \times 22 \times 33$

E How many unique prime factorizations of a number are there? Explain.

ACE Homework starts on page 54.

3.3 Using Prime Factorizations

Sasha and Derrick are looking for the GCF of 24 and 60. Sasha likes using lists to find common factors. Derrick prefers using prime factorization.

Sasha's Method

List all of the factors for each number.

24: 1, 2, 3, 4, 6, 8, 12, 24

60: 1, 2, 3, 4, 5, 6, 10, 12, 15, 20, 30, 60.

List all of the factors both numbers have in common.

1, 2, 3, 4, 6, 12

↑

12 is the GCF.

Derrick's Method

Write the prime factorization of each number.

$24 = 2 \times 2 \times 2 \times 3$

$60 = 2 \times 2 \times 3 \times 5$

Find the longest factor string that both numbers have in common.

$24 = 2 \times 2 \times 2 \times 3$

$60 = 2 \times 2 \times 3 \times 5$

So $2 \times 2 \times 3$, or 12, is the GCF.

- Is each student correct? Explain.
- Will the methods work for any two numbers? Why or why not?

Both students use similar methods to find the LCM of 24 and 60.

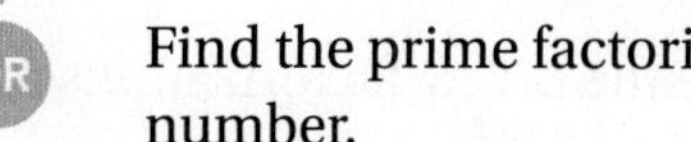

Sasha's Method

List the multiples of each number until you find a common multiple.

24: 24, 48, 72, 96, 120

↑

60: 60, 120

The LCM of 24 and 60 is 120.

OR

Derrick's Method

Find the prime factorization of each number.

$24 = 2 \times 2 \times 2 \times 3$

$60 = 2 \times 2 \times 3 \times 5$

The LCM is the shortest factor string that contains both $2 \times 2 \times 2 \times 3$ and $2 \times 2 \times 3 \times 5$.

The short string $2 \times 2 \times 3$ occurs within both factor strings for 24 and 60. So, we do not have to include this short string twice in the LCM.

$24 = 2 \times 2 \times 2 \times 3$

$60 = 2 \times 2 \times 3 \times 5$

Because the LCM should not repeat any unnecessary factors, I need at most three 2's and one 3 and one 5.

So $2 \times 2 \times 2 \times 3 \times 5$, or 120, is the shortest string.

120 is the LCM of 24 and 60.

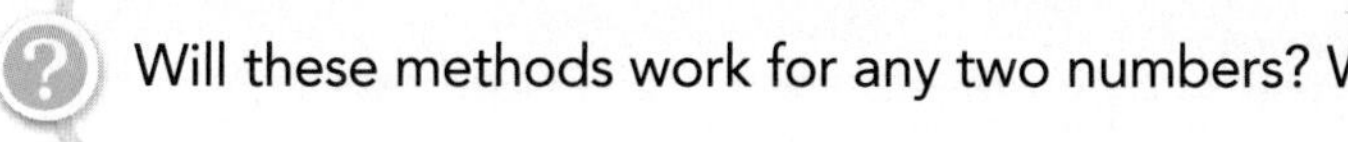

Will these methods work for any two numbers? Why or why not?

Problem 3.3

A
1. Use the prime factorizations of 72 and 120 to find their GCF.
2. Use the prime factorizations of 72 and 120 to find their LCM.

B The GCF of 25 and 12 is 1. Numbers with 1 as the GCF are called **relatively prime.**
1. Find another pair of numbers whose GCF is 1.
2. How can you determine whether the GCF of two numbers is 1 by looking at their prime factorizations?

C
1. Find two pairs of numbers whose LCM is the product of the numbers.
2. Find two pairs of numbers whose LCM is less than the product of the numbers.
3. How can you determine whether the LCM of two numbers is the product of the numbers or is less than the product of the numbers? Explain.

D The prime factorization of a number is $2 \times 5 \times 3^2$.
1. Find two numbers whose LCM is this number.
2. Find two numbers whose GCF is this number.

ACE Homework starts on page 54.

Did You Know?

In mathematics, there are a few relationships so basic that they are called *fundamental theorems.* Among these are the Fundamental Theorem of Calculus, the Fundamental Theorem of Algebra, and one you have found, the Fundamental Theorem of Arithmetic. The Fundamental Theorem of Arithmetic states that every whole number greater than 1 has exactly one prime factorization. (Writing factors in a different order is the same prime factorization.)

3.4 Unraveling the Locker Problem: Putting It All Together

There are 1,000 lockers along a long hall of Westfalls High. The lockers are numbered from 1 to 1,000. When the 1,000 Westfalls High students return from summer vacation, they decide to celebrate the beginning of the school year by working off some energy.

The first student, Student 1, runs down the row of lockers and opens every locker door.

Student 2 closes the doors of Lockers 2, 4, 6, 8, and so on, to the end of the line.

Student 3 *changes the state* of the doors of Lockers 3, 6, 9, 12, and so on, to the end of the line. (*Changes the state* means the student opens the locker door if it is closed and closes the door if it is open.)

Student 4 changes the state of the doors of Lockers 4, 8, 12, 16, and so on.

Student 5 changes the state of every fifth door.

Student 6 changes the state of every sixth door.

This pattern continues until all 1,000 students have had a turn.

When all 1,000 students have finished, which locker doors are open?

Did You Know?

George Polya, a famous mathematician, wrote a book about problem-solving strategies titled *How to Solve It*. He suggests that if you can't solve a problem right away, you might first try to solve a related problem or a simplified version of the problem so that you can look for patterns and strategies to help you. He also suggests drawing pictures. Professor Polya solved some very complicated math problems that way.

Problem 3.4

Use what you learned so far in this Unit to answer these questions.

A Model the Locker Problem for the first 30 students and the first 30 lockers.

1. What patterns do you see as the students put their plan into action?
2. When the 30 students are finished, which locker doors are open? Explain why your answer makes sense. What kind of numbers are these?
3. When the 1,000 students are finished opening and closing the 1,000 lockers, which locker doors are open? Explain why your answer makes sense. What kind of numbers are these?

B

1. Which lockers were touched by exactly two students? Give at least 3 examples. What kind of numbers are these?
2. Which lockers were touched by exactly three students? Give at least 3 examples. What kind of numbers are these?
3. Which lockers were touched by exactly four students?
4. How can you determine exactly how many students have touched a given locker?

C For Questions 1–4, find the number of the first locker touched by both students.

1. Student 6 and Student 8
2. Student 12 and Student 30
3. Student 7 and Student 13
4. Student 100 and Student 120
5. Given two student numbers, how can you determine which locker will be the first locker touched by both students? How can you determine which locker will be the last touched by both students?

D

1. Which students touched both Locker 24 and Locker 36?
2. Which students touched both Locker 100 and Locker 120?
3. Which students touched both Locker 42 and Locker 273?
4. Given two lockers, how can you determine which students touched both?

ACE Homework starts on page 54.

ACE Applications | Connections | Extensions

Applications

To solve a multiplication maze, find a path of numbers from the entrance to the exit so that the product of the numbers equals the puzzle number. No diagonal moves are allowed. Below is the solution of a multiplication maze for 840.

Multiplication Maze 840

For Exercises 1–2, solve each multiplication maze. *Hint:* It may help to find the longest factor string for the puzzle number.

1. **Multiplication Maze 840**

2. **Multiplication Maze 360**

3. Make a multiplication maze for 720. Be sure to record your solution.

4. Mr. Rawlings has 60 cookies. He wants to give each of his 16 grandchildren the same number of cookies. What is the greatest number of whole cookies he can give each child? After he gives his grandchildren their cookies, how many cookies will he have left?

For Exercises 5–13, write the prime factorization of each number in expanded form.

5. 36 **6.** 180 **7.** 525

8. 165 **9.** 293 **10.** 760

11. 216 **12.** 231 **13.** 312

14. Use exponents to rewrite the prime factorizations in Exercises 5–13.

15. **Multiple Choice** What is the prime factorization of 240?

A. 10×24 B. $2 \times 3 \times 5$ C. $2^3 \times 3 \times 5$ D. $2^4 \times 3 \times 5$

16. Jill and Jamahl are comparing their favorite numbers. Jill's number has a prime factorization with six numbers. Jamahl's number has a prime factorization with only three numbers. Jill says this means her number is greater than Jamahl's. Jamahl says that is not necessarily true. Who is correct? Explain.

17. Find all of the numbers less than 100 that have at least one 2 and at least one 5 in their prime factorization. What do you notice about these numbers?

18. **Multiple Choice** Choose the number that is the product of exactly three different prime numbers.

F. 15 G. 20 H. 30 J. 57

19. Find all of the numbers less than 100 that are the product of exactly three different prime numbers.

20. Mr. and Mrs. Fisk have 8 children. Each of those children has 8 children.

   a. How many grandchildren do Mr. and Mrs. Fisk have?

   b. Each grandchild has 8 children. How many great-grandchildren do Mr. and Mrs. Fisk have?

   c. Write an expression with exponents to represent the number of great-grandchildren Mr. and Mrs. Fisk have.

For Exercises 21–26, find the GCF and the LCM of each pair of numbers.

21. 36 and 45 22. 30 and 75 23. 78 and 104

24. 15 and 60 25. 32 and 45 26. 37 and 12

27. a. 180 is the LCM of 12 and a number, N. What are possible values of N?

   b. 14 is the GCF of a number M and 210. What are possible values of M?

For Exercises 28–30, refer to Problem 3.4.

28. Give the numbers of the lockers that were touched by exactly five students.

29. For each part below, find the number of the first locker touched by both students.

a. Student 3 and Student 5

b. Student 12 and Student 20

c. Student 72 and Student 84

d. Student 210 and Student 315

30. For each part below, find the numbers of the students who touched both lockers.

a. Both Locker 13 and Locker 81

b. Both Locker 140 and Locker 210

c. Both Locker 165 and Locker 330

d. Both Locker 196 and Locker 294

Connections

31. Rosa claims the longest string of prime factors for 30 is $2 \times 3 \times 5$. Tyee claims there is a longer string, $1 \times 2 \times 1 \times 3 \times 1 \times 5$. Who is correct? Why?

32. The number 1 is not prime. Why do you think mathematicians decided not to call 1 a prime number?

33. How many factors do each of the following numbers have?

a. 100 **b.** 101 **c.** 102 **d.** 103

e. What patterns do you notice in the factors of these numbers?

For Exercises 34–35, describe the numbers that have both of the given numbers as factors.

34. 2 and 3

35. 3 and 5

36. Suppose 10 and 6 are common factors of two numbers. What other factors must the numbers have in common? Explain.

37. a. Find the multiples of 9 that are less than 100.

    b. Find the multiples of 21 that are less than 100.

    c. Find the common multiples of 9 and 21 that are less than 100.

    d. What is the next common multiple of 9 and 21?

38. Tomas and Sharlina work on weekends and holidays doing odd jobs around the neighborhood. They are paid by the day, not by the hour. They each earn the same whole number of dollars per day. Last month Tomas earned \$184, and Sharlina earned \$207. How many days did each person work? What is their daily pay?

39. Write a mathematical story about the number 648. For example, you might describe its factors and its multiples. You might also give some examples of its relationship to other numbers. Use at least five vocabulary words from this Unit in your story.

40. What is the least prime number greater than 50?

41. Ivan said that if a number ends in 0, both 2 and 5 are factors of the number. Is he correct? Why or why not?

42. What is my number?

    Clue 1 My number is a multiple of 2 and 7.

    Clue 2 My number is less than 100 but greater than 50.

    Clue 3 My number is the product of three different prime numbers.

43. What is my number?

    Clue 1 My number is a perfect square.

    Clue 2 The only prime number in its prime factorization is 2.

    Clue 3 My number is a factor of 32.

    Clue 4 The sum of its digits is odd.

44. What is my number?

Clue 1 My number is a multiple of 5 and is less than 50.

Clue 2 My number is a multiple of 3.

Clue 3 My number has exactly 8 factors.

45. What is my number?

Clue 1 My number is a multiple of 5, but it does not end in 5.

Clue 2 The prime factorization of my number is a string of three numbers.

Clue 3 Two of the numbers in the prime factorization are the same.

Clue 4 My number is greater than the seventh square number.

46. Now it's your turn! Make up a set of clues for a mystery number. You might want to use your favorite number as the mystery number. Include as many ideas from this Unit as you can. Try out your clues on a classmate.

47. There are 50 lockers, numbered 1 through 50, in a short hall at Phillips Middle School. Mr. Giannetti hid treats for his class in one of the lockers. He gave the class the following clues about the locker where the treats are located.

Clue 1 The number is even.

Clue 2 The number is divisible by 3.

Clue 3 The number is a multiple of Mr. Giannetti's lucky number, 7.

In which locker are the treats located?

48. **a.** Find all of the numbers between 1 and 1,000 that have 2 as their only prime factor.

b. What is the next number after 1,000 that has 2 as its only prime factor?

49. The numbers 2 and 3 are *prime numbers*. They are also *consecutive numbers*. Are there other pairs of primes that are consecutive numbers? Why or why not?

50. Which group of numbers, *evens* or *odds*, includes more prime numbers? Why?

Extensions

51. For each part below, use your birth year or the birth year of one of your family members.

a. Find the prime factorization of the birth year.

b. Describe the number to a friend with as much information as you can about it. Here are some ideas to include: Is the number *square, prime, even,* or *odd*? How many *factors* does it have? Is it a *multiple* of some other number?

52. Most years have 365 days, but certain years, called *leap years,* have 366 days. Leap years occur in years divisible by 4, with some exceptions. Years divisible by 100 are *not* leap years, unless they are also divisible by 400. So 1896 was a leap year, but 1900 wasn't. The years 1996, 2000, 2004, 2008, and 2012 were all leap years.

a. A week has 7 days. How many weeks are in each type of year?

b. January 1, 2012, fell on a Sunday. On what dates did the next three Sundays of 2012 occur?

c. What day of the week was January 30, 2012?

d. The year 2012 was a leap year. It had 366 days. What day of the week was January 1, 2013?

e. Find the pattern, over several years, for the days of the week on which your birthday falls.

53. The Greek mathematician Euclid first stated the Fundamental Theorem of Arithmetic. He wrote:

"If a number is the least that is measured by prime numbers, it will not be measured by any prime except those originally measuring it."

What do you suppose Euclid meant?

54. Mr. Barkley has a box of books. He says the number of books in the box is divisible by 2, 3, 4, 5, and 6. How many books could be in the box? Add another condition to the number of books so that there is only one possible solution.

55. a. Barry practiced finding the LCM and GCF by completing the table below. He knows that the LCM is never greater than the product, so he completed the *Product* column to check the reasonableness of his answers.

Numbers	Product	LCM	GCF
10, 15	150	30	5
8, 12	96	24	4
3, 12	36	12	3
9, 10	90	90	1

Barry noticed that he could divide the product by the GCF to find the LCM. He wondered if this was always true. Is Barry's idea always true? Explain. If it is not always true, find a counterexample. If it is always true, explain why it works.

b. What other patterns do you see?

56. David thinks he has a way to predict the number of factors of any number. He writes the prime factorization using exponents and then adds 1 to each exponent. Then he finds the product of these numbers.

Example: $40 = 2^3 \times 5^1$ The exponents are 3 and 1, so multiply $(3 + 1)$ and $(1 + 1)$.

$4 \times 2 = 8$ 40 has 8 factors.

Will David's method work for any number? If so, why? If his method does not work for every number, find a counterexample.

Mathematical Reflections 3

In this Investigation, you found factor strings for numbers, and you saw how you could use the prime factorizations of numbers to find common factors and multiples. The following questions will help you summarize what you have learned.

Think about these questions. Discuss your ideas with other students and your teacher. Then write a summary of your findings in your notebook.

1. a. **Why** is it helpful to write a number as a product of primes?
   b. **Describe** how you can find the prime factorization of a number.
2. a. **When** is it useful to find the LCM or GCF of two or more numbers to solve a problem?
   b. **Describe** a method for finding the LCM of two numbers. Is there another method? Explain.
   c. **Describe** a method for finding the GCF of two numbers. Is there another method? Explain.

Unit Project

Don't forget your favorite number!

What is the prime factorization of your favorite number?

Common Core Mathematical Practices

As you worked on the Problems in this Investigation, you used prior knowledge to make sense of them. You also applied Mathematical Practices to solve the Problems. Think back over your work, the ways you thought about the Problems, and how you used Mathematical Practices.

Nick described his thoughts in the following way:

We think both Sasha and Derrick's method in Problem 3.3 of two numbers work.

In Sasha's method, you list all the factors of each number. Then look for the factors that are common to both sets. The greatest of these common factors is the GCF.

Derrick's method also works since the prime factorization of the GCF must have the largest string of prime factors that is common to the prime factorizations of each number. I like Sasha's method, but my partner prefers Derrick's method.

Common Core Standards for Mathematical Practice

MP3 Construct viable arguments and critique the reasoning of others

- What other Mathematical Practices can you identify in Nick's reasoning?
- Describe a Mathematical Practice that you and your classmates used to solve a different Problem in this Investigation.

Linking Multiplication and Addition: The Distributive Property

Note on Notation You can write a product using a "times sign," as in $12 = 2 \times 6$. You can also show a product with a "raised dot" or with parentheses.

$$12 = 2 \times 6 = 2 \cdot 6 = 2(6)$$

The parentheses mean that the amount inside the parentheses is multiplied by the amount outside the parentheses.

In this unit, you have studied factors and multiples. For example, 12 can be written as the product of two or more numbers, called *factors* of 12. 12 is also a *multiple* of its factors.

Sometimes, you can use an expression as a factor. A **numerical expression** combines numbers using one or more mathematical operations.

$$12 = 2(5 + 1)$$

This example shows the product of 2 and the expression $5 + 1$.

You can also write numbers as the sum of two or more numbers.

$$12 = 10 + 2 \quad \text{or} \quad 12 = 5 + 7 \quad \text{or} \quad 12 = 3 + 4 + 5$$

The expressions 12, $2 \cdot 6$, $10 + 2$, $5 + 7$, $3 + 4 + 5$, and $2(5 + 1)$ are **equivalent expressions.** They have the same numerical value.

You will learn how multiplication and addition are related.

Common Core State Standards

6.NS.B.4 Find the greatest common factor of two whole numbers less than or equal to 100 and the least common multiple of two whole numbers less than or equal to 12. Use the distributive property to express a sum of two whole numbers 1–100 with a common factor as a multiple of a sum of two whole numbers with no common factor.

6.EE.A.1 Write and evaluate numerical expressions involving whole-number exponents.

6.EE.A.2b Identify parts of an expression using mathematical terms (sum, term, product, factor, quotient, coefficient); view one or more parts of an expression as a single entity.

4.1 Reasoning With Even and Odd Numbers

In this Problem you will work with odd and even numbers. An **odd number** is a number that does *not* have 2 as a factor. *Even numbers* are defined in two ways:

- An **even number** is a *multiple of 2*. This definition talks about the number of groups of 2 that make up a given even number.

$$\underbrace{10 = 2 + 2 + 2 + 2 + 2}_{\text{five groups of 2}} \quad \text{or} \quad 10 = 5 \times 2$$

- An **even number** has *2 as a factor*. It is *divisible by 2*. This definition talks about dividing an even number into two equal groups.

$$10 \div 2 = 5 \quad \text{or} \quad \underbrace{10 = 2 \times 5}_{\text{2 is a factor of 10.}} \quad \text{or} \quad 10 = 5 + 5$$

If you represented the even number 10 with square tiles, it might look like this:

You can see the two different definitions of *even number* by rearranging the tiles:

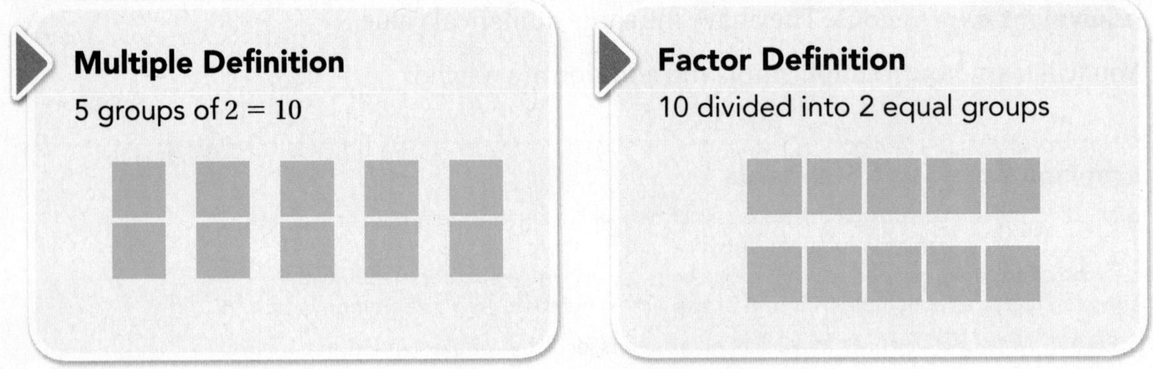

Lila wanted to know more about even and odd numbers. She arranged square tiles in a pattern to make models for whole numbers. Lila's tile models for the numbers from 1 to 7 look like this:

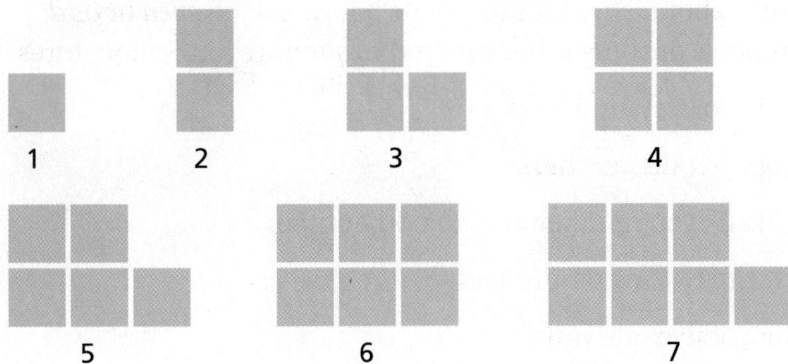

- Which numbers are even? Which numbers are odd?
- How are the models for even numbers different from the models for odd numbers?
- Describe what the models for 50 and 99 would look like.

When you predict what you think will happen in a mathematical situation, you are making a *conjecture*. A **conjecture** is your best guess about an observed pattern or relationship. You can use models, drawings, or other kinds of evidence to support your conjectures.

Make a conjecture about what happens when you add two even numbers. Do you get an even number or an odd number? Explain.

Problem 4.1 asks you to make several conjectures about even and odd numbers.

Problem 4.1

A Make conjectures about whether the results below will be *even* or *odd*. Then use tile models or some other method to support your conjectures.

1. the sum of two even numbers
2. the sum of two odd numbers
3. the sum of an even number and an odd number
4. the product of two even numbers
5. the product of two odd numbers
6. the product of an even number and an odd number

B How can you determine whether a sum of numbers, such as 127 + 38, is even or odd without building a tile model or computing the sum?

C Is 0 an even number or an odd number? How do you know?

ACE Homework starts on page 75.

4.2 Using the Distributive Property

Lila made the conjecture that the sum of two even numbers is an even number. She used square tiles to show why the sum of two even numbers is always even.

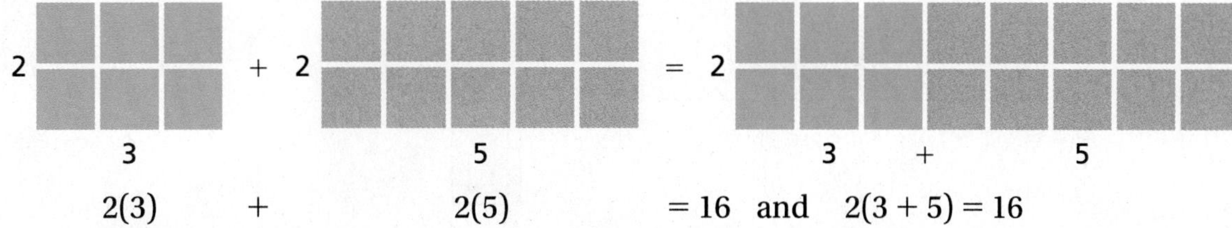

2(3) + 2(5) = 16 and 2(3 + 5) = 16

Alex wondered if this means that 2(3) + 2(5) = 2(3 + 5).

- What do you think? Are Lila and Alex correct? Explain why or why not.

Lila's picture represents an important property of numbers called the *Distributive Property*. The **Distributive Property** connects the operations of addition and multiplication.

2(3) + 2(5) = 2(3 + 5) = 16

sum of two terms — product of two factors

You can write the number 16 as a sum of two quantities, 6 and 10. You can also write the number 16 as the sum of two other quantities, 2(3) and 2(5).

$$16 = 6 + 10 = 2(3) + 2(5)$$

You can write the number 16 as a product of two factors, 2 and 8. You can also write 16 as the product of two other factors, 2 and (3 + 5).

$$16 = 2(8) = 2(3 + 5)$$

The expressions 2(3) + 2(5) and 2(3 + 5) are equivalent expressions.

$$2(3) + 2(5) = 2(3 + 5)$$

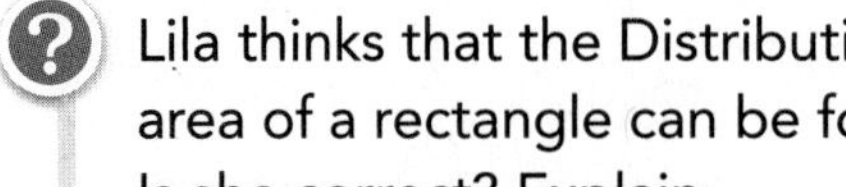

Lila thinks that the Distributive Property explains how the area of a rectangle can be found in two different ways. Is she correct? Explain.

Problem 4.2

A In each diagram below, a large rectangle has been made from two smaller rectangles. In each case, show two different ways to calculate the area of the large rectangle.

1. 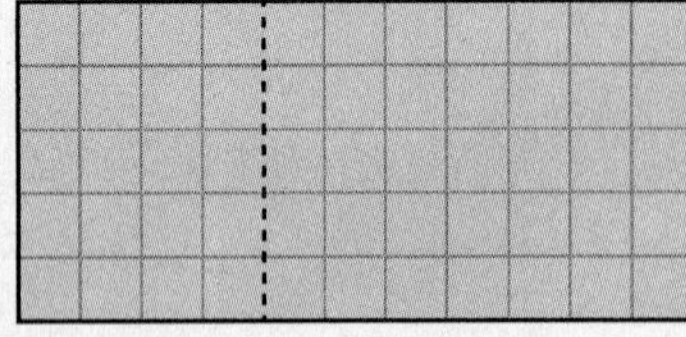

2. 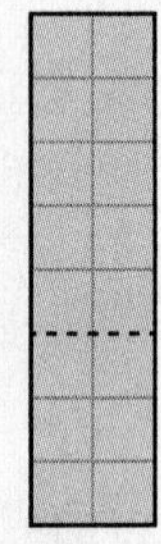

3. 

4. 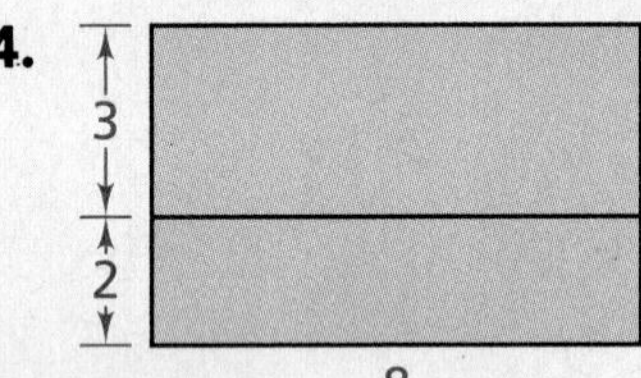

B A large rectangle has an area of 28 square units. It has been divided into two smaller rectangles. One of the smaller rectangles has an area of 4 square units. What are possible whole-number dimensions of the large rectangle? Justify your reasoning.

4
square
units

continued on the next page >

Problem 4.2 continued

C Each of the following numerical expressions represents the area of a rectangle that has been divided into two smaller rectangular pieces. For each expression,

- sketch a rectangle whose area can be represented by the expression.
- write an equivalent expression for the area of the original rectangle.

1. $6(5 + 9)$
2. $4(7) + 4(3)$

D Mrs. Johnson's and Mr. Wei's classes are participating in the Meridian School arts and crafts exhibit. Their spaces will be next to each other. Mrs. Johnson's space will be longer, but it will have the same width as Mr. Wei's space. Ms. Johnson has 48 carpet squares. Mr. Wei has 36 carpet squares.

Mr. Wei's space	Mrs. Johnson's space

1. Use the Distributive Property to find the possible whole-number dimension of the classes' total exhibition space. Explain what each number means in your expressions.
2. What is the greatest width that their exhibition space can have? What is the corresponding depth/length? Which expression represents these dimensions?
3. What is the length of each class's space if you use the greatest width? Do these lengths have any common factors? Explain.
4. Mr. Casey writes the equation $40 = 16 + 24 = a(b + c)$. What whole numbers can he choose for a, b, and c if he wants b and c to have no common factors greater than 1?

continued on the next page >

Problem 4.2 continued

E You can use the area of a rectangle, the Distributive Property, and what you know about place value to find products.

1. Explain how you can use the diagram to find the product 8×27. How does this process represent the Distributive Property?

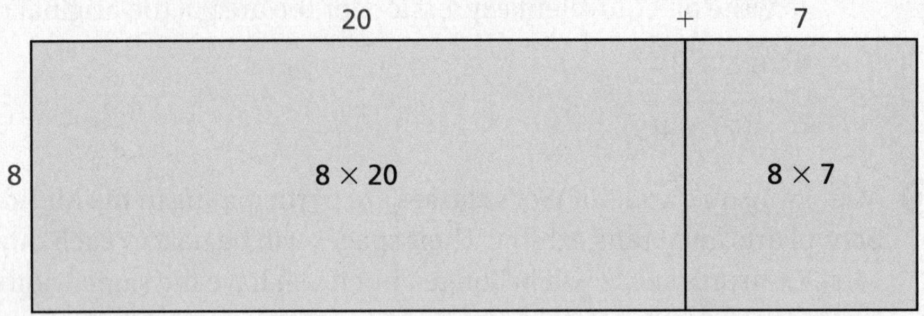

2. Explain how the diagram and the Distributive Property show a way to find the product 32×24.

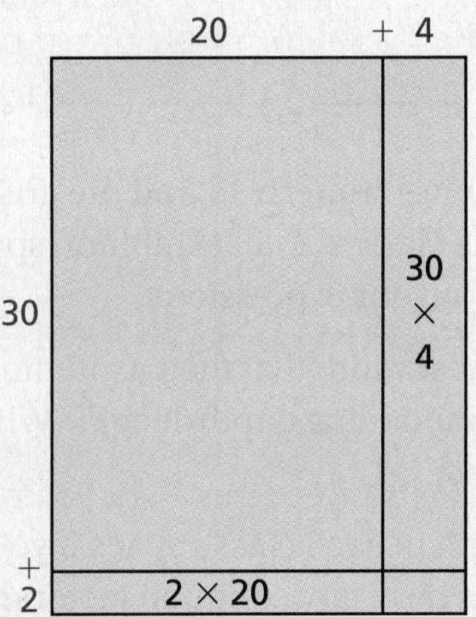

a. Find the missing areas.

b. Write two expressions to find the product 32×24. Simplify the expressions.

c. Explain how finding the area of the rectangle in two different ways is related to the algorithm for finding the product 32×24.

3. How is finding the area of a rectangle related to the Distributive Property?

ACE Homework starts on page 75.

4.3 Ordering Operations

Note on Notation When you multiply a number by a letter variable, you can leave out the multiplication sign or parentheses. So, $3n$ means $3 \times n$ or $3(n)$. This is also true for a product with more than one letter variable. So, ab means $a \times b$ or $a(b)$.

The Distributive Property can be useful when solving problems. The Distributive Property states that if a, b, and c are any numbers, then

$$a(b + c) = a(b) + a(c)$$

- A number can be expressed as both a product and a sum.
- The area of a rectangle can be found in two different ways.

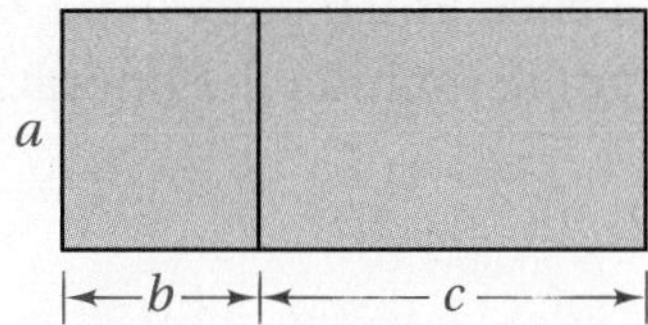

The expression $a(b + c)$ is in **factored form**. The expression $a(b) + a(c)$ is in **expanded form**. The two expressions $a(b + c)$ and $a(b) + a(c)$ are equivalent expressions.

$$\underline{a}(\underline{b + c}) = a(b) + a(c) = \underline{ab} + \underline{ac}$$

factored form (product of two factors) — expanded form (sum of two terms)

In addition to using the Distributive Property, there needs to be an agreement as to which operation should be done first in an expression. In evaluating the expression $3 + 4 \times 6$, Mary thinks you get 42 and Hank thinks you get 27. Who is correct?

Mathematicians know that some numerical situations might be interpreted in more than one way. Therefore, they agreed on an order for simplifying expressions called the **Order of Operations**. When an expression includes more than one operation, you simplify it by following these steps.

1. Work within parentheses.
2. Write numbers written with exponents in standard form.
3. Do all multiplication and division in order from left to right.
4. Do all addition and subtraction in order from left to right.

- Using the Order of Operations, what is $3 + 2(5 + 4)$?

Problem 4.3

A 1. Jenn bought 12 pens for \$2 each and 6 pads of paper for \$3 each. She was in a hurry and forgot to include the operations. She wrote

12 2 6 3

Place parentheses and operation signs to write an expression for the total cost of Jenn's purchase. How much did she spend?

2. Nic bought 12 pens for \$2 each and 12 pads of paper for \$3 each. Write two expressions for how Nic could calculate his total. Write one expression in expanded form and one in factored form.

3. Can Jenn write two expressions for her calculation? Explain.

B Without changing the order of the numbers, how many different numbers can you find by inserting parentheses and/or addition signs between the numbers below? For example, $2(5) + 1 + 3 = 14$.

2 5 1 3

continued on the next page >

Problem 4.3 continued

C Simplify each expression below. Compare your answers with your classmates' answers.

1. $3 + 5 \times 2 + 4$
2. $3 + 5(2 + 4)$
3. $4 + (3 + 7) \div 2 - 2(4)$
4. $3^3 + 5(2 + 3) - 25$
5. $2 + 5^3 \times 10$
6. $4 \div 4 + 7^2$

D When simplifying the expression $3 + 5(2 + 4)$, Kalia applied the Distributive Property first, and then performed the Order of Operations. She wrote,

$$\begin{aligned} 3 + 5(2 + 4) &= 3 + 5(2) + 5(4) \\ &= 3 + 10 + 20 \\ &= 33 \end{aligned}$$

Do you agree with Kalia? Explain.

ACE Homework starts on page 75.

4.4 Choosing an Operation

In Problem 4.3, you used the Distributive Property and the Order of Operations to solve problems. Before you can apply the Distributive Property or the Order of Operations, you need to identify which operations are needed to solve a problem. In Problem 4.4, you will first identify which operations you need. Then you can use what you have learned about the Distributive Property and the Order of Operations to answer the questions.

Problem 4.4

For each of the following situations,

- decide which operations are needed to solve the problem.
- write one or two expressions to represent each problem.
- use the Order of Operations to simplify your expression.
- explain your reasoning.

A Dan is selling fudge to raise money for the school band. Each box of fudge costs $8. One week he sells 15 boxes, and the next week he sells 17 boxes. How much money has Dan made at the end of the two weeks?

B An American football team is on their own 35-yard line. They lose 5 yards on each of the next three plays. At what yard line are they now?

C Leslie is in charge of packing snacks for her class. She has 30 cookies and 20 apples. She wants to put the same number of cookies and the same number of apples in each pack. What are the possible numbers of packs she can make? How many items are in each bag?

D The ferry between an island and the mainland makes one round trip a day. On Monday the ferry carried 83 people to the island and returned 114 people to the mainland. Compare the population of the island at the beginning of the day to the population after the ferry returned.

E Two student clubs plan to share a bus on a trip to the capital. Transportation and lunch for one day costs $12 per student. One club has 25 members and the other club has 18 members. What is the total cost of the trip?

ACE Homework starts on page 75.

Applications

For Exercises 1–4, make a conjecture about whether each result will be *odd* or *even*. Use models, pictures, or other reasoning to support your conjectures.

1. an even number minus an even number

2. an odd number minus an odd number

3. an even number minus an odd number

4. an odd number minus an even number

5. How can you tell whether a number is even or odd? Explain or illustrate your answer in at least two different ways.

6. How can you determine whether the sum of several numbers, such as $13 + 45 + 24 + 17$, is even or odd without actually calculating the sum?

For Exercises 7–9, write expressions for the area of each rectangle in two different ways. Then find the area using each expression.

7.

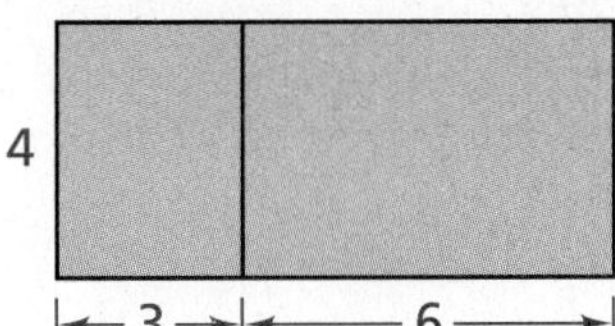

8.

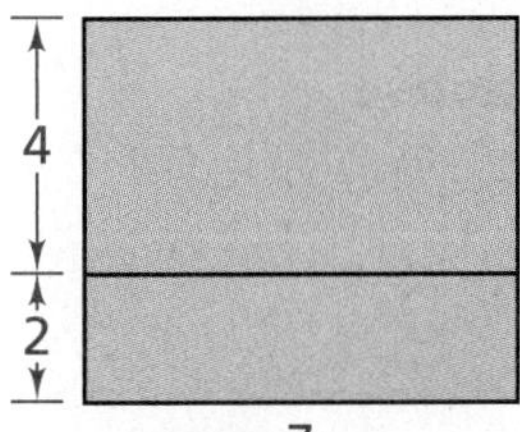

9.

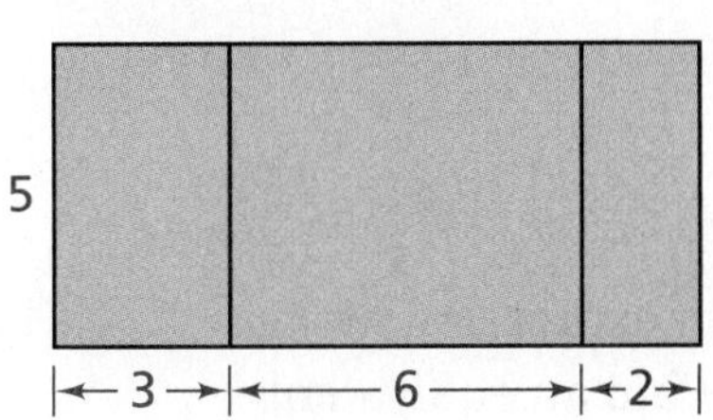

In Exercises 10–12, the dimensions of the rectangles are whole numbers. Find the area of the rectangle composed of the two smaller rectangles. Then find the dimensions of all three rectangles.

10.

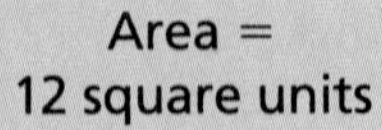

Area =
27 square units

11.

Area =
21 square units

Area =
28 square units

12.

Area =
30 square units

Area =
18 square units

For Exercises 13–16, draw a rectangle with the given width and length. Then use the Distributive Property to write each area as a product and as a sum.

13. 3 and $(4 + 6)$

14. 3 and $(5 + 1 + 3)$

15. N and $(2 + 6)$

16. 5 and $(N + 2)$

For Exercises 17–18, use the area of a rectangle and the Distributive Property to find each product.

17. 9×34

18. 35×18

19. **a.** Write 60 as the sum of two numbers.

b. Write 60 as the product of two numbers.

c. Write 60 as the product of two factors. In your expression, write one of the factors as a sum of two numbers. Find an equivalent way to write this expression.

20. **a.** $90 = 20 + 70$. Use the Distributive Property and the GCF of 20 and 70 to write another related expression for 90. Could you write another expression with a different common factor?

b. $90 = 36 + 54$. Use the Distributive Property and the GCF of 36 and 54 to write another related expression for 90. Could you write another expression with a different common factor?

21. Consider a 3-by-3 grid.

- Choose four numbers, such as 2, 8, 6, and 3. Write the numbers along the border of the grid as shown.

	6	3	Sum
2			
8			
Sum			

- Enter the product of the numbers into the corresponding cells.

	6	3	Sum
2	12	6	
8	48	24	
Sum			

- Add across the rows and columns.

	6	3	Sum
2	12	6	18
8	48	24	72
Sum	60	30	90

a. What is the relationship between the black number in the lower right-hand cell and the red numbers along the edges of the grid?

b. Start a new 3-by-3 grid. Pick another set of numbers for the border. Does the same relationship hold for the lower right-hand cell and the numbers along the edges? Explain.

c. Shalala claims she used the Distributive Property to show that the sum of the numbers in the bottom row was the same as the sum of the numbers in the last column. Do you agree? Explain.

For Exercises 22–23, use rectangles to show that each statement is true.

22. $3(7+2) = 3(7) + 3(2)$

23. $5(6) + 5(2) = 5(6+2)$

For Exercises 24–27, replace *m* with a whole number to make each statement true.

24. $7(4+m) = 49$

25. $8(m-3) = 56$

26. $m \cdot 10 - m \cdot 2 = 8$

27. $m \cdot 10 + m \cdot 13 = 138$

For Exercises 28–31, identify which expression has the greater value.

28.	$3 + 4 \cdot 2$	$(3+4) \cdot 2$
29.	$12 \div 6 \cdot 2$	$12 \div (6 \cdot 2)$
30.	$11 \cdot 2 + 1$	$16 - 5 \cdot 3$
31.	$4 \cdot 3^2$	$3^2 \cdot 3^2$

For Exercises 32–35, insert operation signs to make each equation true.

32. 2 ■ 5 ■ 3 = 17

33. 2 ■ 5 ■ 3 = 13

34. 2 ■ 5 ■ 3 = 30

35. 2 ■ 5 ■ 3 = 7

For Exercises 36–40, insert parentheses and/or addition signs to make each equation true. Remember that parentheses can indicate multiplication.

36. 3 2 4 1 = 9

37. 3 2 4 1 = 13

38. 3 2 4 1 = 21

39. 3 2 4 1 = 12

40. 3 2 4 1 = 10

41. Without changing the order of the numbers below, insert parentheses and/or addition signs so that the computation results in the number described below.

4 3 6 1

a. The number is a multiple of 5.

b. The number is a factor of 36.

42. Andrea thought about how she could rewrite numbers as products and sums in different ways. She came up with the following method.

	First, I find a factor pair of a number.
$36 = 3 \times 12$	3 and 12 are factors of 36.
$= 3 \times (5 + 7)$	Next, I rewrite one factor as a sum. 12 is the sum of 5 + 7.
$= (3 \times 5) + (3 \times 7)$	Next, I use the Distributive Property.
$= 15 + 21$	Last, I find the product in each pair of parentheses.

Use Andrea's method to rewrite each number in different ways.

a. 21 **b.** 24 **c.** 55 **d.** 48

Exercises 43–46 show Devin's work. Devin made some mistakes. Identify where he made each mistake. Then correct his work.

43.

$3^2 \times 2^2 - 3^3$

$= 6 \times 4 - 9$

$= 24 - 9$

$= 15$

44.

$8 + 2 \times 3^2$

$= 8 + 6^2$

$= 8 + 36$

$= 44$

45.

$18 - 6 + 2 \times 3$

$= 18 - 6 + 6$

$= 18 - 12$

$= 6$

46.

$24 \div 6 \times (5 - 1)$

$= 24 \div 6 \times 4$

$= 24 \div 24$

$= 1$

Exercises 47–49 list the steps of an arithmetic trick. Explain why each trick works.

47. **Step 1:** Think of a whole number.

Step 2: Add 15 to the number.

Step 3: Multiply the result by 2.

Step 4: Subtract 30.

The result is double the original number.

48. **Step 1:** Think of a number.

Step 2: Double it.

Step 3: Add 6.

Step 4: Divide by 2.

Step 5: Subtract 3.

The result is the original number.

49. **Step 1:** Think of a number.

Step 2: Add 4.

Step 3: Multiply by 2.

Step 4: Subtract 6.

Step 5: Divide by 2.

Step 6: Subtract the original number.

The result is 1.

For Exercises 50–51, find a number to make each statement true.

50. $12 \times (6 + 4) = (12 \times ■) + (12 \times 4)$

51. $2 \times (n + 4) = (■ \times n) + (■ \times 4)$

For Exercises 52–57, determine whether the number sentence is true. In each case explain how you could answer without calculating. Check your answers by doing the indicated calculations.

52. $50 \times 432 = (50 \times 400) + (50 \times 32)$

53. $50 \times 368 = (50 \times 400) - (50 \times 32)$

54. $50 \times 800 = (50 \times 1000) + (50 \times 200)$

55. $(70 \times 20) + (50 \times 20) = 90 \times 70$

56. $50 + (400 \times 32) = (50 + 400) \times (50 + 32)$

57. $6 \times 17 = 6 \times 20 - 6 \times 3$

58. Sophia used the Order of Operations to simplify $4(5 - 2)$ to 4×3. Jose used the Distributive Property to simplify $4(5 - 2)$ to $20 - 8$. Are they both correct? Explain.

59. **a.** Mr. and Mrs. Lee are adding a swing set to their backyard. Their yard measures $a \times b$ feet. The space for the swing set measures $a \times c$ feet. They want to figure out how much of their yard will be lawn after they add the swing set.

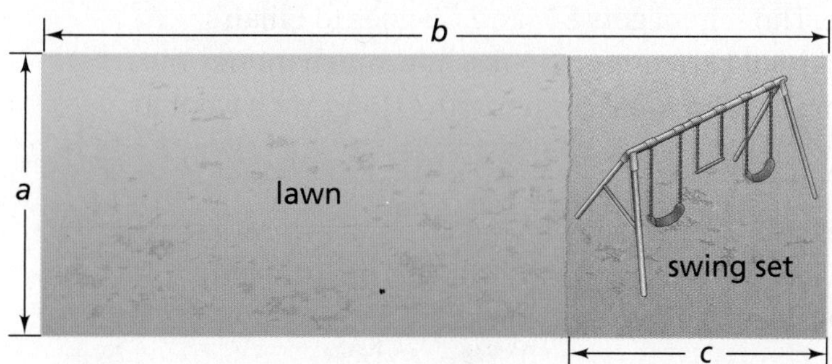

Mrs. Lee said, "The area of the whole yard is $a \times b$. The area for the swing set is $a \times c$. Therefore, the area of the lawn is $a \times b - a \times c$." Is she correct? Explain.

b. Mr. Lee said, "The length of the lawn is $b - c$. The width is a. I know that area = length × width. Therefore, the area of the lawn is $a \times (b - c)$." Is he correct? Explain.

60. The Distributive Property also applies to subtraction.

$$a(b - c) = ab - ac$$

Draw a rectangle to represent $7(10 - 1)$. Use the Distributive Property to write the expression in expanded form. Show that the two expressions are equivalent.

For Exercises 61–65, decide on the operation(s) needed to solve the problem. Then write a mathematical sentence, solve the problem, and explain your reasoning.

61. A pack of baseball cards has 12 trading cards and 2 stickers. In a box of 36 packs, how many stickers and how many trading cards are there?

62. A theater sells a combo pack of popcorn, a soft drink, and a movie ticket for \$12. For groups of five or greater, the theater gives a group discount of \$3 per person. What is the total cost for a class of 30 students?

63. Monday's high temperature was 5 degrees warmer than Sunday's high temperature. Tuesday's high temperature was 8 degrees colder than Monday's high temperature. How does Sunday's high temperature compare to Tuesday's?

64. Elijah is selling coupon books for a school fund-raiser. The coupon books sell for \$11. The school gets \$8, and \$3 goes to Elijah's homeroom. If Elijah sold 24 coupon books, how much money did he collect? How much went to his homeroom? How much went to the school?

65. Samantha charges \$15 to mow a lawn. Each week she mows 1 lawn on Tuesday, 3 lawns on Wednesday, and 2 lawns on Thursday. How much money does she earn in 4 weeks?

Connections

66. Multiple Choice What is my number?

Clue 1: My number has two digits, and each is even.

Clue 2: The sum of my number's digits is 10.

Clue 3: The difference of the two digits of my number is 6.

Clue 4: My number has 4 as a factor.

A. 28 **B.** 46 **C.** 64 **D.** 82

For Exercises 67–74, find the sum, difference, product, or quotient.

67. 50×70

68. 25×70

69. $2{,}200 \div 22$

70. 50×120

71. $39 + 899$

72. $4{,}400 - 1{,}200$

73. $9{,}900 \div 99$

74. $580 + 320$

75. Dot patterns can illustrate the Distributive Property. Write a number sentence suggested by the dot patterns below.

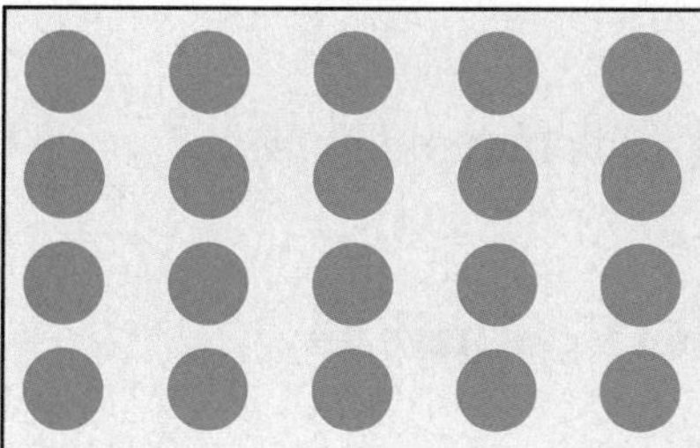

=

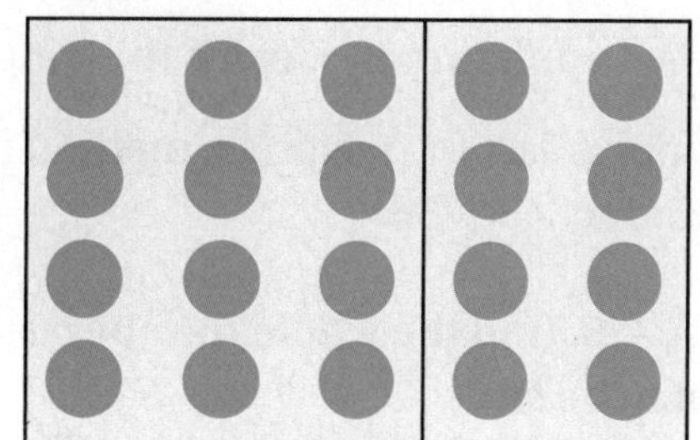

76. To multiply 32×12, Jim used the area of a rectangle.

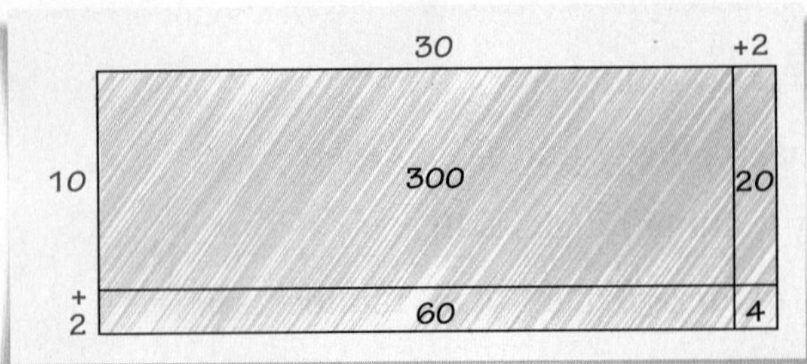

a. How does the diagram relate to finding the product shown below?

$$\begin{array}{r} 32 \\ \times\ 12 \\ \hline 64 \\ +\ 320 \\ \hline 384 \end{array}$$

b. Basilio computed 32×8.

$$32 \times 8 = 16 + 240$$
$$= 256$$

Draw a rectangle to model his thinking.

c. Use Jim's area-of-a-rectangle method and Basilio's method to find the product 45×36.

For Exercises 77–79, find the whole number values that n can have for each statement to be true.

77. $3(n + 2)$ is a multiple of 5.

78. $3(n + 2)$ is a factor of 24.

79. $4n + 6$ is a factor of 20.

Extensions

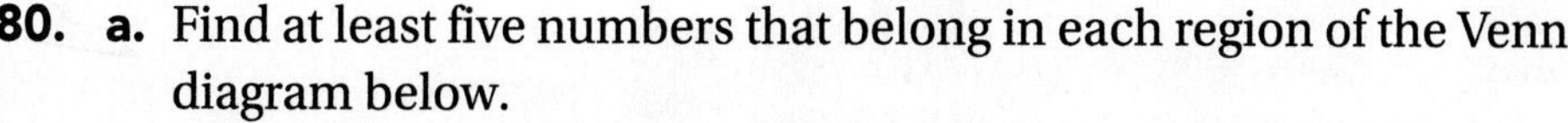

80. **a.** Find at least five numbers that belong in each region of the Venn diagram below.

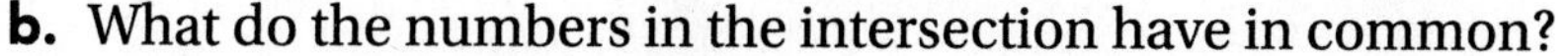

b. What do the numbers in the intersection have in common?

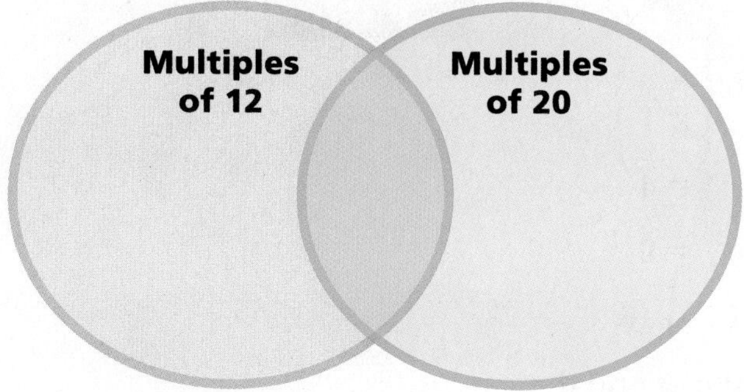

Consecutive numbers are whole numbers in sequence, such as 31, 32, 33 or 52, 53, 54. For Exercises 81–84, think of different consecutive numbers.

81. For any three consecutive numbers, what can you say about odd numbers and even numbers? Explain.

82. **a.** Mirari conjectures that, for any three consecutive numbers, one number would be divisible by 3. Do you think Mirari is correct? Explain.

b. Gia claims that the sum of any three consecutive whole numbers is divisible by 6. Is this true? Explain.

c. Kim claims that the product of any three consecutive whole numbers is divisible by 6. Is this true? Explain.

d. Does the product of any four consecutive whole numbers have any interesting properties? Explain.

83. How many consecutive numbers do you need to guarantee that one of the numbers is divisible by 5?

84. How many consecutive numbers do you need to guarantee that one of the numbers is divisible by 6?

85. Examine the number pattern below.

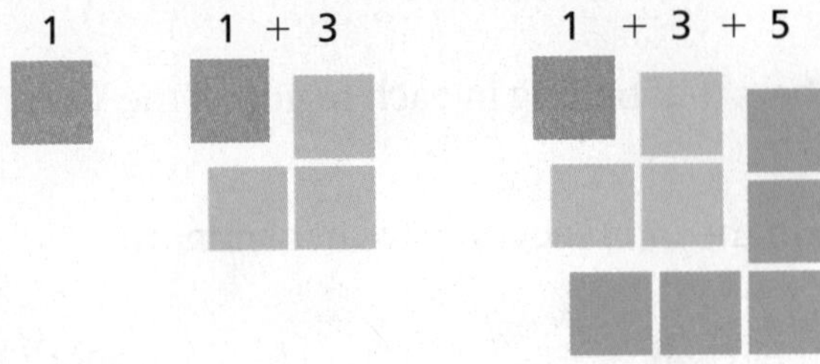

Stage 1: $1 \qquad = 1$

Stage 2: $1 + 3 \qquad = 4$

Stage 3: $1 + 3 + 5 \qquad = 9$

Stage 4: $1 + 3 + 5 + 7 \quad = 16$

a. Find the next four stages and their sums.

b. What is the sum in Stage 20?

c. In what stage will the sum be 576? What is the greatest number added in the sum of this pattern? Explain.

86. Goldbach's Conjecture is a famous conjecture that has never been proven true or false. The conjecture states that every even number, except 2, can be written as the sum of two prime numbers. For example, 16 can be written as $5 + 11$.

a. Write the first six even numbers greater than 2 as the sum of two prime numbers.

b. Write 100 as the sum of two primes.

c. The number 2 is a prime number. Can an even number greater than 4 be written as the sum of two prime numbers if you use 2 as one of the primes? Explain why or why not.

87. The chart below shows the factor counts for the numbers from 975 to 1,000. Each star stands for one factor. For example, the four stars after 989 indicate that 989 has four factors.

975	☆☆☆☆☆☆☆☆☆☆☆☆
976	☆☆☆☆☆☆☆☆☆☆
977	☆☆
978	☆☆☆☆☆☆☆☆
979	☆☆☆☆
980	☆☆☆☆☆☆☆☆☆☆☆☆☆☆☆☆☆☆
981	☆☆☆☆☆☆
982	☆☆☆☆
983	☆☆
984	☆☆☆☆☆☆☆☆☆☆☆☆☆☆☆☆
985	☆☆☆☆
986	☆☆☆☆☆☆☆☆
987	☆☆☆☆☆☆☆☆
988	☆☆☆☆☆☆☆☆☆☆☆☆
989	☆☆☆☆
990	☆☆☆☆☆☆☆☆☆☆☆☆☆☆☆☆☆☆☆☆☆☆☆☆
991	☆☆
992	☆☆☆☆☆☆☆☆☆☆☆☆
993	☆☆☆☆
994	☆☆☆☆☆☆☆☆
995	☆☆☆☆
996	☆☆☆☆☆☆☆☆☆☆☆☆
997	☆☆
998	☆☆☆☆
999	☆☆☆☆☆☆☆☆
1000	☆☆☆☆☆☆☆☆☆☆☆☆☆☆☆☆

a. Boris thinks that numbers that have many factors, such as 975 and 996, must be *abundant numbers.* (Recall that an abundant number is a number whose proper factors have a sum greater than the number.) Is Boris correct? Explain.

b. Doris thinks that there is at least one square number on the list. Is Doris correct? Explain.

88. Evan found a way to find the product of 36×15. He drew this diagram and wrote these computations.

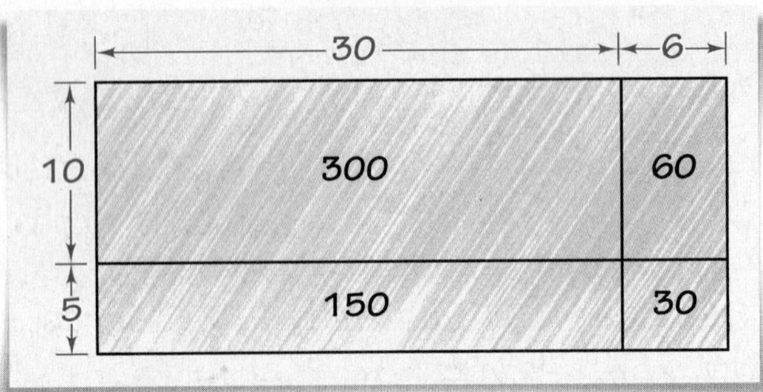

$$36 \times 15 = (30 + 6)(10 + 5) = 300 + 150 + 60 + 30 = 540$$

a. Does Evan's method work for finding 36×15? Explain.

b. Use Evan's method to find $(2 + n)(3 + 5)$.

c. Use Evan's method to find $(n + 2)(a + 3)$.

d. Use Evan's method to find $(a + b)(c + d)$.

89. Use the Distributive Property to prove each statement. *Hint:* You can write an even number as $2n$ and an odd number as $2n + 1$, where n represents any whole number.

a. The sum of two even numbers is even.

b. The sum of two odd numbers is even.

c. The sum of an odd number and an even number is odd.

90. Use a rectangular model to show that the equations below are true.

a. $3(3 + 1 + 7) = 3(3) + 3(1) + 3(7)$

b. $a(b + c + d) = a(b) + a(c) + a(d)$ for any four whole numbers a, b, c, and d.

91. Use the numbers, 1, 2, 3, and 4 exactly once each in any order. Insert operation signs and parentheses to make as many different numbers as you can.

Mathematical Reflections 4

In this Investigation, you have studied an important relationship between multiplication and addition, called the Distributive Property. The following questions will help you summarize what you have learned.

Think about these questions. Discuss your ideas with other students and your teacher. Then write a summary of your findings in your notebook.

1. a. **Explain** what the Distributive Property means for multiplication, addition, and subtraction. Use the area of a rectangle to illustrate your answer.

   b. **Explain** how you can use the Distributive Property to write a number as two equivalent expressions. Give two examples.

2. a. **What** rules for ordering computations with numbers does the Order of Operations convention provide? Why is it important?

   b. **How** do you decide what operation, addition, subtraction, multiplication, or division, is needed to solve a problem?

Unit Project

Don't forget your favorite number!

- Can you use the Distributive Property to express your favorite number in another form?
- What about the Order of Operations?

Common Core Mathematical Practices

As you worked on the Problems in this Investigation, you used prior knowledge to make sense of them. You also applied Mathematical Practices to solve the Problems. Think back over your work, the ways you thought about the Problems, and how you used Mathematical Practices.

Shawna described her thoughts in the following way:

The Order of Operations convention helps me to make sense of an arithmetic statement and make exact calculations when needed in Problem 4.3.

Common Core Standards for Mathematical Practice

MP6 Attend to precision.

- What other Mathematical Practices can you identify in Shawna's reasoning?
- Describe a Mathematical Practice that you and your classmates used to solve a different Problem in this Investigation.

My Favorite Number

At the beginning of this Unit, you chose a favorite number and wrote several things about it in your notebook. As you worked through the Investigations, you used the concepts you learned to write new things about your number.

Now it is time for you to show off your favorite number. Write a story, compose a poem, make a poster, or find some other way to highlight your number.

Your teacher will use your project to determine how well you understand the concepts in this Unit, so be sure to include all the things you have learned while working through the Investigations. You may want to start by looking back through your notebook to find the things you wrote after each Investigation. In your project, be sure you use all the vocabulary your teacher has asked you to record in your notebook for *Prime Time.*

Looking Back

While working on the Problems in this Unit, you investigated some important properties of whole numbers. Finding factors and multiples of numbers and identifying prime numbers helps in answering questions about clocks and calendars, puzzles and games, and rectangular patterns of tiles. Factoring also focuses attention on the properties of even and odd numbers, square numbers, greatest common factors, and least common multiples.

Use Your Understanding: Number Patterns

Test your understanding of multiples, factors, and prime numbers by solving the following problems.

1. The Red Top Taxi Company wants to keep its cars in good operating condition. It has a schedule for regular maintenance checks on each car. Oil is to be changed once every 6 weeks. Brakes are to be inspected and repaired every 10 weeks.
   - **a.** After a new cab is put in service, is there ever a week when that cab is scheduled for both an oil change and a brake inspection? If so, what is the first such time?
   - **b.** Suppose the oil change time is extended to 8 weeks and the brake inspection to 12 weeks. Is there ever a week when the cab is due for both an oil change and a brake inspection? If so, when will such an incident first occur?

2. A university marching band consists of 60 members. The band director wants to arrange the band into a rectangular array for the halftime activities.

   a. In how many ways can she arrange the band? Make a sketch of each arrangement.

   b. How many rectangular arrangements are possible if the band adds one member and becomes a 61-member band?

3. The prime factorization of Tamika's special number is $2 \times 2 \times 3 \times 11$ and the prime factorization of Cyrah's special number is $3 \times 3 \times 5 \times 5$.

   a. What is the least common multiple of the two special numbers?

   b. What is the greatest common factor of the two special numbers?

   c. List all the factors of Tamika's number.

   d. Is Tamika's number even or odd? Is Cyrah's number even or odd?

   e. Is Tamika's number a square number? Is Cyrah's number a square number?

4. Shani gave a clue for her secret number.

   Clue 1: My number is a factor of 90.

   a. Can you determine what Shani's secret number is?

   b. What is the smallest Shani's number can be? What is the largest Shani's number can be?

   c. Brandon says the secret number must also be a factor of 180. Is he correct?

   d. Shani gave a second clue for her secret number.

      Clue 2: My number is prime.

      Now can you determine what the secret number is?

   e. Shani gave a third clue for her secret number.

      Clue 3: Twenty-one is a multiple of my secret number.

      Now can you determine what the secret number is?

For Exercises 5–7, insert parentheses and addition, subtraction, or multiplication signs on the left side of the equality sign to make a true statement.

5. $3 \;\; 2 \;\; 1 = 9$

6. $6 \;\; 4 \;\; 3 \;\; 2 = 26$

7. $5 \;\; 7 \;\; 2 \;\; 7 = 21$

Explain Your Reasoning

In Exercises 1–7 you used knowledge of factors and multiples of a number.

8. What strategies can be used to find

a. all the factors of a number?

b. the least common multiple of two numbers?

c. the greatest common factor of two numbers?

9. How can you decide whether a number is

a. a prime number?

b. a square number?

c. an even number?

d. an odd number?

10. Decide whether each statement is true or false. Explain your reasoning. (A statement is true if it is correct for every pair of numbers. If you can find a counterexample, then the statement is false.)

a. If a number is greater than a second number, then the first number has more factors than the second number.

b. The sum of two odd numbers is even.

c. The product of an even number and an odd number is odd.

d. The least common multiple of two different prime numbers is the product of those numbers.

e. The greatest common factor of two numbers is less than either of those numbers.

11. Explain how the Order of Operations convention and the Distributive Property are useful in performing arithmetic calculations.

English / Spanish Glossary

A

abundant number A number for which the sum of all its proper factors is greater than the number itself. For example, 24 is an abundant number because its proper factors, 1, 2, 3, 4, 6, 8, and 12, add to 36.

número abundante Un número con factores propios que sumados resultan en un número mayor que el número mismo. Por ejemplo, 24 es un número abundante porque la suma de sus factores propios, 1, 2, 3, 4, 6, 8 y 12, es 36.

C

common factor A factor that two or more numbers share. For example, 7 is a common factor of 14 and 35 because 7 is a factor of 14 ($14 = 7 \times 2$) and 7 is a factor of 35 ($35 = 7 \times 5$).

factor común Un factor que comparten dos o más números. Por ejemplo, 7 es factor común de 14 y 35 porque 7 es un factor de 14 ($14 = 7 \times 2$) y 7 es un factor de 35 ($35 = 7 \times 5$).

common multiple A multiple that two or more numbers share. For example, the first few multiples of 5 are 5, 10, 15, 20, 25, 30, 35, 40, 45, 50, 55, 60, 65, and 70. The first few multiples of 7 are 7, 14, 21, 28, 35, 42, 49, 56, 63, 70, 77, 84, 91, and 98. From these lists, we can see that two common multiples of 5 and 7 are 35 and 70.

múltiplo común Un múltiplo comparten dos o más números. Por ejemplo, los primeros múltiplos de 5 son 5, 10, 15, 20, 25, 30, 35, 40, 45, 50, 55, 60, 65 y 70. Los primeros múltiplos de 7 son 7, 14, 21, 28, 35, 42, 49, 56, 63, 70, 77, 84, 91 y 98. Estas listas nos indican que dos múltiplos comunes de 5 y 7 son el 35 y el 70.

composite number A whole number with factors other than itself and 1 (that is, a whole number that is not prime). Some composite numbers are 6, 15, 20, and 1,001.

número compuesto Un número entero con otros factores además del número mismo y 1 (es decir, un número entero que no es primo). Algunos números compuestos son 6, 15, 20 y 1,001.

conjecture A claim about a pattern or relationship based on observations.

conjectura Una afirmación acerca de un patron o relación, basada en observaciones.

consecutive numbers Whole numbers in sequence that follow each other, such as 31, 32, 33 or 52, 53, 54.

números consecutivos Números enteros en una secuencia en que uno sigue al otro, por ejemplo 31, 32, 33 ó 52, 53, 54.

counterexample An example that disproves a claim. If someone claims that a pattern is true for all cases, you only need to find one counterexample to disprove that claim.

contraejemplo Un ejemplo que muestra que un enunciado no es siempre verdadero. Si alguien afirma que un patrón es verdadero en todos los casos, solo se necesita hallar un contraejemplo para refutarlo.

D

deficient number A number for which the sum of all its proper factors is less than the number itself. For example, 14 is a deficient number because its proper factors, 1, 2, and 7, add to 10. All prime numbers are deficient.

número deficiente Un número con factores propios que sumados resultan en un número menor que el número mismo. Por ejemplo, 14 es un número deficiente porque la suma de sus factores 1, 2 y 7 equivale a 10. Todos los números primos son deficientes.

---

determine Academic Vocabulary
To use the given information and any related facts to find a value or make a decision.

related terms *decide, find, calculate, conclude*

sample What is one way to determine the prime factorization of 27?

I could use a factor tree to determine the prime factorization of 27.

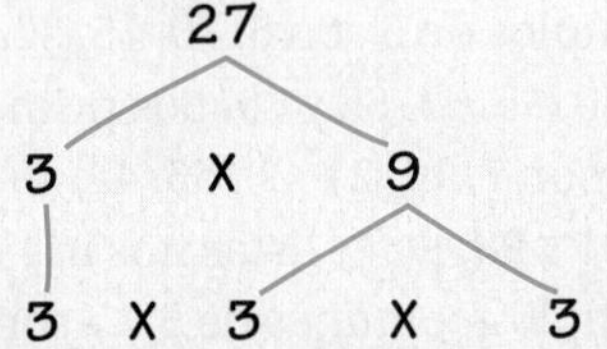

I can also divide 27 by prime numbers until I have a prime quotient. For example, 3 is prime and 27 ÷ 3 = 9. Since 9 is not prime, I continue to divide. 9 ÷ 3 = 3 and 3 is prime. The prime factors for 27 are 3 X 3 X 3.

determinar Vocabulario académico
Usar la información dada y los datos relacionados para hallar un valor o tomar una decisión.

términos relacionados *decidir, hallar, calcular, concluir*

ejemplo ¿Cuál es una manera de determinar la descomposición en factores primos de 27?

Podría usar un árbol de factores para determinar la descomposición en factores primos de 27.

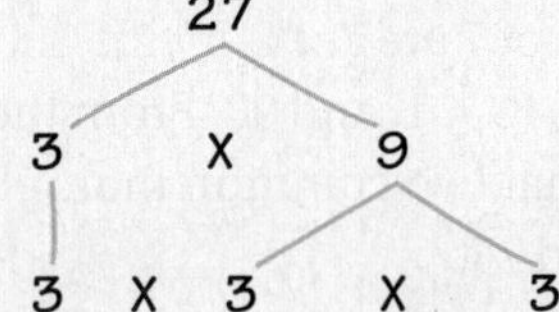

También puedo dividir 27 por números primos hasta obtener el cociente primo. Por ejemplo, 3 es un número primo y 27 ÷ 3 = 9. Puesto que 9 no es un número primo, puedo continuar con la división. 9 ÷ 3 = 3 y 3 es un número primo. Los factores primos de 27 son 3 X 3 X 3.

Distributive Property A mathematical property used to rewrite expressions involving addition and multiplication. The Distributive Property states that for any three numbers a, b, and c, $a(b + c) = ab + ac$. If an expression is written as a factor multiplied by a sum, you can use the Distributive Property to multiply the factor by each term in the sum.

$$4(5 + x) = 4(5) + 4(x) = 20 + 4x$$

If an expression is written as a sum of terms and the terms have a common factor, you can use the Distributive Property to rewrite the expression as the common factor multiplied by a sum. This process is called factoring.

$$20 + 4x = 4(5) + 4(x) = 4(5 + x)$$

propiedad distributiva Una propiedad matemática usada para reescribir expresiones que incluyen la suma y la multiplicación. La propiedad distributiva establece que para tres números cualesquiera a, b, y c, $a(b + c) = ab + ac$. Si una expresión se escribe como la multiplicación de un factor por una suma, la propiedad distributiva puede usarse para multiplicar el factor por cada término de la suma.

$$4(5 + x) = 4(5) + 4(x) = 20 + 4x$$

Si una expresión se escribe como la suma de los términos y los términos tienen un factor común, la propiedad distributiva puede usarse para reescribir o descomponer en factores la expresión como la multiplicación del factor común por una suma. Este proceso se llama descomposición en factores.

$$4(5 + x) = 4(5) + 4(x) = 20 + 4x$$

divisor A number that divides a given number leaving a zero remainder. For example, 5 is a divisor of 20 since $20 \div 5 = 4$ has a remainder of 0. A divisor of a given number is also known as a factor of that number. Another way to determine if 5 is a divisor of 20 is to ask whether there is a whole number that, when multiplied by 5, gives 20. The number is 4: $5 \times 4 = 20$.

divisor Un número que divide a otro número sin dejar ningún resto. Por ejemplo, 5 es un divisor de 20 porque $20 \div 5 = 4$ tiene resto cero. El divisor de un número determinado también se conoce como un factor de ese número. Otra manera de determinar si 5 es un divisor de 20 es preguntando si hay un número entero que, al ser multiplicado por 5, dé 20. El número es 4: $5 \times 4 = 20$.

E

equivalent expressions Expressions that represent the same quantity. For example, $2 + 5$, $3 + 4$, and 7 are equivalent expressions. You can apply the Distributive Property to $2(x + 3)$ to write the equivalent expression $2x + 6$. You can apply the Commutative Property to $2x + 6$ to write the equivalent expression $6 + 2x$.

expresiones equivalentes Expresiones que representan la misma cantidad, como por ejemplo $2 + 5$, $3 + 4$ *y* 7. Puedes aplicar la propiedad distributiva a $2(x + 3)$ para escribir la expresión equivalente $2x + 6$. Puedes aplicar la propiedad conmutativa a $2x + 6$ para escribir la expresión equivalente $6 + 2x$.

even number A multiple of 2. When you divide an even number by 2, the remainder is 0. Examples of even numbers are 0, 2, 4, 6, 8, and 10.

número par Un múltiplo de 2. Cuando divides un número par por 2, el residuo es 0. Los siguientes son ejemplos de números pares: 0, 2, 4, 6, 8 y 10.

expanded form (expression) The form of an expression made up of sums or differences of terms rather than products of factors. The expressions $20 + 30$, $5(4) + 5(21)$, $x^2 + 7x + 12$, and $x^2 + 2x$ are in expanded form.

forma desarrollada (expresión) La forma de una expresión compuesta de sumas o diferencias de términos en vez de productos de factores. Las expresiones $20 + 30$, $5(4) + 5(21)$, $x^2 + 7x + 12$ y $x^2 + 2x$ están representadas en forma desarrollada.

expanded form (number) See *prime factorization.*

forma desarrollada (número en) Ver *descomposición en factores primos.*

explain Academic Vocabulary

To give facts and details that make an idea easier to understand. Explaining can involve a written summary supported by a diagram, chart, table, or a combination of these.

related terms *analyze, clarify, describe, justify, tell*

sample Amara is thinking of a number that is the least common multiple of 5 and 6. What is the number? Explain your reasoning.

Multiples of 5: 5, 10, 15, 20, 25, 30, 35... Multiples of 6: 6, 12, 18, 24, 30, 36, 42... The first common multiple is 30. So, Amara's number is 30.

explicar Vocabulario académico

Dar hechos y detalles que hacen que una idea sea más fácil de comprender. Explicar puede implicar un resumen escrito apoyado por un diagrama, una gráfica, una tabla, o una combinación de éstos.

términos relacionados *analizar, aclarar, describir, justificar, decir*

ejemplo Amara está pensando en un número que es el mínimo común múltiplico de 5 *y* 6. ¿Cuál es el número? Explica tu razonamiento.

Múltiplos de 5: 5, 10, 15, 20, 25, 30, 35... Múltiplos de 6: 6, 12, 18, 24, 30, 36, 42... El primer múltiplo común es 30. Así que el número de Amara es 30.

exponent The small raised number that tells how many times a factor is used. For example, 5^3 means $5 \times 5 \times 5$. The exponent is 3.

exponente El pequeño número elevado que dice cuántas veces se usa un factor. Por ejemplo, 5^3 significa $5 \times 5 \times 5$. El exponente es 3.

exponential form A quantity expressed as a number raised to a power. In exponential form, 32 can be written as 2^5. The exponential form of the prime factorization of 5,000 is $2^3 \times 5^4$.

forma exponencial Una cantidad expresada como un número elevado a una potencia. 32 en forma exponencial se escribe 2^5. La forma exponencial de la descomposición en factores primos de 5,000 es $2^3 \times 5^4$.

F

factor One of two or more whole numbers that are multiplied to get a product. For example, 13 and 4 are both factors of 52 because $13 \times 4 = 52$.

factor Uno de dos o más números enteros que se multiplican para obtener un producto. Por ejemplo, tanto 13 como 4 son factores de 52 porque $13 \times 4 = 52$.

factor pair Two whole numbers that are multiplied to get a product. For example, the pair 13, 4 is a factor pair of 52 because $13 \times 4 = 52$.

par de factores Dos números enteros que se multiplican para obtener un producto. Por ejemplo, el par 13, 4 es un par factor de 52 porque $13 \times 4 = 52$.

factored form The form of an expression made up of products of factors rather than sums or differences of terms. The expressions $2 \times 2 \times 5$, $3(2 + 7)$, $(x + 3)(x + 4)$, and $x(x - 2)$ are in factored form.

forma de factores La forma de una expresión compuesta de productos de factores en vez de sumas o diferencias de términos. Las expresiones $2 \times 2 \times 5$, $3(2 + 7)$, $(x + 3)(x + 4)$ y $x(x - 2)$ están representadas en forma factorizada.

factorization A product of numbers, perhaps with some repetitions, resulting in the desired number. A number can have many factorizations. For example, two factorizations of 60 are 3×20 and $2 \times 2 \times 15$.

descomposición en factores El producto de números, con posibles repeticiones, que resultan en el número deseado. Un número se puede descomponer en factores de varias maneras. Por ejemplo, dos maneras de descomponer 60 en factores son 3×20 y $2 \times 2 \times 15$.

Fundamental Theorem of Arithmetic The theorem stating that, except for the order of the factors, every whole number greater than 1 can be factored into prime factors in only one way. For example, $60 = 2 \times 2 \times 3 \times 5$.

Teorema fundamental de la Aritmética Teorema que enuncia que, excepto por el orden de los factores, todos los números enteros mayores que 1 pueden descomponerse en factores primos de una sola manera. Por ejemplo, $60 = 2 \times 2 \times 3 \times 5$.

G

greatest common factor (GCF) The greatest factor that two or more numbers share. For example, 1, 2, 3, and 6 are common factors of 12 and 30, but 6 is the greatest common factor.

máximo común divisor (M.C.D.) El factor mayor que comparten dos o más números. Por ejemplo, 1, 2, 3 y 6 son factores comunes de 12 y 30, pero 6 es el máximo común divisor.

J

justify Academic Vocabulary
To support your answers with reasons or examples.

related terms *validate, explain, defend*

sample Jeffrey claims that 12 and 14 are relatively prime numbers. Is Jeffrey correct? Justify your answer.

Jeffrey is not correct. The Venn diagram shows that 12 and 14 have both 1 and 2 as common factors. Since 12 and 14 share two factors, they cannot be relatively prime.

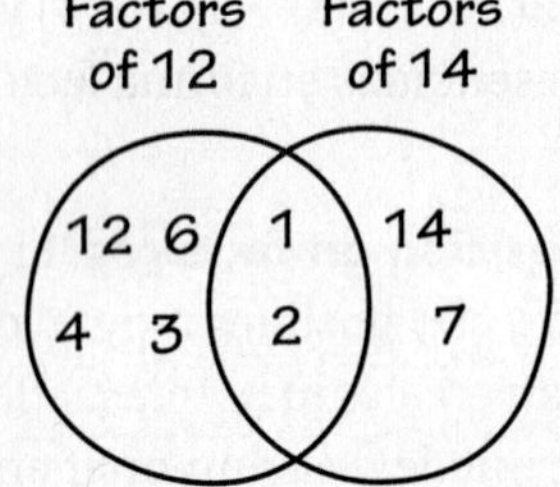

justificar Vocabulario académico
Apoyar tus respuestas con razones o ejemplos.

términos relacionados *validar, explicar, defender*

ejemplo Jeffrey afirma que 12 y 14 son números relativamente primos. ¿Es correcta la afirmación de Jeffrey? Justifica tu respuesta.

La afirmación de Jeffrey no es correcta. El diagrama de Venn muestra que 12 y 14 tienen 1 y 2 como factores comunes. Puesto que 12 y 14 comparten dos factores no pueden ser números relativamente primos.

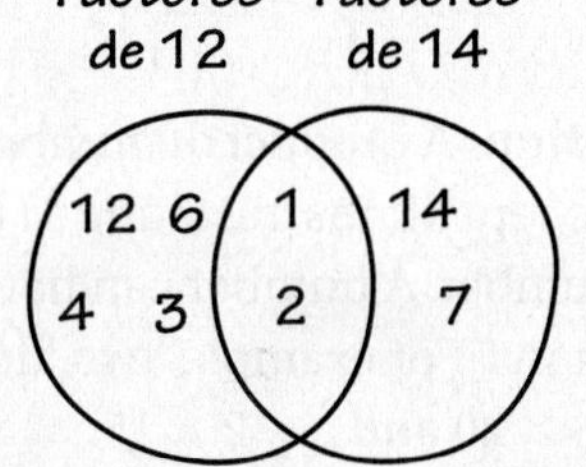

L

least common multiple (LCM) The least multiple that two or more numbers share. Common multiples of 6 and 8 include 24, 48, and 72, but 24 is the least common multiple.

mínimo común múltiplo (M.C.M.) El múltiplo menor que comparten dos o más números. Los múltiplos comunes de 6 y 8 incluyen 24, 48 y 72, pero 24 es el mínimo común múltiplo.

M

multiple The product of a given whole number and another whole number. For example, some multiples of 3 are 3, 6, 9, and 12. Note that if a number is a multiple of 3, then 3 is a factor of the number. For example, 12 is a multiple of 3, and 3 is a factor of 12.

múltiplo El producto de un número entero dado y otro número entero. Por ejemplo, algunos múltiplos de 3 son 3, 6, 9 y 12. Observa que si un número es un múltiplo de 3, entonces 3 es un factor de ese número. Por ejemplo, 12 es un múltiplo de 3, y 3 es un factor de 12.

N

near-perfect number A number for which the sum of all its proper factors is one less than the number. All powers of 2 are near-perfect numbers. For example, 32 is a near-perfect number because its proper factors, 1, 2, 4, 8, and 16, add to 31.

número casi perfecto Un número con factores propios que sumados resultan en uno menos que ese número. Todas las potencias de 2 son números casi perfectos. Por ejemplo, 32 es un número casi perfecto porque sus factores propios 1, 2, 4, 8 y 16 suman 31.

O

odd number A whole number that is not a multiple of 2. When an odd number is divided by 2, the remainder is 1. Examples of odd numbers are 1, 3, 5, 7, and 9.

número impar Un número entero que no es un múltiplo de 2. Cuando un número impar se divide por 2, el residuo es 1. Los siguientes son ejemplos de números impares: 1, 3, 5, 7 y 9.

Order of Operations A set of agreements or conventions for carrying out calculations with one or more operations, parentheses, or exponents.

1. Work within parentheses.
2. Write numbers written with exponents in standard form.
3. Do all multiplication and division in order from left to right.
4. Do all addition and subtraction in order from left to right.

Orden de las operaciones Un conjunto de acuerdos o convenciones para llevar a cabo cálculos con más de una operación, paréntesis o exponentes.

1. Resolver lo que está entre paréntesis.
2. Escribir los números con exponentes en forma estándar.
3. Multiplicar y dividir en orden de izquierda a derecha.
4. Sumar y dividir en orden de izquierda a derecha.

P

perfect number A number for which the sum of all its proper factors is the number itself. For example, 6 is a perfect number because its proper factors, 1, 2, and 3, add to 6.

número perfecto Un número con factores propios que, cuando se suman, dan como resultado ese mismo número. Por ejemplo, 6 es un número perfecto porque la suma de sus factores propios, 1, 2 y 3, es 6.

prime factorization A product of prime numbers, perhaps with some repetitions, resulting in the desired number. For example, the prime factorization of 7,007 is $7 \times 7 \times 11 \times 13$. The prime factorization of a number is unique except for the order of the factors.

descomposición en factores primos Un producto de números primos, con posibles repeticiones, que resulta en el número deseado. Por ejemplo, la descomposición en factores primos de 7,007 es $7 \times 7 \times 11 \times 13$. La descomposición en factores primos de un número es única salvo por el orden de los factores.

prime number A number with exactly two factors, 1 and the number itself. Examples of primes are 11, 17, 53, and 101. The number 1 is not a prime number because it has only one factor.

número primo Un número que tiene exactamente dos factores: 1 y él mismo. Los siguientes son ejemplos de números primos: 11, 17, 53 y 101. El número 1 no es un número primo porque tiene sólo un factor.

proper factors All the factors of a number, except the number itself. For example, the proper factors of 16 are 1, 2, 4, and 8.

factores propios Todos los factores de un número salvo el número mismo. Por ejemplo, los factores propios de 16 son 1, 2, 4 y 8.

R

relatively prime numbers A pair of numbers with no common factors except for 1. For example, 20 and 33 are relatively prime because the factors of 20 are 1, 2, 4, 5, 10, and 20, while the factors of 33 are 1, 3, 11, and 33. Notice that neither 20 nor 33 is itself a prime number.

números relativamente primos Un par de números que no tienen factores comunes excepto por 1. Por ejemplo, 20 y 33 son números relativamente primos porque los factores de 20 son 1, 2, 4, 5, 10 y 20 mientras que los factores de 33 son 1, 3, 11 y 33. Observa que ni el 20 ni el 33 son en sí mismos números primos.

---

represent Academic Vocabulary
To stand for or take the place of something else. Symbols, equations, charts, and tables are often used to represent particular situations.

related terms *symbolize, stand for*

sample Which of the following sets of numbers represents the factors of 16? Explain.

A. {1, 2, 3, 4, 9, 16}

B. {2, 4, 8}

C. {1, 2, 4, 8, 16}

D. {16, 32, 48, 64}

Set C represents the factors of 16. Set A does not represent the factors of 16 since 3 and 9 are not factors of 16. Set B does not include 1 and 16, which are factors of 16. Set D contains multiples of 16 instead of factors of 16.

representar Vocabulario académico
Significar o tomar el lugar de algo más. Con frecuencia se usan símbolos, ecuaciones, gráficas y tablas para representar situaciones particulares.

términos relacionados *simbolizar, significar*

ejemplo ¿Cuál de los siguientes conjuntos de números representa los factores de 16? Explica tu respuesta.

A. {1, 2, 3, 4, 9, 16}

B. {2, 4, 8}

C. {1, 2, 4, 8, 16}

D. {16, 32, 48, 64}

El conjunto C representa los factores de 16. El conjunto A no representa los factores de 16 puesto que 3 y 9 no son factores de 16. El conjunto B no incluye 1 y 16, los cuales son factores de 16. El conjunto D contiene múltiplos de 16 en lugar de factores de 16.

S

square number A number that is a result of the product of a number multiplied by itself. For example, 9 and 64 are square numbers because $9 = 3 \times 3$ and $64 = 8 \times 8$. A square number represents a number of square tiles that can be arranged to form a square.

número al cuadrado Un número que es el resultado del producto de un número multiplicado por sí mismo. Por ejemplo, 9 y 64 son números al cuadrado porque $9 = 3 \times 3$ y $64 = 8 \times 8$. Un número al cuadrado representa un número de mosaicos cuadrados que se pueden colocar para formar un cuadrado.

V

Venn diagram A diagram in which overlapping circles are used to show relationships among sets of objects that have certain attributes. Two examples are shown below.

diagrama de Venn Un diagrama en el que se usan círculos superpuestos para representar relaciones entre conjuntos de objetos que tienen ciertos atributos. A continuación se muestran dos ejemplos. En uno se muestran factores de 24 y factores de 60, y en el otro se muestran múltiplos de 24 y múltiplos de 60.

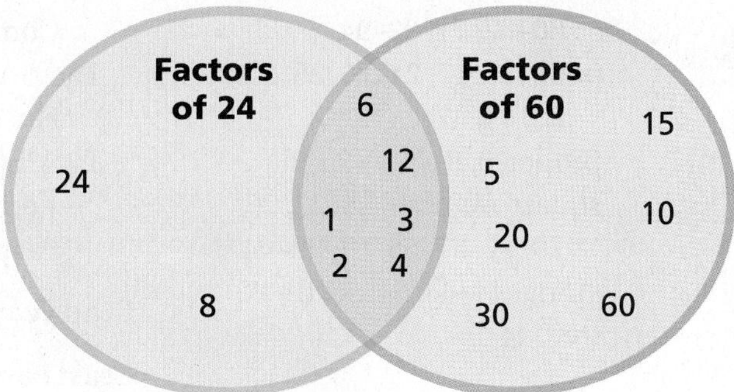

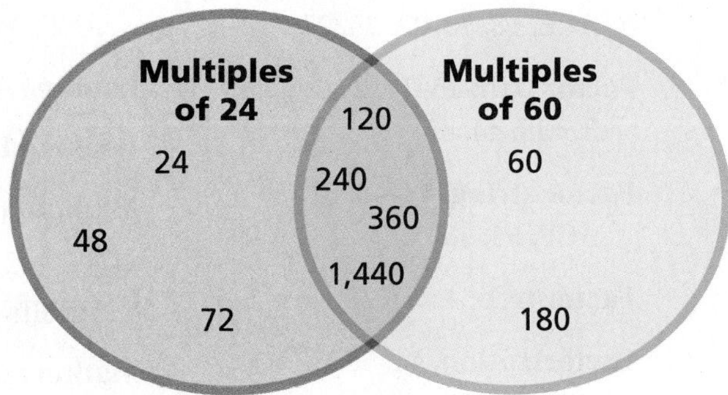

English/Spanish Glossary

Index

Acknowledgments

Cover Design

Three Communication Design, Chicago

Photos

Every effort has been made to secure permission and provide appropriate credit for photographic material. The publisher deeply regrets any omission and pledges to correct errors called to its attention in subsequent editions.

Unless otherwise acknowledged, all photographs are the property of Pearson Education, Inc.

Photo locators denoted as follows: Top (T), Center (C), Bottom (B), Left (L), Right (R), Background (Bkgd)

2TCR Bettmann/Corbis; **3TC** Peter Hvizdak/The Image Works; **3TR** Adrian Peacock/Imagestate Media; **12TR** Declan McCullagh; **22BC** Bettmann/Corbis; **30BR** Ron Chapple/Thinkstock/Alamy; **41C** Sydney Harris.

Data Sources

Information on Prime Numbers on page 12 from THE NEW YORK TIMES, August 8, 2002. Copyright © 2002 The New York Times Company.

Note: Every effort has been made to locate the copyright owner of the material reprinted in this book. Omissions brought to our attention will be corrected in subsequent editions.

CONNECTED MATHEMATICS® 3

Ratios, Rational Numbers, and Equivalence

Lappan, Phillips, Fey, Friel

Comparing Bits and Pieces

Ratios, Rational Numbers, and Equivalence

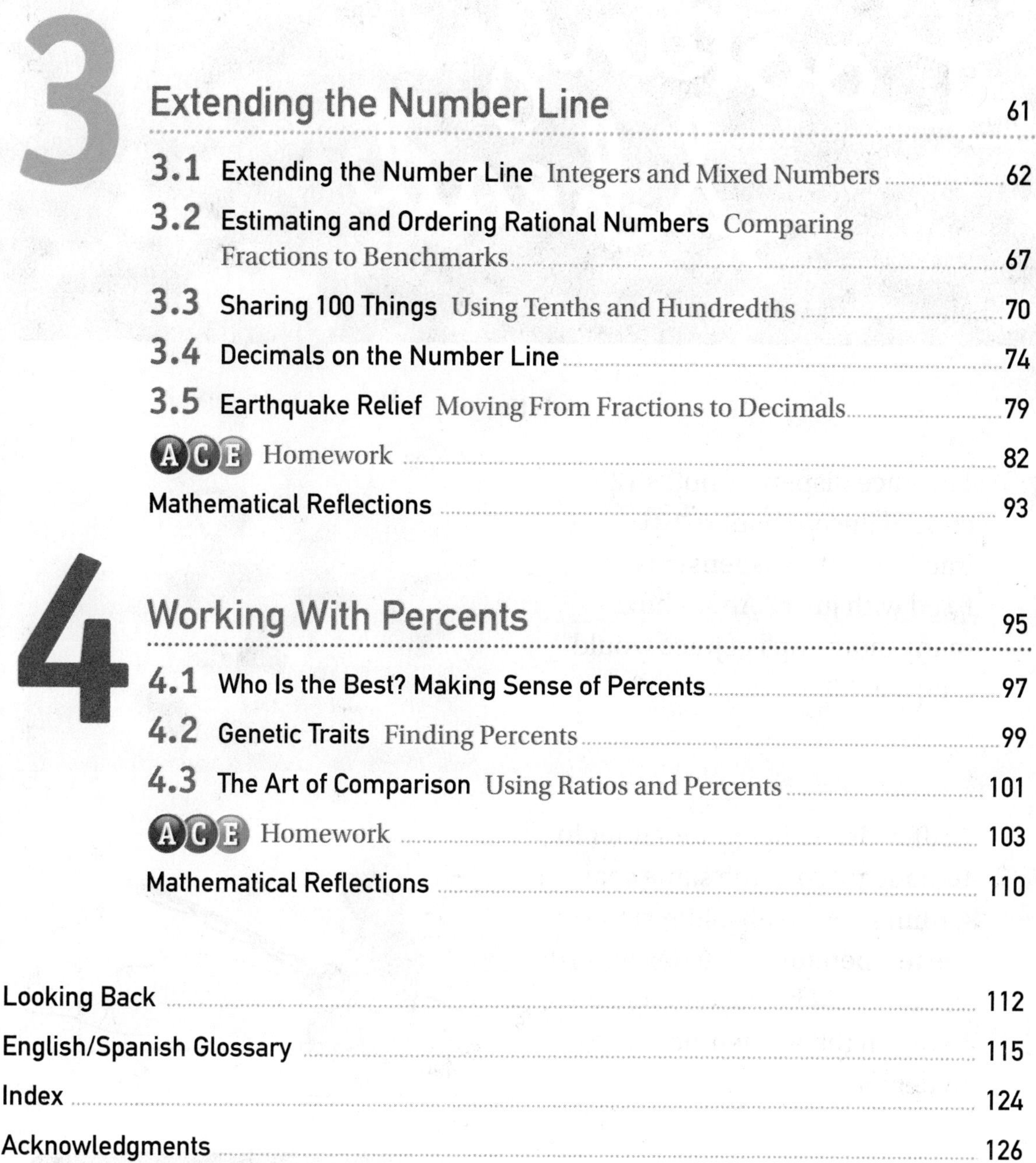

Looking Ahead

The juice dispenser holds 120 cups of juice. About **what** fraction of the dispenser is filled with juice? About how many more cups of juice would it take to fill the dispenser?

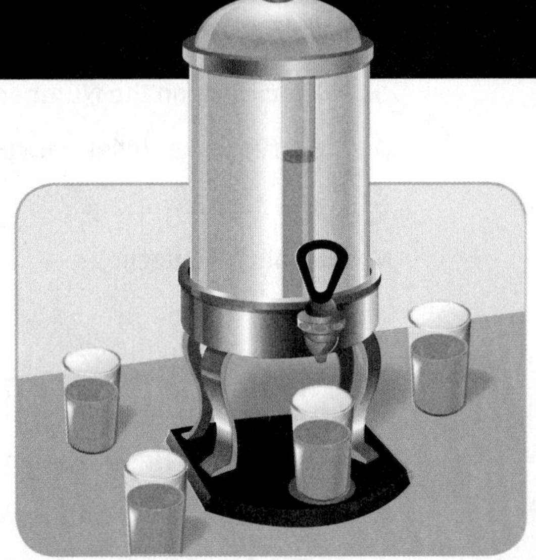

Griffin visited her grandfather in Canada twice in the same year. Griffin says the absolute value of the temperature each day was 10. **What** could be the difference between the two temperatures in degrees?

A survey asked people about their physical characteristics. Out of the 30 people surveyed, 7 people reported having curly hair. **What** percent of the people surveyed have curly hair?

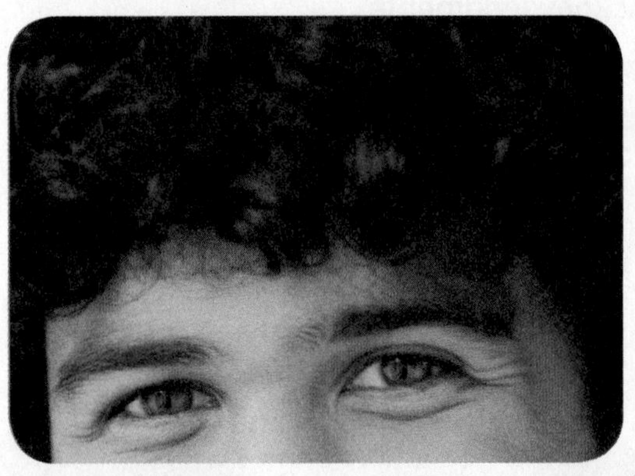

Sometimes whole numbers cannot communicate needed information precisely. You may need to talk about parts of wholes: "What fraction of the students going on this field trip are eighth-graders?" You may also need ways to discuss how to share, divide, or measure things: "What part of the pizza will each person get?" or "How tall are you?" Fractions, decimals, and percents are all ways of expressing quantities or measures.

There are many situations in which you may want to compare numbers. Comparing by subtracting is one way: "I have $2.00 more than my sister." Comparing with ratios gives different information: "I have twice as much money as my sister." Many comparisons in the real world are based on ratios rather than on differences.

In *Comparing Bits and Pieces,* you will develop skills with fractions, decimals, ratios and percents. Your new skills can help you make sense of situations like the ones on the previous page.

Mathematical Highlights

Comparing Bits and Pieces

In *Comparing Bits and Pieces,* you will develop your skills in using fractions, decimals, ratios and percents to measure and to compare quantities.

The Investigations in this Unit will help you understand how to:

- Use ratio language and notation to compare quantities
- Distinguish between fractions as numbers and ratios as comparisons
- Use a variety of scaling and partitioning strategies to reason proportionally
- Think of fractions and decimals as both locations and distances on the number line
- Move flexibly among fraction, decimal, and percent representations
- Find absolute values and opposites, and use them to describe real-world quantities
- Use fraction, decimal, and percent benchmarks to estimate numbers
- Use context, models, drawings, or estimation to reason about situations
- Use equivalence of fractions and ratios to solve problems
- Use rate tables and unit rates to solve problems

As you work on the problems in this Unit, ask yourself questions about situations that involve fractions, decimals, ratios and percents.

What models or diagrams might be helpful in understanding the situation and the relationships among quantities?

Is this a comparison situation? If so, do I use ratios or subtraction?

What strategies can I use to find equivalent forms of these fractions, decimals, ratios, or percents?

What strategies can I use to compare or order a set of fractions, decimals, and percents?

What strategies can I use to reason about numbers greater than or less than 0?

How can I use unit rates or rate table to make comparisons?

Common Core State Standards

Mathematical Practices and Habits of Mind

In the *Connected Mathematics* curriculum you will develop an understanding of important mathematical ideas by solving problems and reflecting on the mathematics involved. Every day, you will use "habits of mind" to make sense of problems and apply what you learn to new situations. Some of these habits are described by the *Common Core State Standards for Mathematical Practices* (MP).

MP1 Make sense of problems and persevere in solving them.

When using mathematics to solve a problem, it helps to think carefully about

- data and other facts you are given and what additional information you need to solve the problem;
- strategies you have used to solve similar problems and whether you could solve a related simpler problem first;
- how you could express the problem with equations, diagrams, or graphs;
- whether your answer makes sense.

MP2 Reason abstractly and quantitatively.

When you are asked to solve a problem, it often helps to

- focus first on the key mathematical ideas;
- check that your answer makes sense in the problem setting;
- use what you know about the problem setting to guide your mathematical reasoning.

MP3 Construct viable arguments and critique the reasoning of others.

When you are asked to explain why a conjecture is correct, you can

- show some examples that fit the claim and explain why they fit;
- show how a new result follows logically from known facts and principles.

When you believe a mathematical claim is incorrect, you can

- show one or more counterexamples—cases that don't fit the claim;
- find steps in the argument that do not follow logically from prior claims.

MP4 Model with mathematics.

When you are asked to solve problems, it often helps to

- think carefully about the numbers or geometric shapes that are the most important factors in the problem, then ask yourself how those factors are related to each other;
- express data and relationships in the problem with tables, graphs, diagrams, or equations, and check your result to see if it makes sense.

MP5 Use appropriate tools strategically.

When working on mathematical questions, you should always

- decide which tools are most helpful for solving the problem and why;
- try a different tool when you get stuck.

MP6 Attend to precision.

In every mathematical exploration or problem-solving task, it is important to

- think carefully about the required accuracy of results; is a number estimate or geometric sketch good enough, or is a precise value or drawing needed?
- report your discoveries with clear and correct mathematical language that can be understood by those to whom you are speaking or writing.

MP7 Look for and make use of structure.

In mathematical explorations and problem solving, it is often helpful to

- look for patterns that show how data points, numbers, or geometric shapes are related to each other;
- use patterns to make predictions.

MP8 Look for and express regularity in repeated reasoning.

When results of a repeated calculation show a pattern, it helps to

- express that pattern as a general rule that can be used in similar cases;
- look for shortcuts that will make the calculation simpler in other cases.

You will use all of the Mathematical Practices in this Unit. Sometimes, when you look at a Problem, it is obvious which practice is most helpful. At other times, you will decide on a practice to use during class explorations and discussions. After completing each Problem, ask yourself:

- What mathematics have I learned by solving this Problem?
- What Mathematical Practices were helpful in learning this mathematics?

Investigation 1: Making Comparisons

People make and do amazing and amusing things all over the world. For instance, the smallest motorized car is so small it has a bumper $\frac{1}{2}$ the thickness of a human hair, and its top speed is 0.011 miles per hour. It's so small it can sit on a fingernail!

On the next page are some more statements about people, places, and things. Notice that numbers are at the heart of each of these claims.

Common Core State Standards

6.RP.A.1 Understand the concept of a ratio and use ratio language to describe a ratio relationship between two quantities.

6.RP.A.3 Use ratio and rate reasoning to solve real-world and mathematical problems, e.g., by reasoning about tables of equivalent ratios, tape diagrams, double number line diagrams, or equations.

6.NS.C.6 Understand a rational number as a point on the number line . . .

Also 6.RP.A.2 and 6.NS.B.4

- The longest plunge over the edge of a waterfall in a kayak by a woman is 82 feet.
- The region of the world with the most biodiversity is the Tropical Andes of South America, where approximately 16% of all known plant species live.
- The winner of the first official backward running race ran one mile in 6 minutes 2.35 seconds.

Many world records use numbers that tell *how many* or *how much.* To make sense of number claims you need understanding and skill in using whole numbers, fractions, decimals, and percents to count, measure, and compare quantities. The goal of this Unit is to extend your ability to use fractions, decimals, percents, and ratios to solve problems, and to explain, compare, or quantify happenings in the world.

1.1 Fundraising
Comparing With Fractions and Ratios

Students at a middle school are organizing three fundraising projects to raise money. The eighth grade will sell calendars. The seventh grade will sell popcorn. The sixth grade will sell posters.

Each grade picks a different goal for its fundraiser. The three grades are competing to see which grade will reach its fundraising goal first.

The fundraising goal for each grade is displayed on a banner in front of the principal's office.

- How can you compare the grades' fundraising goals?

Problem 1.1

A The students wrote some claims about the fundraising goals on slips of paper and gave them to the principal to read over the loudspeaker during the morning announcements. Decide whether each claim is true. Explain your reasoning.

Markus:
The sixth-grade goal is $150 more than the eighth-grade goal.

Kimi:
When the sixth graders meet their goal, they will have raised $\frac{2}{3}$ of the seventh-grade goal.

Lakisha:
The eighth-grade goal is half the sixth-grade goal.

Andres:
For every dollar the eighth graders plan to raise, the sixth graders plan to raise two dollars.

Ben:
For every $60 the sixth graders plan to raise, the seventh graders plan to raise $90.

Eliza:
The sixth-grade goal is 200% of the eighth-grade goal.

Chung:
For every $3 the eighth grade plans to raise, the seventh grade plans to raise $1.

Problem 1.1 continued

B Write three more true comparison statements for the principal to read over the loudspeaker.

C On the first day of the fundraiser, the principal announces one more goal over the loudspeaker—the teachers' fundraising goal. The microphone is not working very well. What do you think the teachers' goal is?

Good morning students, teachers, and staff!
The teachers have joined the school fundraiser.
They will be selling books for summer reading.
They have set a goal of STATIC dollars.

This is 210 dollars more than the STATIC graders, but only $\frac{4}{5}$ as much as the STATIC graders.
For every 60 dollars the teachers plan to raise, the STATIC graders plan to raise 50 dollars.

ACE Homework starts on page 27.

1.2 Fundraising Thermometers

Introducing Ratios

The principal at the middle school shows each grade's fundraising progress on charts that look like thermometers. The principal records the progress shown on the thermometer using fractions and dollar amounts. The fundraiser lasts 10 days. Each day, the principal announces the progress of each grade over the loudspeaker.

The thermometers are all the same length, despite the different goals. Each thermometer is subdivided into 10 equal parts.

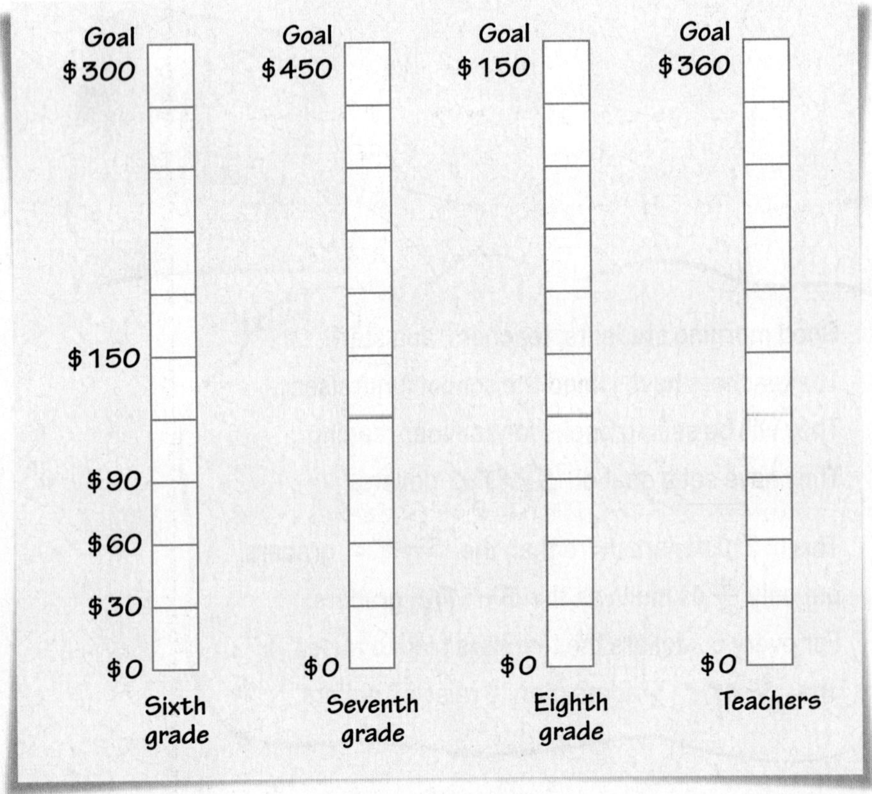

- How can you use the thermometers to make comparisons among the goals?

Problem 1.2

A The principal labeled some of the marks on the four thermometers with dollar amounts. Decide what labels belong on the remaining marks.

B 1. Ben said: *For every $60 the sixth graders plan to raise, the seventh graders plan to raise $90.* He looks at the principal's thermometers and sees that $60 is at the same place on the sixth-grade thermometer as $90 is on the seventh-grade thermometer.

Ben also makes the claim: *For every $30 the sixth graders plan to raise, the seventh graders plan to raise $45.*

Do you agree with this claim? Explain your reasoning.

2. Use the thermometers to write two more *for every* claims that relate the fundraising goals.

C You can write each of the comparisons in Question B as a *ratio*. A **ratio** is a kind of comparison.

Here are two ways that you can rewrite the comparisons in Question B.

The ratio of the sixth-grade goal to the seventh-grade goal is 60 to 90.

The ratio of the sixth-grade goal to the seventh-grade goal is 30 to 45.

1. What do the numbers 60, 90, 30, and 45 mean in each ratio statement?
2. Rewrite your comparisons from Question B part 2 using the word *ratio*.

D 1. The ratios from Ben's statements show the same relationship using different numbers. These ratios are *equivalent*. List some other pairs of equivalent ratios you have found in this Problem.

2. What patterns do you notice in your ratios that can help you find other equivalent ratios?

ACE Homework starts on page 27.

1.3 On the Line

Equivalent Fractions and the Number Line

The sixth graders made their own fundraising thermometer to record their progress. At the end of each day, they compare the total amount they have raised to their goal. The shaded part of the thermometer represents the fraction of the goal the sixth graders have raised. Their challenge is to figure out how to represent dollar amounts as a fraction of $300. They make fraction strips to help them correctly shade their thermometer.

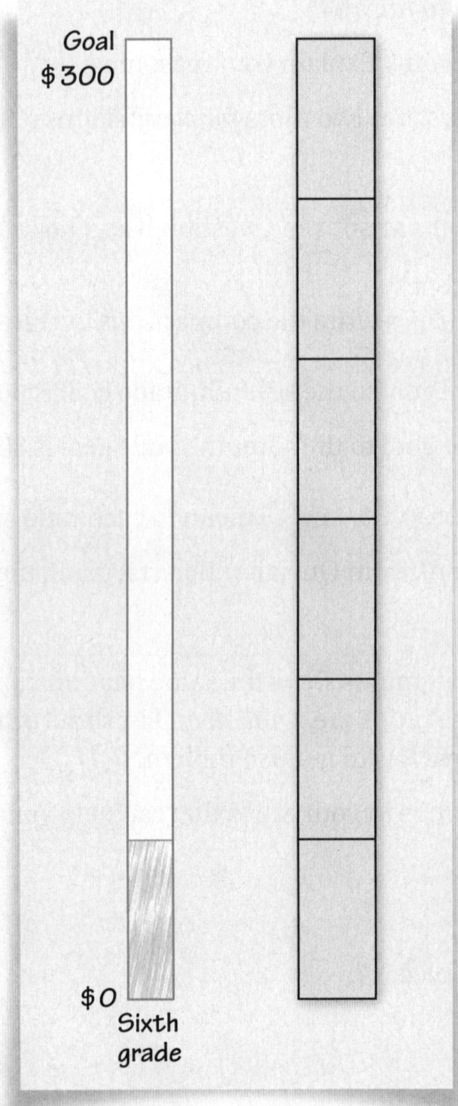

- Have the sixth graders collected more than $\frac{1}{10}$ of their goal? More than $\frac{2}{10}$?
- The thermometer shows the amount they raised on Day 1. What fraction of their goal have they raised?

In this Problem, you will fold fraction strips like those of the sixth graders so that you can measure each day's progress.

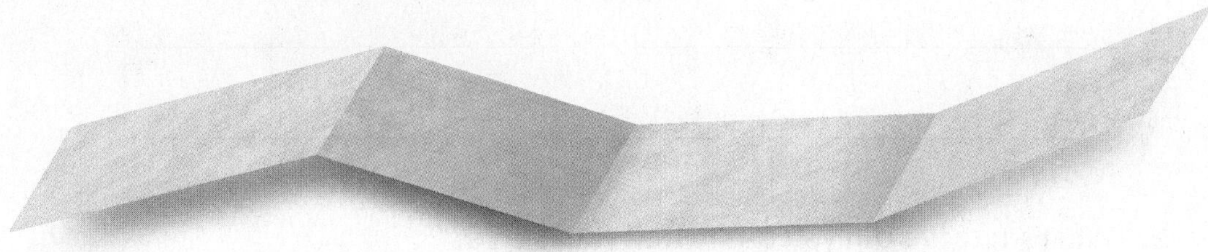

As you fold your strips, think about the strategies you use to make them and about the relationships between the size and number of parts on the various strips.

One important relationship to look for is when the marks on your fraction strips match up, even though the total number of parts on each strip is different. The places where marks match show **equivalent fractions.** Fractions that are equivalent represent the same amount even though their names are different.

What equivalent fractions can you see with these two fraction strips?

- What relationships do you see among your fraction strips?
- What patterns do you see that will help you fold different fraction strips?

Problem 1.3

A **1.** Use strips of paper $8\frac{1}{2}$ inches long. Each strip represents 1 whole. Fold the strips to show halves, thirds, fourths, fifths, sixths, eighths, ninths, tenths, and twelfths. Mark the folds so you can see them easily, as shown below.

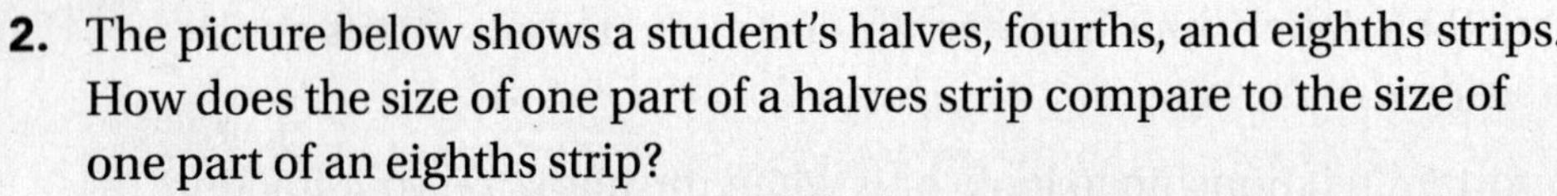

2. What strategies did you use to fold your strips?

B **1.** How can you use the halves strip to fold eighths?

2. The picture below shows a student's halves, fourths, and eighths strips. How does the size of one part of a halves strip compare to the size of one part of an eighths strip?

3. What fraction strips can you make if you start with a thirds strip?

4. Which of the fraction strips you folded have at least one mark that lines up with a mark on a twelfths strip? What equivalent fractions do the matching marks on the strips suggest?

Problem 1.3 continued

C In earlier grades, you used number lines, such as the one below, to show whole numbers.

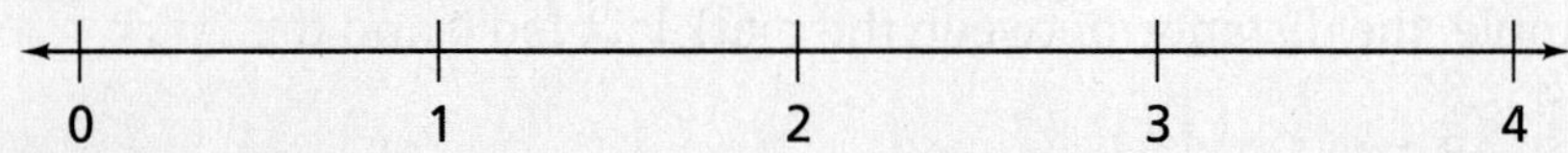

Now you can use fraction strips to mark points between whole numbers.

You start by using a fraction strip to mark and label 0 and 1 on a number line on your paper.

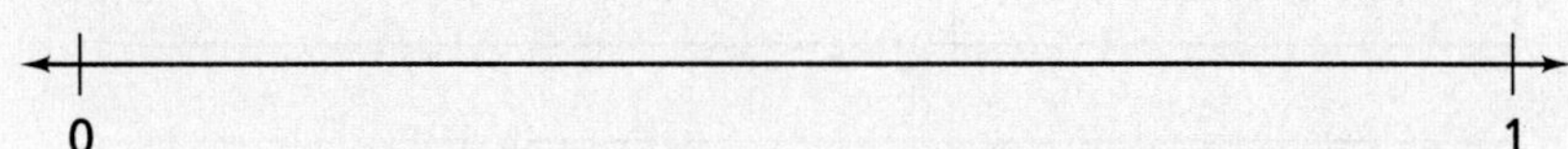

1. Some students began to make a number line using their one-third, one-sixth, one-ninth, and one-twelfth fraction strips. The drawing shows their work so far. One student used the top fraction strip to mark $\frac{2}{3}$ on the number line.

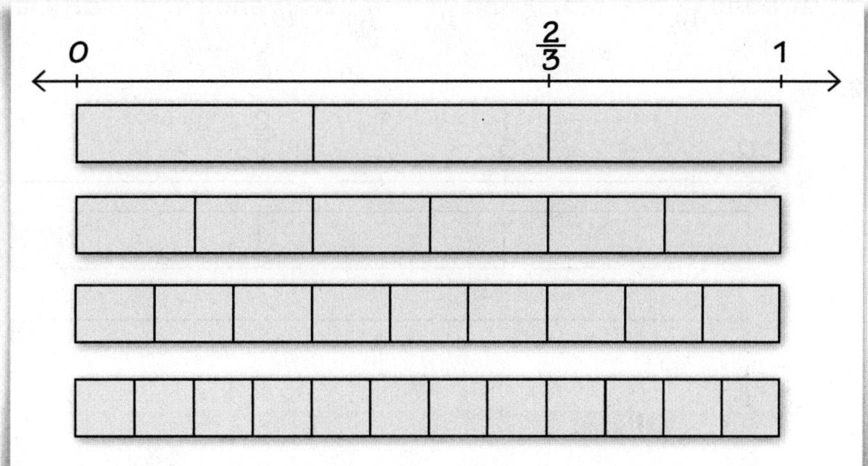

   a. Name three other fractions shown here that are equivalent to $\frac{2}{3}$.

   b. Name another fraction equivalent to $\frac{2}{3}$.

2. If you have used a fraction strip to name a specific point between 0 and 1 on a number line, how can you find equivalent fractions to name this point?

continued on the next page >

Problem 1.3 *continued*

D Some other students began to mark a number line using different fraction strips. Use their drawings to measure distances between points. For example, the distance between the mark labeled 0 and the mark labeled $\frac{3}{5}$ is $\frac{3}{5}$.

1.

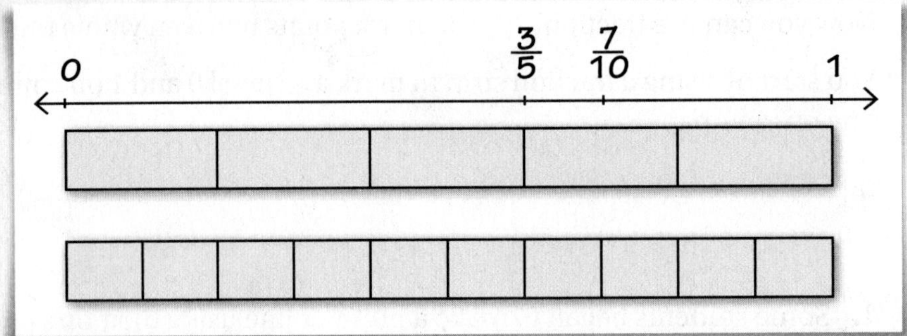

What is the distance between each pair of points?

a. 0 and $\frac{7}{10}$ **b.** $\frac{3}{5}$ and $\frac{7}{10}$ **c.** $\frac{7}{10}$ and 1 **d.** $\frac{3}{5}$ and 1

2.

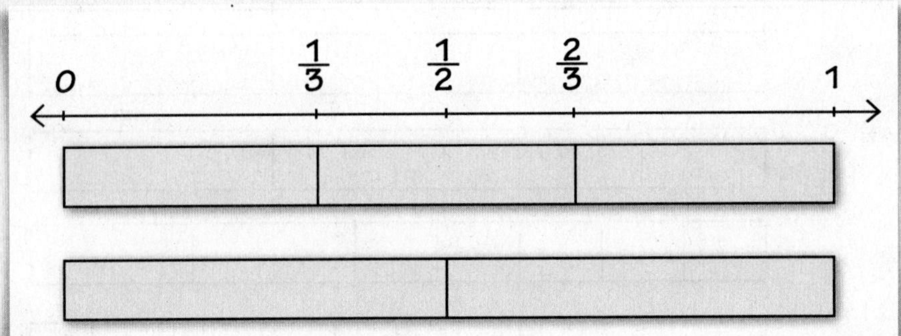

What is the distance between each pair of points?

a. 0 and $\frac{1}{3}$ **b.** $\frac{1}{3}$ and $\frac{1}{2}$ **c.** $\frac{1}{3}$ and $\frac{2}{3}$

d. $\frac{1}{2}$ and $\frac{2}{3}$ **e.** $\frac{1}{2}$ and 1 **f.** $\frac{2}{3}$ and 1

Problem 1.3 continued

E **1.** Name five fractions equivalent to $\frac{4}{12}$.

2. Name five fractions that are near, but not equivalent to, $\frac{4}{12}$.

3. How can fraction strips, number lines, and thinking with numbers help you find equivalent fractions?

4. Matt claims that $\frac{1}{3}$ can indicate a point on a number line as well as distance. Is he correct? Explain.

5. Sally said that the fraction strips remind her of rulers and that you could use fraction strips to measure the progress on the fundraising thermometers. What do you think?

Save your fraction strips to use with Problem 1.4.

ACE Homework starts on page 27.

Did You Know?

Hieroglyphic inscriptions show that, with the exception of $\frac{2}{3}$, Egyptian mathematicians only used fractions with 1 in the numerator. These fractions, such as $\frac{1}{2}$ and $\frac{1}{16}$, are *unit fractions*. The Egyptians expressed other fractions as sums of unit fractions. For example, they expressed the fraction $\frac{5}{12}$ as $\frac{1}{4} + \frac{1}{6}$ (as shown in the second and third pieces of the hieroglyphics below).

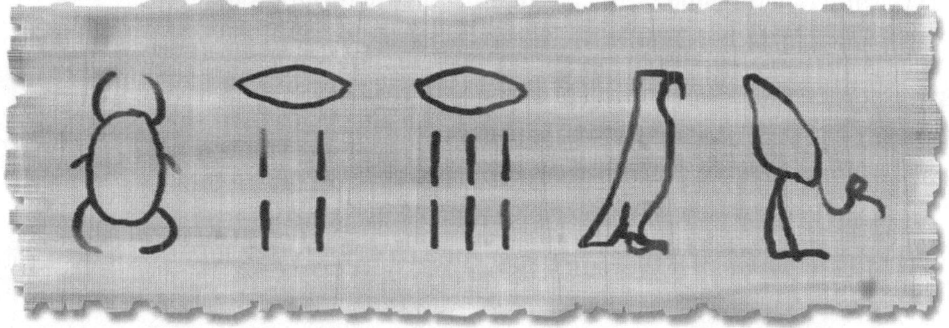

Check with fraction strips to see that $\frac{1}{4} + \frac{1}{6} = \frac{5}{12}$. You studied unit fractions in earlier grades. How do unit fractions appear on fraction strips? On a number line?

1.4 Measuring Progress
Finding Fractional Parts

Here are two claims about the fundraising goals from Problem 1.1.

Ben:

For every $60 the sixth graders plan to raise, the seventh graders plan to raise $90.

Kimi:

When the sixth graders meet their goal, they will have raised $\frac{2}{3}$ of the seventh-grade goal.

Ben and Kimi are each comparing one sixth-grade goal to one seventh-grade goal. Ben uses ratios to make comparisons and Kimi uses fractions to make comparisons.

- Think about some ways in which working with fractions is like and not like working with ratios.

When you use fractions to compare a part to a whole, you often have more than one fraction name for the same quantity. For example, in Problem 1.3, you found that $\frac{1}{5} = \frac{2}{10}$.

In this next problem, you will compare the fundraising progress of a grade to its fundraising goal using fractions.

The thermometers on the next page show the progress of the sixth-grade poster sales after 2, 4, 6, 8, and 10 days. The principal needs to know what fraction of the goal the sixth grade has achieved after each day.

- How can you use your fraction strips to measure the sixth-grade's progress?

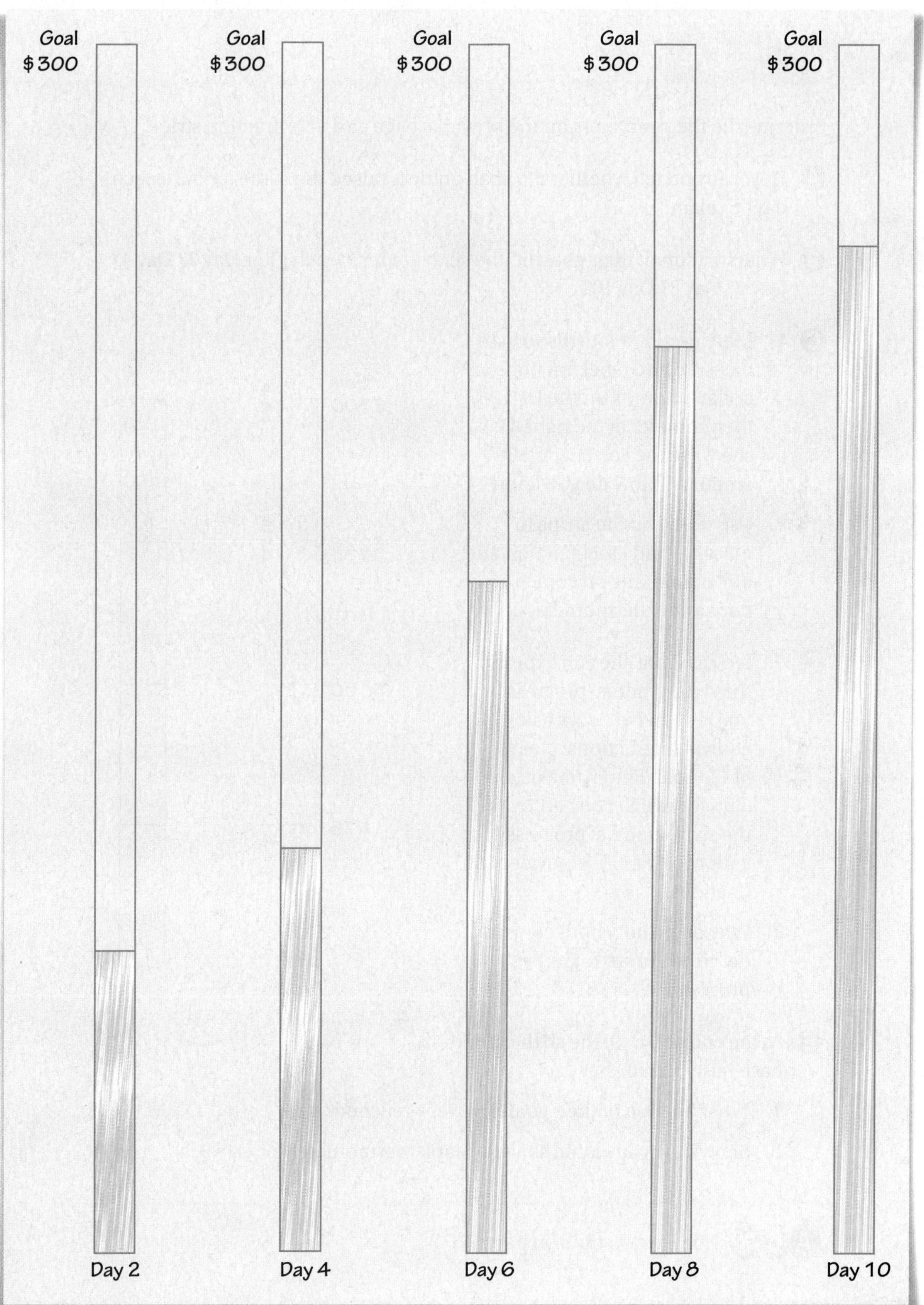
Goal
$300
Day 2
Goal
$300
Day 4
Goal
$300
Day 6
Goal
$300
Day 8
Goal
$300
Day 10

Problem 1.4

Examine the thermometers on the previous page and your fraction strips.

A How can you tell whether the sixth graders raised the same amount each day? Explain.

B What fraction of their goal did the sixth graders reach after Day 2? Day 4? Day 6? Day 8? Day 10?

C 1. Mary used her fourths strip to measure and label fractions and dollar amounts on the Day 2 thermometer at the right. Did she write the correct dollar amounts? How do you know?

2. Use your fraction strips to measure and label fraction and dollar amounts on copies of the remaining thermometers.

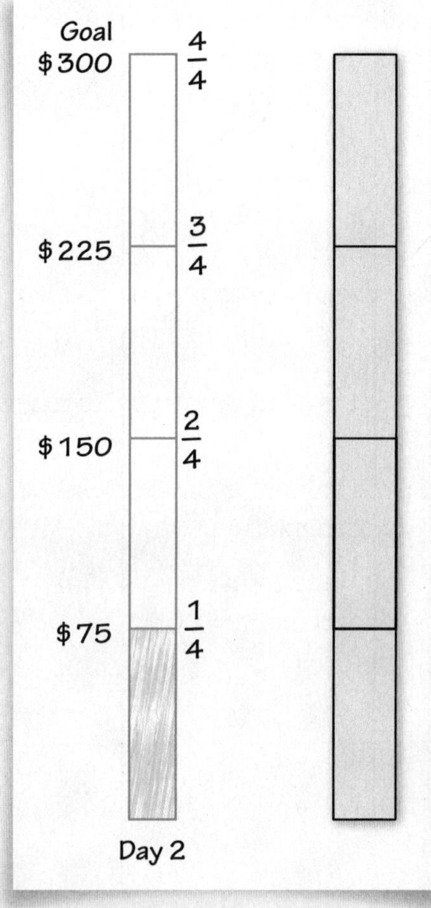

D 1. Jeri says that she can express the sixth-graders' progress on Day 2 in two ways using equivalent fractions: $\frac{1}{4}$ or $\frac{2}{8}$ of the goal. Find some other days for which you can write the sixth-graders' progress with two or more equivalent fractions.

2. Why do $\frac{1}{4}$ and $\frac{2}{8}$ both correctly describe the sixth-graders' progress on Day 2?

E At the end of Day 9, the sixth graders have raised $240.

1. What fraction of their goal have they reached?

2. Show how you would shade a blank thermometer for Day 9.

 Homework starts on page 27.

1.5 Comparing Fundraising Goals
Using Fractions and Ratios

In Problem 1.4, you used fractions to find parts of the sixth-graders' fundraising goal. Fraction strips and pictures such as fundraising thermometers are sometimes called **tape diagrams.** This is because a fraction strip is a long, skinny rectangle, like a long piece of tape.

In this Problem, you will use fractions to find parts of the other goals, and you will use ratios to compare the amounts raised by different grades.

A ratio comparison statement uses both numbers and words to show how two quantities are related. To write ratios, you can use the words *for every*, *to*, or a colon (:). For example, you may write these comparison statements.

For every $60 dollars the sixth graders raise, the seventh graders raise $90.

or

The ratio of the sixth-grade goal to the seventh-grade goal is 60 to 90.

or

The ratio of the sixth-grade goal to the seventh-grade goal is 60 : 90.

You read the colon ":" using the word *to*. Both the word *to* and the colon are common in mathematics.

The fundraising thermometers on the next page show the goals and the progress of each grade and of the teachers after ten days.

- Which situations involve fractions? Ratios? How can you decide?

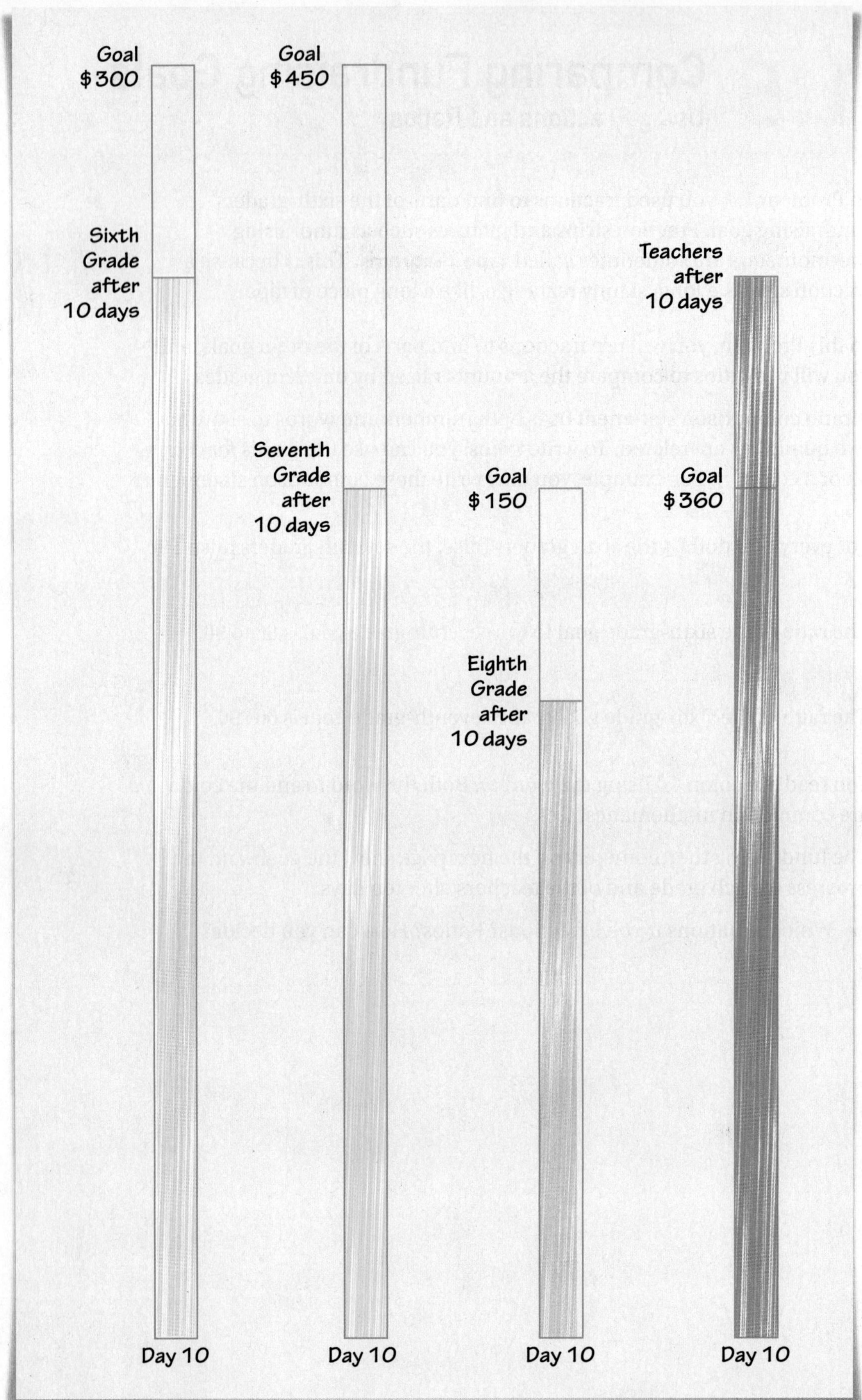
Goal
$300
Sixth
Grade
after
10 days
Day 10
Goal
$450
Seventh
Grade
after
10 days
Day 10
Goal
$150
Eighth
Grade
after
10 days
Day 10
Teachers
after
10 days
Goal
$360
Day 10

Problem 1.5

A **1.** What fraction of its goal did each grade reach by the end of Day 10 of the fundraiser?

2. What fraction of their goal did the teachers reach by the end of Day 10 of the fundraiser?

3. How much money did each group raise?

B Margarita said: "I think the seventh graders raised $300 by the end of Day 10 because I wrote several fractions that are equivalent to what I found with my fraction strips: $\frac{2}{3}$."

$$\frac{2}{3} = \frac{4}{6} = \frac{20}{30} = \frac{60}{90} = \frac{300}{450}$$

Margarita also drew this picture.

150	150	150
$\frac{1}{3}$	$\frac{2}{3}$	$\frac{3}{3}$

1. Explain how Margarita found these equivalent fractions. How does her picture relate to her method of finding equivalent fractions?

2. Use equivalent fractions to show how much money the sixth graders had raised by the end of Day 10.

3. Use equivalent fractions to show how much money the teachers had raised by the end of Day 10.

continued on the next page >

Problem 1.5 continued

C 1. Brian wrote this comparison statement: The ratio of the amount of money raised by the sixth graders to the amount raised by the seventh graders is 250 : 300. Is this a correct statement? Explain.

2. Kate thought of $250 as 25 ten-dollar bills and $300 as 30 ten-dollar bills. She wrote the ratio, 25 : 30. Write a comparison statement using Kate's ratio.

3. Are Brian and Kate's two ratios equivalent? Explain.

4. What ratio would Kate write if she thought of $250 and $300 as numbers of fifty-dollar bills? Would thinking of twenty-dollar bills work? Explain.

5. Write two comparison statements, using equivalent ratios, for amounts of money raised by the sixth grade compared to the eighth grade in the fundraiser.

D On the last day of the fundraiser, the principal announces the results using both fractions and ratios. She has these two sticky notes on her desk.

$$\frac{250}{300} = \frac{5}{6}$$

250 : 300
or
5 : 6

1. What do you think is the meaning of each note?

2. When are fractions useful? When are ratios useful?

ACE Homework starts on page 27.

Applications

1. Another middle school conducted the same type of fundraiser as the middle school in the Problems. The banner below shows the goals for each grade.

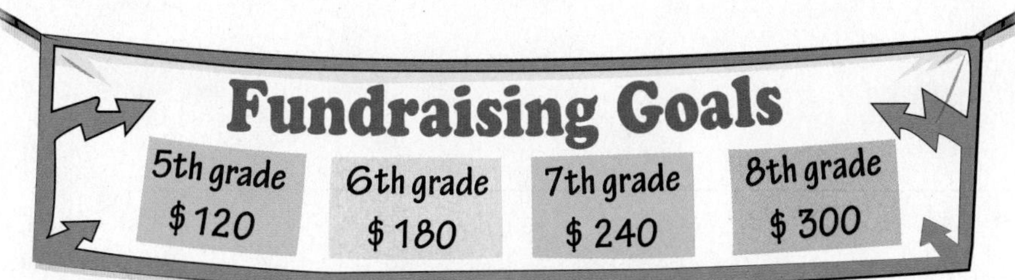

   a. Write three statements that the principal could make when comparing the goals each grade has set.

   b. The teachers set a goal of $225. Write two statements the principal could use to compare this goal to the eighth graders' goal.

2. Bryce and Rachel are collecting canned goods for the local food bank. Bryce's goal is to collect 32 items. Rachel's goal is to collect 24 items. If Rachel and Bryce each meet their goal, what fraction of Bryce's goal does Rachel collect?

3. A sixth-grade class has 12 boys and 24 girls.

   a. Consider this statement: *For every 2 boys, there are 4 girls.* Do you agree with the statement? Explain.

   b. Write two more statements comparing the number of boys in the class to the number of girls.

4. In a different sixth-grade class, the ratio of boys to girls is 3 : 2. How many boys and how many girls could there be in this class? Is there more than one possible answer? Explain.

5. What fraction strips could you make if you started with a fourths strip?

6. Below is a number line labeled using an eighths strip. What other strips could label some of the marks on this number line?

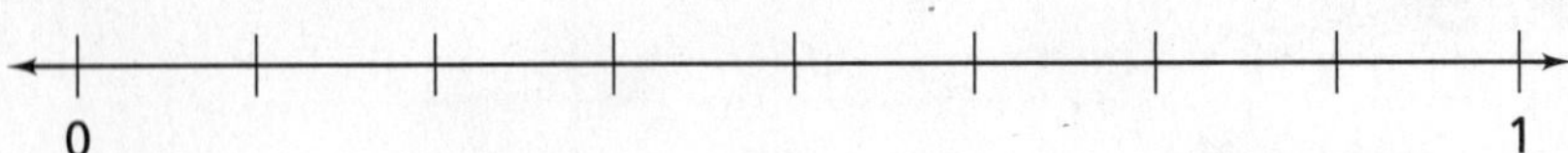

For Exercises 7–9, copy each number line. Make and use fraction strips or use some other method to estimate and name the point with a fraction.

7. 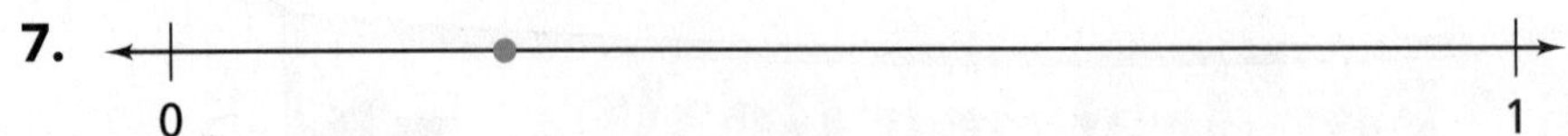

8. 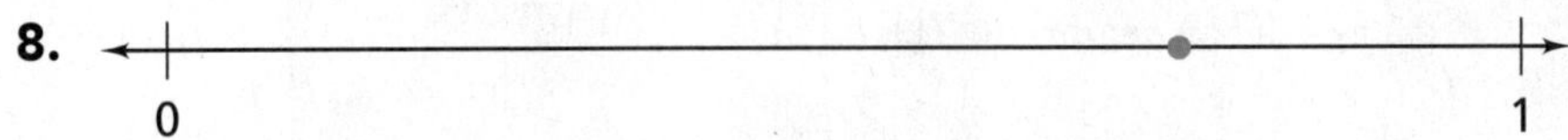

9. 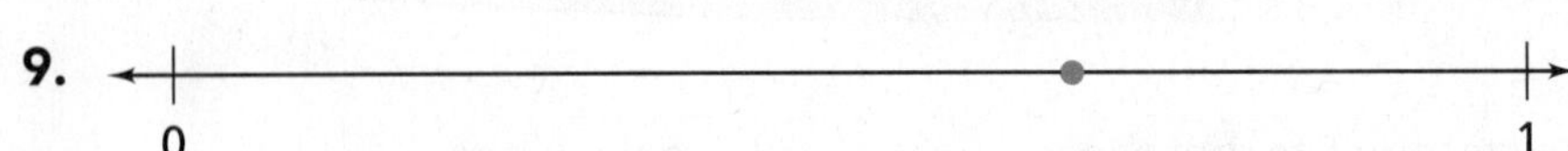

10. These students began to make a number line using different fraction strips as shown in the picture below. One student used the top fraction strip to mark $\frac{9}{12}$ on the number line.

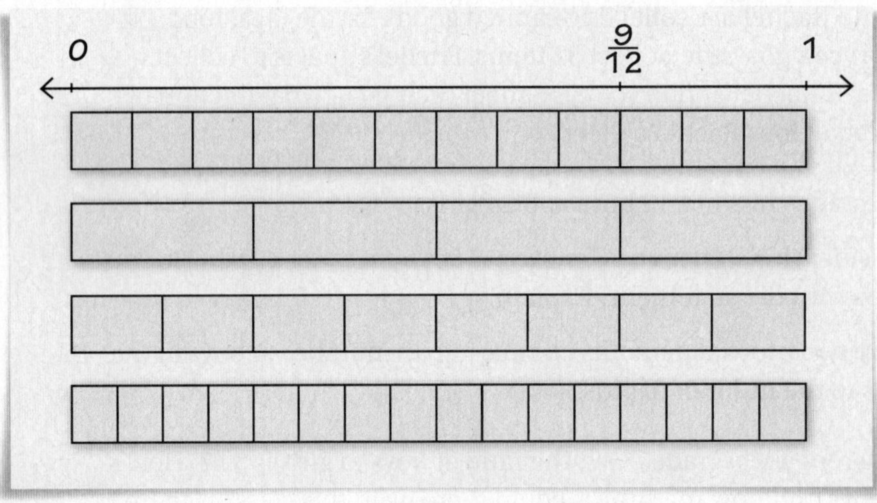

a. Name three other fractions shown here that are equivalent to $\frac{9}{12}$.

b. Name another fraction equivalent to $\frac{9}{12}$.

11. Erin used a fifths strip to mark and label $\frac{1}{5}$, $\frac{2}{5}$, $\frac{3}{5}$, and $\frac{4}{5}$ on her number line, as shown below.

a. Why is no label needed for $\frac{5}{5}$?

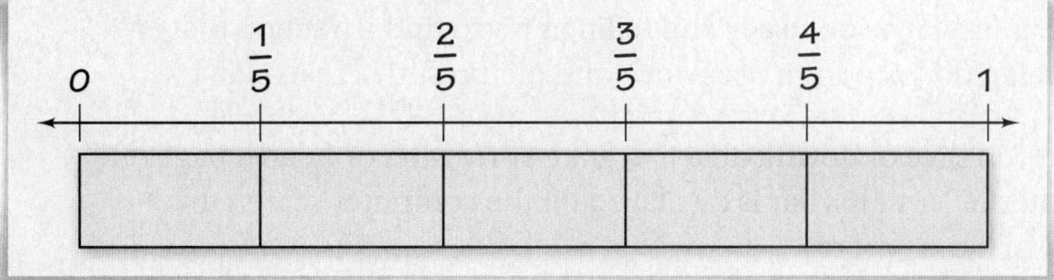

b. Sally marked her fraction strip like this.

$\frac{1}{5}$	$\frac{1}{5}$	$\frac{1}{5}$	$\frac{1}{5}$	$\frac{1}{5}$

She says any two segments on her strip are the same as $\frac{2}{5}$. Do you agree with her? Explain how Sally's thinking is different from the way the number line is marked with $\frac{2}{5}$.

c. If you label marks for $\frac{1}{10}$, $\frac{2}{10}$, $\frac{3}{10}$, $\frac{4}{10}$, $\frac{5}{10}$, $\frac{6}{10}$, $\frac{7}{10}$, $\frac{8}{10}$, $\frac{9}{10}$, and $\frac{10}{10}$ on Erin's number line, which marks now have more than one label? Why is this?

d. If you were to extend your number line to reach from 0 to 2, there would be five fifths for every whole number length. What are some other "for every" statements you can make about a number line from 0 to 2?

For Exercises 12–15, decide whether the statement is correct or incorrect. Explain your reasoning in words or by drawing pictures.

12. $\frac{1}{3} = \frac{4}{12}$

13. $\frac{4}{6} = \frac{2}{3}$

14. $\frac{2}{5} = \frac{1}{3}$

15. $\frac{2}{5} = \frac{5}{10}$

For Exercises 16 and 17, use fraction strips to make marks on a number line to show that the two fractions are equivalent.

16. $\frac{2}{5}$ and $\frac{6}{15}$

17. $\frac{1}{9}$ and $\frac{2}{18}$

18. Write an explanation to a friend telling how to find a fraction that is equivalent to $\frac{3}{5}$. You can use words and pictures to help explain.

19. When you save or download a file, load a program, or open a page on the Internet, a status bar is displayed on the computer screen to let you watch the progress.

a. Use the fraction strips shown to find three fractions that describe the status of the work in progress.

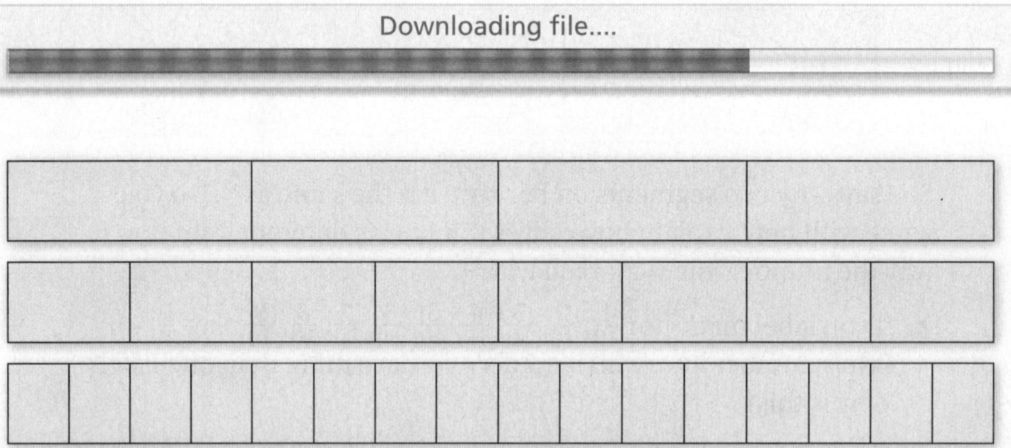

b. Suppose that you are downloading a movie with a file size of 2.8 GB (gigabyte). If the status bar above indicates how much of the movie has been downloaded, how many gigabytes have been downloaded so far?

20. Use your fraction strips to locate and label these numbers on a number line: 0, $\frac{3}{4}$, and $\frac{7}{8}$. Then use your fraction strips to measure the distance between $\frac{3}{4}$ and $\frac{7}{8}$.

For Exercises 21 and 22, fold new fraction strips or use some other method to estimate the fraction of the fundraising thermometer that is shaded.

21. Goal $400

22. Goal $400

For Exercises 23–27, use this illustration of a drink dispenser. The gauge on the front of the dispenser shows how much of the liquid remains in the dispenser. The dispenser holds 120 cups.

23. **a.** About what fraction of the dispenser is filled with liquid?

b. About how many cups of liquid are in the dispenser?

c. About what fraction of the dispenser is empty?

d. About how many more cups of liquid would it take to fill the dispenser?

24. Multiple Choice Which gauge shows about 37 out of 120 cups remaining?

A.  **B.** 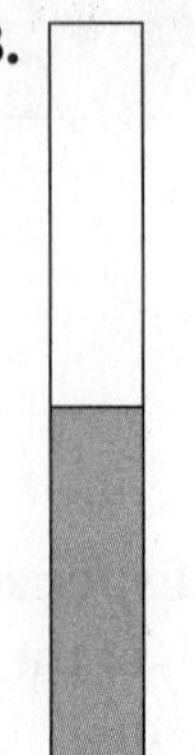 **C.** 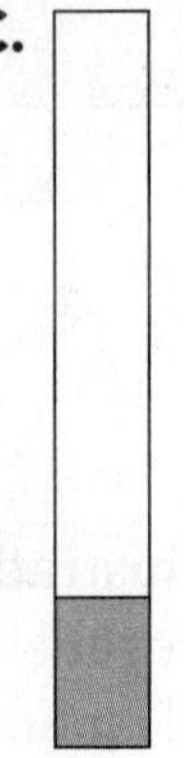 **D.** 

25. Multiple Choice Which gauge shows about 10 out of 120 cups remaining?

F. 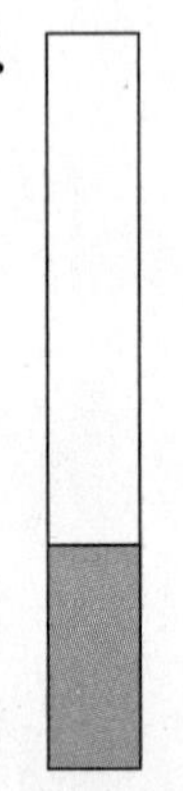 **G.** 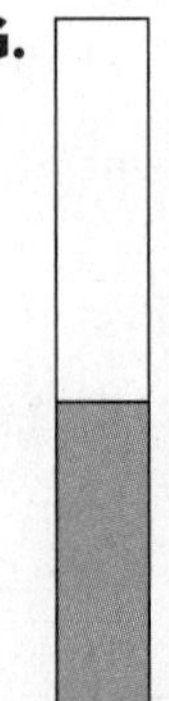 **H.** 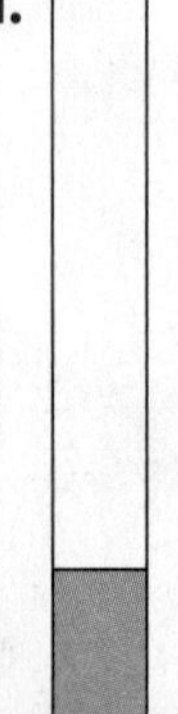 **J.** 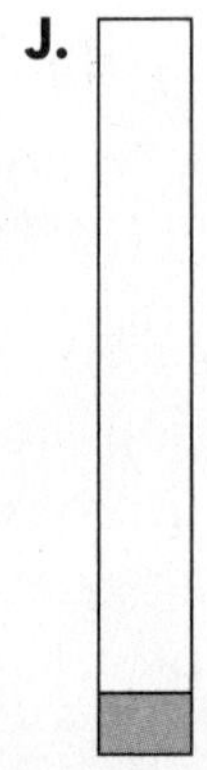

26. In Exercises 24 and 25, about what fraction is shaded in each gauge you chose?

27. For parts (a)–(c), sketch the gauge and, for each dispenser, say whether it can be best described as *almost empty, about half full,* or *almost full.*

a. five sixths $\left(\frac{5}{6}\right)$ of a full dispenser

b. three twelfths $\left(\frac{3}{12}\right)$ of a full dispenser

c. five eighths $\left(\frac{5}{8}\right)$ of a full dispenser

28. If a class collects \$155 toward a fundraising goal of \$775, what fraction represents their progress toward their goal?

For Exercises 29–32, use the graphic below. Christopher downloads two different podcasts each day. Today, one file is loading more slowly than the other.

The Mathcast

45 MB of 60 MB - 22 seconds remaining

Fraction Podcast

20 MB of 30 MB - 1 minute remaining

29. What fraction of each file has downloaded so far?

30. Write a comparison statement for the sizes of the two files.

31. Write a comparison statement for the sizes of the downloaded parts of the two files.

32. How long will it take for each file to download, from beginning to end?

33. Dan, Karim, and Shawn are training for the school cross-country team. One day, they report the distances they ran as comparison statements.

a. Dan says he ran twice as far as Karim. Give three possibilities for the distances each could have run.

b. Karim says that the ratio of the distance he ran to the distance Shawn ran is 4 : 3. Give three possibilities for the distances each could have run.

c. Which boy ran the furthest?

34. Kate, Sue, and Lisa are on the school basketball team. After one game, they report their scoring as comparison statements.

a. Kate and Sue made the same number of successful shots as each other. Kate's successful shots were all 3-pointers. Sue's successful shots were all 2-pointers. Give three possibilities for the numbers of points each could have scored.

b. Lisa says that she made twice as many successful shots as Sue but scored the same number of points. How is this possible?

c. Which girl scored the most points?

d. Which girl made the most shots?

Connections

For Exercises 35–38, explain your answer to each question.

35. Is 450 divisible by 5, 9, and 10?

36. Is 12 a divisor of 48?

37. Is 4 a divisor of 150?

38. Is 3 a divisor of 51?

39. Multiple Choice Choose the number that is *not* a factor of 300.

A. 5

B. 6

C. 8

D. 20

40. Multiple Choice Choose the answer that shows all of the factors of 48.

F. 2, 4, 8, 24, and 48

G. 1, 2, 3, 4, 5, 6, 8, and 12

H. 48, 96, and 144

J. 1, 2, 3, 4, 6, 8, 12, 16, 24, and 48

For Exercises 41–43, use the bar graph below, which shows the number of cans of juice three sixth-grade classes drank.

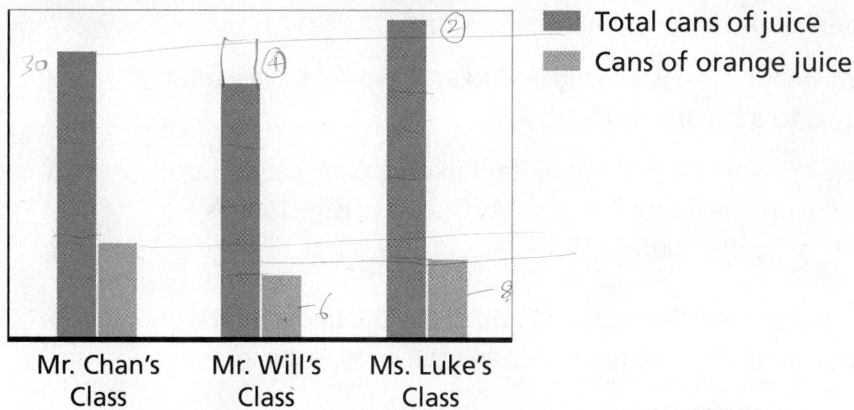

41. In each class, what fraction of the cans were orange juice?

42. In which class would you say orange juice was most popular?

43. a. Students in Mr. Chan's class drank a total of ten cans of orange juice. About how many cans of orange juice did the students in each of the other two classes drink?

b. About how many total cans of juice did each of the three classes drink?

44. a. Miguel says that you can easily separate numbers divisible by 2 into two equal parts. Do you agree? Why or why not?

b. Manny says that if Miguel is correct, then you can easily separate numbers divisible by 3 into three equal parts. Do you agree? Why or why not?

c. Lupe says that if any number is divisible by n, you can easily separate it into n equal parts. Do you agree with her? Explain.

45. a. If you had a fraction strip folded into twelfths, what fractional lengths could you measure with the strip?

b. How is your answer in part (a) related to the factors of 12?

46. a. If you had a fraction strip folded into tenths, what fractional lengths could you measure with the strip?

b. How is your answer in part (a) related to the factors of 10?

47. Ricky found a beetle that is one fourth $\left(\frac{1}{4}\right)$ the length of the fraction strips used in Problem 1.3.

a. How many beetle bodies, placed end to end, would have a total length equal to the length of a fraction strip?

b. How many beetle bodies, placed end to end, would have a total length equal to three fraction strips?

c. Ricky drew 13 paper beetle bodies, end to end, each the same length as the one he found. How many fraction strips long is Ricky's line of beetle bodies?

48. Rachel looked at the two ratios 25 : 30 and 250 : 300. In each ratio she noticed that the first and second numbers have a common factor.

a. What are some common factors of 25 and 30?

b. What are some common factors of 250 and 300?

c. Rachel says that the two numbers in a ratio will always have a common factor. Is she correct?

49. Abby looked at the same ratios (25 : 30 and 250 : 300). In these two equivalent ratios, she noticed that the first numbers have a common factor and the second numbers have a different common factor.

a. What are some common factors of 25 and 250?

b. What are some common factors of 30 and 300?

c. Abby says that the first numbers in two equivalent ratios will always have a common factor. Is she correct?

For Exercises 50 and 51, write a fraction to describe how much pencil is left, compared to a new pencil. Measure from the left edge of the eraser to the point of the pencil.

50.

51.

52. These bars represent trips that Ms. Axler took in her job this week.

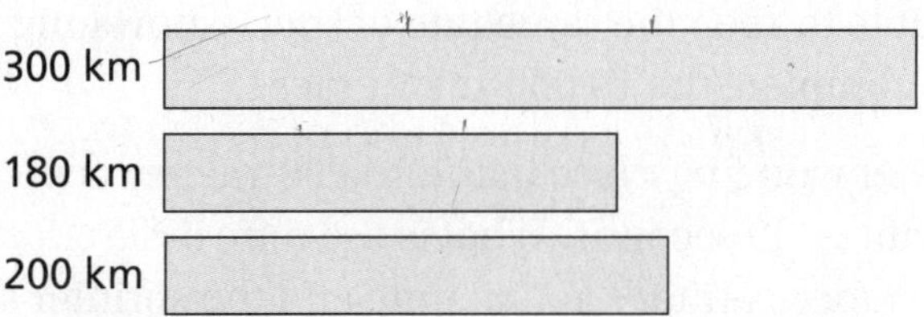

a. Copy each bar and shade in the distance Ms. Axler traveled after going one third of the total distance for each trip.

b. How many kilometers had Ms. Axler traveled when she was at the one-third point in each trip? Explain your reasoning.

53. Brett and Jim sign up to run in the Memorial Day race in their town. There are two different events at this race, a 5K (5 kilometers) and a 10K (10 kilometers). Brett signed up for the 5K and Jim signed up for the 10K.

a. Make fraction strips where each kilometer run is partitioned on equal length fraction strips for both Brett and Jim.

b. Use thermometers to indicate when both Brett and Jim have finished $\frac{3}{5}$ of their races. How many kilometers has each person run at this point?

c. Use the thermometers to indicate when both Brett and Jim are finished with four kilometers of their races. What fraction represents the amount of their respective races they have finished?

d. Write a "for every" claim that relates the distances Brett and Jim have run to their distance goals.

54. A sprinter finished a 100-meter race in a time of 12.63 seconds.

a. If the sprinter were able to keep the same rate of speed, how long would it take him to complete the 10,000-meter race?

b. A long-distance runner won first place in the 10,000-meter race with a time of 37 minutes, 30 seconds. What is the time difference between the long-distance runner's actual time and the sprinter's hypothetical time from part (a)?

55. Multiple Choice Find the least common multiple of the following numbers: 3, 4, 5, 6, 10, and 15.

A. 1 **B.** 15

C. 60 **D.** 54,000

56. Use what you found in Exercise 55. Write the following fractions in equivalent form, all with the same denominator.

$$\frac{1}{3} \quad \frac{1}{4} \quad \frac{1}{5} \quad \frac{1}{6} \quad \frac{1}{10} \quad \frac{1}{15}$$

For Exercises 57–60, find the greatest common factor of each pair of numbers.

57. 12 and 48 **58.** 6 and 9

59. 24 and 72 **60.** 18 and 45

For Exercises 61–64, use your answers from Exercises 57–60 to write a fraction equivalent to each fraction given.

61. $\frac{12}{48}$ **62.** $\frac{6}{9}$ **63.** $\frac{24}{72}$ **64.** $\frac{18}{45}$

Extensions

For Exercises 65–67, write a numerator for each fraction to make the fraction close to, but not equal to, $\frac{1}{2}$. Then, write another numerator to make each fraction close to, but greater than, 1.

65. $\frac{\blacksquare}{22}$ **66.** $\frac{\blacksquare}{43}$ **67.** $\frac{\blacksquare}{17}$

For Exercises 68–70, write a denominator to make each fraction close to, but not equal to, $\frac{1}{2}$. Then, write another denominator to make each fraction close to, but greater than, 1.

68. $\frac{22}{\blacksquare}$ **69.** $\frac{43}{\blacksquare}$ **70.** $\frac{17}{\blacksquare}$

For Exercises 71–74, copy the number line. Use your knowledge of fractions to estimate and name the point with a fraction.

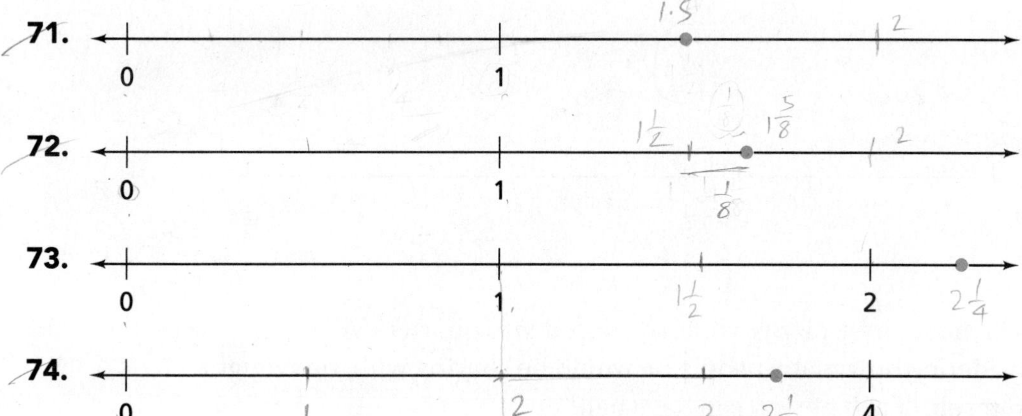

For Exercises 75–80, copy the number line. Estimate and mark where the number 1 belongs on each number line.

75. 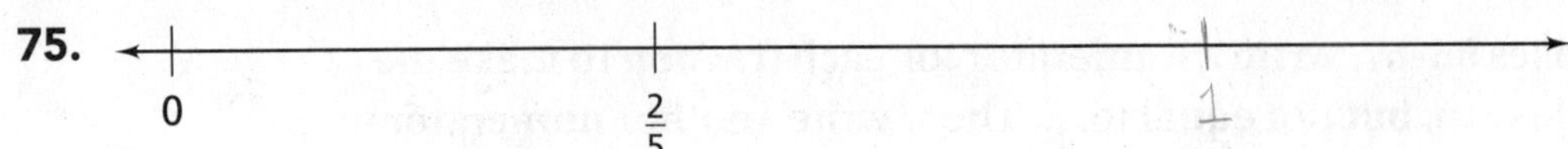

76. 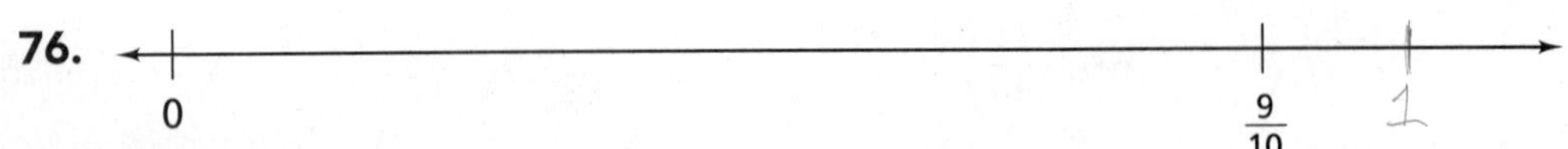

77. 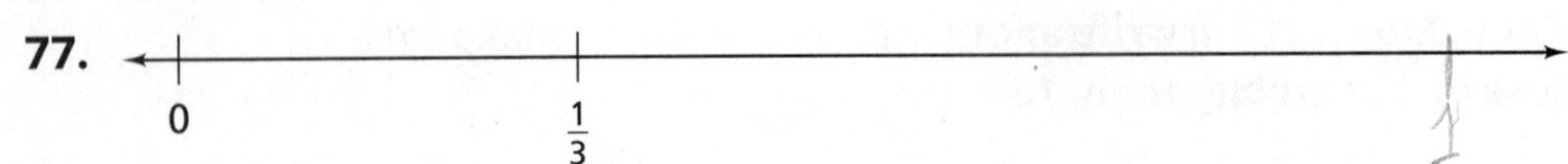

78. 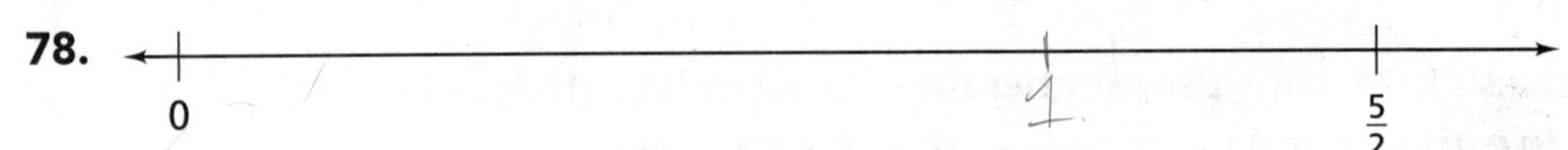

79. 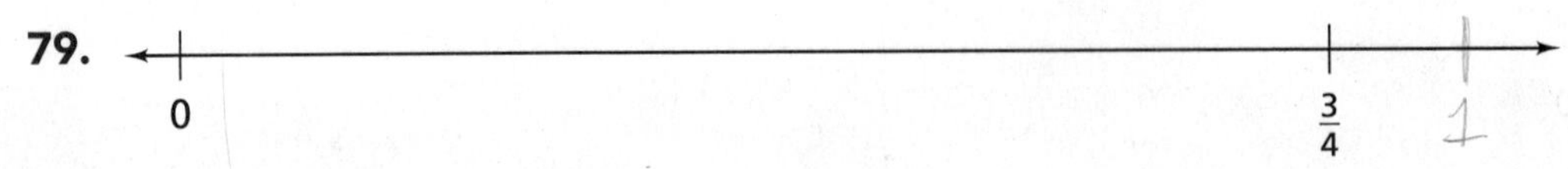

80. 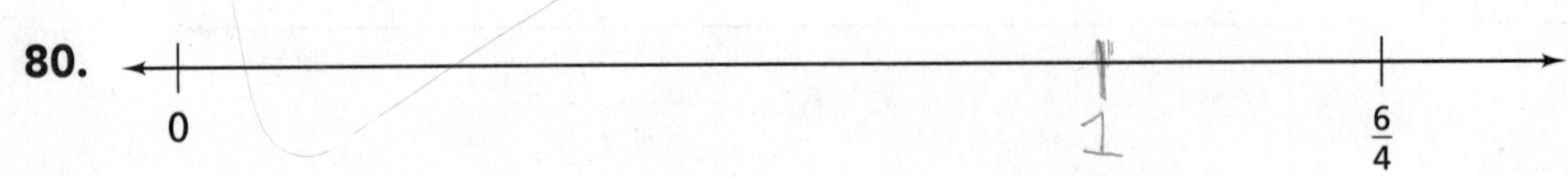

81. Dario made three pizzas, which he sliced into quarters. After considering how many people he would be sharing with, he thought to himself, "Each person can have half."

a. Is it possible that there was only one other person to share with? Explain.

b. Is it possible that Dario was sharing the pizzas with 5 other people? Explain.

c. Is it possible that Dario was sharing the pizzas with 11 other people? Explain.

82. In Problem 1.5, the eighth-grade thermometer is smaller than the sixth- and seventh-grade thermometers. Redraw the eighth-grade thermometer so that it is the same size as the sixth- and seventh-grade thermometers, but still shows the correct fraction for Day 10.

Mathematical Reflections 1

In your work in this Investigation, you wrote comparison statements using fractions and ratios. You also used fraction strips to make a number line and compare fractions. These questions will help you summarize what you have learned.

Think about your answers to these questions. Discuss your ideas with other students and your teacher. Then write a summary of your findings in your notebook.

1. **a. Write** three comparison statements about the same situation, one using difference, one using a fraction, and one using a ratio.

   b. Explain what you think a ratio is.

2. **a. What** does it mean for two fractions to be equivalent? For two ratios to be equivalent?

   b. What are some useful ways of finding equivalent fractions and equivalent ratios?

Common Core Mathematical Practices

As you worked on the Problems in this Investigation, you used prior knowledge to make sense of them. You also applied Mathematical Practices to solve the Problems. Think back over your work, the ways you thought about the Problems, and how you used Mathematical Practices.

Sophie described her thoughts in the following way:

We used fraction strips and number lines as a tool in Problem 1.3 to compare fractions and to find groups of fractions related to each other.

When we lined up the fraction strips, we noticed that equivalent fractions occurred when the fold marks lined up with each other and that these were all names for the same point on the line.

Common Core Standards for Mathematical Practice

MP5 Use appropriate tools strategically

- What other Mathematical Practices can you identify in Sophie's reasoning?
- Describe a Mathematical Practice that you and your classmates used to solve a different Problem in this Investigation.

Connecting Ratios and Rates

In Investigation 1, you used fraction strips as a tool to determine the fraction of each fundraising goal reached and locate points and distances on a number line. You also used ratios to compare quantities and checked to see if they were equivalent. In this Investigation you will continue to explore ratios and ways to write equivalent ratios.

The ratio statements in Investigation 1 were written as "for every" or "to" statements. Ratios can be written in many different ways.

Suppose the cost for ten students to go on a field trip is $120. You can write ratios to show how the quantities are related.

10 students *for every* $120

10 students *to every* $120

10 students : $120

Common Core State Standards

6.RP.A.3 Use ratio and rate reasoning to solve real-world and mathematical problems, e.g., by reasoning about tables of equivalent ratios, tape diagrams, double number line diagrams, or equations.

6.RP.A.3a Make tables of equivalent ratios relating quantities with whole-number measurements, find missing values in the tables . . .

6.RP.A.3b Solve unit rate problems including those involving unit pricing and constant speed.

Also 6.RP.A.1, 6.RP.A.2, 6.NS.B.4

Ratio statements can also be written as "per" statements. For example, "It costs $120 per 10 students to go on the trip." An equivalent comparison statement is "the cost per student to go on a field trip is $12." Now you can say

$12 *for every* 1 student

$12 *for each* student

$12 *per* student

This particular comparison, cost per one student, is called a unit rate. A **unit rate** is a comparison in which one of the numbers being compared is 1 unit.

- If the cost of food is $250 for 50 students, what is the cost per student?

To answer this question, you find the unit rate.

2.1 Equal Shares
Introducing Unit Rates

Often we share food so that each person gets the same amount. This may mean that food is cut into smaller pieces. Think about how to share a chewy fruit worm that is already marked in equal-sized pieces.

The chewy fruit worm below shows four equal segments.

How can you share this 4-segment chewy fruit worm equally among four people?

How many segments of the worm does each person get?

How can you share this 4-segment chewy fruit worm equally among three people?

How many segments of the worm does each person get?

Problem 2.1

In Questions A and B, find the fraction of a chewy fruit worm each person gets.

A 1. Show two ways that four people can share a 6-segment chewy fruit worm. In each case, how many segments does each person get?

2. Show two ways that six people can share an 8-segment chewy fruit worm. In each case, how many segments does each person get?

B 1. Show how 12 people can share an 8-segment chewy fruit worm. How many segments are there for every person?

2. Show how five people can share a 3-segment chewy fruit worm. How much is this per person?

C Jena wants to share a 6-segment chewy fruit worm. The tape diagram below shows the marks she made on the worm so she can share it equally among the members in her CMP group.

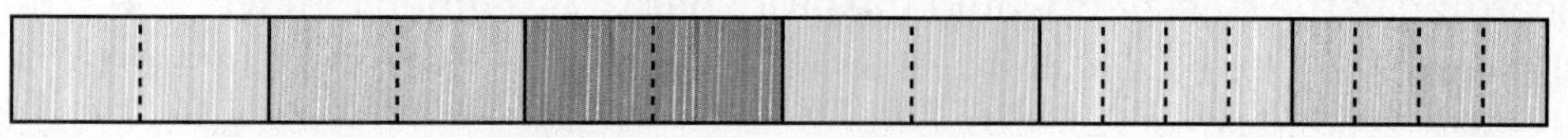

1. How many people are in her group?
2. Is there more than one possible answer to part (1)? Explain.
3. What is the number of segments per person?
4. Write a fraction to show the part of the chewy fruit worm each person gets.

D Would you rather be one of four people sharing a 6-segment chewy fruit worm or one of eight people sharing a 12-segment chewy fruit worm? Explain.

E Look back at your work on this Problem. Describe how you found or used unit rates.

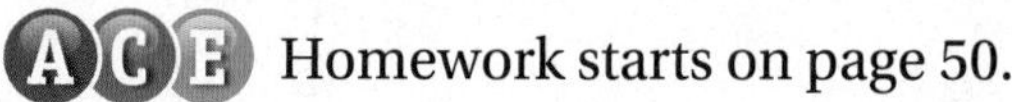

Homework starts on page 50.

2.2 Unequal Shares
Using Ratios and Fractions

Sometimes there are reasons to share quantities *unequally*. Suppose your older brother paid more than half the cost of a video game. You might think it is fair for him to spend more time playing the game. At a party, you might agree that your friend should take the bigger piece of chocolate cake because your friend likes chocolate more than you do.

Two sisters, Crystal and Alexa, are going to a strange birthday party. Instead of birthday cake, pairs of party guests are each served a large chewy fruit worm to share according to their ages. Since the sisters are not the same age, they do not share their fruit worm equally.

Crystal is 12 years old and Alexa is 6 years old. Their chewy fruit worm has 18 segments. According to their ages, Crystal gets 12 segments and Alexa gets 6 segments. The ratio of the girls' shares of the worm, 12 to 6, is equivalent to the ratio of their ages, 12 to 6.

- According to the rule, how would the girls share a 9-segment chewy fruit worm?

Since Crystal's age is two times Alexa's age, Crystal gets twice as many segments as Alexa. The ratio of Crystal's segments to Alexa's segments is 12 to 6 or 2 to 1.

- The ratio 2 to 1 is a unit rate. What do the numbers 2 and 1 mean for the sisters?

In this Problem you will explore situations that involve fractions and ratios.

Problem 2.2

A Draw some chewy fruit worms with different numbers of segments that Crystal and Alexa can share without having to make new cuts.

B **1.** Jared is 10 years old. His brother Peter is 15 years old. What are some chewy fruit worms they can share without having to make new cuts?

2. For each worm you described in part (1), write a ratio comparing the number of segments Jared gets to the number of segments Peter gets.

3. Are the ratios you wrote in part (2) equivalent to each other? Explain.

4. How would you write a unit rate to compare how many segments Jared and Peter get?

C **1.** Caleb and Isaiah are brothers. They share a 14-segment chewy fruit worm according to their age. How old could they be?

Caleb Isaiah

2. Caleb gets 8 out of the 14 segments of the chewy fruit worm, so he gets $\frac{8}{14}$ and Isaiah gets $\frac{6}{14}$ of the worm.

a. From Question A, what fractions of the chewy fruit worm do Crystal and Alexa each get at the birthday party?

b. From Question B, what fractions of the chewy fruit worm do Jared and Peter each get at the birthday party?

c. How does the ratio of segments that Caleb and Isaiah get relate to the fractions of the chewy fruit worm that they each get?

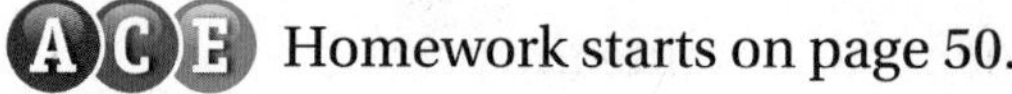

ACE Homework starts on page 50.

2.3 Making Comparisons With Rate Tables

When comparing how to share chewy fruit worms, Crystal recorded how many segments she and her sister would get for different sizes of chewy fruit worms. Crystal thought she could use what she knew about equivalence to make a table showing the amounts.

Comparing Segments

Segments for Alexa	6	3	1	2	$\frac{1}{2}$	10
Segments for Crystal	12	6	2	4	1	20

The table shows that for every segment given to Alexa, Crystal gets two segments. This is Alexa's unit rate. The table also shows that for every $\frac{1}{2}$ segment Alexa is given, Crystal gets one segment. This is Crystal's unit rate.

Crystal sees an ad for chewy fruit worms. She decides she wants the student council to include chewy fruit worms in the fundraising sale.

You can use the information in the advertisement to compute the price for any number of worms you want to buy. One way to figure out the price of a single item from a quantity price is use the information to build a **rate table** of equivalent ratios.

The rate table in Question A shows the price for different numbers of chewy fruit worms. The cost of 30 chewy fruit worms is $3.

Problem 2.3

A **1.** Crystal wants to calculate costs quickly for many different numbers of chewy fruit worms. Copy and complete the rate table below with prices for each of the numbers of chewy fruit worms.

Chewy Fruit Worm Pricing

Number of Worms	1	5	10	15	30	90	150	180
Reduced Price	■	■	■	■	$3	■	■	■

2. How much do 3 chewy fruit worms cost? 300 chewy fruit worms?

3. How many chewy fruit worms can you buy for $50? For $10?

4. What is the unit price of one chewy fruit worm? What is the unit rate?

B The student council also decides to sell popcorn to raise money. One ounce of popcorn (unpopped) kernels yields 4 cups of popcorn. One serving is a bag of popcorn that holds 2 cups of popcorn.

1. Use a rate table to find the number of ounces of popcorn kernels needed to determine the cups of popcorn.

Cups of Popcorn From Ounces of Kernels

Number of Cups of Popcorn	4	■	■	■	■	■	■	■	■	■	■	■
Number of Ounces of Popcorn Kernels	1	2	3	4	5	6	7	8	9	10	11	12

2. How many cups of popcorn can you make from 12 ounces of popcorn kernels? From 30 ounces of popcorn kernels?

3. How many ounces of popcorn kernels are needed to make 40 cups of popcorn? To make 100 cups of popcorn?

4. How many ounces of kernels are needed to make 100 servings?

5. How many ounces of kernels are needed to make 1 cup?

C **1.** How do rate tables help you answer Question A and Question B?

2. How do unit rates help you answer Question A and Question B?

ACE Homework starts on page 50.

Applications

1. Show two ways three people can share a 5-segment chewy fruit worm.

2. Show two ways five people can share a 3-segment chewy fruit worm.

3. Sharon is ready to share the 4-segment chewy fruit worm shown below. She has already made the marks she needs so that she can share it equally among the members of her group.

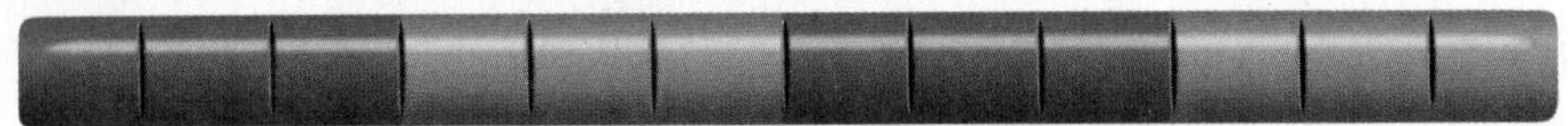

   a. Give two different numbers of people that could be in Sharon's group.

   b. For each answer you gave in part (a), write a ratio comparing the number of people sharing a chewy fruit worm to the number of segments they are sharing. How would you rewrite this as a unit rate?

4. Cheryl, Rita, and four of their friends go to a movie and share a 48-ounce bag of popcorn equally and three 48-inch licorice laces equally. Write a ratio comparing the number of ounces of popcorn to the number of friends. Then, write a unit rate comparing the length of licorice lace for each person.

5. The Lappans buy three large sandwiches to serve at a picnic. Nine people come to the picnic. Show three different ways to cut the sandwiches so that each person gets an equal share.

6. Three neighbors are sharing a rectangular strip of land for a garden. They divide the land into 24 equal-sized pieces. They each get the same amount of land. Write a ratio comparing the number of pieces of land to the number of people. Write the answer in more than one way.

7. For each chewy fruit worm below write the possible ages of the two people sharing the worm by age.

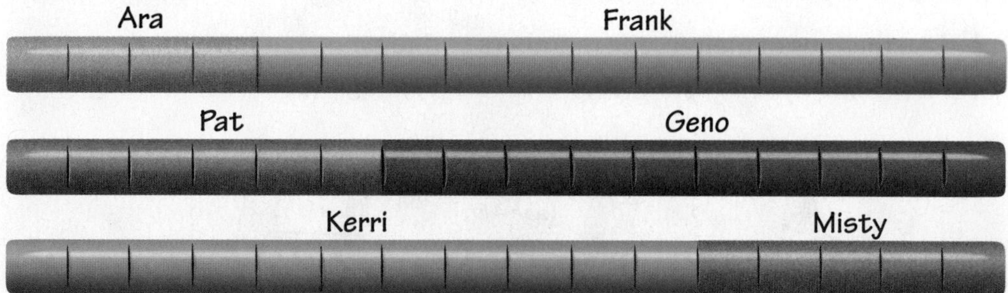

Use this information for Exercises 8–10. At the birthday party in Problem 2.2, the children run relay races. The distance each team member runs depends on the ratio of their ages. For example, a boy who is twice as old as a girl runs twice as far.

8. Crystal is 12 years old and Alexa is 6 years old. If Crystal runs 100 yards, how far does Alexa run? How far do they run altogether?

9. Jared is 10 years old and Peter is 15 years old. Together, they run 150 yards. How far does each brother run?

10. Wynne and Emmett are brother and sister. Wynne runs 180 yards. Emmett runs 120 yards. How old could each of them be?

Use this information for Exercises 11–14. Parents are older than their children. The ratio of a parent's age to a child's age changes as the parent and child get older.

11. Can a parent ever be exactly twice as old as his or her child? Explain.

12. Can a parent ever be exactly three times as old as his or her child? Explain.

13. Can the ratio of a parent's age to his or her child's age ever be exactly 3 : 2? Explain.

14. Can the ratio of a parent's age to his or her child's age ever be exactly 10 : 9? Explain.

15. Crystal and Alexa convince the older members of their family to break up the chewy fruit worms using age ratios. They want to know which family members have the same age ratio as Crystal and Alexa.

a. Use the ages of their family members to find pairs that have the same age ratio as Crystal (age 12) and Alexa (age 6).

b. What do all the ratios that you wrote in part (a) have in common?

For Exercises 16–18, copy and complete the table comparing the chewy fruit worm segments each family member received. State both unit rates in each comparison.

16.

Segments for Alan	48	12	■	1	■	7
Segments for Lisa	24	■	8	■	1	■

17.

Segments for Lisa	24	12	■	1	■	■
Segments for Crystal	6	■	2	■	1	$1\frac{1}{2}$

18.

Segments for Alan	48	24	■	1	■	■
Segments for Crystal	6	■	2	■	1	$1\frac{1}{2}$

For Exercises 19–22, use the family members from Exercise 15, including Crystal and Alexa. Determine which two people have each age ratio.

19. The unit rate is 2 : 1.

20. The unit rate is 4 : 1.

21. The ratio of segments (ages) is 3 : 4.

22. The ratio of segments (ages) is 3 : 2.

For Exercises 23 and 24, Rosco is planning meals for his family. He uses the vertical rate tables.

23. **a.** Complete the rate table for the macaroni and cheese ingredients.

Macaroni and Cheese

Ounces of Macaroni	Cups of Cheese
8	1
■	2
■	3
■	4
■	5
■	6

b. How many ounces of macaroni would you need for 7 cups of cheese?

c. How many cups of cheese would you need for 88 ounces of macaroni?

24. a. Complete the rate table for the spaghetti ingredients.

Spaghetti and Sauce

Ounces of Spaghetti	Ounces of Tomatoes
12	16
6	8
3	■
2	■
1	■

b. What is the unit rate comparing the number of ounces of tomatoes to 1 ounce of spaghetti?

c. What is the unit rate comparing 1 ounce of tomatoes to the number of ounces of spaghetti?

Connections

25. Ursula, Ubaldo, Ulysses, and Dora were trying to come up with different ways to divide a 10-segment chewy fruit worm among the four of them. Which of these strategies would result in sharing equally?

- Ursula's Strategy:

  Give everyone two segments, and then divide the remaining two segments into four equal pieces with each person getting another half of a segment.

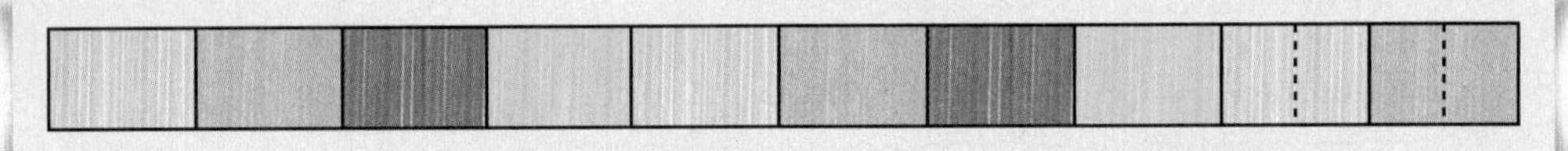

- Ubaldo's Strategy:

  Give each person one segment, then if there's at least four segments left, give each person another segment. Repeat this process until there are less than four segments, then cut the leftover pieces into four equal parts and give each person a part.

- Ulysses' Strategy:

  Give each person two segments, and then use a spinner to pick the winner of the extra two segments.

- Dora's Strategy:

  Forget about the segments. Just cut the worm in half, and then cut each half in half again.

26. If you were going to make segment marks on a chewy fruit worm without any marks, what would be the advantage or disadvantage of using a prime number of segments?

27. A typical container of orange juice concentrate holds 12 fluid ounces (fl oz). The standard recipe is "Mix one can of concentrate with three cans of cold water."

   a. What is the ratio of concentrate to water?

   b. How large of a container will you need to hold the juice?

   c. Olivia has a one-gallon container to fill with orange juice. She uses the standard recipe. How much concentrate does she need? (One gallon is 128 fl oz.)

28. A typical container of lemonade concentrate holds 12 fl oz. The standard recipe is "Mix one can of concentrate with $4\frac{1}{3}$ cans of cold water."

   a. What is the ratio of concentrate to water?

   b. How large of a container will you need to hold the lemonade?

   c. Olivia has a one-gallon container to fill with lemonade. She uses the standard recipe. How much concentrate does she need? (One gallon is 128 fl oz.)

29. Langhus Convenience Store sells multiple sizes of chewy fruit worms. Betsy, Emily, and John are trying to decide which of the deals would give them the most chewy fruit worms for the price.

a. Which argument do you think is the best? Explain.

- Betsy: The small size is the best deal because you get the most amount of worms, 10 more than the medium size, and 18 more than the large size.
- John: The large size is the best deal because you have to pay the least amount of money overall.
- Emily: I used the least common multiple of 4, 8, and 12, which is 24. For $24, I could buy 60 large worms, 54 medium worms, and 56 small worms. The large size is the best deal.

b. How could Betsy, John, and Emily use unit rates to find the best deal?

30. As Johann is working on unit rates in Exercises 16–24, he notices something interesting and says to his teacher, "Whenever you compare two quantities and you write both unit rates, at least one of them will have a fraction in it." Is Johann correct? Explain why you agree or disagree with him.

Extensions

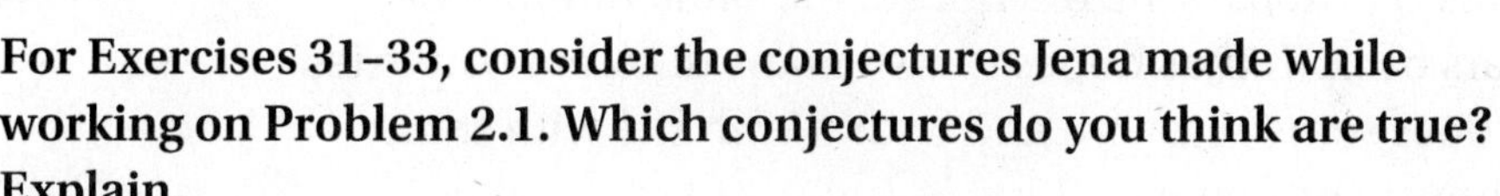

For Exercises 31–33, consider the conjectures Jena made while working on Problem 2.1. Which conjectures do you think are true? Explain.

31. If the number of people is greater than the number of segments, each person will get less than one segment.

32. There are at least two ways to divide any chewy fruit worm so that everyone will get the same amount.

33. If the ratio of people to segments is 1 : 2, then each person will get $\frac{1}{2}$ of a segment.

34. Harold is eight years older than Maynard. On Harold's sixteenth birthday, he notices something interesting about their age ratios. He says, "When I was nine, the ratio of my age to Harold's was 9 : 1. A year later the ratio was 5 : 1. That's when I was ten and Maynard was two. Now on my sixteenth birthday, I'm twice as old as Maynard, which means the ratio of our ages is 2 : 1." Will Harold and Maynard ever have an age ratio 1 : 1? Explain.

35. A women's 4-by-100 meter medley relay team finished in second place. In the relay, each member swims 100 meters using a different stroke. The ages of the team members are 21, 22, 25, and 41.

The age difference between the oldest and youngest swimmer on this team was 20 years!

Suppose they had broken up the distance of 400 meters by age as in Problem 2.2. How far would each person swim in the relay?

36. Mariette, Melissa, and Michelle were given this follow-up question by Mr. Mirasola to Problem 2.3, "If you had $13.75, how many large chewy fruit worms could you buy?"

- Mariette said that she could buy $5\frac{1}{2}$.
- Melissa said that she could buy only 5.
- Michelle said that she could buy only 4.

Mr. Mirasola said, "You are all correct depending on how you think of the ad." How is it possible that they could all be correct?

37. On a recent trip to Canada, Tomas learned that there was an "exchange rate" between U.S. dollars and Canadian dollars. When he exchanged his U.S. dollars, he did not get the same number of Canadian dollars back. Tomas hopes to visit many different countries one day, so he does some research and finds a Web site with some basic money conversions on it.

a. Find the unit rate for each country below.

Currency Exchange Rates

\$20 US ≈ 19 Australian Dollars	\$1 US ≈ ■ AUD	\$■ US ≈ 1 AUD
\$5 US ≈ 4 Euros	\$1 US ≈ ■ Euros	\$■ US ≈ 1 Euro
\$50 US ≈ 49 Swiss Francs	\$1 US ≈ ■ SF	\$■ US ≈ 1 SF
\$3 US ≈ 2 Pounds (UK)	\$1 US ≈ ■ Pounds	\$■ US ≈ 1 Pound
\$4 US ≈ 5 Singapore Dollars	\$1 US ≈ ■ SGD	\$■ US ≈ 1 SGD

Note: Exchange rates often change from day to day; there are Web sites that have the most up-to-date exchange rates.

b. How can you use this information to convert euros to Australian dollars or Swiss francs to Singapore dollars? Explain.

5000 Japanese yen, Ichiyo Higuchi (1872–1896), writer and poet

10 US dollars, Andrew Jackson (1767–1845), seventh President

10 English pounds, Queen Elizabeth II (b. 1926)

20 Australian dollars, Mary Reibey (1777–1855), businesswoman

Mathematical Reflections 2

In this Investigation, you used ratios to share equally and unequally according to certain rules. You used rate tables and unit rates to solve problems. These questions will help you summarize what you have learned.

Think about your answers to these questions. Discuss your ideas with other students and your teacher. Then write a summary in your notebook.

1. **a. How** can you determine a unit rate for a situation?

   b. Describe some ways that unit rates are useful.

2. **a. What** strategies do you use to make a rate table?

   b. Describe some ways that rate tables are useful.

3. **How** are your strategies for writing equivalent ratios the same as or different from writing equivalent fractions?

Common Core Mathematical Practices

As you worked on the Problems in this Investigation, you used prior knowledge to make sense of the Problems. You also applied Mathematical Practices to solve the Problems. Think back over your work, the ways you thought about the Problems, and how you used Mathematical Practices.

Jayden described his thoughts in the following way:

We used rate tables to find the prices for different amounts of chewy fruit worms in Problem 2.3.

In the rate table, we noticed a repeated pattern such as "for every 5 worms we need to pay $.50." Some of us expressed this pattern in the amount of a unit rate: the money per each worm or number of worms per $1.

In figuring out how much we need to pay for 300 worms, we used our rate table and noticed that there is a $3 increase for every 30 worms.

Common Core Standards for Mathematical Practice

MP7 Look for and make use of structure

- What other Mathematical Practices can you identify in Jayden's reasoning?
- Describe a Mathematical Practice that you and your classmates used to solve a different Problem in this Investigation.

Extending the Number Line

In this Unit, you have used fractions to express parts of a whole and ratios to compare quantities. In this Investigation, you will learn about negative fractions and improper fractions. You will also learn about the opposite and absolute value of a number. You will use this information to extend the number line to include negative numbers.

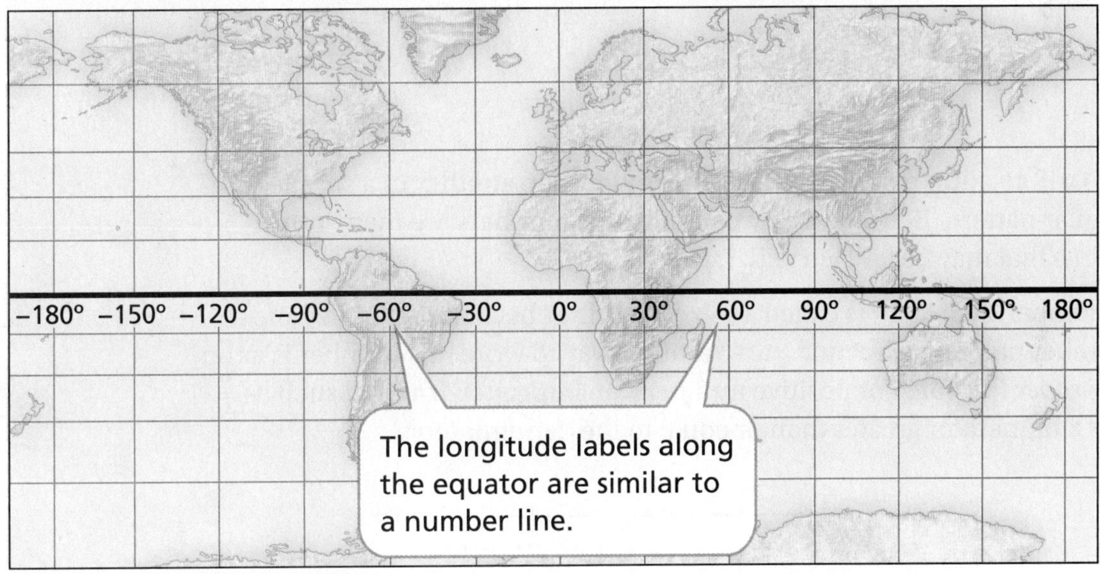

Common Core State Standards

6.NS.C.6a Recognize opposite signs of numbers as indicating locations on opposite sides of 0 on the number line; recognize that the opposite of the opposite of a number is the number itself, e.g., $-(-3) = 3$, and that 0 is its own opposite.

6.NS.C.6c Find and position integers and other rational numbers on a horizontal or vertical number line diagram . . .

6.NS.C.7b Write, interpret, and explain statements of order for rational numbers in real-world contexts.

6.NS.C.7c Understand the absolute value of a rational number as its distance from 0 on the number line; interpret absolute value as magnitude for a positive or negative quantity in a real-world situation.

Also 6.RP.A.1, 6.RP.A.2, 6.RP.A.3, 6.NS.B.3, 6.NS.B.4, 6.NS.C.5, 6.NS.C.6, 6.NS.C.7, and 6.NS.C.7d

As you work through this Investigation, you will combine new information with your previous knowledge of the place-value system of whole numbers to study **decimals.**

In Investigation 2, you used a fraction strip model to show how an item could be shared among a group of people. In this Investigation, you will see how a fraction of an item can be expressed on a grid model. The grid model is also used to write fractions as decimals. In time, you will be able to identify when it is appropriate to express equal shares as a fraction or as a decimal.

3.1 Extending the Number Line

Integers and Mixed Numbers

In Investigation 1, you worked with the part of the number line between 0 and 1, shown below.

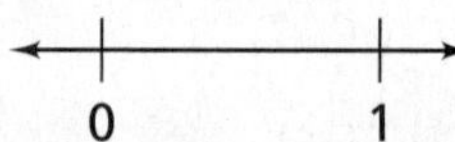

The whole numbers on a number line follow one another in a simple, regular pattern. Between every pair of whole numbers are many other points that may be labeled with fractions.

A number such as $1\frac{1}{2}$ is called a **mixed number** because it has a whole number part and a fraction part. Another way to write this number is as an *improper fraction.* For positive numbers, an **improper fraction** such as $\frac{3}{2}$ has a numerator greater than or equal to the denominator.

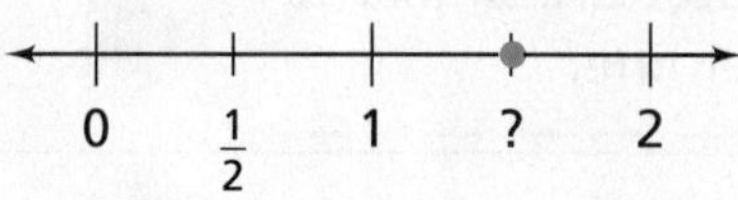

- Why can this point be labeled with two names: $1\frac{1}{2}$ and $\frac{3}{2}$?

There is really nothing improper about these fractions. This is just a name used for fractions that represent more than one whole. You may have used a mixed number or an improper fraction to express the teachers' fundraising success in the previous Investigation.

The number line can be extended in both directions, as shown below. Numbers to the left of zero are marked with a "–" sign and are read as *negative one, negative two,* etc.

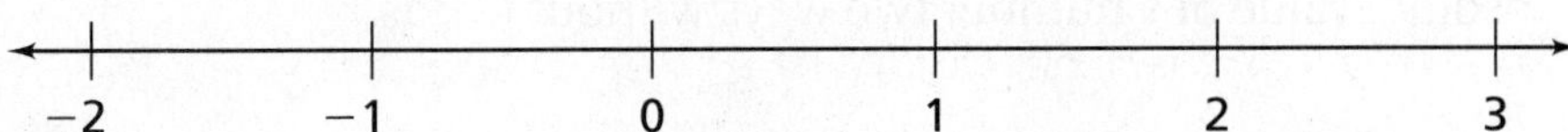

In this Problem, you will use fractions, mixed numbers, and improper fractions. You can represent positive and negative fractions and mixed numbers as points on the number line.

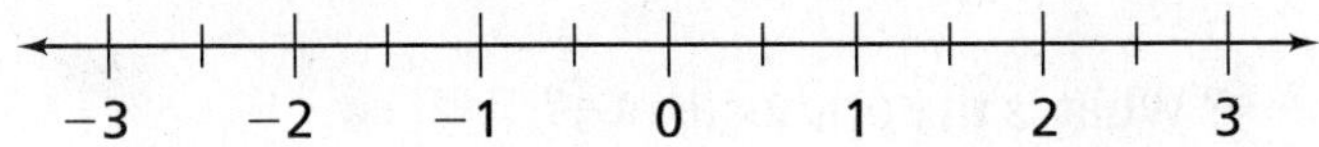

- Betty says that the mark between 2 and 3 should be labeled $\frac{1}{2}$. Do you agree?
- Judi says that the mark between 2 and 3 should be labeled $\frac{5}{2}$. Do you agree?
- What label should you put on the mark between −2 and −3?
- If there were a mark halfway between that mark and −2, what label would you put on it?

On the number line below, 5 and −5 are the same distance from 0 but in opposite directions. Therefore, 5 and −5 are **opposites.** The opposite of 5 is −5. The opposite of −5 is 5. Similarly, the opposite of $2\frac{1}{2}$ is $-2\frac{1}{2}$, and the opposite of $-2\frac{1}{2}$ is $2\frac{1}{2}$.

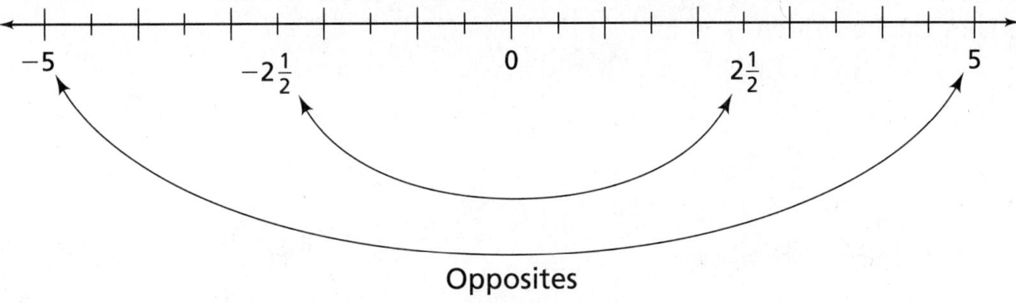

The **absolute value** of a number is its distance from 0 on the number line. Numbers that are the same distance from 0 have the same absolute value. The absolute value of $2\frac{1}{2}$ and the absolute value of $-2\frac{1}{2}$ are both $2\frac{1}{2}$.

You can express the absolute value of a number two ways without words.

Absolute Value Bars		Calculator Notation
$\lvert 2\frac{1}{2} \rvert = 2\frac{1}{2}$	OR	$\text{abs}\left(2\frac{1}{2}\right) = 2\frac{1}{2}$
$\lvert -2\frac{1}{2} \rvert = 2\frac{1}{2}$		$\text{abs}\left(-2\frac{1}{2}\right) = 2\frac{1}{2}$

- What is the opposite of $-\frac{2}{3}$? What is the opposite of $\frac{2}{3}$?
- What is the absolute value of $-\frac{2}{3}$? What is the absolute value of $\frac{2}{3}$?

Zero, whole numbers, fractions, and their opposites are **rational numbers.** The numbers $-\frac{9}{5}$, -3, 0, $\frac{2}{3}$, and $2\frac{1}{3}$ are all rational numbers.

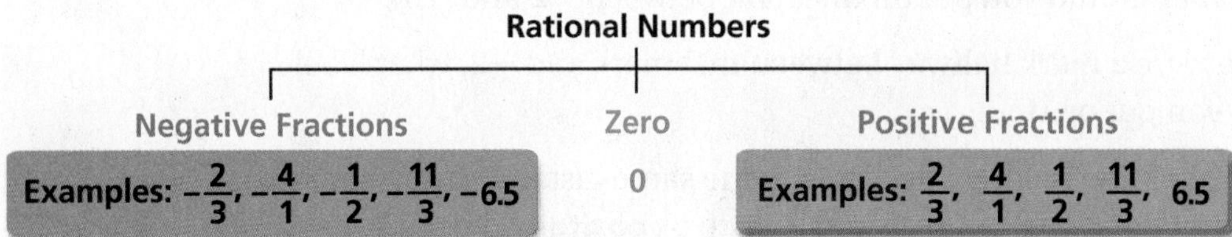

Negative numbers can also be improper fractions. Improper fractions have an absolute value greater than or equal to 1. Both $\frac{7}{5}$ and $-\frac{7}{5}$ are improper fractions. They can be written as $1\frac{2}{5}$ and $-1\frac{2}{5}$.

Problem 3.1

A **1.** On a number line like the one below, mark and label these fractions.

$\frac{1}{4}$ $\frac{2}{4}$ $\frac{3}{4}$ $\frac{4}{4}$ $\frac{5}{4}$ $\frac{6}{4}$ $\frac{7}{4}$ $\frac{8}{4}$ $\frac{9}{4}$ $\frac{0}{4}$ $-\frac{1}{4}$ $-\frac{2}{4}$ $-\frac{3}{4}$ $-\frac{4}{4}$ $-\frac{5}{4}$

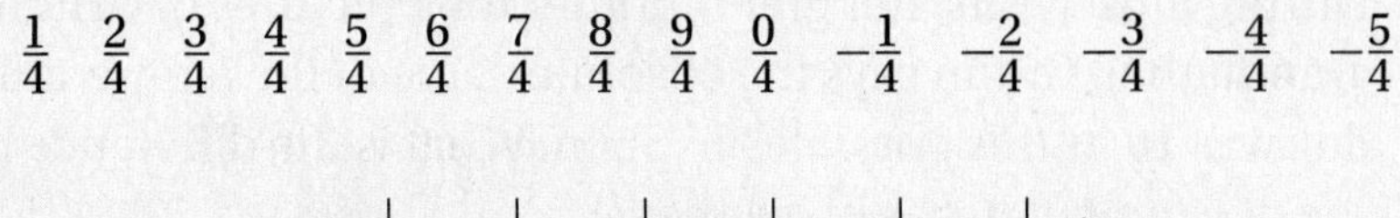

2. Which of the fractions can be written as mixed numbers? Explain.

B **1.** On a new number line, mark and label these numbers.

$\frac{1}{3}$ $1\frac{1}{3}$ $2\frac{2}{3}$ 3 $3\frac{1}{3}$ $-\frac{1}{3}$ $-1\frac{1}{3}$ $-1\frac{2}{3}$

2. Which of these numbers can be written as improper fractions? Explain.

C **1.** What is the opposite of $\frac{1}{2}$?

2. What is the opposite of the opposite of $\frac{1}{2}$?

3. What is the opposite of 0?

4. Write a mathematical sentence for each of the opposite statements in parts (1)–(3).

D **1.** What numbers have an absolute value of 1?

2. How many numbers have an absolute value of $\frac{5}{4}$? What are the numbers?

3. How many numbers have an absolute value of 0?

continued on the next page >

Problem 3.1 continued

E **1. a.** Griffin visited her grandfather in Canada twice in the same year. During those visits, her grandmother took pictures of Griffin with her grandfather. Griffin says the absolute value of the temperature each day was 10. Is this possible? Explain. What is the difference between the two temperatures in degrees?

b. Griffin says the bird's height above and the fish's depth below sea level are opposites. Is this possible? Explain.

2. Aaron is playing a game in which he earns points for a correct answer and loses the same number of points for an incorrect answer.

a. Aaron has zero points. The next question is worth 300 points. Aaron says, "It doesn't matter whether I get the answer right or wrong, the absolute value of my score will be 300." Do you agree? Why or why not?

b. Later in the game, Aaron's score is back to zero. He then answers two more questions and his score is back to zero again. What could be the point values of the last two questions?

ACE Homework starts on page 82.

3.2 Estimating and Ordering Rational Numbers

Comparing Fractions to Benchmarks

When you solve problems involving fractions and decimals, you may find it useful to estimate the size of the numbers. One way is to compare each positive fraction to 0, $\frac{1}{2}$, and 1. These numbers serve as **benchmarks,** or reference points. You also can compare each negative fraction to the opposites of the benchmarks: 0, $-\frac{1}{2}$, and -1. These benchmarks divide the number line below into six equal intervals: the interval between $-1\frac{1}{2}$ and -1, the interval between -1 and $-\frac{1}{2}$, and so on.

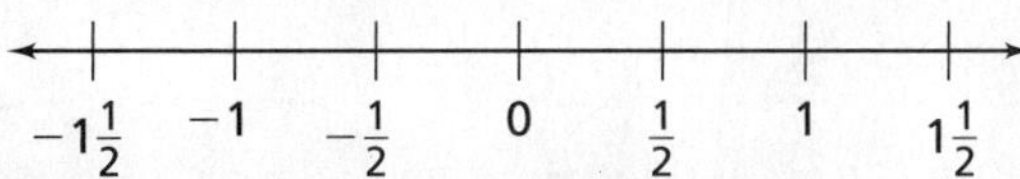

- Name a fraction close to, but not equal to $\frac{1}{2}$. Is it greater than or less than $\frac{1}{2}$?
- Name a fraction close to but not equal to $-\frac{1}{2}$. Is it greater than or less than $-\frac{1}{2}$?
- How can you decide which benchmark is closest to a given rational number?

Problem 3.2

A **1.** Decide in which interval on the number line each fraction below is located.

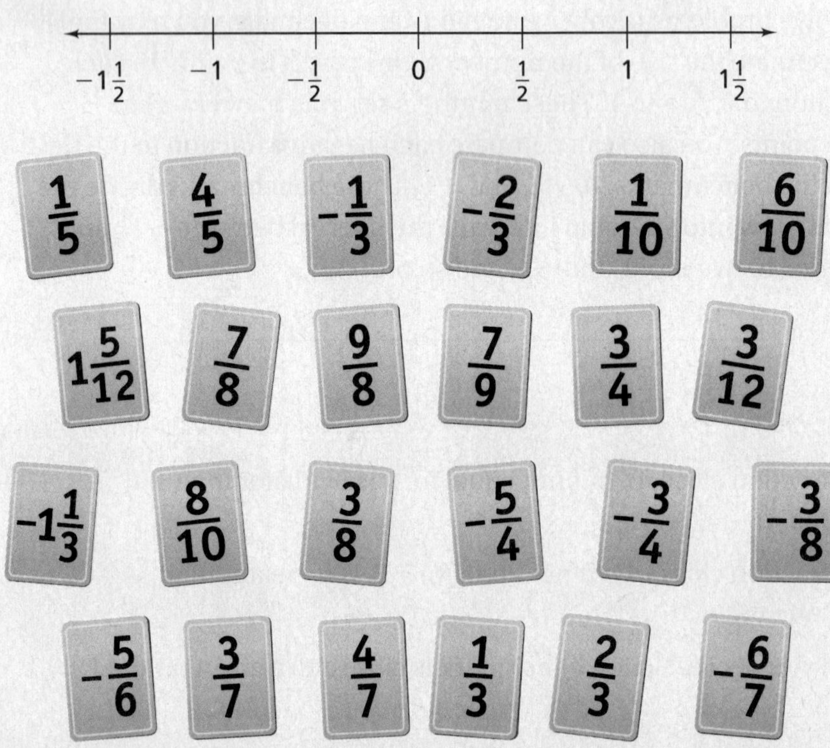

Record your information in a table like the one below that shows which fractions are in each interval.

$-1\frac{1}{2}$ to -1	-1 to $-\frac{1}{2}$	$-\frac{1}{2}$ to 0	0 to $\frac{1}{2}$	$\frac{1}{2}$ to 1	1 to $1\frac{1}{2}$
■	■	■	■	■	■

2. Decide whether each fraction above is closest to $-1\frac{1}{2}$, -1, $-\frac{1}{2}$, 0, $\frac{1}{2}$, 1, or $1\frac{1}{2}$.

Record your information in a way that also includes the possibility that some fractions are exactly halfway between two benchmarks.

Problem 3.2 continued

B Insert a less than (<), greater than (>), or equal to (=) symbol in each sentence below. Explain how the numbers or the number line helped you decide.

1. $-\frac{5}{2}$ ■ 3
2. 0 ■ −3
3. $-\frac{5}{3}$ ■ $-\frac{11}{2}$
4. Callum says that every number is greater than its opposite. Do you agree? Explain.
5. Blake says that he can use absolute value to help order the numbers $-\frac{6}{5}$ and $-\frac{2}{3}$. He says the absolute value of $-\frac{6}{5}$ is greater so it is farther away from zero, and therefore $-\frac{6}{5} < -\frac{2}{3}$. Do you agree? Explain.
6. Will Blake's strategy work for all of the comparisons you did in Questions 1–3? Explain.

C Compare each pair of fractions using benchmarks and other strategies. Then copy the fractions and insert a less than (<), greater than (>), or equal to (=) symbol. Describe your strategies.

1. $\frac{5}{8}$ ■ $\frac{6}{8}$
2. $\frac{5}{6}$ ■ $\frac{5}{8}$
3. $\frac{2}{3}$ ■ $\frac{3}{9}$
4. $\frac{13}{12}$ ■ $\frac{6}{5}$
5. $-\frac{3}{4}$ ■ $\frac{2}{5}$
6. $-1\frac{1}{5}$ ■ $-1\frac{1}{3}$

D The smartphone screen shows deposits to and withdrawals from Brian's checking account.

Online Checking Account

Date	Activity	Amount
10/09/2013	Giancarlo's Steakhouse	-50
10/14/2013	Deposit Broad St.	100
10/21/2013	Barbara's Bookstore	-32
10/23/2013	Deposit Maplewood Ave.	32
10/27/2013	Waterstone Hardware	-30

2:30 PM

1. Which account activities have the same absolute value? What information does this provide for Brian?
2. Brian says that he spent less money on October 27th than he did on October 21st because the absolute value of the account withdrawal is closer to zero. Do you agree? Explain.

ACE Homework starts on page 82.

3.3 Sharing 100 Things
Using Tenths and Hundredths

You see decimals every day, in lots of different places.

- Where might you find each of the decimal numbers below?

Decimals give people a way to write fractions with denominators of 10 or 100 or 1,000 or 10,000 or even 100,000,000,000, as in the table below. These denominators are different forms of **base ten numeration.**

Fraction	Denominator as a Power of 10	Decimal
$\frac{1}{10}$	$\frac{1}{10^1}$	0.1
$\frac{1}{100}$	$\frac{1}{10^2}$	0.01
$\frac{1}{1,000}$	$\frac{1}{10^3}$	0.001
$\frac{1}{10,000}$	$\frac{1}{10^4}$	0.0001
$\frac{1}{100,000}$	$\frac{1}{10^5}$	0.00001
$\frac{1}{1,000,000}$	$\frac{1}{10^6}$	0.000001
⋮	⋮	⋮
$\frac{1}{100,000,000,000}$	?	?

In Investigation 1, you folded fraction strips. One of the strips you made was a tenths strip, similar to the one shown below.

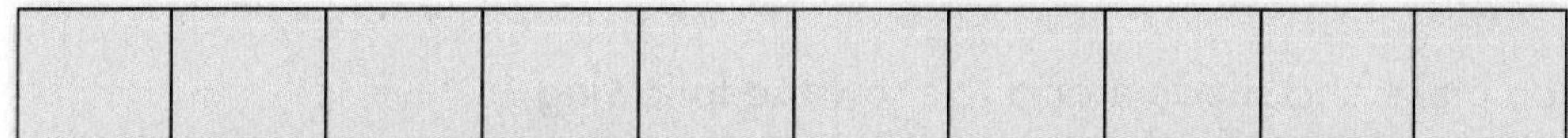

- How could you fold or mark the tenths strip to get a hundredths strip?
- How would you label each part of this new fraction strip?

A tenths grid is also divided into 10 equal parts. You can further divide a tenths grid by drawing horizontal lines to make 100 parts. This is called a hundredths grid.

Tenths Grid

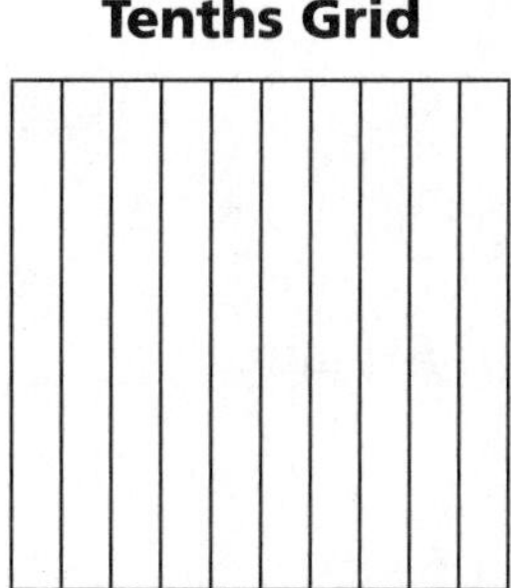

Hundredths Grid

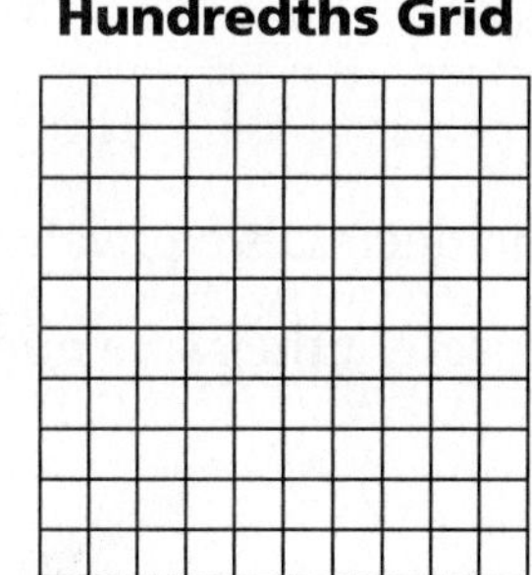

You can represent fractions on grids. You can write fractional parts of 100 as decimal numbers.

Fraction	Decimal	Representation on a Hundredths Grid
$\frac{5}{10}$	0.5	
$\frac{20}{100}$	0.20	
$\frac{2}{100}$	0.02	

How can you make and shade a grid to show the following fractional and decimal amounts?

Fraction	Decimal
$\frac{20}{100}$	0.2
■	0.20
$\frac{250}{1,000}$	■

- What are some fractions and decimals equivalent to $\frac{3}{10}$?
- Do 0.20, 0.02, and 0.2 all represent the same number? Explain.

Problem 3.3

Wendy's mother Ann makes lasagna every year to celebrate the winter holiday season. She makes the lasagna in an enormous 20 inch-by-20 inch square pan.

Ann cuts the lasagna into 100 servings to share with friends, family, neighbors, and co-workers. You may use grids to help answer the following questions.

A Ann gave one pan of lasagna to her ten co-workers.

1. If the co-workers share the lasagna equally, how many servings will each co-worker get? Write each person's share as a fractional and a decimal part of a pan.
2. Ann's pan is 20 inches by 20 inches. Describe each co-worker's share of the lasagna.

B Ann baked three more pans of lasagna. Each pan was shared with a different group of people. For each group below,

- write each person's share as a number of servings.
- write each person's share as a fractional and decimal part of a pan.

1. One pan was shared among Wendy's four favorite teachers.
2. Ann miscalculated and had only one pan to share among all 200 sixth-graders at Wendy's school.
3. One pan went to eight of Ann's neighbors.

continued on the next page >

Problem 3.3 *continued*

C **1.** Four is a good number of people for Ann to share her lasagna with because she does not have to subdivide the 100 servings into even smaller pieces to share equally. What are some other numbers of people that Ann could share with without having to cut her servings into smaller pieces? Describe any patterns you find.

2. What are some numbers of people that force Ann to subdivide the 100 servings into smaller pieces? Explain.

D Sonam compared the decimal numbers 0.1 and 0.09 by thinking about lasagna. She said that 0.1 represents one serving of Ann's lasagna and 0.09 represents 9 servings, so $0.09 > 0.1$. What do you think? Explain your reasoning.

ACE Homework starts on page 82.

3.4 Decimals on the Number Line

In Problem 3.3, you thought about a pan of lasagna that was cut into 100 pieces, and you considered relationships between the fractional and decimal representations for different numbers of servings.

The place value chart on the next page shows the names of each position relative to the decimal point. Think about these questions as you look at it:

- What do you notice about the fraction names of each place value as you move to the right from the decimal point?
- Why are these names useful in writing fractions as decimals?

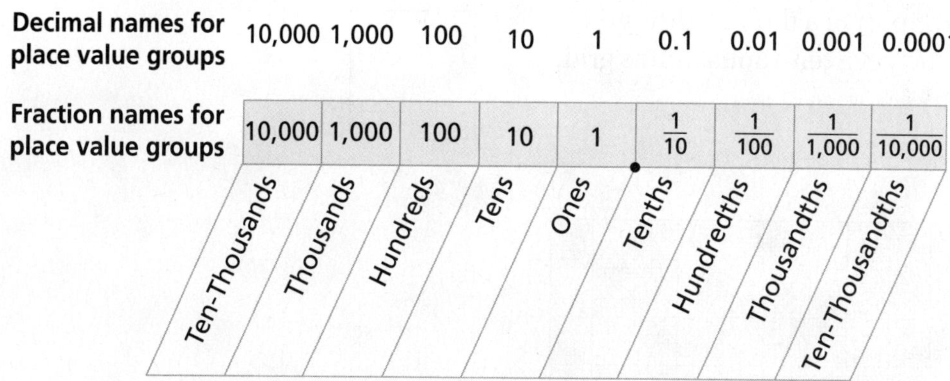

It is often useful to divide a whole into more than 100 pieces. When working with decimals you can always divide the whole into smaller pieces, but you must always use a divisor that is a power of 10.

For example, you made a tenths strip in Investigation 1. You can fold or mark the tenths strip to get a hundredths strip.

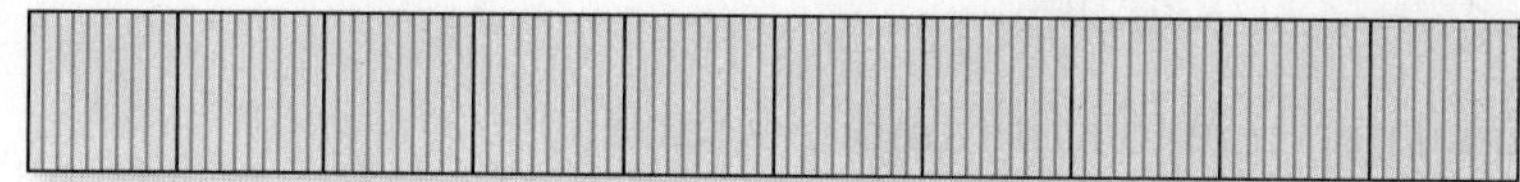

Similarly, you saw the hundredths grids in Problem 3.3. If each square in a hundredths grid is divided into 10 pieces, you get a thousandths grid.

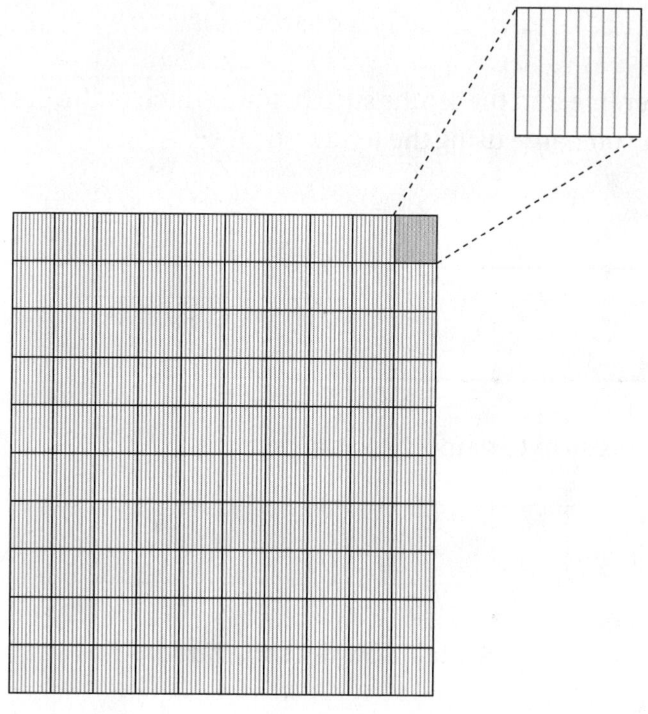

If you divide each part of a thousandths grid into 10 pieces, you get a ten-thousandths grid.

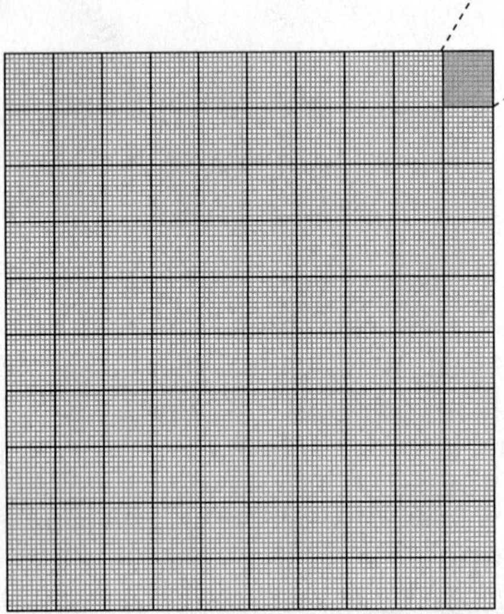

- How can you use decimal notation to write amounts such as $12\frac{1}{2}$ hundredths of a pan of lasagna?

Problem 3.4

A **1.** Use the number line and the tenths strip below. Which of the points $\frac{1}{4}$, $\frac{2}{4}$, $\frac{3}{4}$, and $\frac{4}{4}$ can you name using the tenths strip?

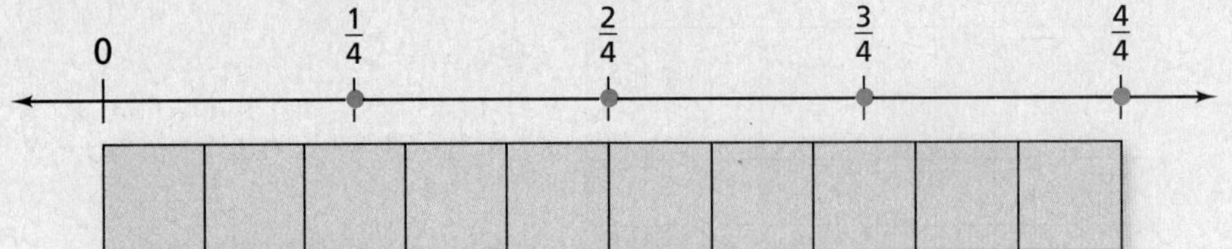

2. Use a hundredths strip to name the same points.

3. Write each fraction as a decimal. How does the hundredths strip help you to do this?

Problem 3.4 continued

B **1.** **a.** Which of the fractions below could be written with tenths or hundredths in the denominator? For each such fraction, write an equivalent decimal.

$\frac{1}{3}$ $\frac{1}{5}$ $\frac{2}{5}$ $\frac{2}{6}$ $\frac{3}{6}$ $\frac{1}{8}$ $\frac{63}{50}$ $\frac{112}{200}$

b. Which fractions cannot be written with tenths or hundredths in the denominator? Justify your answer.

2. Name two other fractions that are easy to write as equivalent decimals, and two that are not easy to write as decimals. Explain.

3. **a.** Which decimal is closest to $\frac{1}{3}$: 0.3, 0.33 or 0.333? Explain.

b. Are any of the decimals 0.3, 0.33, or 0.333 exactly $\frac{1}{3}$? Explain your reasoning.

C Find decimal equivalents for each group of fractions.

1. $-\frac{2}{5}$ $-\frac{3}{5}$ $-\frac{4}{5}$ $-\frac{6}{5}$ **2.** $\frac{2}{8}$ $\frac{3}{8}$ $\frac{4}{8}$ $\frac{5}{8}$ $\frac{6}{8}$ $\frac{7}{8}$ **3.** $\frac{1}{3}$ $\frac{2}{3}$ $\frac{3}{3}$ $\frac{4}{3}$

4. Describe the strategies you used to find decimal equivalents.

D Each number line below has two points labeled with decimal numbers and one with a question mark. In each case, what decimal number should go in place of the question mark?

1. 0.8 ? 0.9

2. 0.3 0.35 ?

3. 0.8 ? 0.9

4. −0.9 ? −0.8

5. 0.499 ? 0.501

continued on the next page >

Problem 3.4 continued

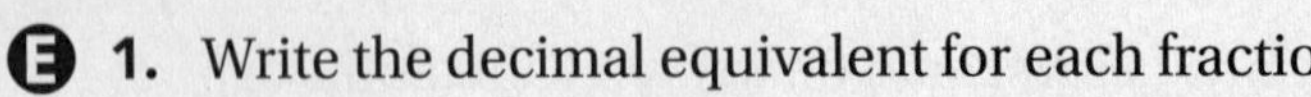

E **1.** Write the decimal equivalent for each fraction.

$-\frac{1}{2}$ $\frac{1}{3}$ $-\frac{1}{4}$ $\frac{1}{5}$ $\frac{1}{6}$ $-\frac{1}{8}$ $\frac{1}{10}$

2. Draw a point for each decimal from part (1) on a number line.

3. How do the fractions $\frac{1}{4}$ and $\frac{1}{8}$ compare? How do the decimal equivalents of $-\frac{1}{4}$ and $-\frac{1}{8}$ compare?

4. How do the fractions $\frac{1}{3}$ and $\frac{1}{6}$ compare? How do the decimal equivalents of $-\frac{1}{3}$ and $-\frac{1}{6}$ compare?

5. Which fraction benchmark is closest to each of the following decimals?

a. 0.18 **b.** -0.46 **c.** -0.225 **d.** 0.099

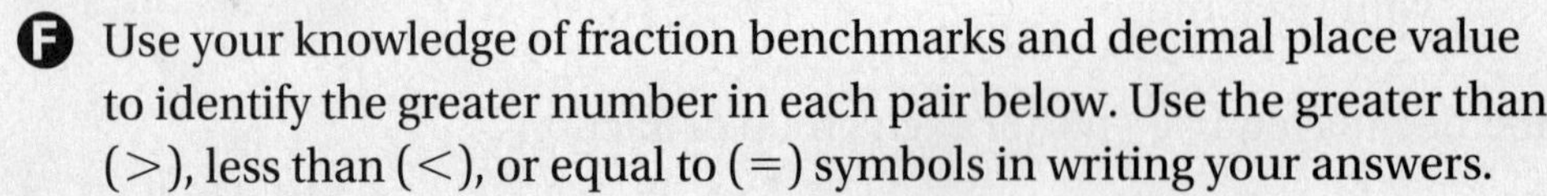

F Use your knowledge of fraction benchmarks and decimal place value to identify the greater number in each pair below. Use the greater than (>), less than (<), or equal to (=) symbols in writing your answers.

1. 0.1 and 0.9 **2.** 0.3 and 0.33 **3.** 0.25 and 0.250

4. 0.12 and 0.125 **5.** -0.1 and 0.1 **6.** -0.3 and -0.27

Choose three pairs of decimals from parts (1)–(6) to complete the following statements.

7. On the number line, __?__ is to the left of __?__.

8. On the number line, __?__ is to the right of __?__.

9. On the number line, __?__ and __?__ share the same point.

Homework starts on page 82.

3.5 Earthquake Relief

Moving From Fractions to Decimals

On January 12, 2010, a 7.0-magnitude earthquake struck the country of Haiti. It destroyed many homes and caused major damage. Many people had no place to live and little clothing and food. In response, people from all over the world collected clothing, household items, and food to send to the victims of the earthquake.

Students at a middle school decided to collect food to distribute to families whose homes were destroyed. They packed what they collected into boxes to send to the families. The students had to solve some problems as they packed the boxes.

As you work on this problem, ask yourself

When is decimal or fraction notation more useful, and why?

Problem 3.5

Each grade was assigned different numbers of families for which to pack boxes. Each grade shared the supplies equally among the families they were assigned. They had bags and plastic containers to repack items for the individual boxes. They also had a digital scale that measured in kilograms (kg) and grams (g).

A **1.** The sixth graders are packing six boxes. How much of each item should the students include in each box? Write your answer as a fraction and as a decimal.

2. Mary says that $\frac{13}{6}$ kg of milk goes in each box. Meleck says that $2\frac{1}{6}$ kg goes in, and he used his benchmark list to rewrite the amount as 2.16 kg. Funda says she divided the amount of milk by 6 and got 2.167 kg. With whom do you agree? Explain why.

3. Scooter said the ratio of numbers of oranges to boxes is 24 to 6. He calculated the number of oranges per box by writing *24 to 6*, then *4 to 1*. Is he correct? Explain.

Problem 3.5 continued

B The seventh graders are packing ten boxes. How much of each item should the students include in each box? Write your answer as a fraction and as a decimal.

C The eighth graders are packing 14 boxes. How much of each item should the students include in each box? Write your answer as a fraction and as a decimal.

D Describe your strategies for solving these problems.

ACE Homework starts on page 82.

Applications | Connections | Extensions

Applications

1. Describe, in writing or with pictures, how $\frac{7}{3}$ compares to $2\frac{1}{3}$.

2. **Multiple Choice** On a number line from 0 to -10, where is $-\frac{13}{3}$ located?

   A. between 0 and -1 **B.** between -4 and -5

   C. between -5 and -6 **D.** between -6 and -7

3. Copy the number line below. Locate and label marks representing $2\frac{1}{4}$, $1\frac{9}{10}$, and $\frac{15}{4}$.

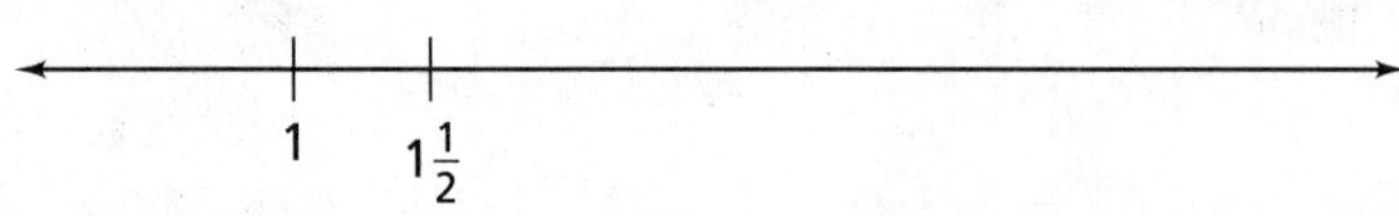

4. For parts (a)–(d), copy the number line below. Locate and label a point representing each fraction described.

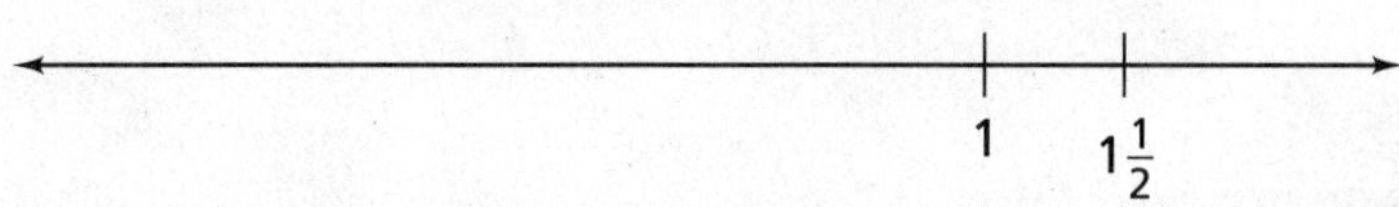

   a. a fraction close to but greater than 1

   b. a fraction close to but less than -1

   c. a fraction close to but greater than $1\frac{1}{2}$

   d. a fraction close to but less than $-1\frac{1}{2}$

For Exercises 5–8, write each mixed number as an improper fraction.

5. $1\frac{2}{3}$ 6. $6\frac{3}{4}$ 7. $-9\frac{7}{9}$ 8. $-4\frac{2}{7}$

For Exercises 9–12, write each improper fraction as a mixed number.

9. $\frac{22}{4}$ 10. $\frac{10}{6}$ 11. $-\frac{17}{5}$ 12. $-\frac{36}{8}$

13. What numbers have an absolute value of $2\frac{1}{2}$?

14. What are some numbers that have an absolute value greater than $2\frac{1}{2}$?

15. A football team has four chances with the ball to gain ten yards and keep going to try to make a touchdown. A team gained 7 yards, lost 2, gained 4, and lost 1.

    a. How many total yards did the team move (forward or backward)?

    b. Did they gain enough to keep the ball? Explain your reasoning.

In many cold places, weather reports often include wind chills, the temperature of how cold it feels outside when you include the wind making it feel colder. For Exercises 16–19, write an inequality statement for the wind chills of the two locations.

16. Lincoln, NE compared to New Albin, IA 15°F ■ 5°F

17. Viroqua, WI compared to Toledo, OH −8°F ■ 6°F

18. Minneapolis, MN compared to Duluth, MN −10°F ■ −25°F

19. Bozeman, MT compared to Rapid City, SD −5°F ■ −3°F

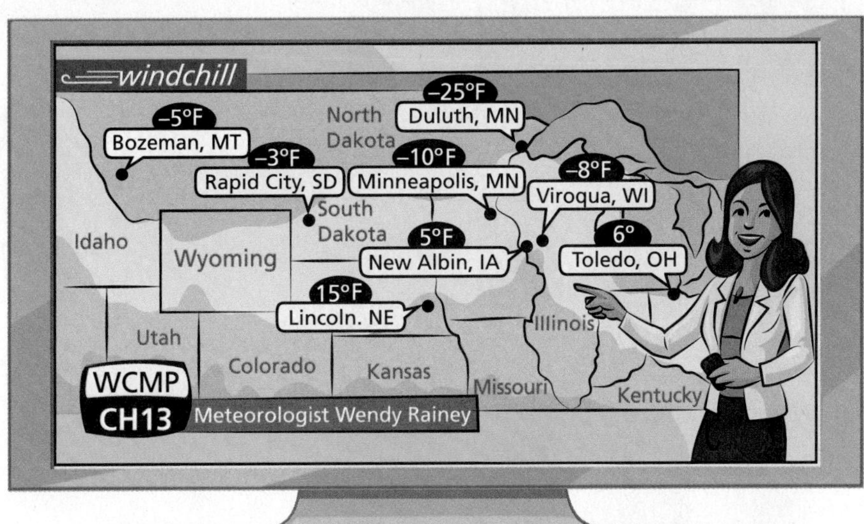

20. Mr. Bergman is having an end-of-the-year trivia contest. Each correct answer is worth 100 points, and each incorrect answer is worth −50 points. At the end of the contest Mr. Bergman is surprised by the final scores.

Blue Team	Orange Team	Purple Team
−50 points	−250 points	−200 points

The Blue team says they win because they have the highest score. The Orange team says that 250 is greater than 50, so they win. Which team should be called the winner? Explain.

21. Mrs. O'Brien's students are playing "The Ordering Game" as a whole class. A student draws five cards numbered −10 to 10. She rearranges the cards in different ways, and the class tries to figure out the reason for the order. In each of the orderings below, what reason was Ashley using for the order? Explain.

Ashley draws these cards.

a. Ordering #1

b. Ordering #2

c. Ordering #3

22. Use Ashley's three ordering methods from the previous problem to order the five cards that Herbert drew. Is there another ordering you could do that Ashley didn't show? Explain.

Herbert's Cards:

23. Franklin Middle School is having an end-of-the-year carnival with different games. One of the games is a bean-bag toss. The object is to get zero, or as close to zero as possible on the toss. Joseph's bag lands on an area labeled -3. Jeremiah's bag lands on an area labeled 2.

Joseph says, "I win because $-3 < 2$."

Jeremiah says, "No, we have to decide whose score is closer to zero. Since $|-3| = 3$ and $|2| = 2$, my score is closer to zero. I win."

Who is correct? Explain.

24. The elevation of different places on Earth is often given as the height above sea level, rounded to the nearest foot. Likewise, there are many places in the world whose elevation is below sea level. These are useful measurements because sea level is relatively constant across the planet.

City	Height above Sea Level
Indio, California	−20 feet
Denver, Colorado	5,280 feet
Wenzuan, China	16,700 feet
New Orleans, LA	−5 feet
Death Valley, California	−300 feet

a. Order the cities in the table from lowest elevation to highest elevation.

b. Order the cities from least to greatest distance from sea level.

c. Did you use absolute value in either part (a) or (b)? Explain.

As Rosemary works through some homework problems, she notices that negative numbers can often be rewritten using positive numbers if you change what you are talking about. For example, a golf score was given as -4 but Rosemary rewrote this as "4 shots under par." For Exercises 25–28, rewrite each negative situation using a positive value.

25. A savings account balance is $-\$15.00$.

26. The elevation of a city is -20 feet.

27. A quarterback ran for -8 yards.

28. The amount of money a lemonade stand made on a rainy day was $-\$10.00$.

For Exercises 29–40, compare each pair of fractions using benchmarks, number lines, and other strategies. Then use a less than (<), greater than (>), or equal to (=) symbol to complete each number sentence.

29. $\frac{8}{10} \blacksquare \frac{3}{8}$ **30.** $\frac{2}{3} \blacksquare \frac{4}{9}$ **31.** $\frac{3}{5} \blacksquare \frac{5}{12}$ **32.** $\frac{1}{3} \blacksquare \frac{2}{3}$

33. $\frac{3}{4} \blacksquare \frac{3}{5}$ **34.** $\frac{3}{2} \blacksquare -\frac{7}{6}$ **35.** $-\frac{8}{12} \blacksquare \frac{6}{9}$ **36.** $\frac{9}{10} \blacksquare \frac{10}{11}$

37. $-\frac{3}{12} \blacksquare -\frac{7}{12}$ **38.** $-\frac{5}{6} \blacksquare -\frac{5}{8}$ **39.** $-\frac{3}{7} \blacksquare -\frac{6}{14}$ **40.** $-\frac{4}{5} \blacksquare -\frac{7}{8}$

For Exercises 41–44, find a rational number between each pair of numbers.

41. $\frac{1}{8}$ and $\frac{1}{4}$ **42.** $\frac{1}{6}$ and $\frac{1}{12}$ **43.** $-\frac{1}{6}$ and $-\frac{2}{6}$ **44.** $-\frac{1}{4}$ and $\frac{2}{5}$

For Exercises 45–50, between which two benchmarks (of 0, $\frac{1}{2}$, 1, $1\frac{1}{2}$, and 2) does each fraction fall? Tell which is the nearer benchmark.

45. $\frac{3}{5}$ **46.** $1\frac{2}{6}$ **47.** $\frac{12}{10}$

48. $\frac{2}{18}$ **49.** $1\frac{8}{10}$ **50.** $1\frac{12}{15}$

51. **Multiple Choice** Which fraction is greatest?

F. $\frac{7}{6}$ G. $\frac{9}{8}$ H. $\frac{13}{12}$ J. $\frac{14}{15}$

52. **Multiple Choice** Find the opposite of each number below. Which one is greatest?

A. $\frac{7}{6}$ B. $\frac{9}{8}$ C. $\frac{13}{12}$ D. $\frac{14}{15}$

A pan of lasagna cut into 100 servings is equally shared among a group of people. For Exercises 53–55, determine the portion of the pan that each person receives given the number of people in each group. Write your answer as both a fractional and a decimal part of a pan.

53. 20 people 54. 40 people 55. 30 people

For Exercises 56–59, write a fraction equivalent to the decimal.

56. 0.08 57. 0.4 58. -0.04 59. -0.84

For Exercises 60–63, write a decimal equivalent to the fraction.

60. $\frac{3}{4}$ 61. $\frac{7}{50}$ 62. $-\frac{13}{25}$ 63. $-\frac{7}{10}$

64. Which is greater, forty-five hundredths or six tenths? Explain. Draw a picture if it helps you explain.

65. Which is greater, 0.6 or 0.60? Explain. Draw a picture if it helps you explain.

For Exercises 66–68, a full one-hundredths grid represents the number 1. What fraction and decimal is represented by each of the shaded parts?

66.

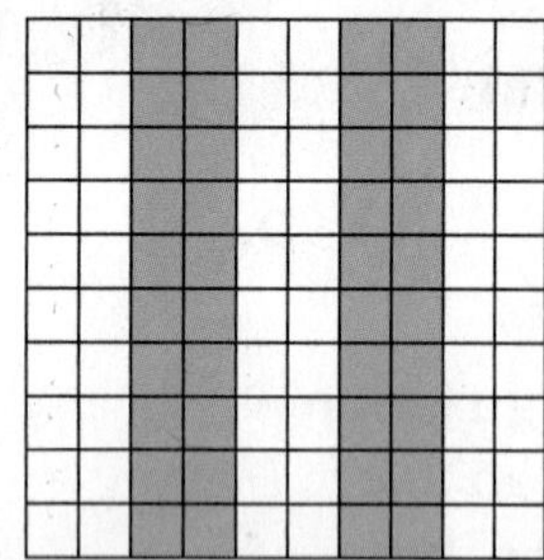

67.

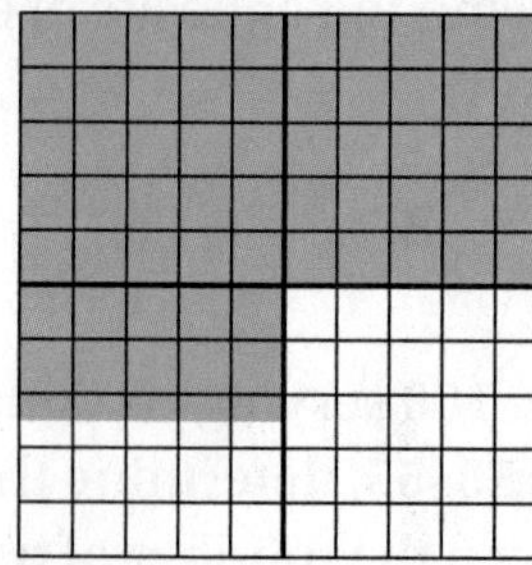

68.

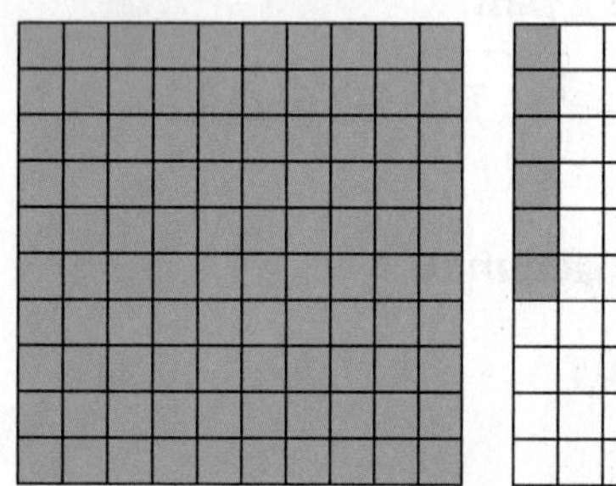

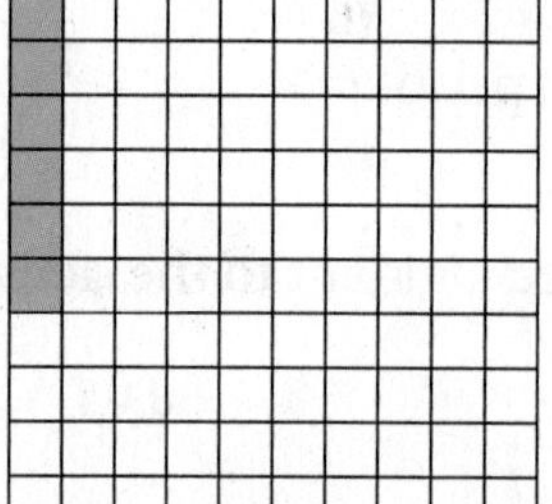

69. Name three fractions whose decimal equivalent is 0.40. Explain how you know each fraction is equivalent to 0.40. Draw a picture if it helps you explain.

For Exercises 70–72, copy the part of the number line given. Then find the "step" by determining the difference from one mark to another. Label the unlabeled marks with decimal numbers.

Sample:

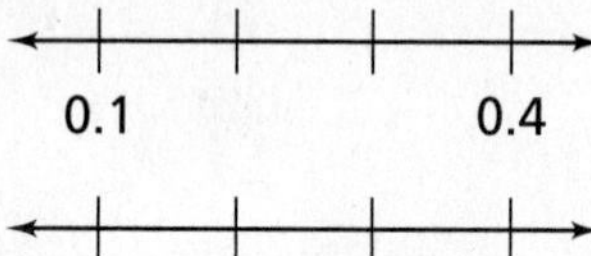

The step is 0.1.

70.

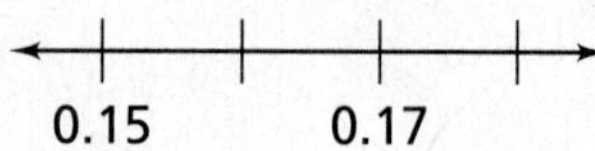

71.

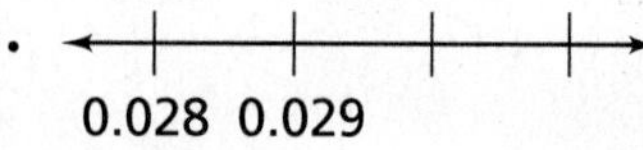

72.

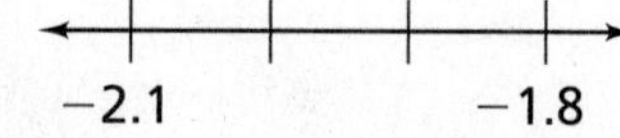

For Exercises 73–76, give the fraction listed that is nearest on the number line to that decimal.

$-\frac{1}{2}$ $-\frac{1}{3}$ $-\frac{1}{4}$ $-\frac{1}{5}$ $-\frac{1}{6}$ $-\frac{1}{8}$ $-\frac{1}{10}$

73. -0.30 **74.** -0.50 **75.** -0.12333 **76.** -0.15

For Exercises 77–82, copy each pair of numbers. Insert $<$, $>$, or $=$ to make a true statement.

77. 0.205 ■ 0.21

78. 0.1 ■ 0.1000

79. -0.04 ■ -0.050

80. -1.03 ■ -0.03

81. $\frac{5}{10}$ ■ 0.6

82. $-\frac{3}{5}$ ■ -0.3

For Exercises 83 and 84, rewrite the numbers in order from least to greatest.

83. $0.33, -0.12, -0.127, 0.2, \frac{45}{10}$

84. $-\frac{45}{10}, \frac{3}{1000}, -0.005, 0.34$

85. Multiple Choice The orchestra at Johnson School is responsible for cleaning up a 15-mile section of highway. There are 45 students in the orchestra. If each orchestra member cleans the same-size section, which of the decimals indicates the part of a mile cleaned by each student?

F. 0.25 **G.** 0.33 **H.** 0.333... **J.** 0.5

86. Pilar divided 1 by 9 on her calculator and found that $\frac{1}{9}$ was approximately 0.1111. Find decimal approximations for each of the following fractions.

a. $\frac{2}{9}$ **b.** $\frac{11}{9}$ **c.** $\frac{6}{9}$ **d.** $\frac{2}{3}$

e. Describe any patterns that you see.

87. Belinda used her calculator to find the decimal equivalent of the fraction $\frac{21}{28}$. When she entered $21 \div 28$, the calculator gave an answer that looked familiar. Why do you think she recognized it?

88. Suppose a new student starts school today and your teacher asks you to teach her how to find decimal equivalents for fractions. What would you tell her? How would you convince the student that your method works?

Connections

For Exercises 89–91, use the following information. Each student activity group at Johnson School agreed to pick up litter along a ten-mile stretch of highway. Draw number lines to show your reasoning.

89. Kelly and Sean work together to clean a section of highway that is $\frac{10}{3}$ miles long. Write this distance as a mixed number.

90. The Drama Club's stretch of highway is very hilly and full of trash. They can clean $1\frac{2}{3}$ miles each day. Jacqueline says that in four days, they will be able to clean $\frac{19}{3}$ miles. Is she correct? Explain.

91. The Chess Club is cleaning a very littered section of highway. Each day the members clean $1\frac{3}{4}$ miles of highway. After four days of hard work, Lakeisha says they have cleaned $\frac{28}{4}$ miles of highway. Glenda says they have cleaned 7 miles of roadway. Who is right? Why?

92. Ten students went to a pizza parlor together. They ordered eight small pizzas.

a. How much pizza will each student get if they share the pizzas equally? Express your answer as a fraction and as a decimal.

b. Explain how you thought about the problem. Draw a picture that would convince someone that your answer is correct.

93. If you look through a microscope that makes objects appear ten times larger, 1 centimeter (cm) on a metric ruler looks like this:

a. Copy this microscope's view of 1 cm. Divide the length for 1 cm into ten equal parts. What fraction of the "centimeter" does each of these parts represent?

b. Now think about dividing one of these smaller parts into ten equal parts. What part of the original "centimeter" does each of the new segments represent?

c. If you were to divide one of these new small parts into ten parts again, what part of the original "centimeter" would each of the new small parts represent?

Extensions

For Exercises 94–96, find every fraction with a denominator less than 50 that is equivalent to the given fraction.

94. $\frac{3}{15}$ **95.** $\frac{8}{3}$ **96.** $1\frac{4}{6}$

97. Find five fractions between $-\frac{8}{10}$ and $-\frac{4}{5}$.

98. Does $\frac{4}{5}$, $\frac{17}{23}$, or $\frac{51}{68}$ represent the greatest part of a whole? Explain your reasoning.

99. Copy the number line below. Place and label marks for 0, $\frac{3}{4}$, $\frac{1}{8}$, and $2\frac{2}{3}$.

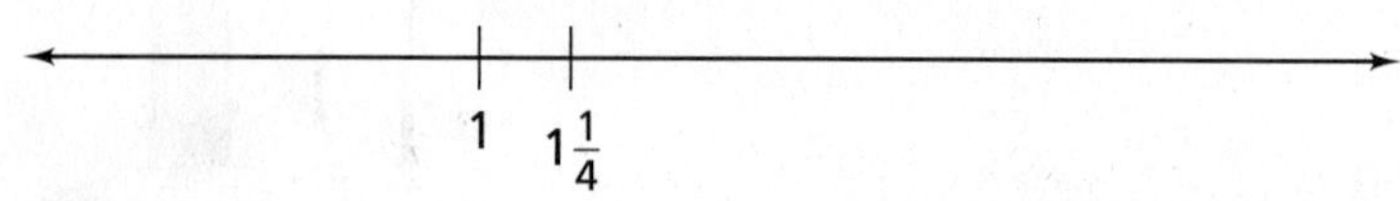

For Exercises 100–105, find an estimate if you cannot find an exact answer. You may find that drawing a number line, a hundredths grid, or some other diagram is useful in solving the problem. Explain your reasoning for each problem.

100. What is $\frac{1}{4}$ of 12? **101.** What is $\frac{3}{4}$ of 8?

102. What is $\frac{2}{9}$ of 3? **103.** What is $\frac{2}{9}$ of 18?

104. What is $\frac{1}{4}$ of 3? **105.** What is $\frac{3}{4}$ of 3?

Mathematical Reflections

In your work in this Investigation, you used number lines to investigate relationships among fractions and decimals and to estimate the size of a number. These questions will help you summarize what you have learned.

Think about your answers to these questions. Discuss your ideas with other students and your teacher. Then write a summary of your findings in your notebook.

1. **a.** Not every fraction refers to a quantity between 0 and 1. Give some examples of numbers that are greater than 1 or less than 0.

   b. **How** is a number and its opposite represented on a number line? Give examples.

2. **a.** **What** are some strategies for deciding which of two numbers is greater? Give examples.

   b. **When** comparing two positive whole numbers with different numbers of digits, such as 115 and 37, the one with more digits is greater. Does this rule work for comparing decimals?

Common Core Mathematical Practices

As you worked on the Problems in this Investigation, you used prior knowledge to make sense of the Problems. You also applied Mathematical Practices to solve the Problems. Think back over your work, the ways you thought about the Problems, and how you used Mathematical Practices.

Elena described her thoughts in the following way:

We thought that Blake was correct in his reasoning in Problem 3.2. He claimed that if the absolute value of a number is larger than the absolute value of another number then the first number is greater since it is further from zero. We tried lots of numbers and they all satisfied this claim.

But then Arthur said we did not try two positive numbers. So we did and it still worked.

Then we noticed that we did not try a positive and a negative number. For example, the absolute value of $-\frac{3}{4}$ is greater than the absolute value of $\frac{1}{2}$ but $-\frac{3}{4}$ is not greater than $\frac{1}{2}$. Blake's conjecture is not true.

Common Core Standards for Mathematical Practice

MP3 Construct viable arguments and critique the reasoning of others

- What other Mathematical Practices can you identify in Elena's reasoning?
- Describe a Mathematical Practice that you and your classmates used to solve a different Problem in this Investigation.

Working With Percents

In this Unit, you have represented quantities as fractions and ratios to answer the questions "How much?" or "How many?" or "Which is better?" When you use a ratio to answer a question, you are making a comparison.

When school construction projects are proposed, voters often must agree on a tax increase to pay for the project. Voters in two neighborhoods were surveyed and asked, "Would you vote *yes* for the construction of a new school gym?" The table shows the results of the survey. Decide which neighborhood is more enthusiastic about building a new school gym.

Neighborhood	Yes	No
Whitehills	31	69
Bailey	17	33

One way to compare the two neighborhoods is to figure out what the numbers in each neighborhood would be if 100 people were surveyed and the rate of support stayed the same. Fractions with 100 in the denominator are useful. You can easily order them and write them as decimals.

Common Core State Standards

6.RP.A.2 Understand the concept of a unit rate a/b associated with a ratio $a : b$ with $b \neq 0$, and use rate language in the context of a ratio relationship.

6.RP.A.3c Find a percent of a quantity as a rate per 100 (e.g., 30% of a quantity means $\frac{30}{100}$ times the quantity); solve problems involving finding the whole, given a part and the percent.

6.RP.A.3d Use ratio reasoning to convert measurement units; manipulate and transform units appropriately when multiplying or dividing quantities.

Also 6.RP.A.1, 6.RP.A.3, 6.RP.A.3b, 6.NS.B.2

Another useful way to express a fraction with a denominator of 100 is to use the percent symbol. A **percent** is a part-to-whole comparison that uses 100 as the whole. The word *percent* means "out of 100." For example, 8% means 8 of 100, or $\frac{8}{100}$, or 8 per 100.

In this Investigation, you will use percents, fractions, and decimals to express relationships and make comparisons. You will develop strategies for estimating and finding percentages equivalent to fractions and ratios.

In Investigation 1, you found the fraction of a fundraising goal each grade achieved. The thermometers could have been marked with percents instead of fractions of the goal to express the same amount.

- What fractions match each of the marked percent values on these thermometers?
- What dollar amounts match each of the marked percent values on these thermometers?

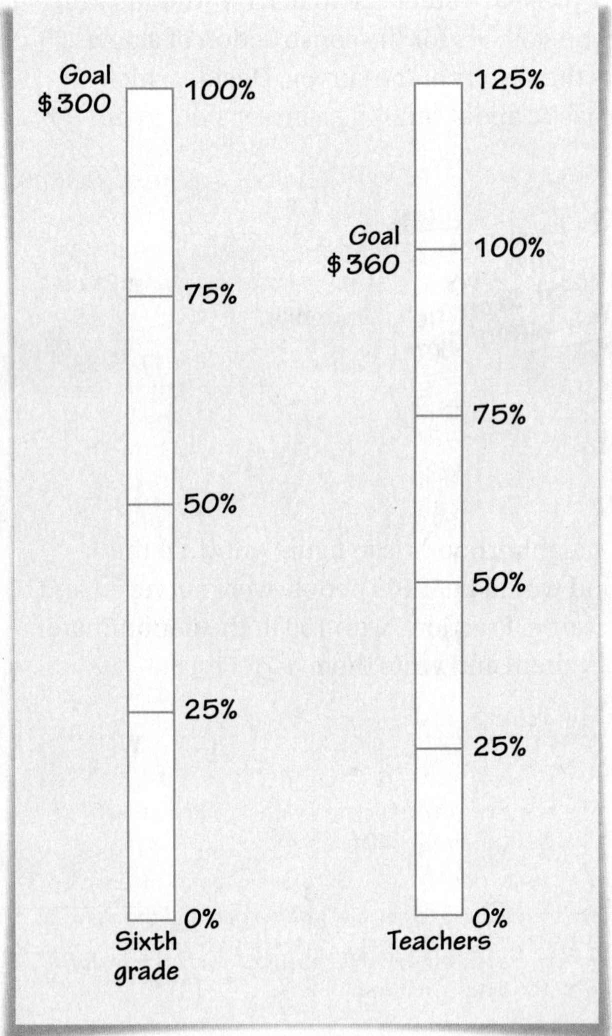

4.1 Who Is the Best?
Making Sense of Percents

Sports statistics are often given in percents. An important statistic for basketball teams is the successful free-throw percent. You will use mathematics to compare the basketball statistics of two well-known men's basketball teams in the National Collegiate Athletic Association (NCAA).

- How are free-throw shooting averages determined for basketball teams?

Problem 4.1

During a recent year, two NCAA basketball teams made 108 out of 126 free-throw attempts and 195 out of 257 attempts. It is difficult to tell which team was better at free throws that year using raw numbers. Therefore, sports announcers often give percents instead of raw numbers.

A Will drew pictures similar to the fund-raising thermometers to help him think about the percent of free throws made by the two teams. Then he got stuck! Help Will use the pictures he drew to decide which team is better at free throws.

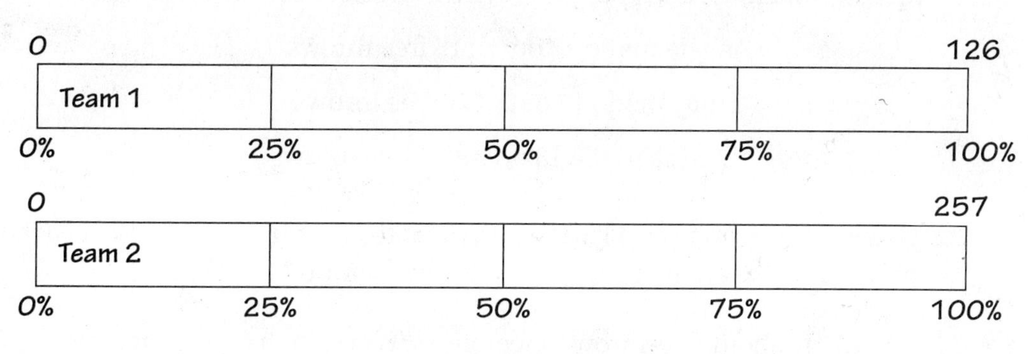

1. For each bar, estimate the number of free throws that should go with each marked percent in the picture.
2. For each team, shade the percent bar to show how many free throws the team made and estimate that percentage. Explain how you did this.
3. At this rate, how many free throws would you expect Team 1 to make in their next 200 free-throw attempts? How many would you expect Team 2 to make in their next 200 free-throw attempts?

continued on the next page >

Problem 4.1 continued

B Alisha said that she could get better estimates of each team's free-throw percentage using the percent bars below. Copy and complete her percent bars to estimate each team's free-throw percentage. Compare your answers to your answers for Question A.

C Will, in Question A, and Alisha, in Question B, each use percent bars to show common percent benchmarks. What benchmarks does each student use?

D **1.** Use percent bars and your own ideas to estimate free-throw percentages for Angela, Emily, and Christina. Who is the best free-throw shooter?

Angela made 12 out of 15 free throws

Emily made 15 out of 20 free throws

Christina made 13 out of 16 free throws

2. Using the rates in part (1), how many free throws would you expect each player to make on the next 30 free-throw attempts?

E After thinking about free-throw percentages, Will said that percents are like fractions. Alisha disagreed and said that percents are more like ratios. Do you agree more with Will or with Alisha? Explain.

ACE Homework starts on page 103.

4.2 Genetic Traits
Finding Percents

Have you ever heard of *genes*? (Not the "jeans" you wear, even though they sound the same.) What color are your eyes? Is your hair curly? Are your earlobes attached? You are born with a unique set of genes that help to determine these traits.

Scientists who study human traits such as eye and hair color are *geneticists*. Geneticists are interested in how common certain human traits are.

Look at the earlobe of a classmate. Is it attached or detached? The type of earlobe you have is a trait determined partly by your genes. Here is a description of four genetic traits:

- A widow's peak is a V-shaped hairline.
- A dimple is a small indentation, usually near the mouth.
- Straight hair does not have natural waves or curls.
- An earlobe is attached if its lowest point is attached directly to the head.

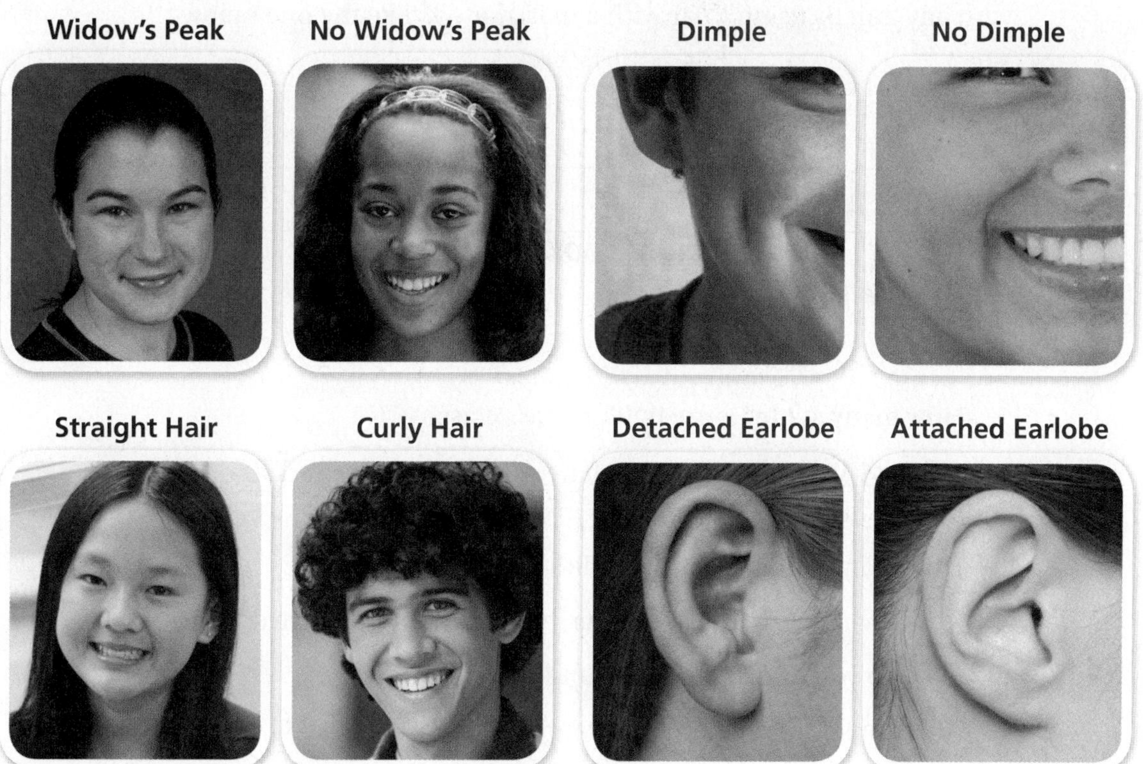

Problem 4.2

A **1.** Copy and complete the table of genetic traits below.

Traits Observed in a Middle School Classroom

Trait	Yes	No	Total
Attached Earlobes	12	■	30
Dimples	7	■	30
Straight Hair	24	■	30
Widow's Peak	17	■	30

2. For each trait, use a percent bar or another strategy to estimate the percent of people in the class who have that trait.

3. Using the percents from part (2) as rates, how many people in a school of 500 are likely to have a widow's peak?

B Marjorie wanted to find the percent of students in her class with dimples. She said that she could get a very good estimate of the percent of students with any trait by using a bar with a mark for 1% like the one below.

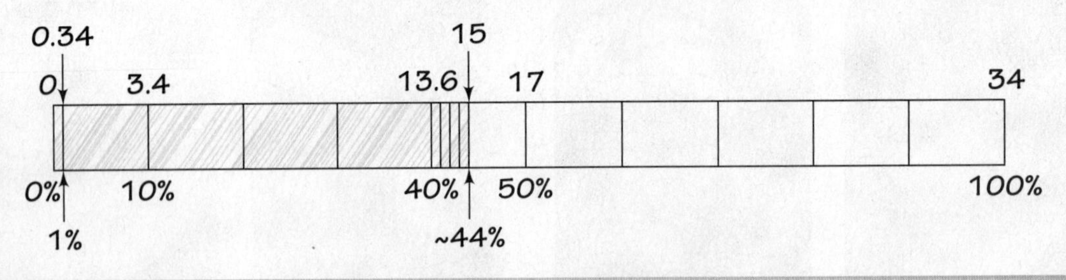

1. How many students are in Marjorie's class?

2. How did Marjorie figure out that 3.4 is at the 10% mark and 13.6 is at the 40% mark?

3. How many students in Marjorie's class have dimples?

4. About what percent of students in Marjorie's class have dimples?

5. How do you think Marjorie found that percent?

6. Are dimples more common in Marjorie's class than in your class? Explain.

C How is using a percent bar like using a rate table?

ACE Homework starts on page 103.

4.3 The Art of Comparison
Using Ratios and Percents

Do you have a favorite work of art? Is it by a famous artist such as Claude Monet, Georgia O'Keefe, or is it by your little sister?

Art museums own more pieces than they can display at one time. This means that art must be stored when it is not hanging in a gallery. A museum curator chooses which works to exhibit.

The Walker Art Center in Minneapolis, Minnesota held an exhibit entitled $\frac{50}{50}$. For the exhibit, the public voted via the Internet on which pieces they wanted the museum to display, and curators chose the remaining pieces.

- What do you think $\frac{50}{50}$ refers to in the title?

Problem 4.3

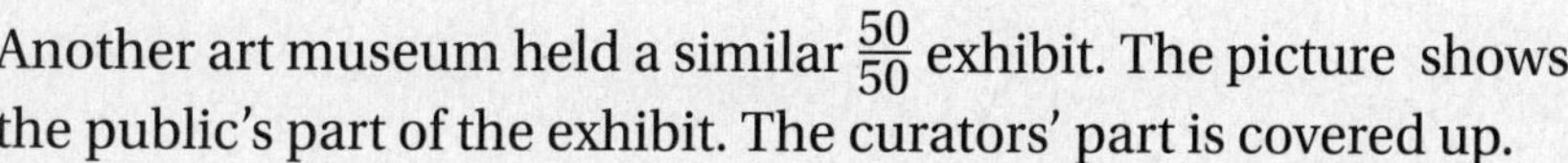

Another art museum held a similar $\frac{50}{50}$ exhibit. The picture shows the public's part of the exhibit. The curators' part is covered up.

A How many works of art do you estimate were in the exhibit? Is there any other information that would help you make a better estimate? Explain.

continued on the next page >

Problem 4.3 continued

B Below is a picture of the complete exhibit. How does this picture change your estimate from Question A?

C The picture in Question B shows you about $\frac{2}{3}$ of each part of the exhibit.

1. Make a drawing to show the size of the whole exhibit.
2. Use your drawing to estimate the number of works in each part.

D 1. Estimate the percent of the exhibit chosen by the public. Estimate the percent chosen by curators.

2. Use the percents from part (1). If there were 200 pieces in the exhibit, how many artworks do you think the public chose? How many do you think the curators chose?

E What title would you choose for this exhibit using percents and ratios?

ACE Homework starts on page 103.

Applications | Connections | Extensions

Applications

1. In a recent year, Team 1 made 191 out of 238 free-throw attempts and Team 2 made 106 out of 160 free-throw attempts. Copy and use the percent bars to answer each question.

0		238
Team 1		
0%		100%

0		160
Team 2		
0%		100%

   a. What fraction benchmark is close to the number of free throws made by each team?

   b. Estimate the percent of free throws made by each team in the season.

   c. If Team 1's free-throw rate does not change, how many free throws will Team 1 make in the next 200 throws? How many free throws will Team 1 make in the next 20 throws?

2. **Multiple Choice** Choose the best score on a quiz.

   A. 15 points out of 25
   B. 8 points out of 14
   C. 25 points out of 45
   D. 27 points out of 50

3. **Multiple Choice** Choose the best score on a quiz.

   F. 150 points out of 250
   G. 24 points out of 42
   H. 75 points out of 135
   J. 75 points out of 150

4. **Multiple Choice** What is the correct percent for a quiz score of 14 points out of 20?

   A. 43%
   B. 53%
   C. 70%
   D. 75%

5. **Multiple Choice** What is the correct percent for a quiz score of 26 points out of 60?

   F. about 43%
   G. about 57%
   H. about 68%
   J. about 76%

For Exercises 6–14, use the data in the table below.

Distribution of Cat Weights

Weight (lb)	Males		Females	
	Kitten	Adult	Kitten	Adult
0–5.9	8	1	7	4
6–10.9	0	16	0	31
11–15.9	2	15	0	10
16–20	0	4	0	2
Total	10	36	7	47

6. a. What fraction of the cats are female?
   b. What fraction of the cats are male?
   c. Write each fraction as a decimal and as a percent.

7. a. What fraction of the cats are kittens?
   b. What fraction of the cats are adults?
   c. Write each fraction as a decimal and a percent.

8. a. What fraction of the kittens are male?
   b. Write the fraction as a decimal and as a percent.

9. What percent of the cats weigh between 11 and 15.9 pounds?

10. What percent of the cats weigh between 0 and 5.9 pounds?

11. What percent of the cats are male kittens and weigh between 11 and 15.9 pounds?

12. What percent of the cats are female and weigh between 6 and 15.9 pounds?

13. What percent of the cats are kittens and weigh between 16 and 20 pounds?

14. What percent of the female cats weigh between 0 and 5.9 pounds?

For Exercises 15–18, use the following information: In a recent survey, 150 dog owners and 200 cat owners were asked what type of food their pets liked. Here are the results of the survey.

Pet Food Preferences

Preference	Dogs	Cats
Human Food Only	75	36
Pet Food Only	45	116
Human and Pet Food	30	48

15. Find the category of food most favored by dogs (Human, Pet, or Human and Pet). Write the data from this category as a fraction, as a decimal, and as a percent of the total dog owners surveyed.

16. Find the category of food most favored by cats. Write the data from this category as a fraction, as a decimal, and as a percent of the total cat owners surveyed.

17. Suppose only 100 dog owners were surveyed with similar results. Estimate the counts in each of the three food categories.

18. Suppose 50 cat owners were surveyed with similar results. Estimate the counts in each of the three food categories.

19. Elisa's math test score, with extra credit included, was $\frac{26}{25}$. What percent is this?

20. Use the data below. Which neighborhood, Elmhurst or Little Neck, is more in favor of building a new sports complex? Explain your reasoning.

Votes on a New Sports Complex

Neighborhood	Yes	No
Elmhurst	43	57
Little Neck	41	9

21. In Problem 4.1, you found free-throw percentages for Angela, Emily, and Christina. Write each girl's free-throw success as a ratio of *percent made* : *percent missed.*

Angela made 12 out of 15 free throws

Emily made 15 out of 20 free throws

Christina made 13 out of 16 free throws

22. A candy manufacturer says on its Web site that it wants to reach a 60 : 40 consumer taste preference for new products. What do you think this means?

23. In some cars, the rear seat folds down to add more space in the trunk. Often, there is a 60 : 40 split in the rear seat instead of 50 : 50. If a rear seat is 60 inches wide with a 60 : 40 split, how wide are the two parts?

24. The 90 : 10 rule says that part of your success in life comes from what happens to you and part comes from how you react to it. Which is 90 and which is 10? Explain.

25. Copy the table and fill in the missing parts.

Percent	Decimal	Fraction
62%	■	■
■	■	$\frac{4}{9}$
■	1.23	■
■	■	$\frac{12}{15}$
■	2.65	■
■	0.55	■
48%	■	■
■	■	$\frac{12}{10}$

Connections

Compare each pair of fractions in Exercises 26–31 using benchmarks or another strategy that makes sense to you. Copy the fractions and insert <, >, or = to make a true statement.

26. $\frac{7}{10}$ ■ $\frac{5}{8}$

27. $\frac{11}{12}$ ■ $\frac{12}{13}$

28. $\frac{12}{15}$ ■ $\frac{12}{14}$

29. $\frac{3}{8}$ ■ $\frac{4}{8}$

30. $\frac{3}{5}$ ■ $\frac{4}{6}$

31. $\frac{4}{3}$ ■ $\frac{15}{12}$

32. Copy the table below and fill in the missing parts.

Fraction	Mixed Number
$\frac{13}{5}$	■
■	$5\frac{2}{7}$
■	$9\frac{3}{4}$
$\frac{23}{3}$	■

33. The following percents are a good set of benchmarks because they have common fraction and decimal equivalents. Copy the table and fill in the missing parts. Use your table to learn these equivalents.

Percent	10%	$12\frac{1}{2}$%	20%	25%	30%	$33\frac{1}{3}$%	50%	$66\frac{2}{3}$%	75%
Fraction	■	■	■	■	■	■	■	■	■
Decimal	■	■	■	■	■	■	■	■	■

Extensions

In Exercises 34–36, determine what fraction is the correct label for the mark halfway between the two marked values on the number line. Write the fraction as a percent and as a decimal.

34.

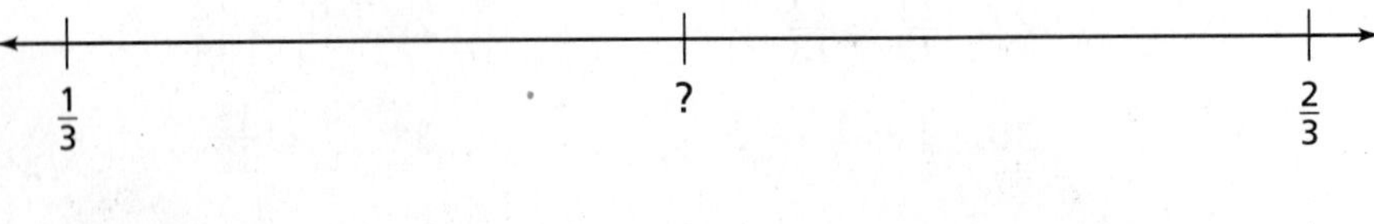

35. $\frac{1}{2}$? $\frac{3}{4}$

36. $\frac{1}{6}$? $\frac{1}{5}$

37. What fraction of the square below is shaded? Explain.

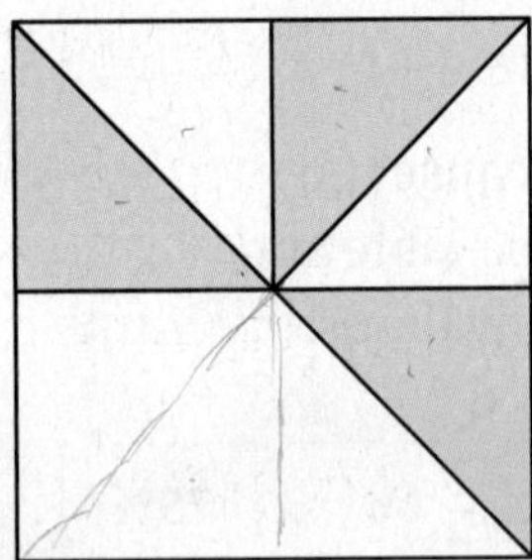

38. In decimal form, what part of the square below is shaded? Explain.

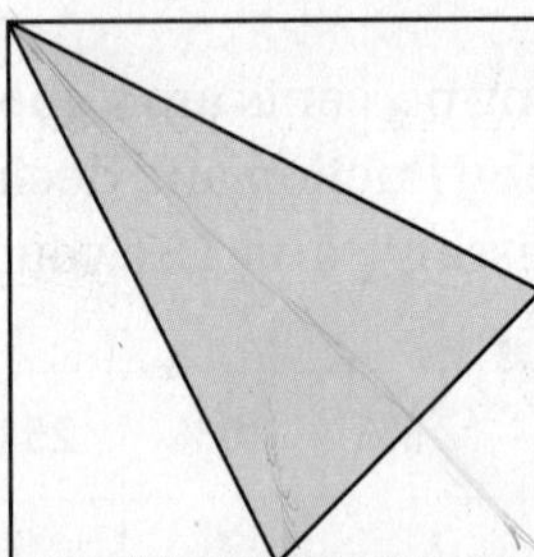

39. What percent of the square below is shaded? Explain.

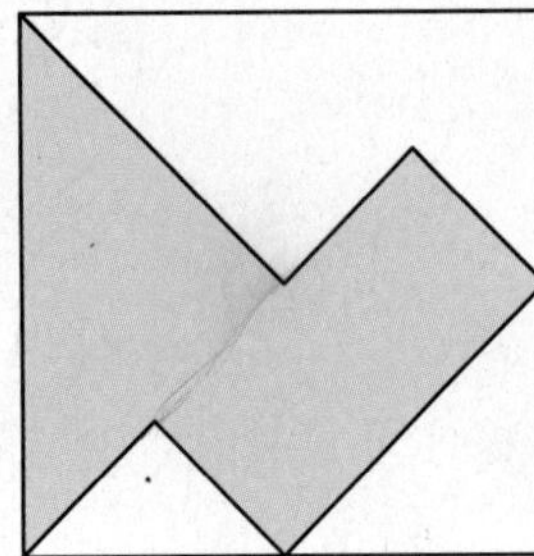

40. A pet store sells digestible mouthwash for cats. To promote the new product, the store is offering $.50 off the regular price of $2.00 for an 8-ounce bottle. What is the percent discount on the mouthwash?

In each of Exercises 41–43, what percent is halfway between the two percents labeled on the percent bar? What number is represented by the percent?

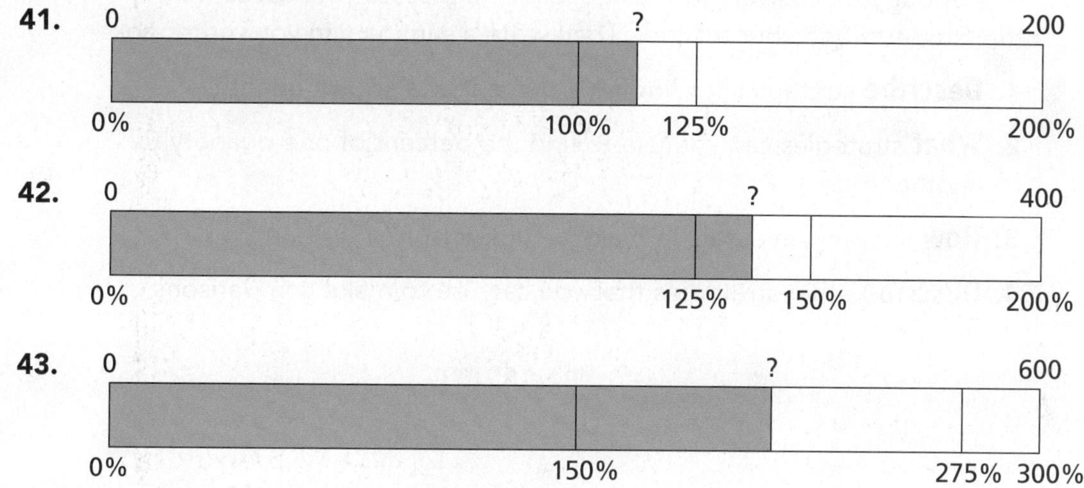

44. A store offers a discount of 30% on all reference books.

a. If a dictionary costs $12 before the discount, what is the dollar amount of the discount?

b. If a book on insect identification originally costs $15, how much will you have to pay for it?

c. If you pay $14 for a math dictionary, what was the original price of the dictionary?

Did You Know?

In the 1400s, the phrase "per cento" stood for "per 100." Writing "per cento" over and over again probably got tiresome. Manuscripts on arithmetic from about 1650 show that people began to replace "per cento" with "per $\frac{0}{0}$" or "p $\frac{0}{0}$." Later, the "per" was dropped and the symbol $\frac{0}{0}$ appeared alone. Then, over time, $\frac{0}{0}$ became %, the symbol used today.

Mathematical Reflections

In this Investigation, you used percent bars, ratios, and fraction reasoning to investigate percents. These questions will help you summarize what you have learned.

Think about your answers to these questions. Discuss your ideas with other students and your teacher. Then write a summary in your notebook.

1. **Describe** strategies for finding a percent of a known quantity.
2. **What** strategies can you use to find the percent of one quantity to another quantity?
3. **How** are percents used to make a comparison?
4. **Describe** other strategies that you can use to make comparisons.

Common Core Mathematical Practices

As you worked on the Problems in this Investigation, you used prior knowledge to make sense of the Problems. You also applied Mathematical Practices to solve the Problems. Think back over your work, the ways you thought about the Problems, and how you used Mathematical Practices.

Ken described his thoughts in the following way:

In Problem 4.2, we talked about how we could find certain common traits in various populations of people.

We used percent bars and rate tables to estimate the percent of people in a class who responded to a survey asking who has attached earlobes, dimples, straight hair, and a widow's peak.

We analyzed the relationships with percent bars and rate tables and drew conclusions based on our representations. We compared the methods. Since the numbers did not quickly scale up to 100, some of us preferred to use the percent bar or division to find the percentage.

Common Core Standards for Mathematical Practice

MP5 Use appropriate tools strategically

- What other Mathematical Practices can you identify in Ken's reasoning?
- Describe a Mathematical Practice that you and your classmates used to solve a different Problem in this Investigation.

Looking Back

In this Unit, you extended your knowledge of fractions, ratios, decimals, and percents. You learned how to

- Use ratios and fractions to make comparisons
- Relate fractions and decimals to their locations on a number line
- Relate fractions, decimals, ratios, and percents to each other
- Compare and order fractions and decimals
- Identify and produce equivalent fractions, decimals, and percents
- Identify and produce equivalent ratios, rate tables, and unit rates

Use Your Understanding: Number Sense

Test your understanding of and skill working with fractions, decimals, and percents by solving the following problems.

1. The diagram shows a puzzle made up of familiar shapes.

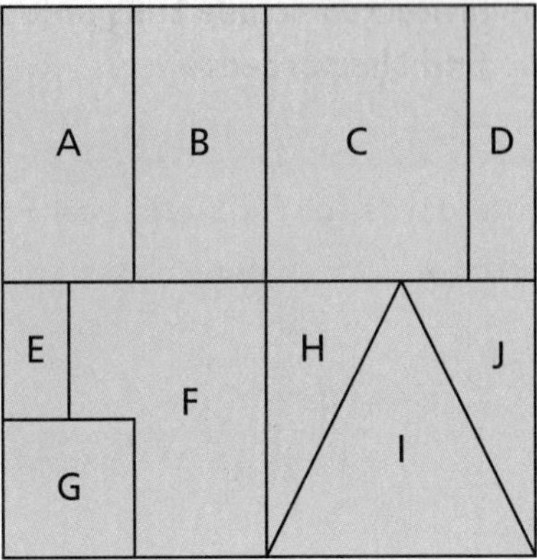

a. What fraction of the puzzle does each piece cover? Use your measurement estimation skills and reasoning to find each fraction.

b. Find two puzzle pieces with sizes in the ratio 2 : 1. Is there more than one possible answer? Explain.

c. What is the ratio of the size of piece C to the size of piece H?

2. Jose draws eight cards from a deck of number cards. He shows the position of each number on a number line as a fraction, as a decimal, and as a percent of the distance between 0 and 1.

The number line below shows the fraction $\frac{1}{4}$ along with its corresponding decimal and percent.

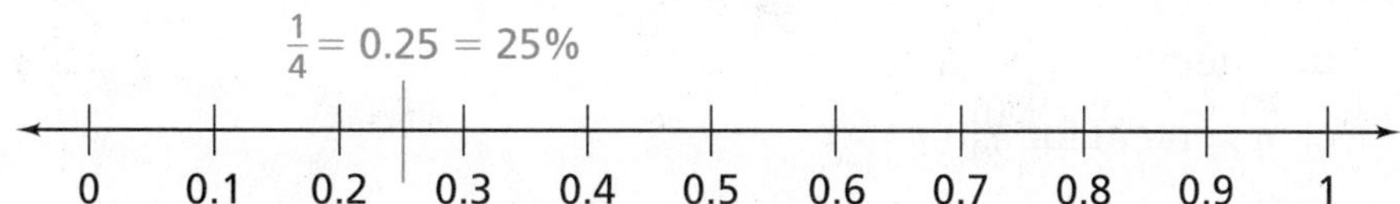

a. Copy the number line and show the position of each of the other numbers.

b. Label each position as a fraction, a decimal, and a percent of the distance between 0 and 1.

Explain Your Reasoning

You have explored relationships among ratios, fractions, decimals, and percents in many different problems. You have learned strategies for working with fractions, decimals, and percents that apply in any situation.

3. Describe a strategy that you can use to compare each pair of numbers.

a. $\frac{5}{8}$ and $\frac{7}{8}$ **b.** $\frac{3}{4}$ and $\frac{3}{5}$ **c.** $\frac{3}{4}$ and $\frac{5}{8}$

d. $\frac{3}{8}$ and $\frac{2}{3}$ **e.** $\frac{3}{4}$ and $\frac{4}{5}$ **f.** $\frac{2}{3}$ and $\frac{5}{8}$

For Exercises 4–6, find each number. Then describe the strategy that you used.

4. a. a fraction equivalent to $\frac{16}{20}$

b. a decimal equivalent to $\frac{16}{20}$

c. a percent for $\frac{16}{20}$

5. a. a decimal equivalent to 0.18

b. a fraction equivalent to 0.18

c. a percent for 0.18

6. a. a fraction for 35%

b. a decimal for 35%

7. A square is shaded so that the ratio of the size of the shaded part to the size of the unshaded part is 3 : 1. Describe a strategy that you can use to find the fraction of the square that is shaded.

8. Two thirds of the students in a sixth-grade class wear glasses. Describe a strategy that you can use to find the ratio of the number of students who wear glasses to the number of students who do not wear glasses.

9. To make chocolate milk, a recipe calls for 12 tablespoons of chocolate syrup for 4 cups of milk. Describe a strategy for finding the amount of chocolate syrup needed to make each quantity of chocolate milk.

a. 1 cup

b. 20 cups

English / Spanish Glossary

A

absolute value The absolute value of a number is its distance from 0 on the number line. Numbers that are the same distance from 0 have the same absolute value.

valor absoluto El valor absoluto de un número es su distancia del 0 en una recta numérica. Se puede interpretar como el valor de un número cuando no importa su signo. Por ejemplo, tanto −3 como 3 tienen un valor absoluto de 3.

B

base ten numeration The common system of writing whole numbers and decimal fractions using digits 0, 1, 2, 3, 4, 5, 6, 7, 8, and 9 and place values that are powers of 10. For example, the base ten numeral 5620.301 represents $5000 + 600 + 20 + 0 + \frac{3}{10} + \frac{0}{100} + \frac{1}{1000}$.

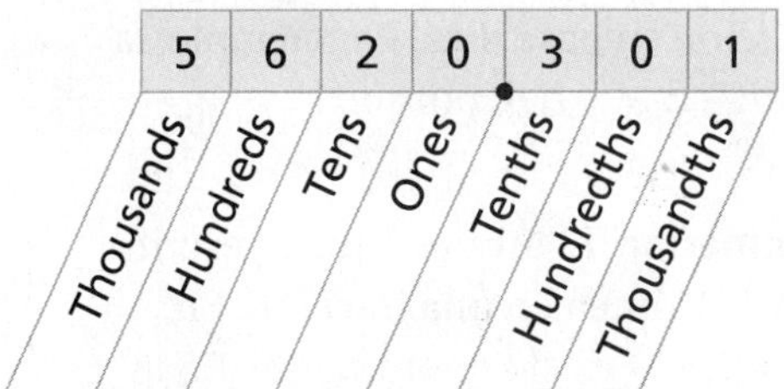

numeración en base diez Un sistema común de escritura de números enteros y fracciones decimales que usa los dígitos 0, 1, 2, 3, 4, 5, 6, 7, 8 y 9, y valores de posición que son potencias de 10. Por ejemplo, el número de base diez 5620.301 representa $5000 + 600 + 20 + 0 + \frac{3}{10} + \frac{0}{100} + \frac{1}{1000}$.

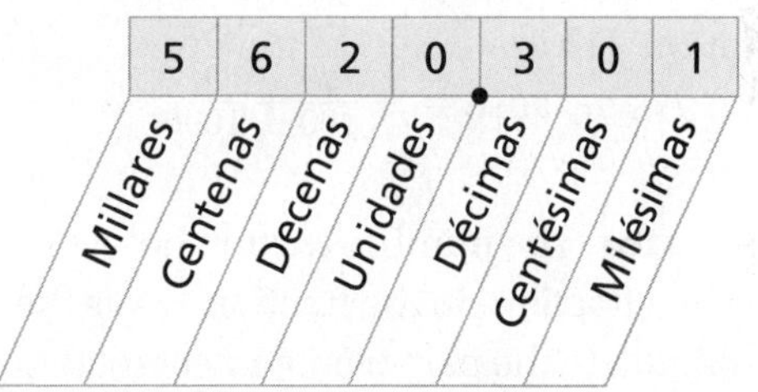

benchmark A reference number that can be used to estimate the size of other numbers. For work with fractions, 0, $\frac{1}{2}$, and 1 are good benchmarks. We often estimate fractions or decimals with benchmarks because it is easier to do arithmetic with them, and estimates often give enough accuracy for the situation. For example, many fractions and decimals—such as $\frac{37}{50}$, $\frac{5}{8}$, 0.43, and 0.55—can be thought of as being close to $\frac{1}{2}$. You might say $\frac{5}{8}$ is between $\frac{1}{2}$ and 1 but closer to $\frac{1}{2}$, so you can estimate $\frac{5}{8}$ to be about $\frac{1}{2}$. We also use benchmarks to help compare fractions and decimals. For example, we could say that $\frac{5}{8}$ is greater than 0.43 because $\frac{5}{8}$ is greater than $\frac{1}{2}$ and 0.43 is less than $\frac{1}{2}$.

punto de referencia Un número que se puede usar como referencia para estimar la magnitud de otros números. Los números 0, $\frac{1}{2}$ y 1 son puntos de referencia convenientes para el trabajo con fracciones. Con frecuencia, estimamos fracciones o números decimales usando puntos de referencia porque resulta más fácil hacer cálculos aritméticos con ellos, y las estimaciones suelen ser lo suficientemente precisas para la situación. Por ejemplo, muchas fracciones y números decimales, como $\frac{37}{50}$, $\frac{5}{8}$, 0.43 y 0.55, se pueden considerar cercanos a $\frac{1}{2}$. Se puede decir que $\frac{5}{8}$ está entre $\frac{1}{2}$ y 1, pero más cerca de $\frac{1}{2}$, por lo que se puede estimar que $\frac{5}{8}$ es aproximadamante $\frac{1}{2}$. También usamos puntos de referencia como ayuda para comparar fracciones y números decimales. Por ejemplo, podemos decir que $\frac{5}{8}$ es mayor que 0.43, porque $\frac{5}{8}$ es mayor que $\frac{1}{2}$ y 0.43 es menor que $\frac{1}{2}$.

C

compare **Academic Vocabulary** To tell or show how two things are alike and different.

related terms: *analyze, relate*

sample Compare the fractions $\frac{2}{3}$ and $\frac{3}{8}$.

I set the fractions strips representing $\frac{2}{3}$ and $\frac{3}{8}$ next to each other to see which fraction was greater. $\frac{2}{3} > \frac{3}{8}$

comparar **Vocabulario académico** Decir o mostrar en qué se parecen y en qué se diferencian dos cosas.

términos relacionados: *analizar, relacionar*

ejemplo Compara las fracciones $\frac{2}{3}$ y $\frac{3}{8}$.

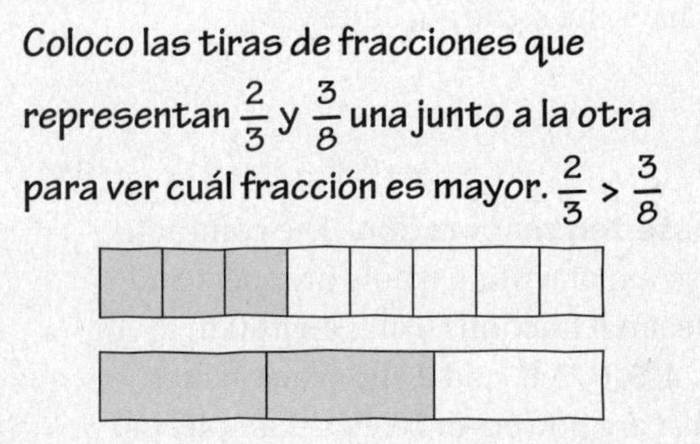

D

decimal a fraction written in base ten numeration. For example, the fraction $\frac{375}{1000} = 0.375$ because $= + \frac{7}{100} + \frac{5}{1000}$.

número decimal Una fracción escrita con numeración en base diez. Por ejemplo, la fracción $\frac{375}{1000} = 0.375$ porque $= + \frac{7}{100} + \frac{5}{1000}$.

denominator The number written below the line in a fraction. In the fraction $\frac{3}{4}$, 4 is the denominator. In the part-whole interpretation of fractions, the denominator shows the number of equal-size parts into which the whole has been split.

denominador El número que se escribe debajo de la línea en una fracción. En la fracción $\frac{3}{4}$, 4 es el denominador. En la interpretación de partes y enteros al hablar de fracciones, el denominador muestra el número de partes de igual tamaño en que se divide el entero.

describe Academic Vocabulary To explain or tell in detail. A written description can contain facts and other information needed to communicate your answer. A diagram or a graph may also be included.

related terms: *express, explain, illustrate*

sample Describe in writing or with pictures how $\frac{5}{4}$ compares to $1\frac{1}{4}$.

I can use fraction strips divided into fourths to show that $1\frac{1}{4}$ is equal to $\frac{5}{4}$.

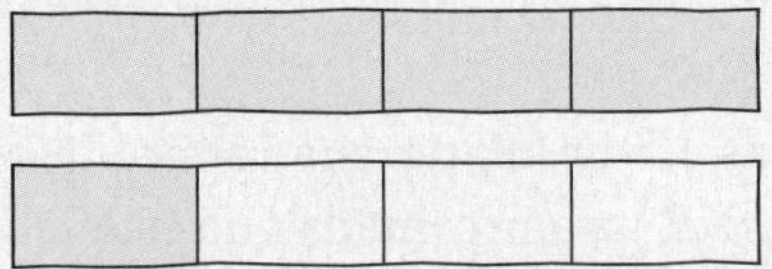

I can also compare using division. 5 divided by 4 is 1 remainder 1. So $\frac{5}{4}$ is the same as $1\frac{5}{4}$.

describir Vocabulario académico Explicar o decir con detalle. Una descripción escrita puede contener datos y otra información necesaria para comunicar tu respuesta. También se puede incluir un diagrama o una gráfica.

términos relacionados: *expresar, explicar, ilustrar*

ejemplo Describe por escrito o mediante un dibujo en qué se parecen o en qué se diferencian $\frac{5}{4}$ y $1\frac{1}{4}$.

Puedo usar tiras de fracciones divididas en cuartos para mostrar que $1\frac{1}{4}$ es igual a $\frac{5}{4}$.

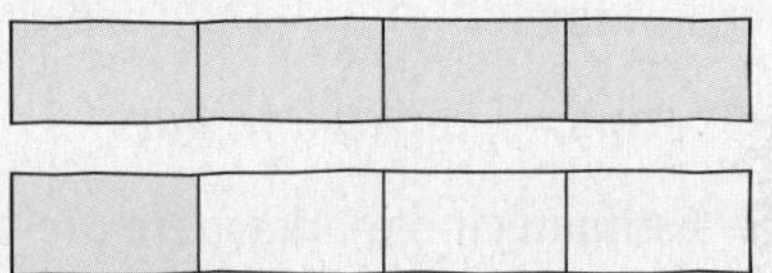

También puedo comparar usando la división. 5 dividido entre 4 es 1 con un residuo de 1. Así, $\frac{5}{4}$ es lo mismo que $1\frac{1}{4}$.

E

equivalent fractions Fractions that are equal in value, but may have different numerators and denominators. For example, $\frac{2}{3}$ and $\frac{14}{21}$ are equivalent fractions. The shaded part of this rectangle represents both $\frac{2}{3}$ and $\frac{14}{21}$.

fracciones equivalentes Fracciones de igual valor que pueden tener diferentes numeradores y denominadores. Por ejemplo, $\frac{2}{3}$ y $\frac{14}{21}$ son fracciones equivalentes. La parte coloreada de este rectángulo representa tanto $\frac{2}{3}$ como $\frac{14}{21}$.

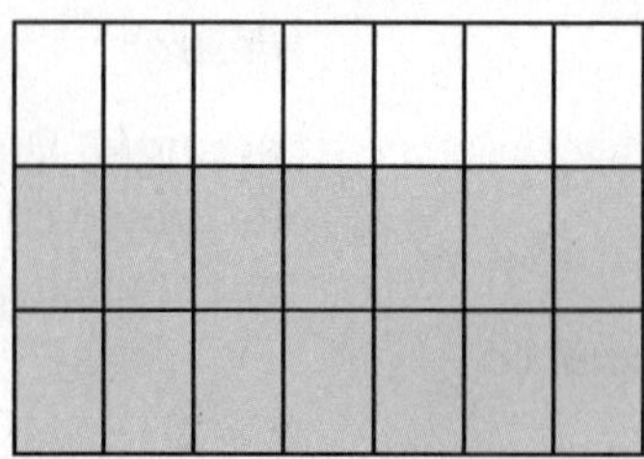

estimate Academic Vocabulary To find an approximate answer that is relatively close to an exact amount.

related terms: *approximate, guess*

sample Estimate and mark where the number 2 should be on the number line below. Explain.

Since $1\frac{1}{5}$ is the same as $\frac{6}{5}$, I divided the space between 0 and $1\frac{1}{5}$ into six parts. This gives me an idea of the length of $\frac{1}{5}$.

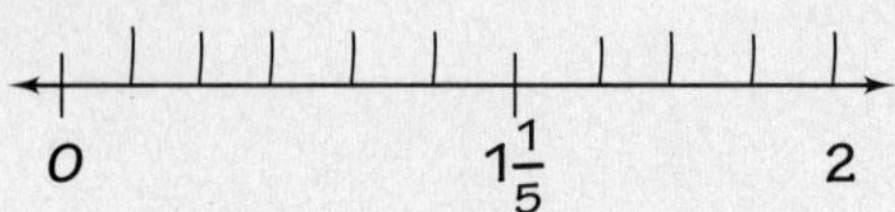

Then I added 4 marks after $1\frac{1}{5}$ to estimate where $1\frac{5}{5}$, or 2, should be on the number line.

estimar Vocabulario académico Hallar una respuesta aproximada que esté relativamente cerca de una cantidad exacta.

términos relacionados: *aproximar, suponer*

ejemplo Haz una estimación y marca dónde debe estar el número 2 en la recta numérica siguiente. Explica tu respuesta.

Puesto que $1\frac{1}{5}$ es lo mismo que $\frac{6}{5}$, divido el espacio entre 0 y $1\frac{1}{5}$ en cinco partes. Esto me da una idea de la longitud de $\frac{1}{5}$.

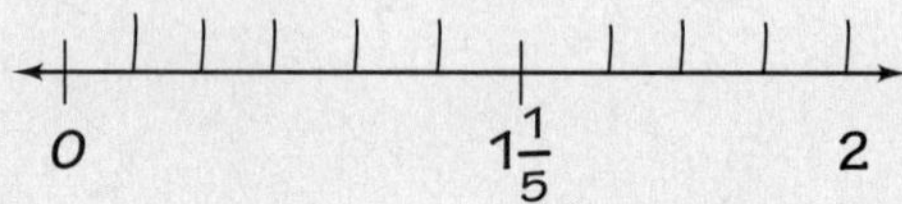

Luego agrego 4 marcas después de $1\frac{1}{5}$ para estimar donde debería estar $1\frac{5}{5}$, ó 2, en la recta numérica.

explain Academic Vocabulary To give facts and details that make an idea easier to understand. Explaining can involve a written summary supported by a diagram, chart, table, or a combination of these.

related terms: *analyze, clarify, describe, justify, tell*

sample Explain why $\frac{9}{10}$ is greater than $\frac{7}{8}$.

I can write the fractions in decimal form and compare digits.

$\frac{9}{10}$	0.900
$\frac{7}{8}$	0.875

Because 9 in the tenths place is greater than 8, $\frac{9}{10}$ is greater than $\frac{7}{8}$. I can also write equivalent fractions with a common denominator and compare the numerators. Since $\frac{9}{10}$ is equivalent to $\frac{36}{40}$ and $\frac{7}{8}$ is equivalent to $\frac{35}{40}$, and 36 is greater than 35, $\frac{9}{10}$ is greater than $\frac{7}{8}$.

explicar Vocabulario académico Dar datos y detalles que hacen que una idea sea más fácil de comprender. Explicar puede incluir un resumen escrito apoyado por un diagrama, una gráfica, una tabla o una combinación de éstos.

términos relacionados: *analizar, aclarar, describir, justificar, decir*

ejemplo Explica por qué $\frac{9}{10}$ es mayor que $\frac{7}{8}$.

Puedo escribir las fracciones en forma decimal y comparar los dígitos.

$\frac{9}{10}$	0.900
$\frac{7}{8}$	0.875

Puesto que 9 en el lugar de los décimos es mayor que 8, $\frac{9}{10}$ es mayor que $\frac{7}{8}$. También puedo escribir fracciones equivalentes con un común denominador y comparar los numeradores. Puesto que $\frac{9}{10}$ es equivalente a $\frac{36}{40}$ y $\frac{7}{8}$ es equivalente a $\frac{35}{40}$ y 36 es mayor que 35, $\frac{9}{10}$ es mayor que $\frac{7}{8}$.

F

fraction A mathematical expression in the form $\frac{a}{b}$ where a and b are numbers. A fraction can indicate a part of a whole object or set, a ratio of two quantities, or a division. For the picture below, the fraction $\frac{3}{4}$ shows the part of the rectangle that is shaded. The denominator 4 indicates the number of equal-size pieces. The numerator 3 indicates the number of pieces that are shaded.

fracción Una expresión matemática que se expresa de esta forma: $\frac{a}{b}$ en la que a y b son números. Una fracción puede indicar una parte de un objeto o de un conjunto de objetos, una razón entre dos cantidades o una división. En el dibujo siguiente, la fracción $\frac{3}{4}$ muestra la parte del rectángulo que está coloreada. El denominador 4 indica la cantidad de piezas de igual tamaño. El numerador 3 indica la cantidad de piezas que están coloreadas.

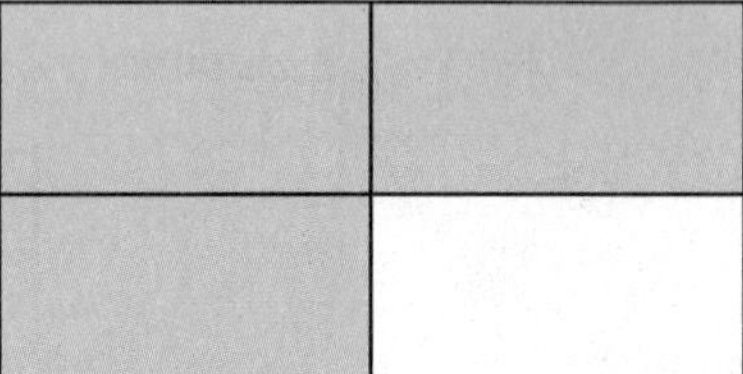

The fraction $\frac{3}{4}$ could also represent three of a group of four items meeting a particular criteria. For example, when 12 students enjoyed a particular activity and 16 students did not (the ratio is 3 to 4). Or, the amount of pizza each person receives when three pizzas are shared equally among four people ($3 \div 4$ or $\frac{3}{4}$ of a pizza per person).

La fracción $\frac{3}{4}$ también puede representar tres dentro de un grupo de cuatro objetos que cumplan con un mismo criterio. Por ejemplo, cuando 12 estudiantes participaron en una determinada actividad y 16 estudiantes no lo hicieron, (la razón es de 3 a 4), o la cantidad de pizza que le toca a cada persona cuando se reparten tres pizzas en partes iguales entre cuatro personas ($3 \div 4$ ó $\frac{3}{4}$ de pizza por persona).

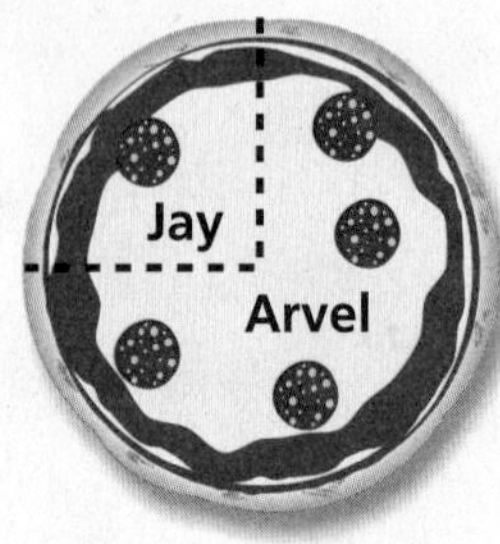

I

improper fraction A fraction in which the absolute value of the numerator is greater than the absolute value of the denominator. The fraction $\frac{5}{2}$ is an improper fraction. The fraction $\frac{5}{2}$ means 5 halves and is equivalent to $2\frac{1}{2}$.

fracción impropia Una fracción cuyo el valor absoluto de numerador es mayor que el valor absoluto de denominador. La fracción $\frac{5}{2}$ es una fracción impropia. La fracción $\frac{5}{2}$ representa 5 mitades y equivale a $2\frac{1}{2}$.

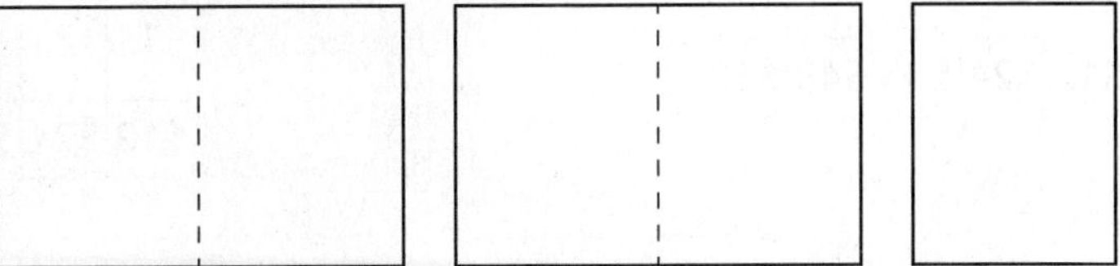

M

mixed number A number that is written with both a whole number and a fraction. A mixed number is the sum of the whole number and the fraction. The number $2\frac{1}{2}$ represents 2 wholes and a $\frac{1}{2}$ and can be thought of as $2 + \frac{1}{2}$.

número mixto Un número que se escribe con un número entero y una fracción. Un número mixto es la suma del número entero y la fracción. El número $2\frac{1}{2}$ representa 2 enteros y un $\frac{1}{2}$, y se puede considerar como $2 + \frac{1}{2}$.

N

numerator The number written above the line in a fraction. In the fraction $\frac{5}{8}$, 5 is the numerator. When you interpret the fraction $\frac{5}{8}$ as a part of a whole, the numerator 5 tells that the fraction refers to 5 of the 8 equal parts.

numerador El número que se escribe sobre la barra en una fracción. En la fracción $\frac{5}{8}$, 5 es el numerador. Cuando se interpreta la fracción $\frac{5}{8}$ como parte de un entero, el numerador 5 indica que la fracción se refiere a 5 de 8 partes iguales.

O

opposites Two numbers whose sum is 0. For example, -3 and 3 are opposites. On a number line, opposites are the same distance from 0 but in different directions from 0. The number 0 is its own opposite.

opuestos Dos números cuya suma da 0. Por ejemplo, -3 y 3 son opuestos. En una recta numérica, los opuestos se encuentran a la misma distancia del 0 pero en direcciones opuestas del 0 en la recta numérica. El número 0 es su propio opuesto.

P

percent "Out of 100." A percent is a fraction in which the denominator is 100. When we write 68%, we mean 68 out of 100, $\frac{68}{100}$, or 0.68. We write the percent sign (%) after a number to indicate percent. The shaded part of this square is 68%.

porcentaje "De 100". Un porcentaje es una fracción en la que el denominador es 100. Cuando escribimos 68%, queremos decir 68 de 100, $\frac{68}{100}$ ó 0.68. Para indicar un porcentaje, escribimos el signo correspondiente (%) después del número. La parte coloreada de este cuadrado es el 68%.

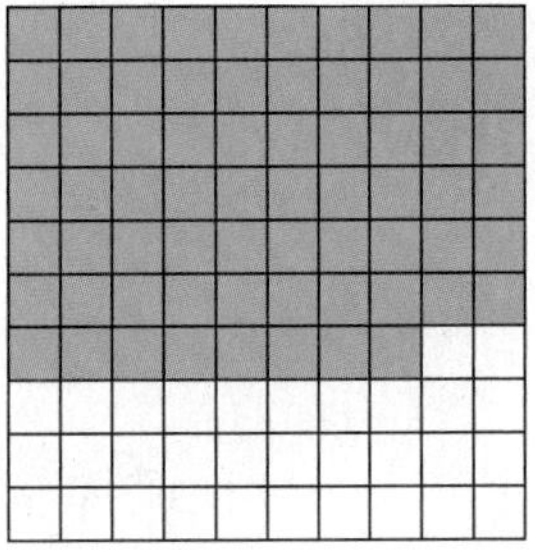

R

rate table A table that shows the value of a single item in terms of another item. It is used to show equivalent ratios of the two items.

Movie Tickets

Number of people	1	2	3	4	5
Total Price	$12	$24	$36	$48	$60

tabla de tasas Una tabla que muestra el valor de un elemento con relación a otro elemento. Se usa para mostrar razones equivalentes de los dos elementos.

Boletos para el cine

Número de personas	1	2	3	4	5
Precio total	$12	$24	$36	$48	$60

ratio A comparison of two quantities expressed with a phrase such as 'the ratio of 3 to 5' which means '3 for every 5.' Such ratio comparisons are often written as common fractions and in the special notation 3 : 5.

$\frac{3}{5}$ 3 to 5 3 : 5

razón Una comparación de dos cantidades que se expresa con frases como "la razón de 3 a 5", que significa "3 de cada 5". Con frecuencia, estas comparaciones se escriben como fracciones comunes $\frac{3}{5}$ y con la notación especial 3 : 5.

$\frac{3}{5}$ 3 a 5 3 : 5

rational number Any number that can be written as the quotient of an integer and a non-zero integer, such as $\frac{3}{4}$, $\frac{13}{4}$, $\frac{3}{1}$, or $-\frac{3}{4}$.

número racional Cualquier número que se puede escribir como el cociente de un entero y de un entero distinto de cero, tales como $\frac{3}{4}$, $\frac{13}{4}$, $\frac{3}{1}$, ó $-\frac{3}{4}$.

T

tape diagram A drawing that looks like a piece of tape, used to model expressions. Also called a bar model.

diagrama con tiras Un dibujo que parece una cinta y que se usa para representar expresiones matemáticas. También se llama modelo de barras.

U

unit fraction A fraction with a numerator of 1. For example, in the unit fraction $\frac{1}{13}$, the part-whole interpretation of fractions tells us that 13 indicates the number of equal-size parts into which the whole has been split and that the fraction represents the quantity of 1 of those parts.

fracción unitaria Una fracción con numerador 1. Por ejemplo, en la fracción unitaria $\frac{1}{13}$, la interpretación de partes y enteros de fracciones nos dice que el 13 indica la cantidad de partes de igual tamaño en las que se divide el entero, y que la fracción representa la cantidad de una de esas partes.

unit rate A unit rate is a rate in which the second number (usually written as the denominator) is 1, or 1 of a quantity. For example, 1.9 children per family, 32 miles per gallon, and $\frac{\text{3 flavors of ice cream}}{\text{1 banana split}}$ are unit rates. Unit rates are often found by scaling other rates.

tasa por unidad Una comparación de dos cantidades mediante la división en la que el valor de la segunda cantidad, el divisor, es 1, ó 1 de una cantidad. Por ejemplo, 1.9 niños por familia, 32 millas por galón, y $\frac{\text{3 sabores de helado}}{\text{1 banana split}}$ son tasas por unidad. Las tasas por unidad se calculan a menudo poniendo a escala otras tasas.

Index

Index

Acknowledgments

Cover Design
Three Communication Design, Chicago

Photographs
Photo locators denoted as follows: Top (T), Center (C), Bottom (B), Left (L), Right (R), Background (Bkgd)

002 Kid Stock/Blend Images/Alamy; **003** Monkey Business Images/Shutterstock; **007** TWPhoto/Corbis; **008** Manchester Evening News; **043** Tom Stewart/Bridge/ Corbis; **058** Ilya Genkin/Fotolia; **070** (TL) Exactostock/SuperStock, (C) Tetra Images/Alamy, (CL) Ed Zurga/Contributor/Getty Images, (TCR) Mbbirdy/E+/ Getty Images, (BCR) only4denn/Fotolia; **079** Ullstein-CARO/Trappe/Glow Images; **099** (CL) Aaron Haupt/Photoresearchers, (TCL) Inti St Clair/Blend Images/Alamy, (TCR) Michael Newman/PhotoEdit,(CR) Custom Medical Stock Photo/Alamy, (BL) RedChopsticks Batch 19/Glow Asia RF/Alamy, (BCL) Kid Stock/Blend Images/Alamy,(BCR) Tatjana Romanova/Shutterstock, (CR) Piotr Marcinski/Fotolia; **104** Juniors Bildarchiv GmbH/Alamy; **106** Pearson Education.

CONNECTED MATHEMATICS® 3

Let's Be Rational

Understanding Fraction Operations

Lappan, Phillips, Fey, Friel

Let's Be Rational

Understanding Fraction Operations

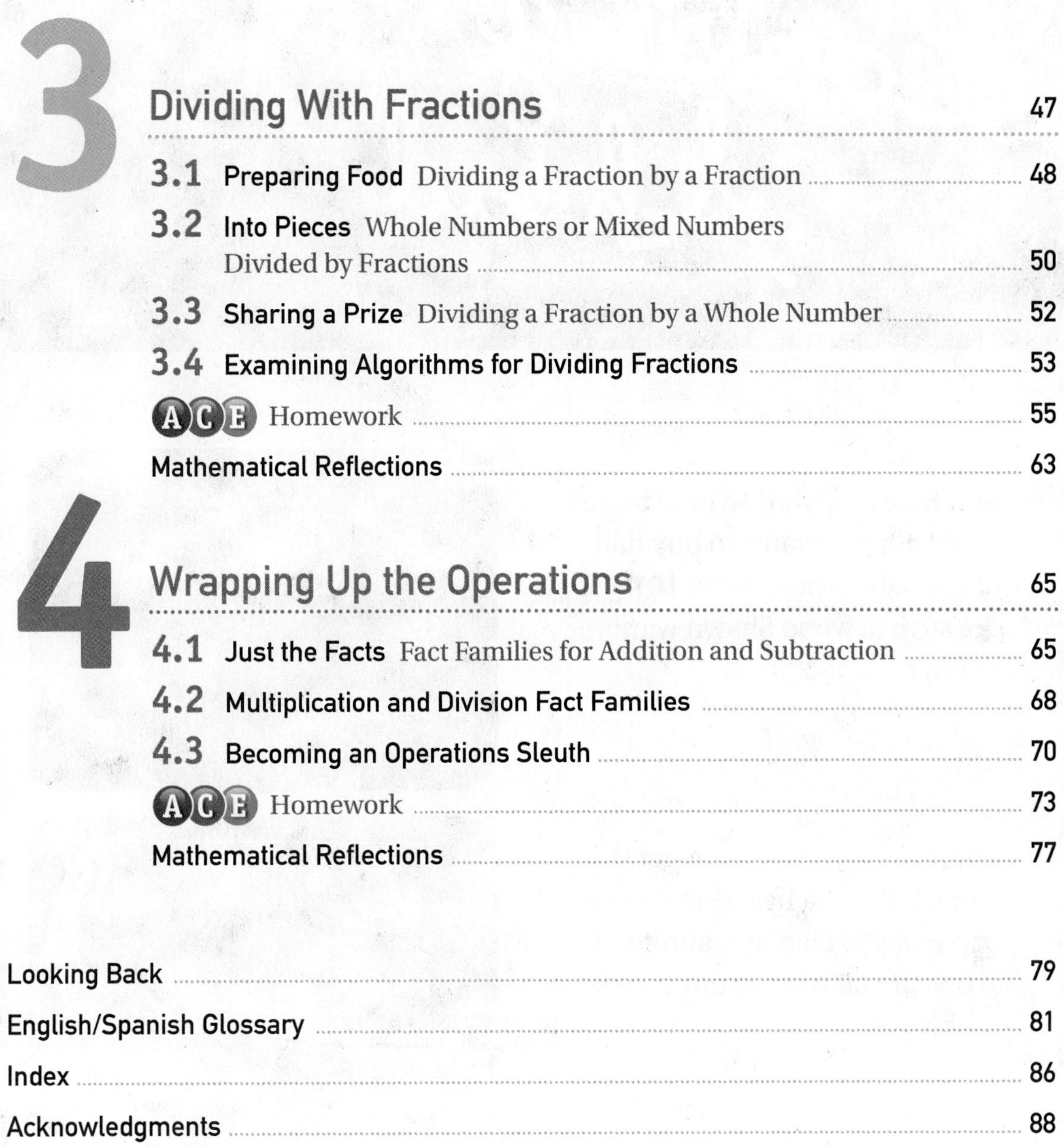

Looking Ahead

Min Ji has a $\frac{7}{8}$-yard strip of balsa wood. Shawn wants to buy half of the balsa wood. **How long** is the strip of wood Shawn wants to buy?

There are 12 rabbits at a pet store. Gabriella has $5\frac{1}{2}$ ounces of parsley to feed the rabbits. **How much** parsley does each rabbit get?

Jimarcus plans to build a fence at the back of his garden. If the fence will be $5\frac{1}{3}$ yards long, **how many** $\frac{2}{3}$-yard sections of fence will he need?

In *Comparing Bits and Pieces,* you learned what fractions, decimals, ratios, and percents mean. You also explored different real-world situations in which these numbers are used.

In *Let's Be Rational,* you will investigate situations such as those described on the previous page. These situations require addition, subtraction, multiplication, or division of fractions, including mixed numbers. You will decide which operation makes sense in each situation.

Knowing strategies for working with all kinds of numbers is very important. If you take part in developing these strategies, they will make more sense to you. You will be able to more easily apply these strategies to other situations.

You may already know some shortcuts for working with fractions. During this Unit, you will think about why those shortcuts, and the strategies you develop with your class, make sense. Remember, it is not enough to answer a problem. The real power is your ability to discuss your ideas and strategies and use them in new situations.

Mathematical Highlights

Understanding Fraction Operations

In *Let's Be Rational,* you will develop an understanding of the four basic arithmetic operations with fractions, including mixed numbers. You will also describe strategies for using these operations when solving problems involving fractions.

You will learn how to

- Use benchmarks and other strategies to make reasonable estimates for results of operations with fractions, including mixed numbers
- Develop ways to model sums, differences, products, and quotients, including the use of areas, fraction strips, and number lines
- Look for rules to generalize patterns in fraction operations
- Use your knowledge of fractions, equivalence of fractions, and properties of numbers to develop algorithms for adding, subtracting, multiplying, and dividing fractions
- Recognize when addition, subtraction, multiplication, or division is the appropriate operation to solve a problem
- Write fact families to show the inverse relationship between addition and subtraction, and between multiplication and division
- Solve problems using operations on fractions, including mixed numbers
- Find values for variables by using operations on fractions, including mixed numbers

When you encounter a new problem, it is a good idea to ask yourself questions. In this Unit, you might ask questions such as:

What models or diagrams might be helpful in understanding the problem situation and the relationships among quantities?

What models or diagrams might help you decide which operation is useful in solving a problem?

What is a reasonable estimate for the answer?

Common Core State Standards

Mathematical Practices and Habits of Mind

In the *Connected Mathematics* curriculum you will develop an understanding of important mathematical ideas by solving problems and reflecting on the mathematics involved. Every day, you will use "habits of mind" to make sense of problems and apply what you learn to new situations. Some of these habits are described by the *Common Core State Standards for Mathematical Practices* (MP).

MP1 **Make sense of problems and persevere in solving them.**

When using mathematics to solve a problem, it helps to think carefully about

- data and other facts you are given and what additional information you need to solve the problem;
- strategies you have used to solve similar problems and whether you could solve a related simpler problem first;
- how you could express the problem with equations, diagrams, or graphs;
- whether your answer makes sense.

MP2 **Reason abstractly and quantitatively.**

When you are asked to solve a problem, it often helps to

- focus first on the key mathematical ideas;
- check that your answer makes sense in the problem setting;
- use what you know about the problem setting to guide your mathematical reasoning.

MP3 **Construct viable arguments and critique the reasoning of others.**

When you are asked to explain why a conjecture is correct, you can

- show some examples that fit the claim and explain why they fit;
- show how a new result follows logically from known facts and principles.

When you believe a mathematical claim is incorrect, you can

- show one or more counterexamples—cases that don't fit the claim;
- find steps in the argument that do not follow logically from prior claims.

MP4 Model with mathematics.

When you are asked to solve problems, it often helps to

- think carefully about the numbers or geometric shapes that are the most important factors in the problem, then ask yourself how those factors are related to each other;
- express data and relationships in the problem with tables, graphs, diagrams, or equations, and check your result to see if it makes sense.

MP5 Use appropriate tools strategically.

When working on mathematical questions, you should always

- decide which tools are most helpful for solving the problem and why;
- try a different tool when you get stuck.

MP6 Attend to precision.

In every mathematical exploration or problem-solving task, it is important to

- think carefully about the required accuracy of results; is a number estimate or geometric sketch good enough, or is a precise value or drawing needed?
- report your discoveries with clear and correct mathematical language that can be understood by those to whom you are speaking or writing.

MP7 Look for and make use of structure.

In mathematical explorations and problem solving, it is often helpful to

- look for patterns that show how data points, numbers, or geometric shapes are related to each other;
- use patterns to make predictions.

MP8 Look for and express regularity in repeated reasoning.

When results of a repeated calculation show a pattern, it helps to

- express that pattern as a general rule that can be used in similar cases;
- look for shortcuts that will make the calculation simpler in other cases.

You will use all of the Mathematical Practices in this Unit. Sometimes, when you look at a Problem, it is obvious which practice is most helpful. At other times, you will decide on a practice to use during class explorations and discussions. After completing each Problem, ask yourself:

- What mathematics have I learned by solving this Problem?
- What Mathematical Practices were helpful in learning this mathematics?

Extending Addition and Subtraction of Fractions

Knowing how to combine and separate quantities is helpful in understanding the world around you. The mathematical names for combining and separating quantities are *adding* and *subtracting*. The result of addition is called a *sum*; the result of subtraction is called a *difference*.

Sometimes when you need to find a sum or difference, you do not need an exact answer. In these situations, making a reasonable estimate is good enough. It is *always* a good idea to estimate, even when you want an exact answer. You can check your exact answer by comparing it to an estimate.

- What is a good estimate for 198 + 605?
- What is a good estimate for 7.9 − 1.04?
- How do these estimates help you check the exact sum and difference?

Common Core State Standards

6.NS.B.4 Find the greatest common factor of two whole numbers less than or equal to 100 and the least common multiple of two whole numbers less than or equal to 12. . .

6.EE.B.7 Solve real-world and mathematical problems by writing and solving equations of the form $x + p = q$ and $px = q$ for cases in which p, q and x are all nonnegative rational numbers.

Also 6.EE.A.2, 6.EE.A.2b, 6.EE.B.5, 6.EE.B.6

1.1 Getting Close
Estimating Sums

Getting Close is a game that will sharpen your estimating skills by using **benchmarks.** A benchmark is a reference number that can be used to estimate the size of other numbers. Examine this set of benchmarks.

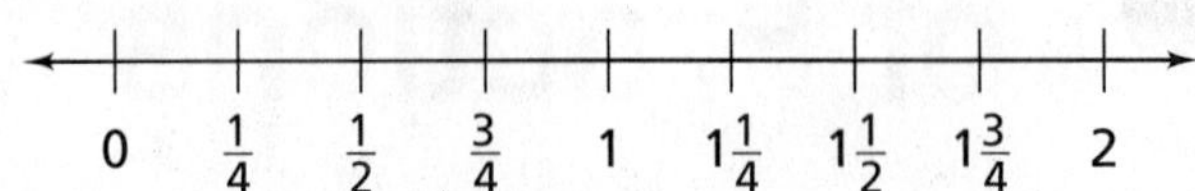

- Which fraction benchmark is $\frac{3}{8}$ closest to?

Raul says that $\frac{3}{8}$ is exactly halfway between $\frac{1}{4}$ and $\frac{1}{2}$. He reasons that $\frac{3}{8}$ is less than $\frac{1}{2}$ because it is less than $\frac{4}{8}$. However, $\frac{3}{8}$ is greater than $\frac{1}{4}$ because it is greater than $\frac{2}{8}$.

- Which benchmark is 0.58 closest to?

Desiree says that since $\frac{1}{2}$ is equal to 0.50, 0.58 is greater than $\frac{1}{2}$. Also, 0.58 is less than 0.75, which equals $\frac{3}{4}$. So 0.58 is between $\frac{1}{2}$ and $\frac{3}{4}$, but it is closer to $\frac{1}{2}$.

- Is Desiree correct?
- Is there another way to find the closest benchmark?

Cetera wonders if she can use benchmarks to estimate the sum of two fractions, such as the sum below.

$$\frac{1}{2} + \frac{5}{8}$$

- Is the sum between 0 and 1 or between 1 and 2?
- Is the sum closest to 0, to 1, or to 2?

You can practice using benchmarks and other strategies to estimate the sum of two numbers during the Getting Close game.

Getting Close Game

Two to four players can play Getting Close.

Materials

- Getting Close fraction or decimal game cards (one set per group)
- A set of four number squares (0, 1, 2, and 3) for each player

Directions

1. All players hold their 0, 1, 2, and 3 number squares in their hand. The game cards are placed facedown in a pile in the center of the table.
2. One player turns over two game cards from the pile. Each player mentally estimates the sum of the numbers on the two game cards.
3. Each player then selects a number square (0, 1, 2, or 3) closest to their estimate and places it facedown on the table.
4. After each player has played a number square, the players turn their number squares over at the same time.
5. Each player calculates the actual sum by hand or with a calculator. The player whose number square is closest to the actual sum gets the two game cards.
   Note: If there is a tie, all players who tied get one game card. Players who have tied may take a game card from the deck if necessary.
6. Players take turns turning over the two game cards.
7. When all game cards have been used, the player with the most game cards wins.

Problem 1.1

Play Getting Close several times. Keep a record of the estimation strategies you find useful. Use these estimation strategies to answer the questions below.

A Suppose you played Getting Close with only these game cards:

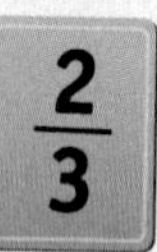

1. Which two cards have the greatest sum? How do you know? Estimate the sum.

2. Which two cards have the least sum? How do you know? Estimate the sum.

B Suppose you played Getting Close with only these game cards:

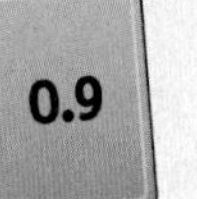

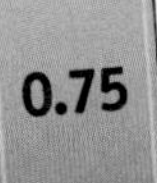

1. Which two cards have the greatest sum? How do you know? Estimate the sum.

2. Which two cards have the least sum? How do you know? Estimate the sum.

C Suppose you played Getting Close with only these game cards:

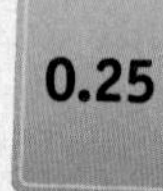

1. Which two cards have the greatest sum? The least sum? How do you know? Estimate the greatest sum and the least sum.

2. How can you estimate the sum of two game cards when one game card is a decimal and one game card is a fraction?

D Estimate each sum to the nearest whole number. Explain how you made each estimate.

1. $\frac{2}{3} + \frac{1}{5}$ 2. $2\frac{1}{3} + 3\frac{2}{3}$ 3. $\frac{3}{4} + \frac{4}{3}$

ACE Homework starts on page 18.

1.2 Estimating Sums and Differences

It is important to know how to find exact sums and differences. It is also important to be able to make good estimates. If an exact answer is not necessary, you can solve problems more quickly by estimating. Estimates help you know whether or not an answer is reasonable.

- What are some situations in which you can estimate a sum or difference instead of finding an exact answer?

Sometimes you should **overestimate,** or give an estimate that is a bit bigger than the actual value. Overestimate to make sure you have enough. Sometimes you should **underestimate,** or give an estimate that is a bit smaller than the actual value. Underestimate to stay below a certain limit.

Problem 1.2

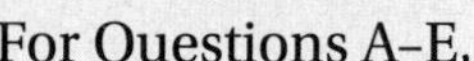

For Questions A–E,

- Answer the question by using estimation. Explain your reasoning.
- Explain how confident you are in your answer.
- For each estimate you make, tell whether it is an overestimate or an underestimate. Explain why you chose to overestimate or underestimate.

A Mrs. Edwards is building a dollhouse for her children. She needs to buy wood for the railing on the balcony.

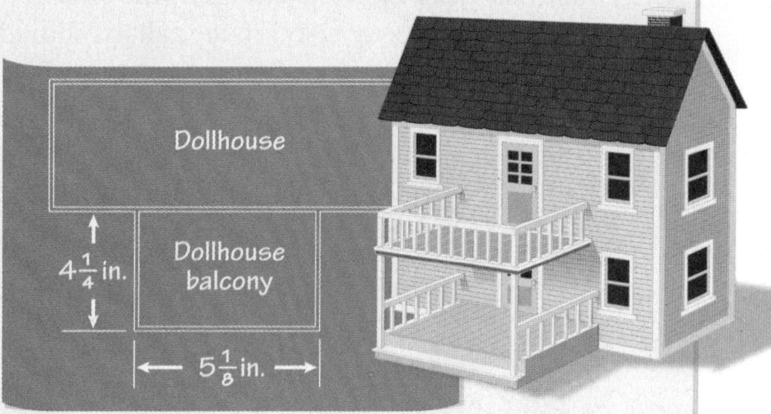

The wood is available in 12-inch, 14-inch, and 16-inch lengths. She does not want to waste wood. What length should she buy?

continued on the next page >

Problem 1.2 continued

B Mr. Cheng is making shades for his office. One window needs $1\frac{1}{3}$ yards of material and the other window needs $1\frac{3}{4}$ yards of material. The fabric store only sells whole-number lengths of this material. How many yards of material should Mr. Cheng buy?

C Mr. Aleman is the treasurer for his local scouting troop. He makes a budget for the troop. He suggests that they spend $\frac{1}{2}$ of their money on field trips, $\frac{1}{3}$ of their money on events, and $\frac{1}{4}$ of their money on scholarships. He wants to save the rest of the troop's money for next year. What do you think of Mr. Aleman's budget?

D Jasmine is making jam to enter in the state fair.

1. Jasmine's raspberry jam recipe calls for $4\frac{1}{3}$ quarts of raspberries. She has picked $3\frac{1}{2}$ quarts of raspberries. About how many more quarts of raspberries should she pick?
2. Jasmine's mixed berry jam recipe calls for $6\frac{2}{3}$ quarts of berries. She has $3\frac{1}{3}$ quarts of strawberries and $2\frac{7}{8}$ quarts of blackberries. Does Jasmine have enough berries? If not, about how many more quarts of berries does she need to pick?

E The gas tank on Priya's pontoon boat can hold 5 gallons. It is completely empty. Priya needs a full tank for the day's activities. She adds $2\frac{1}{4}$ gallons from a gas canister and then takes the boat to a nearby marina to fill it up. She has to pay ahead. Priya wants the tank as full as possible but does not want to overpay. How many gallons should Priya ask for?

ACE Homework starts on page 18.

1.3 Land Sections
Adding and Subtracting Fractions

When Tupelo Township was founded, the land was divided into sections that could be farmed. Each section is a square that is 1 mile long on each side. In other words, each section is 1 square mile of land. There are 640 acres of land in one square-mile section.

Over time, the owners of the sections have bought and sold land, so each section is owned by several owners. You can use **number sentences** to find how much land each owner has.

If a farmer owns 2 acres of land and buys another $1\frac{1}{2}$ acres of land, she will have $2 + 1\frac{1}{2}$, or $3\frac{1}{2}$, acres of land. The number sentence that shows this relationship is

$$2 + 1\frac{1}{2} = 3\frac{1}{2}$$

The *sum* of the parts is the total land the farmer owns, $3\frac{1}{2}$ acres.

If a farmer has $2\frac{1}{2}$ acres of land and then sells $\frac{1}{2}$ of an acre of land, she will own $2\frac{1}{2} - \frac{1}{2}$, or 2, acres of land. The number sentence that shows this relationship is:

$$2\frac{1}{2} - \frac{1}{2} = 2$$

The *difference* is the land the farmer still owns, 2 acres.

This Problem requires you to add and subtract fractions to find exact answers. Remember to estimate to make sure that your answers are reasonable. As you work, use what you know about fractions and finding *equivalent fractions.* Write number sentences to communicate your strategies for solving the Problem.

The diagram below shows two sections of land that are *adjacent,* or side by side, in Tupelo Township. Several people share ownership of each section. The diagram shows the part of a section each person owns.

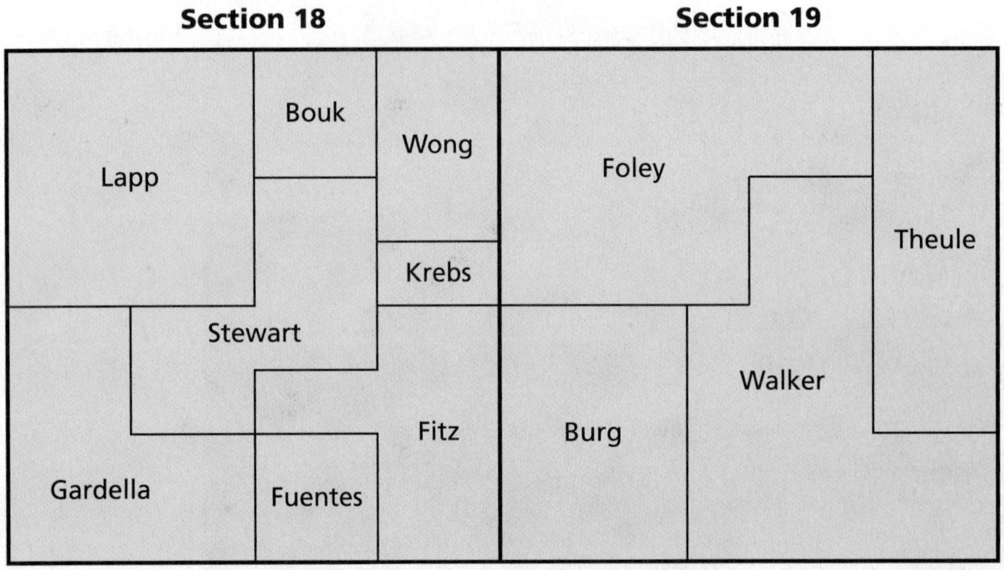

Section 18 **Section 19**

Lapp
Bouk
Wong
Krebs
Stewart
Gardella
Fuentes
Fitz
Foley
Theule
Walker
Burg

- Who owns the most land in Section 18? In Section 19?

Problem 1.3

A What fraction of a section does each person own? Explain how you know.

For Questions B and C,

- Find an approximate answer using estimation.
- Write a number sentence and answer the question.
- Compare your answer to your estimate to make sure your answer is reasonable.
- Identify the meaning of each number and symbol in your number sentence.

B
1. Stewart and Bouck combine their land. What fraction of a section do they now own together?
2. Foley and Burg combine their land. What fraction of a section do they now own together?
3. How much more land does Lapp own than Wong?

C
1. Name a set of owners whose combined land equals $1\frac{1}{2}$ sections.
2. Name a set of owners whose combined land equals $1\frac{3}{4}$ sections.

D
1. Each section of land is one square mile. One square mile is equal to 640 acres. How many acres of land does each person own? Explain your reasoning.
2. Foley, Walker, Burg, and Krebs sell their land for a state park. How many acres are covered by the state park? Explain.
3. After Foley, Walker, Burg, and Krebs sell their land, what fraction of Section 19 remains in private ownership? Explain.

E
1. Which set of owners' combined land does this number sentence represent?

$$1 + \frac{1}{4} + \frac{3}{16} + \frac{1}{16} = 1\frac{1}{2}$$

2. Explain how you know that this sum of fractions is exactly equal to $1\frac{1}{2}$.

ACE Homework starts on page 18.

1.4 Visiting the Spice Shop
Adding and Subtracting Mixed Numbers

All over the world, cooks use spices to add flavor to foods. Because recipe ingredients are often measured using fractions, cooking can involve operating with fractional quantities.

Reyna owns a spice shop in Tupelo Township. Some of her recipes are shown below.

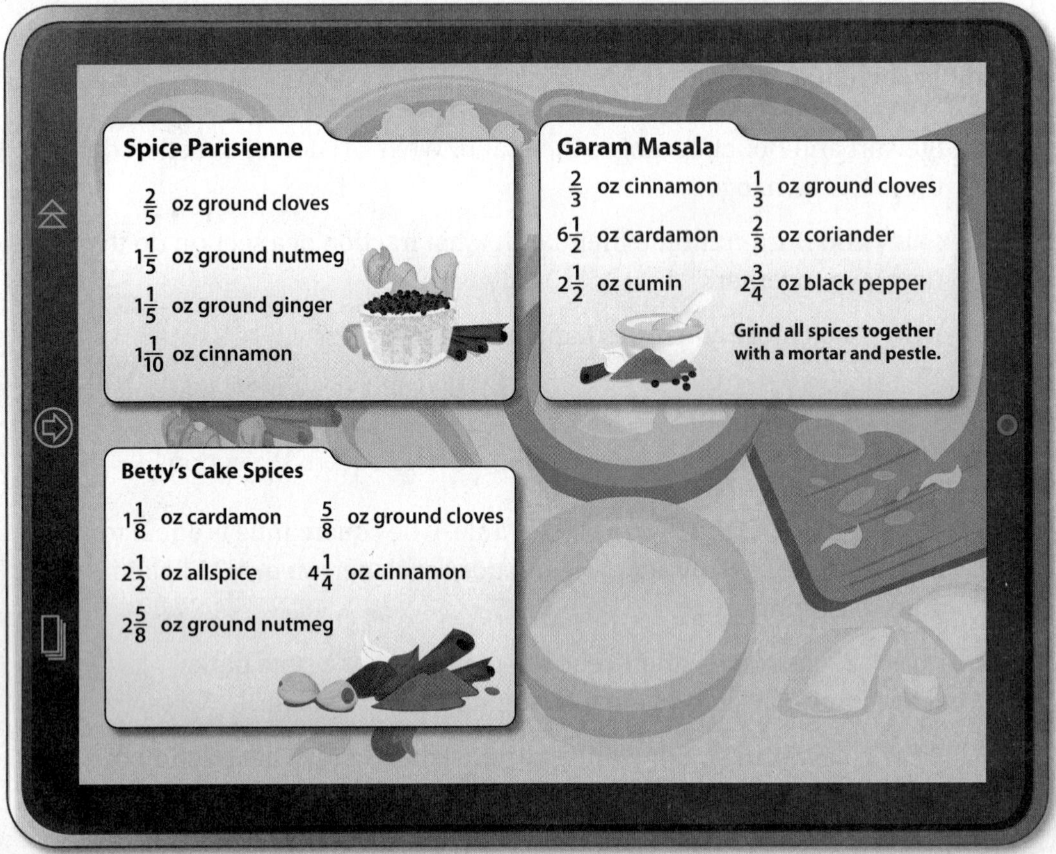

- Which makes a greater amount of spice mix, Betty's Cake Spices recipe, or the Garam Masala recipe? How much more spice mix?

Problem 1.4

A **1.** Latisha buys spices to make one batch of Spice Parisienne. Use estimation to decide whether she buys more or less than 4 ounces of spices. Explain your reasoning.

2. Use estimation to decide which weighs more, one batch of Betty's Cake Spices or one batch of Garam Masala. About how much more does it weigh? Explain.

For Questions B and C,

- Decide which operation you will use to solve each problem.
- Find an approximate answer using estimation.
- Write a number sentence and answer the question.

B Betty buys spices for her famous cake.

1. How many ounces of spice does Betty buy?

2. Tevin is allergic to cinnamon. If Betty removes cinnamon from the recipe for him, how many ounces of spice does she buy?

C Ms. Garza buys spices to make one batch of Garam Masala. When she weighs her spices at home, she only has $10\frac{11}{12}$ ounces of spice. Which spice did Ms. Garza forget?

D Renuka has two pounds of pepper in her cupboard. She knows that there are 16 ounces in one pound. After Renuka makes one batch of Garam Masala, how many ounces of pepper does Renuka have left in her cupboard?

E For each number sentence below, write a spice story. Then find the value for N that makes the sentence true.

1. $3\frac{1}{6} - 1\frac{3}{4} = N$ **2.** $N + \frac{3}{4} = 1\frac{1}{2}$ **3.** $2\frac{2}{3} - N = 1\frac{1}{4}$

F **1.** Describe a strategy for estimating sums and differences of fractions, including mixed numbers.

2. An **algorithm** (AL guh rith um) is a plan, or a series of steps, for doing a computation. Each step in an algorithm should be clear and precise. Describe an algorithm for finding sums and differences of fractions, including mixed numbers.

ACE Homework starts on page 18.

Applications | Connections | Extensions

Applications

For Exercises 1–6, determine whether the number is closest to 0, $\frac{1}{2}$, or 1. Explain your reasoning.

1. $\frac{10}{9}$ **2.** $\frac{9}{16}$ **3.** $\frac{5}{6}$

4. $\frac{48}{100}$ **5.** 0.67 **6.** 0.0009999

For Exercises 7–12, determine whether the sum of the two Getting Close game cards is closest to 0, 1, 2, or 3. Explain.

7. $\frac{7}{8}$ and $\frac{4}{9}$ **8.** $1\frac{3}{4}$ and $\frac{1}{8}$ **9.** $1\frac{1}{3}$ and 1.3

10. 0.25 and $\frac{1}{8}$ **11.** 1.352 and 0.84 **12.** $1\frac{4}{10}$ and 0.375

For Exercises 13–15, you are playing a game called Getting Even Closer. In this game, you have to estimate sums to the nearest $\frac{1}{2}$ or 0.5. Decide if the sum of the two game cards turned up is closest to 0, 0.5, or 1. Explain.

13. 

14. 

15. 

16. Four students were asked the following question: "Can you find two fractions with a sum greater than $\frac{3}{4}$?" Explain whether or not each answer below is correct.

a. $\frac{1}{8} + \frac{2}{4}$ **b.** $\frac{3}{6} + \frac{2}{4}$ **c.** $\frac{5}{12} + \frac{5}{6}$ **d.** $\frac{5}{10} + \frac{3}{8}$

For Exercises 17–20, find two fractions with a sum that is between the two given numbers.

17. 0 and $\frac{1}{2}$ **18.** $\frac{1}{2}$ and 1 **19.** 1 and $1\frac{1}{2}$ **20.** $1\frac{1}{2}$ and 2

21. A new set of Getting Close Cards contains the following numbers:

$$1.05 \qquad 0.7 \qquad \frac{3}{5} \qquad \frac{1}{4} \qquad \frac{9}{10}$$

a. Which two cards have the greatest sum?

b. Which two cards have the least sum?

22. Julio is at the grocery store. He has $10.00. Here is a list of the items he would like to buy.

Use mental computation and estimation to answer parts (a)–(c).

a. Can Julio buy all the items with the money he has? Explain your reasoning.

b. If Julio only has $5.00, what can he buy? Give two possible combinations.

c. What different items can he buy to come as close as possible to spending $5.00?

23. Many sewing patterns have a $\frac{5}{8}$-inch border for sewing the seam. Is a $\frac{5}{8}$-inch border closest to 0, $\frac{1}{2}$, or 1 inch? Explain your reasoning.

24. Soo needs 2 yards of molding to put around the bottom of a stand. He has two pieces of molding. One piece is $\frac{7}{8}$ of a yard long. The other is $\frac{8}{7}$ yards long. Estimate whether or not he has enough molding. Explain.

25. Reggie picked $3\frac{3}{4}$ quarts of blueberries and $4\frac{1}{3}$ quarts of raspberries at a fruit farm. *About* how many total quarts of berries did he pick?

26. You mix $\frac{5}{8}$ of a cup of wheat flour with $1\frac{3}{4}$ cups of white flour. Do you have enough flour for a recipe that calls for $2\frac{1}{2}$ cups of flour? Explain.

27. The Langstons planted a big garden with flowers.

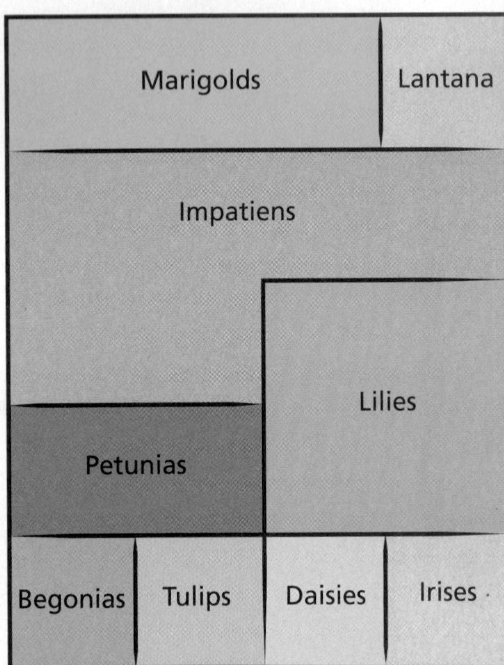

a. About what fraction of the garden is planted with each type of flower?

b. How much more of the garden is planted with lilies than daisies?

c. The Langstons replace the daisies and irises with lilies. What fraction of the garden is planted with lilies? Write a number sentence.

d. In the following sentence, the name of each type of flower represents the fraction of the garden in which the flower is planted.

$$\text{Marigolds} - \text{Begonias} = \text{Petunias} + \text{Tulips}$$

Use fractions to explain whether the sentence is correct or incorrect.

e. Look at the original garden plan. Find three different combinations of plots that total the fraction of the garden planted with impatiens. Write a number sentence for each combination.

For Exercises 28–30, use the sample magazine page shown.

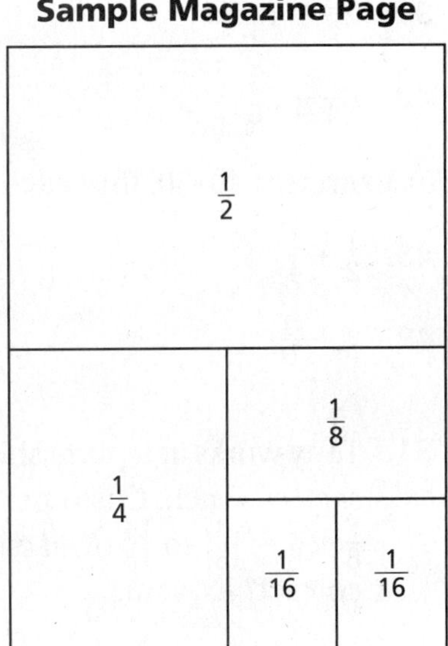

28. A local magazine sells space for ads. It charges advertisers according to the fraction of a page purchased.

a. Advertisers purchase $\frac{1}{8}$ and $\frac{1}{16}$ of page 20. What fraction of the page is used for ads?

b. What fraction of page 20 remains available for other uses? Explain.

29. The Cool Sub Shop is having its grand opening. The owner buys three $\frac{1}{4}$-page ads, four $\frac{1}{8}$-page ads, and ten $\frac{1}{16}$-page ads. What is the total amount of ad space that the owner buys?

30. A local concert promoter purchases $2\frac{3}{4}$ pages of ads. When one of the concerts is canceled, the promoter cancels $1\frac{5}{8}$ pages of ads. How much advertising space is the concert promoter actually using?

31. Rico and his friend eat some lasagna. Rico eats $\frac{1}{9}$ of the lasagna, and his friend eats $\frac{1}{18}$ of the lasagna. How much of the lasagna is left?

32. Sonia finds a $\frac{3}{4}$-full small bag of chips. She eats the rest of the chips in the bag. Then she opens another small bag of chips. Sonia eats $\frac{1}{8}$ of those chips. What fraction of a small bag of chips does Sonia eat altogether?

For Exercises 33–36, find each sum or difference.

33. $1\frac{2}{5} + 1\frac{1}{3}$

34. $2\frac{1}{8} + 3\frac{3}{4} + 1\frac{1}{2}$

35. $11\frac{1}{2} - 2\frac{2}{3}$

36. $8\frac{11}{12} - 2\frac{3}{4}$

For Exercises 37–38, determine which sum or difference is greater. Show your work.

37. $\frac{2}{3} + \frac{5}{6}$ or $\frac{3}{4} + \frac{4}{5}$

38. $\frac{7}{6} - \frac{2}{3}$ or $\frac{3}{5} - \frac{5}{10}$

For Exercises 39–44, find each sum or difference.

39. $2\frac{5}{6} + 1\frac{1}{3}$

40. $15\frac{5}{8} + 10\frac{5}{6}$

41. $4\frac{4}{9} + 2\frac{1}{5}$

42. $6\frac{1}{4} - 2\frac{5}{6}$

43. $3\frac{1}{2} - 1\frac{4}{5}$

44. $8\frac{2}{3} - 6\frac{5}{7}$

For Exercises 45–50, find each sum. Describe any patterns that you see.

45. $\frac{1}{2} + \frac{1}{4}$

46. $\frac{1}{3} + \frac{1}{6}$

47. $\frac{1}{4} + \frac{1}{8}$

48. $\frac{1}{5} + \frac{1}{10}$

49. $\frac{1}{6} + \frac{1}{12}$

50. $\frac{1}{7} + \frac{1}{14}$

51. Tony works at a pizza shop. He cuts two pizzas into eight equal sections each. Customers then eat $\frac{7}{8}$ of each pizza. Tony says that $\frac{7}{8} + \frac{7}{8} = \frac{14}{16}$, so $\frac{14}{16}$ of all of the pizza was eaten. Is Tony's addition correct? Explain.

Connections

52. The rectangle shown represents 150% of a whole. Draw 100% of the same whole.

53. The beans shown represent $\frac{3}{5}$ of the total beans on the kitchen counter. How many total beans are there on the counter?

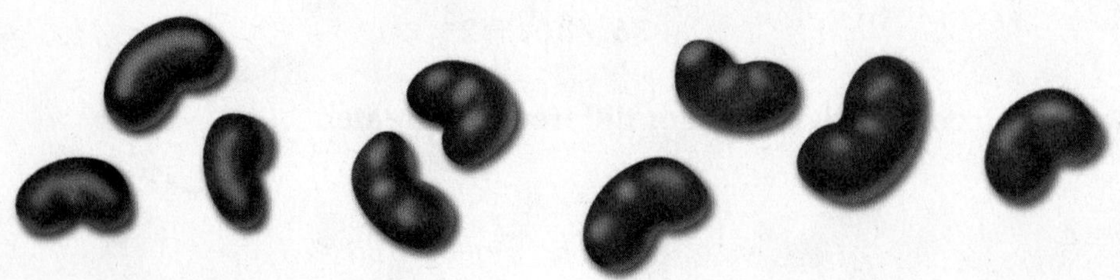

54. The following fractions occur often in our lives. It is useful to quickly recall their decimal and percent equivalents.

$\frac{1}{2}$ $\frac{1}{3}$ $\frac{1}{4}$ $\frac{2}{3}$ $\frac{3}{4}$ $\frac{1}{6}$ $\frac{1}{5}$ $\frac{1}{8}$

a. For each of these important fractions, give the decimal and percent equivalents.

b. Draw a number line. On your number line, mark the point that corresponds to each fraction shown above. Label each point with its fraction and decimal equivalent.

55. **Multiple Choice** Which set of decimals is ordered from least to greatest?

A. 5.603 5.63 5.096 5.67 5.599

B. 5.63 5.67 5.096 5.599 5.603

C. 5.096 5.63 5.67 5.603 5.599

D. 5.096 5.599 5.603 5.63 5.67

56. In which of the following groups of fractions can *all* of the fractions be renamed as a whole number of hundredths? Explain your reasoning for each group.

a. $\frac{3}{2}, \frac{3}{4}, \frac{3}{5}$

b. $\frac{7}{10}, \frac{7}{11}, \frac{7}{12}$

c. $\frac{2}{5}, \frac{2}{6}, \frac{2}{8}$

d. $\frac{11}{5}, \frac{11}{10}, \frac{11}{20}$

57. Suppose you select a number in the interval from $\frac{1}{2}$ to $\frac{3}{4}$ and a number in the interval from $\frac{3}{4}$ to $1\frac{1}{4}$. (Note: The numbers $\frac{1}{2}$ and $\frac{3}{4}$ are included in the interval from $\frac{1}{2}$ to $\frac{3}{4}$. The numbers $\frac{3}{4}$ and $1\frac{1}{4}$ are included in the interval from $\frac{3}{4}$ to $1\frac{1}{4}$.)

a. What is the least possible sum for these two numbers? Explain your reasoning.

b. What is the greatest possible sum for these two numbers? Explain your reasoning.

For a number sentence, the word *solve* means to find the value that makes the number sentence true. Solve Exercises 58–61.

58. $\frac{3}{12} = \frac{N}{8}$

59. $\frac{N}{4} = \frac{6}{8}$

60. $\frac{N}{12} = \frac{2}{3}$

61. $\frac{5}{12} = \frac{10}{N}$

In Exercises 62–64, paint has spilled on the page, covering part of the fraction strips. You can identify important information about each set of strips by looking at what is shown. The question marks indicate equivalent fractions of the strips. Name the equivalent fractions indicated by the question marks.

62.

63.

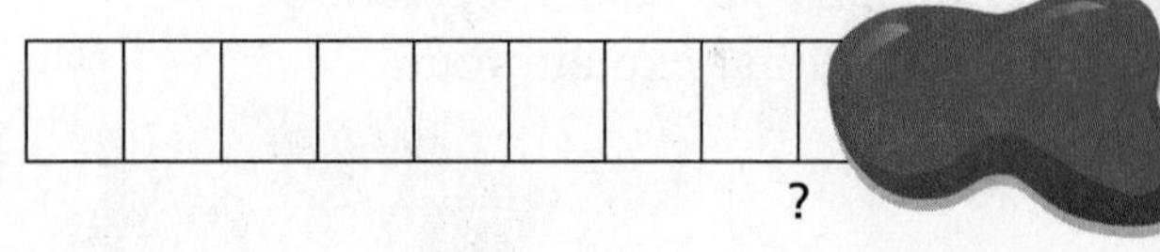

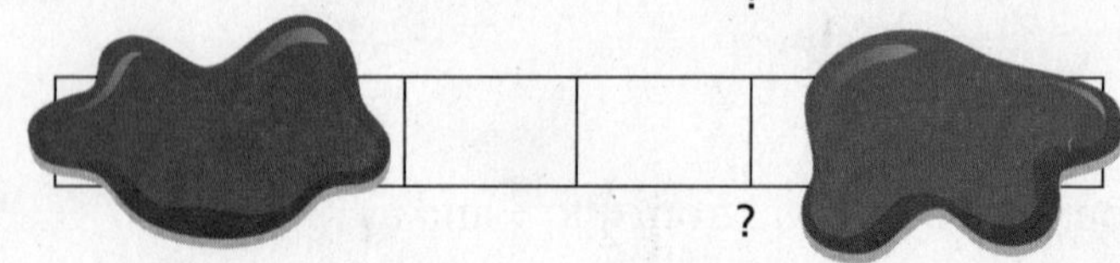

64.

For Exercises 65 and 66, copy each pair of numbers. Insert < , >, or = to make a true statement.

65. 18.156 ▇ 18.17

66. 4.0074 ▇ 4.0008

For Exercises 67 and 68, use the map of Tupelo Township.

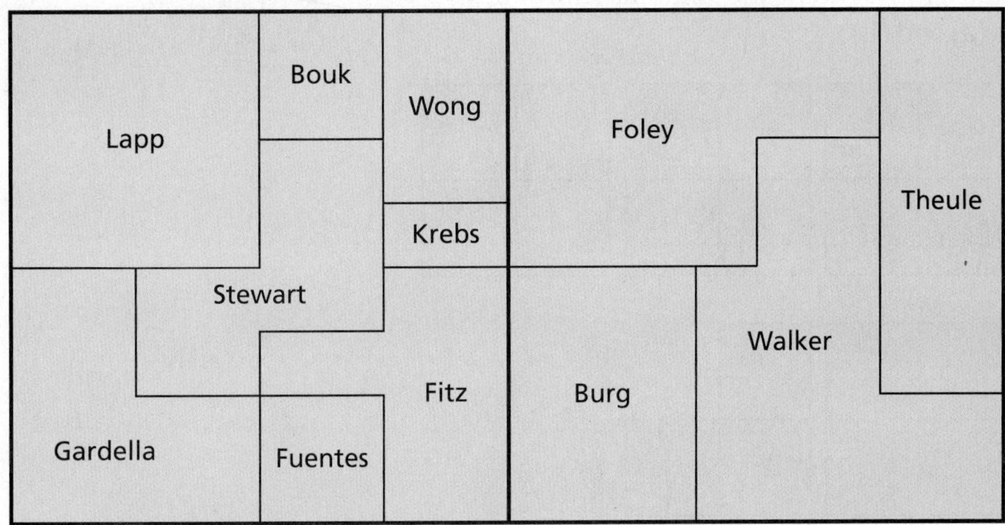

67. Multiple Choice Choose the combination of landowners who together own exactly one hundred percent of a section.

F. Burg, Lapp, Wong, Fuentes, and Bouck

G. Burg, Lapp, Fuentes, Bouck, Wong, Theule, and Stewart

H. Lapp, Fitz, Foley, and Walker

J. Walker, Foley, Fitz, and Fuentes

68. Find two different combinations of landowners whose total land is equal to 1.25 sections. Write number sentences to show your solutions.

69. The figure below represents $\frac{1}{3}$ of a whole.

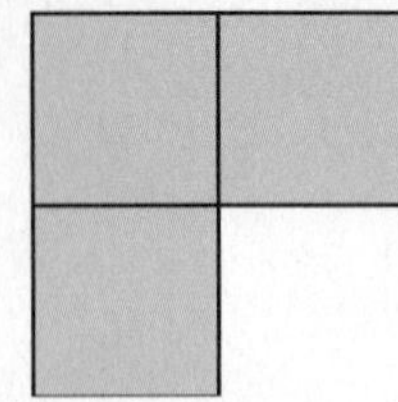

Use the figure to name the amounts shown in parts (a) and (b).

a.

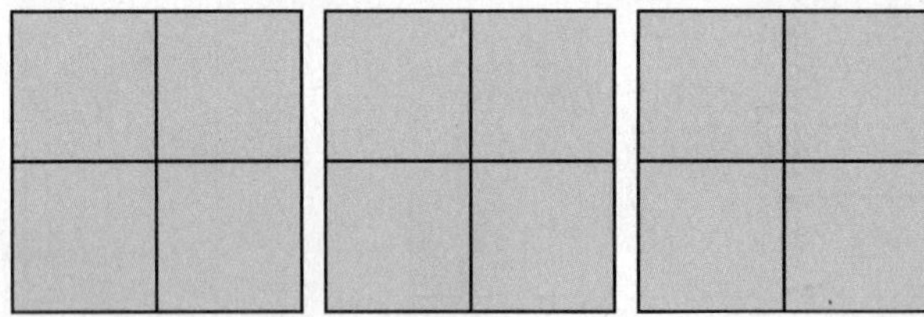

b.

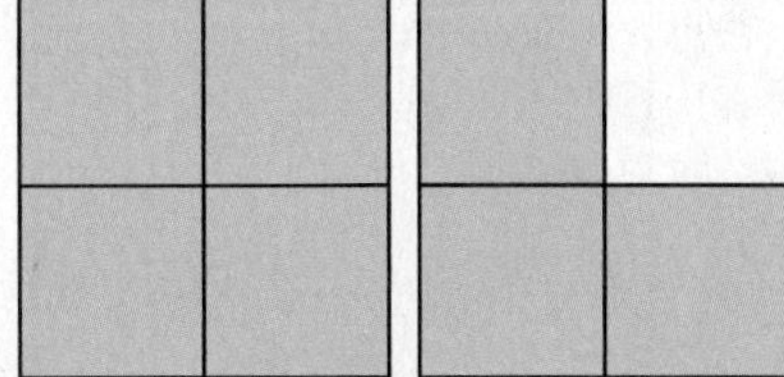

70. The following figure represents one whole.

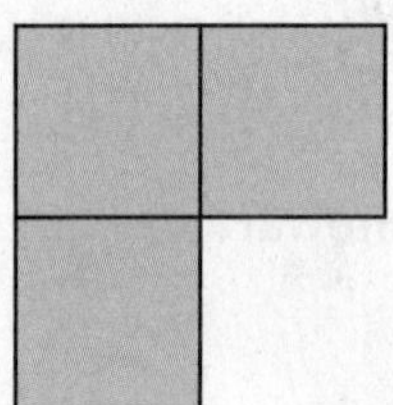

a. Draw a picture to represent $1\frac{1}{3} + \frac{1}{6}$.

b. Draw a picture to represent $2\frac{2}{3} - \frac{4}{3}$.

71. When adding $\frac{7}{15} + \frac{2}{10}$, Maribel writes $\frac{70}{150} + \frac{30}{150}$.

a. Show why $\frac{70}{150} + \frac{30}{150}$ is equivalent to $\frac{7}{15} + \frac{2}{10}$.

b. Write two more addition problems that are equivalent to $\frac{7}{15} + \frac{2}{10}$.

c. Consider the three problems, Maribel's problem and the two you wrote. Which is the easiest to use to find the sum? Why?

Extensions

For Exercises 72–74, use the number line below.

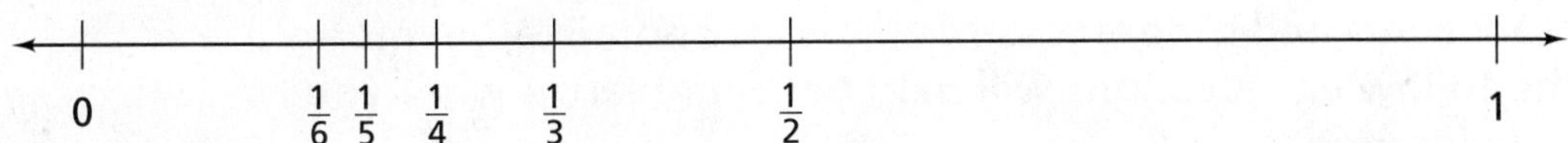

72. Name a fraction between $\frac{1}{3}$ and $\frac{1}{2}$.

73. Name a fraction between $\frac{1}{4}$ and $\frac{1}{3}$.

74. For Exercises 72 and 73, can you find another fraction in each interval? Explain.

75. *The Spartan* magazine charges $160 for each full page of advertising.

a. Identify the cost for each ad size shown below.

$\frac{1}{32}$-page, $\frac{1}{16}$-page, $\frac{1}{8}$-page, $\frac{1}{4}$-page, $\frac{1}{2}$-page, 1-page

b. Use the costs you found. What is the bill for the Cool Sub Shop if the owner purchases three $\frac{1}{4}$-page ads, four $\frac{1}{8}$-page ads, and one $\frac{1}{16}$-page ad?

c. The senior class is raising money for a trip. They have $80 to spend on advertising. Can they purchase two $\frac{1}{8}$-page ads and four $\frac{1}{16}$-page ads? Explain.

d. Find four different sets of ad sizes that the senior class can purchase for $80. Show why your answers are correct.

76. It takes 8 people to clear an acre of weeds in 4 hours.

a. How many acres can 16 people clear in 4 hours?

b. How many acres can 2 people clear in 4 hours?

c. How many people are needed to clear 3 acres in 4 hours?

d. How many people are needed to clear 3 acres in 2 hours?

77. a. Find a number for each *denominator* to make the number sentence below true. If necessary, you may use a number more than once.

$$\frac{1}{\blacksquare} - \frac{1}{\blacksquare} = \frac{1}{\blacksquare}$$

b. Find a different solution for part (a).

Mathematical Reflections 1

In this Investigation, you developed strategies for estimating the sum or difference of fractions and decimals. You then found exact sums and differences of fractions and mixed numbers. The following questions will help you summarize what you have learned.

Think about these questions. Discuss your ideas with other students and your teacher. Then write a summary of your findings in your notebook.

1. a. **What** are some situations in which estimating a sum or difference is useful? **Why** is estimation useful in these situations?

   b. **When** is it useful to overestimate? **When** is it useful to underestimate?

2. **When** should you use addition to solve a problem involving fractions? **When** should you use subtraction?

3. Suppose you are helping a student who has not studied fractions. **Explain** to him or her how to add and subtract fractions. Give an example of the type you think is easiest to explain. Give an example of the type you think is hardest to explain.

Common Core Mathematical Practices

As you worked on the Problems in this Investigation, you used prior knowledge to make sense of them. You also applied Mathematical Practices to solve the Problems. Think back over your work, the ways you thought about the Problems, and how you used Mathematical Practices.

Shawna described her thoughts in the following way:

For Problem 1.1, my group knew that the sum $\frac{3}{4} + \frac{4}{3}$ was closest to the benchmark number 2. We knew this because $\frac{3}{4}$ is a little less than 1, and $\frac{4}{3}$ is a little more than 1. But, we did not know if the sum was greater than 2 or less than 2.

After a while, Mia said that $\frac{4}{3}$ is $\frac{1}{3}$ of a unit away from 1. If you add $\frac{1}{3}$ to $\frac{3}{4}$, it is greater than 1. So $\frac{1}{3} + \frac{3}{4} + \frac{3}{3}$ must be greater than 2.

Common Core Standards for Mathematical Practice

MP6 Attend to precision.

- What other Mathematical Practices can you identify in Shawna's reasoning?
- Describe a Mathematical Practice that you and your classmates used to solve a different Problem in this Investigation.

Building on Multiplication With Fractions

Sometimes, instead of adding or subtracting numbers, you need to multiply them. For example, suppose you take inventory at a sporting goods store. There are thirteen full boxes and one half-full box of footballs in the storeroom. Twelve footballs fit in each full box.

- How can you find the total number of footballs without opening the boxes? Why does multiplication make sense in this situation?

In this Investigation, you will use multiplication to solve problems involving fractions. Remember, to make sense of a situation, you can draw a model or change a fraction to an equivalent form. You can also estimate to see if your answer makes sense.

2.1 How Much of the Pan Have We Sold?

Finding Parts of Parts

Paulo and Shania work at the brownie booth at the school fair. Sometimes they have to find a fractional part of another fraction. For example, a customer might ask to purchase $\frac{1}{3}$ of the brownies in a pan that is $\frac{2}{3}$ full.

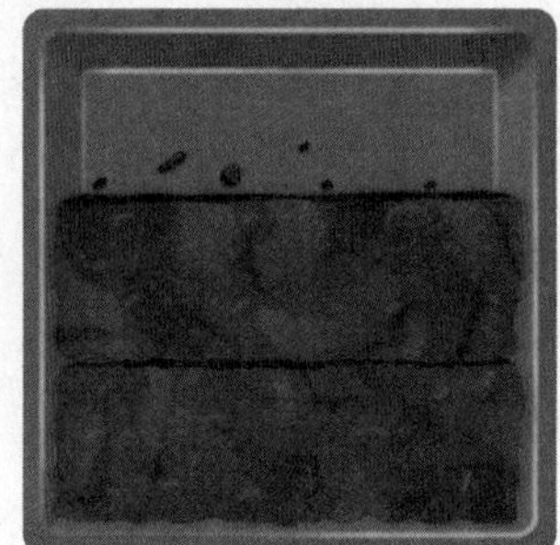

- How much is $\frac{1}{3}$ of $\frac{2}{3}$?

Common Core State Standards

6.EE.A.3 Apply the properties of operations to generate equivalent expressions.

Essential for 6.NS.A.1 Interpret and compute quotients of fractions, and solve word problems involving division of fractions by fractions, e.g., by using visual fraction models and equations to represent the problem.

Problem 2.1

All of the pans of brownies are square. A pan of brownies costs \$12. You can buy any fractional part of a pan of brownies and pay that fraction of \$12. For example, $\frac{1}{2}$ of a pan costs $\frac{1}{2}$ of \$12, or \$6. We can write this as a number sentence using *of*: $\frac{1}{2}$ of $12 = 6$.

A Mr. Williams asks to buy $\frac{1}{2}$ of a pan of brownies that is $\frac{2}{3}$ full.

1. Use a copy of the brownie pan model shown at the right. Draw a picture to show how the brownie pan might look before Mr. Williams buys his brownies.

Model of a Brownie Pan

2. On the same model, use a different color to show the part of the brownies that Mr. Williams buys. Note that Mr. Williams buys a *part of a part* of the brownie pan.
3. What fraction of a whole pan of brownies does Mr. Williams buy? How much does he pay? Write number sentences using *of* to show your thinking.

B Serena buys $\frac{3}{4}$ of another pan that is half full.

1. Draw a picture to show how the brownie pan might look before Serena buys her brownies.
2. Use a different color to show the part Serena buys.
3. What fraction of a whole pan of brownies does Serena buy? How much does she pay? Write number sentences using *of* to show your thinking.

C Draw a brownie pan picture for each example below. Then write a number sentence using *of* for each. Find the part of a whole brownie pan that results.

1. $\frac{1}{3}$ of $\frac{1}{4}$ of a brownie pan
2. $\frac{1}{4}$ of $\frac{1}{3}$ of a brownie pan
3. $\frac{1}{3}$ of $\frac{3}{4}$ of a brownie pan
4. $\frac{3}{4}$ of $\frac{2}{5}$ of a brownie pan

continued on the next page >

Problem 2.1 continued

D The pictures below are models of brownie pan problems. Consider *orange* to be the portion of the brownie pan that is purchased. Consider *blue* to be the portion of the brownie pan that is left in the pan. For each picture, write a number sentence using *of* to describe what fraction of the brownie pan is purchased.

1.

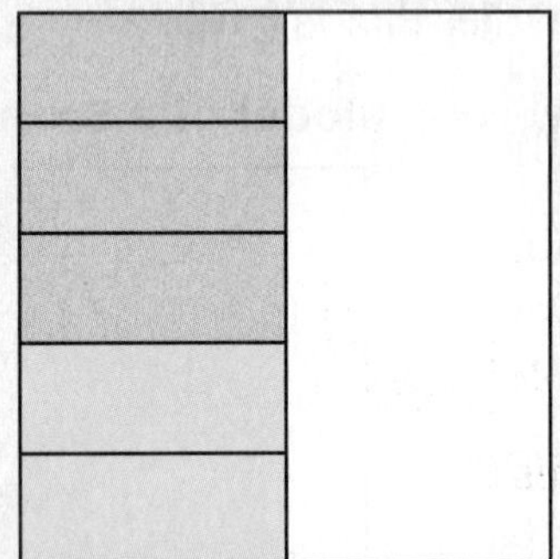

2.

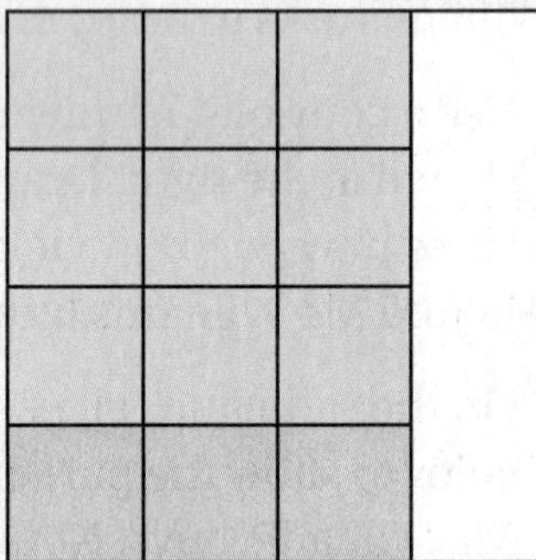

3.

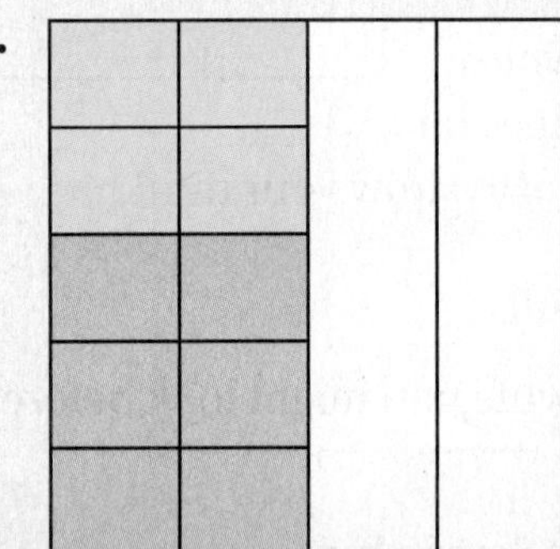

4.

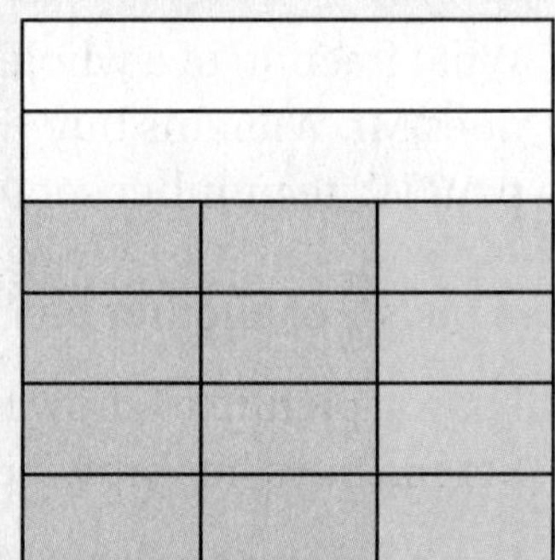

E 1. Draw pictures to check that each of the following number sentences is correct.

a. $\frac{3}{4}$ of $\frac{1}{2} = \frac{3}{8}$

b. $\frac{2}{5}$ of $\frac{4}{5} = \frac{8}{25}$

2. What pattern do you notice in the denominators? How does this pattern relate to your drawings?

3. What pattern do you notice in the numerators? How does this pattern relate to your drawings?

4. Paulo says that when you find a *part of a part*, your answer will always be less than either of the original parts. Is this true? Explain your reasoning.

Homework starts on page 37.

2.2 Modeling Multiplication Situations

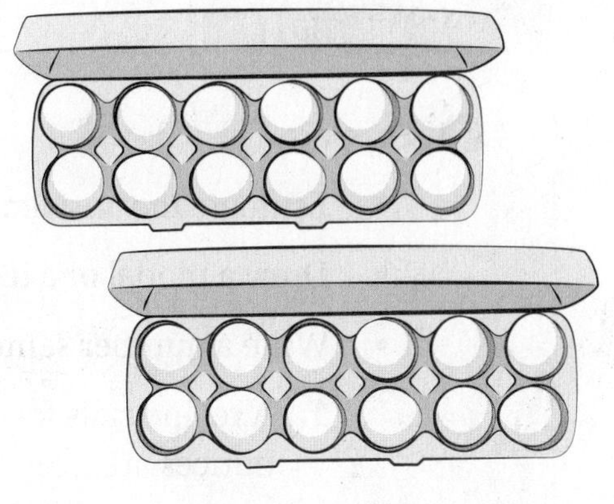

You have used *of* in multiplication statements with whole numbers. For example:

$$2 \text{ groups } of\ 12 = 2 \times 12 = 24$$

In Problem 2.1, you wrote number sentences such as:

$$\frac{3}{4}\ of\ \frac{1}{2} = \frac{3}{8}$$

Mathematicians use multiplication to rewrite number sentences involving fractions. When you multiply a fraction by a fraction, you are finding part of a part:

$$\frac{3}{4} \times \frac{1}{2} = \frac{3}{8}$$

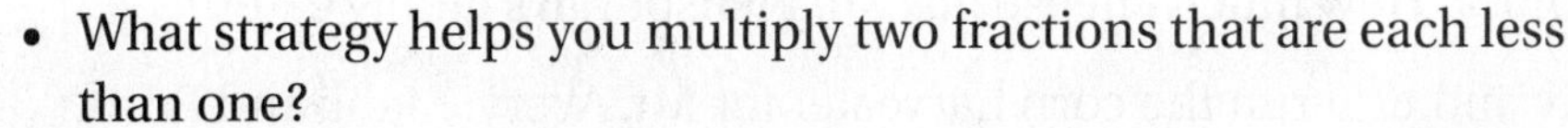

- What strategy helps you multiply two fractions that are each less than one?

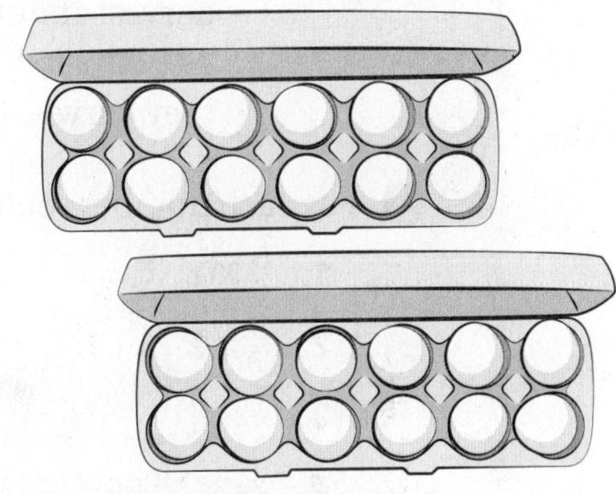

You can also model multiplication situations that involve mixed numbers.

$$\begin{aligned} 2\tfrac{1}{2} \text{ groups } of\ 12 &= 2 \text{ groups } of\ 12\ and\ \tfrac{1}{2} \text{ group } of\ 12 \\ &= 2 \times 12 + \tfrac{1}{2} \times 12 \\ &= 24 + 6 \\ &= 30 \end{aligned}$$

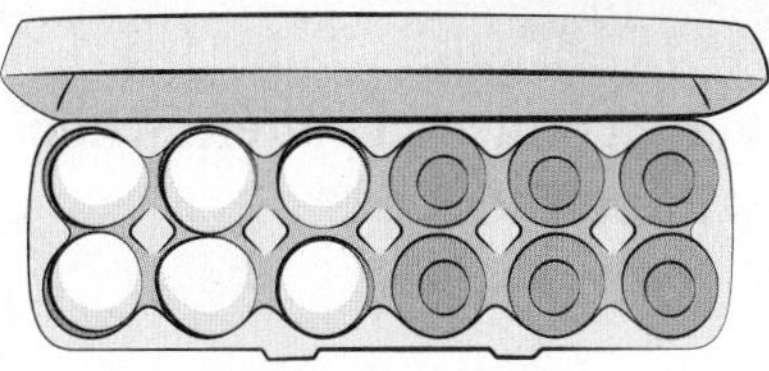

Do you think these multiplication strategies will work for all kinds of fractions?

In this Problem, you will work with multiplication situations that use fractions, whole numbers, and mixed numbers.

Problem 2.2

A For parts (1)–(3):

- Estimate the answer.
- Draw a model or a diagram to find the exact answer.
- Write a number sentence.

1. A recipe calls for $\frac{2}{3}$ of a 16-ounce bag of chocolate chips. How many ounces are needed?
2. Mr. Flansburgh buys a $2\frac{1}{2}$-pound block of cheese. His family eats $\frac{1}{3}$ of the block. How much cheese has Mr. Flansburgh's family eaten?
3. Malik and Erin run the corn harvester for Mr. Avery. Malik and Erin harvest about $2\frac{1}{3}$ acres' worth of corn each day. They only have $10\frac{1}{2}$ days to harvest the corn. How many acres' worth of corn can they harvest for Mr. Avery?

B For each number sentence below, write a story problem and find the answer.

1. $\frac{5}{6} \times 1$
2. $\frac{3}{7} \times 2$
3. $\frac{1}{2} \times \frac{9}{3}$
4. $\frac{9}{10} \times \frac{10}{7}$

C Jacinta notices a pattern when she multiplies fractions. Her pattern is written below.

> When you multiply with fractions, the product is less than each of the two factors.

Is Jacinta's pattern correct for the fractions you worked with in Questions A and B? Explain your reasoning.

D Describe a strategy for multiplying any two fractions.

ACE Homework starts on page 37.

2.3 Changing Forms

Multiplication With Mixed Numbers

You have developed some strategies for modeling multiplication and finding products of fractions. This Problem will give you a chance to formulate your strategies into algorithms. Before you begin a problem, always ask yourself:

- About how large will the product be?

Problem 2.3

A **1.** Takoda and Yuri are computing $\frac{1}{2} \times 2\frac{2}{3}$. What is a reasonable estimate for this product?

2. Takoda and Yuri each use a different strategy.

Takoda's Strategy

I used what I know about fractions to rewrite $2\frac{2}{3}$ as $\frac{8}{3}$ to make the problem easier to solve.

$$\begin{aligned}\frac{1}{2} \times 2\frac{2}{3} &= \frac{1}{2} \times \frac{8}{3}\\ &= \frac{8}{6}\\ &= 1\frac{2}{6}\\ &= 1\frac{1}{3}\end{aligned}$$

Yuri's Strategy

I wrote $2\frac{2}{3}$ as $\left(2 + \frac{2}{3}\right)$ and used the Distributive Property to make the problem easier to solve.

$$\begin{aligned}\frac{1}{2} \times 2\frac{2}{3} &= \frac{1}{2} \times \left(2 + \frac{2}{3}\right)\\ &= \left(\frac{1}{2} \times 2\right) + \left(\frac{1}{2} \times \frac{2}{3}\right)\\ &= 1 + \frac{2}{6}\\ &= 1\frac{2}{6}\\ &= 1\frac{1}{3}\end{aligned}$$

a. Does each strategy work? How do you know?

b. How are the strategies similar? How are they different?

3. Use both strategies to solve $1\frac{1}{3} \times \frac{4}{5}$. Then check your answer with a drawing.

continued on the next page >

Problem 2.3 continued

B For each problem below:

- Estimate the product.
- Use a multiplication strategy to find the exact product.
- Be sure to show your work.

1. $3\frac{4}{5} \times \frac{1}{4}$
2. $\frac{3}{4} \times 16$
3. $2\frac{1}{2} \times 1\frac{1}{6}$
4. $1\frac{1}{3} \times 3\frac{6}{7}$
5. $1\frac{1}{5} \times 2\frac{1}{4}$
6. $12 \times 4\frac{4}{9}$

C 1. Lisa tries to use Yuri's strategy to find $4\frac{1}{2} \times 1\frac{1}{3}$. She writes:

$$4 \times 1 + \frac{1}{2} \times \frac{1}{3} = 4\frac{1}{6}$$

Yuri says that $4\frac{1}{6}$ is too small. Do you agree with Lisa or Yuri? Explain your reasoning.

2. Yuri tries to help Lisa. Yuri writes:

$$4 \times 1\frac{1}{3} + \frac{1}{2} \times 1\frac{1}{3}$$

How is this different from what Lisa wrote?

D Describe an algorithm for multiplying any two fractions, including mixed numbers.

ACE Homework starts on page 37.

Did You Know?

When you reverse the placement of the numbers in the numerator and the denominator of a fraction, a new fraction is formed. This new fraction is the **reciprocal** of the original. For example, $\frac{8}{7}$ is the reciprocal of $\frac{7}{8}$, and $\frac{12}{17}$ is the reciprocal of $\frac{17}{12}$, or $1\frac{5}{12}$. Notice that the product of a fraction and its reciprocal is 1. Why is this?

Applications

1. A pan of brownies is $\frac{7}{10}$ full. Tyreese buys $\frac{2}{5}$ of the brownies.
   a. Draw a picture of how the brownie pan looks before and after Tyreese buys his brownies.
   b. What fraction of a whole pan of brownies does Tyreese buy?

2. a. Draw brownie-pan models to show whether or not $\frac{2}{3}$ of $\frac{3}{4}$ of a pan of brownies is the same amount as $\frac{3}{4}$ of $\frac{2}{3}$ of a pan of brownies.
   b. If the brownie pans are the same size, how do the amounts of brownies from part (a) compare?
   c. Describe the relationship between $\frac{2}{3}$ of $\frac{3}{4}$ and $\frac{3}{4}$ of $\frac{2}{3}$.

3. Ms. Vargas owns $\frac{4}{5}$ of an acre of land in Tupelo Township. She wants to sell $\frac{2}{3}$ of her land to her neighbor.
   a. What fraction of an acre does Ms. Vargas want to sell? Draw a picture to illustrate your thinking.
   b. Write a number sentence that can be used to solve the problem.

4. Find each answer.
   a. $\frac{1}{2}$ of $\frac{1}{3}$
   b. $\frac{1}{2}$ of $\frac{1}{4}$
   c. $\frac{1}{2}$ of $\frac{2}{3}$
   d. $\frac{1}{2}$ of $\frac{3}{4}$
   e. Describe any patterns that you see in parts (a)–(d).

5. Answer each part without finding the exact answer. Explain your reasoning.
   a. Is $\frac{3}{4} \times 1$ greater than or less than 1?
   b. Is $\frac{3}{4} \times \frac{2}{3}$ greater than or less than 1?
   c. Is $\frac{3}{4} \times \frac{2}{3}$ greater than or less than $\frac{2}{3}$?
   d. Is $\frac{3}{4} \times \frac{2}{3}$ greater than or less than $\frac{3}{4}$?

For Exercises 6–9, write a number sentence. Use a fraction that is both positive and less than 1.

6. a fraction and a whole number with a whole number product

7. a fraction and a whole number with a product less than 1

8. a fraction and a whole number with a product greater than 1

9. a fraction and a whole number with a product between $\frac{1}{2}$ and 1

10. Shonice is making snack bags for her daughter's field hockey team. She puts $\frac{3}{4}$ cup of pretzels, $\frac{2}{3}$ cup of popcorn, $\frac{1}{3}$ cup of peanuts, and $\frac{1}{4}$ cup of chocolate chips in each bag.

a. She wants to make 12 snack bags. How much of each ingredient does she need?

b. Shonice decides that she would like to make snack bags for her card club. There are 15 people in the card club. How much of each ingredient will she need?

11. **a.** When Sierra gets home, $\frac{3}{4}$ of a sandwich is left in the refrigerator. She cuts the remaining part into three equal parts and eats two of them. What fraction of the whole sandwich did she eat?

b. Write a number sentence to show your computation.

12. Mr. Jablonski's class is making fudge for a bake sale. Mr. Jablonski has a recipe that makes $\frac{3}{4}$ pound of fudge. There are 21 students in the class. Each student uses the recipe to make one batch of fudge. How many pounds of fudge do the students make?

13. Estimate each product. Explain your reasoning.

a. $\frac{2}{3} \times 8\frac{5}{6}$ **b.** $\frac{2}{3} \times 14\frac{1}{2}$ **c.** $2\frac{1}{2} \times \frac{2}{3}$

14. Esteban is making turtle brownies. The recipe calls for $\frac{3}{4}$ bag of caramel squares. One bag has 24 caramel squares in it.

a. How many caramel squares should Esteban use to make one batch of turtle brownies?

b. Esteban decides to make two batches of turtle brownies. Write a number sentence to show how many bags of caramel squares he will use.

15. Isabel is adding a sun porch onto her house. She finds that covering the entire floor requires 12 rows of tiles with $11\frac{1}{3}$ tiles in each row. Write a number sentence to show how many tiles Isabel needs.

16. Judi is making a frame for a square painting. The square painting is $11\frac{3}{8}$ inches on each side.

To make sure that she has enough wood, Judi wants to buy two extra inches of wood for each corner. How much wood should Judi buy?

17. Find each product.

a. $\frac{1}{3} \times 18$

b. $\frac{2}{3} \times 18$

c. $\frac{5}{3} \times 18$

d. $1\frac{2}{3} \times 18$

e. What patterns do you see in these products?

18. Carolyn is making cookies. The recipe calls for $1\frac{3}{4}$ cups of brown sugar. If she makes $2\frac{1}{2}$ batches of cookies, how much brown sugar does she need?

For Exercises 19–27, use an algorithm for multiplying fractions to determine each product.

19. $\frac{5}{12} \times 1\frac{1}{3}$

20. $\frac{2}{7} \times \frac{7}{8}$

21. $3\frac{2}{9} \times \frac{7}{3}$

22. $2\frac{2}{5} \times 1\frac{1}{15}$

23. $10\frac{3}{4} \times 2\frac{2}{3}$

24. $1\frac{1}{8} \times \frac{4}{7}$

25. $\frac{11}{6} \times \frac{9}{10}$

26. $\frac{9}{4} \times 1\frac{1}{6}$

27. $\frac{5}{2} \times \frac{8}{11}$

Connections

28. Bianca and Yoko work together to mow the lawn. Suppose Yoko mows $\frac{5}{12}$ of the lawn and Bianca mows $\frac{2}{5}$ of the lawn. How much lawn still needs to be mowed?

29. Joe and Ashanti need $2\frac{2}{5}$ bushels of apples to make applesauce. Suppose Joe picks $1\frac{5}{6}$ bushels of apples. How many more bushels need to be picked?

30. Roshaun and Lea go to an amusement park. Lea spends $\frac{1}{2}$ of her money, and Roshaun spends $\frac{1}{4}$ of his money. Is it possible for Roshaun to have spent more money than Lea? Explain your reasoning.

31. Min Ji uses balsa wood to build airplane models.

After completing a model, she has a strip of balsa wood measuring $\frac{7}{8}$ yard left over. Shawn wants to buy half of the strip from Min Ji. How long is the strip of wood Shawn wants to buy?

32. Aran has a bag of pretzels for a snack. He gives half of the pretzels to Jon. Then, Jon gives Kiona $\frac{1}{3}$ of his portion. What fraction of the bag of pretzels does each person get?

33. Mr. Mace's class is planning a field trip, and $\frac{3}{5}$ of his students want to go to Chicago. Of those who want to go to Chicago, $\frac{2}{3}$ want to go to Navy Pier. What fraction of the class wants to go to Navy Pier?

34. In Vashon's class, three fourths of the students are girls. Four fifths of the girls in the class have brown hair.

  a. What fraction represents the girls in Vashon's class with brown hair?

  b. How many students do you think are in Vashon's class? Explain your reasoning.

35. Violeta and Mandy are making beaded necklaces. They have beads of various colors and sizes. As they design patterns, they want to find out how long the final necklace will be. They have the following bead widths to work with:

Widths of Beads

Bead	Width
Small Trade Neck	$\frac{1}{4}$ inch
Medium Trade Neck	$\frac{3}{8}$ inch
Large Trade Neck	$\frac{7}{16}$ inch

  a. Mandy makes the necklace below. She uses 30 small Trade Neck beads, 6 medium Trade Neck beads, and 1 large Trade Neck bead. How long is Mandy's necklace?

  b. Violeta wants to make a 16-inch necklace by alternating medium and large Trade Neck beads. She only has 8 medium Trade Neck beads. If she uses 8 medium Trade Neck beads and 8 large Trade Neck beads, will her necklace be 16 inches long?

36. **Multiple Choice** Which of the numbers below, when multiplied by $\frac{4}{7}$, will be greater than $\frac{4}{7}$?

A. $\frac{1}{7}$ **B.** $\frac{7}{7}$ **C.** $\frac{17}{7}$ **D.** $\frac{4}{7}$

37. **Multiple Choice** Which of the numbers below, when multiplied by $\frac{4}{7}$, will be less than $\frac{4}{7}$?

F. $\frac{1}{7}$ **G.** $\frac{7}{7}$ **H.** $\frac{17}{7}$ **J.** $\frac{8}{7}$

38. **Multiple Choice** Which of the numbers below, when multiplied by $\frac{4}{7}$, will be exactly $\frac{4}{7}$?

A. $\frac{1}{7}$ **B.** $\frac{7}{7}$ **C.** $\frac{17}{7}$ **D.** $\frac{4}{7}$

For Exercises 39–42, find each product.

39. $\frac{1}{3}$ of $\frac{2}{3}$

40. $\frac{5}{6}$ of 3

41. $\frac{2}{3}$ of $\frac{5}{6}$

42. $\frac{2}{5}$ of $\frac{5}{8}$

43. **a.** How many minutes are in 1 hour?

b. How many minutes are in $\frac{1}{2}$ hour?

c. How many minutes are in 0.5 hour?

d. How many minutes are in 0.1 hour?

e. How many minutes are in 1.25 hours?

f. How many hours are in 186 minutes? Express this as a mixed number and as a decimal.

44. Terry wants to make $\frac{1}{2}$ of a batch of chocolate chip cookies. Rewrite her recipe so that she only needs $\frac{1}{2}$ as much of each ingredient.

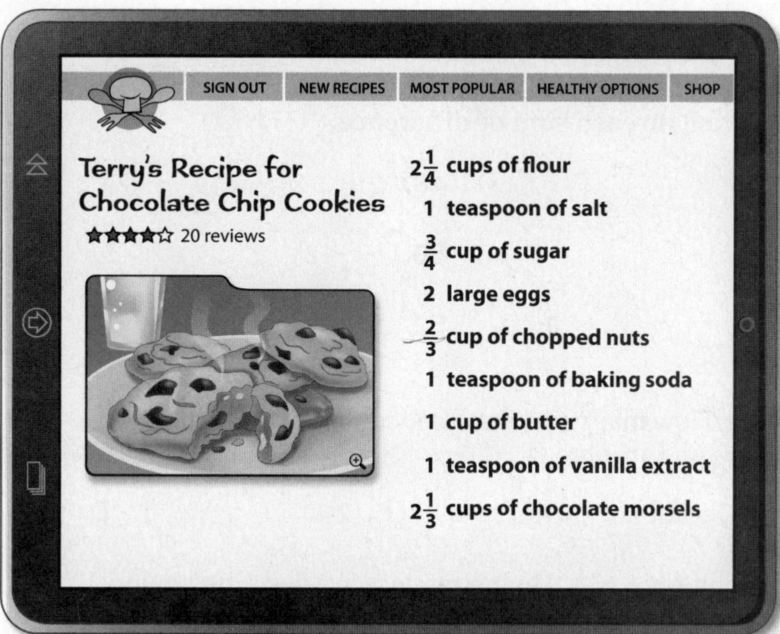

45. Terry finds a recipe for chewy brownie cookies.

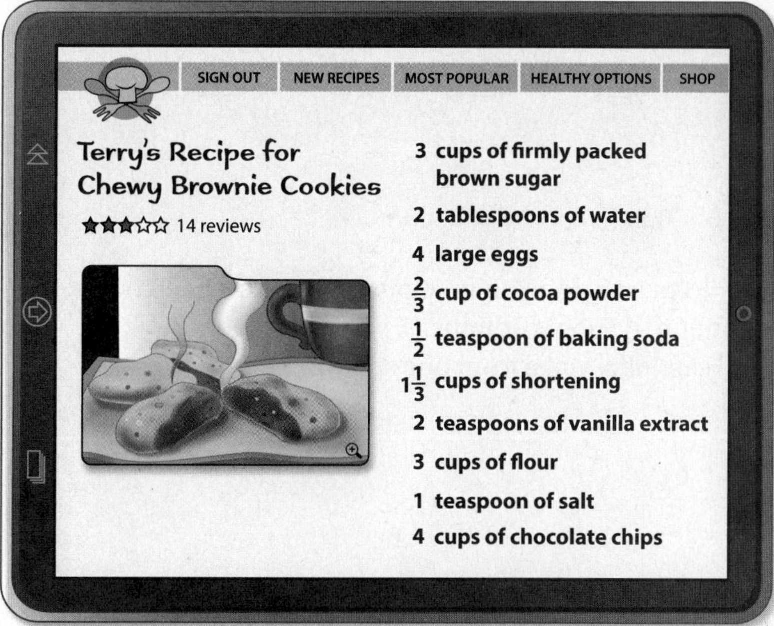

She wants to bake only $\frac{1}{4}$ of the number of cookies the recipe will make. Rewrite her recipe so that it will make $\frac{1}{4}$ as many chewy brownie cookies.

46. Estimate each product to the nearest whole number (1, 2, 3, . . .).

a. $\frac{1}{2} \times 2\frac{9}{10}$ **b.** $1\frac{1}{2} \times 2\frac{9}{10}$ **c.** $2\frac{1}{2} \times \frac{4}{7}$ **d.** $3\frac{1}{4} \times 2\frac{11}{12}$

e. For each of parts (a)–(d), will the actual product be greater than or less than your whole-number estimate? Explain.

For Exercises 47–52, calculate each sum or difference.

47. $2\frac{2}{3} + 3\frac{5}{6}$

48. $2\frac{8}{10} + 2\frac{4}{5} + 1\frac{1}{2}$

49. $4\frac{3}{10} + 2\frac{2}{6}$

50. $5\frac{5}{8} - 2\frac{2}{3}$

51. $6\frac{7}{10} - 3\frac{4}{5}$

52. $8 - 3\frac{14}{15}$

53. Multiple Choice How many tiles are needed to make a rectangle that is $4\frac{1}{3}$ tiles long by $\frac{1}{2}$ tile wide?

A. $2\frac{1}{3}$ **B.** $2\frac{1}{6}$ **C.** 2 **D.** $2\frac{1}{4}$

54. Three students multiply $6 \times \frac{1}{5}$. Their strategies are described below. The students' answers are $\frac{6}{5}$, 1.2, and $1\frac{1}{5}$. Match each answer to the strategy that is most likely to produce it. Explain your reasoning.

a. Fala draws six shapes, each representing $\frac{1}{5}$, and fits them together.

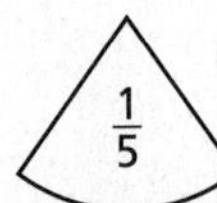

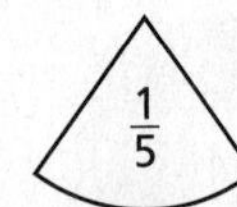

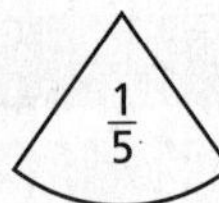

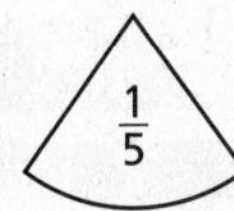

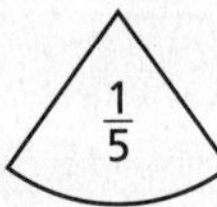

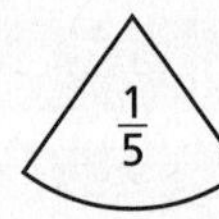

b. Jorell writes $\frac{6}{1} \times \frac{1}{5}$.

c. Hiroshi writes 6×0.2.

55. Multiple Choice John is making bows to put on wreaths. Each bow uses $2\frac{1}{3}$ yards of ribbon. A spool contains 15 yards of ribbon. How many whole bows can John make from one spool?

F. 6 **G.** 7 **H.** 12 **J.** 35

Extensions

For Exercises 56 and 57, find each product.

56. $\frac{2}{3} \times \frac{1}{2} \times \frac{3}{4}$

57. $\frac{5}{8} \times \frac{1}{2} \times \frac{2}{3}$

Mathematical Reflections 2

In this Investigation, you explored situations that required you to multiply fractions. You also developed an algorithm for multiplying fractions. The following questions will help you summarize what you have learned.

Think about these questions. Discuss your ideas with other students and your teacher. Then write a summary of your findings in your notebook.

1. **Explain** and **illustrate** what *of* means when you find a fraction *of* another number. What operation do you use when you find parts of parts?

2. a. If you forget the algorithm for multiplying fractions, **how** might you use rectangular models to help you multiply fractions?

   b. **Describe** an algorithm for multiplying any two fractions.

   c. **Describe** when it might be useful to estimate a product.

3. Use examples to **explain** the following statement:

   When you multiply a fraction by another fraction, your answer might be less than both factors, more than one of the factors, or more than both factors.

Common Core Mathematical Practices

As you worked on the Problems in this Investigation, you used prior knowledge to make sense of them. You also applied Mathematical Practices to solve the Problems. Think back over your work, the ways you thought about the Problems, and how you used Mathematical Practices.

Nick described his thoughts in the following way:

In Problem 2.1, we used a square brownie pan model to show what $\frac{3}{4}$ of $\frac{1}{2}$ looks like. We used the picture to find how much $\frac{3}{4}$ of $\frac{1}{2}$ is. We wrote the number sentence '$\frac{3}{4}$ of $\frac{1}{2} = \frac{3}{8}$' to represent the amount of brownies that we were finding.

This is called an area model for multiplication. The length marked along one side of the pan stands for one fraction. The length along a perpendicular side stands for the second fraction being multiplied. The answer is the area of overlap inside the pan.

Common Core Standards for Mathematical Practice

MP4 Model with mathematics.

- What other Mathematical Practices can you identify in Nick's reasoning?
- Describe a Mathematical Practice that you and your classmates used to solve a different Problem in this Investigation.

Dividing With Fractions

So far in *Let's Be Rational,* you have solved problems using addition, subtraction, and multiplication. In Investigation 3, you will solve problems that require division of fractions. As you work on these problems, think about similarities and differences among the problems.

In the number sentence $21 \div 7 = 3$, 21 is the *dividend,* 7 is the *divisor,* and 3 is the result, or *quotient.*

You can use the vocabulary of division problems as placeholders in a division number sentence. The division sentence below shows how these quantities relate to one another.

$$\text{dividend} \div \text{divisor} = \text{quotient}$$

First, you need to understand what division of fractions means. Then you can calculate quotients when the divisor or the dividend, or both, is a fraction.

Common Core State Standards

6.NS.A.1 Apply and extend previous understandings of multiplication and division to divide fractions by fractions.

6.EE.A.2b Identify parts of an expression using mathematical terms (sum, term, product, factor, quotient, coefficient); view one or more parts of an expression as a single entity.

When you do the division $12 \div 5$, what does the answer mean?

The answer should tell you how many fives are in 12 wholes. Because a whole number of fives will not fit into 12, you might write

$$12 \div 5 = 2\frac{2}{5}$$

Then, what does the fractional part of the answer mean?

The answer means you can make 2 fives and $\frac{2}{5}$ of *another* five.

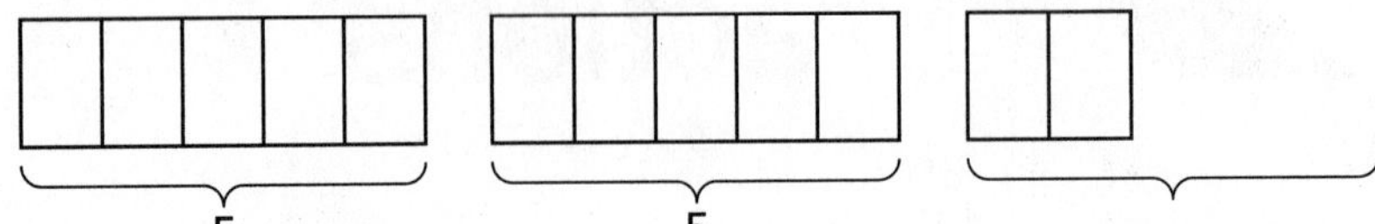

You can check your work by seeing that the related number sentence is true.

$$5 \times 2\frac{2}{5} = 12$$

In the division problem above, the divisor and dividend are both whole numbers. In Problem 3.1, you will explore division problems in which the divisor and dividend are both fractions. You will answer questions such as the following.

- How many $\frac{1}{4}$'s are in $\frac{1}{2}$?
- How can you draw a model to show this?
- How can you write this as a division number sentence?
- What does the answer to this division problem mean?
- What does it mean to divide a fraction by a fraction?

3.1 Preparing Food

Dividing a Fraction by a Fraction

At Humboldt Middle School football games, the students and teachers run a concession stand to raise money. Mrs. Drake's class is hosting a cookout. The students sell hamburgers to raise money.

Problem 3.1

For each question, do the following.

- Solve the problem.
- Draw a model to help explain your reasoning.
- Write a number sentence showing your calculations.
- Explain what your answer means.

A Mrs. Drake is grilling the hamburgers. Some people like big patties, some medium patties, and some small patties.

1. How many $\frac{1}{8}$-pound patties can she make from $\frac{7}{8}$ of a pound of hamburger?
2. How many $\frac{2}{8}$-pound patties can she make from $\frac{7}{8}$ of a pound of hamburger?
3. A teacher brings $2\frac{3}{4}$ pounds of hamburger to make $\frac{1}{4}$-pound patties. How many patties can he make?

B

1. Sam has $\frac{3}{4}$ of a can of hot chocolate mix for drinks to keep everyone warm. To make a cup of hot chocolate, Sam adds hot water to one scoop of hot chocolate mix. The scoop holds $\frac{1}{24}$ of a can. How many cups of hot chocolate can Sam make?
2. Tom decided not to use the $\frac{1}{24}$ scoop used by Sam. Instead, he uses a scoop that is $\frac{1}{8}$ of a can of hot chocolate mix. Tom and Sam each start with the same amount, $\frac{3}{4}$ of a can of hot chocolate mix. Who can make more cups of hot chocolate? Explain.

C Describe a strategy for dividing a fraction by a fraction.

ACE Homework starts on page 55.

3.2 Into Pieces

Whole Numbers or Mixed Numbers Divided by Fractions

Suppose you ask, "How many $\frac{3}{4}$'s are in 14?" You can write this question as a division expression, $14 \div \frac{3}{4}$. Then you can represent it on a number line. Sam starts to use the number line below, but does not know what to do next. What should Sam do?

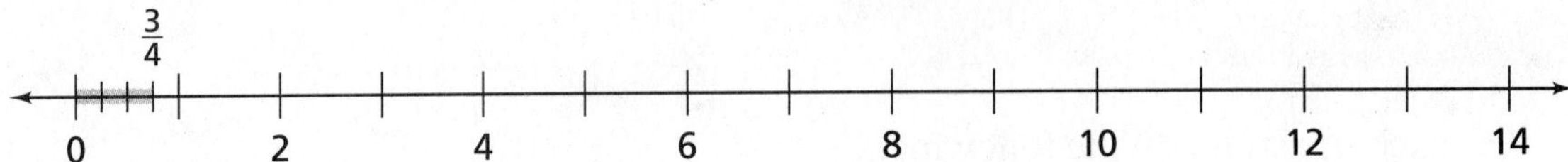

- Can you make a whole number of $\frac{3}{4}$'s out of 14 wholes? If not, what does the fractional part of the answer mean?
- What does it mean to divide a whole number or mixed number by a fraction?

Problem 3.2

For each part of Question A below, do the following.

- Solve the problem.
- Draw a model to help explain your reasoning.
- Write a number sentence that shows your reasoning.

A 1. Naylah plans to make small cheese pizzas to sell at the school carnival. She has nine blocks of cheese. How many pizzas can she make if each pizza needs the given amount of cheese?

a. $\frac{1}{3}$ block **b.** $\frac{1}{4}$ block

c. $\frac{1}{5}$ block **d.** $\frac{2}{3}$ block

e. $\frac{3}{3}$ block **f.** $\frac{4}{3}$ block

2. The answer to part (d) above is a mixed number. What does the fractional part of the answer mean?

continued on the next page >

Problem 3.2 continued

B Use your ideas from Question A to write questions that the following expressions could fit. Then do the calculations. Be sure to label your answers.

1. $12 \div \frac{2}{3}$
2. $12 \div \frac{5}{6}$
3. $12 \div \frac{7}{6}$
4. $12 \div 1\frac{1}{3}$

C 1. Jasmine has $5\frac{1}{4}$ cups of frosting. She wants to put $\frac{3}{8}$ cup of frosting on each cupcake she makes. About how many cupcakes can she frost?

2. Chris needs $3\frac{1}{2}$ cups of flour. His only clean measuring cup holds $\frac{1}{3}$ cup. How many $\frac{1}{3}$ cups of flour does Chris need?

D Describe a strategy for dividing a whole number or a mixed number by a fraction.

ACE Homework starts on page 55.

3.3 Sharing a Prize

Dividing a Fraction by a Whole Number

At a recent school carnival, teams of students competed in contests. The members of each winning team shared prizes donated by store owners. Sharing the prizes leads to a new kind of division.

- What does it mean to divide a fraction by a whole number?

Problem 3.3

A Ms. Li gave peanuts as a prize for a relay race. The members of the winning team share the peanuts equally among themselves. What fraction of a pound of peanuts does each team member get in each situation? Use diagrams and number sentences to explain your reasoning.

1. Four students share $\frac{1}{2}$ pound of peanuts.
2. Three students share $\frac{1}{4}$ pound of peanuts.
3. Two students share $\frac{3}{4}$ pound of peanuts.
4. Four students share $1\frac{1}{2}$ pounds of peanuts.

B Find each quotient and explain how you thought about it.

1. $\frac{2}{3} \div 5$
2. $\frac{3}{2} \div 2$
3. $\frac{2}{5} \div 3$
4. $\frac{4}{5} \div 4$

C Write a story problem that can be represented by $\frac{8}{3} \div 4$. Explain why the division makes sense.

D Describe a strategy for dividing a fraction by a whole number.

ACE Homework starts on page 55.

3.4 Examining Algorithms for Dividing Fractions

In Problems 3.1, 3.2, and 3.3, you solved a variety of division problems. In Problem 3.4, you will develop an algorithm to handle all of them. You begin by dividing division problems into categories.

What is an algorithm you can use to divide any two fractions, including mixed numbers?

Problem 3.4

A For each division expression below, do the following.

- Estimate the quotient.
- Calculate the exact value of the quotient.
- State what the answer to the division expression means.

1. $\frac{1}{3} \div 9$	**2.** $12 \div \frac{1}{6}$	**3.** $\frac{5}{6} \div \frac{1}{12}$
4. $5 \div 1\frac{1}{2}$	**5.** $\frac{1}{2} \div 3\frac{2}{3}$	**6.** $\frac{3}{4} \div \frac{3}{4}$
7. $5 \div \frac{2}{3}$	**8.** $\frac{1}{6} \div 12$	**9.** $3 \div \frac{2}{5}$
10. $3\frac{1}{3} \div \frac{2}{3}$	**11.** $5\frac{2}{3} \div 1\frac{1}{2}$	**12.** $\frac{9}{5} \div \frac{1}{2}$

continued on the next page >

Problem 3.4 continued

B **1.** Sort the expressions from Question A into two groups:

- Group 1. Problems that require little work to evaluate.
- Group 2. Problems that require much work to evaluate.

2. Explain why you put each expression into the group you chose.

C Write two new division expressions involving fractions for each of your groups. Explain why each expression goes with one group.

D Write an algorithm for division involving *any* two fractions, including mixed numbers.

E Use your division algorithm to divide.

1. $9 \div \frac{4}{5}$

2. $1\frac{7}{8} \div 3$

3. $1\frac{2}{3} \div \frac{1}{5}$

4. $2\frac{5}{6} \div 1\frac{1}{3}$

F April notices that sometimes a quotient is less than one and sometimes a quotient is greater than one. What is the relationship between the dividend and the divisor in each case?

ACE Homework starts on page 55.

Applications | Connections | Extensions

Applications

1. A latte (LAH tay) is the most popular drink at Antonio's Coffee Shop.

Antonio makes only one size of latte, and he uses $\frac{1}{3}$ cup of milk in each drink. How many lattes can Antonio make with the amount of milk in containers (a)–(c)? If there is a remainder, what does it mean?

a. $\frac{7}{9}$ cup **b.** $\frac{5}{6}$ cup **c.** $3\frac{2}{3}$ cups

2. Write a story problem that can be solved using $1\frac{3}{4} \div \frac{1}{2}$. Explain how the calculation matches your story.

3. The Easy Baking Company makes muffins. They make several sizes, ranging from very small to very large. There are 20 cups of flour in the packages of flour they buy. How many muffins can they make from a package of flour if each muffin takes one of the following amounts of flour?

a. $\frac{1}{4}$ cup **b.** $\frac{2}{4}$ cup **c.** $\frac{3}{4}$ cup

d. $\frac{1}{10}$ cup **e.** $\frac{2}{10}$ cup **f.** $\frac{7}{10}$ cup

g. $\frac{1}{7}$ cup **h.** $\frac{2}{7}$ cup **i.** $\frac{6}{7}$ cup

j. Explain how the answers for $20 \div \frac{1}{7}$, $20 \div \frac{2}{7}$, and $20 \div \frac{6}{7}$ are related. Show why this makes sense.

For Exercises 4–7, find each quotient.

4. $6 \div \frac{3}{5}$

5. $5 \div \frac{2}{9}$

6. $3 \div \frac{1}{4}$

7. $4 \div \frac{5}{8}$

For Exercises 8–10, find each quotient. Describe any patterns that you see.

8. $5 \div \frac{1}{4}$

9. $5 \div \frac{1}{8}$

10. $5 \div \frac{1}{16}$

For Exercises 11–13, answer the question. Then draw a picture or write a number sentence to show why your answer is correct. If there is a remainder, tell what it means for the given situation.

11. Bill wants to make 22 small pizzas for a party. He has 16 cups of flour. Each pizza crust takes $\frac{3}{4}$ cup of flour. Does he have enough flour?

12. It takes $18\frac{3}{8}$ inches of wood to make a frame for a small photo. Ms. Jones has 3 yards of wood. How many frames can she make?

13. There are 12 rabbits at a pet store. The manager lets Gabriella feed vegetables to the rabbits. She has $5\frac{1}{4}$ ounces of parsley today. She wants to give each rabbit the same amount. How much parsley does each rabbit get?

14. Anoki is in charge of giving prizes to teams at a mathematics competition. With each prize, he also wants to give all the members of the team equal amounts of mints. How much will each team member get if Anoki has the given amounts of mints?

a. $\frac{1}{2}$ pound of mints for 8 students

b. $\frac{1}{4}$ pound of mints for 4 students

c. $\frac{3}{4}$ pound of mints for 3 students

d. $\frac{4}{5}$ pound of mints for 10 students

e. $1\frac{1}{2}$ pounds of mints for 2 students

15. Maria uses $5\frac{1}{3}$ gallons of gas to drive to work and back four times.

a. How many gallons of gas does Maria use in one round trip to work?

b. Maria's car gets 28 miles to the gallon. How many miles is her round trip to work?

16. **Multiple Choice** Nana's recipe for applesauce makes $8\frac{1}{2}$ cups. She serves the applesauce equally among her three grandchildren. How many cups of applesauce will each one get?

A. $\frac{3}{2}$ cups

B. $25\frac{1}{2}$ cups

C. $\frac{9}{6}$ cups

D. none of these

For Exercises 17–19, find each quotient. Draw a picture to prove that each quotient makes sense.

17. $\frac{4}{5} \div 3$

18. $1\frac{2}{3} \div 5$

19. $\frac{5}{3} \div 5$

20. Multiple Choice Which of the following diagrams represents $\frac{1}{3} \div 4$?

A. 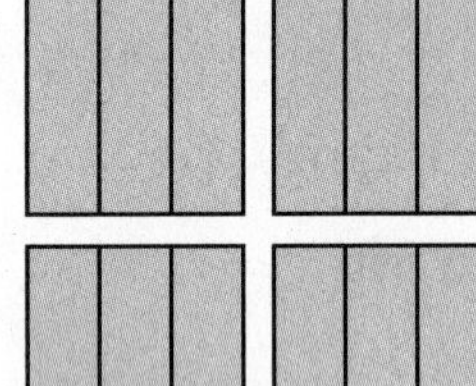

B. 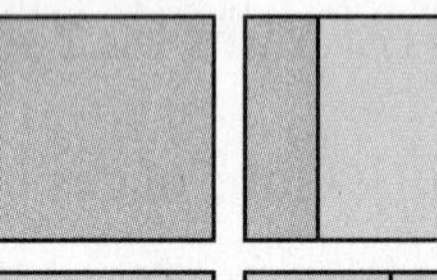

C.

D. 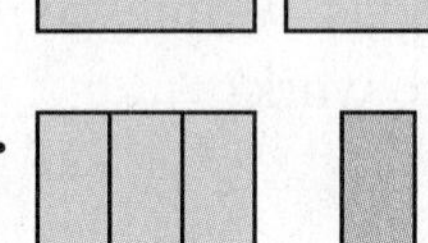

21. Multiple Choice Which of the following diagrams represents $4 \div \frac{1}{3}$?

F. 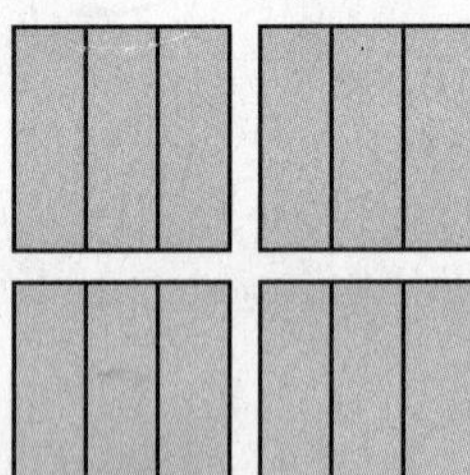

G. 

H. 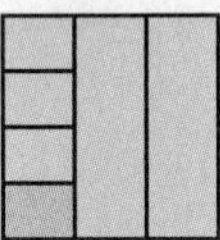

J. 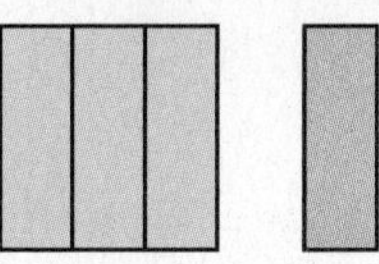

For Exercises 22–25, is each quotient greater than or less than one? Explain your reasoning.

22. $\frac{7}{9} \div \frac{1}{9}$

23. $\frac{2}{3} \div \frac{1}{9}$

24. $\frac{1}{18} \div \frac{1}{9}$

25. $1 \div \frac{1}{9}$

For Exercises 26–34, find the quotient.

26. $\frac{5}{6} \div \frac{1}{3}$

27. $\frac{2}{3} \div \frac{1}{9}$

28. $1\frac{1}{2} \div \frac{3}{8}$

29. $10 \div \frac{2}{3}$

30. $5 \div \frac{3}{4}$

31. $\frac{6}{7} \div 4$

32. $\frac{3}{10} \div 2$

33. $\frac{2}{5} \div \frac{1}{3}$

34. $2\frac{1}{2} \div 1\frac{1}{3}$

35. For Exercises 29 and 31 above, write a story problem to fit the computation.

Connections

For Exercises 36–39, find two equivalent fractions. (For example, $\frac{12}{15}$ and $\frac{24}{30}$ are equivalent fractions.) One fraction should have a numerator greater than the one given. The other fraction should have a numerator less than the one given.

36. $\frac{4}{6}$

37. $\frac{10}{12}$

38. $\frac{12}{9}$

39. $\frac{8}{6}$

40. Toshi has to work at the car wash for 3 hours. So far, he has worked $1\frac{3}{4}$ hours. How many more hours will it be before he can leave work?

For Exercises 41–44, find each sum or difference.

41. $\frac{9}{10} + \frac{1}{5}$

42. $\frac{5}{6} + \frac{7}{8}$

43. $\frac{2}{3} + 1\frac{1}{3}$

44. $12\frac{5}{6} - 8\frac{1}{4}$

For Exercises 45–48, find each product.

45. $\frac{2}{7} \times \frac{1}{3}$

46. $\frac{3}{4} \times \frac{7}{8}$

47. $1\frac{1}{2} \times \frac{1}{3}$

48. $4\frac{2}{3} \times 2\frac{3}{4}$

49. Kendra jogs $2\frac{2}{5}$ km on a trail and then sits down to wait for Louis. Louis has jogged $1\frac{1}{2}$ km on the same trail.

How much farther will Louis have to jog to reach Kendra?

50. The marks on each number line are spaced so that the distance between any two consecutive tick marks is the same. Copy each number line and label the marks.

a. 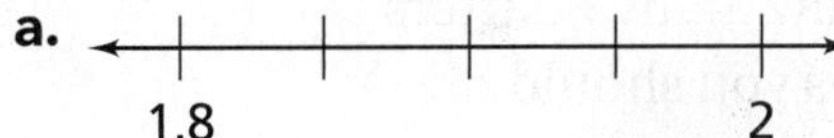

b. 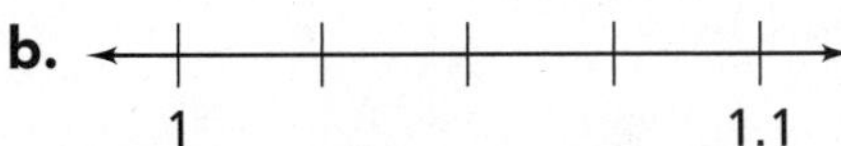

c.

2.93 2.95

d. 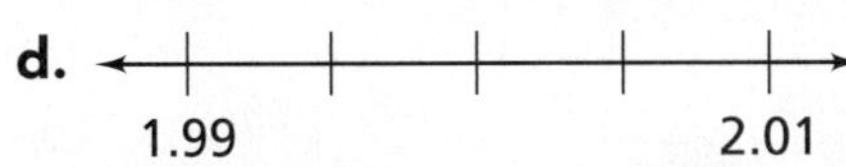

e. Explain how you determined what the labels should be.

Use the cartoon below to answer Exercises 51–53.

51. How many slices of the pizza will have olives?

52. How many slices of the pizza will be plain?

53. What fraction of the pizza will have onions and green peppers?

Extensions

54. Dante says there is an easy way to find out how many quarters are in some whole number of dollars. He says you should divide the number of dollars by $\frac{1}{4}$. Vanna says she knows an easier way. You just need to multiply the number of dollars by 4. With whom do you agree? Explain.

Use the table of equivalent measures below to solve Exercises 55–59.

Measurement	Equivalent Measurement
1 cup	16 tablespoons
1 quart	4 cups
1 quart	2 pints
1 gallon	4 quarts
1 tablespoon	3 teaspoons

55. Brian is missing his measuring cup. He needs to measure out $\frac{1}{2}$ cup of vegetable oil. How many tablespoons should he use?

56. To measure out $\frac{1}{2}$ cup of vegetable oil, how many teaspoons does Brian need?

57. What fraction of a quart is $\frac{1}{2}$ cup?

58. What fraction of a gallon is $\frac{1}{2}$ cup?

59. Suppose you need to measure out exactly one gallon of water. The only measuring scoops you have are $\frac{1}{2}$ cup, 1 cup, and 1 pint. Which scoop would you use? How would you make sure you had exactly one gallon?

Mathematical Reflections 3

In this Investigation, you developed strategies for dividing when fractions are involved. You developed algorithms to use for division problems involving fractions or mixed numbers. The following questions will help you summarize what you have learned.

Think about these questions. Discuss your ideas with other students and your teacher. Then write a summary of your findings in your notebook.

1. When solving a problem, **how** do you recognize when division is the operation you need to use?

2. **a.** **How** is dividing a whole number by a fraction similar to or different from dividing a fraction by a whole number?

b. **Explain** your strategy for dividing one fraction by another fraction. Does your strategy also work for divisions where the dividend or divisor is a whole number or a mixed number? Explain.

3. When dividing a whole number by a whole number greater than 1, the quotient is always less than the dividend. For example, $15 \div 3 = 5$, and 5 is less than 15 (the dividend). Use examples to help **explain** the following statement:

When you divide a fraction by another fraction, your answer might be greater than the dividend or less than the dividend.

Common Core Mathematical Practices

As you worked on the Problems in this Investigation, you used prior knowledge to make sense of them. You also applied Mathematical Practices to solve the Problems. Think back over your work, the ways you thought about the Problems, and how you used Mathematical Practices.

Hector described his thoughts in the following way:

In Problem 3.4, we solved and sorted all sorts of division problems. Then, we found an algorithm that works for all of them. If you make a mixed number into an improper fraction, you can use the same division algorithm all of the time.

We came up with two algorithms. The first was finding common denominators and then dividing the numerators. The second was multiplying the dividend by the denominator of the divisor. Then divide the result by the numerator of the divisor.

Both algorithms consistently give the correct answer. We looked for patterns. Then we made sure those patterns worked for all division with fractions problems.

Common Core Standards for Mathematical Practice

MP8 Look for and express regularity in repeated reasoning.

- What other Mathematical Practices can you identify in Hector's reasoning?
- Describe a Mathematical Practice that you and your classmates used to solve a different Problem in this Investigation.

Wrapping Up the Operations

4.1 Just the Facts
Fact Families for Addition and Subtraction

In Investigation 1, you wrote addition and subtraction sentences to show calculations you did. For each addition sentence you write, there are related number sentences that show the same information. These sets of number sentences form a related set of facts called a *fact family.*

- How could you write a number sentence showing a relationship among 7, 2, and 9?
- Is there more than one correct number sentence?

Below are two fact families. The family on the left has all values included. The family on the right has a missing value.

	Example 1	Example 2
Addition Sentence	$2 + 3 = 5$	$2 + n = 5$
Related Number Sentences	$3 + 2 = 5$ $5 - 3 = 2$ $5 - 2 = 3$	$n + 2 = 5$ $5 - n = 2$ $5 - 2 = n$

- How are the three additional sentences related to the original sentence?

Common Core State Standards

6.EE.A.2 Write, read, and evaluate expressions in which letters stand for numbers.

6.EE.B.6 Use variables to represent numbers and write expressions when solving a real-world or mathematical problem; understand that a variable can represent an unknown number . . .

6.EE.B.7 Solve real-world and mathematical problems by writing and solving equations of the form $x + p = q$ and $px = q$ for cases in which p, q and x are all nonnegative rational numbers.

You can also create fact families with fractions.

- What number sentences can you write showing a relationship among $\frac{1}{2}$, $\frac{1}{4}$, and $\frac{3}{4}$?

Ravi says that when he is thinking about fact families, he thinks about a picture like a section in Tupelo Township. The parts of the large rectangle represent the *addends*. The entire large rectangle represents the total acreage, or the *sum*.

- The total area of the rectangle below is 42 acres. What number sentence does this model represent?

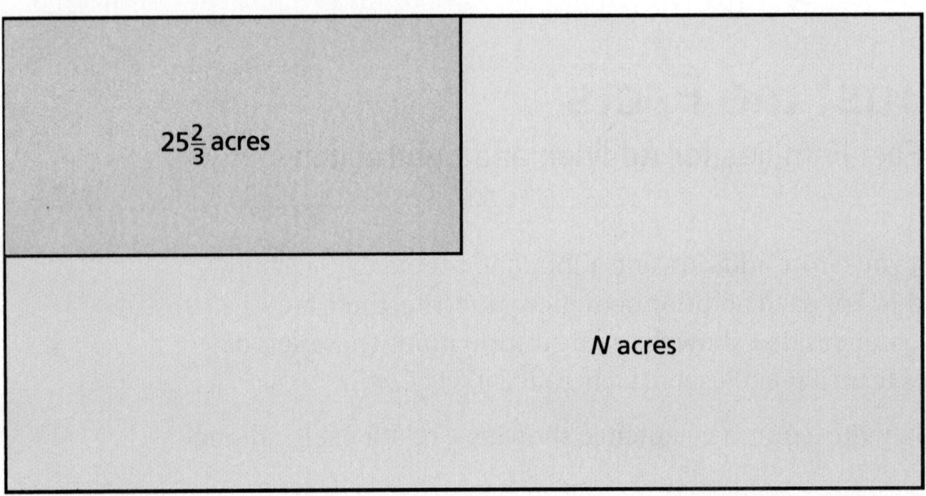

- What are some other ways of writing the relationship between $25\frac{2}{3}$, N, and 42 acres?

The model shows that any sum can be broken down, *or decomposed*, into two (or more) parts. The parts are the addends. In Ravi's model, the total acreage, the sum, is 42 acres. The parts, N acres and $25\frac{2}{3}$ acres, are the addends.

Below are two fact families expressing relationships among fractions.

	Example 1	Example 2
Addition Sentence	$\frac{3}{4}+\frac{1}{8}=\frac{7}{8}$	$\frac{6}{8}+N=\frac{7}{8}$
Related Number Sentences	$\frac{1}{8}+\frac{3}{4}=\frac{7}{8}$ $\frac{7}{8}-\frac{3}{4}=\frac{1}{8}$ $\frac{7}{8}-\frac{1}{8}=\frac{3}{4}$	$N+\frac{6}{8}=\frac{7}{8}$ $\frac{7}{8}-\frac{6}{8}=N$ $\frac{7}{8}-N=\frac{6}{8}$

- How are these fact families different from each other?
- How do you know that the three related sentences below the top row are true?

In Problem 4.1 you will create fact families and use them to find unknown numbers.

Problem 4.1

A For each number sentence, write a complete fact family and find the value of *N*.

1. $\frac{5}{10}-\frac{2}{5}=N$
2. $3\frac{3}{5}+1\frac{2}{3}=N$
3. Describe the relationship between addition and subtraction. Use the fact families in parts (1) and (2) as examples.

B For each number sentence, find the value of *N*.

1. $N+1\frac{2}{3}=5\frac{5}{6}$
2. $\frac{3}{4}+N=\frac{17}{12}$
3. $N-\frac{1}{2}=\frac{3}{8}$
4. How can fact families help you find the value of *N* in parts (1)–(3)?

ACE Homework starts on page 73.

4.2 Multiplication and Division Fact Families

In Problem 4.1 you wrote fact families made up of related addition and subtraction sentences. You can also use fact families to show relationships between multiplication and division.

	Example 1	Example 2
Multiplication Sentence	$4 \times 5 = 20$	$17 \times N = 51$
Related Number Sentences	$5 \times 4 = 20$ $20 \div 5 = 4$ $20 \div 4 = 5$	$N \times 17 = 51$ $51 \div N = 17$ $51 \div 17 = N$

In Problem 4.1, you saw Ravi's rectangular model for adding area. For multiplication, Ravi uses words instead of a model to help him decide on the correct rearrangements. Any multiplication sentence, whether involving fractions or whole numbers, can be written in the form below.

$$(\text{factor 1}) \times (\text{factor 2}) = \text{product}$$

- How might you rearrange the sentence above but still keep the same relationship between factor 1, factor 2, and the product?
- How might you rearrange the sentence $\frac{2}{3} \times N = \frac{1}{2}$ to complete the following table?

	Example 1	Example 2
Multiplication Sentence	$\frac{1}{2} \times \frac{1}{3} = \frac{1}{6}$	$\frac{2}{3} \times N = \frac{1}{2}$
Related Number Sentences	$\frac{1}{3} \times \frac{1}{2} = \frac{1}{6}$ $\frac{1}{6} \div \frac{1}{3} = \frac{1}{2}$ $\frac{1}{6} \div \frac{1}{2} = \frac{1}{3}$	

- In Example 2 in the table above, which rearrangement is most helpful for finding the value of N?

Problem 4.2

Now it is your turn to write fact families.

A Write a complete fact family for each of the following sentences.

1. $\frac{2}{3} \times \frac{1}{5} = \frac{2}{15}$
2. $\frac{3}{4} \times \frac{5}{8} = \frac{15}{32}$
3. $\frac{9}{40} \div \frac{3}{5} = \frac{3}{8}$
4. $\frac{4}{15} \div \frac{2}{5} = \frac{2}{3}$

B Write a complete fact family for each of the following equations. Use your fact family to find the value of *N*.

1. $\frac{3}{8} \times N = \frac{21}{80}$
2. $\frac{2}{3} \times N = \frac{10}{15}$
3. $1 \div N = \frac{2}{3}$
4. $\frac{8}{15} \div N = \frac{2}{3}$

C Marla says she can use the idea of *decomposing* a product to find the unknown factor, *N*, in $15 = 2 \times N$. She rearranges this multiplication sentence as the division sentence $15 \div 2 = N$. Does Marla's strategy work? Explain why or why not.

D Below are sets of three numbers. Some of these sets can be related using addition and subtraction. Some can be related using multiplication and division. For each set, identify what the relation is. Then write a complete fact family.

1. $\frac{3}{5}, \frac{1}{3}, \frac{14}{15}$
2. $\frac{3}{4}, \frac{4}{3}, 1$
3. $1\frac{1}{2}, 2\frac{2}{3}, 4\frac{1}{6}$
4. $\frac{3}{2}, 3, \frac{9}{2}$

ACE Homework starts on page 73.

4.3 Becoming an Operations Sleuth

In *Let's Be Rational* you have revisited and deepened your skills with the operations addition, subtraction, multiplication, and division. In the real world, problems do not come with labels saying *add, subtract, multiply,* or *divide.* You need to use your mathematics knowledge to identify which operation will be helpful to solve a problem.

Think about the operations you would use in the following situations.

The sixth-grade class is taking a field trip to the state capital. There are 389 students in the sixth grade, but 29 did not get the permission slip signed by their parents. The principal needs to know how many sixth-grade students have permission to go on the field trip.

A varsity softball team has 15 players. The junior varsity team has 10 players. The fan club is buying the teams new uniforms. The fan club wants to know how many uniforms they need to buy.

There are 360 students going on a field trip. Each school bus carries 30 students. The school office needs to know how many buses to send.

The school auditorium has 30 rows of 50 seats each. You want to find out how many seats are in the auditorium.

- Which situations require you to add? Which require you to subtract?
- Which require you to multiply? Which require you to divide?
- How do you know?

In Problem 4.3 you will examine situations that require computations with fractions. In each case your first task is to determine what operations will help you solve the problem.

Problem 4.3

For each of the Questions below, do the following.

- Decide which operation you need to find an answer. Explain how you identified the operation.
- When you use more than one operation, explain the order in which you use them.
- Write the number sentence(s) you use.
- Find the answer.

A Sammy the turtle can walk $\frac{1}{8}$ of a mile in an hour. How many hours will it take him to walk $1\frac{1}{4}$ miles?

B Jimarcus plans to build a fence $5\frac{1}{3}$ yards long at the back of his garden. How many $\frac{2}{3}$-yard sections of fence will he need?

C Sasha bought $3\frac{1}{2}$ pints of blueberries to make jelly. She ate $\frac{3}{4}$ of a pint of berries on her way home. How many pints of berries does she have left to make jelly?

D Judi uses $2\frac{3}{4}$ pounds of potatoes every week. How many pounds of potatoes does she use in $3\frac{1}{2}$ weeks?

continued on the next page >

Problem 4.3 continued

E At a bake sale, Leslie sold $2\frac{1}{2}$ dozen sweet rolls. Christie sold sweet rolls but did not keep track of what she sold. She started with 5 dozen sweet rolls and had $1\frac{2}{3}$ dozen left at the end of the sale. Who sold more sweet rolls? How many more did she sell?

F Raymar ate $\frac{1}{4}$ of a pan of brownies. His brother Kalen ate $\frac{1}{4}$ of the rest of the pan of brownies. What part of the whole pan did Kalen eat?

G Mrs. Larnell is making snack packs for a class picnic. She puts $\frac{1}{4}$ pound of apples, $\frac{1}{8}$ pound of nut mix, and $\frac{1}{16}$ pound of chocolate in each student's pack. There are 24 students in the class. What is the total weight of the snack packs? Is there more than one way to solve this problem?

H A grandmother is making clothes for her three granddaughters. She will make a jacket and one other item for each granddaughter. The three other items will be exactly the same. A jacket takes $1\frac{5}{8}$ yards of fabric. She has ten yards of material in all. She is trying to figure out how much fabric she has for each of the three extra items.

Let N represent the fabric needed for one extra item. Explain why each of the sentences below does or does not describe the situation. (More than one sentence may apply.)

1. $3\left(1\frac{5}{8} + N\right) = 10$
2. $10 - 4\frac{7}{8} = 3N$
3. $3 \times 1\frac{5}{8} + N = 10$
4. $10 \div 1\frac{5}{8} = N$

ACE Homework starts on page 73.

Applications | Connections | Extensions

Applications

For each of Exercises 1–4, write a complete fact family.

1. $\frac{1}{16} + \frac{1}{12} = N$
2. $\frac{5}{4} - \frac{4}{5} = N$
3. $N - 1\frac{1}{3} = 2\frac{2}{3}$
4. $N + \frac{4}{3} = \frac{1}{3}$

For Exercises 5–10, find the value for *N* that makes each number sentence true.

5. $\frac{2}{3} + \frac{3}{4} = N$
6. $\frac{3}{4} + N = \frac{4}{5}$
7. $N - \frac{3}{5} = \frac{1}{4}$
8. $\frac{2}{2} - \frac{2}{4} = N$
9. $\frac{3}{8} - N = \frac{1}{4}$
10. $\frac{3}{4} + N = \frac{5}{8}$

11. Find the value for m that makes this number sentence true:
$\frac{1}{2} + \frac{9}{10} + m = 2$.

12. Find values for m and n that make this number sentence true:
$\frac{1}{2} + \frac{9}{10} + m + n = 2$.

13. Find the value for m that makes this number sentence true:
$\frac{1}{2} + \frac{9}{10} = 2 - m$.

For Exercises 14 and 15, write a complete multiplication and division fact family for the operation given.

14. $\frac{2}{3} \times \frac{5}{7} = \frac{10}{21}$
15. $\frac{3}{4} \div 1\frac{1}{2} = \frac{1}{2}$

Solve Exercises 16–21.

16. $N \times \frac{1}{5} = \frac{2}{15}$

17. $N \div \frac{1}{5} = \frac{2}{3}$

18. $\frac{1}{2} \times N = \frac{1}{3}$

19. $\frac{1}{5} \div N = \frac{1}{3}$

20. $1\frac{3}{4} \div N = \frac{1}{4}$

21. $2\frac{2}{3} \div N = 8$

22. Find the value for m that makes each number sentence true.

a. $\frac{2}{3} \times \frac{4}{5} \times m = \frac{1}{3}$

b. $\frac{4}{5} \times \frac{2}{3} \times m = \frac{1}{3}$

c. $\frac{2}{3} \times \frac{4}{5} = \frac{1}{3} \div m$

23. Gregory is building a pen for his new puppy. He needs the pen to be $9\frac{1}{2}$ feet by $6\frac{3}{4}$ feet. How many feet of fencing does he need?

24. Sam goes to the market to buy hamburger for a cookout. He buys $3\frac{3}{4}$ pounds of hamburger. How many $\frac{1}{4}$-pound patties can he make?

25. a. Kalisha made two dozen large buns. She ate $\frac{1}{2}$ of a bun and gave her mother and father one each. How many buns does she have left?

b. She is going to cut the remaining buns into thirds for a party. How many $\frac{1}{3}$-size buns will she have?

26. Eun Mi raked $\frac{1}{3}$ of her mother's lawn. Her brother, Yeping, raked $\frac{1}{3}$ of the rest of the lawn. What part of the whole lawn still needs raking?

27. Monday through Friday a grocery store buys $\frac{2}{3}$ bushel of apples per day from a local grower. Saturday the grocer buys $1\frac{1}{3}$ bushels of apples. If the grocer buys apples for four weeks, how many bushels of apples does he buy?

28. Kalin walks at a steady rate of $3\frac{2}{3}$ miles per hour. The beach is $4\frac{1}{4}$ miles from his home. How long will it take Kalin to walk from his home to the beach and back to his home?

Connections

29. **a.** Find the value for N that makes this number sentence true:

$\left(\frac{1}{4}+\frac{1}{3}\right)N=\frac{1}{2}$.

b. Find the value for N that makes this number sentence true:

$\frac{1}{4}+\frac{1}{3}N=\frac{1}{2}$.

c. Why are the correct answers for part (a) and part (b) different from each other?

For Exercises 30–38, find each missing number.

30. $2 \times ■ = 1$	**31.** $\frac{1}{2} \times ■ = 1$	**32.** $3 \times ■ = 1$
33. $\frac{1}{3} \times ■ = 1$	**34.** $■ \times \frac{2}{3} = 1$	**35.** $\frac{3}{4} \times ■ = 1$
36. $■ \times \frac{5}{2} = 1$	**37.** $1\frac{1}{4} \times ■ = 1$	**38.** $\frac{7}{12} \times ■ = 1$

For Exercises 39–41, find the missing numbers in each pair of number sentences. What is the relationship between each pair of numbers?

39. $3 \div ■ = 9$	**40.** $3 \div ■ = 12$	**41.** $2\frac{1}{2} \div ■ = 5$
$3 \times ■ = 9$	$3 \times ■ = 12$	$2\frac{1}{2} \times ■ = 5$

For Exercises 42–43, estimate which sum or difference is greater. Then compute the answers to compare with your estimates. Show your work.

42. $\frac{1}{8}+\frac{5}{6}$ or $\frac{1}{6}+\frac{5}{8}$

43. $\frac{5}{6}-\frac{1}{8}$ or $\frac{5}{8}-\frac{1}{6}$

44. Find the value for N that makes this number sentence true:

$3 \times \left(N+\frac{1}{3}\right)=2$

45. Find the value for N that makes this number sentence true:

$\left(N+\frac{1}{2}\right) \times 1\frac{1}{2}=2\frac{1}{4}$

46. In the number sentence below, find values for m and n that make the sum exactly 3.

$$\frac{5}{8}+\frac{1}{4}+\frac{2}{3}+m+n=3$$

Extensions

For Exercises 47–50, find the value of N that makes each number sentence true.

47. $\frac{1}{2} + N = \frac{1}{2}$

48. $\frac{1}{2} - N = \frac{1}{2}$

49. $\frac{1}{2} \times N = \frac{1}{2}$

50. $\frac{1}{2} \div N = \frac{1}{2}$

51. Mathematicians call the number 0 the *additive identity*. They call the number 1 the *multiplicative identity*. Based on your work in Exercises 47–50, what do you think *identity* means?

For Exercises 52–55, find the value of N that makes each number sentence true.

52. $\frac{1}{2} + N = 0$

53. $\frac{2}{3} + N = 0$

54. $\frac{1}{2} \times N = 1$

55. $\frac{2}{3} \times N = 1$

56. Mathematicians have a special name for each value of N you found in Exercises 52–55. Each N is the additive or multiplicative *inverse* of the number you started with.

- An *additive inverse* is the number you add to another number to get 0.
- A *multiplicative inverse* is the number you multiply by another number to get 1.

a. Does every number have an additive inverse?

b. Does every number have a multiplicative inverse?

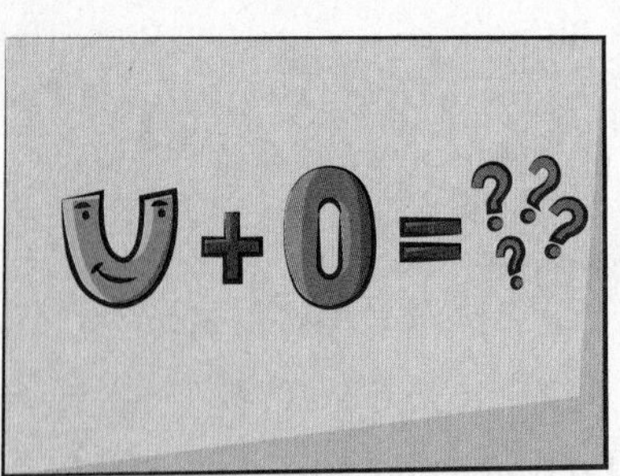

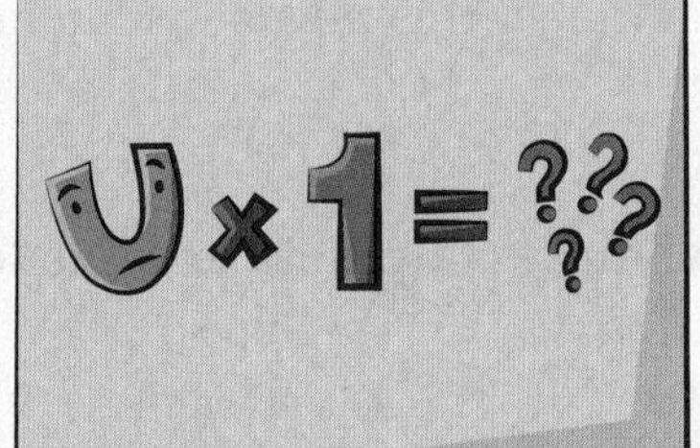

Mathematical Reflections 4

In this Investigation, you explored relationships among addition, subtraction, multiplication and division. The following questions will help you summarize what you have learned.

Think about these questions. Discuss your ideas with other students and your teacher. Then write a summary of your findings in your notebook.

1. **How** do you decide which operation to use when you are solving a problem?
2. **How** is the relationship between addition and subtraction like the relationship between multiplication and division? **How** is it different?
3. While working with fact families, you thought about *decomposing* numbers.
   a. **What** does it mean to decompose a number?
   b. **How** do fact families help you figure out the value for N in a sentence such as $N \div 2\frac{1}{2} = 1\frac{1}{4}$?

Common Core Mathematical Practices

As you worked on the Problems in this Investigation, you used prior knowledge to make sense of them. You also applied Mathematical Practices to solve the Problems. Think back over your work, the ways you thought about the Problems, and how you used Mathematical Practices.

Tori described her thoughts in the following way:

In Problem 4.3, we had to figure out whether to add, subtract, multiply, or divide. Sometimes we used a combination of operations. We had to read each problem really carefully.

Sometimes we drew a picture to represent what the problem was asking. This helped us figure out which operation to use. For example, if the problem called for combining quantities, we used addition.

This was a good way to end because in real life, you don't get told which operation to use. You need to figure it out.

Common Core Standards for Mathematical Practice

MP2 Reason abstractly and quantitatively.

- What other Mathematical Practices can you identify in Tori's reasoning?
- Describe a Mathematical Practice that you and your classmates used to solve a different Problem in this Investigation.

Looking Back

During this Unit, you developed strategies for estimating and computing with fractions and mixed numbers. You learned how to determine which situations call for which operations when working with fractions and mixed numbers. You developed algorithms for adding, subtracting, multiplying, and dividing fractions. You learned how to solve problems with fractions. Use what you have learned to solve the following examples.

Use Your Understanding: Fraction Operations

1. The Scoop Shop sells many types of nuts. Lily asks for this mix:
   - $\frac{1}{2}$ pound peanuts
   - $\frac{1}{6}$ pound hazelnuts
   - $\frac{1}{3}$ pound almonds
   - $\frac{3}{4}$ pound cashews
   - $\frac{1}{4}$ pound pecans

   a. Mixed nuts cost \$5.00 per pound. What is Lily's bill?

   b. What fraction of the mix does each type of nut represent?

   c. Diego does not like cashews, so he asks for Lily's mix without the cashews. What is Diego's bill?

   d. Taisha is making small bowls of nuts for a party. Each bowl can hold $\frac{1}{4}$ cup of nuts. Taisha has $3\frac{3}{8}$ cups of nuts. How many full bowls can she make?

2. Shaquille likes dried fruit. He wants a mix of peaches, cherries, pineapple chunks, and apple rings. The following chart shows how much The Scoop Shop has of each fruit. It also shows how much of each fruit Shaquille buys.

The Scoop Shop's Stock	Shaquille's Order
$1\frac{1}{2}$ pounds dried peaches	$\frac{1}{3}$ of the stock
$\frac{4}{5}$ pound dried cherries	$\frac{1}{2}$ of the stock
$\frac{3}{4}$ pound dried pineapple chunks	$\frac{2}{3}$ of the stock
$2\frac{1}{4}$ pounds dried apple rings	$\frac{3}{5}$ of the stock

a. How many pounds of dried fruit does Shaquille buy?

b. Dried fruit costs $6.00 per pound. What is Shaquille's bill?

Explain Your Reasoning

When you solve a problem or make a decision, it is important to be able to support each step of your reasoning.

3. What operations did you use to calculate Lily's bill?

4. How did you find the fraction of Lily's mix that each type of nut represented?

5. Jacob says that $4 \div \frac{1}{3} = 12$ and $4 \div \frac{2}{3} = 6$. Why is the answer in the second number sentence half of the answer in the first number sentence?

6. Use the following problems to show the steps involved in the algorithms for each operation on fractions. Be prepared to explain your reasoning.

a. $\frac{5}{6} + \frac{1}{4}$ **b.** $\frac{3}{4} - \frac{2}{3}$ **c.** $\frac{2}{5} \times \frac{3}{8}$ **d.** $\frac{3}{8} \div \frac{3}{4}$

English / Spanish Glossary

A

algorithm A set of rules for performing a procedure. Mathematicians invent algorithms that are useful in many kinds of situations. Some examples of algorithms are the rules for long division or the rules for adding two fractions.

To add two fractions, first change them to equivalent fractions with the same denominator. Then add the numerators and put the sum over the common denominator.

algoritmo Un conjunto de reglas para realizar un procedimiento. Los matemáticos inventan algoritmos que son útiles en muchos tipos de situaciones. Algunos ejemplos de algoritmos son las reglas para una división larga o las reglas para sumar dos fracciones. El siguiente es un algoritmo escrito por un estudiante de un grado intermedio.

Para sumar dos fracciones, primero transfórmalas en fracciones equivalentes con el mismo denominador. Luego suma los numeradores y coloca la suma sobre el denominador común.

B

benchmark A reference number that can be used to estimate the size of other numbers. For work with fractions, 0, $\frac{1}{2}$, and 1 are good benchmarks. We often estimate fractions or decimals with benchmarks because it is easier to do arithmetic with them, and estimates often give enough accuracy for the situation. For example, many fractions and decimals—such as $\frac{37}{50}$, $\frac{5}{8}$, 0.43, and 0.55—can be thought of as being close to $\frac{1}{2}$. You might say $\frac{5}{8}$ is between $\frac{1}{2}$ and 1 but closer to $\frac{1}{2}$, so you can estimate $\frac{5}{8}$ to be about $\frac{1}{2}$. We also use benchmarks to help compare fractions and decimals. For example, we could say that $\frac{5}{8}$ is greater than 0.43 because $\frac{5}{8}$ is greater than $\frac{1}{2}$ and 0.43 is less than $\frac{1}{2}$.

punto de referencia Un número "bueno" que se puede usar para estimar el tamaño de otros números. Para trabajar con fracciones, 0, $\frac{1}{2}$ y 1 son buenos puntos de referencia. Por lo general estimamos fracciones o decimales con puntos de referencia porque nos resulta más fácil hacer cálculos aritméticos con ellos, y las estimaciones suelen ser bastante exactas para la situación. Por ejemplo, muchas fracciones y decimales, como por ejemplo $\frac{37}{50}$, $\frac{5}{8}$, 0.43 y 0.55, se pueden considerar como cercanos a $\frac{1}{2}$. Se podría decir que $\frac{5}{8}$ está entre $\frac{1}{2}$ y 1, pero más cerca de $\frac{1}{2}$, por lo que se puede estimar que $\frac{5}{8}$ es alrededor de $\frac{1}{2}$. También usamos puntos de referencia para ayudarnos a comparar fracciones. Por ejemplo, podríamos decir que $\frac{5}{8}$ es mayor que 0.43, porque $\frac{5}{8}$ es mayor que $\frac{1}{2}$ y 0.43 es menor que $\frac{1}{2}$.

E

equivalent fractions Fractions that are equal in value, but may have different numerators and denominators. For example, $\frac{2}{3}$ and $\frac{14}{21}$ are equivalent fractions. The shaded part of this rectangle represents both $\frac{2}{3}$ and $\frac{14}{21}$.

fracciones equivalentes Fracciones de igual valor, que pueden tener diferentes numeradores y denominadores. Por ejemplo, $\frac{2}{3}$ y $\frac{14}{21}$ son fracciones equivalentes. La parte sombreada de este rectángulo representa tanto $\frac{2}{3}$ como $\frac{14}{21}$.

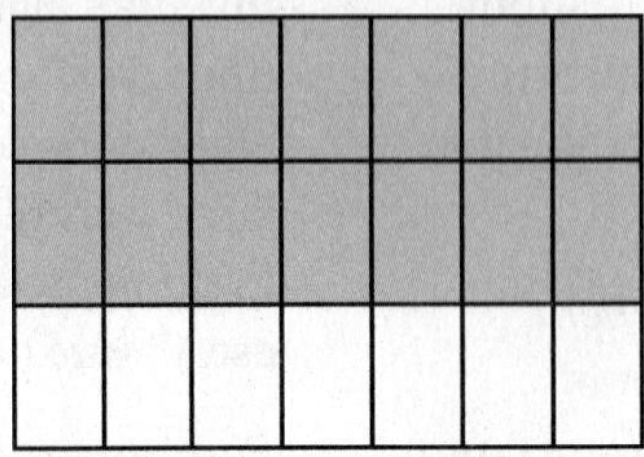

explain Academic Vocabulary To give facts and details that make an idea easier to understand. Explaining can involve a written summary supported by a diagram, chart, table, or a combination of these.

related terms *analyze, clarify, describe, justify, tell*

sample Explain why the answer to $12 \div \frac{3}{4}$ is equal to one third of the answer to $12 \div \frac{1}{4}$.

> Because $\frac{3}{4} = 3 \times \frac{1}{4}$, it takes three $\frac{1}{4}$s to make every $\frac{3}{4}$. There are forty-eight $\frac{1}{4}$s in 12, but there are only sixteen $\frac{3}{4}$s in 12.

explicar Vocabulario académico Dar datos y detalles que hacen que una idea sea más fácil de comprender. Explicar puede incluir un resumen escrito apoyado por un diagrama, una gráfica, una tabla o una combinación de éstos.

términos relacionados *analizar, aclarar, describir, justificar, decir*

ejemplo Explica por qué el resultado de $12 \div \frac{3}{4}$ es igual a un tercio del resultado de $12 \div \frac{1}{4}$.

> Porque $\frac{3}{4} = 3 \times \frac{1}{4}$, se requieren tres $\frac{1}{4}$ para formar cada $\frac{3}{4}$. Hay cuarenta y ocho $\frac{1}{4}$ en 12, pero sólo hay dieciséis $\frac{3}{4}$ en 12.

F

fact family A set of related addition–subtraction sentences or multiplication–division sentences. For example, the set of numbers, 3, 5, and 15, is part of this multiplication–division fact family:

$3 \times 5 = 15$ $5 \times 3 = 15$

$15 \div 5 = 3$ $15 \div 3 = 5$

If you have one fact from a family, you can use the addition–subtraction or multiplication–division relationship to write the three related facts that are also part of the family. For example, with $2 + 3 = 5$, you can use the relationship between addition and subtraction to write the related number sentences $3 + 2 = 5$, $5 - 3 = 2$, and $5 - 2 = 3$.

familia de operaciones Conjunto de oraciones relacionadas de suma y resta o de multiplicación y división. Por ejemplo, los números 3, 5 y 15, son parte de esta familia de operaciones de multiplicación y división:

$3 \times 5 = 15$ $5 \times 3 = 15$

$15 \div 5 = 3$ $15 \div 3 = 5$

Si conoces una operación de una familia de operaciones, puedes usar la relación entre la suma y la resta, y entre la multiplicación y la división, para escribir las otras tres operaciones relacionadas que son parte de esa familia. Por ejemplo, con $2 + 3 = 5$, puedes usar la relación entre la suma y la resta para escribir las oraciones numéricas relacionadas $3 + 2 = 5$, $5 - 3 = 2$ y $5 - 2 = 3$.

M

model Academic Vocabulary To represent a situation using pictures, diagrams, number sentences, or experiments.

related terms *represent, demonstrate*

sample Yolanda has one half of an apple pie. She eats one third of the half of a pie. Model this situation using a number sentence or a picture.

I can write one third as $\frac{1}{3}$ and one half as $\frac{1}{2}$, so one third of one half can be written as $\frac{1}{3} \times \frac{1}{2}$. Because $\frac{1}{3} \times \frac{1}{2} = \frac{1}{6}$, she eats $\frac{1}{6}$ of the entire pie.

I can also fold a whole fraction strip into halves, then fold each half into thirds.

$\frac{1}{2}$			$\frac{1}{2}$		
$\frac{1}{6}$	$\frac{1}{6}$	$\frac{1}{6}$	$\frac{1}{6}$	$\frac{1}{6}$	$\frac{1}{6}$

Yolanda eats $\frac{1}{6}$ of the entire pie.

demostrar Vocabulario académico Representar una situación con dibujos, diagramas, oraciones numéricas o experimentos.

término relacionado *representar*

ejemplo Yolanda tiene la mitad de una tarta de manzana. Se come un tercio de la mitad de la tarta. Demuestra esta situación con una oración numérica o un dibujo.

Puedo escribir un tercio como $\frac{1}{3}$ y la mitad como $\frac{1}{2}$, así que un tercio de una mitad puede escribirse como $\frac{1}{3} \times \frac{1}{2}$. Debido a que $\frac{1}{3} \times \frac{1}{2} = \frac{1}{6}$, ella se come $\frac{1}{6}$ de la tarta entera.

También puedo doblar una tira de fracciones por el medio para obtener mitades y doblar cada mitad en tres tercios.

$\frac{1}{2}$			$\frac{1}{2}$		
$\frac{1}{6}$	$\frac{1}{6}$	$\frac{1}{6}$	$\frac{1}{6}$	$\frac{1}{6}$	$\frac{1}{6}$

Yolanda se come $\frac{1}{6}$ de la tarta entera.

N

number sentence A mathematical statement that gives the relationship between two expressions that are composed of numbers and operation signs. For example, $3 + 2 = 5$ and $6 \times 2 > 10$ are number sentences; $3 + 2$, 5, 6×2, and 10 are expressions.

oración numérica Enunciado matemático que describe la relación entre dos expresiones compuestas por números y signos de operaciones. Por ejemplo, $3 + 2 = 5$ y $6 \times 2 > 10$ son oraciones numéricas; $3 + 2$, 5, 6×2 y 10 son expresiones.

O

overestimate To make an estimate that is slightly greater than the actual value.

estimación por exceso Una estimación que es un poco mayor que el valor real.

R

reason Academic Vocabulary To think through using facts and information.

related terms *think, examine, logic*

sample To find the number of $\frac{1}{2}$-cup servings in 6 cups, Jenni says it is necessary to multiply 6 by $\frac{1}{2}$. Zach says that 6 must be divided by $\frac{1}{2}$ to find the number of servings. Do you agree with Jenni or Zach? Explain how you reasoned.

I agree with Zach because you want to know how many halves there are in 6. This question is answered by division: $6 \div \frac{1}{2} = 12$. Multiplying 6 by $\frac{1}{2}$ separates it into 2 equal parts of 3 each. That is not what is asked for in the question.

razonar Vocabulario académico Pensar algo con cuidado usando operaciones e información.

términos relacionados *pensar, examinar, lógico*

ejemplo Para hallar el número de porciones de $\frac{1}{2}$ taza que hay en 6 tazas, Jenni dice que se debe multiplicar 6 por $\frac{1}{2}$. Zach dice que hay que dividir 6 por $\frac{1}{2}$ para hallar el número de porciones. ¿Estás de acuerdo con Jenni o con Zach? Explica tu razonamiento.

Estoy de acuerdo con Zach porque se desea saber cuántas mitades hay en 6. Esta pregunta se responde usando la división: $6 \div \frac{1}{2} = 12$. Multiplicar 6 por $\frac{1}{2}$ lo separa en 2 partes iguales de 3 cada una. Esto no es lo que se pide en la pregunta.

recall Academic Vocabulary To remember a fact quickly.

related terms *remember, recognize*

sample Mateo wants to add 0.3 to $\frac{1}{2}$. What fact can you recall about $\frac{1}{2}$ or 0.3 that will help him find the sum? Explain.

I recall that $\frac{1}{2}$ is equivalent to the decimal 0.5. When both numbers are in decimal form, they can be added easily. Mateo can add $0.5 + 0.3$ to get 0.8.

I also recall that 0.3 is the same as $\frac{3}{10}$ and $\frac{1}{2}$ is equivalent to $\frac{5}{10}$. Mateo can add $\frac{3}{10} + \frac{5}{10}$ to get $\frac{8}{10}$ which is the same as 0.8.

recordar Vocabulario académico Acordarse de una operación rápidamente.

términus relacionados *acordarse, reconocer*

ejemplo Mateo quiere sumar 0.3 y $\frac{1}{2}$. ¿Qué operación con $\frac{1}{2}$ ó 0.3 puedes recordar para ayudarlo a hallar la suma? Explica tu respuesta.

Recuerdo que $\frac{1}{2}$ es equivalente al número decimal 0.5. Cuando ambos números están en forma decimal, pueden sumarse con facilidad. Mateo puede sumar $0.5 + 0.3$ para obtener 0.8.

También recuerdo que 0.3 igual $\frac{3}{10}$ y $\frac{1}{2}$ es equivalente a $\frac{5}{10}$. Mateo puede sumar $\frac{3}{10} + \frac{5}{10}$ para obtener $\frac{8}{10}$, que es igual a 0.8.

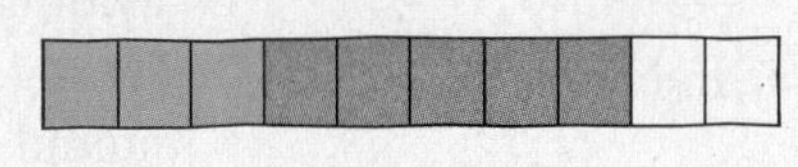

reciprocal A factor by which you multiply a given number so that their product is 1. For example, $\frac{3}{5}$ is the reciprocal of $\frac{5}{3}$, and $\frac{5}{3}$ is the reciprocal of $\frac{3}{5}$ because $\frac{3}{5} \times \frac{5}{3} = 1$. Note that the reciprocal of $1\frac{2}{3}$ is $\frac{3}{5}$ because $1\frac{2}{3} \times \frac{3}{5} = 1$.

recíproco Un factor por el cual multiplicas un dado de manera que su producto sea 1. Por ejemplo, $\frac{3}{5}$ es el recíproco de $\frac{5}{3}$, y $\frac{5}{3}$ es el recíproco de $\frac{3}{5}$, porque $\frac{3}{5} \times \frac{5}{3} = 1$. Observa que el recíproco de $1\frac{2}{3}$ es $\frac{3}{5}$, porque $1\frac{2}{3} \times \frac{3}{5} = 1$.

U

underestimate To make an estimate that is slightly less than the actual value.

estimación por defecto Una estimación que es un poco menor que el valor real.

Index

Acknowledgments

Cover Design
Three Communication Design, Chicago

Photographs
Photo locators denoted as follows: Top (T), Center (C), Bottom (B), Left (L), Right (R), Background (Bkgd)

002 Serguei Liachenko/Fotolia; **003** Christy Thompson/Shutterstock; **013** Gigra/Fotolia; **040** Serguei Liachenko/Fotolia; **061** ©2001 Hilary B. Price/King Features Syndicate; **074** Photoexpert117/Fotolia.

CONNECTED MATHEMATICS® 3

Two-Dimensional Measurement

Lappan, Phillips, Fey, Friel

Covering and Surrounding

Two-Dimensional Measurement

Looking Ahead

Suppose you are building a rectangular storm shelter for a national park. You have 24 square meters of flooring. **What** are the dimensions of a rectangle that would give your shelter the greatest perimeter? The least perimeter?

Suppose you need to make sails shaped as triangles and quadrilaterals for a schooner (SKOON ur). **What** measurements do you need to make to find how much cloth you need for the sails?

Suppose you are making a custom package with rectangular lateral faces and triangular bases. **How** much cardboard do you need to build the package?

You can describe the size of something in different ways. You can use words such as long, short, thin, or wide. Other words like big or small may also give a general description of size. When you want to be more specific, you can use numbers. Numbers require units of measurement, such as centimeters, square feet, or cubic inches.

All these questions involve size. In this Unit, you will learn mathematical ideas and techniques that can help you answer questions about size.

Mathematical Highlights

Two-Dimensional Measurement

In *Covering and Surrounding*, you will explore areas and perimeters of figures. Attention is given especially to quadrilaterals and triangles. You will also explore surface area and volume of rectangular prisms.

The Investigations in this Unit will help you

- Analyze what it means to measure area and perimeter
- Relate perimeter to surrounding a figure and area to covering a figure
- Develop strategies, procedures, and formulas, stated in words or symbols, for finding areas and perimeters of rectangles, parallelograms, and triangles
- Investigate relationships between perimeter and area, including that one can vary while the other stays fixed
- Analyze how the area of a triangle and the area of a parallelogram are related to the area of a rectangle
- Use nets that are made from rectangles and triangles to find surface areas of prisms
- Find the volume of rectangular prisms with fractional side lengths
- Use perimeter, area, surface area, and volume to solve problems.

When you encounter a new problem, it is a good idea to ask yourself questions. In this Unit, you might ask questions such as:

What attributes of a shape are important to measure?

Is an exact answer required?

How do I recognize whether area or perimeter of a figure is involved?

What am I looking for when I find area? When I find perimeter?

What relationships involving area, perimeter, or both, will help solve the problem?

How can I determine the surface area of a prism from a net or a three-dimensional representation of the prism?

What is the difference between area of a two-dimensional figure and surface area of a prism?

Common Core State Standards

Mathematical Practices and Habits of Mind

In the *Connected Mathematics* curriculum you will develop an understanding of important mathematical ideas by solving problems and reflecting on the mathematics involved. Every day, you will use "habits of mind" to make sense of problems and apply what you learn to new situations. Some of these habits are described by the *Common Core State Standards for Mathematical Practices* (MP).

MP1 Make sense of problems and persevere in solving them.

When using mathematics to solve a problem, it helps to think carefully about

- data and other facts you are given and what additional information you need to solve the problem;
- strategies you have used to solve similar problems and whether you could solve a related simpler problem first;
- how you could express the problem with equations, diagrams, or graphs;
- whether your answer makes sense.

MP2 Reason abstractly and quantitatively.

When you are asked to solve a problem, it often helps to

- focus first on the key mathematical ideas;
- check that your answer makes sense in the problem setting;
- use what you know about the problem setting to guide your mathematical reasoning.

MP3 Construct viable arguments and critique the reasoning of others.

When you are asked to explain why a conjecture is correct, you can

- show some examples that fit the claim and explain why they fit;
- show how a new result follows logically from known facts and principles.

When you believe a mathematical claim is incorrect, you can

- show one or more counterexamples—cases that don't fit the claim;
- find steps in the argument that do not follow logically from prior claims.

MP4 Model with mathematics.

When you are asked to solve problems, it often helps to

- think carefully about the numbers or geometric shapes that are the most important factors in the problem, then ask yourself how those factors are related to each other;
- express data and relationships in the problem with tables, graphs, diagrams, or equations, and check your result to see if it makes sense.

MP5 Use appropriate tools strategically.

When working on mathematical questions, you should always

- decide which tools are most helpful for solving the problem and why;
- try a different tool when you get stuck.

MP6 Attend to precision.

In every mathematical exploration or problem-solving task, it is important to

- think carefully about the required accuracy of results; is a number estimate or geometric sketch good enough, or is a precise value or drawing needed?
- report your discoveries with clear and correct mathematical language that can be understood by those to whom you are speaking or writing.

MP7 Look for and make use of structure.

In mathematical explorations and problem solving, it is often helpful to

- look for patterns that show how data points, numbers, or geometric shapes are related to each other;
- use patterns to make predictions.

MP8 Look for and express regularity in repeated reasoning.

When results of a repeated calculation show a pattern, it helps to

- express that pattern as a general rule that can be used in similar cases;
- look for shortcuts that will make the calculation simpler in other cases.

You will use all of the Mathematical Practices in this Unit. Sometimes, when you look at a Problem, it is obvious which practice is most helpful. At other times, you will decide on a practice to use during class explorations and discussions. After completing each Problem, ask yourself:

- What mathematics have I learned by solving this Problem?
- What Mathematical Practices were helpful in learning this mathematics?

Designing Bumper Cars: Extending and Building on Area and Perimeter

Most people enjoy rides at amusement parks and carnivals such as merry go rounds, Ferris wheels, roller coasters, and bumper cars. A company called Midway Amusement Rides (MARS for short) builds rides for amusement parks and carnivals. To do well in their business, MARS designers have to use mathematical thinking.

1.1 Designing Bumper-Car Rides

Area and Perimeter

Bumper cars are a popular ride at amusement parks and carnivals. Bumper cars ride on a smooth floor with bumper rails surrounding it. MARS makes their bumper-car floors from 1 meter-by-1 meter square tiles. The bumper rails are built from 1 meter sections.

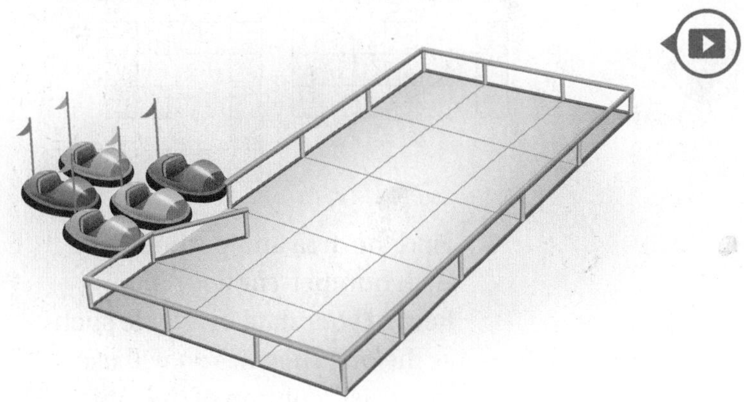

Common Core State Standards

6.NS.C.8 Solve real-world and mathematical problems by graphing points in all four quadrants of the coordinate plane . . .

6.EE.A.3 Apply the properties of operations to generate equivalent expressions.

6.EE.C.9 Use variables to represent two quantities in a real-world problem that change in relationship to one another; write an equation to express one quantity, thought of as the dependent variable, in terms of the other quantity, thought of as the independent variable. Analyze the relationship between the dependent and independent variables using graphs and tables, and relate these to the equation.

Also 6.EE.A.2, 6.EE.A.2a, 6.EE.A.2c, 6.EE.B.6, 6.G.A.1

Two measures tell you important facts about the size of the bumper-car floor plans. The number of tiles needed to cover the floor is a measure of **area.** The number of rail sections needed to surround the floor is a measure of **perimeter.** The bumper-car floor you just saw had the shape of a rectangle. Next, you will see bumper-car floors that are not rectangles.

Problem 1.1

When a customer places an order, the designers at MARS use square tiles to model possible floor plans. MARS receives the customer orders below. Experiment with square tiles and then sketch some designs on grid paper for the customer to consider.

A 1. Lone Star Carnivals in Texas wants a bumper-car ride that covers 36 square meters of floor space and has lots of rail sections. Sketch two or three possible floor plans.

2. Badger State Shows in Wisconsin requests a bumper-car ride with 36 square meters of floor space and 26 meters of rail sections. Sketch two or three floor plans for this request.

B The designers at MARS created four designs for bumper-car rides.

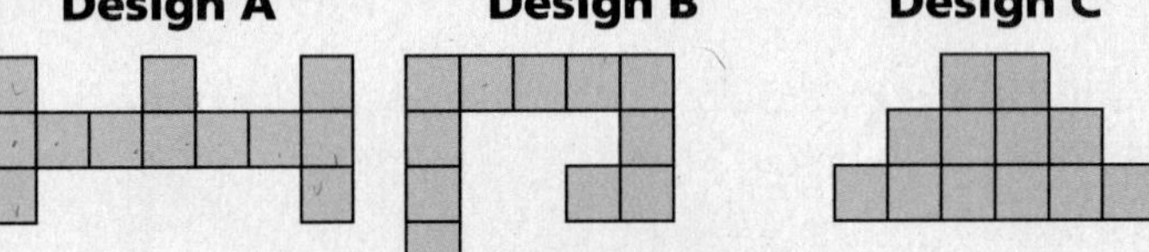

1. Find the area and perimeter of each bumper-car floor plan. Record your data in a table such as the one shown. You will use the "Cost" column of the table in part (3).

Bumper-Car Floor Plans

Design	Area	Perimeter	Cost
A	■	■	■
B	■	■	■

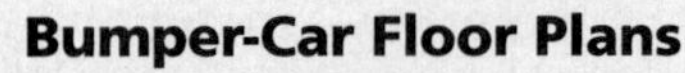

2. Which of the designs can be made from the same number of floor tiles? Will those designs have the same number of rail sections? Explain.

3. The designers at MARS charge $25 for each rail section and $30 for each floor tile. For the designs with the same floor area, which design costs the most? Which design costs the least? Explain.

4. Rearrange the tiles in Design B to form a rectangle. Can you make more than one rectangle? If so, are the perimeters the same? Explain.

continued on the next page >

Problem 1.1 continued

C Riverview School orders a bumper-car ride in the shape of a rectangle for their fundraising festival. The MARS company sends the school Designs I, II, and III.

1. What is the area of each design? Explain how you found the area.
2. What is the perimeter of each design? Explain how you found the perimeter.

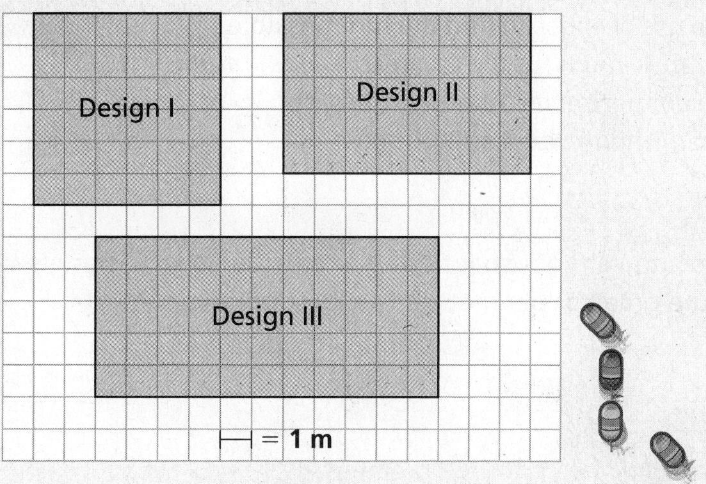

3. The dimensions of a rectangle are called **length** ℓ and **width** w. Look for patterns throughout Problem 1.1 to help you answer the questions below.

   a. Use words to describe a formula for finding the perimeter of a rectangle. Write the formula using symbols. Explain why it works.

   b. Use words to describe a formula for finding the area of a rectangle. Write the formula using symbols. Explain why it works.

   c. Find the perimeter and area of a rectangle with a width of 6 centimeters and a length of 15 centimeters.

Homework starts on page 14.

1.2 Building Storm Shelters
Constant Area, Changing Perimeter

Sometimes, during fierce winter storms, people are stranded in the snow. To prepare for this kind of emergency, parks often provide shelters at points along hiking trails.

When you make a floor plan for anything from a bumper-car ride to a storm shelter, you need to consider the use of space to find the best possible plan. Sometimes you want the greatest, or *maximum*, possible area or perimeter. At other times, you want the least, or *minimum*, area or perimeter.

If a rectangular floor space has a fixed area, what rectangle will have the greatest perimeter? The least perimeter?

Problem 1.2

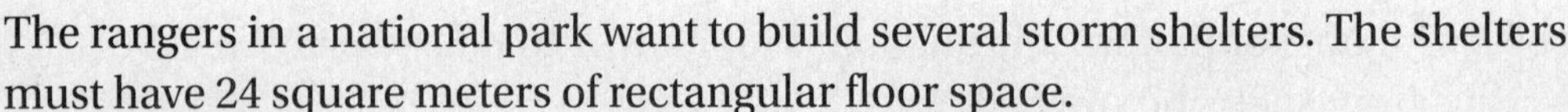

The rangers in a national park want to build several storm shelters. The shelters must have 24 square meters of rectangular floor space.

A Experiment with different rectangles that have whole-number dimensions. Sketch each possible floor plan on grid paper. Record your data in a table such as the one started below. Look for patterns, and describe the data.

Shelter Floor Plans

Rectangle	Length	Width	Perimeter	Area
1 m × 24 m	1 m	24 m	50 m	24 m^2

B Suppose the walls are made of flat rectangular panels that are 1 meter wide and have the needed height.

1. What determines how many wall panels are needed, area or perimeter? Explain your reasoning.
2. Which design would require the most panels? Explain.
3. Which design would require the fewest panels? Explain.

continued on the next page >

Problem 1.2 *continued*

C **1.** Use your table to make a graph, such as the one below, to compare lengths and perimeters of various rectangles with an area of 24 square meters.

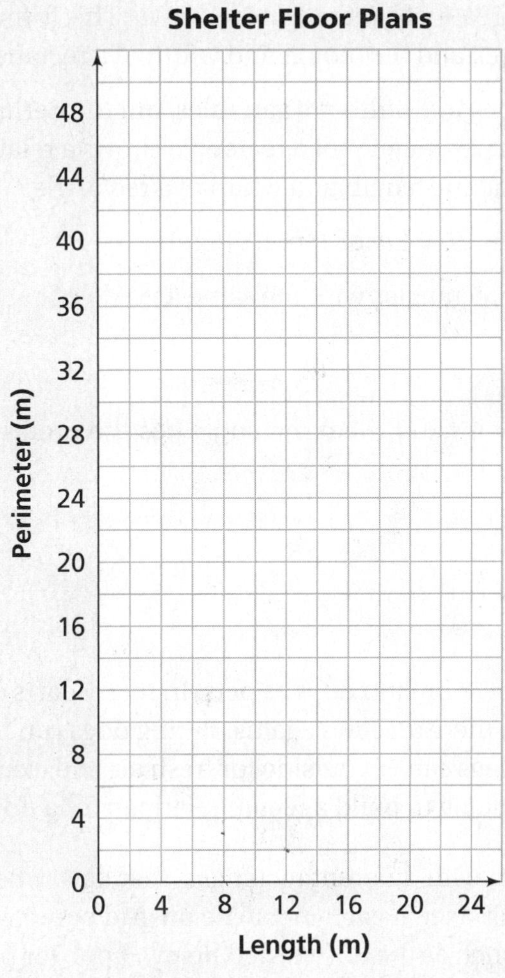

2. Describe the shape of the graph. How do the patterns that you saw in your table show up in the graph?

D **1.** Suppose you build a storm shelter with 36 square meters of rectangular floor space. Which design has the least perimeter? Which has the greatest perimeter? Explain your reasoning.

2. In general, describe the rectangle that has the greatest perimeter for a *fixed,* or unchanging, area. Describe the rectangle that has the least perimeter for a fixed area.

ACE Homework starts on page 14.

1.3 Fencing in Spaces

Constant Perimeter, Changing Area

In Problem 1.2, the length and width of rectangles changed, but the area was fixed. In this situation, length ℓ and width w are variables. The **formula,** or rule, for the area A of a rectangle is $A = \ell w$. This formula shows a relationship between area and the length and width of a rectangle.

In the next Problem, length and width are variables, but the perimeter is fixed. The formula for the perimeter P of a rectangle shows a relationship between the perimeter and the length and width of a rectangle:

$$P = 2\ell + 2w \text{ or } P = 2(\ell + w)$$

You have discovered that rectangles with the same area do not always have the same perimeter.

When the perimeter is fixed, what rectangle has the greatest area? The least area?

Problem 1.3

Americans have over 78 million dogs as pets. In many parts of the country, particularly in cities, there are laws against letting dogs run free. Many people build pens so their dogs can get outside for fresh air and exercise. Suppose you have 24 meters of fencing to build a rectangular pen for a dog.

A 1. Experiment with different rectangles that have whole-number dimensions. Sketch each rectangle on grid paper. Record your data in a table such as the one started below. Look for patterns, and describe the data.

Dog Pen Floor Plans

Rectangle	Length	Width	Perimeter	Area
1 m × 11 m	1 m	11 m	24 m	11 m^2

2. Which rectangle has the least area? Which rectangle has the greatest area?
3. Which design would you choose to build a pen for your dog? Explain your reasoning.

continued on the next page >

Problem 1.3 continued

B **1.** Use your table to make a graph, such as the one below, to compare the lengths and areas of various rectangles with a perimeter of 24 meters.

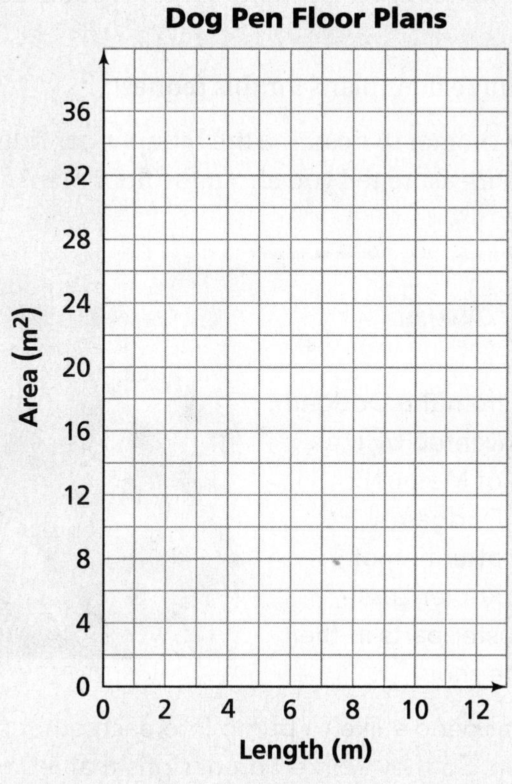

2. Describe the shape of the graph. How do the patterns that you saw in your table show up in the graph?

3. How is this graph similar to the graph you made in Problem 1.2? How is it different?

C **1.** Suppose you have 36 meters of fencing to surround a rectangular pen. Which rectangle has the least area? Which rectangle has the greatest area? Explain your reasoning.

2. In general, describe the rectangle that has the least area for a fixed perimeter. Describe the rectangle that has the greatest area for a fixed perimeter.

ACE Homework starts on page 14.

Applications | Connections | Extensions

Applications

1. Coney Island Park wants a bumper-car ride with 24 square meters of floor space and 22 meters of rail section. The floor plans do not have to be rectangular.

   a. Sketch at least three floor plans for this request.

   b. Use area and perimeter to describe the bumper-car ride plan. What does each measure tell you about the floor plan?

Did You Know?

Bumper cars came from the Dodgem, a rear-steering car invented by Max and Harold Stoeher of Methuen, Massachusetts. The Dodgem's popularity drew the attention of cousins Joseph and Robler Lusse, who made roller coaster parts in their Philadelphia machine shop.

The Lusses knew that people like to bump into each other and also want to choose who to bump. So they worked on designs that let a bumper car go from forward to reverse without going through neutral. They filed the first of 11 patents in 1922 for their bumper car.

For Exercises 2–4, experiment with tiles or square grid paper. Sketch your final answers on grid paper.

2. Draw two different shapes, each with an area of 16 square units. What is the perimeter of each shape?

3. Draw two different shapes, each with a perimeter of 16 units. What is the area of each shape?

4. Draw two different shapes, each with an area of 6 square units and perimeter of 12 units.

5. Use the designs below from Problem 1.1. Each design has an area of 12 square meters. Are the perimeters of the two designs the same? Explain your reasoning.

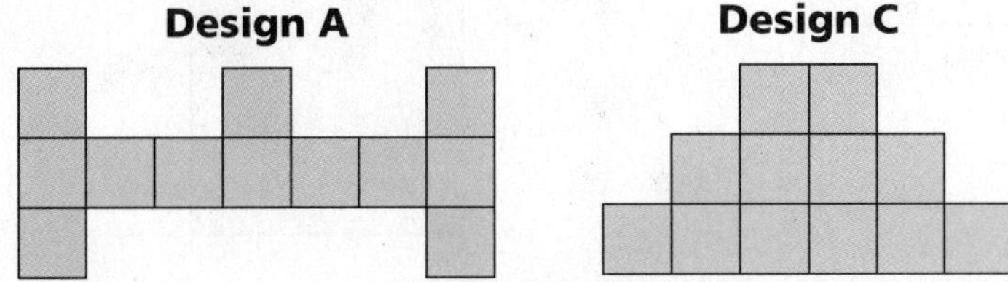

6. Copy the design below onto grid paper. Add six squares to make a new design with a perimeter of 30 units. Explain how the perimeter changes as you add new tiles to the figure.

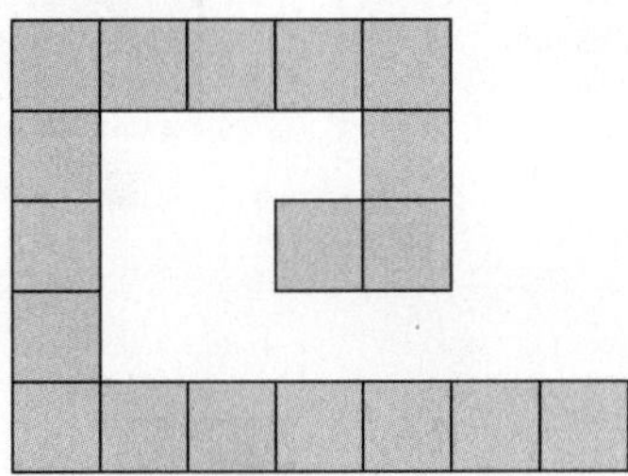

For Exercises 7–10, find the area and perimeter of each bumper-car floor plan.

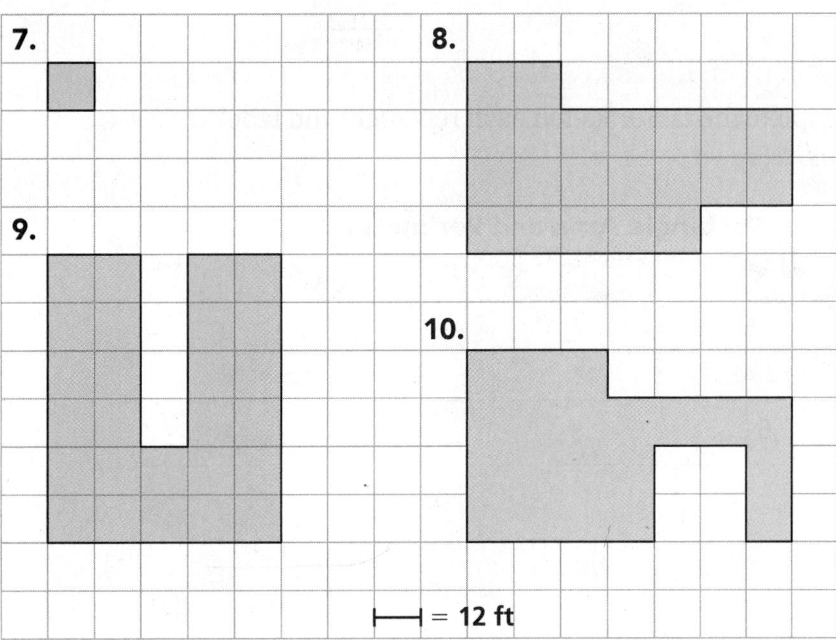

For Exercises 11–16, find the area and perimeter of each rectangle.

11.

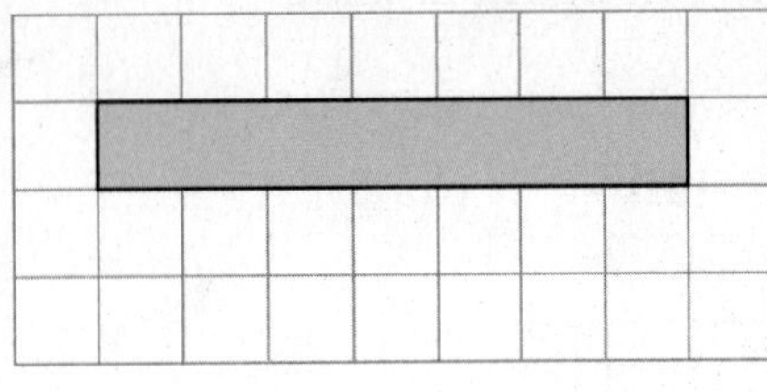

12.

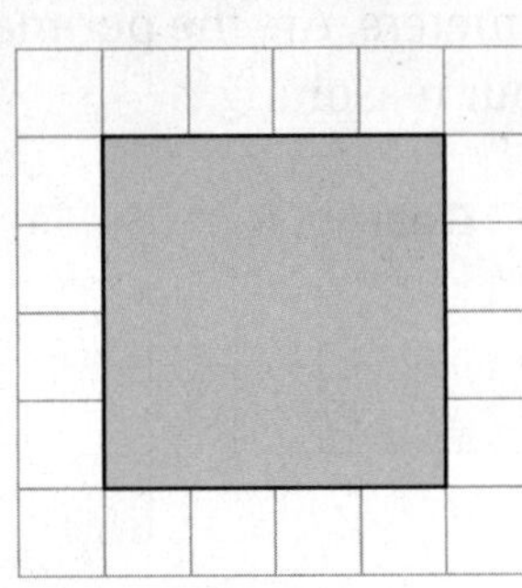

13.

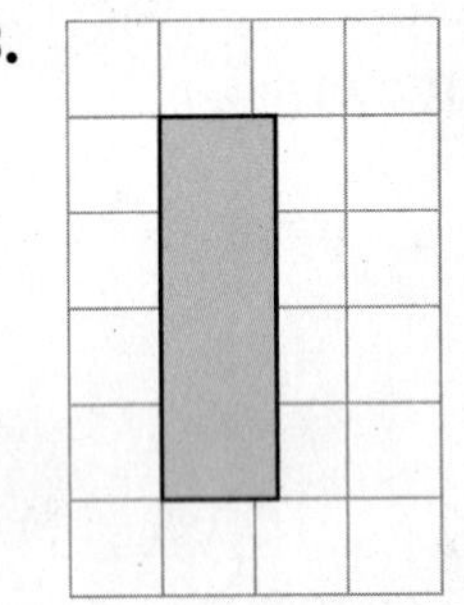

14.

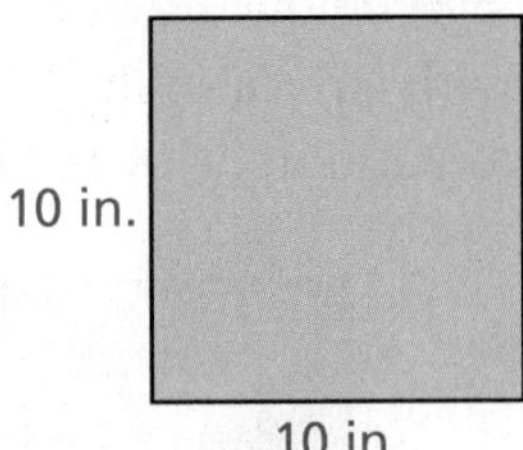

15.

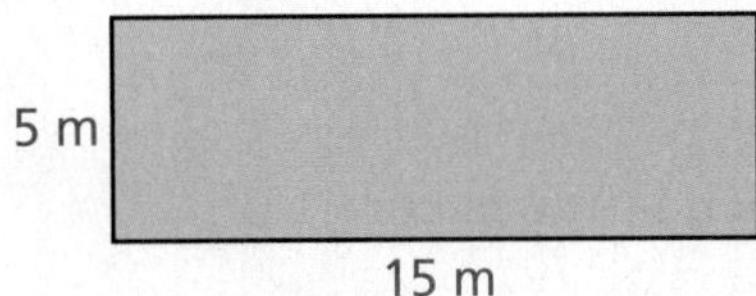

16.

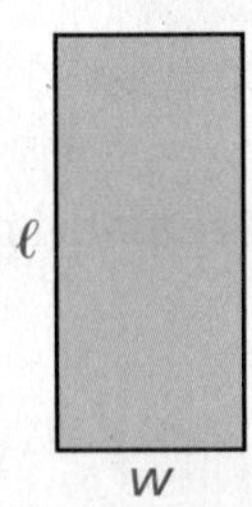

17. Copy and complete the table. Sketch each rectangle and label its dimensions.

Rectangle Area and Perimeter

Rectangle	Length (in.)	Width (in.)	Area (in.^{2})	Perimeter (in.)
A	5	6	■	■
B	4	13	■	■
C	$6\frac{1}{2}$	8	■	■

For Exercises 18 and 19, find the area and perimeter of each figure.

18.

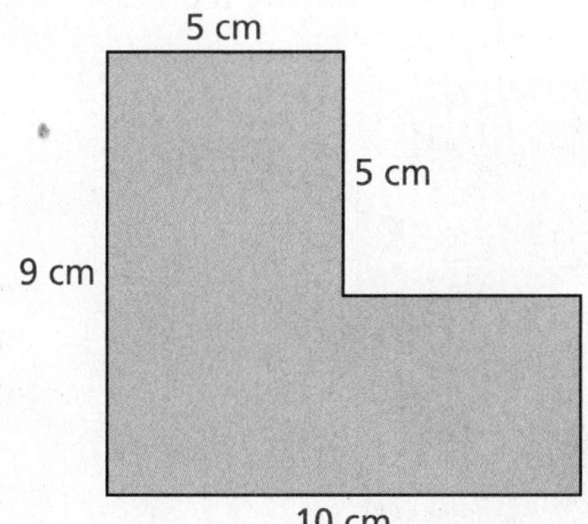

19.

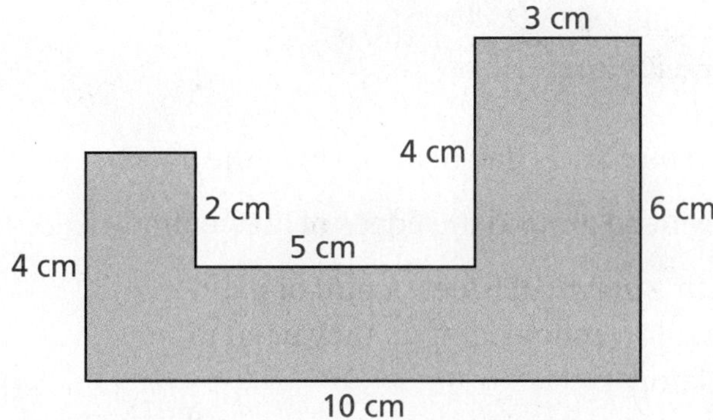

20. A student is tired of counting the individual rail sections around the outside of each bumper-car track. She starts to think of them as one long rail. She wraps a string around the outside, as shown.

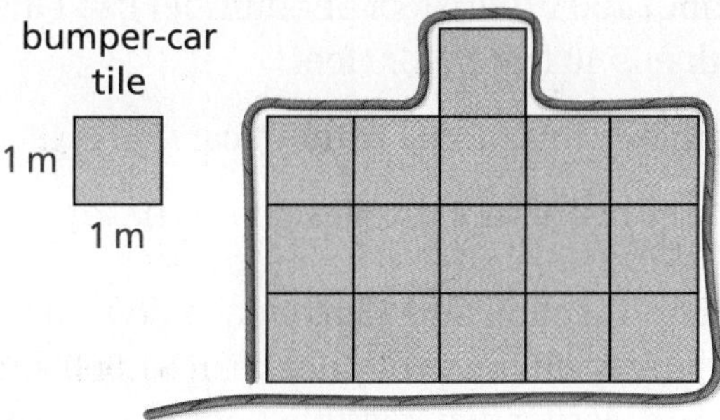

a. What do you think she does next?

b. How does this string method compare to counting the individual rail sections?

c. Can she use the string method to find the area? Explain your reasoning.

21. Karl and his dad are building a playhouse for Karl's younger sister. The floor of the playhouse will be a rectangle that is 6 feet by $8\frac{1}{2}$ feet.

a. How much carpeting do Karl and Karl's dad need to cover the floor?

b. How much molding do they need around the edges of the ceiling?

c. The walls are rectangles with a height of 6 feet. A pint of paint covers about 50 square feet. How much paint do they need to paint the inside walls? Explain.

d. Make your own plan for a playhouse. Figure out how much carpeting, paint, and molding you would need to build the playhouse.

22. MARS sells a deluxe model of bumper-car rides for $95 per square foot. Most rides require about 100 square feet per bumper car. One ride design is a rectangle that is 40 feet by 120 feet.

a. How much does it cost to buy this model without cars?

b. What is the maximum number of cars this design can have?

23. MARS charges $25 for each rail section and $30 for each floor tile. An amusement park company is willing to pay between $1,000 and $2,000 for a bumper-car floor. Design two possible floor plans. Find the area, perimeter, and cost for each.

24. Multiple Choice Each tile in this figure is 1 square centimeter. Which result is *not* possible to get by adding one tile to this figure?

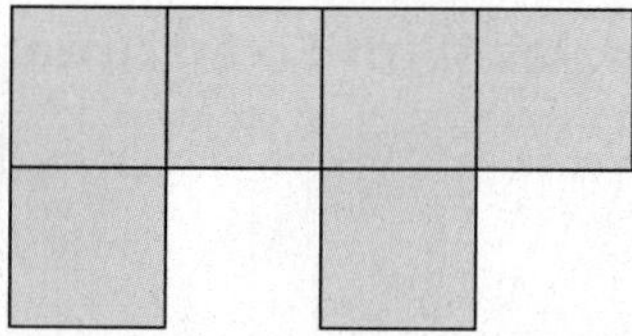

A. The area increases by 1 square centimeter and the perimeter increases by 1 centimeter.

B. The area increases by 1 square centimeter and the perimeter remains the same.

C. The area increases by 1 square centimeter and the perimeter decreases by 2 centimeters.

D. The area increases by 1 square centimeter and the perimeter increases by 2 centimeters.

25. Nu is designing a rectangular sandbox. The bottom is 16 square feet. Which dimensions require the least amount of material for the sides of the sandbox?

26. Alyssa is designing a garage with a rectangular floor area of 240 square feet.

a. List the length and width, in feet, of all the possible garages Alyssa can make. Use whole-number dimensions.

b. Which rectangles are reasonable for a garage floor? Explain.

In Exercises 27–29, the area of a rectangle is given. For each area, follow the steps below.

a. Sketch all the rectangles with the given area and whole-number side lengths. Record the length, width, area, and perimeter in a table.

b. Sketch a graph of the length and perimeter. Use the graph from Problem 1.2 as a reference.

c. Describe how you can use the table and graph to find the rectangle with the greatest perimeter and the rectangle with the least perimeter.

27. 30 square meters **28.** 20 square meters **29.** 64 square meters

30. The graph shows the lengths and perimeters for rectangles with a fixed area and whole-number dimensions.

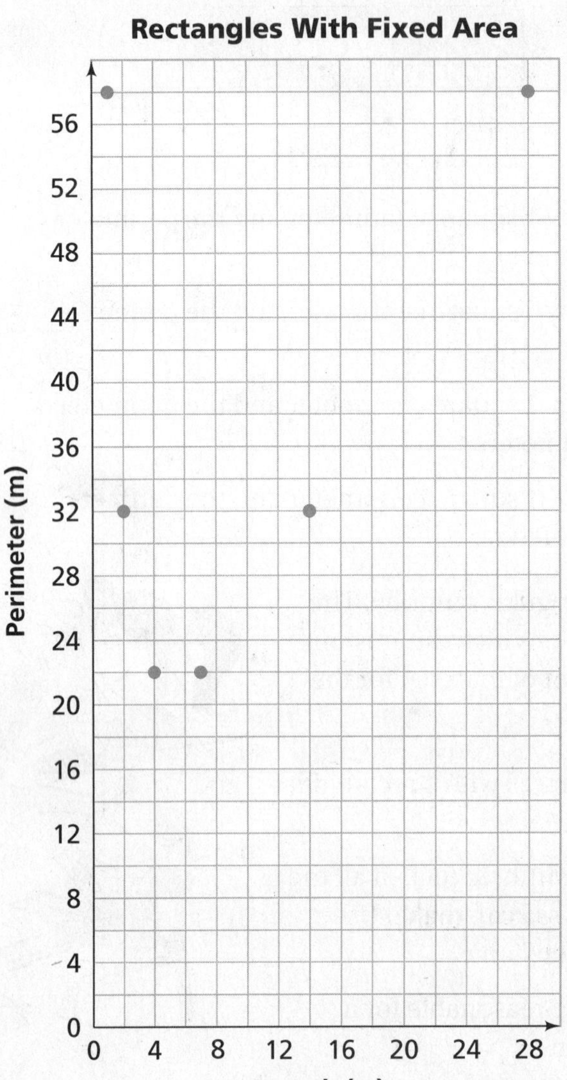

a. What is the perimeter of a rectangle with a length of 2 meters? What is its width?

b. Describe the dimensions and shape of the rectangle that has the greatest perimeter represented in the graph.

c. Describe the dimensions and shape of the rectangle that has the least perimeter represented in the graph.

d. What is the fixed area? Explain your reasoning.

31. The graph shows the lengths and areas for rectangles with a fixed perimeter and whole-number dimensions.

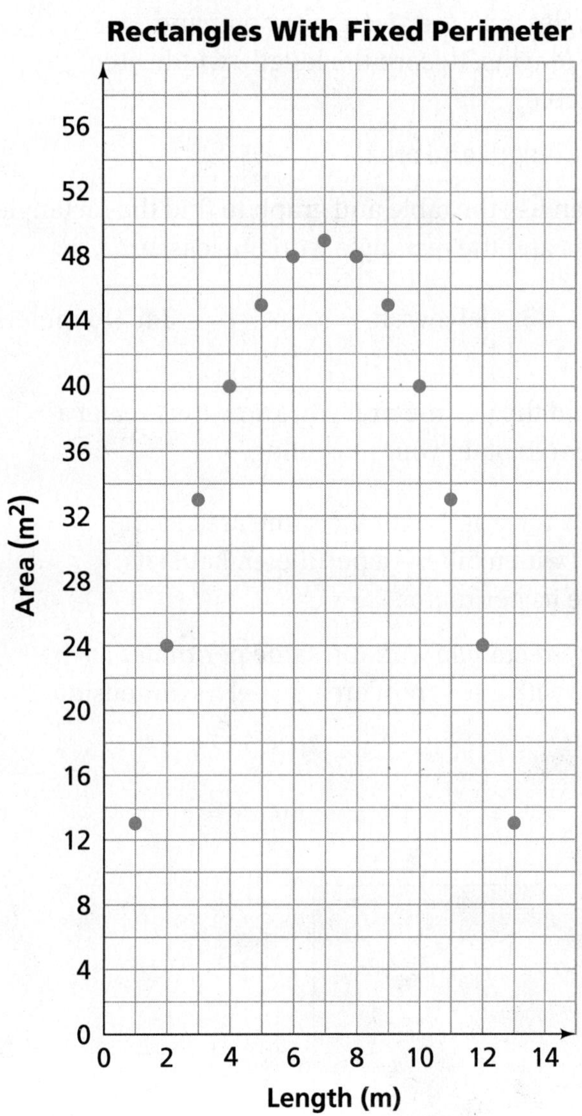

a. What is the area of a rectangle with a length of 2 meters? What is its width?

b. Describe the dimensions and shape of the rectangle that has the greatest area represented in the graph.

c. Describe the dimensions and shape of the rectangle that has the least area represented in the graph.

d. What is the fixed perimeter? Explain your reasoning.

For Exercises 32–34, the perimeter of a rectangle is given. For each perimeter, follow the steps below.

a. Sketch all the rectangles with the given perimeter and whole-number side lengths. Record the length, width, area, and perimeter in a table.

b. Sketch a graph of the length and area.

c. Describe how you can use the table and graph to find the rectangle with the greatest area and the rectangle with the least area.

32. 8 meters **33.** 20 meters **34.** 15 meters

35. Diego says, "You can find the perimeter if you know the area of a rectangle." Do you agree? Explain your reasoning.

36. **a.** On grid paper, draw a rectangle with the same area as the rectangle below, but with a different perimeter. Label its dimensions and give its perimeter.

b. On grid paper, draw a rectangle with the same perimeter as the rectangle below, but with a different area. Label its dimensions and give its area.

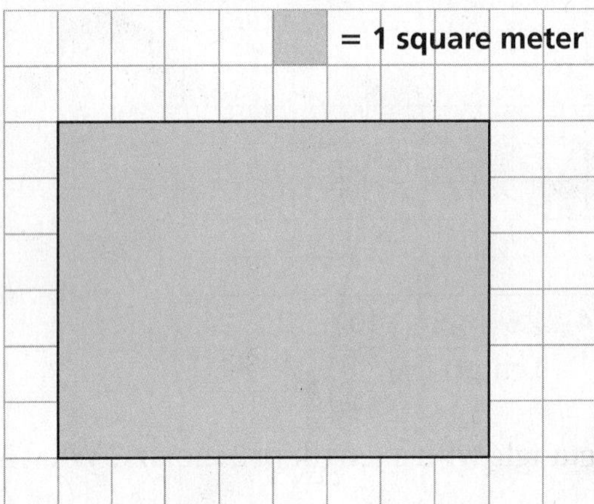

Connections

37. Multiple Choice How many square feet are in one square yard?

A. 1 square foot **B.** 3 square feet

C. 9 square feet **D.** 27 square feet

38. Describe a flat surface in your home or classroom with an area of about 1 square foot. Describe another surface with an area of about 1 square yard.

For Exercises 39–44, determine whether or not the measures in each pair are the same. If not, tell which measure is greater. Explain your reasoning.

39. 1 square yard or 1 square foot

40. 5 feet or 60 inches

41. 12 meters or 120 centimeters

42. 12 yards or 120 feet

43. 50 centimeters or 500 millimeters

44. 1 square meter or 1 square yard

45. Billie drew a 4-by-6 rectangle on grid paper. She started at a corner and cut a path to the opposite corner. Then she slid the piece over to the opposite edge, making the straight edges match.

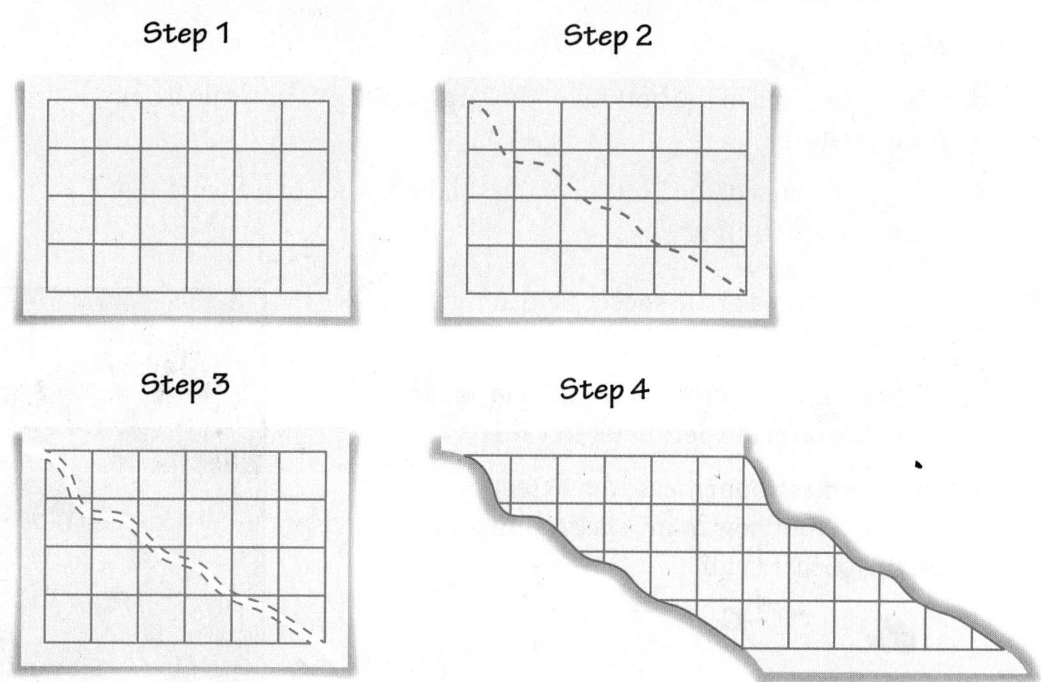

Are the area and perimeter of her new figure the same as, less than, or greater than the area and perimeter of the original figure? Explain.

46. For each area, sketch all the possible rectangles with whole-number dimensions on grid paper.

a. 18 square units **b.** 25 square units **c.** 23 square units

d. Explain how the factors of a number are related to the rectangles you sketched for parts (a)–(c).

For Exercises 47–50, find each product.

47. $4\frac{1}{4} \times 7\frac{2}{5}$ **48.** $12\frac{1}{4} \times 4$ **49.** $10\frac{5}{8} \times 2\frac{1}{4}$ **50.** $\frac{15}{6} \times \frac{7}{12}$

51. The product of two numbers is 20.

a. Suppose one number is $2\frac{1}{2}$. What is the other number?

b. Suppose one number is $1\frac{1}{4}$. What is the other number?

c. Suppose one number is $3\frac{1}{3}$. What is the other number?

52. Midge and Jon are making brownies. They use a 10 inch-by-10 inch baking pan. They want to cut the brownies into equal-sized pieces. For each number of brownies in parts (a)–(c), do the following.

- Sketch the cuts you would make to get the given number of pieces.
- Give the dimensions of one piece.

a. 25 pieces **b.** 20 pieces **c.** 30 pieces

d. What is the area of the bottom of the largest piece of brownie from parts (a)–(c)?

e. What is the area of the bottom of the smallest piece of brownie from parts (a)–(c)?

53. a. What is the area of the soccer field at right in square feet? What is the perimeter in feet?

b. What is the area of the soccer field in square yards? What is the perimeter in yards?

c. Jamilla's classroom measures 15 feet by 25 feet. About how many classrooms will fit on this soccer field?

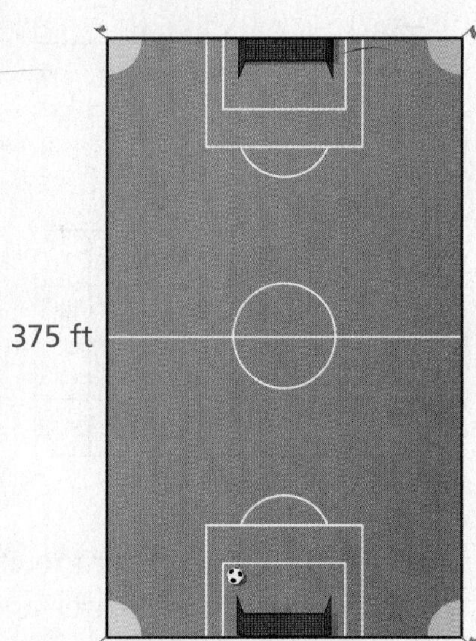

54. a. Find the area of the following rectangle.

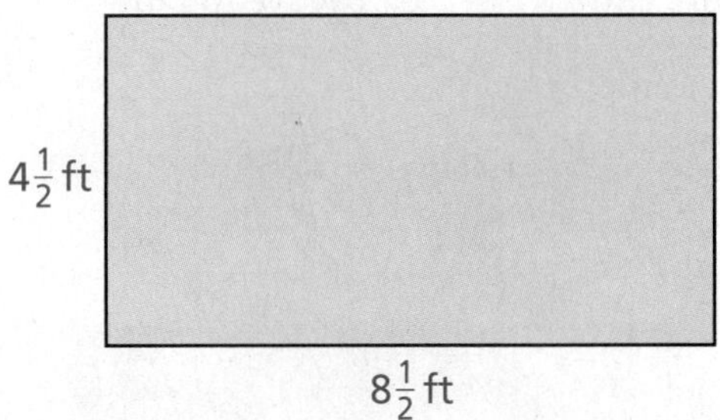

b. Amy says to find the area, you just multiply the length times the width:

area = $8\frac{1}{2}$ feet × $4\frac{1}{2}$ feet, or $38\frac{1}{4}$ square feet

Nathan divides the rectangle into four smaller rectangles. He says the area of the larger rectangle is the sum of the areas of smaller rectangles and writes the following:

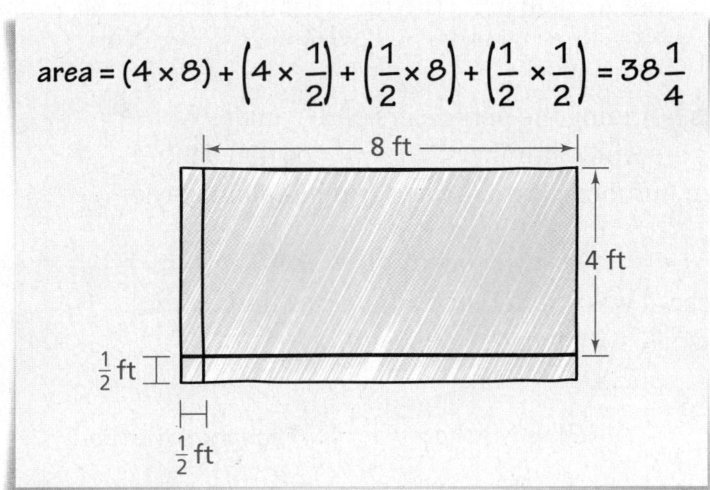

Which method is correct? Explain your reasoning.

55. The area of a square is 169 square centimeters. What is its perimeter? Explain how you found your answer.

56. The area of a rectangle is 120 square centimeters. Can you find its perimeter? Explain.

57. Multiple Choice The area of a storm shelter is 24 square meters. The length is $5\frac{1}{3}$ meters. What is the width of the storm shelter in meters?

F. $4\frac{1}{2}$ m **G.** $4\frac{1}{3}$ m **H.** $4\frac{1}{4}$ m **J.** $4\frac{1}{5}$ m

58. You can seat four people for dinner at a square table, one person on each side. With two square tables put together, you can seat six people.

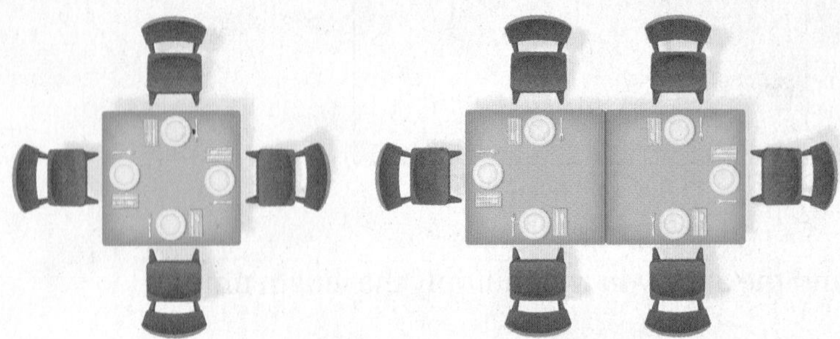

How would you arrange 36 square tables to make a rectangular table that seats the greatest number of people? Explain your reasoning.

59. For parts (a)–(c), list the dimensions of all the rectangles that you can make from the given number of square tiles.

a. 60 tiles **b.** 61 tiles **c.** 62 tiles

d. How can you use your work in parts (a)–(c) to list the factors of 60, 61, and 62?

60. A group of students is finding the perimeters of rectangles whose lengths and widths are whole numbers. They notice that all the perimeters are even numbers. Is this always true? Explain why or why not.

61. Stella, Gia, and Richard wrote different formulas for finding the perimeter of a rectangle with length ℓ and width w.

Stella's Method	Gia's Method	Richard's Method
$P = 2(\ell + w)$	$P = 2\ell + 2w$	$P = \ell + w + \ell + w$

Who is correct? Explain your reasoning.

62. A rectangle has a length of 5 inches and a width of $7\frac{1}{2}$ inches. What is the perimeter of the rectangle?

63. A rectangle has a perimeter of 196 meters and a length of 50 meters. What is the width of the rectangle? Explain how you found the width.

64. Matt wrote the following formulas for the area A and the perimeter P of a square with side length s.

$$A = s^2$$
$$P = 4s$$

Sophia says these formulas are not correct because a square is a special rectangle and these formulas do not look like the formulas for the area and perimeter of a rectangle. Who is correct? Explain your reasoning.

65. Use a formula to find the area and perimeter of a square if its side length is 11 inches.

66. Use a formula to find the area and perimeter of a square if its side length is $12\frac{1}{2}$ inches.

67. If the area of a square is 144 square centimeters, what is its side length? Explain your reasoning by using a formula.

Did You Know?

A *golden rectangle* is a rectangle that has special side lengths. The ratio of a golden rectangle's short side to long side is approximately 1 to 1.62. There are many examples of the golden ratio in nature. Some artists use golden rectangles in sculptures, paintings, and architecture because they are appealing to the eye. People in finance use the golden ratio in a strategy called Fibonacci retracement.

Mathematicians have also studied the golden ratio because of its interesting properties. They noticed that the ratio of (length + width) to width is the same as the ratio of width to length. The ratio is approximately 1.62 to 1.

68. You can find the golden ratio in the dimensions of a Nautilus shell.

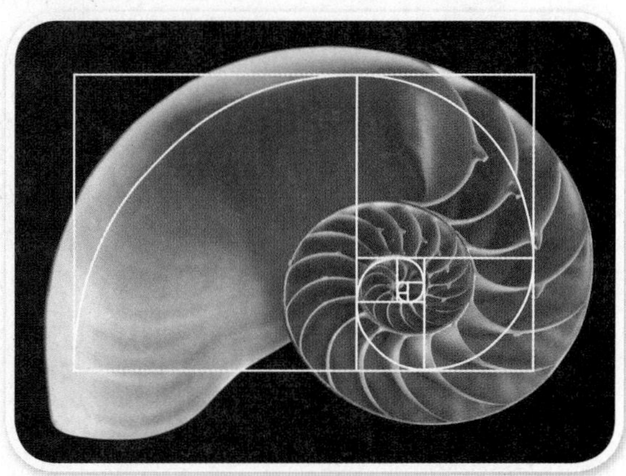

a. Examine the picture. Find at least three nonsquare rectangles. Write the ratio of length to width for each rectangle. Express each ratio as a decimal.

b. The Nautilus shell is very popular among people who collect seashells. Why do you think the Nautilus shell is so popular?

69. The Parthenon is an example of a mathematical approach to architecture. The photograph below shows several examples of golden rectangles.

a. Measure the dimensions of the three golden rectangles in the photograph in centimeters. Write the ratio of length to width for each rectangle. Write each ratio as a fraction and then as a decimal. Compare the ratios to each other and to the golden ratio.

b. The height of the Parthenon was about 64 feet. What must its width be to be considered a golden rectangle?

Extensions

70. Suppose a square sheet of paper has a perimeter of 1 meter.

a. What is the length of each side (in meters)?

b. Suppose you fold the square sheet in half. What new shape do you have? What are the lengths of the shape's four sides in meters? What is the perimeter?

c. Suppose you fold over the top $\frac{1}{4}$ of the square. What new shape do you have? What are the lengths of the shape's four sides in meters? What is the perimeter?

d. Suppose you fold over only the top $\frac{1}{8}$ of the square. What new shape do you have? What are the lengths of the shape's four sides in meters? What is the perimeter?

e. What do you predict the perimeter of the shape would be if you were to fold over $\frac{1}{16}$ of the square?

71. Design a rectangle with an area of 18 square centimeters such that its length is twice its width.

72. Suppose you know the perimeter of a rectangle. Can you find its area? Explain why or why not.

73. Shapes that are not rectangles can also be made from tiles. A *pentomino* (pen TAWM in oh) is a shape made from five identical square tiles connected along their edges.

- Make this pentomino with your tiles:

- For each part, sketch the new figure on grid paper and show where you would add the tile(s).

a. Sara claims you can add one tile to the pentomino and not increase the perimeter of the figure. Is Sara correct? Explain your reasoning.

b. Add tiles to the pentomino to make a new figure with a perimeter of 18 units.

c. What is the least number of tiles you can add to the pentomino to make a new figure with a perimeter of 18 units?

d. What is the greatest number of tiles you can add to the pentomino to make a new figure with a perimeter of 18 units? Describe the shape of the figure.

74. Turning or flipping a pentomino does not make a different pentomino, so these two figures are considered the same.

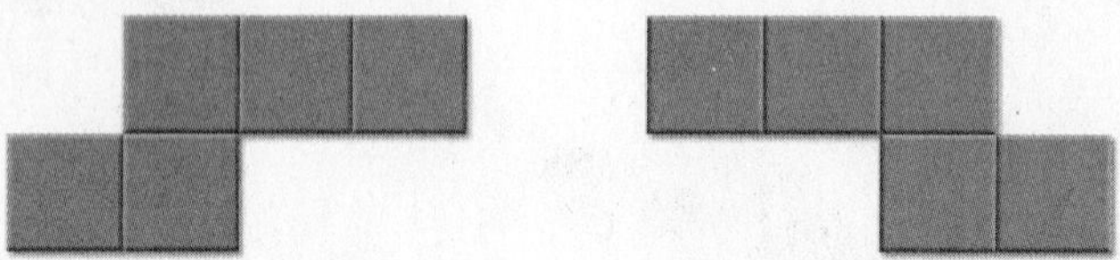

a. Find all the possible different pentominos. Sketch them on grid paper.

b. How do you know that you have found all the possible pentominos?

c. Which pentomino has the least perimeter? Which pentomino has the greatest perimeter?

In Exercises 75–77, Brevort Township wants to find the area and perimeter of two of its most popular lakes by using a transparent grid.

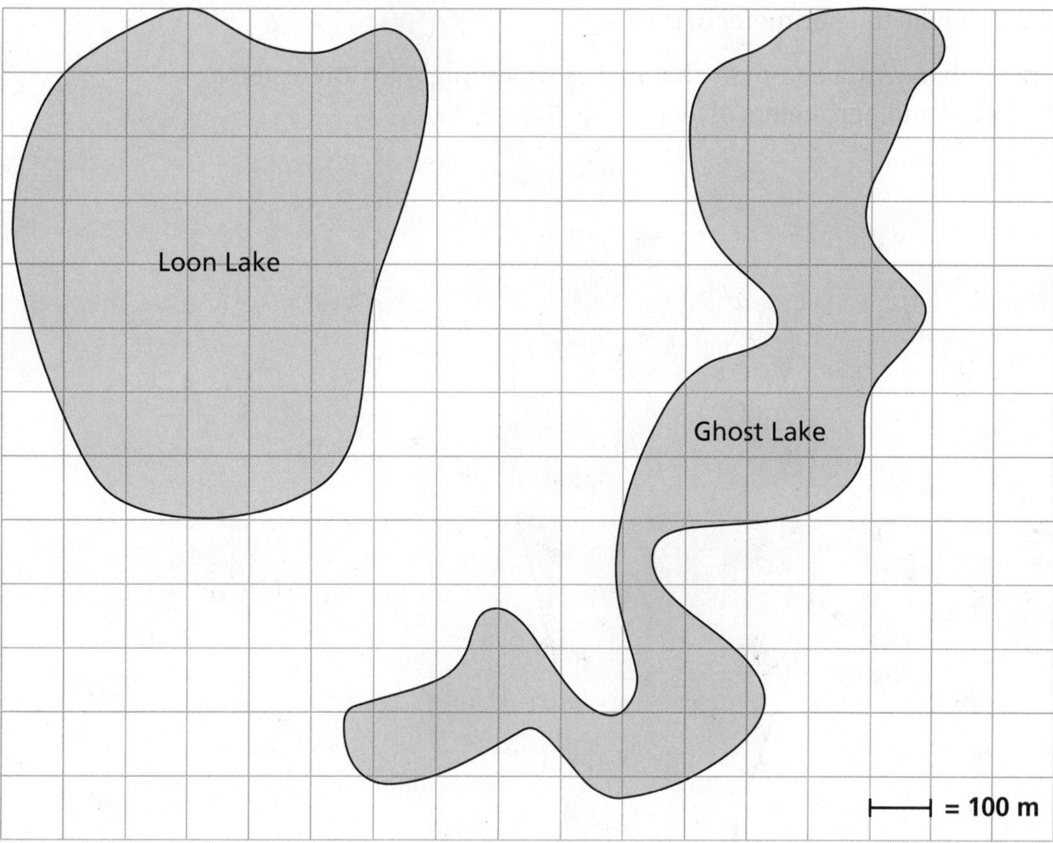

75. a. Estimate the area of each lake.

b. How could you get a more accurate estimate?

76. a. How could you find the perimeter of each lake?

b. Estimate the perimeter of each lake.

77. Use your estimates to answer the following questions. Explain your reasoning.

a. Naturalists claim that water birds need long shorelines for nesting and fishing. Which lake better supports water birds?

b. Sailboaters and waterskiers want a lake with room to cruise. Which lake works better for boating and skiing?

c. Which lake can better handle swimming, boating, and fishing all at the same time?

d. Which lake has more space for lakeside campsites?

78. A tracing of a foot is shown below on centimeter grid paper.

a. Estimate the area of the foot.

b. Estimate the perimeter of the foot.

c. Explain why a company that makes shoes might be interested in areas and perimeters of feet.

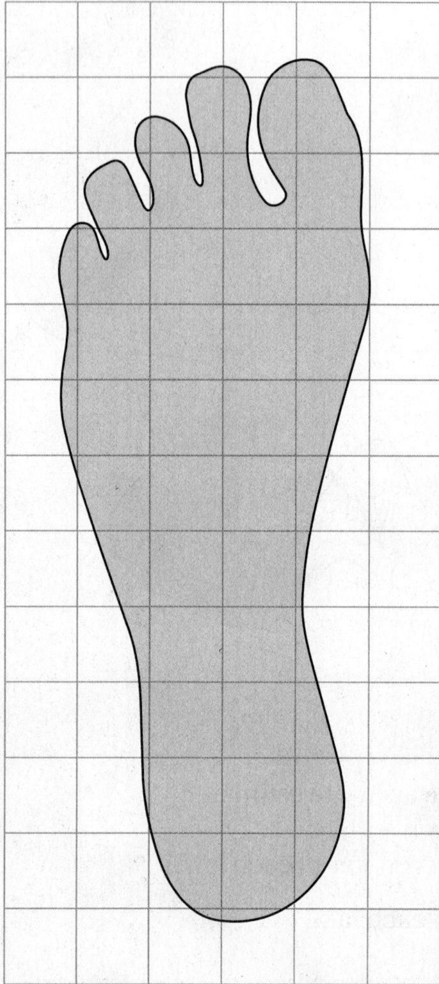

Mathematical Reflections 1

In this Investigation, you revisited strategies for finding the area and perimeter of a rectangle. You examined the areas and perimeters of figures made from square tiles. You also found that some arrangements of tiles have the same area but different perimeters. Other arrangements of the tiles have the same perimeter but different areas. The following questions will help you summarize what you have learned.

Think about these questions. Discuss your ideas with other students and your teacher. Then write a summary of your findings in your notebook.

1. a. **Explain** what area and perimeter of a figure means.
   b. **Describe** a strategy for finding the area and perimeter of any two-dimensional shape.
   c. **Describe** how you can find the area of a rectangle. Explain why this method works.
   d. **Describe** how you can find the perimeter of a rectangle. Explain why this method works.
2. a. Consider all the rectangles with the same area. Describe the rectangle with the least perimeter. Describe the rectangle with the greatest perimeter.
   b. Consider all the rectangles with the same perimeter. Describe the rectangle with the least area. Describe the rectangle with the greatest area.
   c. **Explain** how graphing relationships between length and perimeter or length and area helps explain patterns between area and perimeter.

Common Core Mathematical Practices

As you worked on the Problems in this Investigation, you used prior knowledge to make sense of them. You also applied Mathematical Practices to solve the Problems. Think back over your work, the ways you thought about the Problems, and how you used Mathematical Practices.

Ken described his thoughts in the following way:

In Problem 1.3, we made different rectangular shapes with a perimeter of 24 meters. We started by looking at our rectangles with different dimensions. We arranged these into a table. We noticed a pattern in our table.

The dimensions started to repeat at a certain point. The area increased to this repeated rectangle and then started to decrease. The rectangle with the dimensions where the repeat starts has the greatest area. John also noticed that the rectangle that has a shape closest to a square will have the greatest area. Our pattern worked with a perimeter of 36 meters, too.

Common Core Standards for Mathematical Practice

MP7 Look for and make use of structure.

- What other Mathematical Practices can you identify in Ken's reasoning?
- Describe a Mathematical Practice that you and your classmates used to solve a different Problem in this Investigation.

Measuring Triangles

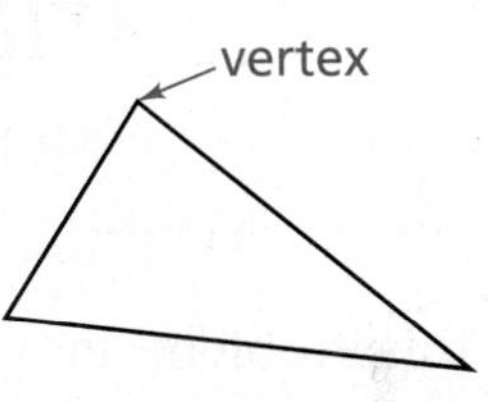

In Investigation 1, you studied rectangles and other figures that are examples of polygons. A **polygon** is a shape composed of line segments, called *sides*, that are joined together. A **vertex** (plural *vertices*) of a polygon is where two sides of the polygon meet.

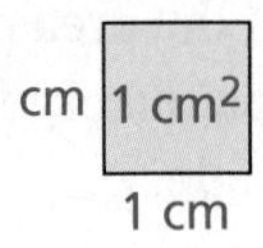

When you find the area of a polygon, you measure the enclosed space inside the polygon. Area is the number of square units that will "cover" the enclosed space. In this Investigation, you will mostly use square centimeters. A square centimeter is 1 centimeter by 1 centimeter. It has an area of 1 square centimeter.

- Draw one diagonal in the square to form two triangles. What is the area of each triangle?
- Is the perimeter of each of the triangles greater than, less than, or equal to 3 centimeters? Explain your thinking.

You can find the area of a figure by drawing it on a grid (or covering it with a transparent grid) and counting squares. In Investigation 1, you found a formula for finding the area and perimeter of a rectangle without counting squares. Now you will look for formulas for finding the area and perimeter of triangles using what you know about rectangles.

Common Core State Standards

6.EE.A.2a Write expressions that record operations with numbers and with letters standing for numbers.

6.EE.B.6 Use variables to represent numbers and write expressions when solving a real-world or mathematical problem; understand that a variable can represent an unknown number, or, depending on the purpose at hand, any number in a specified set.

6.G.A.1 Find the area of right triangles, other triangles, special quadrilaterals, and polygons by composing into rectangles or decomposing into triangles and other shapes; apply these techniques in the context of solving real-world and mathematical problems.

Also 6.EE.A.2, 6.EE.A.2c, 6.EE.A.3, 6.EE.A.4, 6.EE.C.9

First, it is important to review a few definitions. An angle whose measure is 90 degrees is a **right angle.** Right angles are sometimes indicated with a small red square. Two lines that form a right angle are **perpendicular lines.**

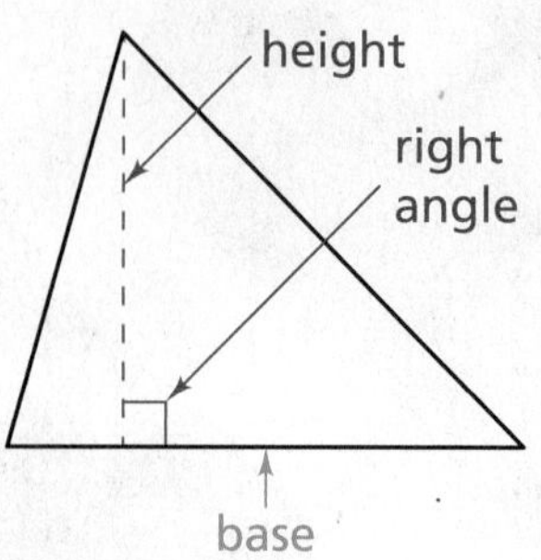

Triangles often seem to rest on one side. This side is usually called the **base.** Any of a triangle's three sides can serve as a base. The **height** of a triangle is the perpendicular distance from the vertex opposite the base to the base.

2.1 Triangles on Grids

Finding Area and Perimeter of Triangles

For this Problem several triangles are drawn on grid paper.

As you find the area of each triangle in this Problem, think about the patterns you observe that will help you write a formula for finding the area of any triangle.

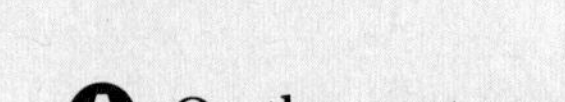

Problem 2.1

A On the next page, six triangles labeled A–F are drawn on a centimeter grid.

1. Find the perimeter of each triangle. Describe the strategies you use.
2. Find the area of each triangle. Describe the strategies you use.

B Look at triangles A–F again. Using the grid lines, draw the smallest possible rectangle around each triangle.

1. Find the area of each rectangle you drew. Record your data in a table with the areas of the triangles from Question A, part (2).
2. Compare the area of the rectangle to the area of the triangle. Describe a pattern that tells how the two are related.

C
1. Use your results from Question B to write a formula to find the area of any triangle. Explain why your formula works.
2. Use your formula to find the area of a triangle with a base of 8 inches and a height of $3\frac{1}{2}$ inches.

ACE Homework starts on page 42.

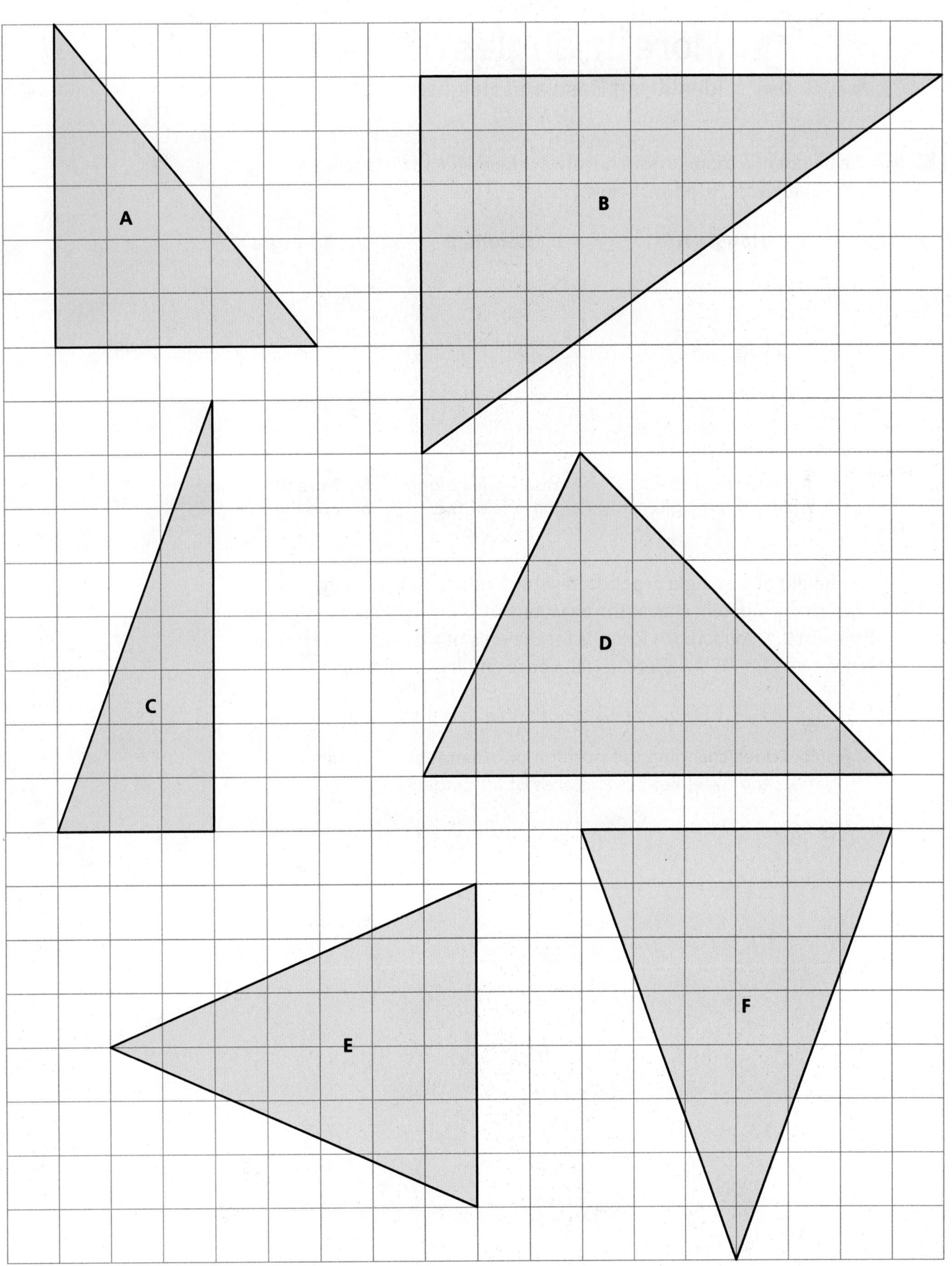
A
B
C
D
E
F

2.2 More Triangles
Identifying Base and Height

The height of a triangle does not always lie inside the triangle. (See Triangles A, B, and C below.)

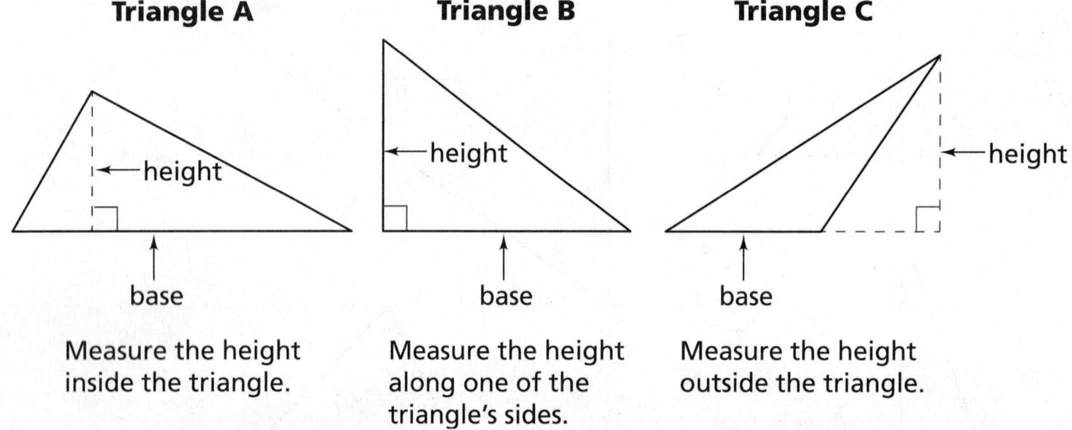

The height of a triangle depends on which side is chosen as the base. Choosing a different side as the base may result in a different height. In Problem 2.1, you found a formula for the area of a triangle. The formula is given by $A = \frac{1}{2}b \times h$. Here, b is the base and h is the height.

How does changing the position or orientation of a triangle affect the base, height, and area of a triangle?

Problem 2.2

A **1.** For each triangle, choose one side to use as the base. Use transparent centimeter grid paper to help you find the area of each triangle. Explain how you found the area. Include any calculations that you used.

Triangle D

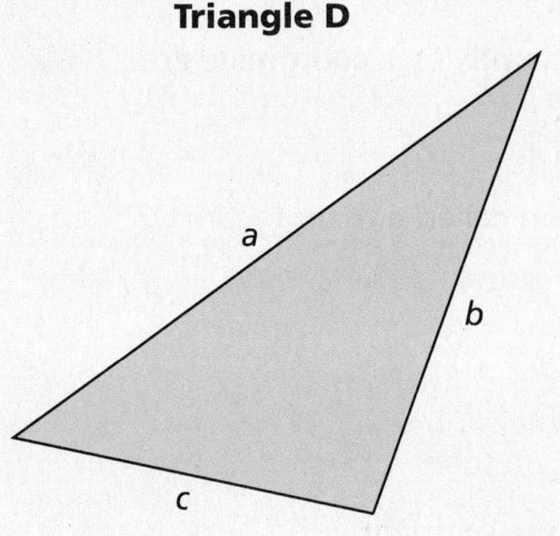

Triangle E

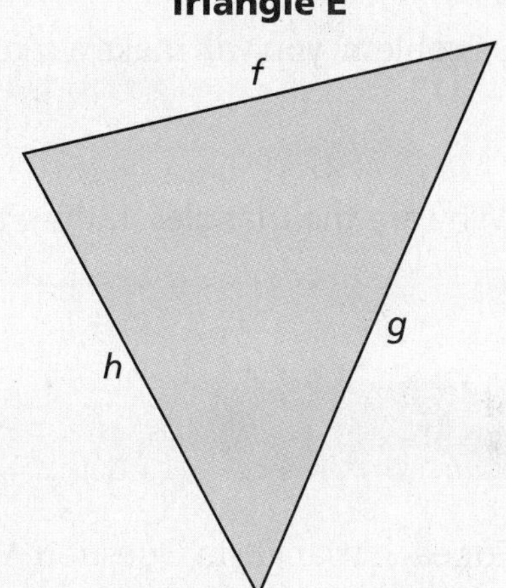

2. Find the area of each triangle in two other ways, using each of the other two sides as the base. Record the base, height, and area in a table.

Triangle D			Triangle E		
Base (cm)	Height (cm)	Area (cm²)	Base (cm)	Height (cm)	Area (cm²)
a			*f*		
b			*g*		
c			*h*		

B **1.** Does changing the side you choose as the base of a triangle change the area? Explain.

2. When finding the area of a triangle, are there advantages or disadvantages to choosing a particular side as the base? Explain.

C Maria claims that if a triangle's height falls outside the triangle, the formula for area will not work. Is Maria correct? Explain.

Homework starts on page 42.

2.3 Making Families of Triangles
Maintaining the Base and the Height

The word *family* can be used to describe relationships among objects.

- For example, if Tamar says that the fractions $\frac{1}{2}$, $\frac{2}{4}$, $\frac{3}{6}$, and $\frac{4}{8}$ form a family of fractions, what might she mean?

In this Problem, you will make a triangle family on a coordinate grid.

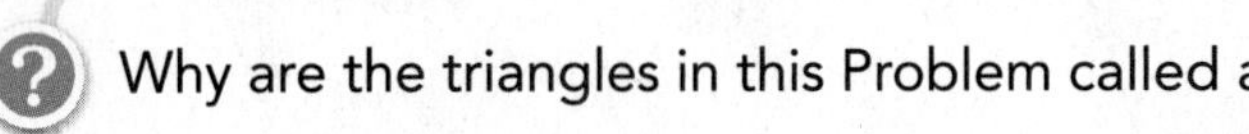

Why are the triangles in this Problem called a triangle family?

Problem 2.3

For each triangle in Question A, draw a segment 6 centimeters long on a separate piece of grid paper. Use the segment as a base for the triangle.

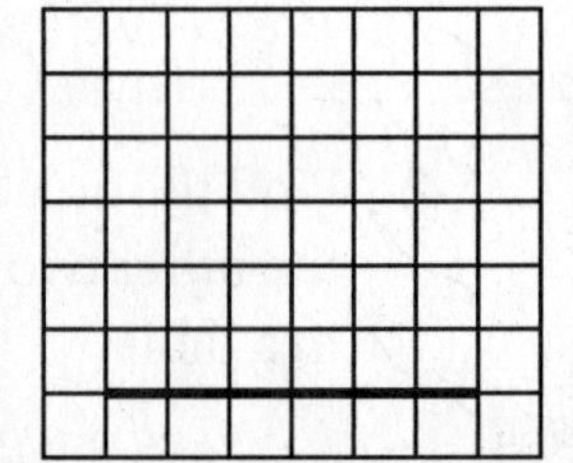

A 1. Sketch a right triangle with a height of 4 centimeters.

2. Sketch a different right triangle with a height of 4 centimeters.

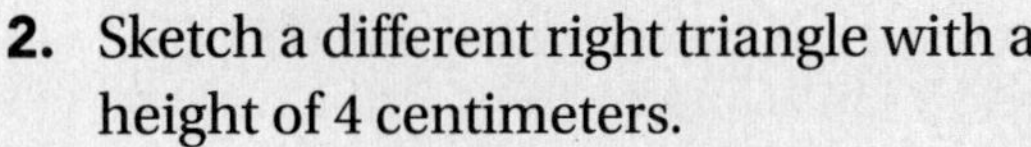

3. Sketch an isosceles triangle with a height of 4 centimeters. An **isosceles triangle** is a triangle with exactly two equal sides.

4. Sketch a scalene triangle with a height of 4 centimeters. A **scalene triangle** is a triangle with no equal sides.

5. Find the area of each triangle that you made.

B 1. What do these four triangles have in common?

2. Why do you think these four triangles can be called a triangle family?

C 1. Use grid paper to make a new triangle family that has a different base and height from the triangle family you have already made. What are the base, height, and area of each triangle in your triangle family?

2. What can you say about triangles that have the same base and height?

Homework starts on page 42.

2.4 Designing Triangles Under Constraints

In this Problem, you will use what you know about triangles to draw triangles that meet given conditions (constraints).

? What conditions for a triangle produce triangles that have the same area? Do those triangles have the same shape?

Problem 2.4

For each description, draw two triangles that are *not* congruent. (Two figures are *congruent* if they have the same size and the same shape.) If you cannot draw more than one triangle for each description, explain why. Make your drawings on centimeter grid paper.

A The triangles both have a base of 5 centimeters and a height of 6 centimeters. Do the two triangles have the same area?

B The triangles both have an area of 15 square centimeters. Do the two triangles have the same perimeter?

C The triangles both have sides of length 3 centimeters, 4 centimeters, and 5 centimeters. Do the two triangles have the same area?

D The triangles are right triangles and both have a 30-degree angle. Do the two triangles have the same area? Do they have the same perimeter?

ACE Homework starts on page 42.

Applications

For Exercises 1–6, the triangles are drawn on centimeter grid paper. Calculate the area and perimeter of each triangle. Explain how you found your answers for Exercises 1, 4, and 5.

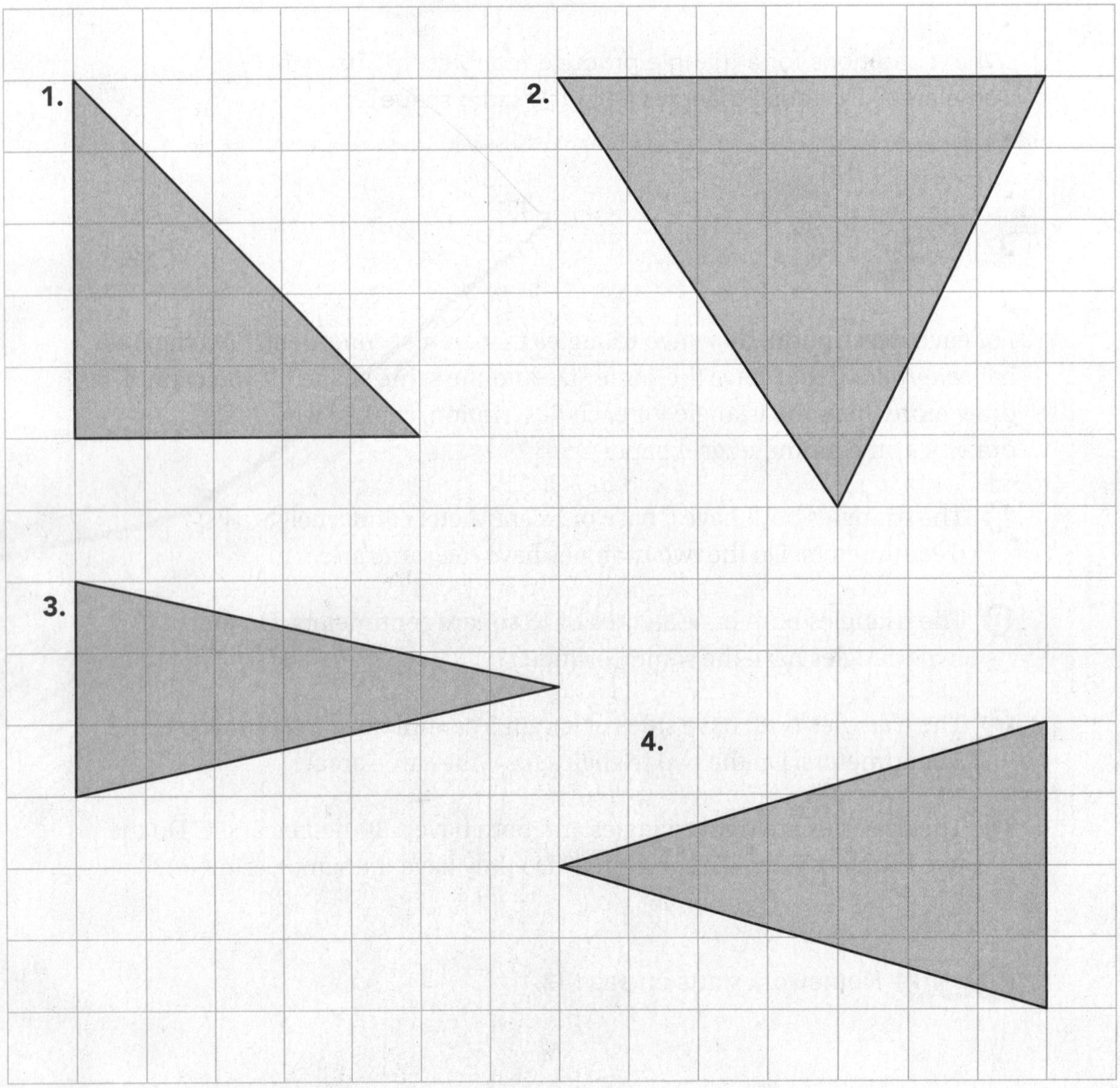

1.

2.

3.

4.

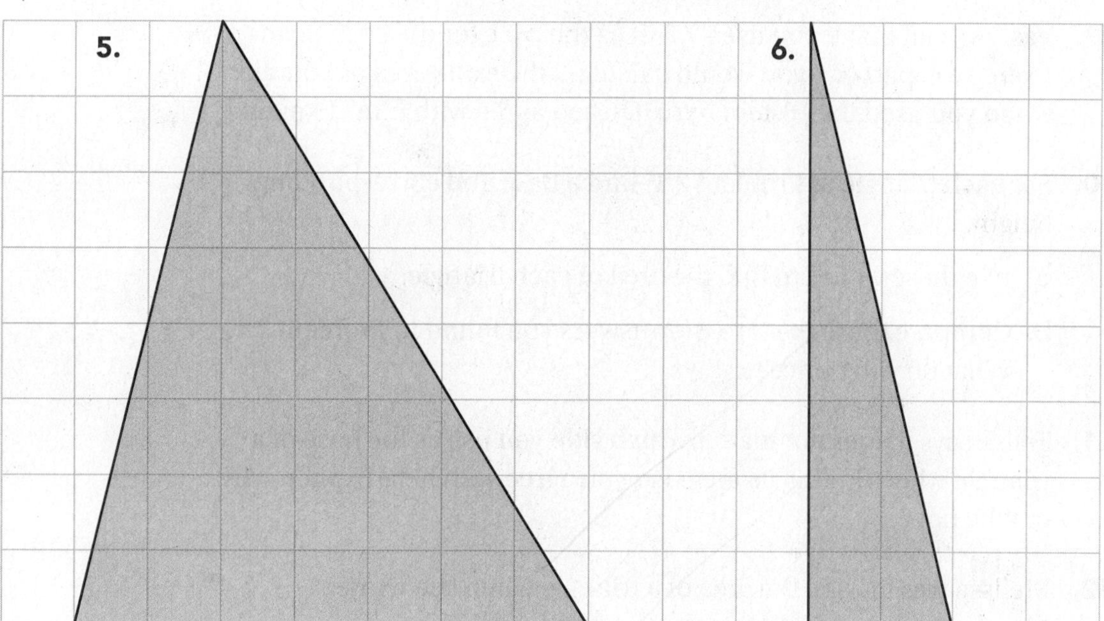

7. Ian tried to find a formula for the area of a right triangle with height h and base b. He cut off half of the triangle's height and rearranged it to make a rectangle. He then claimed he could find the area of the triangle.

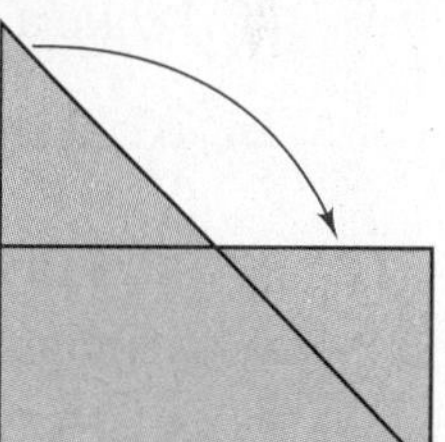

a. What formula did he write? Is it the same as the formula you found?

b. The area of a triangle is 30 square centimeters and its height is 10 centimeters. Use the formula to find the length of the base.

c. Will Ian's method work for any triangle? Explain.

8. Find the area of each figure.

a.

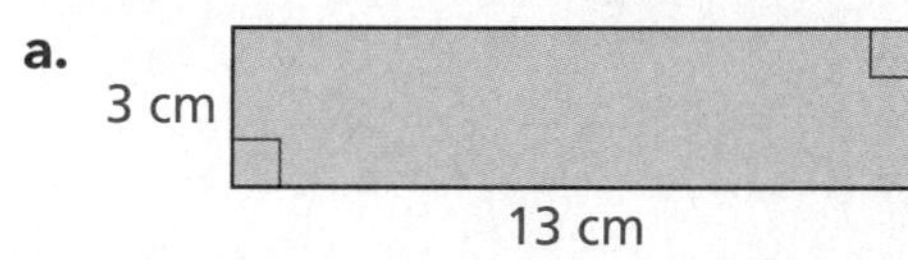

b.

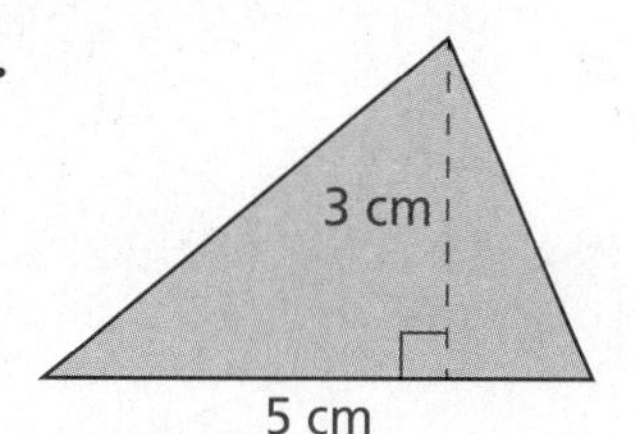

c.

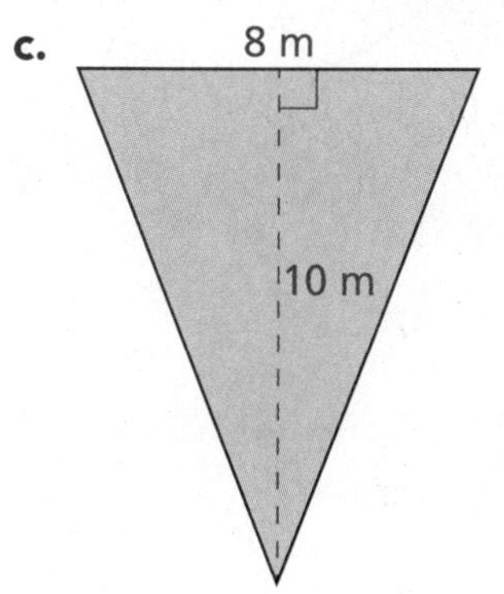

d.

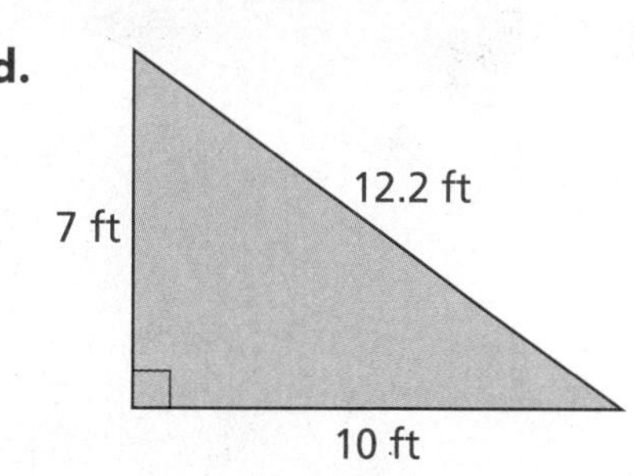

9. Vashon said that if you used 7 feet as the base for the triangle in Exercise 8, part (d), you would calculate the same area as you did when you used the 10-foot base. Do you agree with him? Explain.

10. For each triangle in Problem 2.1, find a base and corresponding height.
    a. Use these values to find the area of each triangle.
    b. Compare these areas to the answers you found in Problem 2.1. What do you notice?

11. Talisa says it does not matter which side you use as the base of a triangle when finding its area. Do you agree with her? Explain why or why not.

12. Melissa was finding the area of a triangle when she wrote

$$\text{area} = \tfrac{1}{2}\left(3 \times 4\tfrac{1}{2}\right)$$

    a. Make a sketch of a triangle she might have been working with.
    b. What is the area of the triangle?

13. What is the height of a triangle whose area is 4 square meters and whose base is $2\frac{1}{2}$ meters?

For Exercises 14–17, find the perimeter and area of each figure.

14.
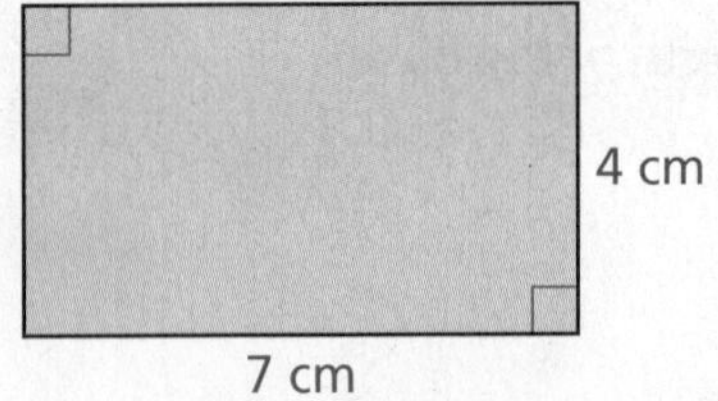

15.
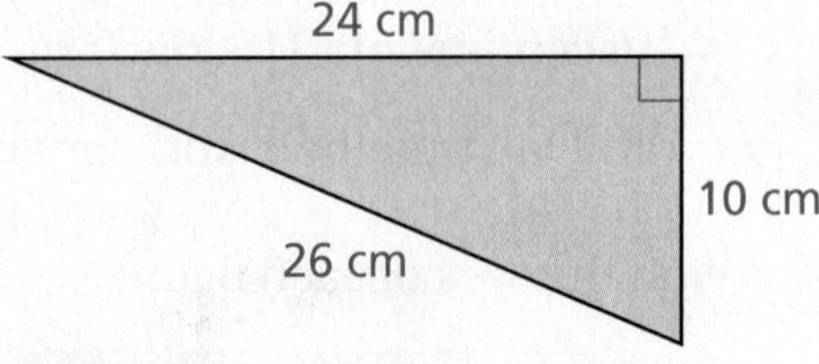

16.
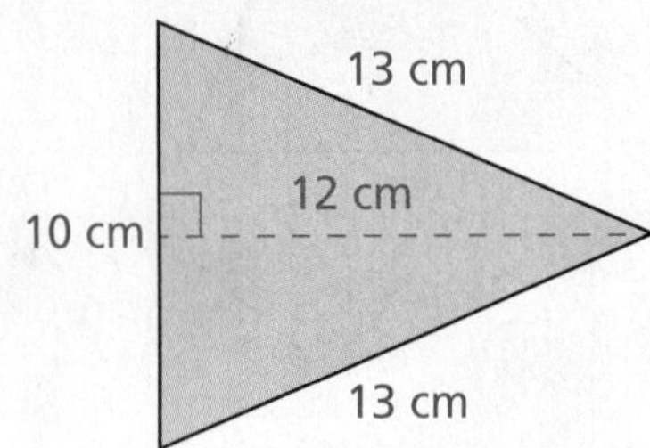

17.
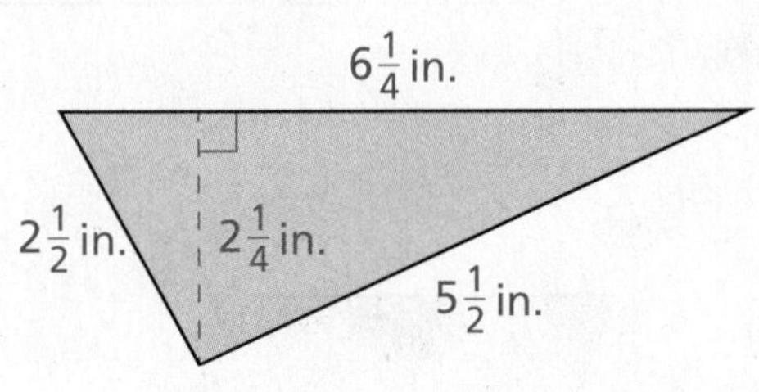

18. Keisha says these right triangles have different areas. Do you agree with her? Explain why or why not.

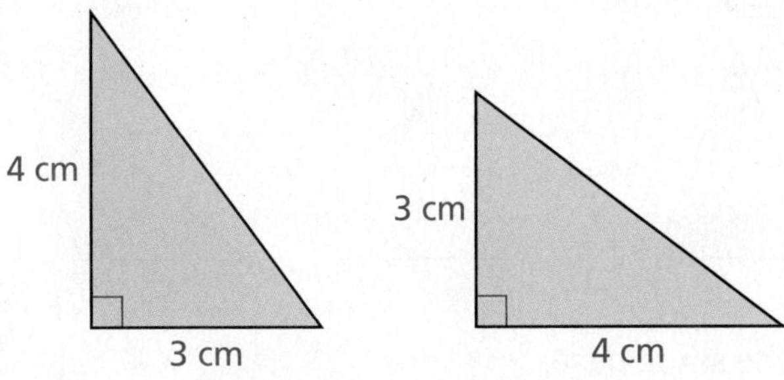

For Exercises 19–21, find the area of each triangle.

19.

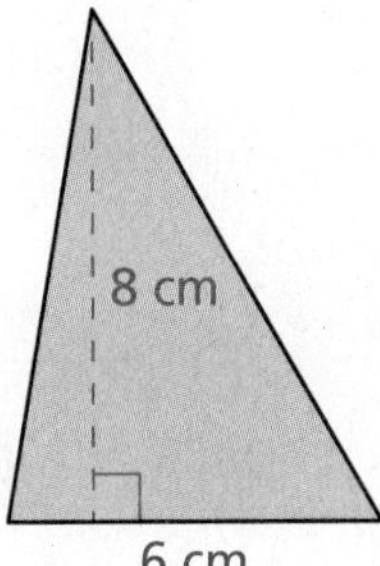

20.

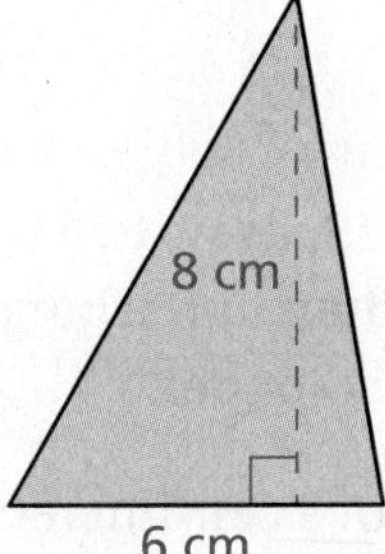

21.

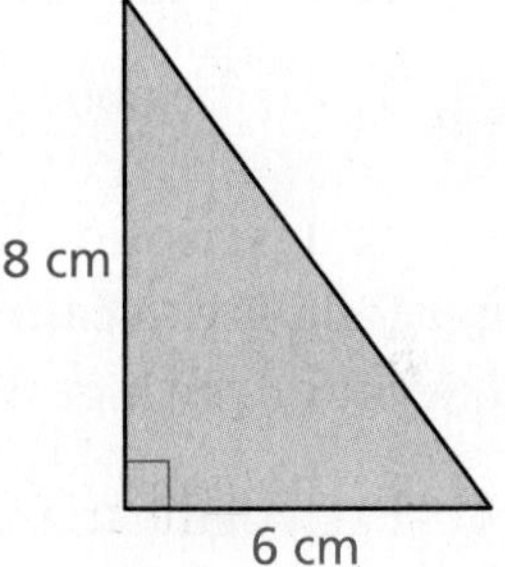

22. Tomas says that scalene, isosceles, and right triangles have different areas because they look different. Marlika disagrees and says that if they have the same base and the same height, their areas will be the same. Do you agree with Tomas or with Marlika? Explain.

23. Multiple Choice Which is the best statement about this family of triangles?

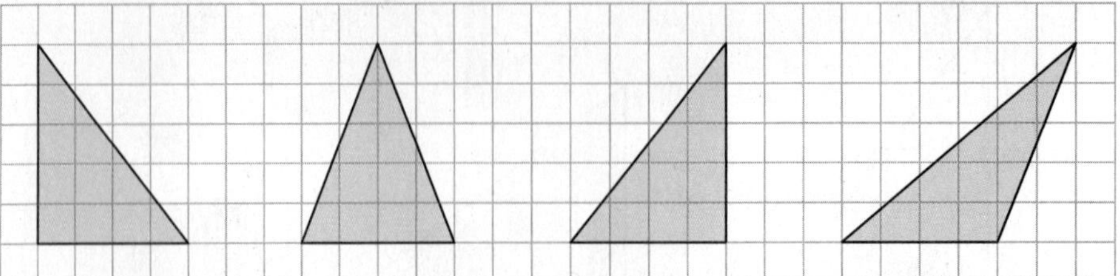

A. The triangles have the same base.

B. The triangles have the same area.

C. The triangles have three vertices each.

D. All the above statements are true.

For each description in Exercises 24–26, draw two triangles that are *not* congruent. If you cannot draw more than one triangle, explain why. Make your drawings on centimeter grid paper.

24. Each of the triangles has a base of 8 centimeters and a height of 5 centimeters. Do the triangles have the same area?

25. Each of the triangles has an area of 18 square centimeters. Do the triangles have the same perimeter?

26. Each of the triangles has sides 6 centimeters, 8 centimeters, and 10 centimeters long. Do the triangles have the same area?

Connections

For Exercises 27–32, find the area and perimeter of each polygon. Explain how you found your answers for Exercises 28, 31, and 32.

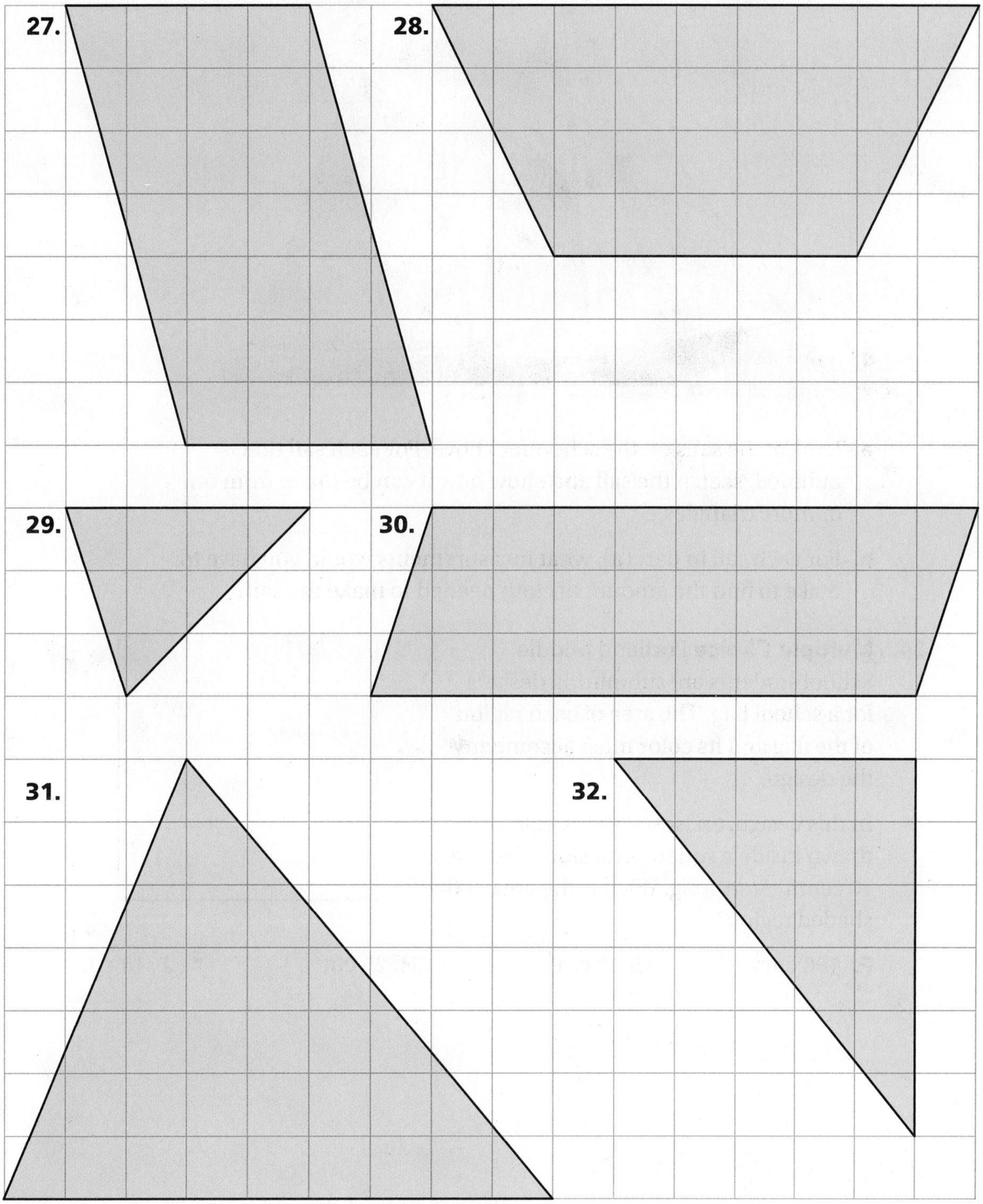

27.

28.

29.

30.

31.

32.

33. A schooner (SKOON ur) is a sailing ship with two or more masts. The sails of a schooner have interesting shapes. Many sails are triangular or can be made by putting two or more triangles together.

a. Look at the sails on the schooner above. For each sail that is outlined, sketch the sail and show how it can be made from one or more triangles.

b. For each sail in part (a), what measurements would you have to make to find the amount of cloth needed to make the sail?

34. Multiple Choice Portland Middle School students are submitting designs for a school flag. The area of each region of the flag and its color must accompany the design.

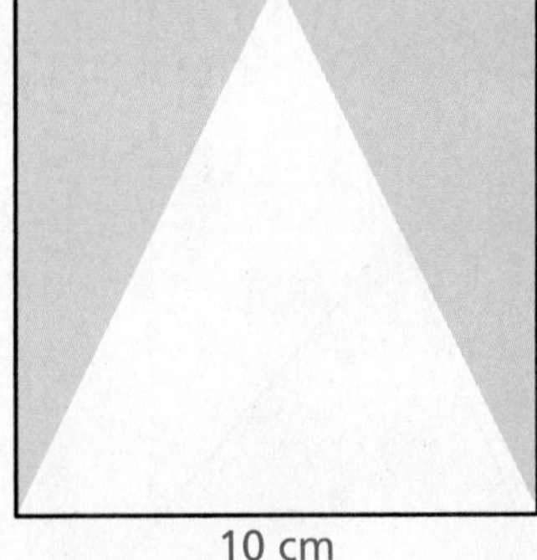

In this design, an isosceles triangle is drawn inside a square with sides that are 10 centimeters long. What is the area of the shaded region?

F. 100 cm^2 **G.** 50 cm^2 **H.** 25 cm^2 **J.** 10 cm^2

35. The garden club is making glass pyramids to sell as terrariums (tuh RAYR ee um; a container for a garden of small plants). They need to know how much glass to order.

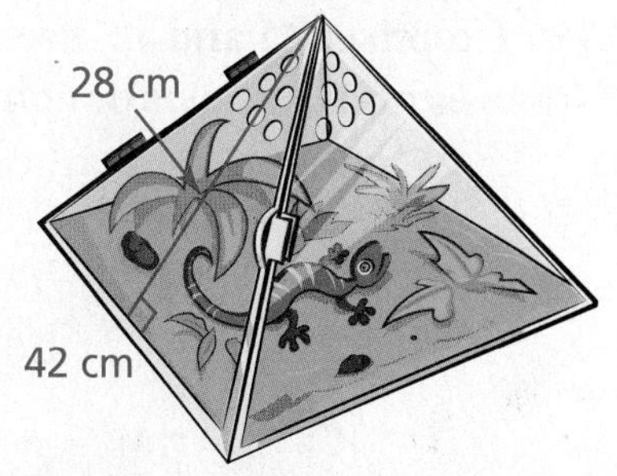

The four faces (sides) of the terrarium are isosceles triangles. Each triangle has a base of 42 centimeters and a height of 28 centimeters. The square bottom of the terrarium is also glass. How much glass is needed for each terrarium?

For Exercises 36–39, a game company decides to experiment with new shapes for dartboards. For each problem, subdivide the shape into the given regions. Explain your strategies.

36. a square with four regions representing $\frac{1}{10}$ of the area, $\frac{1}{5}$ of the area, $\frac{3}{10}$ of the area, and $\frac{2}{5}$ of the area

37. an **equilateral triangle** (a triangle with all sides equal) with four regions, each representing $\frac{1}{4}$ of the area

38. a rectangle with four regions representing $\frac{1}{3}$ of the area, $\frac{1}{6}$ of the area, $\frac{3}{12}$ of the area, and $\frac{1}{4}$ of the area

39. a rectangle with four regions representing $\frac{1}{2}$ of the area, $\frac{1}{4}$ of the area, $\frac{3}{16}$ of the area, and $\frac{1}{16}$ of the area

Extensions

40. Explain how you could calculate the area and perimeter of this regular hexagon. A **regular polygon** is a polygon with all of its sides equal and all of its angles equal.

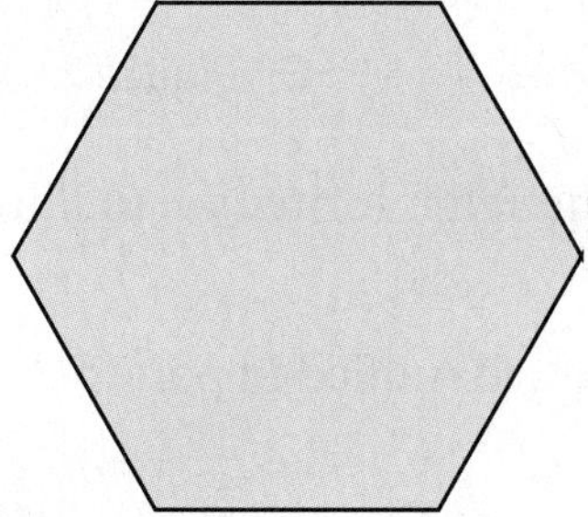

For Exercises 41 and 42, use Figures 1–4. All the figures are made from squares and isosceles or equilateral triangles.

Figure 1

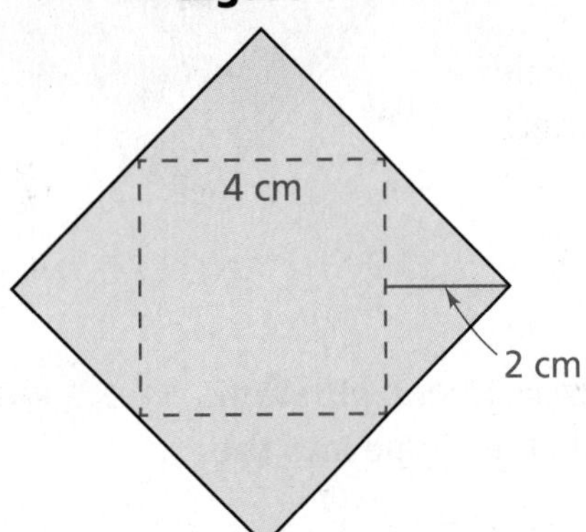

Figure 2

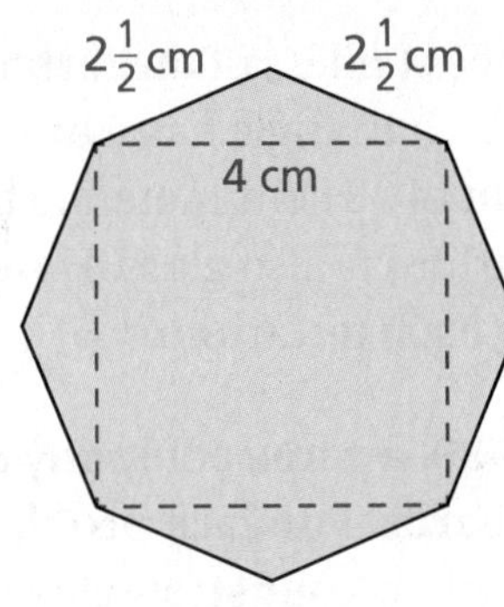

Figure 3

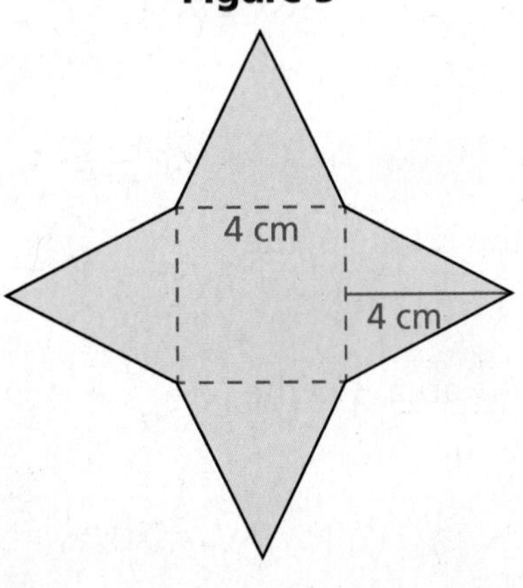

Figure 4

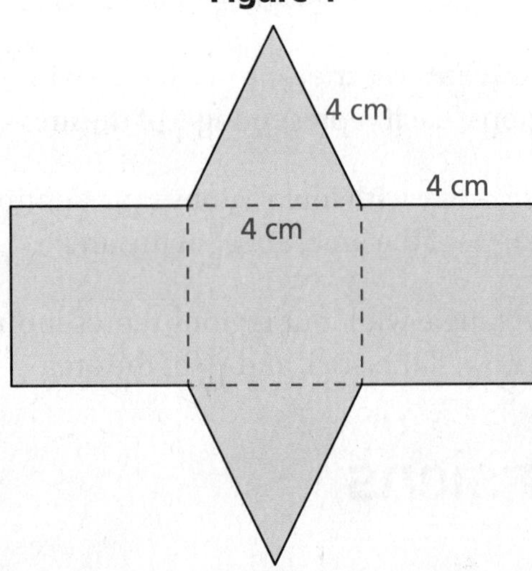

41. Multiple Choice Which polygon would make a pyramid when folded along the dashed lines? (A pyramid is the shape shown in Exercise 35.)

A. Figure 1 **B.** Figure 2 **C.** Figure 3 **D.** Figure 4

42. a. For which figure(s) is there enough information to find the area of the polygon?

b. Find the area of each figure you identified in part (a).

Mathematical Reflections 2

In this Investigation, you discovered strategies for finding the areas and perimeters of triangles by relating them to what you know about rectangles. The following questions will help you summarize what you have learned.

Think about these questions. Discuss your ideas with other students and your teacher. Then write a summary of your findings in your notebook.

1. a. **Describe** how to find the area of a triangle. Explain why your method works.

   b. **Describe** how to find the perimeter of a triangle. Explain why your method works.

2. a. **Does** the choice of the base affect the area of a triangle? Does the choice of the base affect the perimeter of a triangle? Explain why or why not.

   b. **What** can you say about the area and perimeter of two triangles that have the same base and height? Give evidence to support your answer.

3. **How** is finding the area of a triangle related to finding the area of a rectangle? How is finding the perimeter of a triangle related to finding the perimeter of a rectangle?

Common Core Mathematical Practices

As you worked on the Problems in this Investigation, you used prior knowledge to make sense of them. You also applied Mathematical Practices to solve the Problems. Think back over your work, the ways you thought about the Problems, and how you used Mathematical Practices.

Shawna described her thoughts in the following way:

In our group, we would enclose a triangle in the smallest possible rectangle. We then noticed that the area of the triangle is half the area of the rectangle. However, we did not know how find a formula. Gia, however, noticed that the sides of the rectangle are the base and height of the triangle. We had to make sketches on grid paper to convince ourselves that this was always true.

Common Core Standards for Mathematical Practice
MP8 Look for and express regularity in repeated reasoning.

- What other Mathematical Practices can you identify in Shawna's reasoning?
- Describe a Mathematical Practice that you and your classmates used to solve a different Problem in this Investigation.

Measuring Parallelograms

You have developed strategies for finding the area and perimeter of rectangles and of triangles. In this Investigation, you will develop strategies for finding the area and perimeter of parallelograms. Rectangles are a special type of parallelogram. This means that everything that is true for parallelograms is also true for rectangles.

When you work with rectangles, you use the measurements length and width. For triangles, you use the side lengths, the base, and the height. Like triangles, parallelograms are often described by side length, base, and height.

3.1 Parallelograms and Triangles

Finding Area and Perimeter of Parallelograms

As you work with parallelograms, look for ways to use triangles and rectangles to find the area of a parallelogram.

Common Core State Standards

6.NS.C.8 Solve real-world and mathematical problems by graphing points in all four quadrants of the coordinate plane. Include use of coordinates and absolute value to find distances between points with the same first coordinate or the same second coordinate.

6.G.A.1 Find the area of right triangles, other triangles, special quadrilaterals, and polygons by composing into rectangles or decomposing into triangles and other shapes; apply these techniques in the context of solving real-world and mathematical problems.

6.G.A.3 Draw polygons in the coordinate plane given coordinates for the vertices; use coordinates to find the length of a side joining points with the same first coordinate or the same second coordinate. Apply these techniques in the context of solving real-world and mathematical problems.

Also 6.EE.A.2, 6.EE.A.2a, 6.EE.A.2c, 6.EE.B.6, 6.EE.C.9

Here are three parallelograms with the base and height of two parallelograms marked.

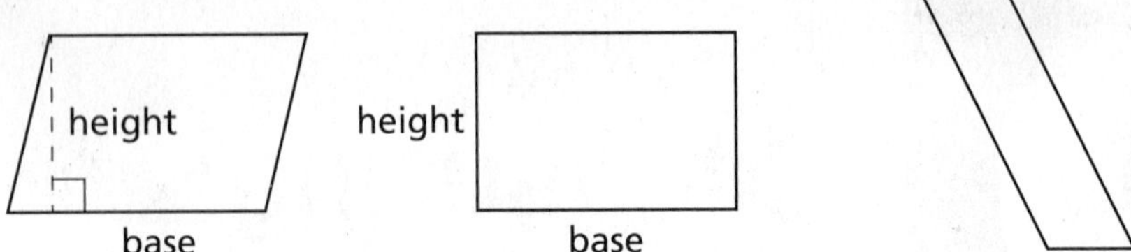

- What do you think the base and the height of a parallelogram mean?
- How can you mark and measure the base and height of the third parallelogram?

Problem 3.1

The centimeter grid on the next page shows six parallelograms labeled A–F.

A 1. Find the perimeter of each parallelogram.

2. Describe a strategy for finding the perimeter of a parallelogram.

B 1. Find the area of each parallelogram.

2. Describe the strategies you used to find the areas.

C 1. For each parallelogram, record the base, height, and area in a table. Describe any patterns you see in the data.

2. Draw one diagonal in each parallelogram as shown below. Add columns to your table recording the base, height, and area of each triangle you make.

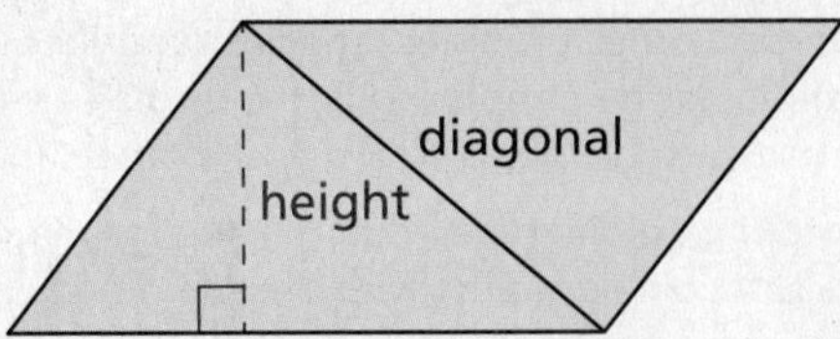

3. Describe any patterns in your table that show how the area of each parallelogram and the area of its triangles are related.

continued on the next page >

Problem 3.1 *continued*

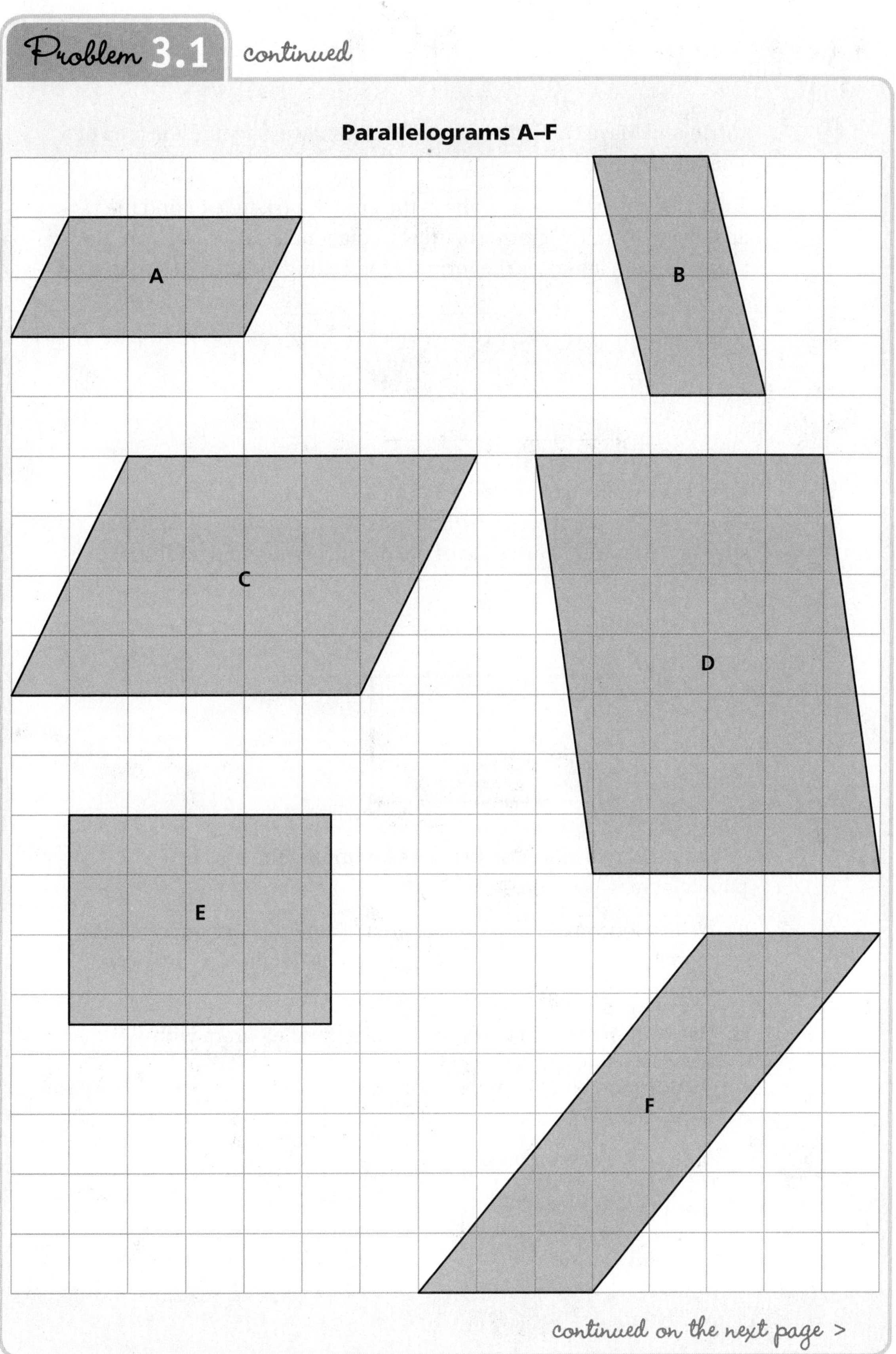

continued on the next page >

Problem 3.1 continued

D **1.** Torrin and Maya came up with two different ways to find the area of a parallelogram.

Torrin uses what he knows about the area of a triangle to find the area of any parallelogram. He draws a diagonal and a height on the parallelogram and uses the formula for finding the area of a triangle.

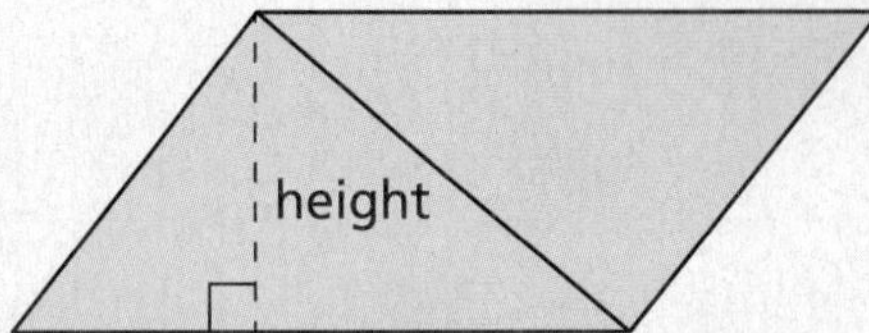

Maya uses what she knows about the area of a rectangle to find the area of the parallelogram. She makes a drawing to show how she cut a triangle off one side of the parallelogram and added it to the other side.

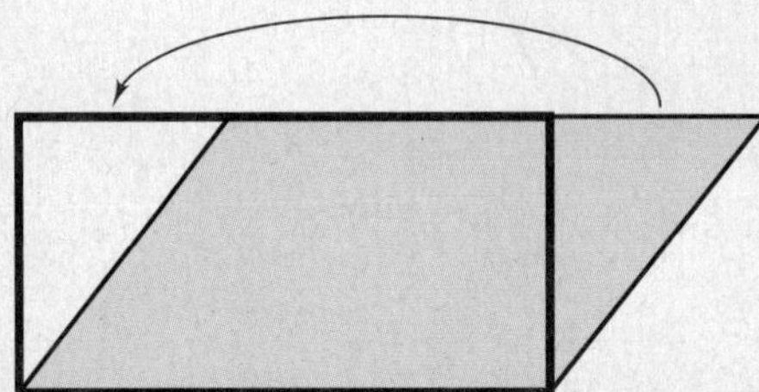

Will they get two different formulas for finding the area of a parallelogram? Explain.

2. **a.** Write a formula for finding the area of a parallelogram. Use b to represent the base and h to represent the height. Explain why your formula works.

b. Use your method to find the area of a parallelogram with $b = 7\frac{2}{3}$ inches and $h = 12$ inches.

 Homework starts on page 64.

3.2 Making Families of Parallelograms

Maintaining the Base and the Height

In the last Problem, you found a formula for the area of a parallelogram:

$$A = b \times h,$$

where A is the area, b is the base, and h is the height.

In this Problem, you will continue to explore the relationship between the area of a parallelogram and its base and height.

Is the area of a parallelogram affected by changing which side is called the base?

Problem 3.2

Parallelograms F and G are shown.

A 1. Find the area of each parallelogram twice using a different side as the base each time.

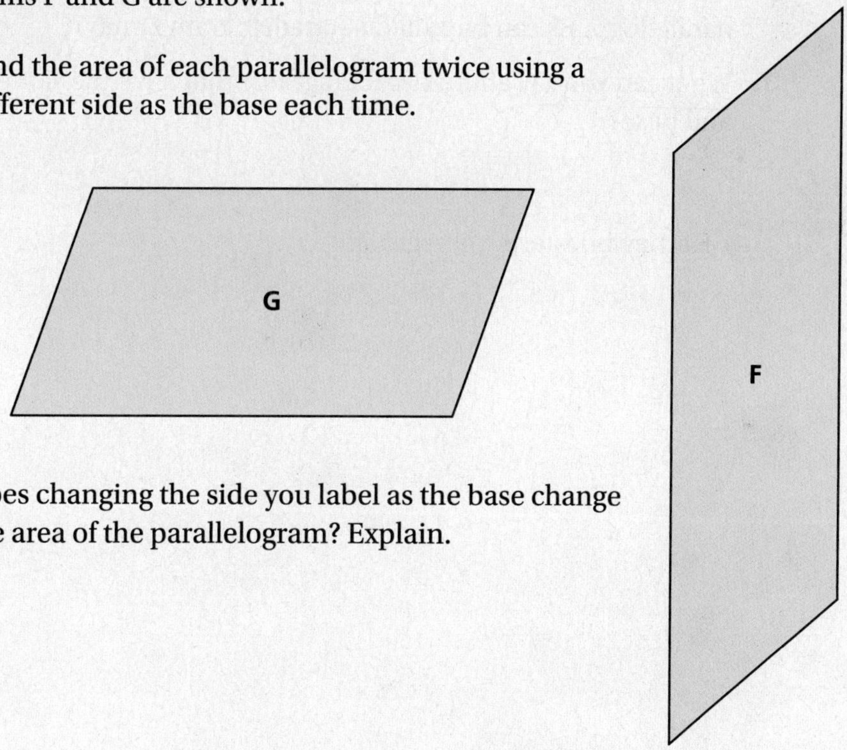

G

F

2. Does changing the side you label as the base change the area of the parallelogram? Explain.

continued on the next page >

Problem 3.2 continued

For each parallelogram in Question B, part (1), follow the steps below.

- Draw a segment 6 centimeters long on a separate piece of centimeter grid paper.
- Use the segment as a base for the parallelogram.

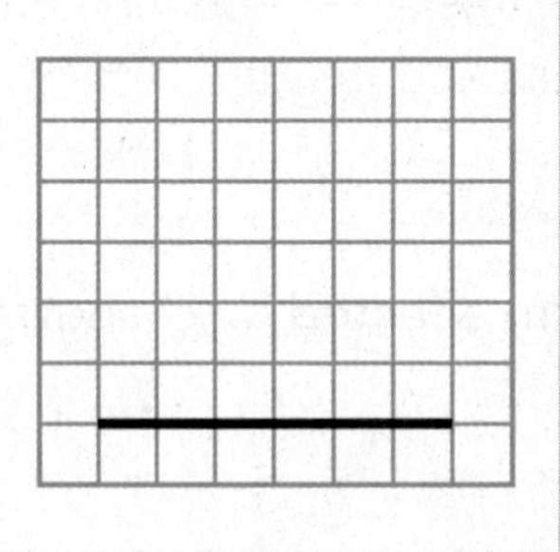

B **1.** Sketch four different parallelograms with a height of 4 centimeters.

2. Find the area of each parallelogram. Why do you think these four parallelograms can be called a parallelogram family?

3. What can you say about parallelograms that have the same height and base?

ACE Homework starts on page 64.

3.3 Designing Parallelograms Under Constraints

You will now draw parallelograms that meet given conditions. Sometimes you will be able to draw more than one parallelogram that satisfies the conditions.

Problem 3.3

For each description, draw two figures that are *not* congruent to each other. If you cannot draw a second figure, explain why. Make your drawings on centimeter grid paper.

A Draw two rectangles that each have an area of 18 square centimeters. If you can draw two different rectangles, do they have the same perimeter? Explain.

B Draw two rectangles that are each 3 centimeters by 8 centimeters. If you can draw two different rectangles, do they have the same area? Explain.

C Draw two parallelograms that each have a base of 7 centimeters and a height of 4 centimeters. If you can draw two different parallelograms, do they have the same area? The same perimeter? Explain.

D Draw two parallelograms that each have four 6-cm-long sides. If you can draw two different parallelograms, do they have the same area? Explain.

E Draw two parallelograms that each have an area of 30 square centimeters. If you draw two different parallelograms, do they have the same perimeter? Explain.

Homework starts on page 64.

3.4 Polygons on Coordinate Grids

You can design construction projects and artwork with the help of computer programs. To use some of these programs, it is helpful to describe polygons and other shapes by naming *coordinates* of key points.

Points on a coordinate grid are labeled with a pair of points called **coordinates.** The first number, or **x-coordinate,** tells the horizontal distance from the *y*-axis. The second or **y-coordinate** tells the vertical distance from the *x*-axis. For example, vertex *A* on the pentagon below has coordinates (10, 7).

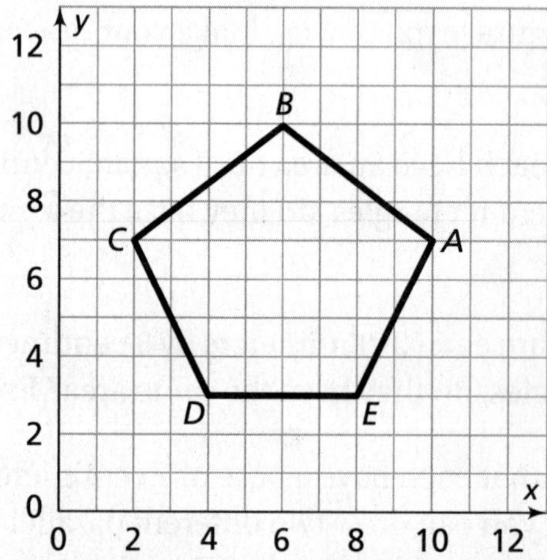

- What are the coordinates of vertices *B, C, D,* and *E*?

Problem 3.4

The Midway Amusement Rides Company (MARS) is working on new polygon designs for bumper-car floor plans. They use a computer program that places the polygons on a coordinate grid.

A The diagram on the next page shows four polygons on a coordinate grid.

1. Describe each triangle or quadrilateral as precisely as possible.
2. For each figure, give the coordinates of all vertices.

continued on the next page >

Problem 3.4 continued

3. When is it possible to find the side lengths of a polygon using the coordinates? Find at least one example on each figure. For each example, use the coordinates to find the side lengths.
4. Find the area of each polygon.
5. If each figure is moved to a different location on the grid, what will change and what will not change? Explain.

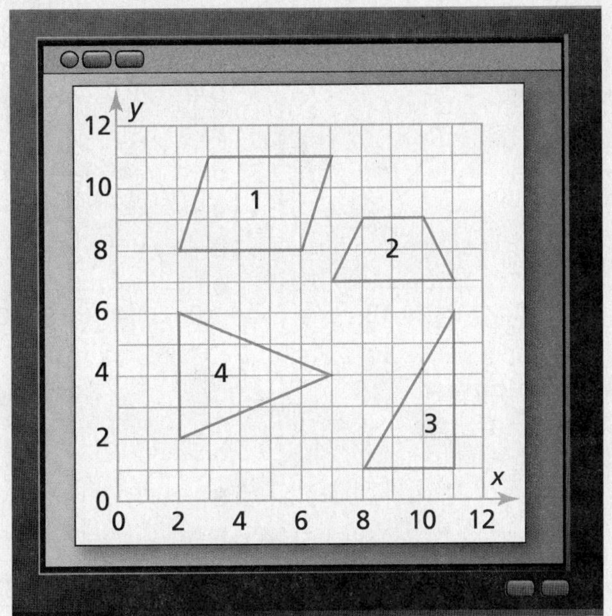

B For each polygon listed in Question B, follow the steps below.

- Find all of the coordinates of the vertices of the polygon.
- Draw the polygon on a coordinate grid.
- Find the area of the polygon.

1. A square with vertices $A(2, 1)$, $B(5, 1)$, $C(x_1, y_1)$, and $D(x_2, y_2)$.
2. An isosceles triangle with vertices $P(1, 3)$, $Q(1, 7)$, and $R(12, y)$.
3. A rectangle with vertices $E(9, 3)$, $F(9, 7)$, $G(4, 7)$, and $H(x, y)$.
4. A parallelogram with vertices $J(3, 2)$, $K(6, 4)$, $L(6, 11)$, and $M(x, y)$.

continued on the next page >

Problem 3.4 continued

C Below are four figures on a coordinate graph. One of the vertices in each figure is missing a coordinate.

Rectangle

(x, 10) (10, 10)

(4, 6) (10, 6)

Right Triangle

(x, 10)

(4, 6) (10, 6)

Parallelogram

(x, 10) (20, 10)

(4, 6) (10, 6)

Rectangle

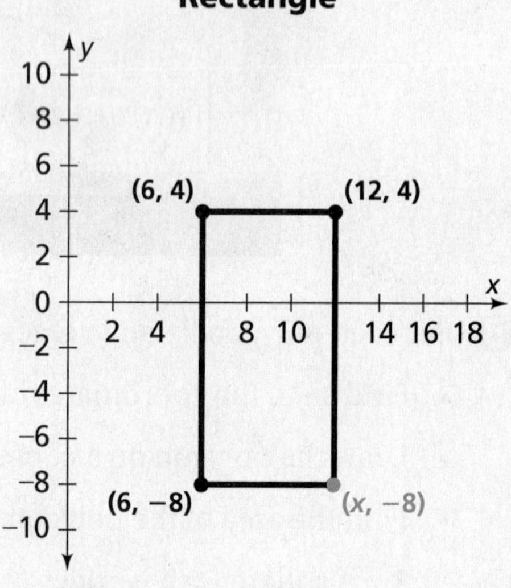

1. For each figure, find the missing coordinate.
2. The bases of all the figures have the same length. Are the areas the same? Explain.
3. Are the perimeters of the figures the same? Explain.

continued on the next page >

Problem 3.4 continued

D Here are three different polygons on a coordinate grid. All three polygons could be broken down into triangles and/or rectangles.

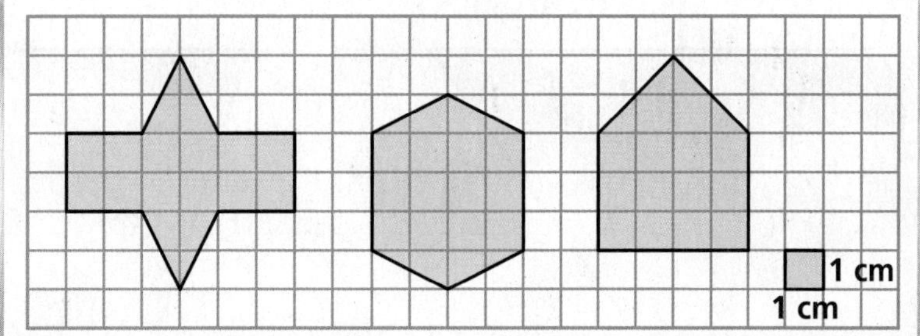

1. Find the area of each polygon. Explain how you found each area.
2. After studying these polygons, Angie insists that all three polygons have same area. Do you agree with her? Explain your reasoning.
3. Design another polygon that has the same area as the hexagon.

ACE Homework starts on page 64.

Applications | Connections | Extensions

Applications

For Exercises 1–7, find the area and perimeter of each parallelogram. Explain how you found your answers for parallelograms 2, 6, and 7.

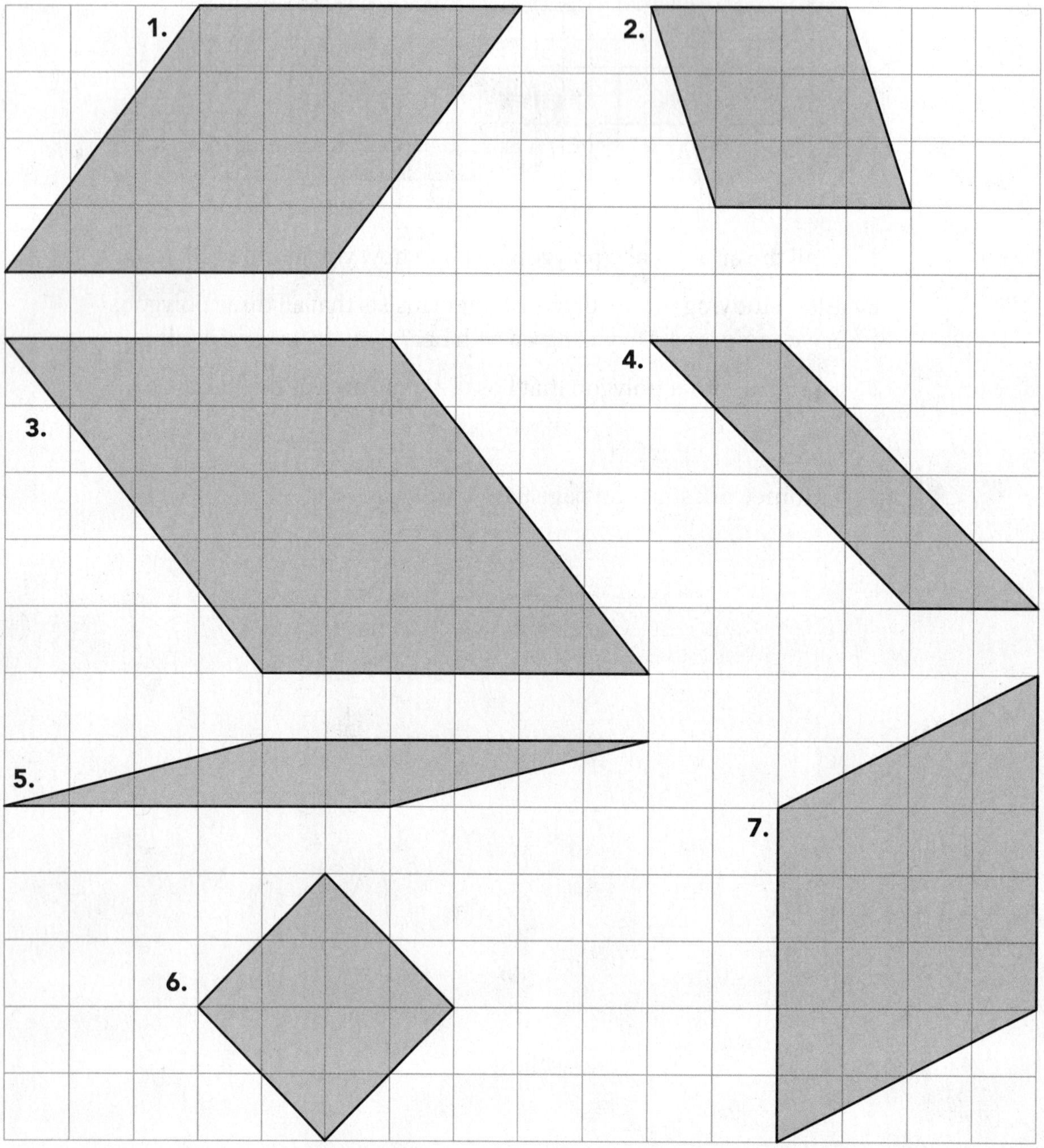

1.

2.

3.

4.

5.

6.

7.

8. On the grid is a family of parallelograms.

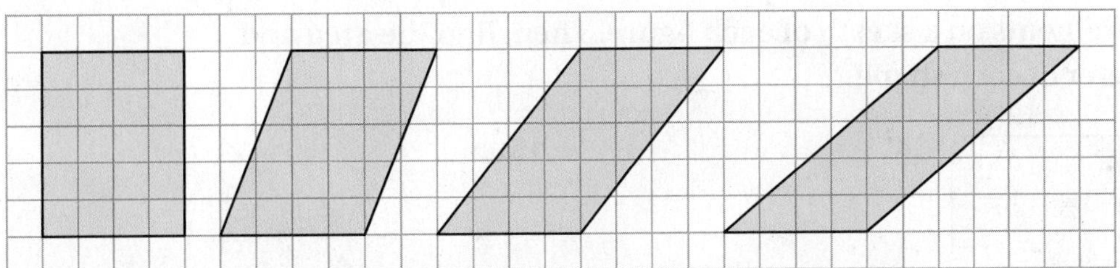

a. Find the base, height, and area of each of the parallelograms.

b. What patterns do you see?

c. Why do you think these parallelograms belong to a family of parallelograms?

9. a. The base of a parallelogram is $9\frac{1}{2}$ centimeters and its height is $11\frac{1}{2}$ centimeters. What is the area of the parallelogram?

b. The base of a rectangle is $9\frac{1}{2}$ centimeters and its height is $11\frac{1}{2}$ centimeters. What is the area of the rectangle?

c. Do the parallelogram in part (a) and the rectangle in part (b) have the same perimeter? Explain.

For Exercises 10–13, find the area and perimeter of each figure.

10.

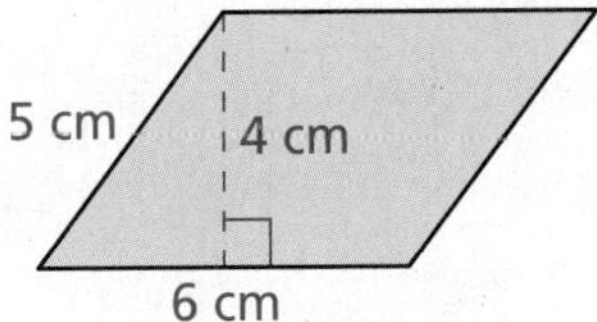

11.

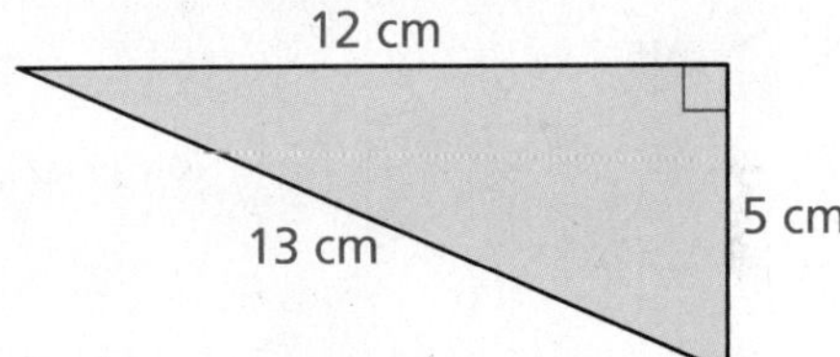

12.

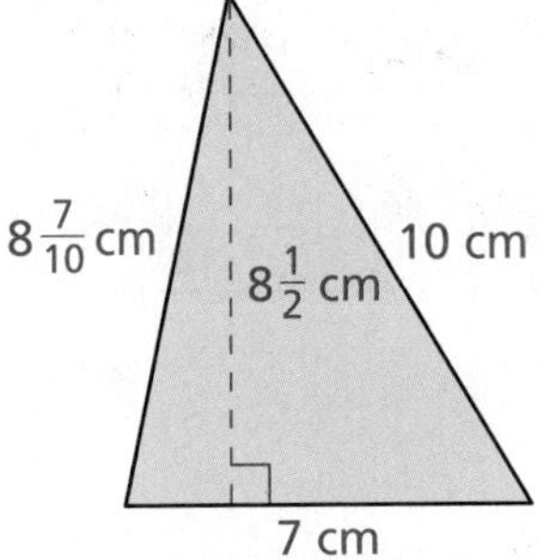

13.

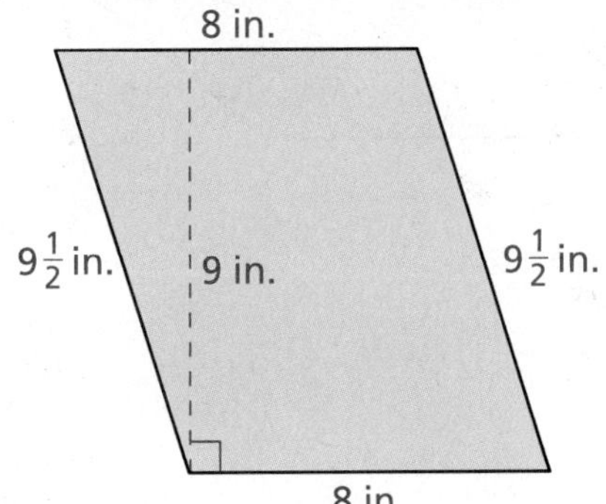

For Exercises 14–19, make the measurements (in centimeters) that you need to find the area and perimeter of each shape. Write your measurements on a sketch of each figure. Then, find the area and perimeter of each shape.

14.

15.

16.

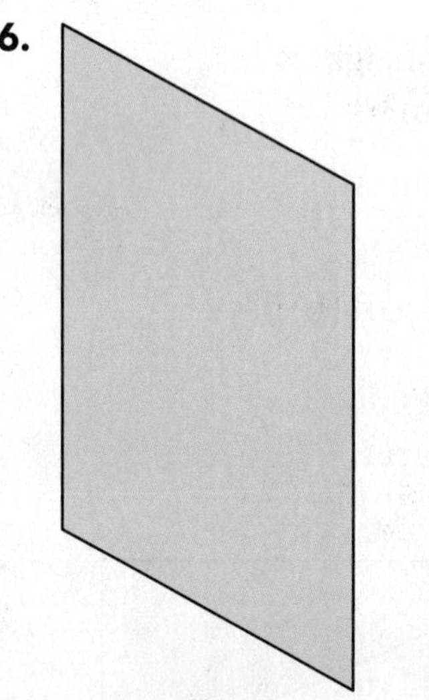

17.

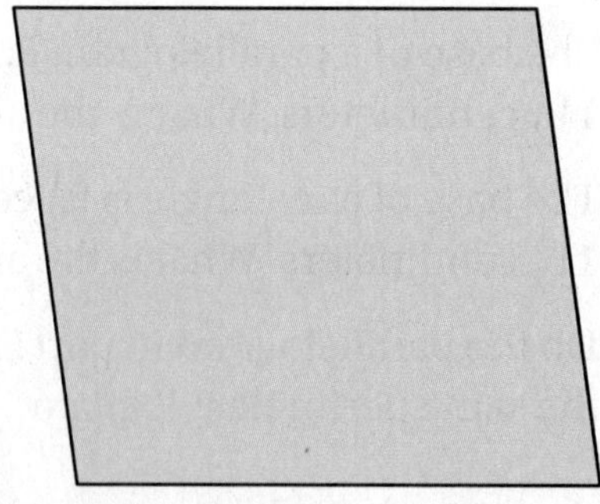

18.

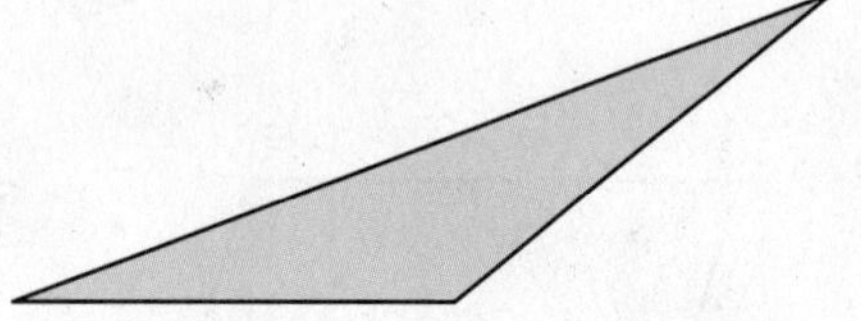

19.

20. Denzel decides the shape of Tennessee is approximately that of a parallelogram, as shown below.

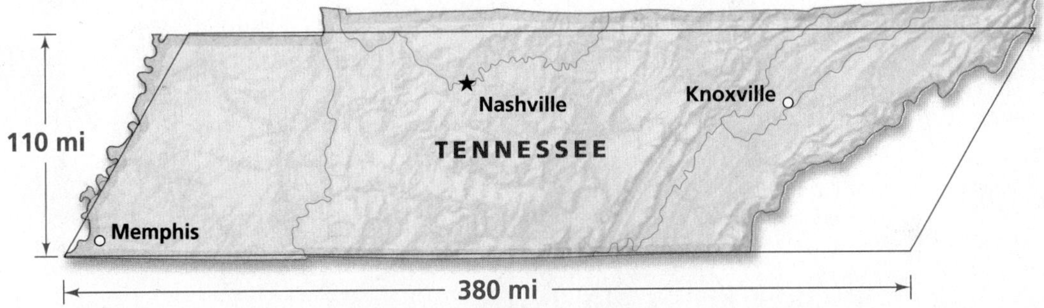

a. Use the distances on the map to estimate the area of Tennessee.

b. Suppose the actual area of Tennessee is 42,144 square miles. How does your estimate compare to the actual area? Explain.

21. Explain why these three parallelograms have the same area.

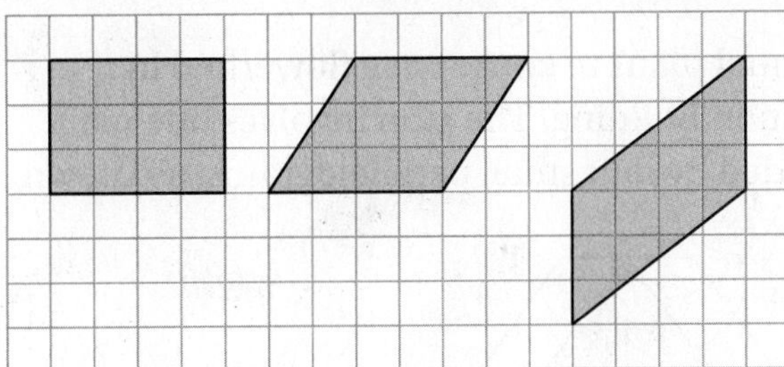

For Exercises 22–27, follow the steps below.

a. Sketch the described parallelogram.

b. Label its base and height.

c. Explain whether or not you can draw more than one parallelogram that will meet the given conditions.

22. The base is 8 centimeters and the perimeter is 28 centimeters.

23. The base is 4.5 centimeters and the area is 27 square centimeters.

24. The parallelogram is nonrectangular with a base of 10 centimeters and a height of 8 centimeters.

25. The base is 6 centimeters and the area is 30 square centimeters.

26. The area is 24 square centimeters.

27. The perimeter is 24 centimeters.

28. a. An equilateral triangle can be divided into equal-size triangles using line segments parallel to the opposite sides. Each segment connects two midpoints. How many parallelograms can you find in the figure?

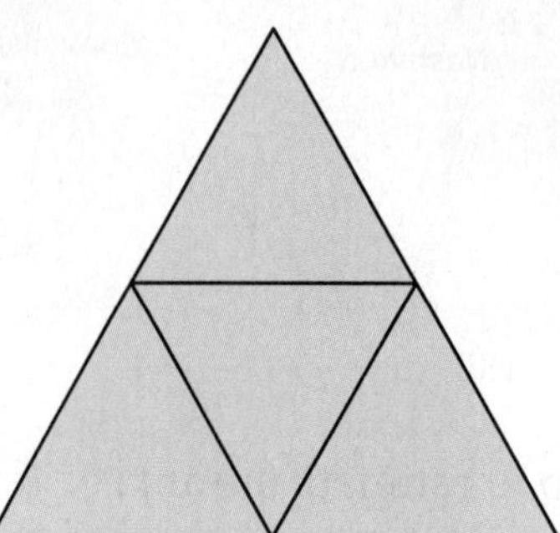

b. Are the parallelograms you found the same size?

c. Suppose the area of the large triangle is 16 square units. What is the area of one of the parallelograms?

29. The Akland Middle School plans to construct a flowerbed in front of the Administration Building. The plan involves one main parallelogram surrounded by four small parallelograms, as shown.

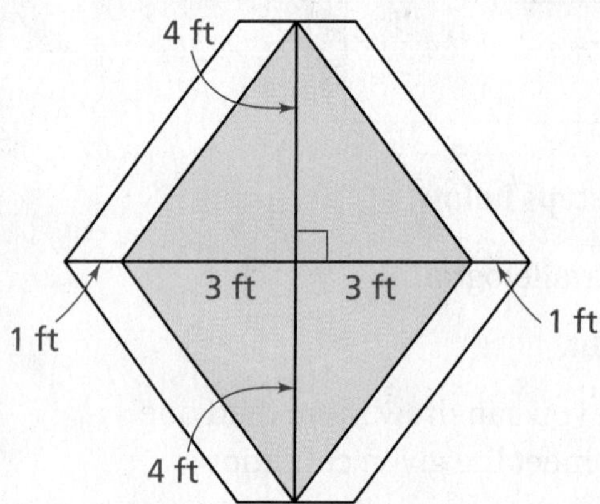

a. Find the area of one of the small parallelograms.

b. Find the area of the main parallelogram.

30. Mr. Lee wants to install ceiling tiles in his recreation room. The room measures 24 feet by 18 feet. Each ceiling tile is 2 feet by 3 feet. How many ceiling tiles will he need?

31. The Lopez family bought a plot of land in the shape of a parallelogram. It is 100 feet wide (across the front) and 200 feet deep (the height). Their house covers 2,250 square feet of land. How much land is left for grass?

32. The Luis Park District set aside a rectangular section of land to make a park. After talking with students, the park district decided to make an area for skateboarding, an area with playground equipment, and an area with a basketball court, as shown.

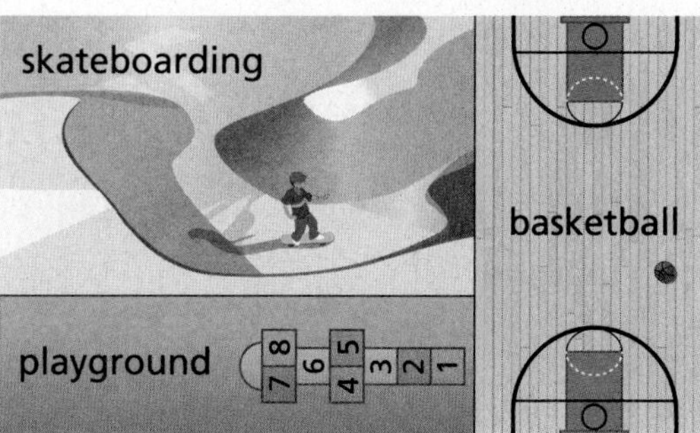

a. The skateboarding area takes up $\frac{2}{3}$ of the length and $\frac{2}{3}$ of the width of the park. What fraction of the area of the park does the skateboarding area occupy?

b. The basketball court is 35 feet by 60 feet. Use this information and what you know about the skateboarding area to find the area and the perimeter of the playground area.

33. Quilters use shapes such as triangles, squares, rectangles, and parallelograms when designing quilts. This is a pattern of a 10 inch-by-10 inch quilt square on inch grid paper.

a. Each parallelogram in the quilt is made from how many square inches of fabric?

b. How many square inches of fabric are needed to make the five squares in the quilt square?

c. The squares and the parallelograms will be sewn onto gray fabric. How many square inches of the gray fabric will be visible?

34. The coordinate grid at the right shows four polygons.

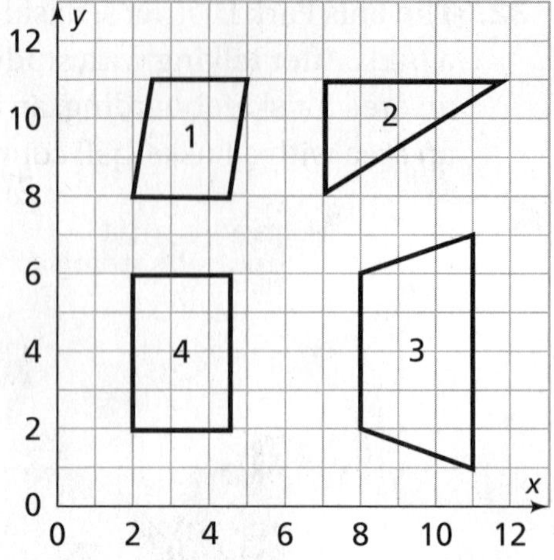

a. Give the coordinates of all vertices of each polygon.

b. Use the coordinates to find the lengths of as many sides (horizontal and vertical) as you can.

c. Describe as precisely as possible each type of triangle or quadrilateral shown.

35. The coordinate grid at the right shows four polygons.

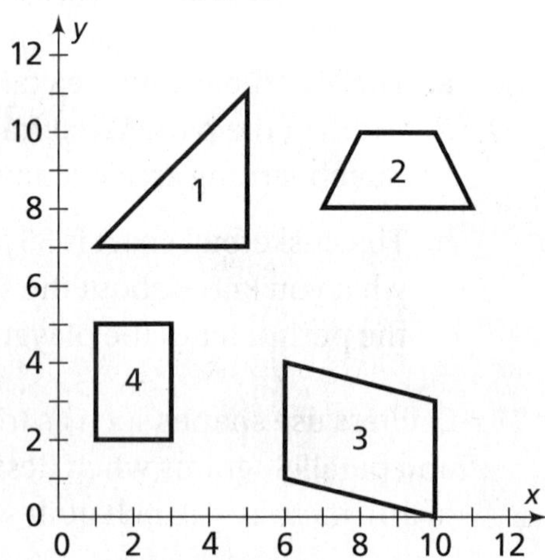

a. Give the coordinates of all vertices of each polygon.

b. Use the coordinates to find the lengths of as many sides as you can.

c. Describe as precisely as possible each type of triangle or quadrilateral shown.

36. Don made a puzzle. He listed points that would make a polygon on a grid, but he left out some coordinates. Find the missing coordinates.

a. A square with vertices $A(x, 2)$, $B(5, 6)$, $C(1, 6)$, and $D(m, n)$.

b. A right triangle with a right angle at $P(1, 3)$ and vertices $Q(1, 7)$ and $R(5, y)$.

c. A rectangle with vertices $E(3, 9)$, $F(7, 9)$, $G(7, 4)$, and $H(x, y)$.

d. A parallelogram with vertices $J(3, 2)$, $K(5, 1)$, $L(5, 11)$, and $M(x, y)$.

37. Use the polygons from Exercise 36.

a. Find the lengths of the horizontal and vertical sides of each polygon.

b. Find the area of each polygon.

38. a. Find the area of each figure.

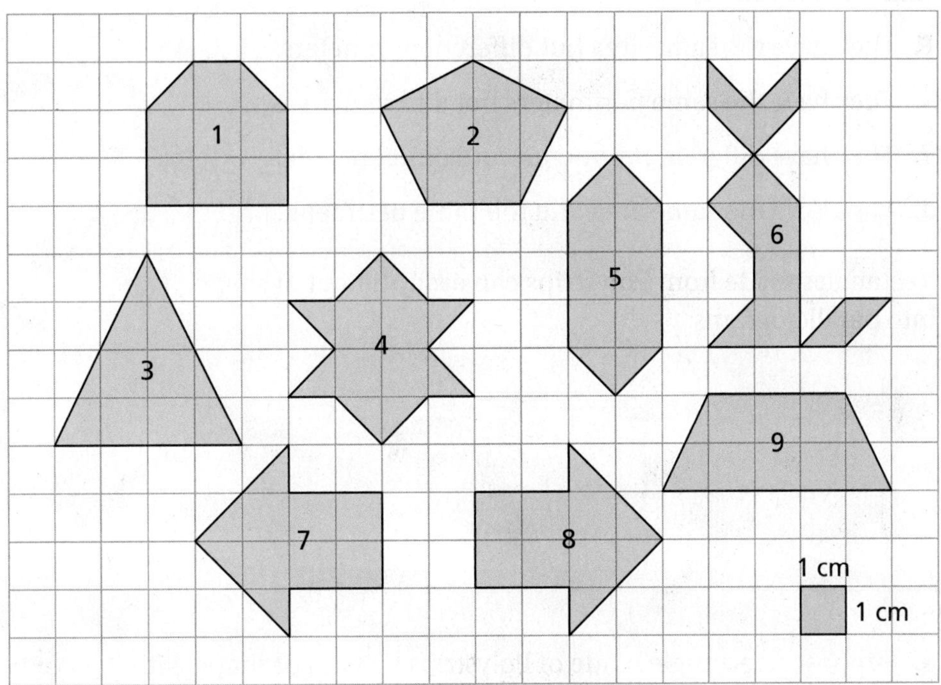

b. Design another figure that has twice the area of the following figure.

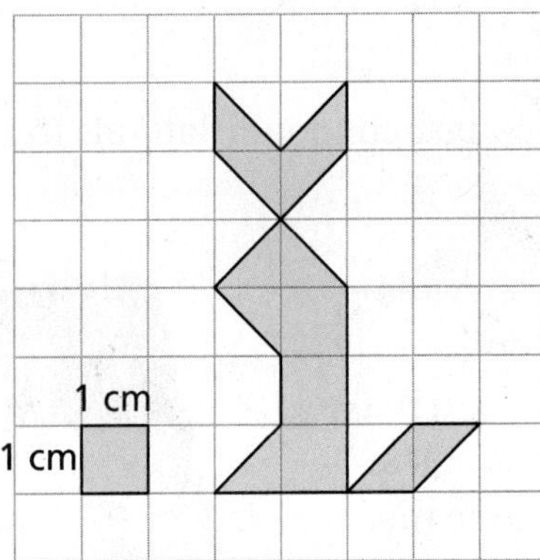

Connections

39. Multiple Choice Which set of numbers is ordered from greatest to least?

A. 0.215, 0.23, 2.3, $\frac{2}{3}$

B. $\frac{2}{3}$, 0.215, 0.23, 2.3

C. $\frac{2}{3}$, 0.23, 0.215, 2.3

D. 2.3, $\frac{2}{3}$, 0.23, 0.215

40. Multiple Choice Two quadrilaterals are congruent. Which statement is correct?

F. They have the same area but different perimeters.

G. They have the same perimeters but different areas.

H. They have different perimeters and different areas.

J. They have the same area and the same perimeter.

41. Rectangles made from Polystrips can easily tilt out of shape into parallelograms.

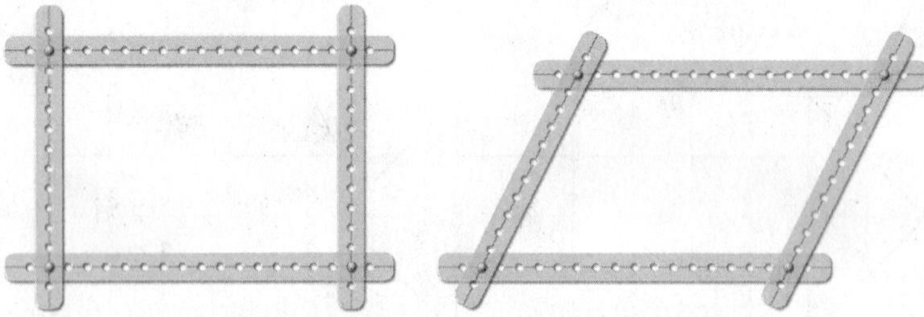

a. Suppose a rectangle made of Polystrips tilts out of shape with the sides staying the same length. How will the angles, area, and perimeter of the new figure compare to the original?

b. What relationships among the sides and angles of rectangles are also true of parallelograms?

42. Give two examples of a pair of congruent quadrilaterals that you have seen in real life.

43. Rapid City is having its annual citywide celebration. The city wants to rent a bumper-car ride. The pieces used to make the floor are 4 foot-by-5 foot rectangles. The ride covers a rectangular space that is 40 feet by 120 feet.

a. How many rectangular floor pieces are needed?

b. How much would it cost Rapid City to rent the floor and the bumper cars? (You will need to decide how many bumper cars are appropriate.)

Extensions

44. You saw earlier that for some parallelograms and triangles, the height may be outside the figure being measured.

a. Sketch an example of a parallelogram with the height outside the parallelogram. Explain why the area of the parallelogram can still be calculated by multiplying the base times the height.

b. Sketch an example of a triangle with the height outside the triangle. Explain why the area of the triangle can still be calculated by multiplying $\frac{1}{2}$ times the base times the height.

45. Vlasy and Anastasia are trying to think of ways to find the area of the parallelogram below.

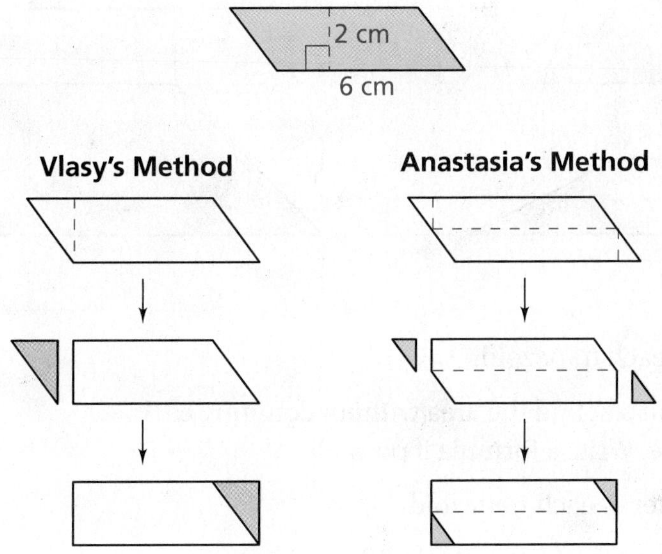

a. Are Vlasy's and Anastasia's methods correct? Explain why they are correct or not correct.

b. Compare these strategies to those you developed in class to find the area of a parallelogram.

c. Will these methods work for any parallelogram? Explain.

46. A *trapezoid* is a quadrilateral with exactly one pair of parallel sides. Use these six trapezoids. Make a table to summarize what you find in parts (a) and (c).

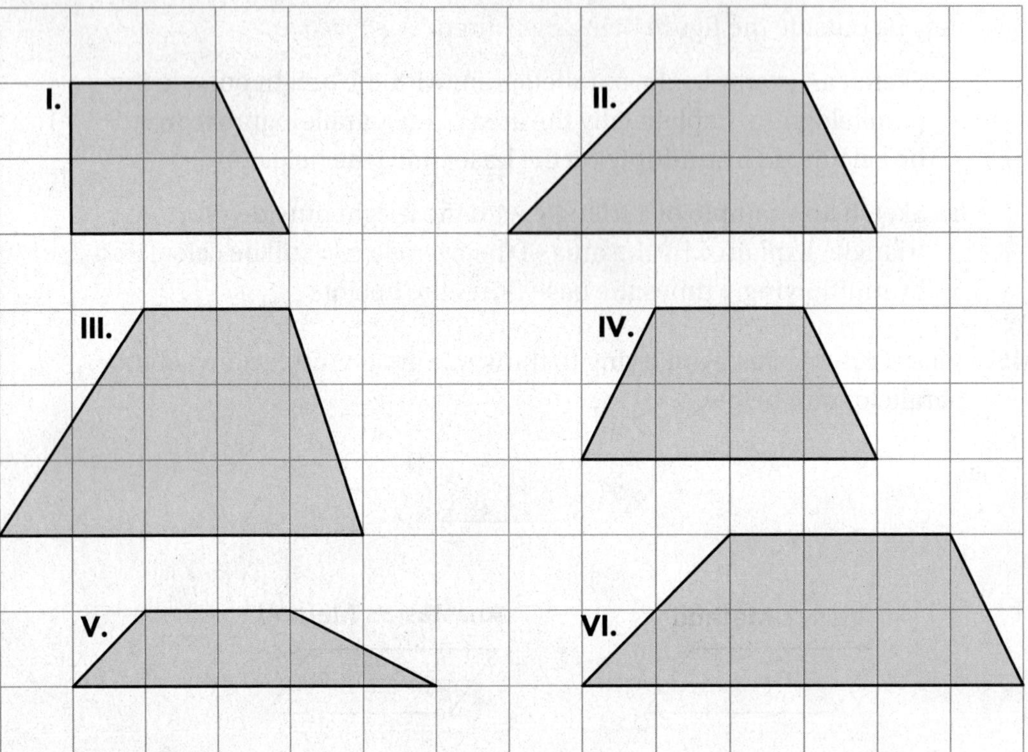

a. Find the area of each trapezoid.

b. Describe how you can find the area without counting each individual square. Write a formula if possible.

c. Find the perimeter of each trapezoid.

d. Summarize your method for part (c) with a rule or a description.

47. Find the area and perimeter of the figure.

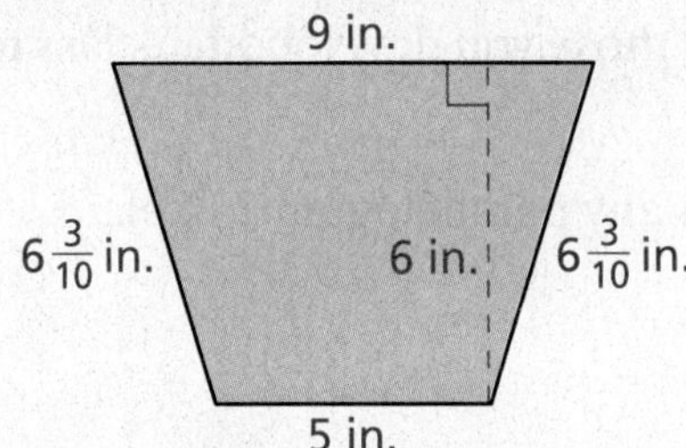

48. Auntie Judi promised to make a patchwork quilt for Amy. Amy wanted a snowflake quilt made from the block pattern below. Auntie Judi told Amy that she needed twelve patchwork blocks of this design and asked her to buy enough fabric to make it. Each block is square, 20 centimeters by 20 centimeters.

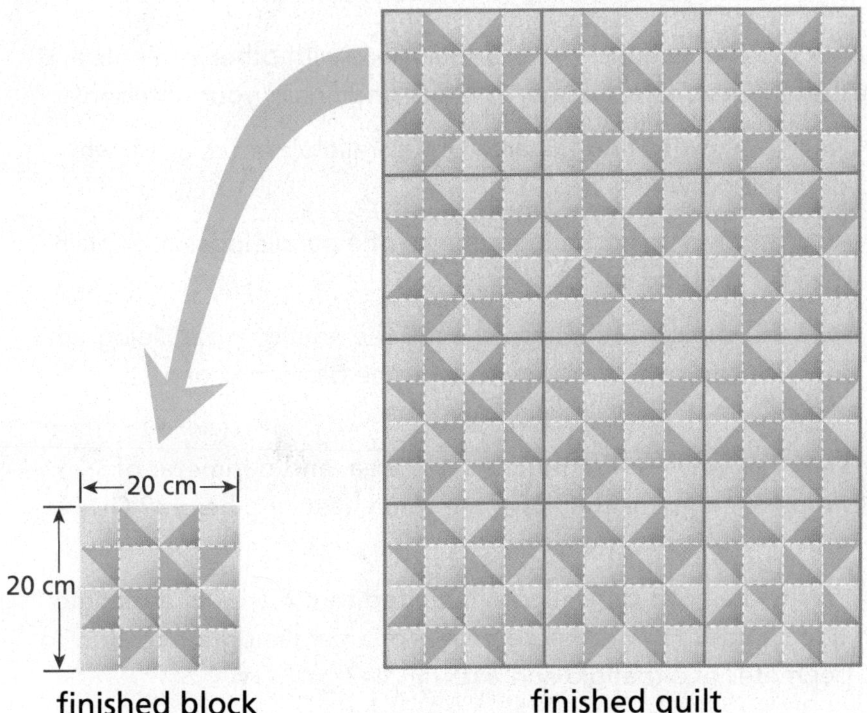

a. How much yellow fabric does Amy need for one patchwork block?

b. How much green fabric does she need for one patchwork block?

c. What is the area of the entire snowflake quilt?

d. In the whole quilt, what is the total area of the yellow fabric? The total area of green fabric?

Mathematical Reflections 3

In this Investigation, you developed strategies for finding the area and perimeter of parallelograms. The following questions will help you summarize what you have learned.

Think about these questions. Discuss your ideas with other students and your teacher. Then write a summary of your findings in your notebook.

1. a. **Describe** how to find the area of a parallelogram. Explain why your method works.

   b. **Describe** how to find the perimeter of a parallelogram. Explain why your method works.

2. a. **Does** the choice of the base change the area of a parallelogram? Does the choice of the base change the perimeter of a parallelogram? Explain why or why not.

   b. **What** can you say about the shape, area, and perimeter of two parallelograms that have the same base and height? Give evidence to support your answer.

3. **How** is the area of a parallelogram related to the area of a triangle and a rectangle? How is the perimeter of a parallelogram related to the perimeter of a triangle and a rectangle?

Common Core Mathematical Practices

As you worked on the Problems in this Investigation, you used prior knowledge to make sense of them. You also applied Mathematical Practices to solve the Problems. Think back over your work, the ways you thought about the Problems, and how you used Mathematical Practices.

Sophie described her thoughts in the following way:

> We used different strategies for finding the area of the polygons in Problem 3.4, Question D. My partner used the grid. He subdivided the polygons into rectangles and triangles. He counted units on the grid to find the measurements he needed. He used these measurements to calculate the areas of the triangles and rectangles.
>
> I put the polygons on a coordinate grid. Next, I subdivided each polygon into rectangles and triangles. Then, I subtracted the coordinates of the vertices of the horizontal and vertical sides to find the necessary measurements. I used these measurements to calculate the areas of the sub-parts.
>
> Another member enclosed the polygon in a rectangle. We all got the same answer. We all felt that it was quicker to either decompose or enclose the polygon on the grid than move it to a coordinate grid. Besides, the polygons were already on a grid.

Common Core Standards for Mathematical Practice

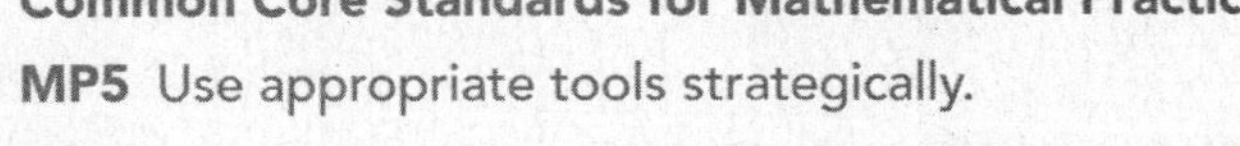

MP5 Use appropriate tools strategically.

- What other Mathematical Practices can you identify in Sophie's reasoning?
- Describe a Mathematical Practice that you and your classmates used to solve a different Problem in this Investigation.

Measuring Surface Area and Volume

Several universities offer degrees in packaging. Designing packages is interesting and complex. Package designers must consider many things including choice of material, cost, post-use recycling, shipping and distribution, and design appeal.

Packaging engineers draw patterns, or nets, that can be folded to form packages. A **net** is a two-dimensional pattern that can be folded to form a three-dimensional figure. These patterns help determine the amount of material needed to construct the packages.

- What other things might a packaging engineer consider when designing a package?

The diagram below shows one possible net being folded into a three-dimensional cube.

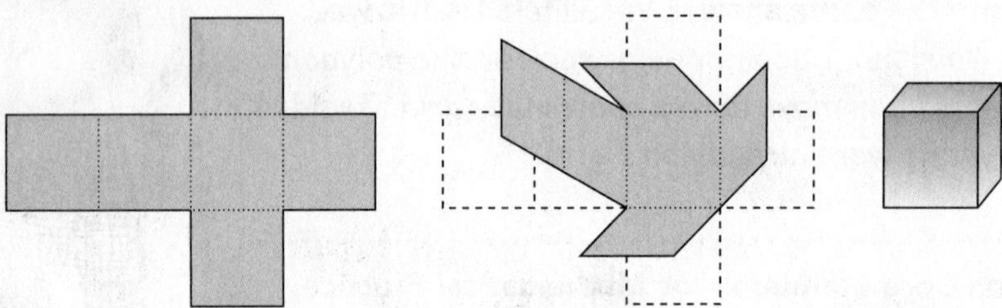

Common Core State Standards

6.EE.A.4 Identify when two expressions are equivalent . . .

6.G.A.2 Find the volume of a right rectangular prism with fractional edge lengths by packing it with unit cubes of the appropriate unit fraction edge lengths, and show that the volume is the same as would be found by multiplying the edge lengths of the prism. Apply the formulas $V = l\,w\,h$ and $V = b\,h$ to find volumes of rectangular prisms with fractional edge lengths in the context of solving real-world and mathematical problems.

6.G.A.4 Represent three-dimensional figures using nets made up of rectangles and triangles, and use the nets to find the surface area of these figures. Apply these techniques in the context of solving real-world and mathematical problems.

Also 6.EE.A.2, 6.EE.A.2a, 6.EE.A.2c, 6.EE.B.6, 6.EE.C.9, 6.G.A.1

The three-dimensional shape on the previous page is called a **unit cube** because all of its **edges** are 1 unit long. The cube is also an example of a rectangular prism.

- How many faces does this cube have? How many edges?

A **prism** is a three-dimensional shape with two parallel and congruent **faces** called **bases.** The other faces are called *lateral (side) faces* and are parallelograms.

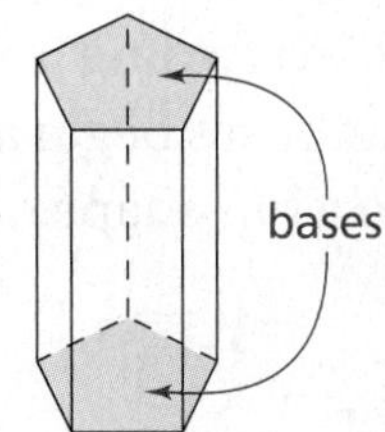

A **rectangular prism** has bases that are rectangles. The **length** and **width** of a rectangular prism are the length and width of its rectangular base. The **height** is the distance from the bottom of the prism to its top. The length, width, and height of a rectangular prism are its dimensions.

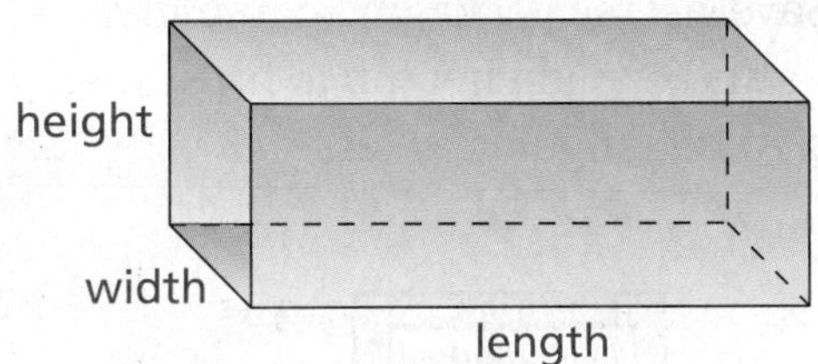

- Is the base of a prism always on the bottom?
- Can only two faces of a rectangular prism be the bases?
- What everyday objects have you seen that are rectangular prisms?

In a right prism, the lateral faces are rectangles. In an **oblique prism,** the lateral faces are nonrectangular. In this Investigation, you may assume that a prism is a right prism unless stated or pictured otherwise.

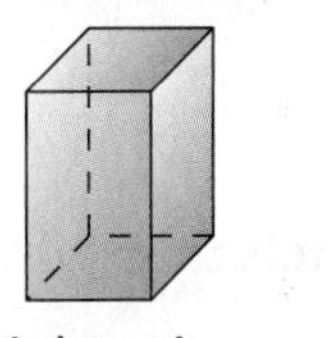
right prism

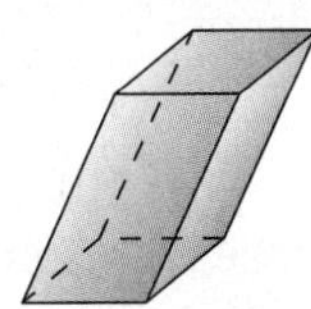
oblique prism

The **surface area** of a box is the total area of all its faces.

- What is the total surface area of a unit cube?

In this Investigation, you will experiment with various three-dimensional shapes made from two-dimensional nets.

4.1 Making Rectangular Boxes

The most common type of package is the rectangular box. Rectangular boxes hold everything from cereal to shoes to pizza to paper clips. Most rectangular boxes begin as flat sheets of cardboard, which are cut and then folded into a box shape.

How can you determine the surface area of a rectangular box?

Amy is a packaging engineer at the Save-a-Tree packaging company. Mr. Shu asks Amy to come to his class and explain her job to his students. She gives the class some tasks to design rectangular boxes.

Problem 4.1

A On grid paper, draw at least three different nets that will fold into a box shaped like a unit cube.

1. What is the total area of each net, in square units?
2. Design a net that forms any other rectangular prism.

continued on the next page >

Problem 4.1 continued

B An engineer at the Save-a-Tree packaging company drew the nets below. He lost the notes that indicated the dimensions of the boxes.

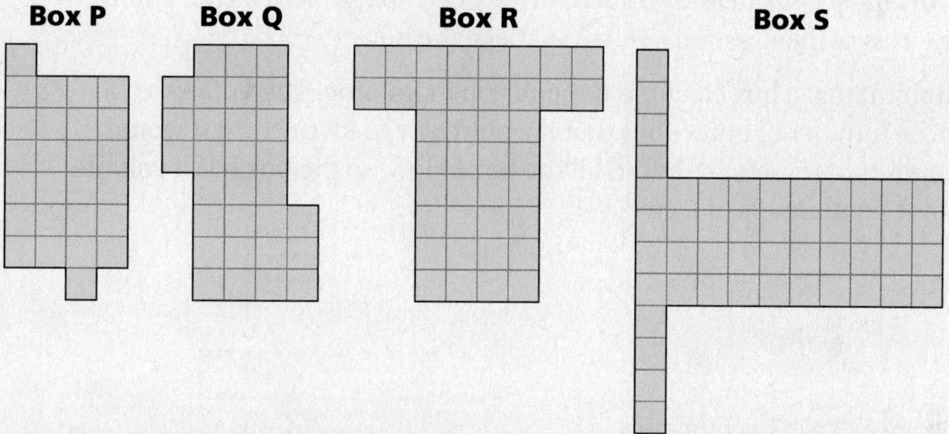

Using a copy of the diagram above,

- Draw in fold lines.
- Cut out each pattern and fold it to form a box.

1. What are the dimensions of each box?
2. How are the dimensions of each box related to the dimensions of its faces?
3. What is the surface area of each box?
4. How many unit cubes does it take to fill each box?
5. Design a net for a box that has a different shape than Box P but holds the same number of cubes as Box P.

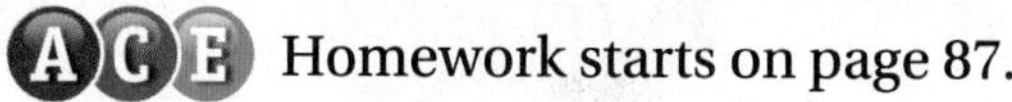

ACE Homework starts on page 87.

4.2 Filling the Boxes

Finding Volume

Finding the right box for a product requires thought and planning. A company must consider how much the box can hold as well as the amount and the cost of the material needed to make the box.

The amount that a box can hold depends on its volume. The **volume** of a box is the number of unit cubes that it would take to fill the box. It would take three 1-centimeter cubes to fill the box below, so the box has a volume of 3 cubic centimeters or 3 cm^3.

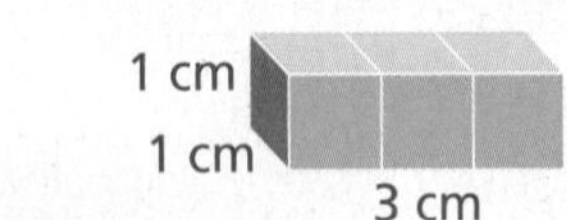

volume = 3 cubic centimeters

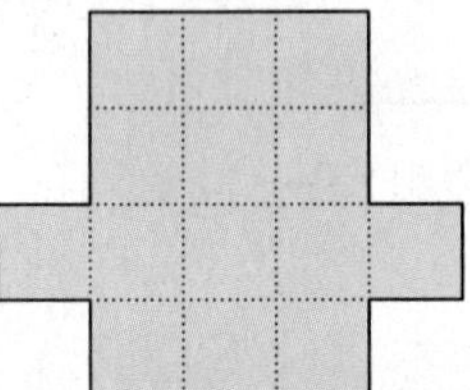

surface area = 14 square centimeters

- What is the volume of each rectangular box in Problem 4.1, Question B?

Problem 4.2

A These rectangular prisms are made from centimeter cubes.

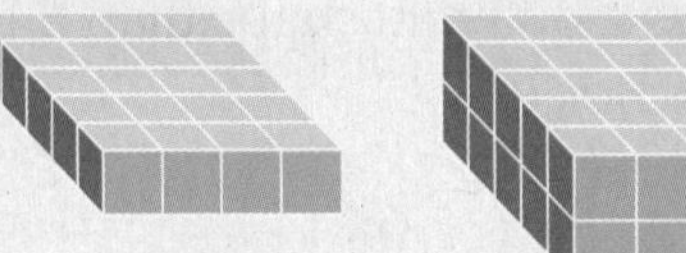

1. What are the length, width, and height of each prism? Record your data in a table.
2. What is the volume of each prism? Describe how you found it.
3. What is the surface area of each prism? Describe how you found it.

continued on the next page >

Problem 4.2 continued

B Natasha and Kurt use different strategies to find the volume of a rectangular box.

Kurt finds the volume by multiplying the length by the width by the height. He uses the diagram below to illustrate his strategy.

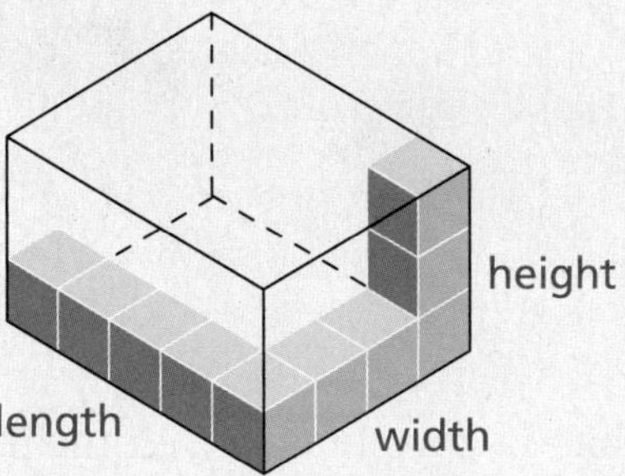

Natasha finds the volume of a rectangular prism by multiplying the area of the base by the height. She uses the following diagram to illustrate her strategy.

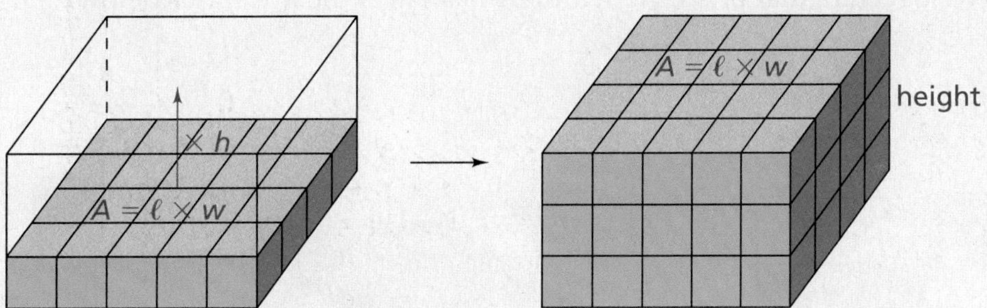

1. Is either of these strategies correct for finding volume? Explain.
2. For each correct method, write a formula for finding the volume of a rectangular prism. Explain what each of the letters in your formulas represents. Compare your formulas.
3. Use your formulas to find the volume of a rectangular prism with a length of 12 centimeters, a width of 10 centimeters, and a height of 7 centimeters.
4. Dushane says that the formulas for Natasha's and Kurt's methods do not work for cubes because the volume of a cube with side length ℓ is ℓ^3. Do you agree with Dushane? Explain your reasoning.

continued on the next page >

Problem 4.2 continued

C Durian wants to compute the volume of the box below.

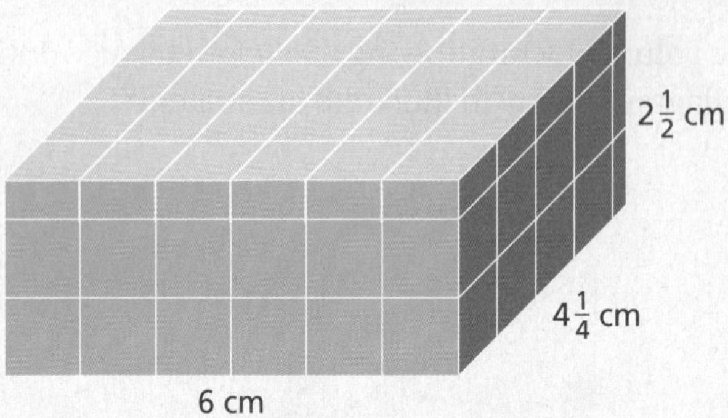

1. Durian claims that the formulas for volume do not work. He says that he cannot fit unit centimeter cubes exactly into the box because the side lengths are not whole numbers. Is he correct? Explain.
2. Find the volume of the box.

D Use rectangular prisms I, II, and III to answer the questions below.

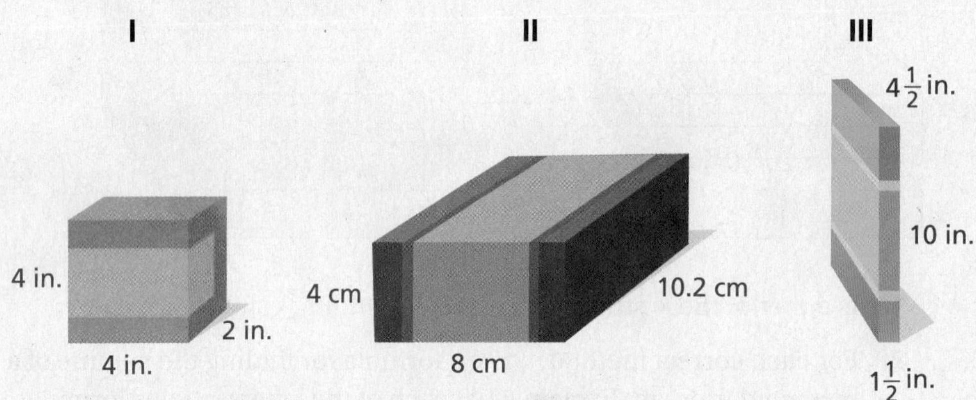

1. What is the volume of each prism? Explain how you found it.
2. What is the surface area of each prism? Explain how you found it.
3. If all the edges of each prism are taped (with no overlap), how much tape is needed for each prism? Explain.

ACE Homework starts on page 87.

4.3 Designing Gift Boxes
Finding Surface Area

A prism is named for the shape of its base—triangular, rectangular, pentagonal, hexagonal, etc. You can draw a net that will fold up to a three-dimensional figure for every kind of prism. Drawing these nets will help you to find the surface area of nonrectangular prisms.

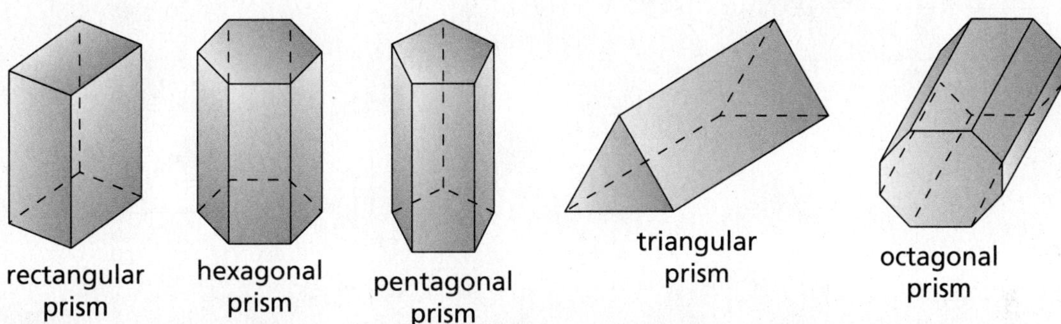

A **pyramid** is a three-dimensional shape with one base that can be any polygon. The lateral sides of a pyramid are triangles that meet at a vertex opposite the base.

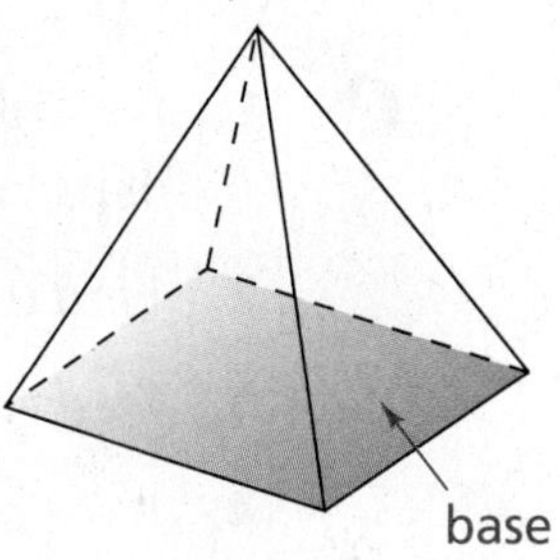

The Save-a-Tree packaging company is sponsoring a contest for students to design gift boxes. Each school submits two designs along with the amount of material required for those designs.

Problem 4.3

Star Middle School has designed the following nets for the contest.

Using a copy of the diagram, cut out each net and fold it into a gift box.

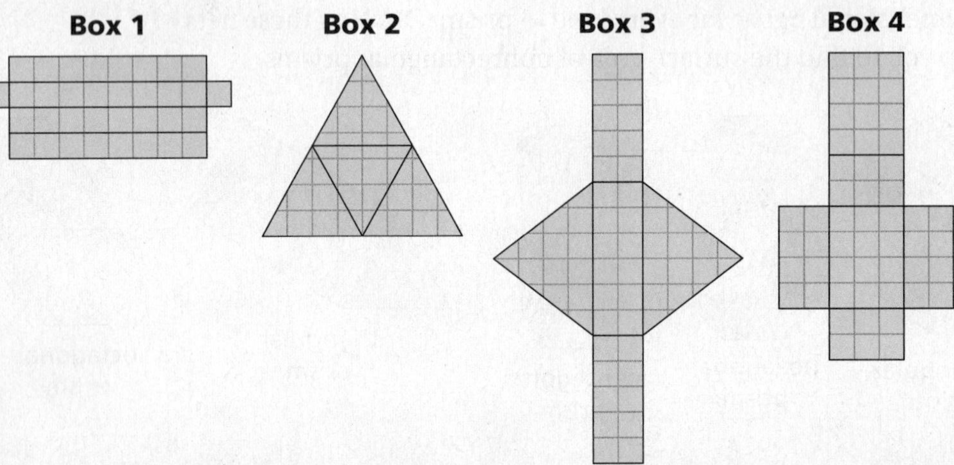

A 1. Describe the shape of each box including the shapes and dimensions of its faces.

2. Find the surface area of each box. Show your work.

3. Describe a method for finding the surface area of any box.

4. If the school wanted to seal all the edges with colored tape (with no overlap) to add some decoration, how much tape is needed for each box? How did you determine the amount?

5. Which design should the school submit? List both the advantages and disadvantages of your choices.

B Valley View Middle School submitted the two boxes at right.

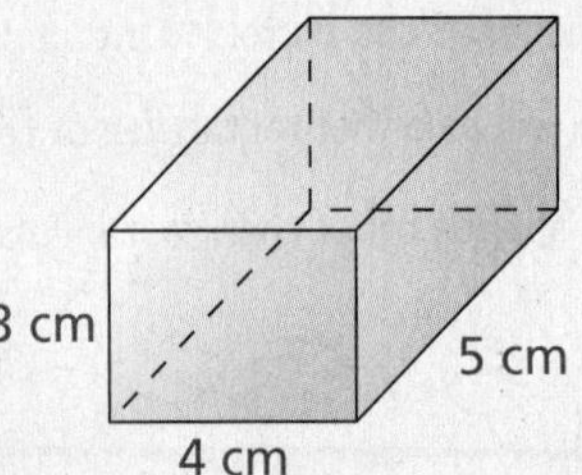

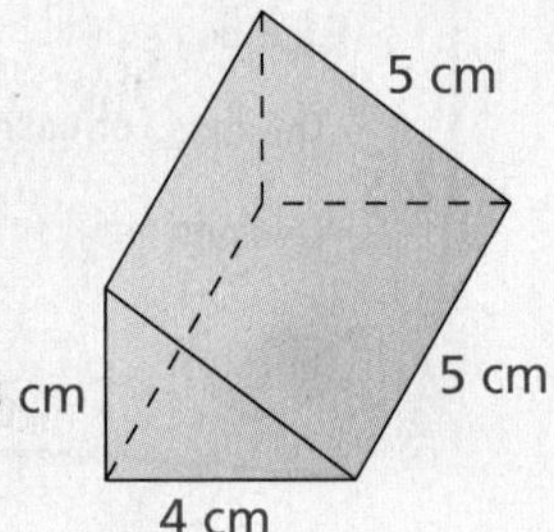

1. Describe how you could determine the surface area of each box, then find the surface area of each box.

2. Sketch a net that would fold up to make each box.

ACE Homework starts on page 87.

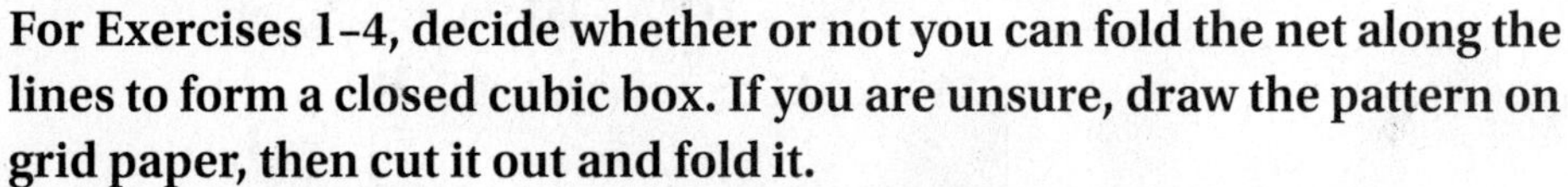

Applications | Connections | Extensions

Applications

For Exercises 1–4, decide whether or not you can fold the net along the lines to form a closed cubic box. If you are unsure, draw the pattern on grid paper, then cut it out and fold it.

1. 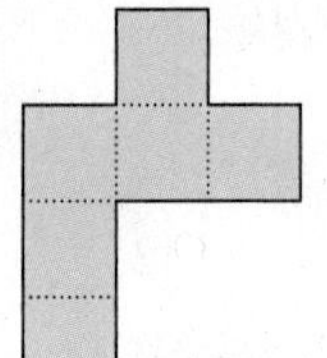

2. 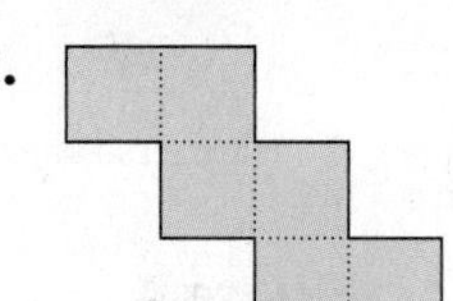

3. 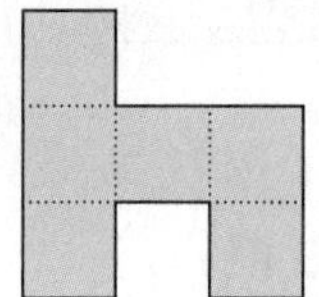

4. 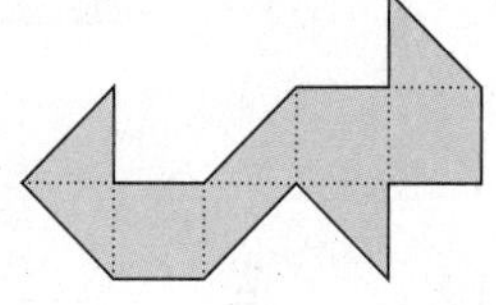

5. For Figures 1–3, answer the questions below.

Figure 1

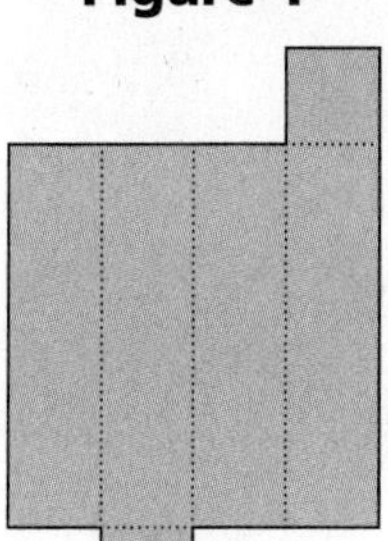

Figure 2

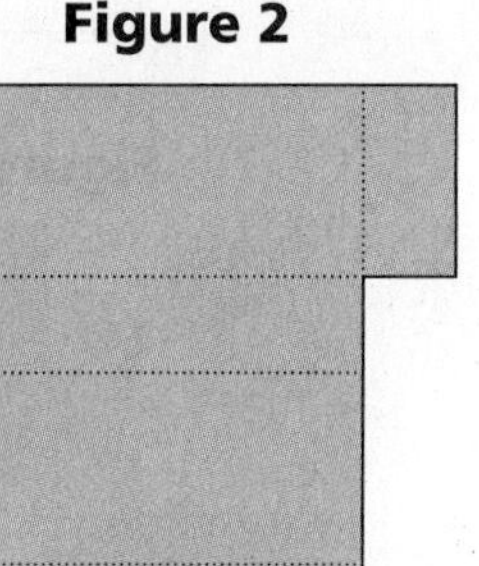

Figure 3

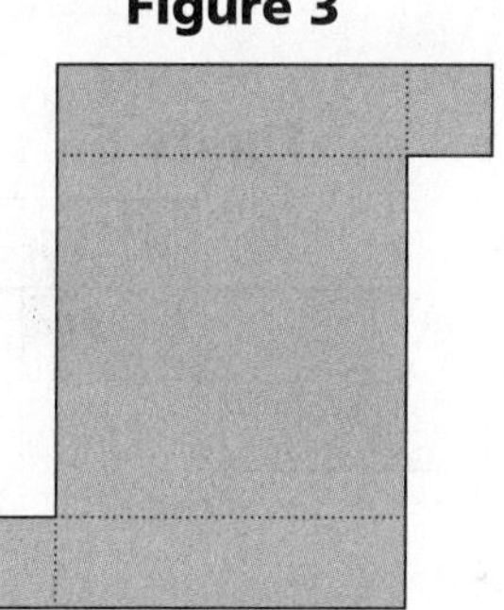

a. Which of these nets could be folded along the lines to form a closed rectangular box?

b. For the figures that form a closed rectangular box, use the unit square shown to help you find the dimensions of the box.

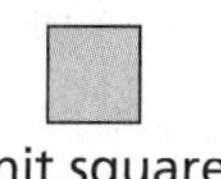
unit square

c. For the figures that form a closed rectangular box, find the total area, in square units, of all of the faces of the box.

d. For the figures that form a closed rectangular box, find the number of unit cubes it would take to fill the box.

6. a. What are the dimensions of the box at the right?

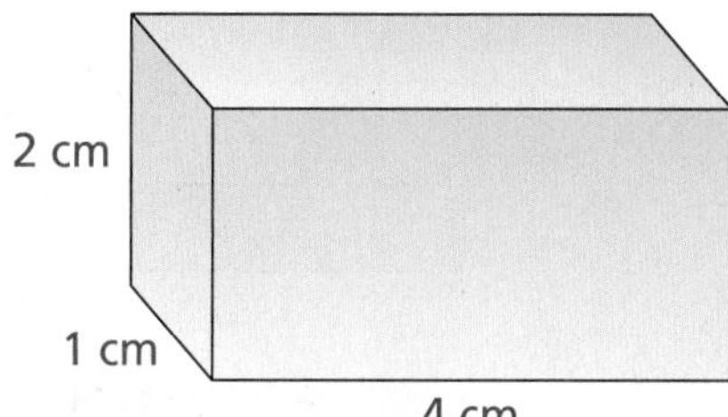

b. On centimeter grid paper, sketch two nets for the box.

c. Find the area, in square centimeters, of each net.

d. Find the total area of all the faces of the box. How does your answer compare with the areas you found in part (c)?

7. Which pattern(s) below can be folded along the lines to form a closed rectangular box? Explain your reasoning.

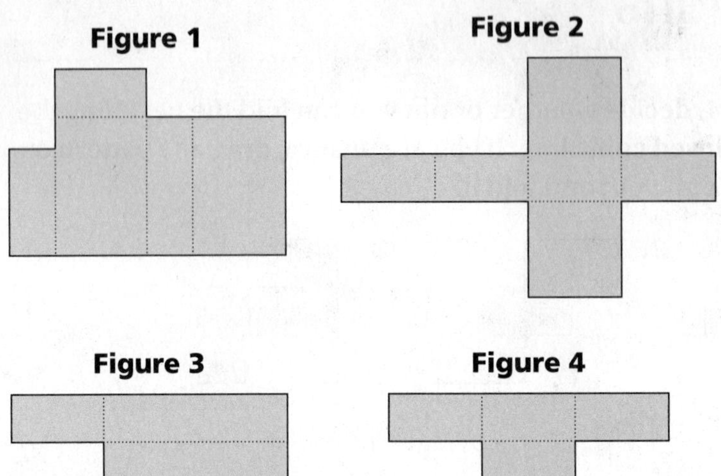

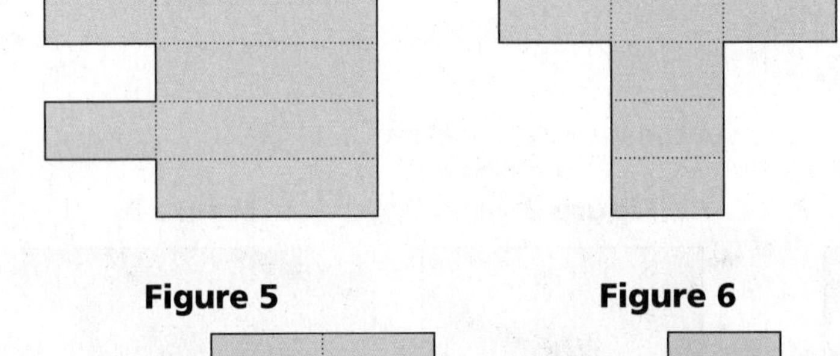

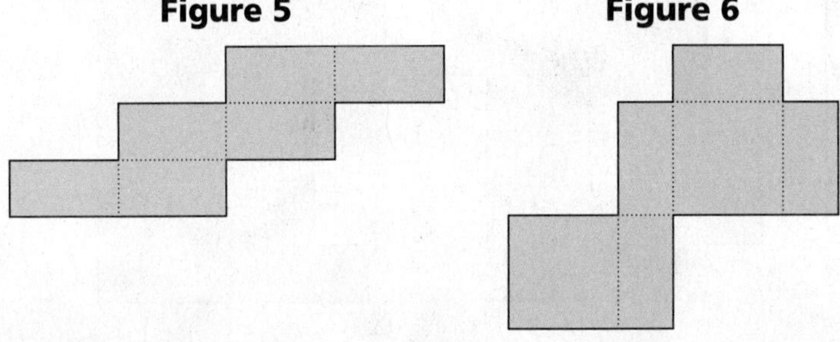

8. Which net(s) could you fold into a cube?

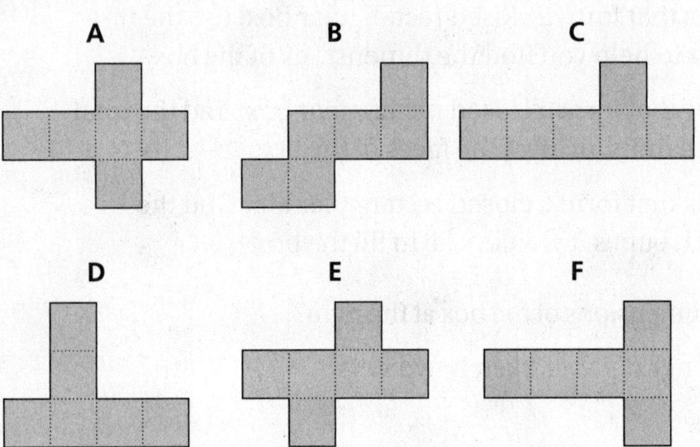

9. Can you fold this net along the lines to form an open cubic box (a box without a top)? Explain your reasoning.

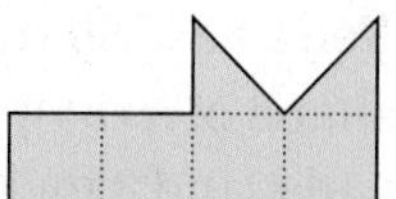

For Exercises 10–13, use each box's description.

- Make a sketch of the box and label its dimensions.
- Draw a net for the box on grid paper.
- Find the area of each face.
- Find the total area of all the faces.

10. a rectangular box with dimensions 2 cm × 3 cm × 5 cm

11. a rectangular box with dimensions $2\frac{1}{2}$ cm × 2 cm × 1 cm

12. a cubic box with side lengths of $3\frac{2}{3}$ in.

13. a cubic box that holds 125 unit cubes

14. An open box is a box without a top.

a. On grid paper, sketch nets for three different open cubic boxes.

b. On grid paper, sketch nets for three different open rectangular boxes (not cubic boxes) with square ends.

c. Find the area of each net you found in parts (a) and (b).

For Exercises 15–17, a rectangular prism is built with $\frac{1}{2}$-inch cubic blocks.

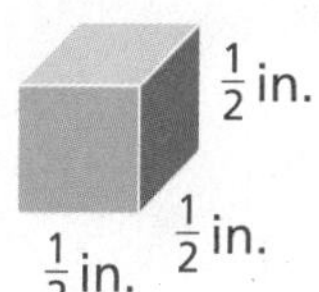

- Find the length, width, and height of each prism.
- How many $\frac{1}{2}$-inch cubes are needed to fill the box?
- What is the volume of each prism in cubic inches?
- Find the surface area of each prism.

15.

16.

17.

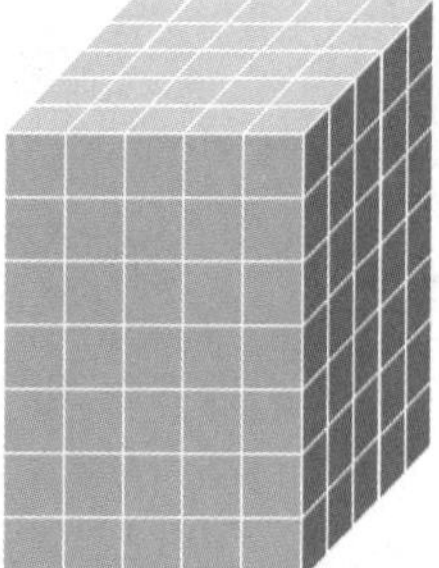

18. Keira has 750 square inches of wrapping paper. Her package is in the shape of a right rectangular prism that is 15 inches long, 12 inches wide, and 8 inches high. Does she have enough paper to cover her package? Explain your reasoning.

19. Mr. Bergstedt's sixth-grade class has a netted butterfly cage in the shape of a pyramid. The four lateral faces are all congruent triangles.

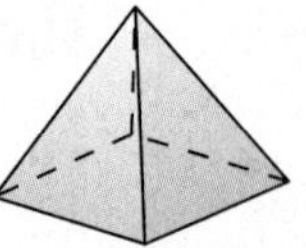

a. What shape is the base of the pyramid?

b. If you know just the length of a side of the base, do you have enough information to find the surface area of the pyramid? Explain your reasoning.

For Exercises 20–23, find the volume and surface area of each rectangular prism.

20.

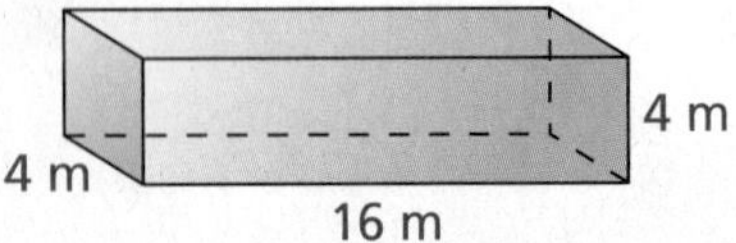

21.

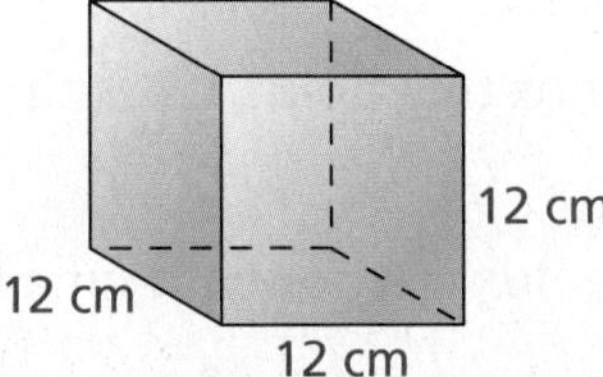

22.

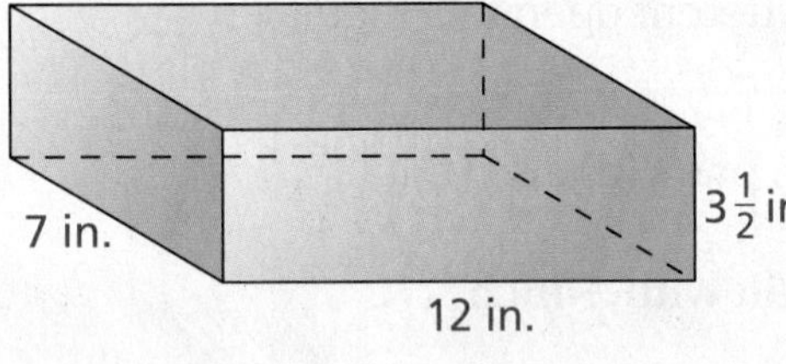

23.

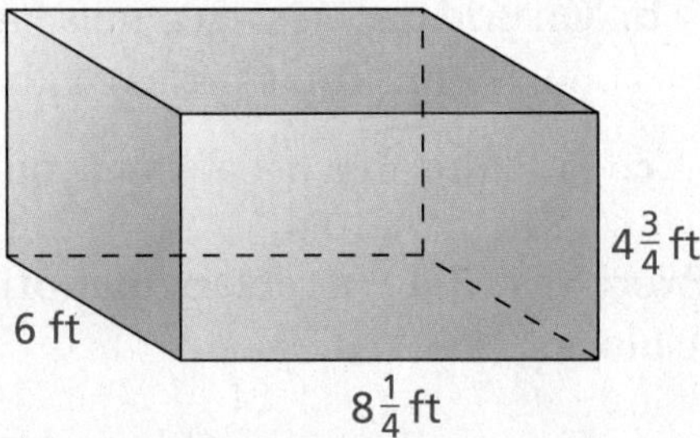

24. Brenda and Stephanie are filling a 3 foot-by-4 foot sandbox to a depth of 3 inches of sand. Stephanie is wondering how much sand they used. Brenda says that to find the volume, you multiply the length, width, and height. Is Brenda's work correct? Explain your reasoning.

Brenda's Work

volume = $\ell \times w \times h$
$= 3 \times 4 \times 3$
$= 36$
The amount of sand is 36 cubic feet.

25. Lumber is often sold by the "board foot," which is a piece of wood that measures 1 foot by 1 foot by 1 inch.

a. What is the volume, in cubic inches, of a piece of wood that is 1 board foot?

b. How many board feet are in a cubic foot?

c. Greg buys a 6 inch-by-6 inch piece of wood that is 4 feet long. Does this have a volume equal to, less than, or greater than the volume of a board foot? Find the difference of the two volumes.

26. Use the diagram at the right.

a. Find the volume of the shoe box.

b. Draw another rectangular prism with different dimensions but the same volume.

c. Does your prism from part (b) have the same surface area as the original prism? Explain.

27. Andrea has 1-inch, $\frac{1}{2}$-inch, and $\frac{1}{4}$-inch blocks. She wants to build a rectangular prism that is $2\frac{1}{2}$ inches by $3\frac{1}{2}$ inches by 4 inches.

a. Andrea wants to build the prism using blocks of the same size. What size blocks could she use?

b. For each block size you chose in part (a), how many blocks would Andrea need?

c. Is it possible to describe the volume of this prism in cubic inches? If so, what is the volume in cubic inches? If not, why is this not possible?

28. Multiple Choice Which set of dimensions describes the rectangular prism with the greatest volume?

A. $3\frac{1}{2}$ in. $\times$ 2 in. $\times$ 5 in.

B. 3 in. $\times$ 2 in. $\times$ $4\frac{1}{2}$ in.

C. 4 in. $\times$ 2 in. $\times$ 4 in.

D. $2\frac{1}{4}$ in. $\times$ 2 in. $\times$ 6 in.

29. What strategies can you use to determine which prism from Exercise 28 has the greatest volume?

30. Megan uses 216 cubic blocks to make a rectangular prism 9 blocks long and 3 blocks tall. Each block measures $\frac{1}{4}$ inch on each side.

a. How many blocks wide is the prism?

b. What are the prism's dimensions in inches?

c. What is the prism's volume in cubic inches?

d. Megan uses all of the blocks to make a new prism that is 6 blocks tall. She could have made several prisms with different bases. Give three possible sets of dimensions for the new prism's base.

31. a. Determine the surface areas of the four nets shown below.

b. Which net(s) could you fold into a rectangular prism?

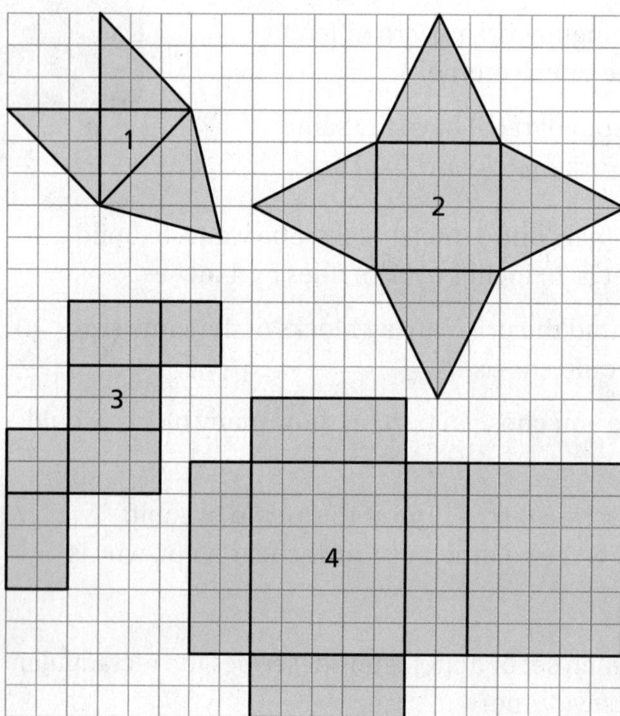

32. Match the nets A, B, and C with the corresponding rectangular prisms D, E, and F.

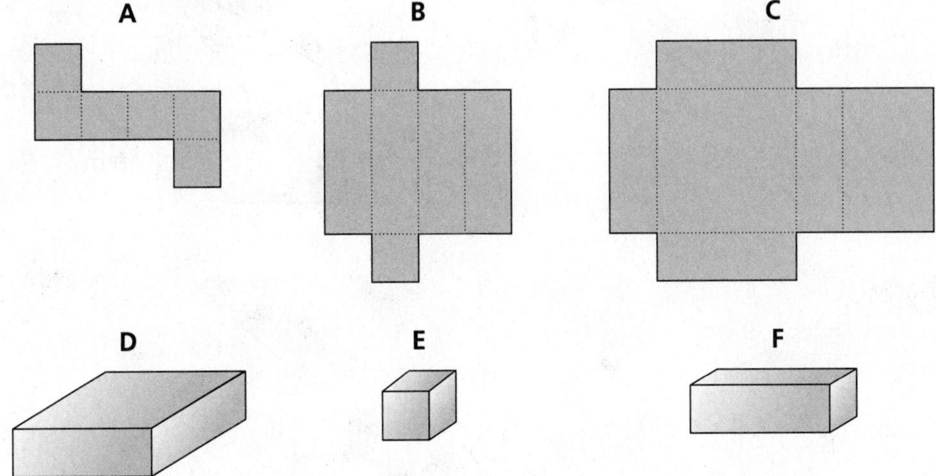

For Exercises 33–35, name the two-dimensional shapes used to make the faces of each object. Tell how many of each shape there are.

33. a rectangular prism, such as a shoebox

34. a triangular prism, such as a tent

35. a rectangular pyramid, such as the structures built by the Egyptians

For Exercises 36–39, sketch a net for each figure.

36.

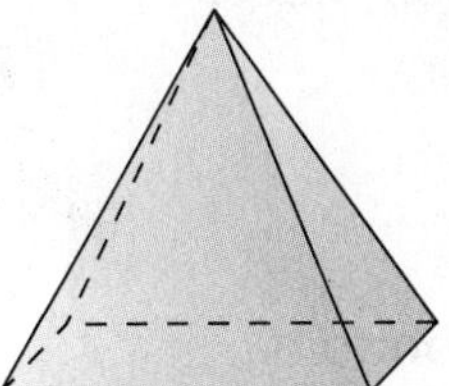

37.

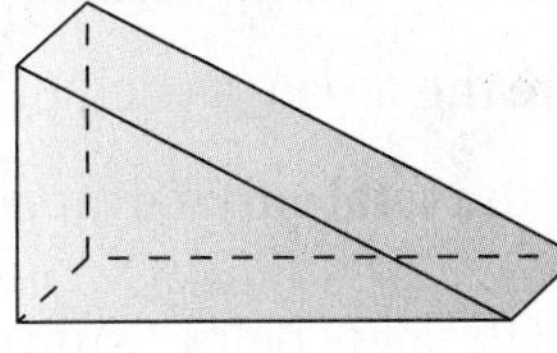

38.

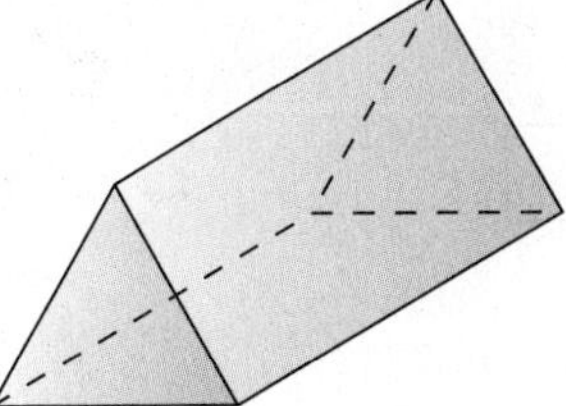

39.

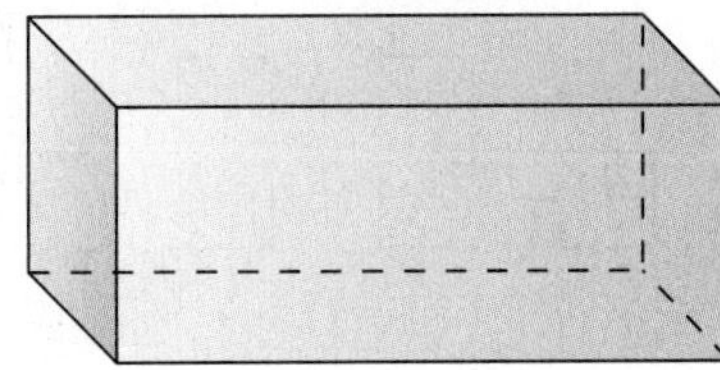

For Exercises 40–43, find the surface area of each object.

40.

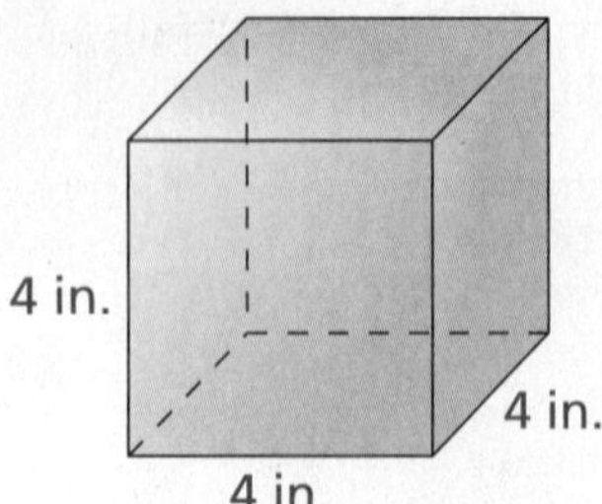

41.

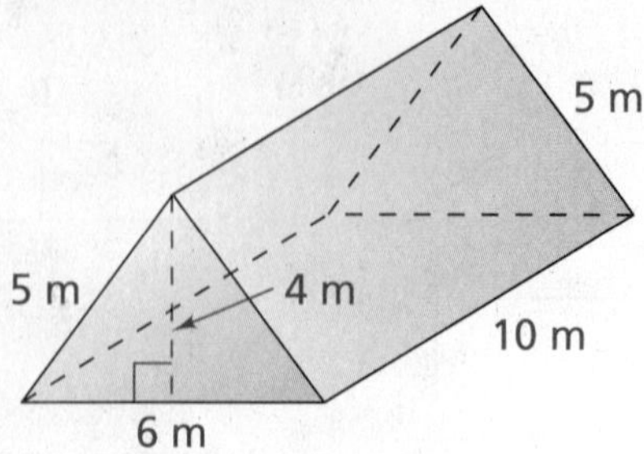

42.

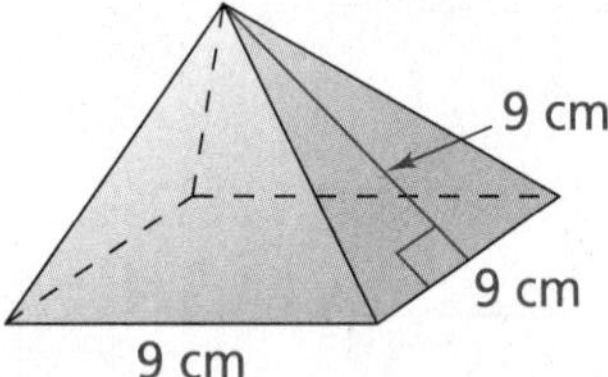

43.

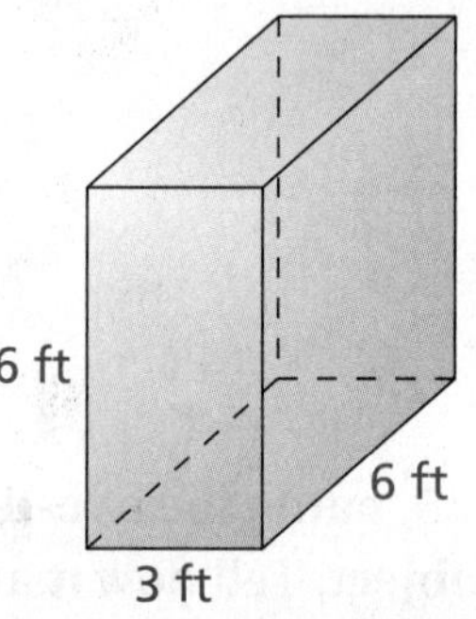

44. Suppose you wanted to tape all the edges of the rectangular prism from Exercise 43. What length of tape would you need?

45. A container in the shape of a rectangular prism has two rectangular faces that measure 4 feet by 6 feet and another side that has a length of 12 feet.

a. What are the measurements of each of the faces of the container?

b. What are the areas of each of the faces of the container?

c. What is the total surface area of the container?

46. For each of the nets below, suppose the shaded face is the bottom face of the cube. When folded, which face will be on top?

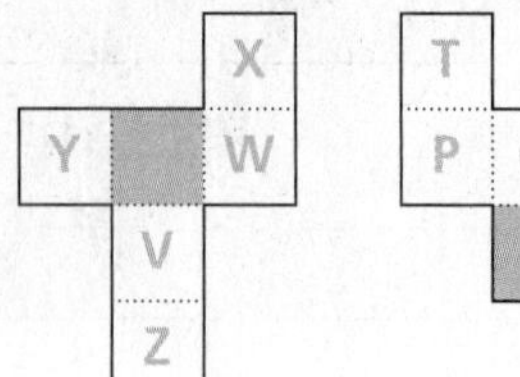

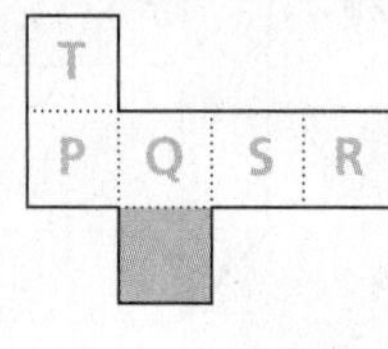

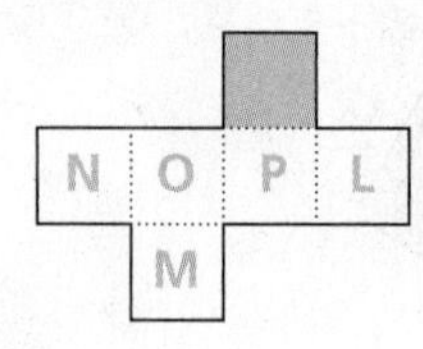

Connections

For Exercises 47–51, use the following information: A *hexomino* is a shape made of six identical squares connected along their sides. The nets for a closed cubic box are examples of hexominos. Below are five different hexominos.

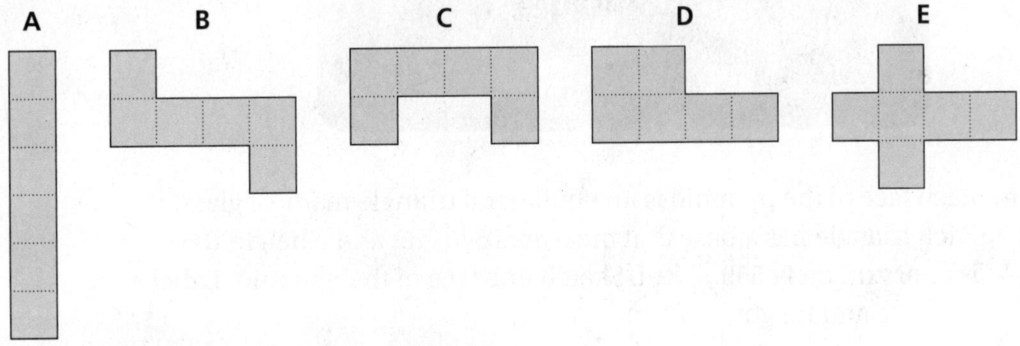

47. Find the perimeter of each hexomino shown above.

48. Which hexominos can you fold to form a closed cubic box?

49. From which hexominos can you remove one square to make a net for an open cubic box? For each hexomino you select, draw a diagram showing which square can be removed.

50. To which hexominos can you add one square without changing the perimeter? For each hexomino you select, draw a diagram. Explain why the perimeter does not change.

51. To which hexominos can you add two squares without changing the perimeter? For each hexomino you select, draw a diagram. Explain why the perimeter does not change.

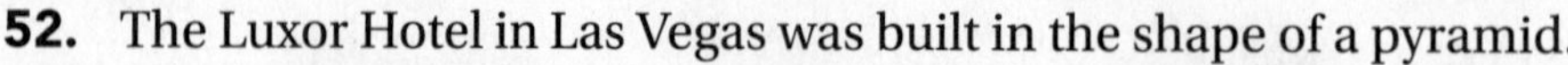

52. The Luxor Hotel in Las Vegas was built in the shape of a pyramid.

a. Each face of the pyramid is an equilateral triangle made of glass. Each triangle has a base that measures 646 feet and a height that is approximately $559\frac{9}{20}$ feet. Sketch one face of the pyramid. Label the base and height.

b. Estimate the area of the glass used to cover one triangular face.

c. If lights are strung along the three edges of one triangular face, how many feet of lights are needed?

53. A group of students were trying to find the volume, V, and surface area, S.A., of a rectangular prism with length ℓ, width w, and height h.

a. One student said that, to find the volume, you multiply the area of the base by the height. Another student said you multiply the length times the width times the height. Who is correct?

b. For finding surface area, the group has three different methods:

Method 1: S.A. = the sum of the areas of faces

Method 2: S.A. = $2(\ell w + \ell h + hw)$

Method 3: S.A. = $2\ell w + 2\ell h + 2hw$

Are they all correct? Explain.

c. Choose a correct formula from part (a) and a correct formula from part (b). Find the volume and surface area of a rectangular prism with a length of $3\frac{1}{4}$ inches, a width of 7 inches, and a height of $10\frac{2}{3}$ inches.

d. Which formula did you use to find the volume? To find the surface area? Why did you choose these formulas?

54. **a.** Matt wrote the following formulas for the volume, V, and surface area, S.A., of a cube with side length s:

$$V = s^3$$

$$\text{S.A.} = 6s^2$$

Sophia says these formulas are not correct because a cube is a special rectangular prism. She says that these formulas do not look like the formulas for the volume and surface area of a rectangular prism. Who is correct? Explain your reasoning.

b. Suppose the side length of the cube is 11 centimeters. What is the volume of the cube?

c. Suppose the side length of the cube is 11 centimeters. What is the surface area of the cube?

55. Demetri is shipping a package and wants to reinforce the box with tape. He tapes every edge once (with no overlap).

a. Suppose the box is 12 inches by 10 inches by 8 inches. How much tape does Demetri use?

b. Demetri thinks he can use a formula to find out how much tape he needs. He uses the formula $4 \cdot (\ell + w + h)$.

Demetri's friend Peter thinks he has another way to determine the amount of tape needed. Peter's formula is $4 \cdot \ell + 4 \cdot w + 4 \cdot h$.

Who is correct? Explain.

Extensions

56. When shipping a first-class package with the U.S. Postal Service, the maximum size is 108 inches. "Size" is calculated by adding the length (the longest dimension) of the package to the girth (the perimeter of the package's base, perpendicular to the length).

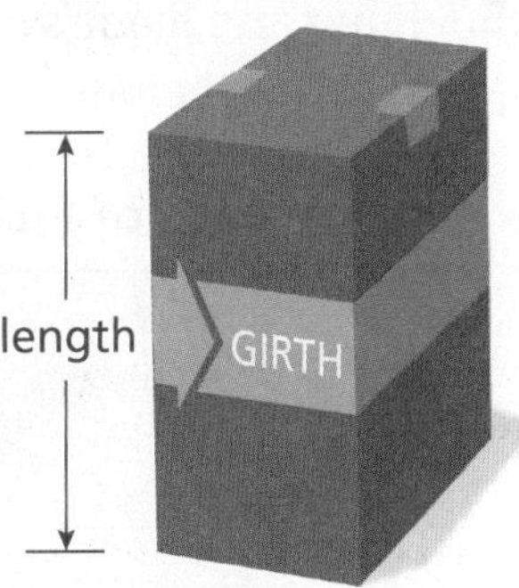

a. Pat is shipping a box that has a base of 10 inches by 15 inches. How tall can the box be for him to ship it first class via the U.S. Postal Service?

b. Samantha is looking for a box that is a rectangular prism with a square base. Darlene suggests using a box that is 30 inches long by 30 inches wide and 9 inches tall. Will Samantha be able to ship that box first class via the U.S. Postal Service? Explain your reasoning.

For Exercises 57–59, Rita made sculptures by gluing together one-inch cubes. She wants to put each sculpture in the smallest possible box. The box must be a rectangular prism. What are the dimensions of the box for each sculpture?

57. 

58. 

59. 

For Exercises 60–62, add a square to each net so that the result would fold into a cube. Draw at least two possible locations for the additional square for each figure.

60. 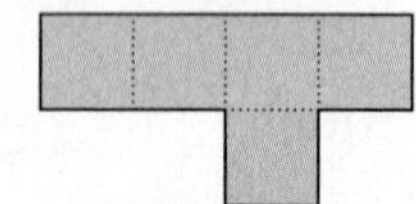

61. 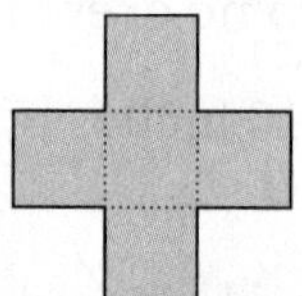

62. 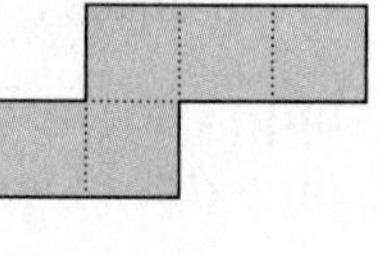

For Exercises 63–65, determine which prism has the greater volume.

63. Abigail and Beatrice both have prisms with heights of 20 inches. Abigail's base is a right triangle with legs that are 3 inches long and 4 inches long. Beatrice's base is a rectangle that is 3 inches by 4 inches.

64. Charlie and Diane's bases are the same, but Charlie's prism is half as tall as Diane's.

65. Elliot and Fiona's prisms are the same height. The base of each prism is shown below.

Base of Fiona's Prism

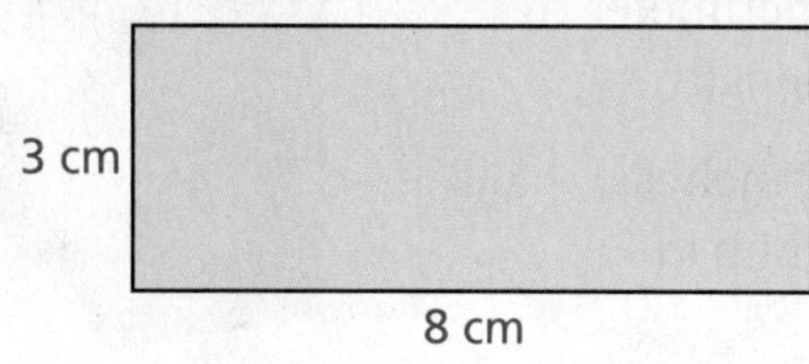

Base of Elliot's Prism

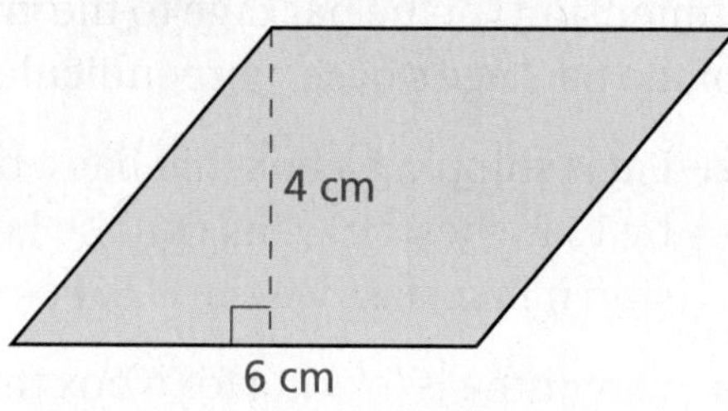

For Exercises 66–69, use centimeter grid paper to draw a net that satisfies the conditions.

66. a prism with a volume of 18 cubic centimeters

67. a prism with a surface area of 62 square centimeters

68. a prism with a volume of 216 cubic centimeters and a surface area of 216 square centimeters

69. a prism with a volume of 250 cubic centimeters and a surface area of 250 square centimeters

70. Every prism has polygonal bases and rectangular sides. For each prism below, describe the shape of each face, and tell how many of each face there are.

a. rectangular prism

b. triangular prism

c. pentagonal prism

d. hexagonal prism

e. decagonal prism

f. Suppose the base of a prism has n sides. How many faces, and what shapes, would you see in the net of the prism?

71. An icosahedron is an object with 20 faces that are all equilateral triangles. The net of an icosahedron is shown below. Suppose each equilateral triangle has a base of 15 centimeters and a height of 13 centimeters. What is the surface area of the icosahedron?

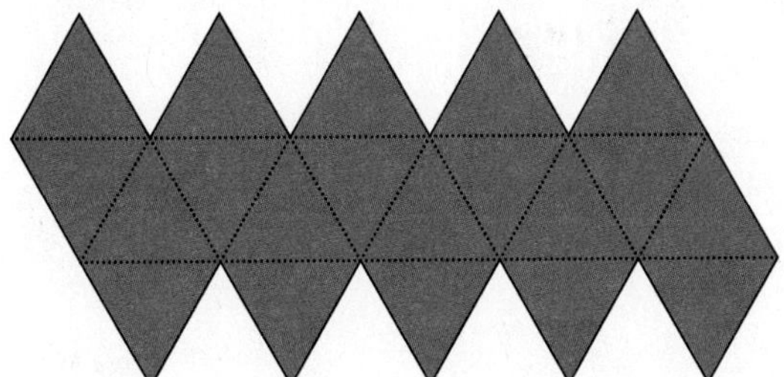

Mathematical Reflections 4

In this Investigation, you revisited strategies for finding the area and perimeter of a rectangle. You examined the areas and perimeters of figures made from square tiles. You also found that some arrangements of tiles have the same area but different perimeters. Other arrangements of the tiles have the same perimeter but different areas. The following questions will help you summarize what you have learned.

Think about these questions. Discuss your ideas with other students and your teacher. Then write a summary of your findings in your notebook.

1. a. **What** information do you need to find the volume of a rectangular prism? Describe a strategy to find the volume of a rectangular prism.

   b. **What** information do you need to find the surface area of a rectangular prism? Describe a strategy to find the surface area of a rectangular prism.

2. a. **Describe** a strategy for finding the surface area of three-dimensional shapes made from rectangles and triangles.

   b. **How** does knowing the area of two-dimensional figures help you find the surface area of a three-dimensional shape?

Common Core Mathematical Practices

As you worked on the Problems in this Investigation, you used prior knowledge to make sense of them. You also applied Mathematical Practices to solve the Problems. Think back over your work, the ways you thought about the Problems, and how you used Mathematical Practices.

Nick described his thoughts in the following way:

Our teacher challenged us to find the dimensions of each box using only the nets. Finding the dimensions using the nets was not obvious. We knew we couldn't simply cut out the net and fold it up into a box. We had to think about the features of a rectangular box. Then we had to locate the faces on the grid. We also used the fact that opposite faces are congruent. Once we outlined the faces of the box, we were able to find its dimensions.

Common Core Standards for Mathematical Practice

MP2 Reason abstractly and quantitatively.

- What other Mathematical Practices can you identify in Nick's reasoning?
- Describe a Mathematical Practice that you and your classmates used to solve a different Problem in this Investigation.

Unit Project

Design an Aquarium

Your school is planning to have an aquarium of schooling fish. The aquarium will be on display at the school entrance. The school holds a contest for the best aquarium design. The design theme is *School for Fish.*

Your task is to design an aquarium to represent a school for fish. The design should contain miniature items related to some aspect of your school day.

You will need to make an argument for why your design should be chosen. Use what you know about your school and what you learned from this Unit to design your aquarium.

Part 1: The Design

Your design must satisfy the following requirements:

- The aquarium has the shape of a rectangular prism.
- The floor area of the aquarium is rectangular and has dimensions of 5 feet by 3 feet.
- The four sides of the aquarium must be made of glass.
- The height of the aquarium will depend on the tallest miniature or (live or artificial) plant in the aquarium.
- The bottom of the aquarium must be covered with 3 centimeters of gravel. You may consider using different kinds of gravel.

- The aquarium must provide an appropriate amount of space in which the fish can swim. The amount of space may vary depending on the species of fish.
- Your design must take into consideration maintenance requirements for the aquarium (e.g., a porous filter media).

Part 2: Write a Report

Your design package must be neat, clear, and easy to follow.

1. Draw a floor plan of your aquarium on centimeter grid paper. Use shapes such as triangles, quadrilaterals, or other polygons to indicate the locations of the miniatures and plants. Label your design items in black and white.

   Determine the scale for your blueprint: 1 cm = ___. Write the scale at the corner of your blueprint. Use the scale for all elements of your design.

2. Make two flat patterns that can be folded to represent two of the miniatures.

3. Provide the following information in your report. Include the calculations you used to determine the information.
   - the dimensions of the aquarium
   - the amount of gravel
   - the volume of water needed to fill the tank
   - the number of fish
   - the amount of available space in which the fish can swim
   - the area needed for plants and artifacts
   - the amount of glass needed for the sides
   - the surface area of the two miniatures for which you made flat patterns

Extension Question

Write a letter to the school board. Explain why they should choose your design for the aquarium. Justify the choices you made about the size and quantity of the items in your aquarium.

Looking Back

Working on the Problems in this Unit helped you to understand area and perimeter. You learned

- Efficient strategies for estimating and calculating the area and perimeter of figures such as triangles, rectangles, and parallelograms
- To investigate the relationship between area and perimeter of simple polygons
- To investigate the relationship between the surface area of a prism and the areas of triangles, rectangles, and parallelograms

Use Your Understanding: Area and Perimeter

Test your understanding and skill in working with area and perimeter on these problems.

1. The diagram shows a hexagon drawn on a centimeter grid.

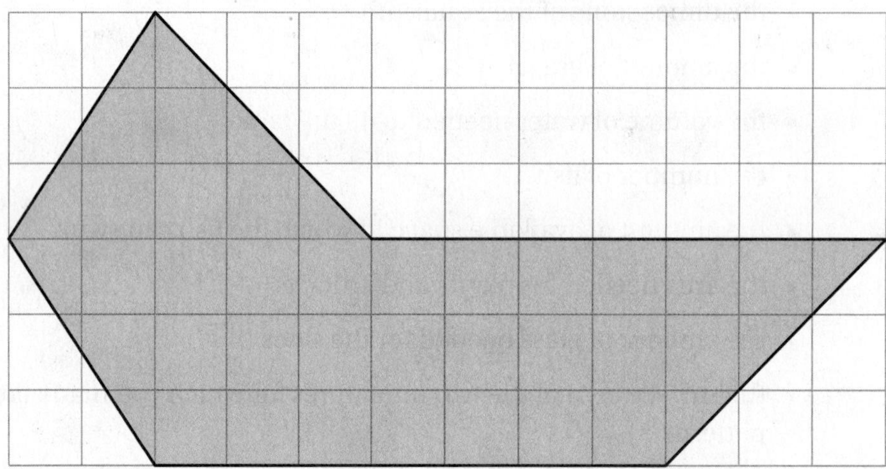

   a. Find the area of the hexagon.

   b. Describe two different strategies for calculating the area.

2. Amy has a gift for her mother that she needs to wrap. She designs a gift box in the shape of a rectangular prism. The dimensions of the prism are 6 inches by 6 inches by 7.5 inches.

a. What is the volume of the gift box?

b. What is the surface area of the gift box?

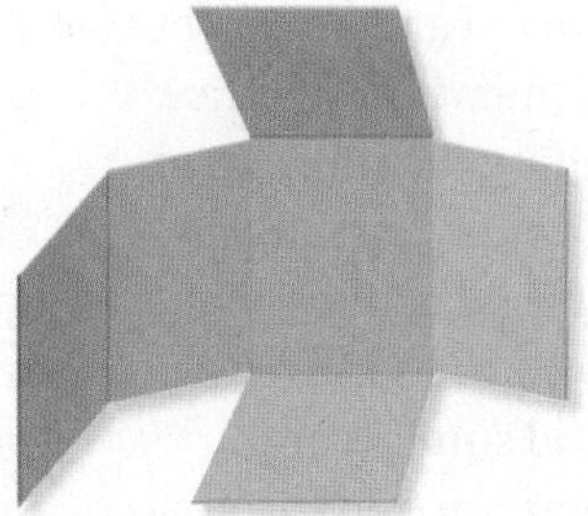

3. What is the surface area of the triangular prism below?

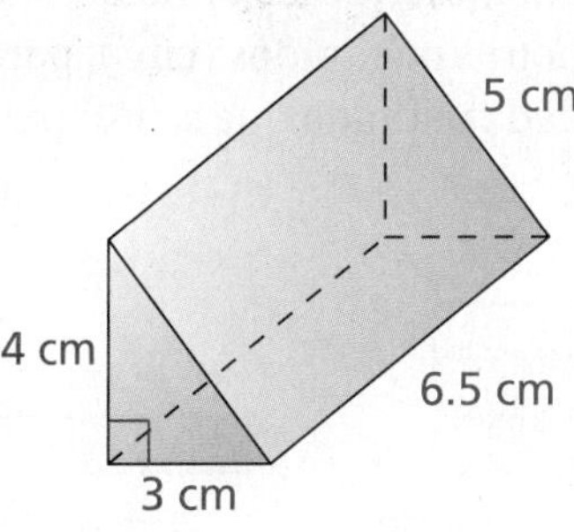

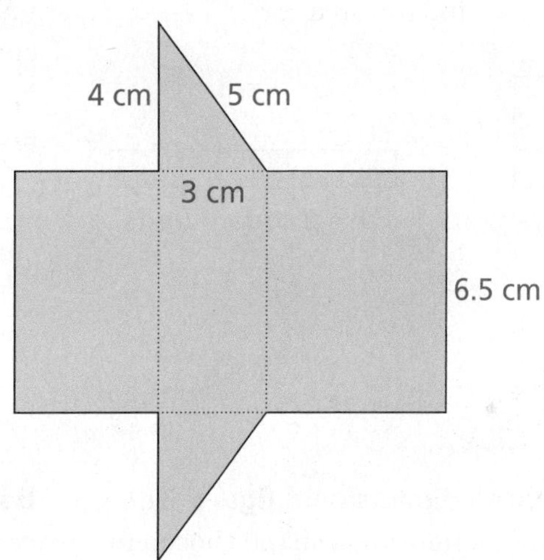

Explain Your Reasoning

4. Give a formula for finding the area and perimeter of each figure.

a. rectangle **b.** triangle **c.** parallelogram

5. Explain why the formulas you wrote for Problem 4 work.

6. Explain the role that a square or rectangle plays in developing the area of a triangle and the area of a parallelogram.

7. Give a formula for finding the surface area and volume of a rectangular prism. Explain why the formulas work.

English / Spanish Glossary

A

area The measure of the amount of surface enclosed by the boundary of a figure. To find the area *A* of a figure, you can count how many unit squares it takes to cover the figure. You can find the area of a rectangle by multiplying the length by the width. This is a shortcut method for finding the number of unit squares it takes to cover the rectangle. If a figure has curved or irregular sides, you can estimate the area. Cover the surface with a grid and count whole grid squares and parts of grid squares. When you find the area of a shape, write the units, such as square centimeters (cm^2), to indicate the unit square that was used to find the area.

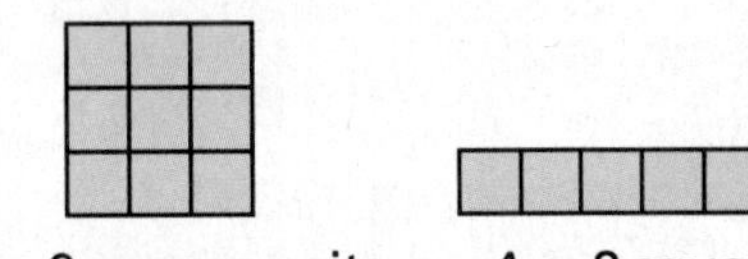

A = 9 square units　　A = 8 square units

área La medida de la cantidad de superficie encerrada por los límites de una figura. Para hallar el área de una figura, puedes contar cuántas unidades cuadradas se necesitan para cubrir la figura. Puedes hallar el área de un rectángulo multiplicando el largo por el ancho. Este es un método más corto para hallar el número de unidades cuadradas que se necesitan para cubrir el rectángulo. Si una figura tiene lados curvos o irregulares, puedes estimar el área. Para ello, cubre la superficie con una cuadrícula y cuenta los cuadrados enteros y las partes de cuadrados en la cuadrícula. Cuando halles el área de una figura, escribe las unidades, por ejemplo, centímetros cuadrados (cm^2), para indicar la unidad cuadrada que se usó para hallar el área.

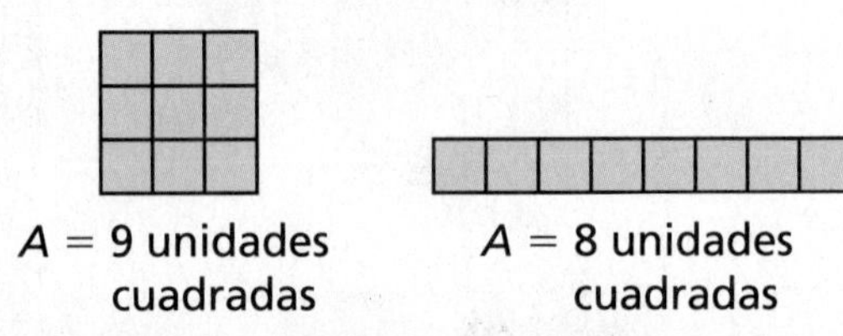

B

base of a three-dimensional figure The face of a three-dimensional shape chosen to be the "bottom" face.

base de una figura tridimensional La cara de una figura tridimensional que se elige como la cara inferior.

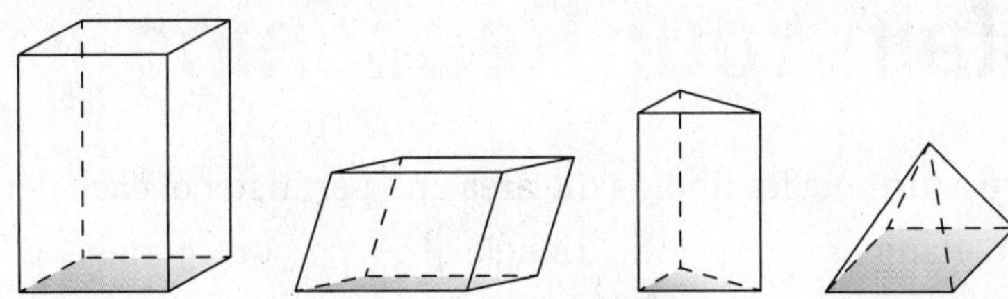

base of a two-dimensional figure See *measurements of two-dimensional figures.*

base de una figura bidimensional Ver *medidas de las figuras bidimensionales.*

C

coordinates An ordered pair of numbers used to locate a point on a coordinate grid. The first number in a coordinate pair is the value for the *x*-coordinate, and the second number is the value for the *y*-coordinate. A coordinate pair for the graph shown below is (0, 60).

coordenadas Un par ordenado de números que se usa para localizar un punto en una gráfica de coordenadas. El primer número del par de coordenadas es el valor de la coordenada *x* y el segundo número es el valor de la coordenada *y*. Un par de coordenadas para la gráfica que se muestra es (0, 60).

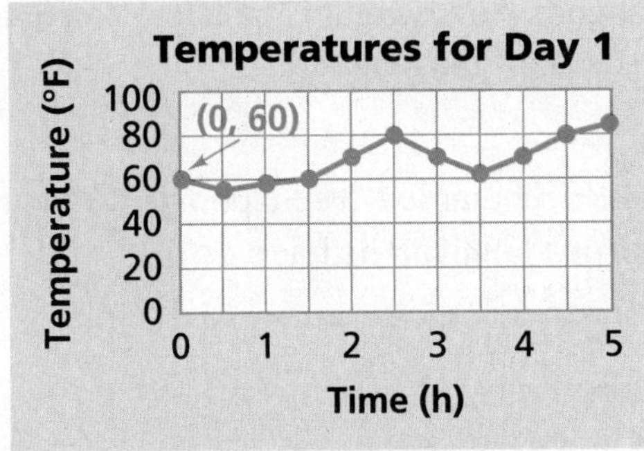

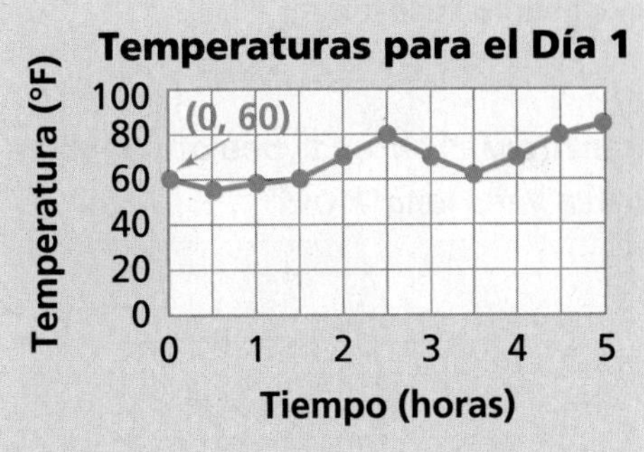

E

edge A line segment formed where two faces of a three-dimensional shape meet.

arista El segmento de recta que se forma en el lugar en donde se encuentran dos caras de una figura tridimensional.

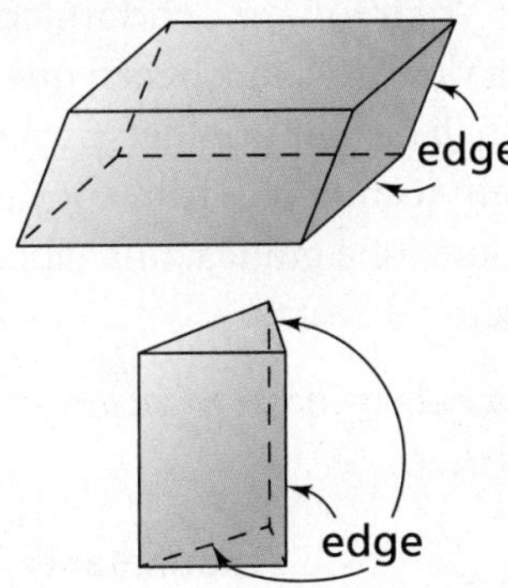

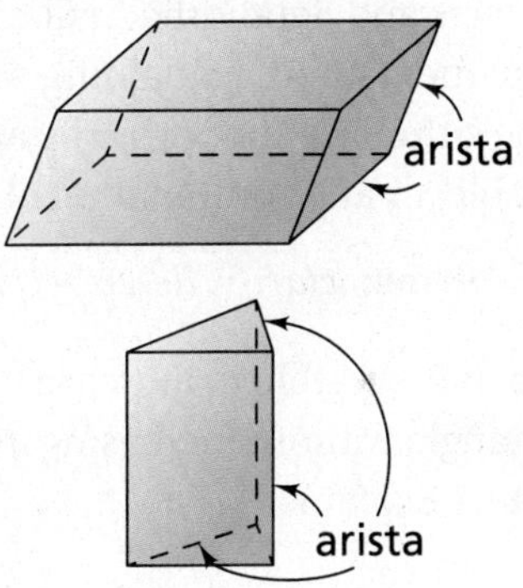

equilateral triangle A triangle with all three sides the same length.

triángulo equilátero Un triángulo que tiene los tres lados de la misma longitud.

experiment Academic Vocabulary
To try several different or new ways to discover something unknown or to demonstrate something known.

related terms: *explore, examine, discover*

sample Experiment to see if you can draw an isosceles, a right, and an equilateral triangle with the same base length.

I can draw all three types of triangles with a base length of 3.

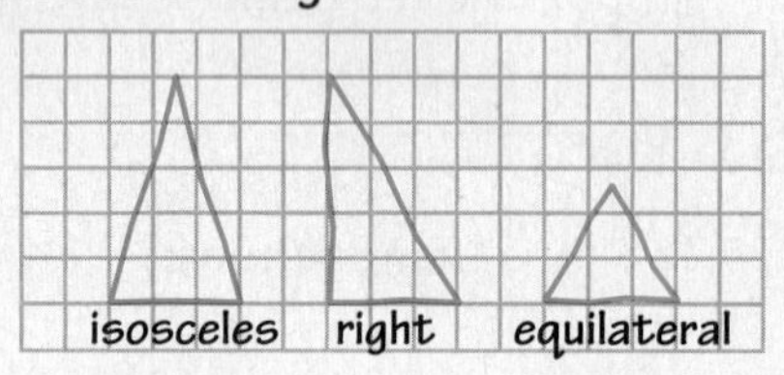

experimentar Vocabulario académico
Intentar varias o nuevas maneras de descubrir algo desconocido o demostrar algo conocido.

términos relacionados: *explorar, examinar, descubrir*

ejemplo Experimenta para ver si puedes dibujar un triángulo isósceles, un triángulo rectángulo y un triángulo equilátero con una base de la misma longitud.

Puedo dibujar los tres tipos de triángulos con una longitud de base de 3.

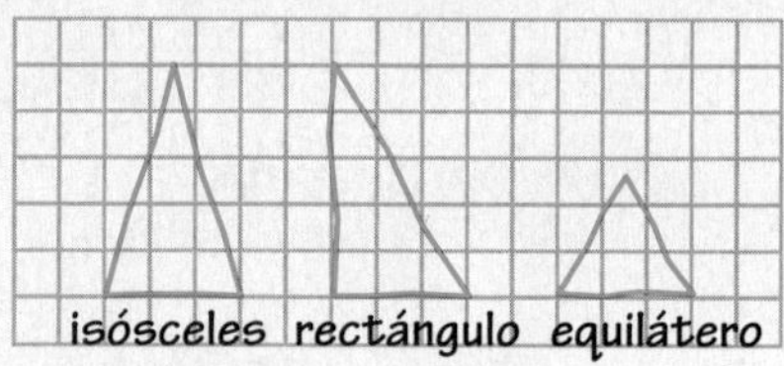

explain Academic Vocabulary
To give facts and details that make an idea easier to understand. Explaining can involve a written summary supported by a diagram, chart, table, or any combination of these.

related terms: *clarify, describe, justify, tell*

sample Is it possible to increase the area of a rectangle without increasing its perimeter? Explain.

I can increase the area of a rectangle from 8 square units to 9 without increasing the perimeter of 12.

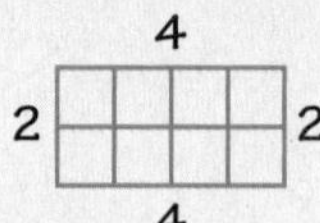

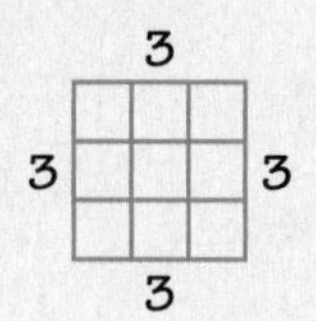

explicar Vocabulario académico
Dar datos y detalles que hacen que una idea sea más fácil de comprender. Explicar puede implicar un resumen escrito apoyado por un diagrama, una gráfica, una tabla, o una combinación de estos.

términos relacionados: *aclarar, describir, justificar, decir*

ejemplo ¿Es posible aumentar el área de un rectángulo sin aumentar su perímetro? Explica tu respuesta.

Puedo aumentar el área de un rectángulo de 8 unidades cuadradas a 9 sin aumentar el perímetro de 12 unidades.

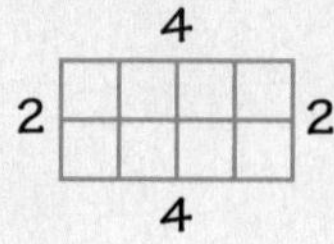

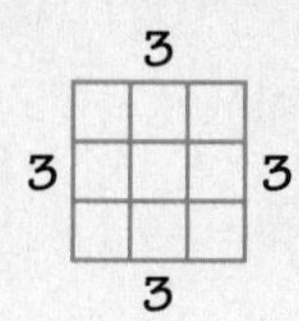

F **face** A flat two-dimensional surface of a three-dimensional shape.

cara Una superficie plana y bidimensional de una figura tridimensional.

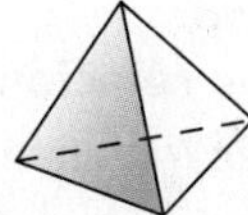
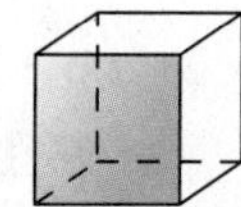
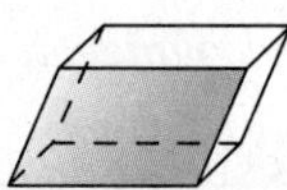

formula A rule containing variables that represents a mathematical relationship. An example is the formula for finding the area of a rectangle: $A = \ell w$, where ℓ represents the length and w represents the width.

fórmula Una regla que contiene variables que representa una relación matemática. Un ejemplo es la fórmula para hallar el área de un rectángulo: $A = \ell a$, donde ℓ representa la longitud y a el ancho.

H **height of a three-dimensional figure** See *measurements of three-dimensional figures.*

altura de una figura tridimensional Ver medidas de las figuras tridimensionales.

height of a two-dimensional figure See *measurements of two-dimensional figures.*

altura de una figura bidimensional Ver *medidas de las figuras bidimensionales.*

English / Spanish Glossary

I

identify Academic Vocabulary
To match a definition or a description to an object or to recognize something and be able to name it.

related terms: *name, find, recognize, locate*

sample Identify the triangles shown below that have the same area. Explain.

A.
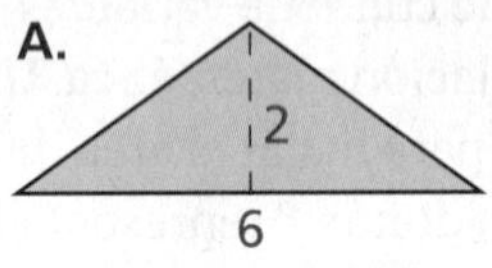

B.
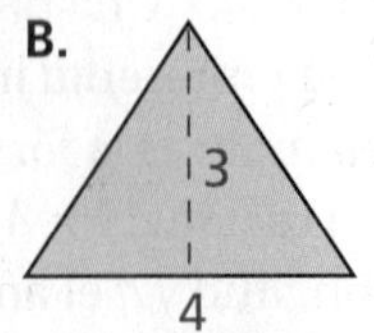

C.
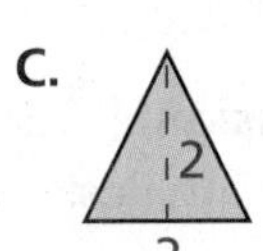

D.
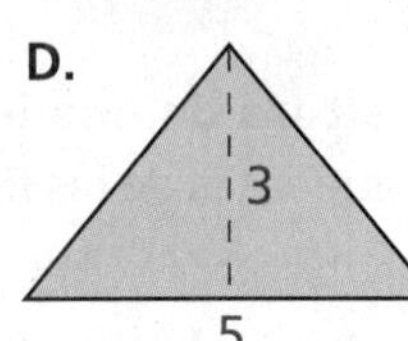

Triangles A and B have the same area. The area of Triangle A is $\frac{1}{2}(2)(6) = 6$. The area of Triangle B is $\frac{1}{2}(3)(4) = 6$. The area of Triangle C is 2, and the area of Triangle D is 7.5.

identificar Vocabulario académico
Relacionar una definición o una descripción con un objeto, o bien, reconocer algo y ser capaz de nombrarlo.

términos relacionados: *nombrar, hallar, reconocer, localizar*

ejemplo Identifica los triángulos que se muestran a continuación que tienen la misma área. Explica tu respuesta.

A.
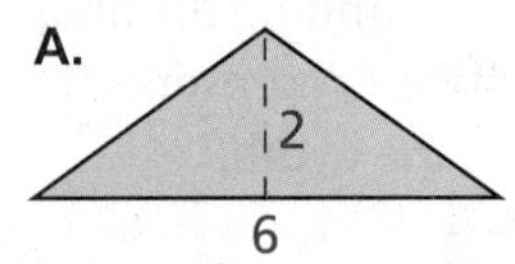

B.
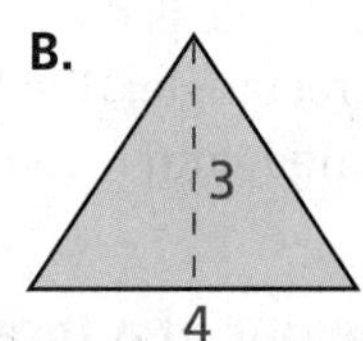

C.
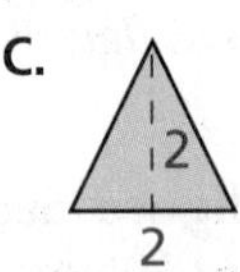

D.
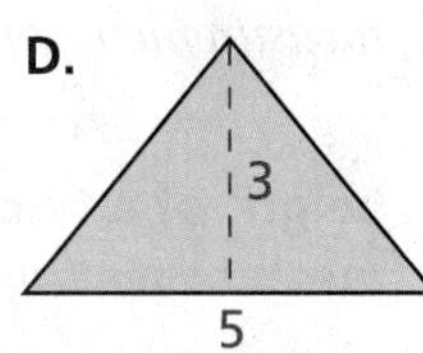

Los triángulos A y B tienen la misma área. El área del Triángulo A es $\frac{1}{2}(2)(6) = 6$. El área del Triángulo B es $\frac{1}{2}(3)(4) = 6$. El área del Triángulo C es 2, y el área del Triángulo D es 7.5.

isosceles triangle A triangle with two sides the same length.

triángulo isósceles Un triángulo que tiene dos lados de la misma longitud.

L

length of a three-dimensional figure See *measurements of three-dimensional figures.*

longitud de una figura tridimensional Ver *medidas de las figuras tridimensionales.*

length of a two-dimensional figure See *measurements of two-dimensional figures.*

longitud de una figura bidimensional Ver *medidas de las figuras bidimensionales.*

M **measurements of three-dimensional figures** Dimensions, such as length, width, and height, which describe the size of three-dimensional figures. If the base of the figure is a rectangle, *length* and *width* refer to the length and width of the figure's rectangular base. The *height* of a three-dimensional figure is the vertical distance from the bottom of the figure to its top.

medidas de las figuras tridimensionales Dimensiones como la longitud, el ancho y la altura, que describen el tamaño de las figuras tridimensionales. Si la base de la figura es un rectángulo, la *longitud* y el *ancho* se refieren a la longitud y al ancho de la base rectangular de la figura. La *altura* de una figura tridimensional es la distancia vertical desde la parte de abajo de la figura hasta la parte de arriba.

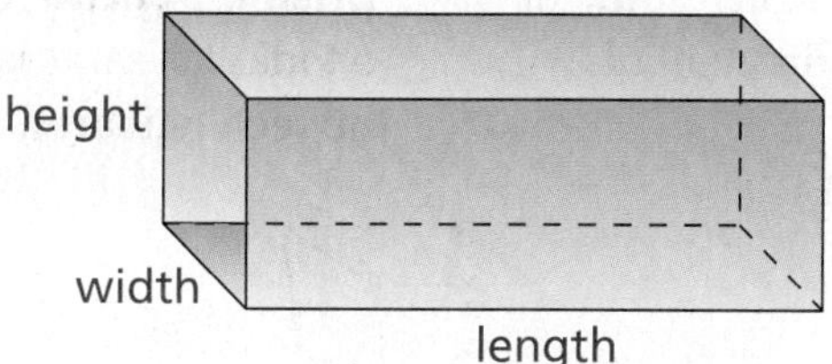

measurements of two-dimensional figures Dimensions, such as length, width, base, and height, which describe the size of two-dimensional figures. The longest dimension or the dimension along the bottom of a rectangle is usually called the length, and the other dimension is called the width, but it is not incorrect to reverse these labels. The word base is used when talking about triangles and parallelograms. The base is usually measured along a horizontal side, but it is sometimes convenient to think of one of the other sides as the base. For a triangle, the height is the perpendicular distance from a vertex opposite the base to the line containing the base. For a parallelogram, the height is the perpendicular distance from a point on the side opposite the base to the base. You need to be flexible when you encounter these terms, so you are able to determine their meanings from the context of the situation.

medidas de las figuras bidimensionales Dimensiones como la longitud, el ancho, la base y la altura, que describen el tamaño de las figuras bidimensionales. La dimensión más larga, o la dimensión de la parte inferior de un rectángulo, generalmente se llama *longitud* y la otra dimensión se llama *ancho*, sin embargo no es incorrecto intercambiar estos nombres. La palabra *base* se usa cuando se habla de triángulos y de paralelogramos. La base se mide a lo largo de un lado horizontal pero a veces es conveniente pensar en uno de los otros lados como la base. En un triángulo, la altura es la distancia perpendicular que hay desde el vértice opuesto a la base, hasta la base. En un paralelogramo, la altura es la distancia perpendicular que hay desde un punto en el lado opuesto a la base, hasta la base. Tienes que ser flexible cuando encuentres estos términos para que puedas determinar su significado dentro del contexto de la situación.

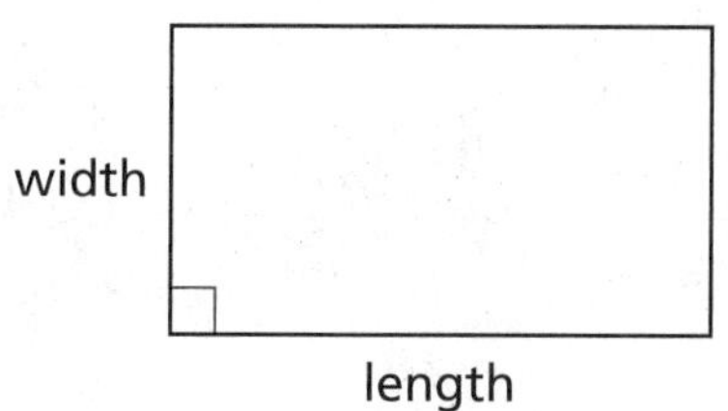

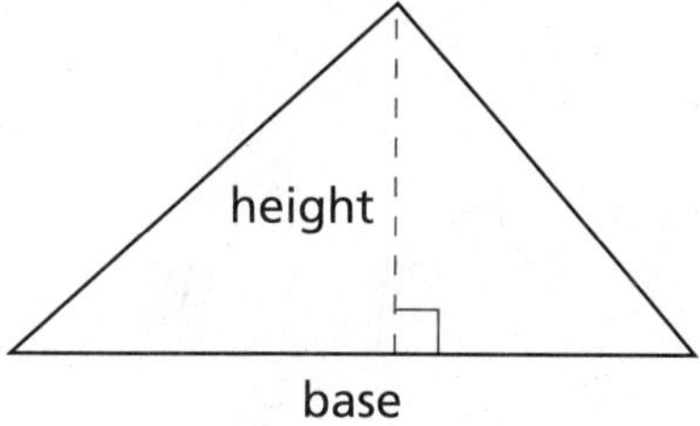

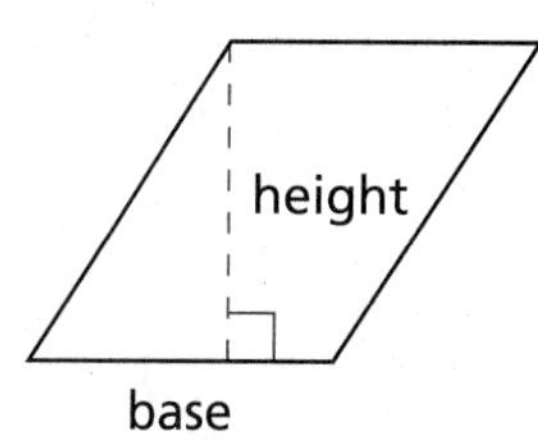

N

net A two-dimensional pattern that can be folded into a three-dimensional figure.

modelo plano Un patrón bidimensional que se puede doblar para formar una figura tridimensional.

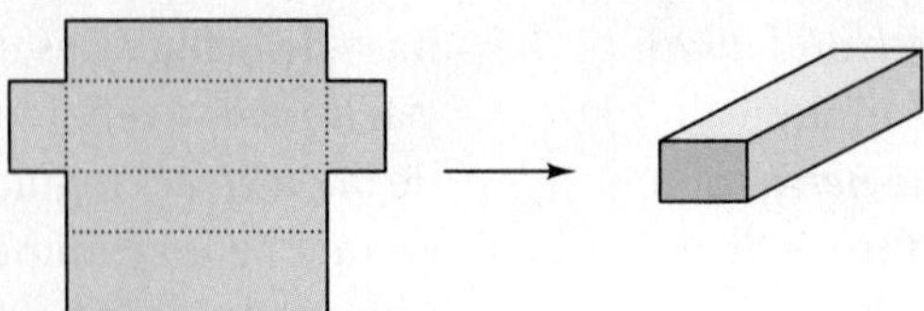

O

oblique prism A prism for which some or all of the lateral faces are nonrectangular parallelograms.

prisma oblicuo Un prisma en el que algunas o todas las caras laterales son paralelogramos no rectangulares.

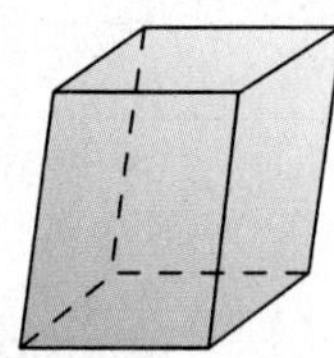

P

perimeter The measure of the distance around a two-dimensional figure. Perimeter is a measure of length. To find the perimeter P of a figure, you count the number of unit lengths it takes to surround the figure. When you find the perimeter of a shape, write the units (such as centimeters, feet, or yards) to indicate the unit that was used to find the perimeter. The perimeter of the square below is 12 units, because 12 units of length surround the figure. The perimeter of the rectangle is 18 units. Notice that the rectangle has a greater perimeter, but a lesser area, than the square.

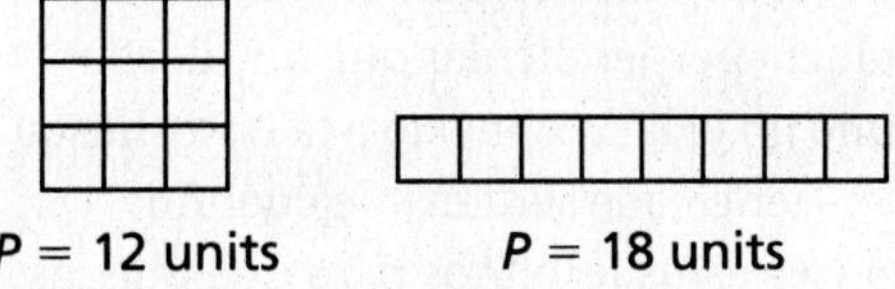

P = 12 units P = 18 units

perímetro La medida de la distancia alrededor de una figura bidimensional. El perímetro es una medida de longitud. Para hallar el perímetro P de una figura, cuentas el número de unidades de longitud que se requieren para rodear la figura. Cuando halles el perímetro de una figura, escribe las unidades (por ejemplo, centímetros, pies o yardas) para indicar la unidad que se usó al hallar el perímetro. El perímetro del cuadrado que se muestra es de 12 unidades, porque 12 unidades de longitud rodean la figura. El perímetro del rectángulo es de 18 unidades. Observa que el rectángulo tiene un perímetro mayor, pero un área más pequeña, que la del cuadrado.

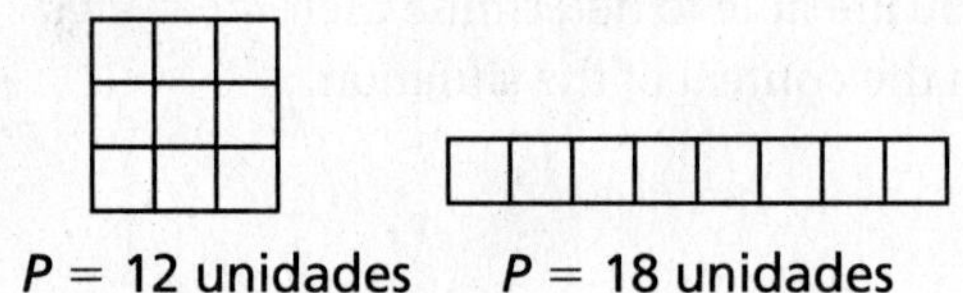

P = 12 unidades P = 18 unidades

perpendicular lines Lines that meet at right angles. The length and width of a rectangle are perpendicular to each other and the base and height of a triangle are perpendicular to each other. In diagrams, perpendicular lines are often indicated by drawing a small square where the lines meet.

rectas perpendiculares Rectas que se intersecan y forman ángulos rectos. La longitud y el ancho de un rectángulo son perpendiculares entre sí. La base y la altura de un triángulo también son perpendiculares entre sí. En los diagramas, las rectas perpendiculares generalmente se representan dibujando un cuadrado pequeño en el lugar en donde coinciden las rectas.

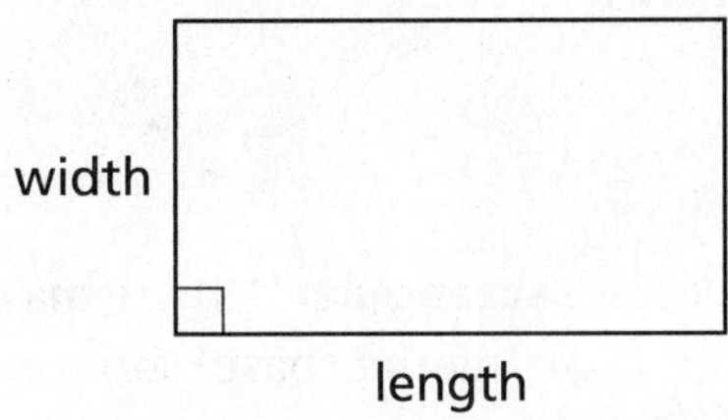

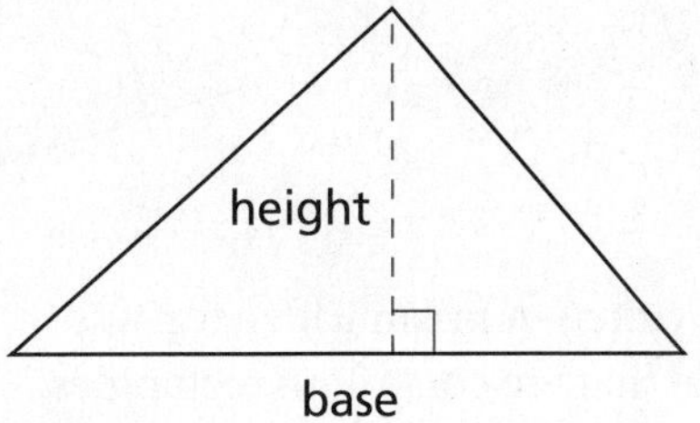

polygon A shape formed by three or more line segments, called *sides*. Each segment meets exactly two other segments, but only at their endpoints.

polígono Una figura formada por tres o más segmentos de recta llamados *lados*. Cada segmento se interseca exactamente con otros dos segmentos, pero solamente en los extremos.

Polygons

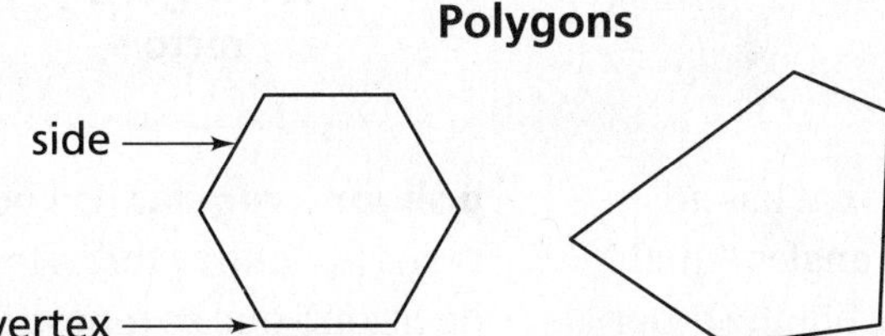

prism A three-dimensional shape with a top and bottom (base) that are congruent polygons and lateral faces that are parallelograms.

prisma Una figura tridimensional que tiene una parte superior y una parte inferior (base) que son polígonos congruentes, y cuyas caras laterales son paralelogramos.

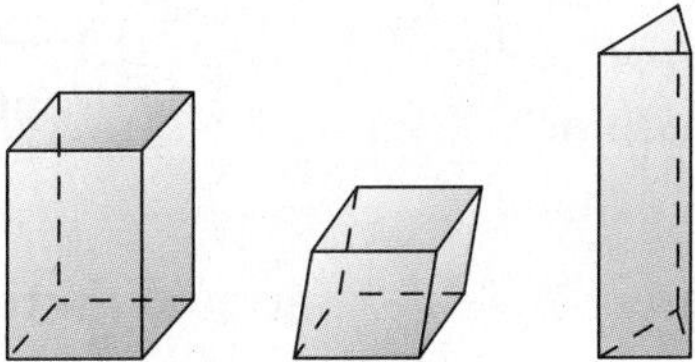

pyramid A three-dimensional shape with one polygonal base and lateral faces that are all triangles that meet at a vertex opposite the base.

pirámide Un figura tridimensional con una base que es un polígono y cuyas caras laterales son triángulos que coinciden en un vértice opuesto a la base.

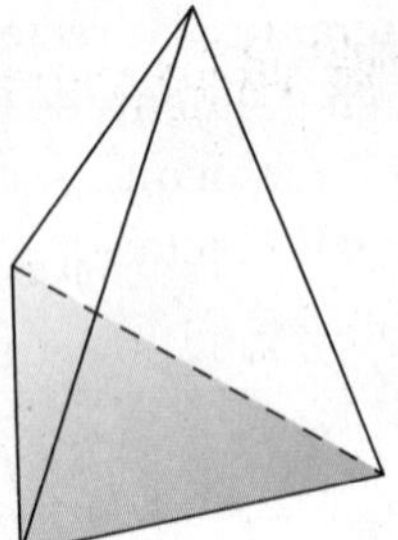
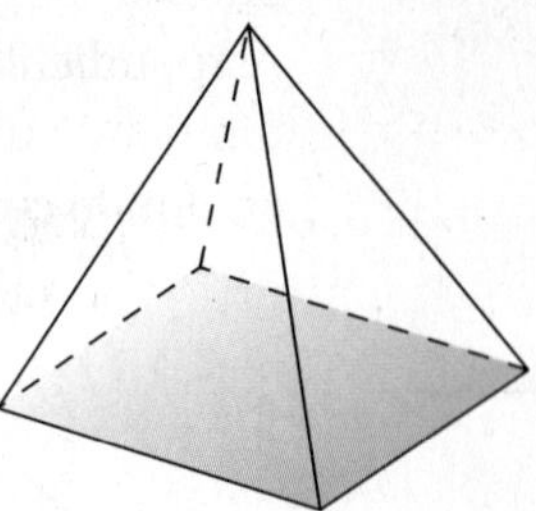
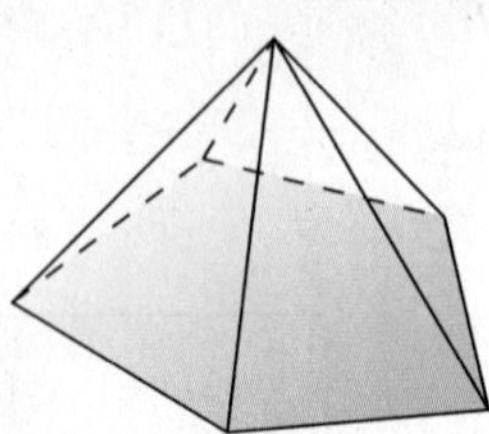

R

rectangular prism A prism with a top and bottom (base) that are congruent rectangles.

prisma rectangular Un prisma cuyas partes superior e inferior (base) son rectángulos congruentes.

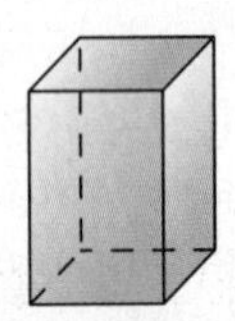

right rectangular prism

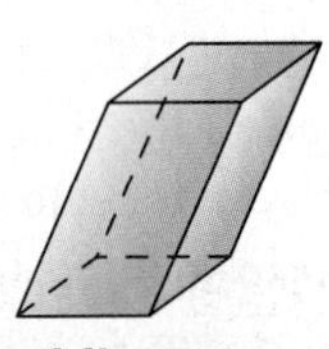

oblique rectangular prism

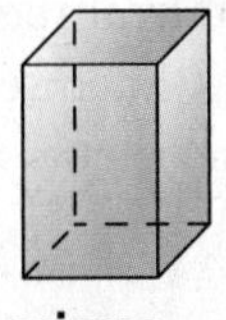

prisma rectangular recto

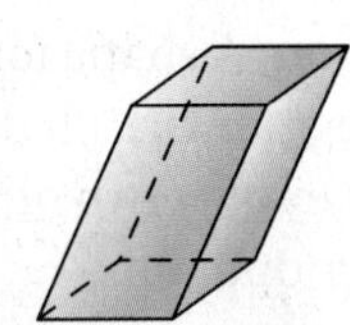

prisma rectangular oblicuo

regular polygon A polygon that has all of its sides equal and all of its angles equal. The hexagon below is regular, but the other hexagon is not regular, because its sides and its angles are not equal.

polígono regular Un polígono que tiene todos los lados y todos los ángulos iguales. El hexágono que se muestra a continuación es regular, pero el otro no lo es porque sus lados y sus ángulos no son iguales.

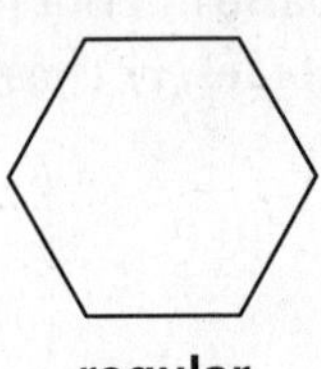

regular

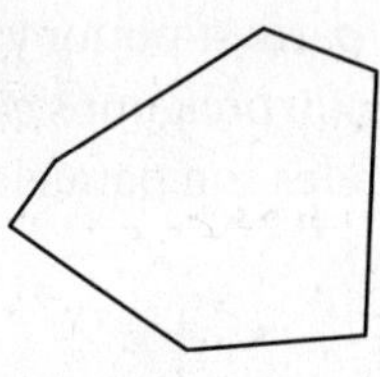

not regular

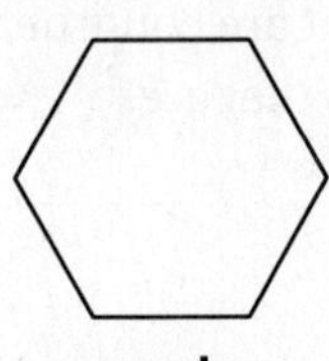

regular

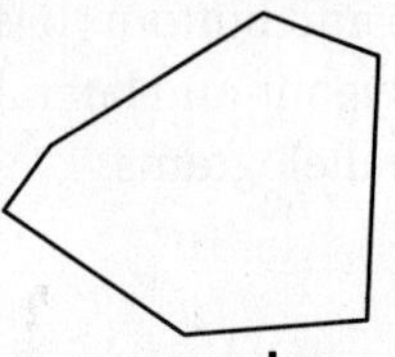

no regular

right angle An angle that measures 90°. A rectangle has four right angles.

ángulo recto Un ángulo que mide 90°. Un rectángulo tiene cuatro ángulos rectos.

right prism A prism whose vertical faces are rectangles. The bases are congruent polygons.

prisma recto Un prisma cuyas caras verticales son rectángulos. Las bases son polígonos congruentes.

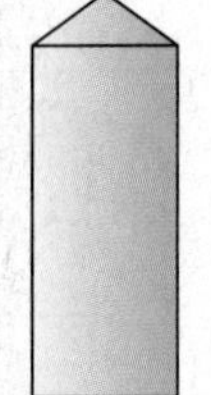
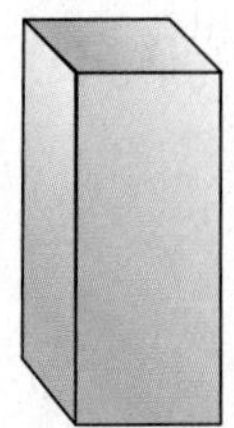
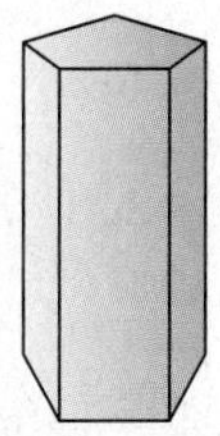
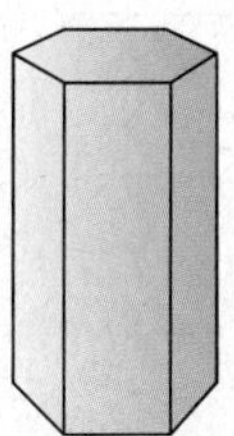

S

scalene triangle A triangle with no sides equal.

triángulo escaleno Un triángulo que no tiene lados iguales.

summarize Academic Vocabulary
To go over or review the most important points.

related terms: *explain, demonstrate, present*

sample Summarize what you know about isosceles, right, and equilateral triangles.

An isosceles triangle has at least 2 sides with equal lengths. A right triangle has one right angle. An equilateral triangle is a triangle with 3 equal side lengths.

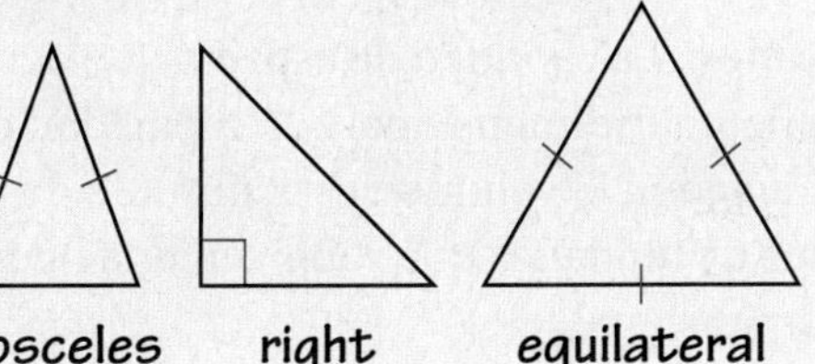

resumir Vocabulario académico
Repasar o revisar los puntos más importantes.

términos relacionados: *explicar, demostrar, presentar*

ejemplo Haz un resumen de lo que sabes sobre los triángulos isósceles, los triángulos rectángulos y los triángulos equiláteros.

Un triángulo isósceles tiene al menos 2 lados con longitudes iguales. Un triángulo rectángulo tiene un ángulo recto. Un triángulo equilátero es un triángulo con 3 lados de longitudes iguales.

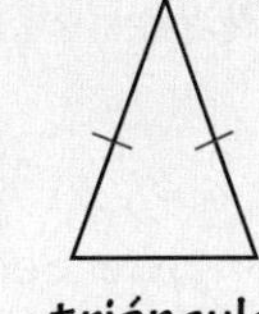
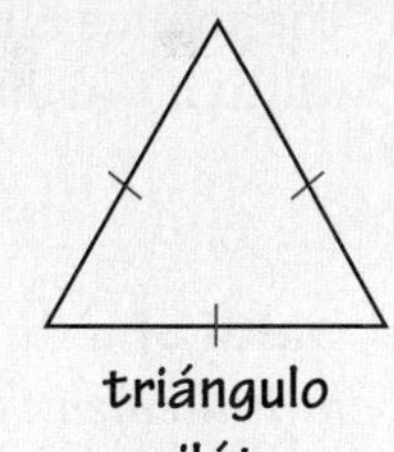

triángulo isósceles — triángulo rectángulo — triángulo equilátero

surface area The area required to cover a three-dimensional shape.

área total El área que se necesita para cubrir una figura tridimensional.

U

unit cube A cube whose edges are 1 unit long. It is the basic unit of measurement for volume.

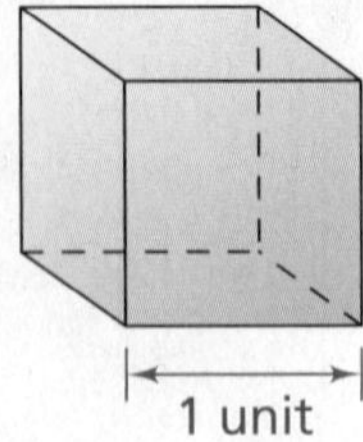

cubo de unidades Un cubo cuyas aristas miden 1 unidad de longitud. Es la unidad básica de medición para el volumen.

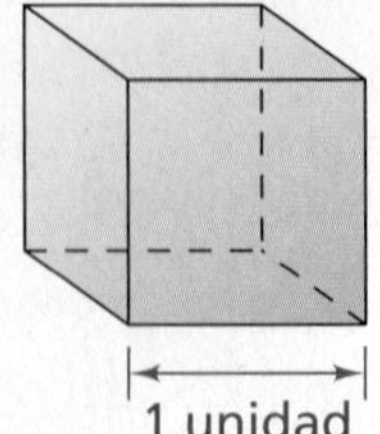

V

vertex A corner of a polygon. For example, *G, H, I, J,* and *K* are all vertices in the pentagon below. All angles have vertices: For example, in the hexagon below, angle *AFE* has a vertex at *F.*

vértice La esquina de un polígono. Por ejemplo, *G, H, I, J* y *K* son vértices del pentágono que se muestra a continuación. Todos los ángulos tienen vértices. Por ejemplo, para este hexágono, el ángulo *AFE* tiene un vértice en *F.*

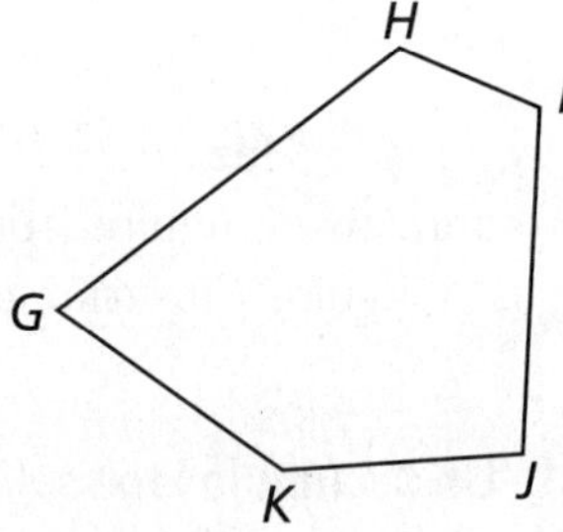

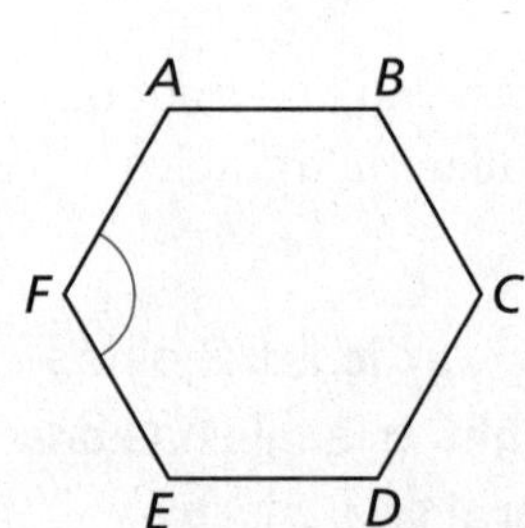

volume The amount of space occupied by or the capacity of a three-dimensional shape. The volume is the number of unit cubes that will fit into a three-dimensional shape.

volumen La cantidad de espacio que ocupa una figura tridimensional o la capacidad de dicha figura. El volumen es el número de cubos de unidades que caben en una figura tridimensional.

W

width of a three-dimensional figure See *measurements of three-dimensional figures.*

ancho de una figura tridimensional Ver *medidas de las figuras tridimensionales.*

width of a two-dimensional figure See *measurements of two-dimensional figures.*

ancho de una figura bidimensional Ver *medidas de las figuras bidimensionales.*

X

***x*-coordinate** See *coordinates.*

coordenada *x* Ver *coordenadas.*

Y

***y*-coordinate** See *coordinates.*

coordenada *y* Ver *par de coordenadas.*

Index

Acknowledgments

Cover Design

Three Communication Design, Chicago

Photographs

Photo locators denoted as follows: Top (T), Center (C), Bottom (B), Left (L), Right (R), Background (Bkgd)

002 (T) Thomas Aichinger/VWPics/SuperStock, (C) Sherman Hines/Masterfile Corporation; **003** Ann Jones/Iconica/Getty Images; **010** Thomas Aichinger/VWPics/SuperStock; **014** Universal Images Group (Lake County Discovery Museum)/Alamy; **027** Christian Delbert/Shutterstock; **028** Izzet Keribar/Lonely Planet Images/Getty Images; **048** Sherman Hines/Masterfile Corporation; **096** B.S.P.I./Encyclopedia/Corbis; **099** Georgi Pavlov/Fotolia.

Data Sources

Grateful acknowledgement is made to the following for copyrighted material:

Automobile Magazine

From *"A Short History of Bumper Cars"* by Seth Gussow from AUTOMOBILE MAGAZINE (p 14)

American Pet Products Association

Data from *"2011-2012 National Pet Owners Survey"* from the American Pet Products Association (APPA). (p 12)

CONNECTED MATHEMATICS® 3

Decimal Ops

Computing With Decimals and Percents

Lappan, Phillips, Fey, Friel

Decimal Ops

Computing With Decimals and Percents

3 Multiplying and Dividing Decimals 42

4 Using Percents 74

Looking Ahead

Every year, students volunteer to clean up local highways. The sections they clean are measured with a trundle wheel. Vijay cleans 0.287 of a mile. He later cleans 0.02 of a mile. **How much** does Vijay clean altogether?

Sweety's Ice Cream Shop sells ice cream by weight. They charge $6.95 per pound. If your dish of ice cream weighs 0.42 pounds, **how much** will it cost?

A bean plant grows 15% of its height each day. Today, after 10 days, the bean plant is 27 inches tall. **What** was its height yesterday?

Knowing when and how to estimate and to compute with all types of numbers is important. You already know about working with fractions and with whole numbers. In this Unit, you will use what you know to make sense of computing with decimals.

In *Let's Be Rational*, you studied the operations of addition, subtraction, multiplication, and division with fractions. In *Decimal Ops*, you will study the same operations with decimals. You will need to decide which operation makes sense in a given situation. For example, suppose a swim team competes in a 200-meter relay race. They finish the race in 3.5 minutes. How could you determine how fast, on average, each team member swam?

You will then use all of your knowledge to develop strategies for working with percents in everyday situations.

Remember that finding the right answers is only one part of the work you do in math. You must also be able to make sense of and describe your strategies for finding these answers.

Mathematical Highlights

Decimal Ops

In *Decimal Ops*, you will learn how to make sense of and use the four operations (+, −, ×, ÷) on decimal numbers. You will also improve your understanding of and skill in working with percents.

You will learn how to

- Add, subtract, multiply, and divide decimals
- Estimate the results of decimal operations
- Know when to use each operation in a situation involving decimals
- Relate operations on decimals to problems involving unit rates
- Use percents to solve problems

When you encounter a new problem, it is a good idea to ask yourself questions. In this Unit, you might ask questions such as:

Which operations on decimals or percents will help in solving this problem?

What algorithms will help with the calculations?

About **how much** will the sum, difference, product, or quotient be?

What do the decimals and/or percents in the problem tell me about the situation?

Common Core State Standards

Mathematical Practices and Habits of Mind

In the *Connected Mathematics* curriculum, you will develop an understanding of important mathematical ideas by solving problems and reflecting on the mathematics involved. Every day, you will use "habits of mind" to make sense of problems and apply what you learn to new situations. Some of these habits are described by the *Common Core State Standards for Mathematical Practice* (MP).

MP1 Make sense of problems and persevere in solving them.

When using mathematics to solve a problem, it helps to think carefully about

- data and other facts you are given and what additional information you need to solve the problem;
- strategies you have used to solve similar problems and whether you could solve a related simpler problem first;
- how you could express the problem with equations, diagrams, or graphs;
- whether your answer makes sense.

MP2 Reason abstractly and quantitatively.

When you are asked to solve a problem, it often helps to

- focus first on the key mathematical ideas;
- check that your answer makes sense in the problem setting;
- use what you know about the problem setting to guide your mathematical reasoning.

MP3 Construct viable arguments and critique the reasoning of others.

When you are asked to explain why a conjecture is correct, you can

- show some examples that fit the claim and explain why they fit;
- show how a new result follows logically from known facts and principles.

When you believe a mathematical claim is incorrect, you can

- show one or more counterexamples—cases that don't fit the claim;
- find steps in the argument that do not follow logically from prior claims.

MP4 Model with mathematics.

When you are asked to solve problems, it often helps to

- think carefully about the numbers or geometric shapes that are the most important factors in the problem, then ask yourself how those factors are related to each other;
- express data and relationships in the problem with tables, graphs, diagrams, or equations, and check your result to see if it makes sense.

MP5 Use appropriate tools strategically.

When working on mathematical questions, you should always

- decide which tools are most helpful for solving the problem and why;
- try a different tool when you get stuck.

MP6 Attend to precision.

In every mathematical exploration or problem-solving task, it is important to

- think carefully about the required accuracy of results; is a number estimate or geometric sketch good enough, or is a precise value or drawing needed?
- report your discoveries with clear and correct mathematical language that can be understood by those to whom you are speaking or writing.

MP7 Look for and make use of structure.

In mathematical explorations and problem solving, it is often helpful to

- look for patterns that show how data points, numbers, or geometric shapes are related to each other;
- use patterns to make predictions.

MP8 Look for and express regularity in repeated reasoning.

When results of a repeated calculation show a pattern, it helps to

- express that pattern as a general rule that can be used in similar cases;
- look for shortcuts that will make the calculation simpler in other cases.

You will use all of the Mathematical Practices in this Unit. Sometimes, when you look at a Problem, it is obvious which practice is most helpful. At other times, you will decide on a practice to use during class explorations and discussions. After completing each Problem, ask yourself:

- What mathematics have I learned by solving this Problem?
- What Mathematical Practices were helpful in learning this mathematics?

Decimal Operations and Estimation

Whole numbers, decimals, and percents are numbers used to report news, sports, and economics. In this Unit, you will consider everyday situations in which decimals are used, such as:

A sixth grader might win a 100-meter dash race with a time of 13.36 seconds.

Gas stations charge rates such as $4.079 per gallon. Gas purchases are measured in amounts such as 11.2 gallons.

In most of the United States, consumers pay sales taxes such as 6%, 7.25%, or even 8% of the purchase price.

To solve problems involving numbers, you often need to decide which operations are needed. In this Investigation, you will develop skills in recognizing when a situation involves addition, subtraction, multiplication, or division. You will also practice estimating the results of computations with decimals.

Common Core State Standards

6.RP.A.1 Understand the concept of a ratio and use ratio language to describe a ratio relationship between two quantities.

6.RP.A.2 Understand the concept of a unit rate a/b associated with a ratio $a : b$ with $b \neq 0$, and use rate language in the context of a ratio relationship.

6.RP.A.3b Solve unit rate problems including those involving unit pricing and constant speed.

Also 6.RP.A.3 and essential for 6.NS.B.3

1.1 Out to Lunch

Matching Operations and Questions

Draymond's mother gave him $20 to take his brother and sister to lunch. They ordered a pizza for $13.95 and three drinks that cost $2.25 each.

- Does Draymond have enough money to pay the bill?
- Which operations should Draymond use to find the cost of the lunch?

Questions such as these are common. In Problem 1.1, you will decide which operation or operations are needed, and you will use those operations as you work through the Problem.

Problem 1.1

For Questions A–E,

- Identify the operation(s) you need to use to answer the Question.
- Explain how you decided which operation(s) to use.

- Use mental arithmetic, a calculator, or some other method to find the exact answer(s).
- Write a number sentence.

A
1. The world record for the women's 400-meter race is 47.6 seconds. The world record for the men's 400-meter race is 43.18 seconds. How much faster is the men's world record time than the women's world record time?
2. Suppose that the men's and women's world-record holders were to run in an 800-meter race at their winning speeds. The women's record-holder runs 400 meters and tags the men's record-holder, who runs the last 400 meters. How long would it take them to run the total distance of 800 meters?
3. If the women's world record-holder ran the 400-meter race at a constant speed, how long did it take her to run each 100-meter segment of the race?

Problem 1.1 continued

B Pedro buys 7.5 gallons of gasoline for $28.49. How much does each gallon of gasoline cost?

C Chakara makes a rectangular tablecloth that is 3.5 meters long and 1.5 meters wide. What is the area of the tablecloth?

D A gas station sells gasoline for $4.10 per gallon. Elizabeth has a discount card. For each gallon of gas that she buys, she gets $.30 off the regular price. How much does it cost Elizabeth to buy 9.8 gallons of gasoline?

E Raman buys two packages of chicken wings. One package weighs 1.28 pounds, and the other weighs 2.63 pounds. The price of chicken wings is $3.25 per pound. What is the total cost of the chicken wings?

ACE Homework starts on page 14.

1.2 Getting Close
Estimating Decimal Calculations

In the introduction to Problem 1.1, Draymond ordered a pizza for $13.95 and three drinks that cost $2.25 each. Draymond could have *estimated* whether his order would cost more than the $20 his mother gave him.

- What estimation strategy could Draymond use to be sure he can pay the bill?

Estimating helps you know about what answer to expect. If your estimate and your actual calculation are not close, you may have made a mistake.

In this Problem, you will practice making estimates. When you **estimate**, you find an approximate answer.

Problem 1.2

A Tat Ming shops for party food. The register below shows Tat Ming's purchases.

1. Estimate Tat Ming's bill. What operation(s) did you use?
2. Tat Ming estimates that his bill is about $10. How do you think he arrived at that estimate?
3. The cashier told Tat Ming that his bill was $34.75.
   - **a.** How do you know that total is unreasonable?
   - **b.** What error do you think the cashier made in ringing up the bill?

4. Use a calculator, mental arithmetic, or another method to find the exact total. Was your estimate in part (1) close enough to be helpful? Explain.

B Maria wants to buy a new bicycle that costs $129.89. She has saved $78 of her babysitting money. She owes her brother $5. Maria's grandfather gave her $25 for her birthday. She finds $13.73 in her piggy bank. She expects to make another $12 for babysitting this weekend.

1. How much money will Maria have after she babysits this weekend? Estimate to the nearest $5.
2. Use a calculator, mental arithmetic, or some other method to find the exact amount of money that Maria will have. How close is your estimate to the exact amount?
3. Does Maria have enough money to buy the bicycle? If so, how much money will she have left after she buys the bicycle? If not, how much more money does she need?

Problem 1.2 continued

C Latisha wants to replace the carpet in her bedroom with hardwood flooring. Hardwood flooring costs $23.95 per square meter. A diagram of the room is below.

1. Latisha estimates the cost of the flooring. Explain how Latisha found the numbers she used in her estimates.

Estimate A	Estimate B	Estimate C
$3 \times 4 = 12$	$3 \times 4 = 12$	$4 \times 4 = 16$
Area $\approx$ 12 m^2	Area $\approx$ 13 m^2	Area $\approx$ 16 m^2
$12 \times 20 = 240$	$13 \times 25 = 325$	$16 \times 25 = 400$
Cost $\approx$ $240	Cost $\approx$ $325	Cost $\approx$ $400

2. Which of Latisha's strategies seems most reasonable? Explain your reasoning.
3. Latisha decides that she wants to place a rug over one fourth of the floor. Estimate the area of the rug. Explain how you estimated.
4. Latisha also considers replacing the carpeting in her room with tile. Covering her entire room with tile would cost $350. Estimate the cost per square meter of the tile.

ACE Homework starts on page 14.

1.3 Take a Hike
Connecting Ratios, Rates, and Decimals

The Madison Middle School Outdoor Club went on a three-day hiking trip in a national park. The club members made a table to show the distance traveled and time spent hiking for each of the three days.

Outdoor Club Hiking Trip

Day	Distance Traveled (miles)	Time (hours)
1	9	4
2	12	5
3	6.4	2.5

- How can you use the data above to compare the walking rates for each of the three days?

In *Comparing Bits and Pieces*, you learned about *unit rates*. You expressed each person's share of a chewy fruit worm as a unit rate. A **unit rate** is a comparison of two quantities in which one of the quantities being compared is 1 unit. In this Problem, you will use a calculator to find unit rates, such as the distance the hikers traveled per hour. You can express these unit rates in decimal form.

Problem 1.3

A The table above gives information about the Outdoor Club's hiking trip. Use a calculator or some other method to find the unit rate for the speed at which the Outdoor Club hikers traveled for each day of the hiking trip. Compare the unit rates you found.

B Before the trip, the hikers made some trail mix. A recipe for trail mix calls for a *ratio* of 3 cups of raisins to 4 cups of peanuts.

1. What is the ratio of raisins to peanuts as a unit rate? Express this in both fraction and decimal form.
2. How many cups of raisins should the hikers have used if they had 2 cups of peanuts? 3 cups of peanuts? 5 cups of peanuts? Explain your reasoning.

Problem 1.3 continued

C Abril and her dad bought ice cream after the trip. They found two different flavors and package sizes.

1. For each of the two ice cream packages, what is the price per quart? The number of quarts per dollar?
2. Use each kind of unit rate from part (1) to compare the values of the two packages.
3. Each ice cream flavor offers an 8-quart package with the same unit price as the smaller container. For each flavor, what does the larger package cost? Explain your reasoning.

ACE Homework starts on page 14.

Did You Know?

Have you ever heard someone use the phrase "in a jiffy"? A *jiffy* is a real unit of measurement that represents 0.01 second. A *unit of measurement* is a label for a specific, measurable quantity, such as *mile*, *liter*, or *week*. Units of measurement appear in other common sayings as well, such as "in a *shake*" (a shake is equal to 10 nanoseconds). In his Gettysburg Address, President Abraham Lincoln talked about a time "Four score and seven years ago." A *score* is equal to 20 years.

Applications

For Exercises 1–7,

- **Write a number sentence for the problem.**
- **Estimate the answer.**
- **Use mental arithmetic, a calculator, or some other method to find the exact answer.**
- **Explain how your estimate helps you check the exact answer.**

1. Billie buys materials for a project at a fabric store. She has $16.95 to spend. She buys fabric for $8.69, craft glue for $1.95, and craft paper for $4.29. How much money does she have left after she pays for the items?

2. Greg's home is 1.8 miles from his school. There is a music store halfway between school and his home. Today, Greg wants to stop at the store after school. Right now, he is 0.36 miles away from school.

   a. How far is the music store from Greg's school?

   b. How much farther does Greg need to walk to get to the store?

   c. How many miles does he have left to walk home?

3. A local farm grows strawberries, blueberries, and raspberries. Customers can pick their own fruit at the farm for $2.95 per pound.

   a. The Payne family picks 10.5 pounds of raspberries. How much do they have to pay?

   b. A week later, the Paynes pick 6.75 pounds of blueberries and 5.2 pounds of strawberries. How much do they have to pay?

4. The drink dispenser in a fast-food restaurant holds 250 liters of lemonade. How many 0.6-liter drinks can be dispensed before a refill is needed?

5. Chris, Kiona, Seiko, and Dwayne each run 100 meters in a relay race. Chris runs his part of the race in 12.35 seconds, Kiona takes 13.12 seconds, and Seiko takes 11.91 seconds.

   a. The team wants to break the school record of 48.92 seconds. How fast will Dwayne have to run?

   b. The team sets a new record of 47.65 seconds for the relay race. On average, how many meters did the team members run per second?

   c. On average, how long did it take each team member to run 100 meters?

6. Every year, students at Memorial High School volunteer to clean up local highway roadsides. Each club at the school cleans a section of the highway.

   A club member uses a trundle wheel to measure out each student's part of the highway. A trundle wheel can measure distances in thousandths of a mile.

   a. Carmela signs up to clean 1.5 miles for the cross-country team. After she cleans 0.25 of a mile, it starts to rain. How much does she have left to clean?

   b. Rashard cleans 0.25 of a mile for the chorus. He cleans another 0.375 of a mile for the math club. How much does Rashard clean altogether?

   c. Vijay, a member of the chess club, cleans 0.287 of a mile. He later cleans another 0.02 of a mile. How much does he clean altogether?

   d. Janet cleans 0.005 of a mile past her goal of 0.85 of a mile for the debate team. She claims she cleaned nine tenths of a mile. Is she correct? Explain.

Each time a trundle wheel makes one revolution, a counter clicks. The total number of clicks is the same as the number of whole units of distance. The wheel is marked in subdivisions for more precise measures.

7. Karen, Lou, and Jeff each buy a miniature tree. They measure the heights of their trees once a month from December to April. The heights are recorded in the table.

Miniature Tree Heights (meters)

	December	January	February	March	April
Karen's Tree	0.794	0.932	1.043	1.356	1.602
Lou's Tree	0.510	0.678	0.84	1.34	1.551
Jeff's Tree	0.788	0.903	1.22	1.452	1.61

a. Whose tree was tallest in December?

b. Whose tree was tallest at the end of April?

c. Whose tree grew the most during the first month?

d. Whose tree grew the most from December to April?

To make estimation with decimals easier, you can think about whole numbers or fractions that are close to the decimals in value. For Exercises 8–17, identify a common fraction that is equal to or close to each decimal.

8. 0.2

9. 0.25

10. 0.4

11. 0.5

12. 0.6

13. 0.67

14. 0.8

15. 0.875

16. 0.9

17. 0.78

For Exercises 18–23, write a whole number, mixed number, or fraction that could replace each decimal in an estimation task.

18. 3.14

19. 12.96

20. 0.42

21. 473.2

22. 0.33

23. 4.25

24. On a cross-country trip, the Anderson family planned to average 500 miles and 10 hours of driving each day.

    a. On average, how many miles per hour did the Andersons plan to drive?

    b. At the rate from part (a), how far would the Andersons travel if they drove for 8 hours? For 12 hours?

    c. How long would it take the Andersons to drive 450 miles at the rate from part (a)?

25. Elliot buys a 5-pound package of ground beef for $12.50.

    a. What is the unit price of the ground beef?

    b. At the same unit price, how much would 8 pounds of ground beef cost?

    c. Varna buys a package of ground beef for $7.50 at the same unit price. What is the weight of the package?

26. Suppose 50 members of the sixth-grade class raise a total of $740 during a poster sale.

    a. What unit rate best describes this result?

    b. There are 60 students in the seventh-grade class. The seventh graders match the sixth graders' fundraising rate by selling t-shirts. How much money does the seventh-grade class raise?

Connections

27. Draymond and his siblings ordered a pizza for $13.95 and three drinks for $2.25 each. After lunch, they bought ice cream cones for $2.75 each. Draymond calculated the total cost of the meal.

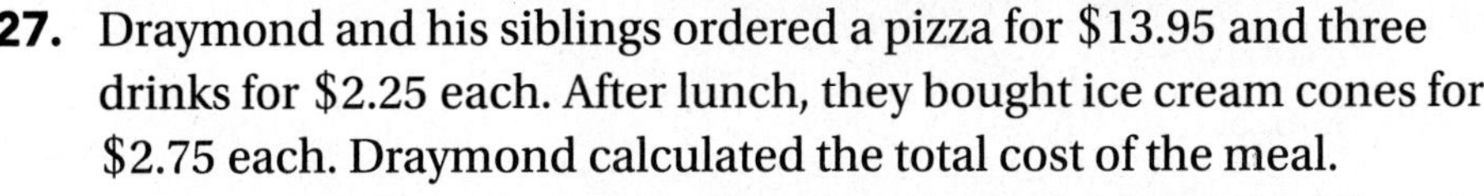

$$13.95 + 3(2.25) + 3(2.75) = 13.95 + 3(5.00)$$
$$= 13.95 + 15$$
$$= 28.95$$

    a. Describe how Draymond's calculations differ from the standard Order of Operations.

    b. Why did Draymond still find the correct total?

For Exercises 28–31,

- **Name each geometric figure.**
- **Find the perimeter of each figure.**
- **Write a number sentence that you could use to estimate each perimeter using only mental arithmetic.**

28.

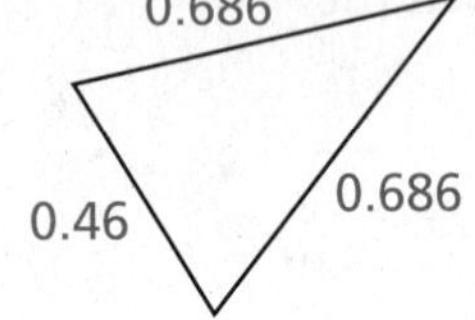

29.

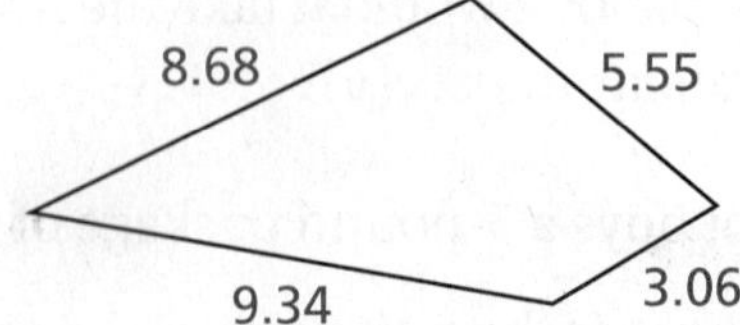

30.

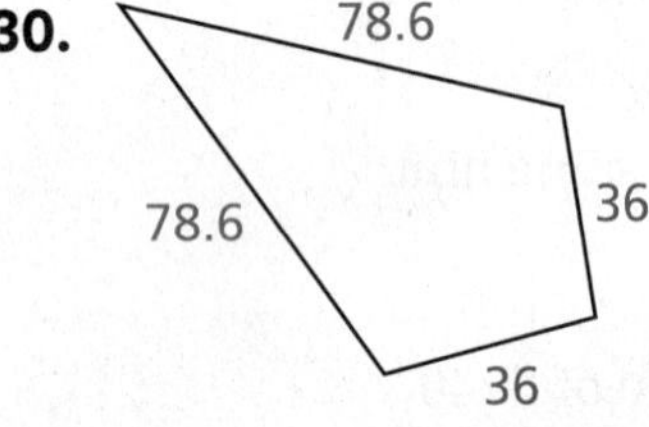

31.

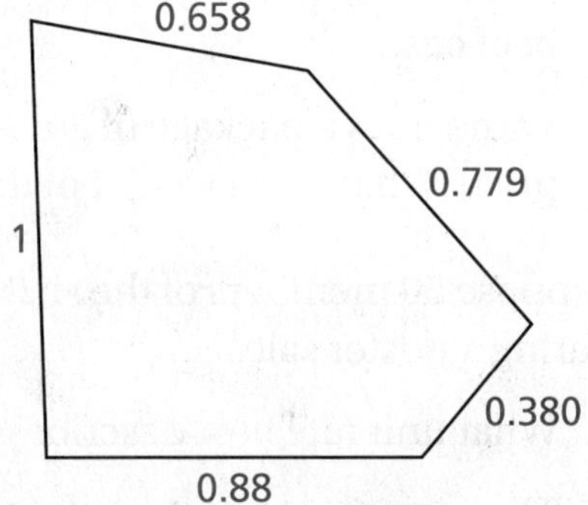

32. Multiple Choice Which of these numbers is greatest? Explain how you know.

A. 81.9 **B.** 81.90 **C.** 81.900 **D.** 81.91

33. Multiple Choice Which group of decimals is ordered from least to greatest?

F. 5.6, 5.9, 5.09, 5.96, 5.139

G. 0.112, 1.012, 1.3, 1.0099, 10.12

H. 2.8, 2.109, 2.72, 2.1, 2.719

J. 0.132, 0.23, 0.383, 0.3905, 0.392

34. Match each number with a point on the number line below.

0.5 3.05 0.350 3.50 1.95 1.095

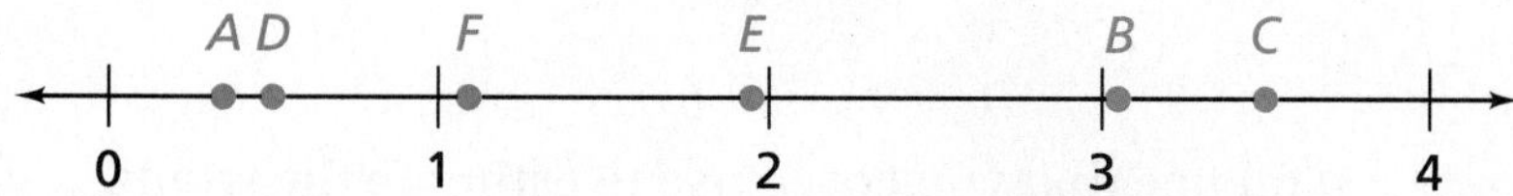

35. For each set below, record the products. If you are unsure of the correct result, check your work with a calculator. What patterns do you see?

Set A
21 × 100
21 × 10
21 × 1
21 × 0.1
21 × 0.01
21 × 0.001

Set B
2.1 × 100
2.1 × 10
2.1 × 1
2.1 × 0.1
2.1 × 0.01
2.1 × 0.001

Set C
0.21 × 100
0.21 × 10
0.21 × 1
0.21 × 0.1
0.21 × 0.01
0.21 × 0.001

For Exercises 36–41,

- **Find each sum or difference.**
- **Then rewrite each sum or difference as a decimal number.**

36. $\frac{2}{5} + \frac{1}{2}$

37. $\frac{3}{4} + \frac{3}{10}$

38. $1\frac{1}{2} + \frac{7}{10}$

39. $2\frac{4}{5} - \frac{3}{4}$

40. $\frac{3}{5} - \frac{1}{2}$

41. $4\frac{3}{8} - 1\frac{3}{4}$

For Exercises 42–47, tell whether the number is closest to 0, $\frac{1}{2}$, or 1. Explain your reasoning.

42. 0.07

43. 1.150

44. 0.391

45. 0.0999

46. 0.99

47. 0.599

For Exercises 48–51, write each fraction as an equivalent decimal.

48. $\frac{273}{10}$ **49.** $\frac{273}{100}$ **50.** $\frac{273}{1,000}$ **51.** $\frac{273}{10,000}$

For Exercises 52–55,

- **Write a simpler number sentence that you could use to estimate the result.**
- **Estimate using mental math.**
- **Compare your estimate to the exact result.**
- **Explain any significant differences.**

52. $715 + 1,129$

53. $1,543 - 512$

54. 53×48

55. $8,114 \div 92$

56. Draymond and his siblings ordered a pizza for \$13.95 and three drinks for \$2.25 each. To find the cost of the meal, Draymond entered $13.95 + 3 \times 2.25$ into a calculator. The calculator shows the total below. What error is the calculator making?

38.14

For Exercises 57–59, tell whether each pair of number sentences gives the same result. How can you tell without actually doing the arithmetic?

57. $3.5(4.6 + 0.94)$ and $3.5(4.6) + 0.94$

58. $4.61(3.2) + 3.05(3.2)$ and $7.66(3.2)$

59. $3.48(7.2 - 2.8)$ and $3.48(7.2) - 3.48(2.8)$

Extensions

60. To add 3 dollars and 35 cents to 5 dollars and 78 cents, write each amount as a decimal. Since $3.35 + 5.78 = 9.13$, the total is 9 dollars and 13 cents.

Can you add 2 hours 45 minutes to 3 hours 57 minutes by using decimal numbers $(2.45 + 3.57)$? Explain your reasoning.

61. You can add 13 meters 47 centimeters to 4 meters 72 centimeters by using decimal numbers. Since $13.47 + 4.72 = 18.19$, the total length is 18 meters 19 centimeters.

Can you add 3 feet 7 inches and 5 feet 6 inches by using decimal numbers $(3.7 + 5.6)$? Explain your reasoning.

62. Mark says that 3.002 must be less than 3.0019 since 2 is less than 19. Explain why he is wrong.

63. There are 16 ounces in 1 pound.

a. How many pounds are in 256 ounces?

b. How many ounces are in 0.125 pounds? 3.375 pounds?

64. Jose uses the bread recipe below.

a. How much flour does Jose need to make three batches of the recipe?

b. He has no flour at home. How many 5-pound bags of flour should Jose buy to make three batches of the recipe?

c. There are 2,000 pounds in 1 ton. How many batches of the bread recipe could Jose make with 1 ton of flour?

Mathematical Reflections 1

In this Investigation, you solved problems involving measurements and amounts of money written as decimals. You developed strategies for identifying the operations needed to answer questions about decimal numbers. You also estimated answers to decimal problems. The following questions will help you summarize what you have learned.

Think about these questions. Discuss your ideas with other students and your teacher. Then write a summary of your findings in your notebook.

1. **How** do you know when solving a problem that involves decimals requires addition? Subtraction? Multiplication? Division?
2. **Describe** a strategy that you use when estimating with decimals. Explain why it is helpful to you.
3. **What** is a unit rate? Describe how unit rates are useful.

Common Core Mathematical Practices

As you worked on the Problems in this Investigation, you used prior knowledge to make sense of them. You also applied Mathematical Practices to solve the Problems. Think back over your work, the ways you thought about the Problems, and how you used Mathematical Practices.

Elena described her thoughts in the following way:

In Problem 1.3, Question C, we found unit rates. Since we were going to compare the unit rates, we needed our answers to be exact.

The unit price for chocolate chip ice cream was \$2.50 for 1 quart of ice cream (or $\frac{2}{5}$ quart per \$1). We found this unit rate pretty easily.

The numbers were difficult to compute for cherry vanilla, so we used our calculators. To find the unit price per quart for cherry vanilla, we found the quotient $4 \div 1.75$. We used our calculators to find that the unit price was about \$2.29 per 1 quart.

We used a mathematical tool to find that 1 quart of cherry vanilla is about 21¢ cheaper than 1 quart of chocolate chip.

Common Core Standards for Mathematical Practice
MP5 Use appropriate tools strategically

- What other Mathematical Practices can you identify in Elena's reasoning?
- Describe a Mathematical Practice that you and your classmates used to solve a different Problem in this Investigation.

Adding and Subtracting Decimals

This Investigation has two goals. The first goal is to develop algorithms for adding and subtracting decimals. The second goal is to sharpen estimation skills and number sense. In each Problem, you will use what you know about operations with fractions to make sense of decimal operations.

2.1 Getting Things in the Right Place

Adding Decimals

Sally Jane and her friend Zeke stopped at the Quick Shop to buy snacks. They picked out a bag of pretzels for \$.89 and a bottle of cider for \$1.97. At the checkout, the clerk said that the computers were down. He then calculated their bill himself. The clerk wrote some numbers on a piece of paper. He told Sally Jane and Zeke that they owed \$10.87 for their snacks and \$.66 more for tax.

Common Core State Standards

6.NS.B.3. Fluently add, subtract, multiply, and divide multi-digit decimals using the standard algorithm for each operation.

6.EE.B.5 Understand solving an equation or inequality as a process of answering a question: which values from a specified set, if any, make the equation or inequality true? . . .

6.EE.B.6 Use variables to represent numbers and write expressions when solving a real-world or mathematical problem; understand that a variable can represent an unknown number . . .

6.EE.B.7. Solve real-world and mathematical problems by writing and solving equations of the form $x + p = q$ and $px = q$ for cases in which p, q and x are all nonnegative rational numbers.

Also 6.EE.A.2, 6.EE.A.2a

Sally Jane pulled out her smart phone and got a total of $2.86 before tax. But she could not convince the clerk that he was wrong.

- How do you think the clerk might have arrived at the total of $10.87?
- How would you explain that the correct amount cannot be $10.87, without simply saying, “The calculator says $2.86”?

It seems as if the Quick Shop clerk did not understand place value for whole numbers and decimals.

Sally Jane explained to the clerk that she could tell by estimation that the answer could not be more than $3.

- Does Sally’s estimate make sense?
- How does place value play a role in the clerk’s error?

In this Problem, you will use equivalence of fractions and decimals to think about place value. You will use your understanding of place value to add and subtract decimals.

Some of the cards shown below have decimal numbers and some have fractions. Sorting these cards will help you think about place value.

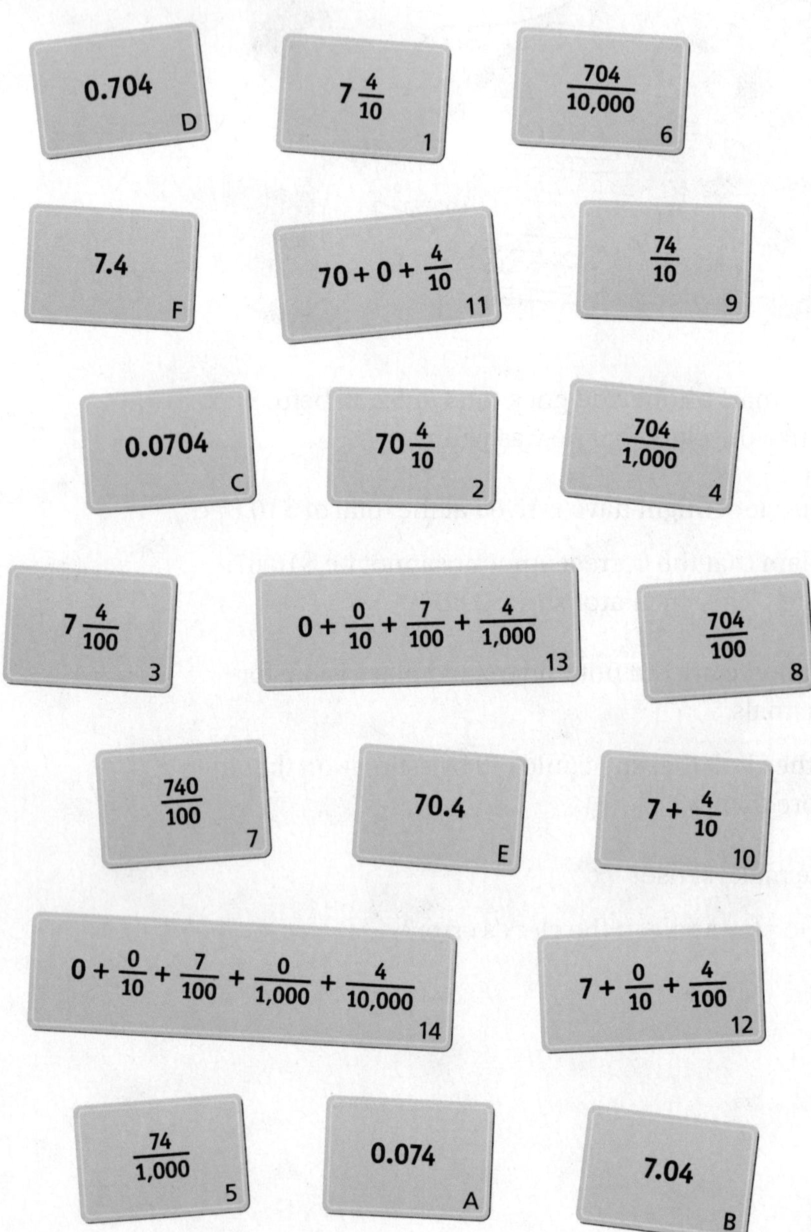

Problem 2.1

A 1. Sort the cards on the previous page into groups of numbers with equivalent values.

2. Order the groups of cards from least to greatest values.

3. Use blank cards to write at least one new card with an equivalent value that belongs in each group.

B Isaac and Madeline are using decimal cards to practice finding sums of decimals. Isaac chose two cards and said they have a sum of 0.0778.

0.074 (A)	0.0704 (C)

Madeline disagreed. She said, "If you use the equivalent expanded form for each decimal, the answer will be

$$0 + \frac{0}{10} + \frac{14}{100} + \frac{4}{1000} + \frac{4}{10000}."$$

$0 + \frac{0}{10} + \frac{7}{100} + \frac{4}{1{,}000}$ (13)	$0 + \frac{0}{10} + \frac{7}{100} + \frac{0}{1{,}000} + \frac{4}{10{,}000}$ (14)

1. Who is correct, Isaac or Madeline? Explain.

2. What is the correct answer in decimal form? In fraction form?

continued on the next page >

Problem 2.1 continued

C Use your knowledge of place value and fractions to find the following sums.

1. 70.4 + 7.04
2. 7.4 + 7.04
3. 0.704 + 0.704
4. 0.704 + 7.4
5. Find two decimal cards that sum to each value.

   a. 14.44 b. 77.8 c. 7.744 d. 0.778

D Sally Jane said, "You can add decimals the same way that you add whole numbers. You just need to line up the decimal points to make sure that numbers with the same place value are added."

$$\begin{array}{r} 7.4 \\ +0.704 \\ \hline 8.104 \end{array}$$

1. How did Sally Jane get each digit in the answer 8.104?
2. Lee Ann said, "It helps to put two zeros after the 4 in 7.4 to be sure that everything lines up right."

$$\begin{array}{r} 7.400 \\ +0.704 \\ \hline 8.104 \end{array}$$

   a. Why is 7.4 equal to 7.400?

   b. Explain how Lee Ann's suggestion might be helpful.

E Use your knowledge of place value and fractions to:

- Estimate the answers for each decimal sum.
- Calculate exact values for each decimal sum.

1. 1.1999 + 2.02
2. 1.762 + 6.9
3. 0.243 + 0.7
4. 3.47 + 8

Problem 2.1 continued

F Four students calculated the sum 2.561 + 15.74 + 92.03 and got various answers. Study their work to see if any of their sums are correct. For those that are not correct, identify the errors they made.

1. Mike

$$\begin{array}{r} 2.561 \\ 15.74 \\ +92.03 \\ \hline 133.38 \end{array}$$

2. Sam

$$\begin{array}{r} 2.561 \\ 15.740 \\ +92.030 \\ \hline 109.231 \end{array}$$

3. Miley

$$\begin{array}{r} 2.561 \\ 15.740 \\ +92.030 \\ \hline 110.331 \end{array}$$

4. Jackie

$$\begin{array}{r} 2.561 \\ 15.74 \\ +92.03 \\ \hline 110.331 \end{array}$$

G Describe a systematic procedure or algorithm you can use for finding the sum of two (or more) decimal numbers.

ACE Homework starts on page 34.

2.2 What's the Difference?

Subtracting Decimals

In Problem 2.1, you found that when you add decimals, you add digits with the same place value. Similar reasoning applies to subtraction of decimals.

The questions of this Problem ask you to extend your understanding of, and skill in working with, decimal subtraction.

How do you subtract one decimal number from another?

Problem 2.2

A For parts (1)-(4), find each difference. You may choose to use the Decimal Cards from Problem 2.1. You will need the Decimal Cards for part (5).

1. 70.4 − 7.4

2. 7.4 − 7.04

3. 0.704 − 0.074

4. 70.4 − 7.04

5. Find two cards whose difference is the given value.

a. 0.6336 **b.** 6.336 **c.** 0.0036

Problem 2.2 continued

B Use your knowledge of place value and fractions for the following problems to:

- Estimate the answers for each decimal difference.
- Calculate the exact value for each decimal difference.

1. 3.724 − 0.49

2. 6.899 − 2.9

3. 7.5097 − 1.008

4. 12 − 3.45

C Four students calculated the difference 25.638 − 17.45 and got different answers. Which are correct? For those that are not correct, find the errors. Explain how using estimation might have caught the errors.

1. Juana

```
  25.638
- 17.450
  18.288
```

2. Adam

```
  25.638
- 17.450
   8.188
```

3. Blanca

```
  25.638
- 17.450
  12.228
```

4. Jonathan

```
  25.638
-  17.45
  23.993
```

D Describe a systematic procedure or algorithm you can use for finding the difference of any two decimal numbers.

ACE Homework starts on page 34.

2.3 Connecting Operations

Fact Families

For whole numbers and fractions, addition and subtraction facts are related. For example, the numbers 4, 8, and 12 are related by four equations using addition and subtraction.

Addition Sentence	$4 + 8 = 12$
Related Number Sentences	$8 + 4 = 12$ $12 - 8 = 4$ $12 - 4 = 8$

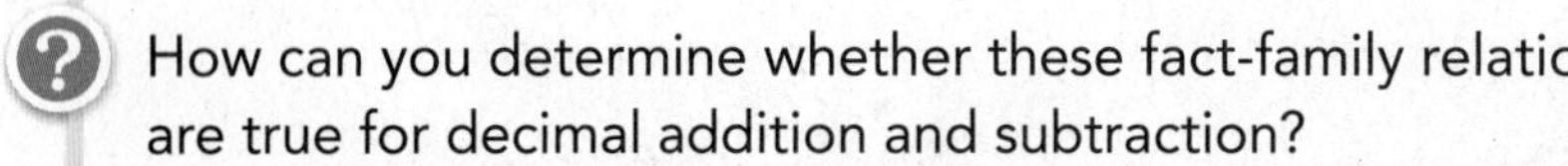

Problem 2.3

Use what you know about decimals to see whether fact-family ideas apply to operations with decimals. Use a calculator if necessary.

A Write fact families for these equations. Check to see whether each related number sentence is true.

1. $0.02 + 0.103 = 0.123$ **2.** $1.82 - 0.103 = 1.717$

B Are the addition and subtraction relationships you see in whole-number fact families also true for addition and subtraction of decimals? Explain your reasoning.

C Fact-family reasoning often helps when solving equations. Use the number line below to write two sentences relating 0.02, 0.123, and x. Then find the value of x.

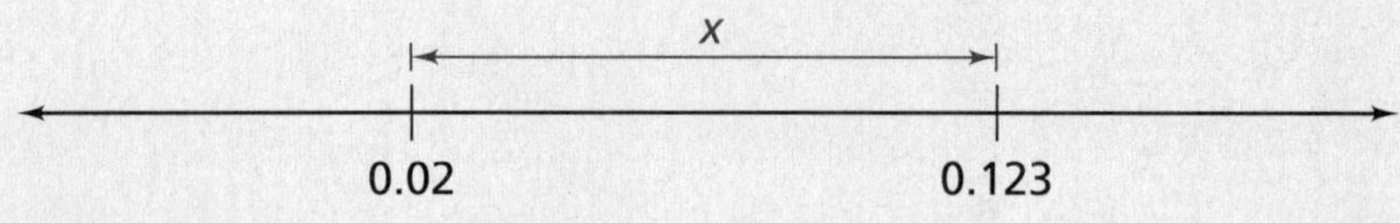

Problem 2.3 continued

D Use fact-family reasoning to find values of n that make these mathematical sentences true. Then check your answers.

1. $n + 2.3 = 6.55$
2. $n - 6.88 = 7.21$
3. $2n + 1.55 = 6.4$

E Suppose you have a five-dollar bill to buy fruit as shown in the photo below. You decide to buy three apples, four pears, and some bananas.

1. How many bananas can you buy without going over your total of $5?
2. After purchasing your fruit, how much change will you get back from your five-dollar bill?
3. Write a sentence to show your thinking for part (2). Did you use fact families in answering the question? Explain.

ACE Homework starts on page 34.

Applications | Connections | Extensions

Applications

For Exercises 1–4, find the sum of each pair of cards without using a calculator. Show your work and explain how an estimation strategy suggests that your answer is probably correct.

1. 3.42 | 5.8

2. 5.012 | 0.93

3.  10.437 | 4.0034

4. 0.403 | 0.07

5. During the Memorial High School highway clean-up project, Ms. Palkowski cleaned 0.125 of a mile for the teachers' team and then 0.4 of a mile for the science club. How much did she clean altogether?

6. **Multiple Choice** Which is the correct decimal sum?

   A. $\begin{array}{r} 81.9 \\ +\,0.62 \\ \hline 88.1 \end{array}$ **B.** $\begin{array}{r} 81.9 \\ +\,0.62 \\ \hline 82.52 \end{array}$ **C.** $\begin{array}{r} 81.9 \\ +\,0.62 \\ \hline 0.1439 \end{array}$ **D.** $\begin{array}{r} 81.9 \\ +\,0.62 \\ \hline 8.81 \end{array}$

7. Find each sum.

   a. $4.9 + 3\frac{3}{4}$ **b.** $91.678 + 2.34 + 12.001$ **c.** $2.75 + 3\frac{2}{5}$

8. Place decimal points in 102 and 19 so that the sum of the two numbers is 1.21.

9. Place decimal points in 34, 4, and 417 so that the sum of the three numbers is 7.97.

For Exercises 10–15, find each difference without using a calculator. Show your work and explain how an estimation strategy suggests that your answer is probably correct.

10. $5.2 - 0.12$

11. $4.54 - 2.9$

12. $0.095 - 0.0071$

13. $2.057 - 1.99$

14. $10 - 1.068$

15. $5.63 - 4.05 + 9.2$

16. Place decimal points in 431 and 205 so that the difference of the two numbers is 16.19.

17. Find the value of *n* that make each sentence true. Then write the addition and subtraction fact family for the sentence.

a. $22.3 + 31.65 = n$

b. $18.7 - 4.24 = n$

18. Find the value of *n* that makes each sentence true. Use fact families to help.

a. $2.3 + n = 3.42$

b. $n - 11.6 = 3.75$

19. Find the missing numbers.

a. $\begin{array}{r} 36.03 \\ +\ n \\ \hline 45.218 \end{array}$

b. $\begin{array}{r} n \\ +\ 0.488 \\ \hline 13.762 \end{array}$

c. $0.45 + n + 0.4 = 2.62$

d. $75.4 - 10.801 + n = 77.781$

20. Owen had a sinus infection. The thermometer below shows his temperature when he ran a fever.

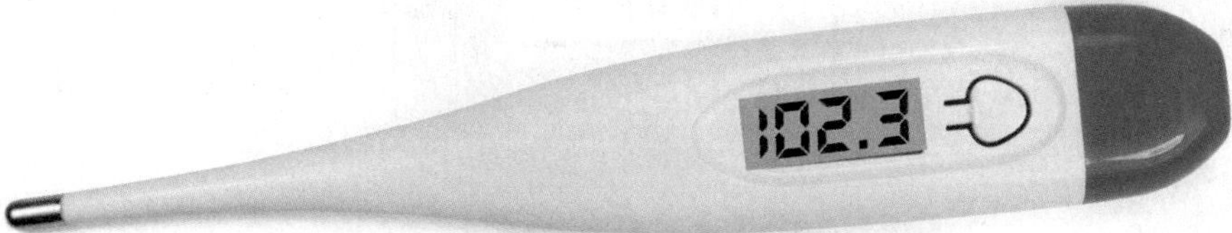

After he took some medicine, his temperature dropped 3.4°F overnight.

a. What was Owen's temperature in the morning?

b. How far above a normal temperature of 98.6°F was Owen's temperature even after medicine and a night's sleep?

Connections

For Exercises 21–26, perform each calculation.

21. $5(10 + 7)$ **22.** $4^3 \cdot 2$ **23.** $10(42)$

24. $\frac{24}{6}$ **25.** 3^3 **26.** $2(10 - 8) + 8$

For Exercises 27–30, write the calculation needed to answer the given question and explain how you know you've chosen the right operation.

27. A world-class athlete ran 200 meters in 19.19 seconds. Suppose that he ran the first half of that race (around a curve) in 10.75 seconds. How long did it take him to run the second half of the race (on a straightaway)?

28. A female world-record-holder ran 200 meters in 22.58 seconds. She and the runner in Exercise 27 complete a two-person relay race of 400 meters. How long would it take them to run the relay race if they were to run at their individual winning speeds?

29. Yvonne plans to frame a poster she bought at a concert. The frame will be rectangular with base 0.45 meters and height 0.95 meters. What total length of frame material will she need?

30. Multiple Choice The average number of points per game for two star high-school basketball players are shown below.

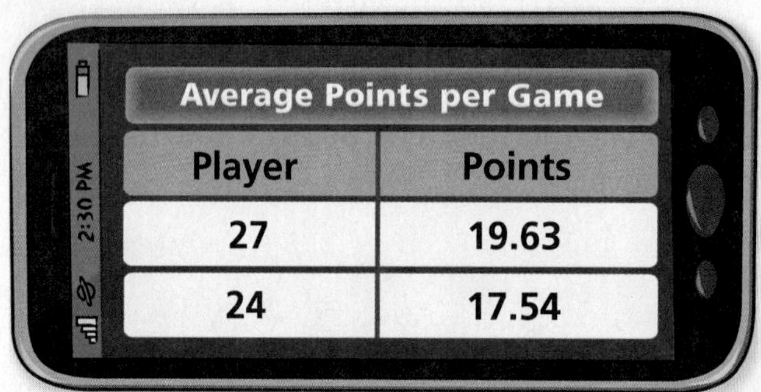

Average Points per Game

Player	Points
27	19.63
24	17.54

The high-school basketball team averages 70.9 points per game. What is the average number of points per game scored by all the other players together?

A. 14.18 **B.** 17.54 **C.** 19.63 **D.** 33.73

31. Find the missing lengths in the figure below. Then find the perimeter of the figure. All measurements are in inches.

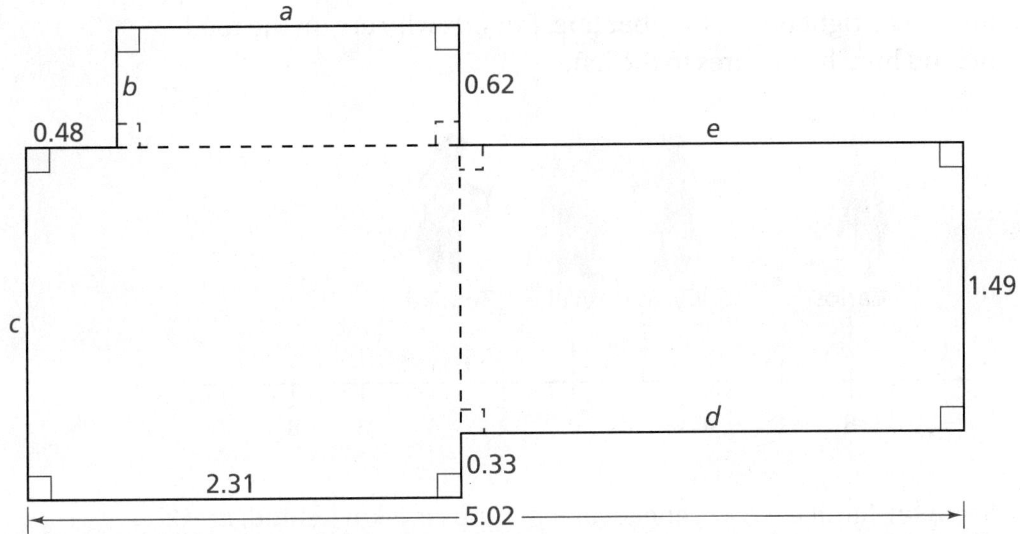

32. The perimeter of a parallelogram is 15.42 cm. The length of one of its sides is 2.93 cm. What are the lengths of its other sides?

33. Write these times as decimal parts of an hour.

a. 45 minutes
b. 24 minutes
c. 90 minutes

For Exercises 34–39, find each sum or difference in fraction form.

34. $\frac{4}{5} + \frac{3}{4}$

35. $2\frac{3}{5} + \frac{3}{8}$

36. $1\frac{2}{3} + 3\frac{5}{6}$

37. $\frac{8}{3} - \frac{4}{5}$

38. $1\frac{4}{5} - \frac{1}{2}$

39. $4\frac{2}{8} - 1\frac{3}{4}$

40. Rewrite Exercises 34–39 with decimal numbers and find the results of the operations using the decimal equivalents. Compare your decimal answers to the fraction answers.

41. Will likes to keep track of his Memorial High School friends during the highway clean-up project. He thinks of himself as being at 0 on the number line. He pictures friends who are on the road ahead of him to the right on the number line. Friends who are on the road behind him, he pictures to the left.

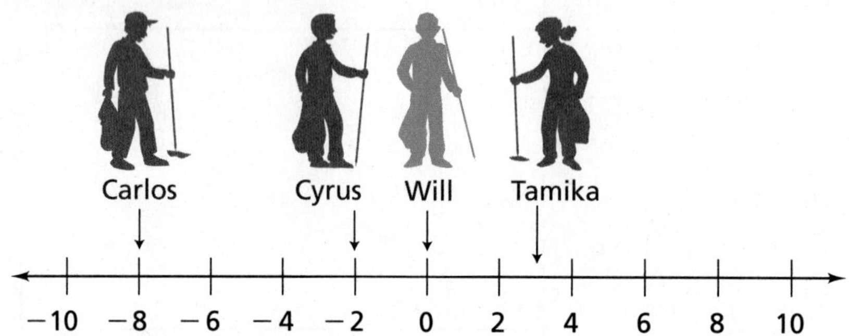

Sample: Tamika is 3 km ahead, at +3. Cyrus is 2 km behind, at −2.

a. Justin is located the same distance from Will as Will is from Tamika. Justin and Tamika are on opposite sides of Will. Mark Justin's position on a copy of the number line above.

b. Carlos is at the location shown on the number line. Is Carlos ahead of or behind Will? By how many kilometers?

c. Write three numbers that show locations behind Will.

d. Write three numbers that show locations ahead of Will.

Extensions

42. **a.** Use the numbers 2, 9, 7, and 4 only once each. Write the greatest possible number of the form 3.■■■■.

b. Use the numbers 2, 9, 7, and 4 only once each. Write the least possible number of the form 3.■■■■.

c. Write all numbers of the form 3.■■■■ that are greater than 3.795.

d. Write all numbers of the form 3.■■■■ that are less than 3.73 but greater than 3.4399.

For Exercises 43–46, use 1, 2, 3, or 4 to form decimal numbers so that each sum or difference is as close as possible to the given number. You may use the same digit more than once. For example, you may write 0.33. The symbol ≈ means "is approximately equal to."

43. 0.■■ + 0.■■ $\approx \frac{1}{3}$

44. 0.■■ + 0.■■ ≈ 0.9

45. 0.■■ − 0.■■ $\approx \frac{2}{7}$

46. 0.■■ − 0.■■ ≈ 0.125

For Exercises 47 and 48, use 1, 2, 3, or 4 to form decimal numbers so that each calculation is correct. You may use the same digit more than once in a number.

47. 0.■■ + 0.■■ = 0.75

48. 0.■■ − 0.■■ = 0.3

Mathematical Reflections 2

In this Investigation, you used your understanding of fractions and place value to develop algorithms for adding and subtracting decimals. The following questions will help you summarize what you have learned.

Think about these questions. Discuss your ideas with other students and your teacher. Then write a summary of your findings in your notebook.

1. **How** does interpreting decimals as fractions help you make sense of adding and subtracting decimals? Give an example to show your thinking.
2. **How** does the place-value interpretation of decimals help you add and subtract decimals? Give an example to show your thinking.
3. **Describe** algorithms for adding and subtracting any two decimal numbers.

Common Core Mathematical Practices

As you worked on the Problems in this Investigation, you used prior knowledge to make sense of them. You also applied Mathematical Practices to solve the Problems. Think back over your work, the ways you thought about the Problems, and how you used Mathematical Practices.

Tori described her thoughts in the following way:

In Problem 2.3, we used fact families to find some unknown values. These families show how the same numbers are related to each other in different ways. It is easy to see this with whole numbers. $8 + 4 = 12$ and $12 - 4 = 8$ show the same relationship between 4, 8, and 12.

But this fact-family idea works for all numbers.

When we had to find N in $N - 6.88 = 7.21$, we could write $7.21 + 6.88 = N$. So, $N = 14.09$.

Common Core Standards for Mathematical Practice

MP7 Look for and make use of structure

- What other Mathematical Practices can you identify in Tori's reasoning?
- Describe a Mathematical Practice that you and your classmates used to solve a different Problem in this Investigation.

Multiplying and Dividing Decimals

Festivals celebrating food, arts and crafts, music, cars and motorcycles, and ethnic traditions occur all over the country. Vendors may sell food, drinks, or crafts. The rental fee a vendor might pay is based on the size and location of the rented booth.

Suppose a PTA group from Treetops Middle School plans to raise funds by selling iced tea at the county fair. Vendor booths are rectangular in shape. They measure 12 feet from front to back, but they vary in width.

- How can you find the area of a booth that is 17.5 feet wide?
- If a booth rents for $1.95 per square foot, how can you find the area of a space that rents for $200?

Common Core State Standards

6.NS.A.1 Interpret and compute quotients of fractions, and solve word problems involving division of fractions by fractions, e.g., by using visual fraction models and equations to represent the problem.

6.NS.B.2 Fluently divide multi-digit numbers using the standard algorithm.

6.NS.B.3 Fluently add, subtract, multiply, and divide multi-digit numbers using the standard algorithm for each operation.

6.EE.B.7 Solve real-world and mathematical problems by writing and solving equations of the form $p + x = q$ and $px = q$ for cases in which p, q, and x are nonnegative rational numbers.

Answering the questions about booth rentals involves multiplication and division of decimals. The easiest way to calculate the solutions is with a calculator. Understanding algorithms for decimal multiplication and division is helpful, too.

3.1 It's Decimal Time(s)

Multiplying Decimals I

When you encounter new types of problems to solve in mathematics, it often helps to use a strategy that has worked on similar problems. The key to finding algorithms for multiplying and dividing decimals is to connect those decimal operations with what you already know about working with fractions.

You can write 0.4 × 0.3 as $\frac{4}{10} \times \frac{3}{10}$. The area model below shows how to find the fractional answer of this product.

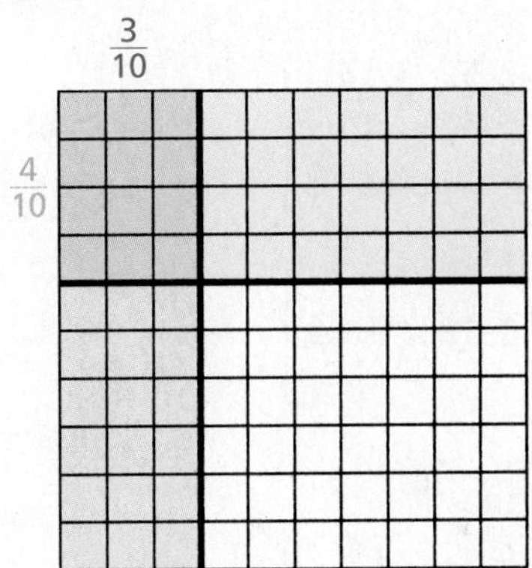

- What decimal is represented by this area model?
- How does thinking about fraction multiplication help you find a decimal answer for the product 0.4 × 0.3?
- How might an area model help you find the product 0.4 × 2.3?

Problem 3.1

A **1.** Which expressions below are equivalent? Explain.

a. 0.04×3.2

b. $\frac{4}{100}\left(3 + \frac{2}{10}\right)$

c. $\frac{4}{100} \times \frac{32}{10}$

d. 1.28

e. 0.04×0.32

f. $\frac{128}{1000}$

2. Use what you know about fraction multiplication to compute the decimal answer for the product 0.04×3.2.

B **1.** Sort the cards shown below into groups of equivalent expressions.

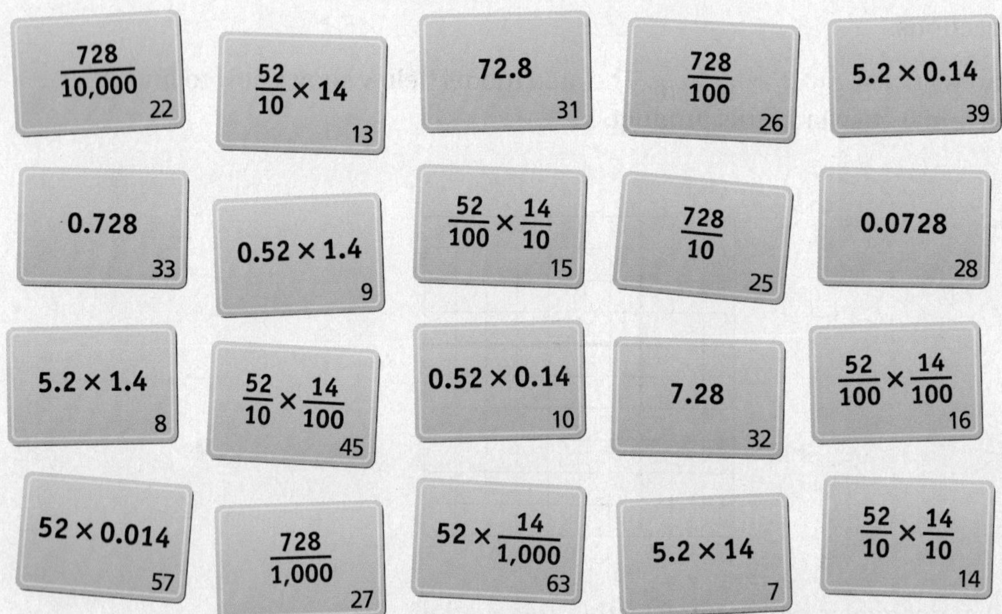

2. Explain how you decided which expressions are equivalent.

3. Order the groups of cards from least to greatest value.

4. What is the least product? What is the greatest product?

5. For each group of equivalent expression, identify and write down patterns that can help you efficiently multiply any two decimal numbers.

Problem 3.1 continued

C In parts (1)–(9) below, the products involve the digits 2, 3, and 1. Using the fact that $21 \times 11 = 231$, predict where the decimal point goes by inspecting the factors being multiplied. Explain your reasoning.

1. 2.1×11
2. 2.1×1.1
3. 2.1×0.11
4. 2.1×0.011
5. 0.21×11
6. 0.021×1.1
7. 0.021×0.11
8. 0.21×0.011
9. 0.021×0.011

D When Ingrid was asked to calculate 6.7×0.9, she first found $67 \times 9 = 603$. Her thinking is shown below.

> One factor is 6.7 and the other factor is a bit less than 1. So the answer will be a bit less than 6.7. It must be 6.03.

Apply estimation like Ingrid's to place the decimal point in the products below.

1. If $12 \times 43 = 516$, what is 1.2×4.3?
2. If $18 \times 23 = 414$, what is 0.18×2.3?

E Using what you learned from Questions A–D, describe an algorithm for multiplying decimals. Explain why you think your algorithm works.

ACE Homework starts on page 57.

3.2 It Works Every Time
Multiplying Decimals II

Use your algorithm to work out two more decimal products with numbers of your choosing. When students in one *Connected Mathematics* class finished work on Problem 3.1, they wrote a summary of their ideas. The students came up with two different strategies.

To multiply decimals such as 6.5×1.43, all the students agreed on the first step.

(1) Ignore the decimal points and multiply the whole numbers.

$65 \times 143 = 9295$

Estimation Strategy

(2) Estimate the decimal product.

$6 \times 1.5 = 9$

(3) Use the estimate to place the decimal point in the answer.

$6.5 \times 1.43 = 9.295$

OR

(1) Ignore the decimal points and multiply the whole numbers.

$65 \times 143 = 9295$

Count-the-Decimal-Places Strategy

(2) Examine the number of decimal places in the question. In the expression 6.5×1.43, the first factor has one decimal place, *5 tenths*, and the second factor has two decimal places, *43 hundredths.*

(3) Add the number of decimal places in the factors, and make the product have that same number of decimal places. In the example, this means the product should have 3 decimal places, *295 thousandths*.

$6.5 \times 1.43 = 9.295$

- How does an estimate help students choose 9.295 and not 92.95?
- Why do three decimal places make sense for the answer, when the factors have only one and two places?
- Which of the algorithms make(s) sense to you? Explain.

Problem 3.2

A

1. Estimate the decimal product 4.09×9.1. Then find the exact product. Do you agree that the estimation strategy will always give correct results? Explain.
2. How does the connection between decimals and fractions explain the count-the-decimal-places strategy? Why will it work for any product of decimals?
3. Find each decimal product. Which method of placing the decimal point do you find most helpful? Explain.
   - **a.** 5.2×4.1
   - **b.** 0.00052×0.0041
   - **c.** 5.2005×4.1001

B Estimate each of these decimal products. Then use a multiplication algorithm to find the exact result. Show your work.

1. $\begin{array}{r} 1.56 \\ \times\ 2.3 \\ \hline \end{array}$
2. $\begin{array}{r} 27.35 \\ \times\ 4.5 \\ \hline \end{array}$
3. $\begin{array}{r} 1.508 \\ \times\ 2.34 \\ \hline \end{array}$
4. $\begin{array}{r} 6.5 \\ \times\ 1.42 \\ \hline \end{array}$

ACE Homework starts on page 57.

3.3 How Many Times?
Dividing Decimals I

The connection between common fractions and decimals suggested a way to multiply decimals. Similarly, you can use what you know about fraction division to develop an algorithm for decimal division.

Each number in a division problem has a name to help you explain your thinking. The number you are dividing by is the *divisor*. The number into which you are dividing is the *dividend*. The answer is the *quotient*.

The calculation *18 divided by 3 equals 6* can be written like this:

$$18 \div 3 = 6$$

$$\text{dividend} \div \text{divisor} = \text{quotient}$$

You can also write the above calculation in two other ways.

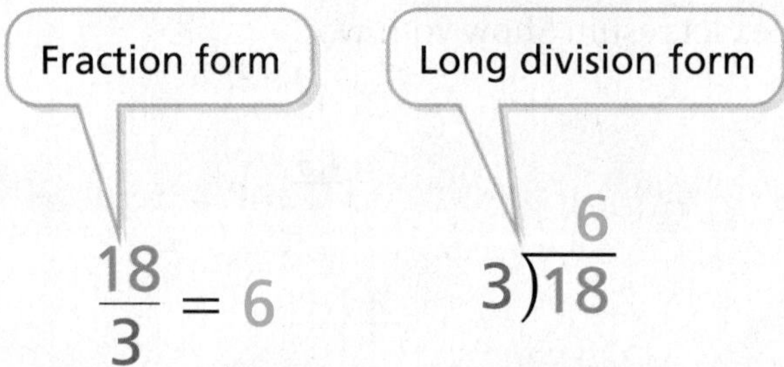

- Which of the three forms do you prefer to use? Why?

Problem 3.3

To find a quotient of decimals, you can think of the decimals as fractions.

A **1.** How might you complete the work below to find the quotient? Explain.

$$4.2 \div 0.84 = \frac{\blacksquare}{100} \div \frac{84}{100}$$

$$= \frac{\blacksquare}{84}$$

$$= \blacksquare$$

Problem 3.3 continued

2. Abe says that he uses multiplication to check his answers for division problems. He says, "$4.2 \div 0.84 = n$ means that 0.84 goes into 4.2, n times. So, $0.84 \times n = 4.2$." Do you agree with Abe's reasoning? Does your answer for Question A, part (1), make Abe's multiplication sentence true? Explain.

B 1. Kevin claims he has found a different strategy for dividing decimals. His strategy starts by writing the division as a *single fraction*. How could you complete Kevin's work to find the quotient $7.5 \div 1.25$? Explain.

$$7.5 \div 1.25 = \frac{7.5}{1.25}$$
$$= \frac{■}{125}$$
$$= ■$$

2. Use the strategy of rewriting *both* 7.5 and 1.25 as fractions, and then dividing the fractions. Does this give the same answer as Kevin's strategy? Why or why not?

3. Why do both strategies end up as a division of whole numbers?

C Use either of the division methods described in Questions A and B to find each quotient.

1. $0.75 \div 0.125$
2. $7.5 \div 0.0125$
3. $0.78 \div 0.13$
4. $6.3 \div 0.009$

D Describe the algorithm *you* would use for division of decimals. Explain why your strategy works.

ACE Homework starts on page 57.

3.4 Going the Long Way

Dividing Decimals II

The *Connected Mathematics* students who figured out algorithms for decimal multiplication finished their work on Problem 3.3 and wrote summaries of their ideas about division.

To divide decimal numbers such as $7.8 \div 0.13$, you have a choice of two methods. In each case you end up doing a whole-number division.

Common Denominator Strategy

You can write *both* the dividend and the divisor as fractions with a common denominator.

$$\frac{780}{100} \div \frac{13}{100}$$

Then find the quotient of the numerators.

$$\frac{780}{13} = 60$$

OR

Equivalent Fraction Strategy

You can write the division as *one* fraction involving decimals and then use equivalent fractions like this:

$$7.8 \div 0.13 = \frac{7.8}{0.13}$$

That fraction is equivalent to $\frac{780}{13}$.

$$\frac{780}{13} = 60$$

In the example above, it may be easy to see what the quotient will be. When you work with multi-digit numbers, however, you may need to use other strategies.

Suppose two boys who live near a golf course search for lost golf balls. They collect 6,324 balls and package them for resale.

- How many packs of 12 golf balls can be made from a supply of 6,324 balls?
- If 6,324 golf balls are packed in 12 boxes, how many balls will be in each box?
- What number sentence (or sentences) describes this situation?

Problems such as this involve *long division* of whole numbers. In Problem 3.4, you will revisit this idea. You will use long division of whole numbers in the process of dividing decimals.

Problem 3.4

A **1.** The work below shows one strategy for carrying out long division to find the quotient 6,324 ÷ 12. Explain each step.

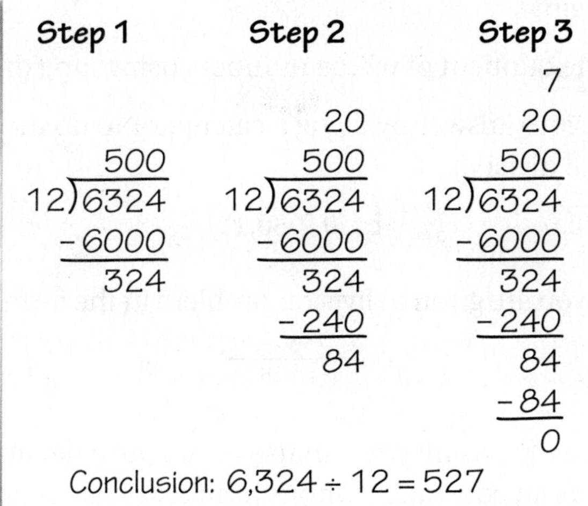

continued on the next page >

Problem 3.4 continued

2. Use your reasoning from part (1) or some other long-division algorithm to find each quotient. Explain how you could use fact-family thinking to check each division with a related multiplication.

   a. 6,440 ÷ 184 **b.** 118,750 ÷ 250 **c.** 64,575 ÷ 205

B Division problems that involve decimals are sometimes written in a short form, such as the one shown for whole numbers in Question A. For example, you might write 15.6 ÷ 3.12 as $3.12\overline{)15.6}$.

1. Use what you know about the connection between decimals and common fractions to explain why the quotient $3.12\overline{)15.6}$ is the same as $312\overline{)1560}$.

2. For each of the following decimal divisions:
   - Write the division as a whole-number division that will give the same result.
   - Explain how you know that your new problem is equivalent to the original.
   - Find the quotient of whole numbers using long division.
   - Check your answer by using a calculator to do the equivalent decimal division.

   a. $5.72\overline{)28.6}$ **b.** $0.7\overline{)30.1}$ **c.** $0.732\overline{)32.94}$

3. Suppose you are given a division problem in the form

   $$\text{divisor}\overline{)\text{dividend}}.$$

   Describe a procedure you can use to rewrite a decimal division problem as an equivalent whole-number division problem.

ACE Homework starts on page 57.

3.5 Challenging Cases
Dividing Decimals III

Converting decimal division into an equivalent whole-number division is a useful strategy. It allows you to solve an unfamiliar problem with a method that you already know. But this strategy doesn't work all of the time.

Here are two whole-number divisions that don't work out nicely:

$$\begin{array}{r} 30 \\ 24\overline{)\,738} \\ \underline{720} \\ 18 \end{array} \quad \text{and} \quad 95\overline{)76}$$

Your calculator would show you that 738 ÷ 24 = 30.75 and 76 ÷ 95 = 0.8.

Here's a way to think about 738 ÷ 24 without using a calculator:

> Suppose that 24 workers at a supermarket each buy Top Prize lottery tickets, with a promise to share winnings equally. If they win a prize of $738 (after taxes), each share can be found by dividing $738 by 24.

The traditional long-division algorithm gives a quotient of $30 and a remainder of $18.

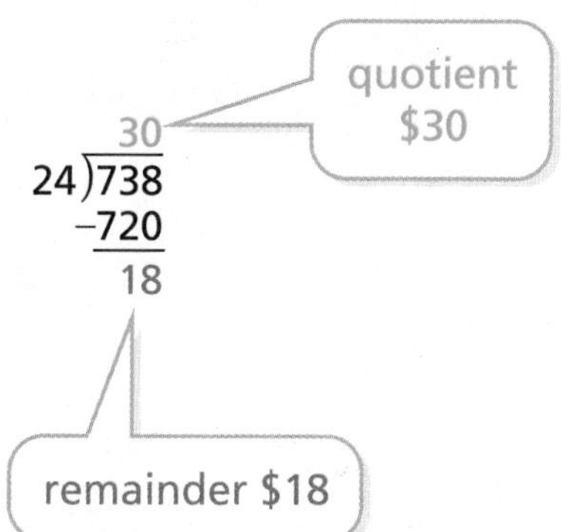

In mixed-number form, the quotient 738 ÷ 24 is $30\frac{18}{24}$, or $30\frac{3}{4}$.

You can think about the remainder of $18 in a way that leads to a decimal quotient.

$18 is equal to 180 dimes, and 180 ÷ 24 = 7 dimes, with remainder 12 dimes. Record that result like this:

12 dimes is equal to 120 pennies, and 120 ÷ 24 = 5 pennies with no remainder. Record that result like this:

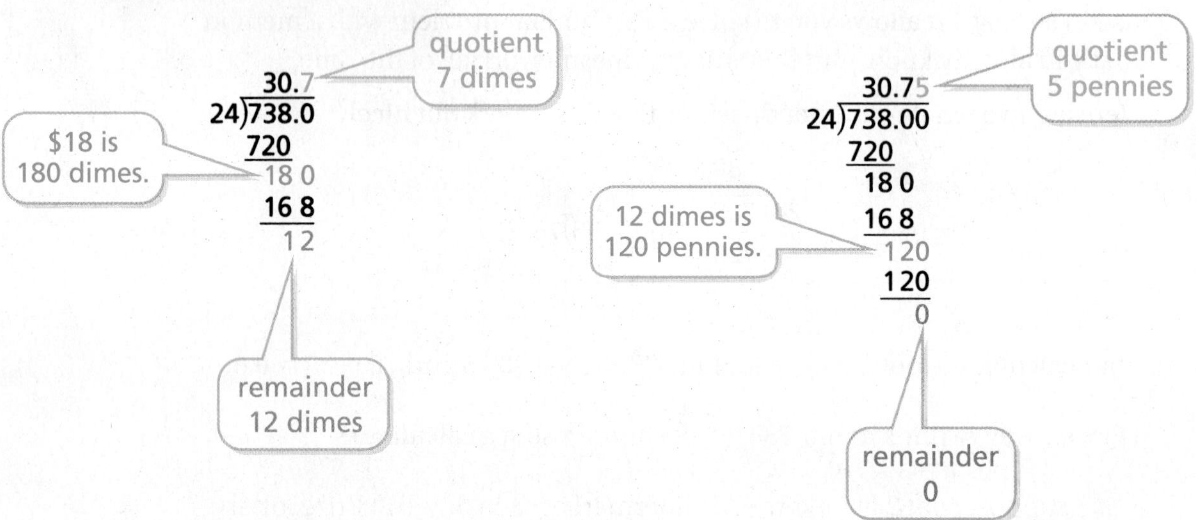

So, each Top Prize winner gets $30.75.

- On the previous page, the remainder was 18 whole dollars. In the above division process, what does "180" mean? What does "12" mean?
- The remainder in the left-hand column above was 12 tenths. What does "120" mean?
- How does 30.75 compare to the fraction answer on the previous page?
- Why is 738 ÷ 24 equal to 738.0 ÷ 24?
- Why is 738 ÷ 24 equal to 738.00 ÷ 24?

Problem 3.5

A **1.** For each problem below:

- Adapt the division strategy on the previous page to find the quotient.
- Estimate each quotient to check your answer.

a. $25\overline{)765}$ **b.** $18\overline{)225}$

c. $24\overline{)609}$ **d.** $30\overline{)890}$

2. In part (1), the quotient $25\overline{)765}$ can by written as $\frac{765}{25}$, which is equal to $30\frac{15}{25}$, or $30\frac{3}{5}$. Write each quotient in part (1) as an equivalent fraction or mixed number. Compare the fraction and decimal answers.

3. When you were asked to calculate $890 \div 30$, something different happened. How does your fraction answer help you to understand your decimal answer?

B You can use the strategy for dealing with whole-number divisions that do not result in a zero remainder to deal with problems such as $95\overline{)76}$.

1. What thinking is shown in the following work?

$$\begin{array}{r} 0.8 \\ 95\overline{)76.0} \\ \underline{76.0} \\ 0 \end{array}$$

2. The quotient $95\overline{)76}$ can be written as a fraction, $\frac{76}{95}$. Explain why this fraction is equivalent to the decimal shown in part (1).

3. Use the strategy shown in part (1) to find each quotient.

a. $52\overline{)39}$ **b.** $72\overline{)40}$

4. Write each division in part (3) as an equivalent fraction.

continued on the next page >

Problem 3.5 continued

C In *Comparing Bits and Pieces*, you learned that every fraction can be written as a decimal by dividing the numerator by the denominator. Now you know how to do that division without using a calculator. The decimal representation for $\frac{39}{52}$ is 0.75, which is a **terminating decimal.** Terminating decimals have a remainder of zero.

The decimal representation for $\frac{40}{72}$ is 0.55555..., or $0.\overline{5}$, which is a **repeating decimal.** This means that the remainder never becomes zero, because a digit or group of digits in the quotient repeats over and over.

1. For each of the fractions below,
   - Predict whether the decimal representation will be a terminating decimal or a repeating decimal.
   - Do the division to find the decimal equivalent to each fraction.
   - If possible, write an equivalent fraction with a denominator that is 10, 100, or some other power of 10.

   a. $\frac{6}{15}$ **b.** $\frac{6}{16}$ **c.** $\frac{6}{18}$ **d.** $\frac{6}{22}$

2. How can you predict for which fractions the equivalent decimal will be a terminating decimal? A repeating decimal?

D For each of the decimal divisions below,

- Rewrite the problem as a whole-number division.
- Estimate the solution.
- Find an exact decimal answer.

1. $0.76 \div 0.95$ **2.** $7.6 \div 0.95$ **3.** $0.76 \div 9.5$

E Summarize your approach to dealing with whole-number or decimal division problems that require exact decimal answers.

ACE Homework starts on page 57.

Applications | Connections | Extensions

Applications

1. For each decimal multiplication problem below,
   - Write each decimal factor as an equivalent fraction.
   - Find the product of the two fractions.
   - Write the product in equivalent decimal form.

   a. 0.3×1.4 b. 1.2×3.54
   c. 1.04×0.6 d. 23.2×0.45
   e. 0.54×1.2 f. 4.20×5.6

2. Use the fact that $17 \times 13 = 221$ to find each product.

   a. 1.7×13 b. 0.17×1.3 c. 17×0.13

For Exercises 3–6, use the given information to find each product.

3. If $34 \times 8 = 272$, what is 3.4×0.8? What is 0.34×0.08?

4. If $32 \times 517 = 16{,}544$, what is 3.2×5.17?

5. If $7263 \times 32 = 232{,}416$, what is 7.263×3.2?

6. If $2405 \times 5317 = 12{,}787{,}385$, what is 2.405×53.17?

7. **Multiple Choice** Which product is greater than 1?

   A. 2.4×0.75 B. 0.66×0.7 C. 9.8×0.001 D. 0.004×0.8

8. **Multiple Choice** Which product is greatest?

   F. 0.6×0.4 G. 0.06×0.04 H. 0.06×0.4 J. 0.6×0.04

9. Show how to calculate each of these products using a multiplication algorithm for whole numbers. Estimate each product to check your answer.

   a. 325×24
   b. 580×73
   c. 5.84×73
   d. 3.17×2.8
   e. 29×732
   f. 2.9×7.32

For Exercises 10–13, identify the errors in each calculation and find the correct product.

10.
```
  472
  x19
 4248
 +472
 4720
```

11.
```
  327
 x123
  981
  654
 +327
 1962
```

12.
```
  47.2
  x1.9
  4248
 +4720
 896.8
```

13.
```
    571
   x342
      2
   2800
+150000
 152802
```

For Exercises 14–19, estimate each product. Then compute the exact result without using a calculator.

14. 0.6×0.8

15. 2.1×1.45

16. 3.822×5.2

17. 0.9×1.305

18. 5.13×2.9

19. 4.17×6.72

20. You type 2.7×4.63 into your calculator. The calculator screen is damaged, and it shows 12501. Where does the decimal point belong?

21. Sweety's Ice Cream Shop sells ice cream by weight. They charge $6.95 per pound. If your dish of ice cream weighs 0.42 pounds, how much will it cost?

22. Aaron plans to buy new flooring for his office. His office floor is a rectangle that is 7.9 meters by 6.2 meters.

a. How many square meters of floor space does his office have?

b. Suppose flooring costs $5.90 per square meter. How much will the new flooring for Aaron's office cost?

23. Ten-year-old Chi learned a lot of math from his older brother, Shing. One day, Shing told him that when you multiply a number by 10, "you just add a zero."

a. With Shing's idea in his mind, Chi says, "To find 10×20, I just add a zero. So, $20 + 0 = 20$." How would you correct him?

b. After Chi realizes that "adding zero" actually means "putting an extra zero at the end," he says,

"10×0.02 equals 0.020 by putting an extra zero at the end."

Is he right this time? How would you rephrase "putting an extra zero at the end" in case the other number is a decimal number? Explain why your suggestion works.

c. How can you find the result of multiplying by 100; 1,000; or 10,000 using a similar strategy?

24. For each decimal division problem below,

- Write the dividend and divisor as fractions with common denominators.
- Estimate the quotient of the two fractions.
- Find the exact value of the quotient.

a. 4.2 ÷ 2.1 **b.** 16.1 ÷ 2.3 **c.** 0.56 ÷ 0.08

d. 7.6 ÷ 0.04 **e.** 25.9 ÷ 1.85 **f.** 36 ÷ 2.4

25. Write these decimal divisions as equivalent whole-number divisions. Then find the quotients.

a. $3.2\overline{)44.8}$ **b.** $0.17\overline{)2.55}$ **c.** $4.75\overline{)114}$ **d.** $0.014\overline{)350}$

For Exercises 26 and 27, estimate each answer. Then write each division in equivalent fraction form with whole-number numerator and denominator. Finally, compute the quotients. Look for patterns in your answers.

26. a. 36 ÷ 12 **b.** 3.6 ÷ 12

c. 3.6 ÷ 1.2 **d.** 3.6 ÷ 0.12

e. 3.6 ÷ 120 **f.** 0.36 ÷ 0.12

27. a. 124 ÷ 32 **b.** 1,240 ÷ 320

c. 12,400 ÷ 3,200 **d.** 12,400 ÷ 3.2

e. 1.24 ÷ 3.2 **f.** 1.24 ÷ 0.32

28. Here are three decimal divisions that are closely related. Do they all have the same result? Why or why not?

a. 27.5 ÷ 55 **b.** 2,750 ÷ 5.5 **c.** 0.275 ÷ 0.55

29. Write the complete multiplication-division fact family for $0.84 \div 0.06 = 14$. Use a calculator, or some other method that you prefer, to check each equation in the family.

30. Find the value of N that makes each equation true.

a. $3.2 \times N = 0.96$ b. $0.7 \times N = 0.042$ c. $N \times 3.21 = 9.63$

d. $N \div 0.8 = 3.5$ e. $2.75 \div N = 5.5$ f. $5.3N + 7.25 = 70.85$

31. Find each quotient.

a. $15\overline{)630}$ b. $75\overline{)9{,}900}$ c. $230\overline{)40{,}250}$

For Exercises 32–39, use long division to find each quotient.

32. $43 \div 8.6$

33. $418.6 \div 80.5$

34. $254 \div 40$

35. $107.5 \div 125$

36. $12.012 \div 5.6$

37. $45.13 \div 0.125$

38. $1.2 \div 4.8$

39. $1.99 \div 10$

40. Check the work in these divisions. Identify and correct any errors present in the work shown.

a.

```
      5
    100
14)1470  Answer:105
  -1400
     70
    -70
      0
```

b.

```
          4
          7
         40
30)1422.0  Answer: 51
  -1200
    222
   -210
     12.0
    -12.0
        0
```

For Exercises 41–47, write the operations needed to answer the questions. Then perform the operations without using a calculator. Finally, show how to estimate the answers to see that your exact answers make sense.

41. Sandy cuts lawns in her neighborhood during the summer. When Sandy bought 4.5 gallons of gasoline for the mower, the pump showed a charge of $18. What was the gasoline price in dollars per gallon?

42. Garden plots in the Portland Community Garden are rectangles limited to 45 square meters. Christopher and his friends want a plot that has a width of 7.5 meters. What length will give a plot that has the maximum area allowed?

43. The world record for the men's 4×400-meter relay race is 2:54.29, set in 1993.

a. Why does that figure equal 174.29 seconds?

b. What was the average time (in seconds) of each of the four runners?

44. The Ironman Triathlon is a speed and endurance race that combines swimming (2.4 miles), biking (112 miles), and running (26.2 miles). One famous Ironman competition occurs each year in Hawaii, where the race began in 1978.

a. What is the total distance covered in an Ironman race?

b. The best men's time for the Hawaiian Ironman race is 8.07 hours. What was the average speed of that Ironman winner?

c. The best women's time for the Hawaiian Ironman race is 8.9 hours. What was the average speed of that Ironman winner?

45. Ironman racers are allowed a maximum of 2 hours and 20 minutes to complete the 2.4-mile swim.

a. Why is that time limit equal to $2\frac{1}{3}$ hours?

b. Write that time limit as an improper fraction.

c. Use your answer to part (b) to write the time limit as a decimal.

d. How fast does a racer have to swim to meet the time limit exactly?

46. Loren is putting brick along both edges of the 21-meter walkway to his house. Each brick is 0.26 meters long. Loren is placing the bricks end to end.

a. How many bricks does he need?

b. If bricks cost \$.15 apiece, how much will the brick border cost?

47. Angie is making wreaths to sell at a craft show. She has 6.5 yards of ribbon. Each wreath has a bow made from $1\frac{1}{3}$ yards of ribbon. How many bows can she make?

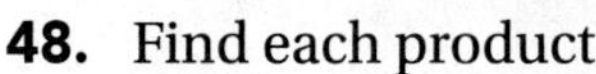

Connections

48. Find each product.

a. 3×10

b. 3×10^2

c. 3×10^3

d. 50×10^4

e. 502×10^5

f. 520×10^6

g. What pattern helps you multiply a whole number by a power of 10?

49. Simplify each expression.

a. $5(10 + 7)$

b. $5(17)$

c. $5(100 - 1)$

d. $50(99)$

e. 3^3

f. $4^3 \cdot 2$

g. $2(10 - 8) + 8$

h. $\frac{2}{10}(20 - 1)$

i. $\frac{2}{10}(19)$

j. $\frac{2}{10}(12.75 + 6.25)$

50. Find each product or quotient.

a. $\frac{7}{3} \times \frac{4}{9}$

b. $\frac{2}{5} \times 15$

c. $3 \times \frac{4}{9}$

d. $2\frac{2}{3} \times \frac{1}{2}$

e. $4 \times 2\frac{2}{3}$

f. $1\frac{1}{2} \times 2.3$

g. $\frac{2}{3} \div \frac{1}{6}$

h. $2\frac{2}{3} \div \frac{1}{2}$

i. $4 \div 2\frac{1}{2}$

j. $3\frac{2}{5} \times 10$

51. Midge wants to buy a carpet for her new room. She finds three carpets that she likes, but they are different sizes and have different prices. She writes down the information about each size and price so that she can decide at home.

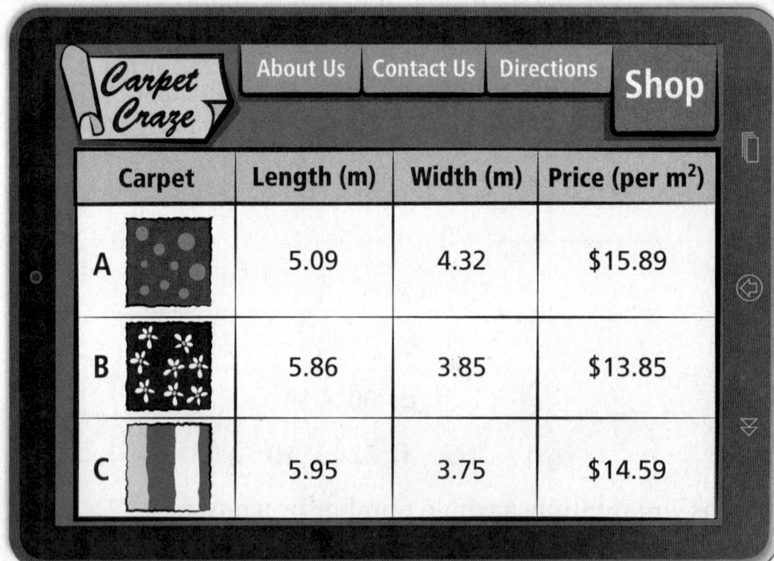

Carpet	Length (m)	Width (m)	Price (per m²)
A	5.09	4.32	$15.89
B	5.86	3.85	$13.85
C	5.95	3.75	$14.59

a. Which carpet is longest?

b. Which carpet has the greatest area?

c. What is the total cost of each carpet? Which carpet costs the most? Which carpet costs the least?

52. Find a length and width for a rectangle with the given area.

a. 56 ft^2

b. 5.6 ft^2

c. 0.56 ft^2

53. Find the decimal equivalent of each fraction or mixed number.

a. $\frac{2}{6}$

b. $\frac{13}{39}$

c. $\frac{5}{15}$

d. $\frac{11}{9}$

e. $1\frac{6}{27}$

f. $\frac{22}{18}$

54. Copy the table below, and write each fraction as a decimal.

Fraction	Decimal
$\frac{1}{9}$	■
$\frac{2}{9}$	■
$\frac{3}{9}$	■
$\frac{4}{9}$	■
$\frac{5}{9}$	■
$\frac{6}{9}$	■
$\frac{7}{9}$	■
$\frac{8}{9}$	■

a. Describe the pattern you see in the table.

b. Use the pattern to write a decimal representation for each fraction. Use your calculator to check your answers.

i. $\frac{9}{9}$ **ii.** $\frac{10}{9}$ **iii.** $\frac{15}{9}$

c. What fraction is equivalent to each decimal? Note that 1.222... can be written as 1 + 0.222...

i. 1.2222... **ii.** 2.7777...

55. For parts (a)–(d), copy the number line and label each tick mark.

a.
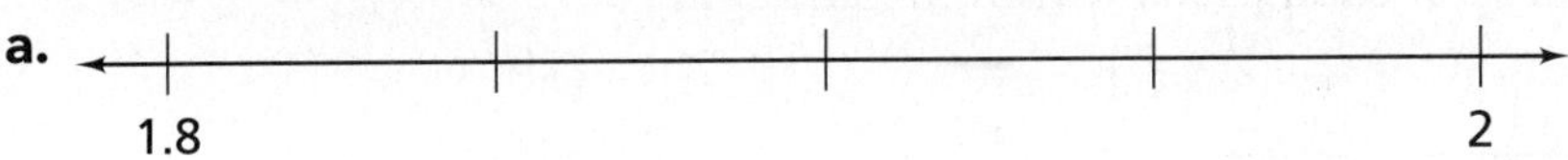

b.
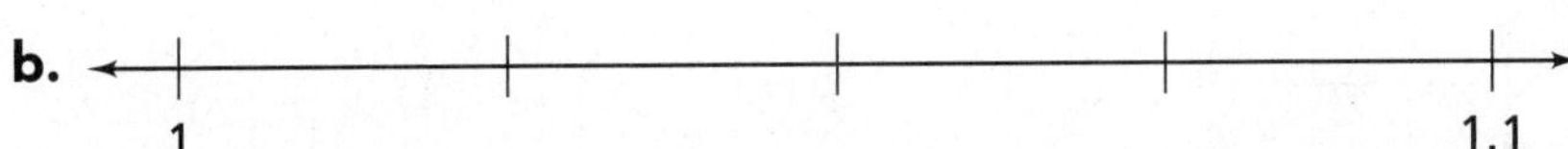

c.
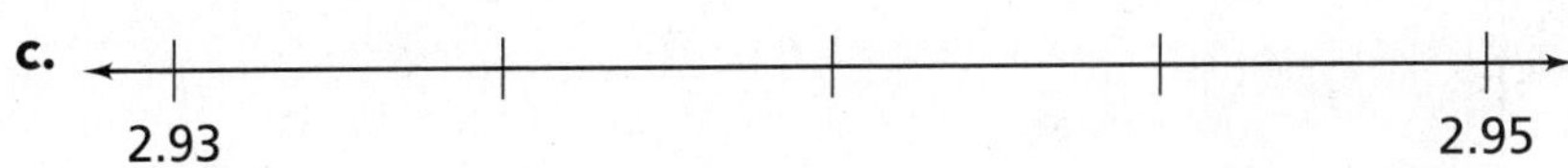

d.
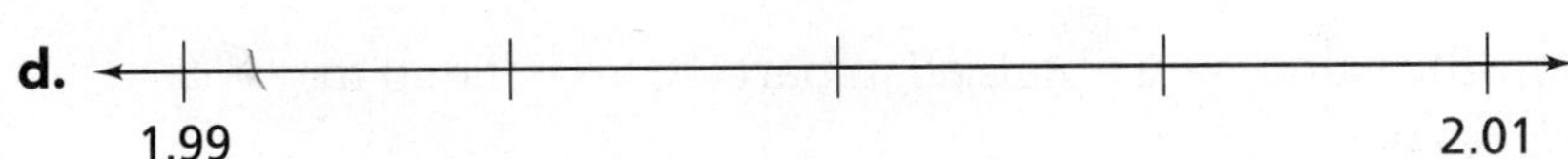

e. Explain your strategy for answering parts (a)–(d).

For Exercises 56–59, find the area of each shape.

56.

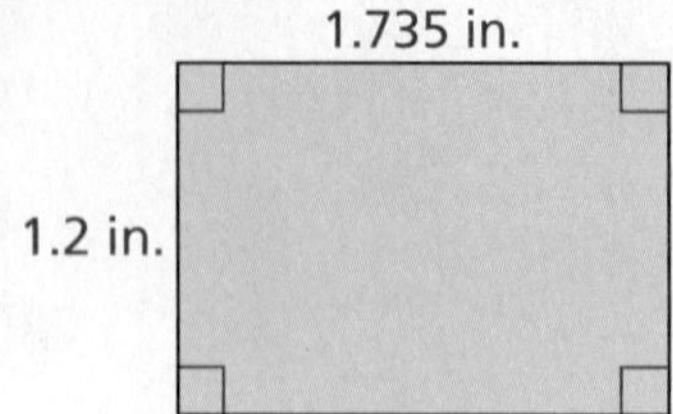

57.

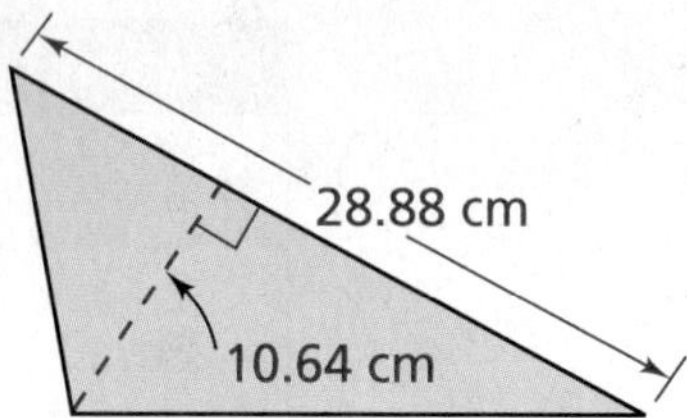

58.

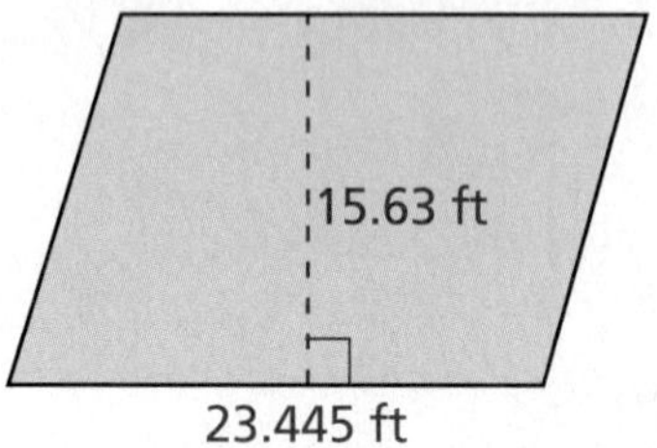

59.

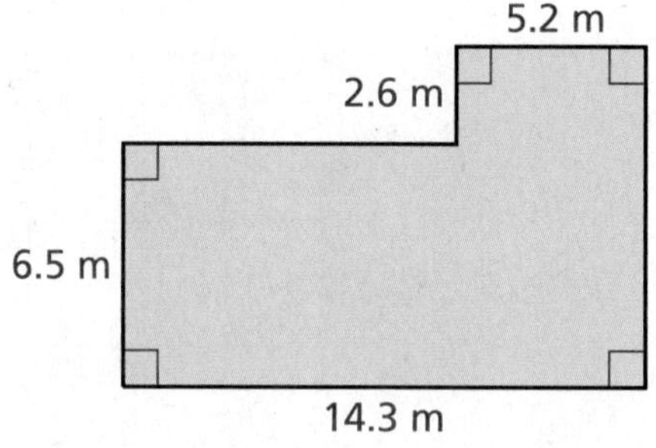

60. **a.** Find the area of the orange square.

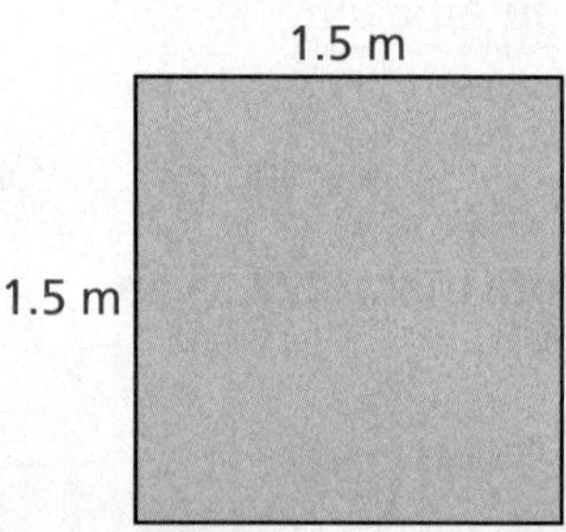

b. Find the area of each piece within the larger square.

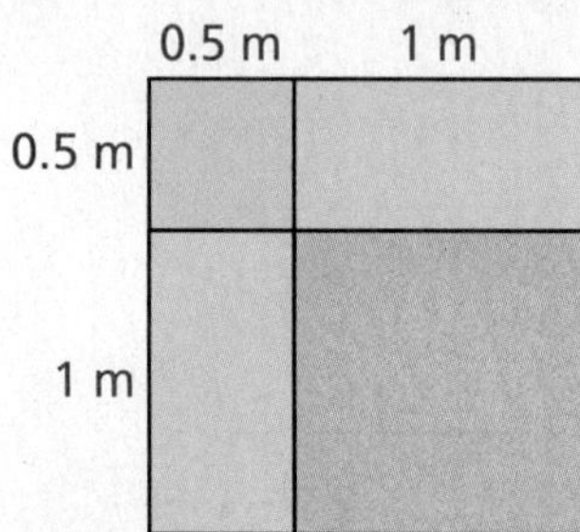

c. Explain how the values you obtained in part (b) are related to your answer to part (a).

61. Multiple Choice Which quotient is greater than 1?

A. $\frac{1}{4} \div \frac{3}{8}$ **B.** $\frac{19}{5} \div 5$ **C.** $1\frac{2}{3} \div 2\frac{2}{9}$ **D.** $3 \div \frac{19}{7}$

62. Use the Order of Operations and algorithms for decimal arithmetic to simplify each expression.

a. $0.3 + 0.4 \div 2$ **b.** $1.5 \times 2 - 1.5$ **c.** $\frac{3.5 - 1.3}{2 + 0.2}$

63. Akiko's dog has three puppies. They weigh 2.6 pounds, 2.74 pounds, and 3.1 pounds. How much more does the heaviest puppy weigh than the lightest puppy?

64. On some television game shows, players can lose points for incorrect answers. For example, if a player starts with 0 points and gets a 100-point question wrong, he or she has −100 (read as "negative one hundred") points.

a. The picture above shows Kate's score right now. Suppose she gets three 50-point questions wrong. What will Kate's score be at that point in the game?

b. The picture shows Lola's score right now. Suppose she gets three 100-point questions wrong. What will Lola's score be then?

c. Use Hiro's score from the picture above. Suppose he gets a 100-point question right and then gets a 200-point question wrong. How many points does Hiro need to get to 0 points?

d. The picture shows John's score after getting one question right and one question wrong. What are the possible point values of the questions?

Extensions

65. Tanisha and Belinda estimated the product 5.2×100.4 in two different ways. Without finding the exact result of 5.2×100.4, can you tell whose estimation is closer to the exact answer? Explain.

Tanisha

I round 5.2 to 5. I multiply 5 x 100.4 because I know that 5 x 0.4 is 2. So, my estimation is 500 + 2, or 502.

Belinda

I prefer to round 100.4 to 100 and find 5.2 x 100 instead. Moving the decimal point two places to the right, I find the estimation is 520.

66. Find each product.

a. $1.2 \times \frac{31}{40}$ **b.** $0.45 \times 1.7 \times 0.34$ **c.** $0.14 \times 74.3 \times 2.125$

67. **a.** Write a fraction equivalent to $\frac{3.7}{23}$ without decimals.

b. Write a fraction equivalent to $\frac{1.6}{4}$ without decimals.

c. Use your equivalent fractions from parts (a) and (b) to find $\frac{3.7}{23} \times \frac{1.6}{4}$.

68. Copy this calculation. Replace the boxes with numbers to make the calculation correct. You may need to insert a decimal point in the top line.

```
      1 5 2 ■
  ×       ■.9
  -----------
    1 3 7 1 ■
  + 3 ■ 4 8
  -----------
    4 ■.1 9 6
```

69. One morning, Janet was feeling very sleepy toward the end of class when her teacher multiplied two decimal numbers and got 24.9344. Later, when Janet looked at her notebook, she realized that she had forgotten to put the decimal points of the two numbers in her notebook. Here is what she had written:

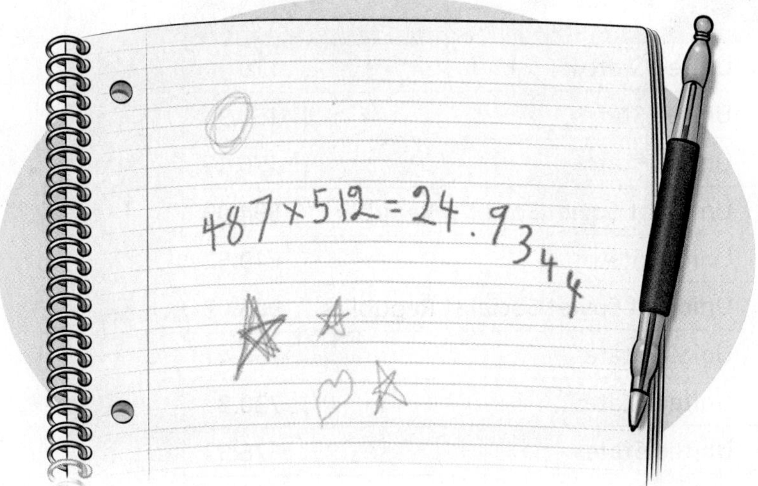

a. Where do you think the decimal points should be in the factors?

b. Is there more than one possibility? Explain.

70. Consider ways to complete marking this number line.

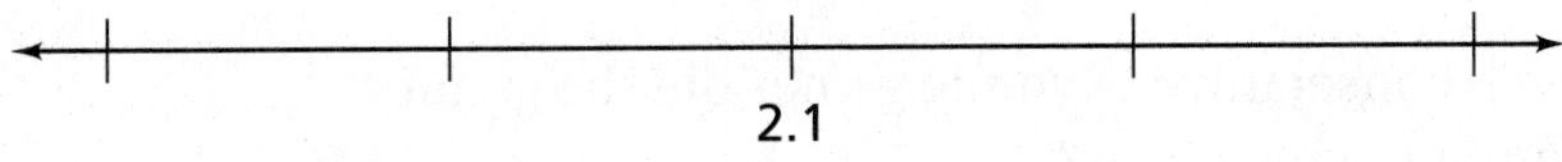

a. Give four different ways to label the unlabeled marks on the number line.

b. Find the average of the five numbers in each of your answers in part (a). Do you see a pattern? Explain.

c. Can you label the unlabeled marks on the number line so that the sum of the five numbers will be 10? Explain.

71. For parts (a)–(d), use the table. Give evidence to support your conclusions. You may want to make a table of the differences in scores between each pair of consecutive years.

Olympic Diving (Men's 3-Meter Springboard)

Year	Winner (country)	Score
1960	United States	170
1964	United States	150.9
1968	United States	170.15
1972	Union of Soviet Socialist Republics	594.09
1976	United States	619.52
1980	Union of Soviet Socialist Republics	905.02
1984	United States	754.41
1988	United States	730.8
1992	United States	676.53
1996	China	701.46
2000	China	708.72
2004	China	787.38
2008	China	572.9
2012	Russia	555.9

a. Between which consecutive Olympic games did the greatest change in winning score occur?

b. Between which consecutive Olympic games did the next greatest change in winning score occur?

c. Between which consecutive Olympic games did the least change in winning score occur?

d. The same athlete won the 3-meter springboard competition in 1984 and 1988. What is the average of his scores?

72. Leah filled her gas tank at the start of a trip and noted that her mileage indicator read 15,738.1 miles. When her mileage indicator read 16,167.6, she needed gas again. It took 18.2 gallons of gas to fill the tank. How many miles did her car go on each gallon of gas?

Each of the shapes in Exercises 73–75 has the same area as the rectangle below.

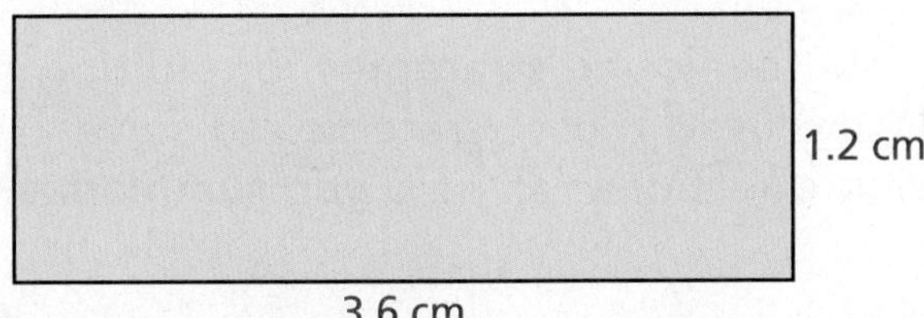

Use this information to find the length of each side labeled *n*.

73.

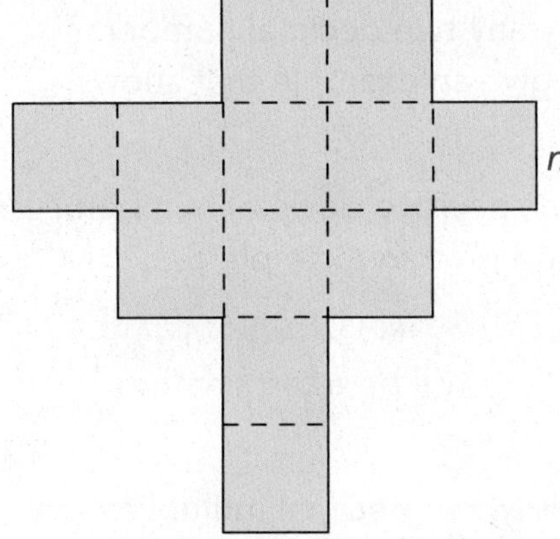

74.

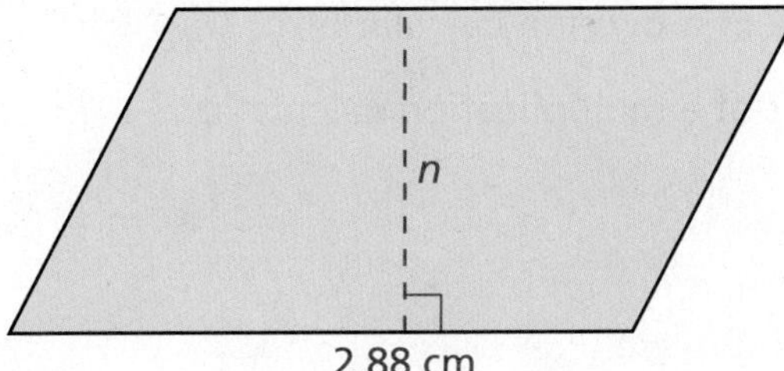

75.

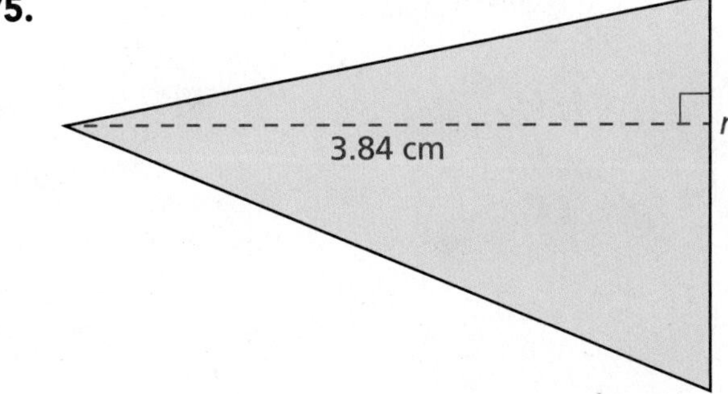

Mathematical Reflections 3

In this Investigation, you developed strategies for multiplying and dividing decimals and used those strategies to solve problems. The following questions will help you summarize what you have learned.

Think about these questions. Discuss your ideas with other students and your teacher. Then write a summary of your findings in your notebook.

1. **What** algorithm can be used to multiply any two decimal numbers? Explain why your algorithm works, and give an example that shows how it works.
2. **a.** **What** algorithm can be used to divide any two decimal numbers? Explain why your algorithm works, and give an example that shows how it works.

   b. **How** can you predict whether a quotient will be a terminating decimal or a repeating decimal?
3. **a.** **What** is the fact-family connection between decimal multiplication and division?

   b. **How** can you check the result of a division calculation?

   c. **How** can you check the result of a multiplication calculation?

Common Core Mathematical Practices

As you worked on the Problems in this Investigation, you used prior knowledge to make sense of them. You also applied Mathematical Practices to solve the Problems. Think back over your work, the ways you thought about the Problems, and how you used Mathematical Practices.

Jayden described his thoughts in the following way:

In Problem 3.5, we had to do long divisions BY HAND! Writing a decimal division as a whole-number division is the easy part. The division process is long and complicated.

None of the divisions came out even, so we had to add zeroes after the decimal point and keep going.

One good thing about it is that I finally see why sometimes the divisions end when the remainder is zero. Also, when I see that a remainder repeats, I know that the digits in the quotient repeat.

Common Core Standards for Mathematical Practice
MP6 Attend to precision

- What other Mathematical Practices can you identify in Jayden's reasoning?
- Describe a Mathematical Practice that you and your classmates used to solve a different Problem in this Investigation.

Using Percents

When you buy something in a store, you often pay sales tax on the purchase price. When the store has a sale, the manager posts signs advertising a discount. Discounts and tax rates are commonly expressed as percents. For discounts, you might see percents like 25%, 30%, or 50%. For sales tax, you might see percents such as 5%, 6.25%, or 8%. Understanding how to compute and use percents can make you a smarter consumer.

Item Name	Price	Tax	Total
pencil	1.00	0.06	1.06
doodle pad	5.90		
eraser	0.50		

Credit	Debit
Check	Cash
Print Receipt	

Subtotal	7.40
Tax	
Order total	
Cash	

Common Core State Standards

6.RP.A.3c Find a percent of a quantity as a rate per 100 (e.g., 30% of a quantity means $\frac{30}{100}$ times the quantity); solve problems involving finding the whole, given a part and the percent.

6.NS.B.3 Fluently add, subtract, multiply, and divide multi-digit decimals using the standard algorithm for each operation.

6.EE.A.3 Apply the properties of operations to generate equivalent expressions.

6.EE.B.7 Solve real-world and mathematical problems by writing and solving equations of the form $x + p = q$ and $px = q$ for cases in which p, q and x are all nonnegative rational numbers.

Also 6.RP.A.3, 6.EE.B.6

4.1 What's the Tax on This Item?

A percent is a special way of writing a fraction with a denominator of 100. You can think of percent as meaning "out of 100."

For example, a sales tax of 6% means that for every dollar an item costs, a person pays an additional six hundredths of a dollar. This is equal to 6 cents, or \$.06.

$$\begin{aligned} \$1.00 + (6\% \text{ of } \$1.00) &= \$1.00 + \$.06 \\ &= \$1.06 \end{aligned}$$

Another way to think about this is to remember that \$1.00 is 100 pennies.

$$\begin{aligned} 100 \text{ pennies} + (6\% \text{ of } 100 \text{ pennies}) &= 100 \text{ pennies} + 6 \text{ pennies} \\ &= 106 \text{ pennies} \\ &= \$1.06 \end{aligned}$$

- At a 6% tax rate, what would be the total cost for an item priced at \$5?
- At a 6% tax rate, what would be the total cost for an item priced at 50¢?

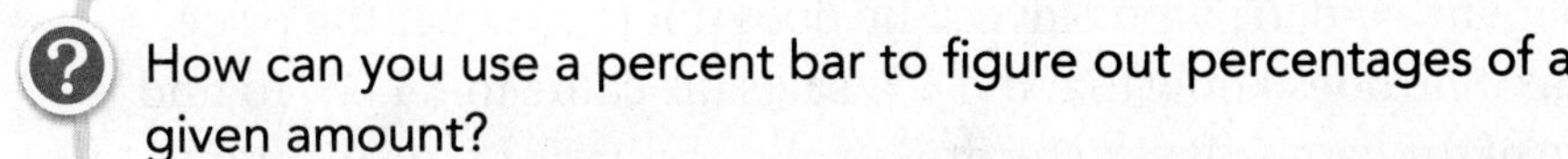
How can you use a percent bar to figure out percentages of a given amount?

Problem 4.1

Write a number sentence for each question. Then answer the question.

A Jill wants to buy an album of music that is priced at $7.50. The sales tax is 6%. What will be the total cost of the album?

Try to find more than one way to solve this problem. Explain the different methods you find.

2:30 PM
Franklin and the Androids
Methodic Melodics
$7.50
BUY
1,067 Ratings
I'm a Robot
Cold Cold Heart
Automatic Love

B States have different sales tax rates. Find the *total cost* of each item below.

1. a $2.00 magazine if the sales tax rate is 7%
2. a $5.00 book if the sales tax rate is 6.5%
3. a $.50 comic book if the sales tax rate is 7.5%

Note: When a percent calculation for sales tax does not come out to a whole number of cents, the standard practice is to round up the tax to the next penny.

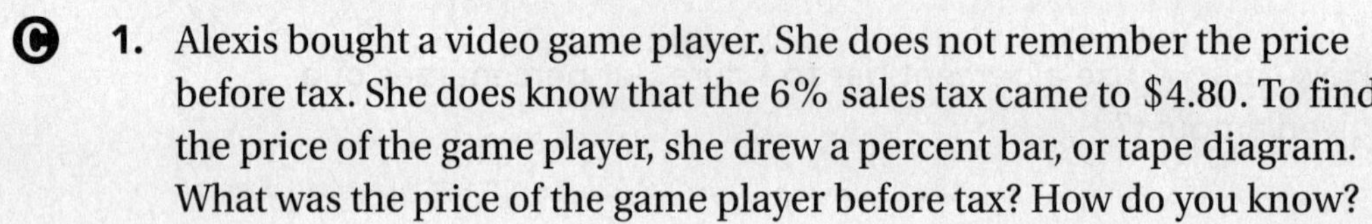

C 1. Alexis bought a video game player. She does not remember the price before tax. She does know that the 6% sales tax came to $4.80. To find the price of the game player, she drew a percent bar, or tape diagram. What was the price of the game player before tax? How do you know?

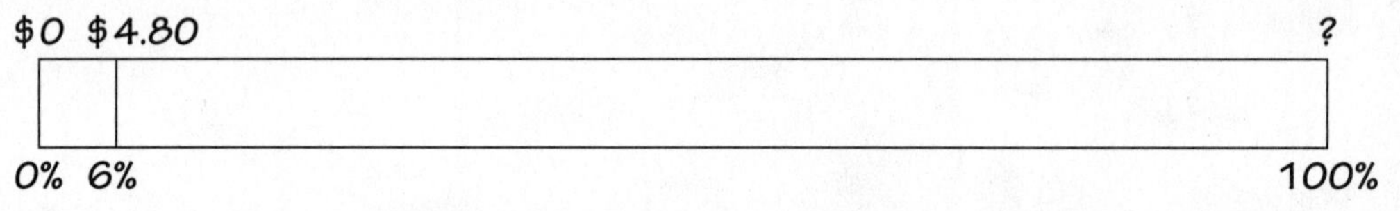

2. Frank bought a new video game. The 5% sales tax was $.75. What was the price of the game before tax?
   a. Draw a tape diagram to illustrate the problem.
   b. Find the price (before tax) of the game. Explain how you know.

Problem 4.1 continued

3. Nic paid a total of $25.68 for a game, including 7% tax. What was the price before tax?

   a. Draw a tape diagram to illustrate the problem.

   b. Find the game price before tax. Explain how you know.

D After Susan did many price-plus-tax calculations, she noticed that all of the problems could be done two different ways.

1. Susan said to find the total cost of a $250 bicycle and the 7% tax, you could figure 7% of $250 and then add that amount to $250. The information she knows is shown on the percent bar.

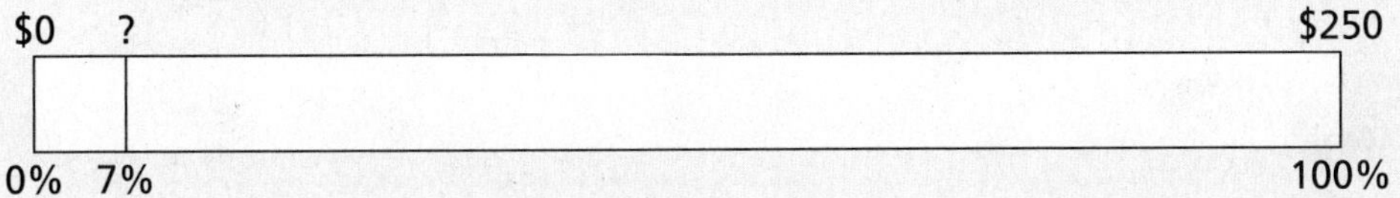

   Write a sentence that starts "Total cost =" to show how to use this method to find the total cost.

2. The other way to do this is simply to multiply 1.07(250). Write a sentence that starts "Total cost =" to show how to use this method to find the total cost.

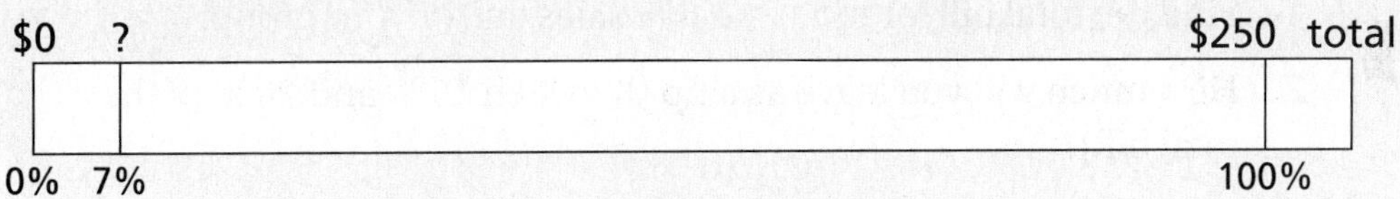

3. Are both methods correct? Why or why not?

ACE Homework starts on page 87.

4.2 Computing Tips

At most restaurants, customers pay their server a tip for providing good service. A typical tip is 15% to 20% of the price of the meal.

- What could be the tip on a restaurant bill of $14?
- How might this percent bar, or tape diagram, help you figure out the tip on a $14 bill?

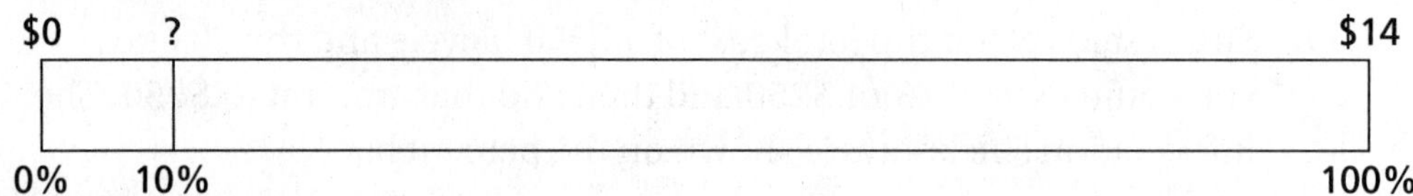

Problem 4.2

Try to find more than one way to answer each of the following questions about restaurant tipping. Record your thinking in number sentences. Be prepared to explain your different methods.

A Have each member of your group use the menu from Larry's Lunch Place to make up a lunch order. Write a list of all the items ordered by your group.

1. Find the total bill for food and 6% sales tax for your group.
2. How much will you leave as a tip (between 15% and 20% of the total bill)?
3. Suppose that your group members decide to share the cost of the meal equally. What is each person's share of the cost, including tip?

Problem 4.2 continued

Larry's Lunch Place

Appetizers

Chicken Tenders $7.99
Hummus Plate $6.99

Soups and Salads

Soup of the Day or Clam Chowder
Cup $2.99
Bowl $5.29

Garden Salad
Small $2.99
Large $5.99

Sandwiches

(served with two sides)
BLT $7.29
Veggie BLT $7.29
Tuna Salad $7.29
Deli Sandwich (turkey, ham, or roast beef) $7.29
Grilled Cheese $5.29

Burgers

(served with two sides)
Hamburger $7.99
Bacon Cheeseburger $8.29
Double Cheeseburger $10.29

Sides: French fries, sweet potato fries, mac'n'cheese, chips, baked beans, potato salad, or cole slaw

Drinks

Cola, Diet Cola, Citrus Surprise ... $1.99
Fresh Brewed Iced Tea $1.00
Lemonade $1.99

Desserts

Chocolate Pudding $2.25
Pecan Pie $3.95

continued on the next page >

Problem 4.2 continued

B Many people use benchmarks for determining tips. Gil explains his strategy: "I always figure out 10% of the bill, and then I use this information to calculate a 15% or 20% tip."

1. Find 10% and 5% of $20.00. How are the two percents related?
2. Find 10% and 20% of $24.50. How are the two percents related?
3. Find 10% of $17.35. Use this to find 15% and 20% of $17.35. Explain your reasoning in each case.

C The sales tax in Kadisha's state is 5%. Kadisha says she computes a 15% tip by multiplying the tax shown on her bill by 3. For a bill with a tax charge of $.38, Kadisha's tip is $.38 × 3 = $1.14.

1. Why does Kadisha's method work?
2. Use a similar method to compute a 20% tip. Explain your reasoning.
3. When people leave a 15% or 20% tip, they often round up to the nearest multiple of 5 or 10 cents. If Kadisha always rounds up, what is a 20% tip on her bill?

D A customer left Jerome $2.50 as a tip for service. That tip is 20% of the total bill for the food.

1. How much is the food bill?
2. Draw a percent bar or tape diagram to illustrate this problem and its solution.
3. Explain the reasoning you used to answer part (1).

E After Katrina did many price-plus-tip calculations, she noticed that all of the problems could be done two ways. For example, one way to find the total cost of a $25 meal + 20% tip uses a multiplication and an addition. The other way uses a single multiplication.

1. Write a sentence starting "Total price =" for each of these ways.
2. How are these two sentences related?

ACE Homework starts on page 87.

4.3 Percent Discounts

Newspapers often have coupons for discounts. A discount coupon for shampoo is shown here.

The regular price for the shampoo is $5.00. Alicia wants to figure out what percent discount $1.50 is of $5.00.

- How can you write the discount as a fraction of the regular price with denominator 100?
- How can you write the discount as a percent of the regular price?
- How could the percent bar below help you find what $1.50 is as a percent of the regular price?

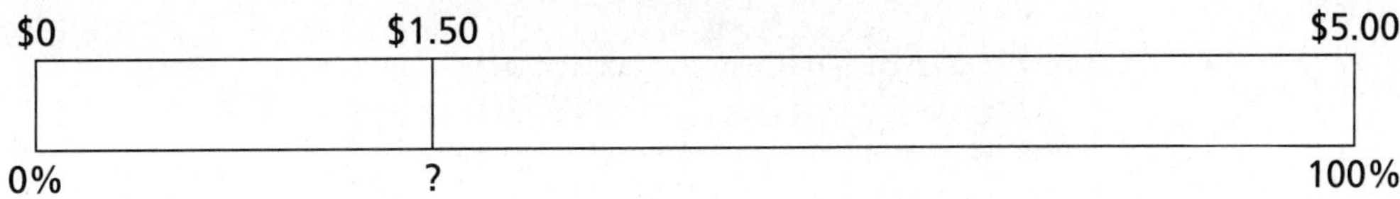

Problem 4.3

Use what you know about percents to answer the following questions about discounts. Record your reasoning in number sentences. Be prepared to explain your thinking.

A What percent discount do you get with the coupon shown here? Try to find more than one way to solve this problem.

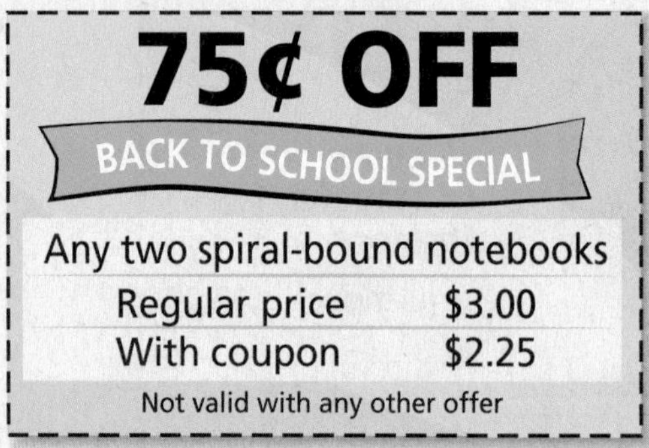

B What percent discount do you get with the coupon shown here? Try to find more than one way to solve this problem. Be prepared to explain your methods.

C A 25% discount on a skateboard is $24.75. What is the cost before the discount?

Problem 4.3 continued

D Rita, Masako, and Kazuko each got discounts on some items they bought.

1. At a music store, Rita got a $12 discount on an item originally priced at $48. What percent discount did she get?
2. Masako had a $25-off coupon on a purchase of $100 or more at a department store. She bought a jacket with a price of $125. What is the percent discount on her purchase?
3. Describe the calculations you used to answer parts (1) and (2). Explain why your methods work.
4. Masako's sister Kazuko also had a $25-off coupon. She bought a rain jacket for $110 at the same store.
   a. Which sister got the greater percent discount?
   b. How can you answer part (a) without actually calculating any discount percents?

E Aladar used a 20%-discount coupon to buy a new smartphone priced at $95. When he got to the telecom store, he learned that they were having a 30%-off sale.

The clerk calculated the 30% discount first and then applied the 20%-off coupon to the discounted amount.

1. What should be the final price (without sales tax)?
2. Is that final price the same as a 50% discount? Explain.

ACE Homework starts on page 87.

4.4 Putting Operations Together

The Columbus Boys and Girls Club, CBGC, offers after-school tutoring and computer-use time. The Club also provides opportunities to compete on sports teams, perform in musicals and dramatic shows, and take field trips for education and entertainment.

Problem 4.4

The following questions came up in operating the Club. For each question, follow the directions below.

- Choose numbers and operations that will give the answer.
- Write mathematical expressions that show the required calculations.
- Use a calculator, mental arithmetic, or paper and pencil algorithms to find exact answers.
- Answer the question in one or more complete sentences.

A One group of boys and girls planned to operate a lawn-mowing service as a fundraiser for the Club. They decided to set the price for any lawn by measuring the area to be mowed.

1. What is the area in square meters of the lawn shown below?

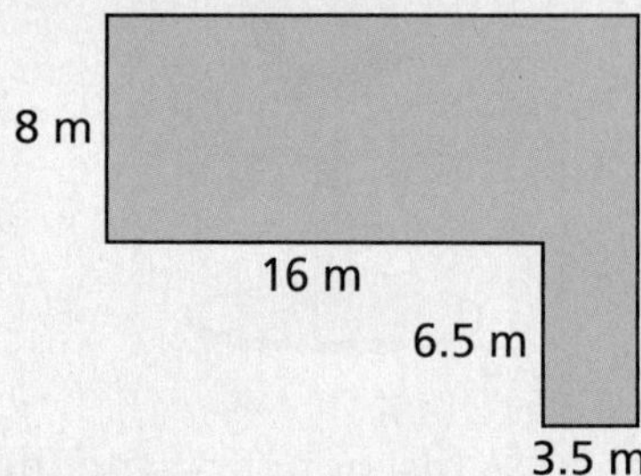

2. The boys and girls who had experience mowing lawns thought the job was worth about $25. What is the price in dollars per square meter?
3. Using the price per square meter from part (2), what should the boys and girls charge to mow a lawn with area 200 square meters?

Problem 4.4 continued

B The CBGC pays college and high school students $5.75 per hour to tutor the younger boys and girls.

1. If one of those tutors works 3.4 hours on Monday and 2.7 hours on Thursday, what will the tutor earn for the week?
2. If the Club has a tutoring budget of $250 per week, how many tutoring hours can be provided?
3. Danny is tutoring Abe. Below are the results of two check-up quizzes.
   a. Write the score of Abe's first quiz (21 out of 30) as a percent.
   b. Abe is pleased with his improvement on the second check-up. He says he has made a 10% improvement. Danny says the new score is not a 10% increase *over the old score.* Who is correct? Explain.

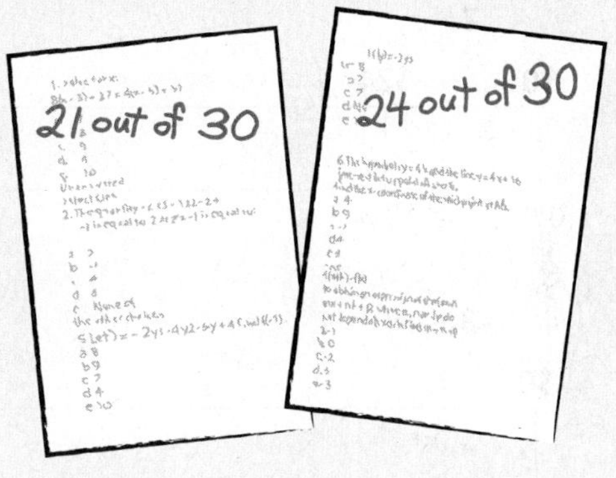

   c. Abe now has 45 out of a total of 60 points on check-up quizzes. There is one more quiz to come in this Unit. It is also out of 30 points. What does he have to score on this last quiz to raise his check-up quiz grade to 80% overall?

C At the end of the summer, the Club had enough money from the lawn-mowing group and other fundraising efforts to pay for a bus ride and admission to an amusement park.

1. Suppose 325 club members want to go, and each bus holds 60 club members. How many buses are needed for the trip?
2. Suppose the bus company charges $2.95 per mile for each bus. What is the cost per bus for the 124-mile round trip? What is the cost for all buses combined?
3. Suppose the bus company charges 6% sales tax. What are the tax and the total bill?
4. Suppose the trip takes 3 hours and 15 minutes of driving time for the 124-mile round trip. What is the average speed of the buses in miles per hour?

continued on the next page >

Problem 4.4 *continued*

D Write and solve a problem that could be represented by each percent bar or number sentence below.

1.

2.

3.

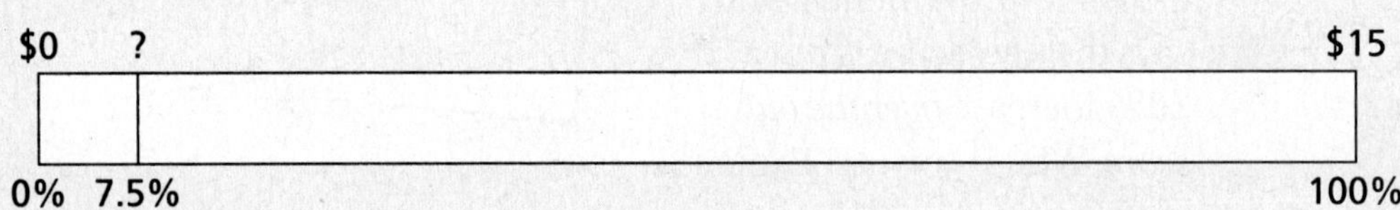

4. $20.25 = 1.35P$

5. $\frac{20}{120} = r$

ACE Homework starts on page 87.

Applications

1. Find three examples of percents used in everyday life. Newspapers, magazines, radio, the Internet, and television are good places to look. Write down each example, or cut it out and tape it to your paper. For each example, describe how percents are used and what they mean.

2. Hot dogs at a carnival cost $2.99 each plus 7% tax. What is the total cost for one hot dog?

3. A class conducts a survey of 1,000 students.

   a. The survey reveals that 20% of the students speak Spanish. How many students speak Spanish?

   b. At one time or another, 6% of the students have forgotten their locker combinations. How many students have forgotten their locker combinations?

   c. Of the Grade 6 students surveyed, 12% bring their lunch to school. Suppose 24 sixth graders do this. How many Grade 6 students are at the school?

4. Arif and Keisha go to a restaurant for dinner. Their meals total $13.75. The tax is 5%.

   a. How much tax is added to the bill?

   b. Arif and Keisha want to leave a 15% tip based on the bill and the tax combined. How much should they leave? Explain.

   c. Arif ordered a more expensive meal than Keisha. After the tax and tip were figured, he decided he should pay $3.00 more than Keisha. How much should each pay?

5. Jen and Sarah go to lunch at the Green Grill. Their meals total \$28.00. The tax is 6%.

   a. What is the total cost including tax?

   b. Jen and Sarah want to leave a 20% tip based on the cost before tax. How much tip should they leave?

   c. Describe two strategies that Jen and Sarah can use to figure the amount of the tip.

6. Marilyn carries a tip-calculator card with her. It lists the amounts for 15% and 20% tips on whole-dollar values up to \$100.00. Her daughter notices a pattern. She says, "For each dollar the cost increases, the tips in the 15% column increase by \$.15."

   a. Explain why this pattern occurs for 15%-tip values.

   b. For each dollar increase, what is the amount of increase in the 20% column?

   c. The tip-calculator card only goes up to \$100.00. How can you use the card if your restaurant bill totals \$325.00?

7. Jason stops at a ball-toss game at the carnival. The sign reads, "Three balls for 40¢ or six balls for 60¢." What percent does he save by buying one set of six balls instead of two sets of three balls?

8. The Science Supply Store is having a sale. All graduated cylinders are 25% off. Mrs. Delmar buys four graduated cylinders that were originally \$8.00 each and six that were originally \$9.50 each.

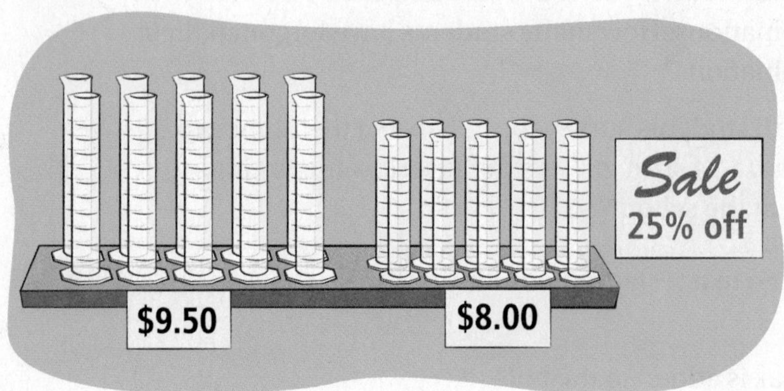

   a. How much money will Mrs. Delmar save?

   b. What percent of the original price will Mrs. Delmar pay?

   c. Suppose the sales tax is 4%. What is Mrs. Delmar's total cost?

The questions in Exercises 9–11 involve discounts at a store that is having a hat sale. All regular-priced hats are 20% off. Shirley, Lisa, and Sandy each find a hat to buy.

9. Shirley's beach hat was originally $24.95. What is the sale price?

10. Sandy finds a sun visor that was originally $12.50. What is the sale price?

11. Lisa finds a hat that is already marked down. The price tag shows that the original price was $36.00. The marked-down price is $27.00. What percent has the hat been marked down? Explain.

12. Inline skates are on sale for 35% off the regular price.

a. What fraction off is this discount?

b. The original price of one pair of inline skates is $124.99. What is the sale price?

c. A tax of 5% is computed on the sale price. What is the total cost of the inline skates?

13. The price per gallon of gasoline changes often. Most drivers pay close attention to those changes. Find the percent change in price for each of these cases.

a. increase from $4.00 per gallon to $4.20 per gallon

b. increase from $3.00 per gallon to $3.75 per gallon

c. decrease from $3.75 per gallon to $3.00 per gallon

Connections

14. Theo does $\frac{3}{10}$ of his homework. What percent is equal to $\frac{3}{10}$? What percent of his homework does Theo still have to do?

15. **Multiple Choice** In a survey, 75% of 400 parents said they give their children fruit as a snack. How many of the parents surveyed gave that response?

    A. 150 **B.** 200 **C.** 225 **D.** 300

16. If $2.4 \div 0.2 = 12$, is $2.4 \div 0.5$ greater than or less than 12? Explain.

17. If $0.25 \times 0.8 = 0.2$, is 0.25×0.7 greater than or less than 0.2? Explain.

18. A certain bean plant grows 15% of its height each day.

    a. Express this percent as a decimal.

    b. Today, after 10 days, the bean plant is 27 inches tall. How tall was it yesterday?

19. **Multiple Choice** Ike's Bikes requires 25% of the cost as a down payment for a new mountain bike. What fraction of the cost is this percent?

    F. $\frac{9}{35}$ **G.** $\frac{5}{21}$ **H.** $\frac{8}{32}$ **J.** $\frac{7}{24}$

20. Four friends order a square pizza. Marisa says she isn't very hungry and only wants 10% of the pizza. Tomarr is very hungry and says he will eat 50% of the pizza. Jon says he will eat 35%, and Kwan says she will eat 15%. Is this possible? Explain your reasoning.

21. The Running Shoe Company advertised that they would award a number of prizes equal to 1% of the total number of entries in a contest. They received 1,600 entries. How many prizes should they award?

In Exercises 22 and 23, a paint spill covers up part of the fraction strips. Use what is showing to reason about each set of strips. Find a fraction for each question mark.

22.

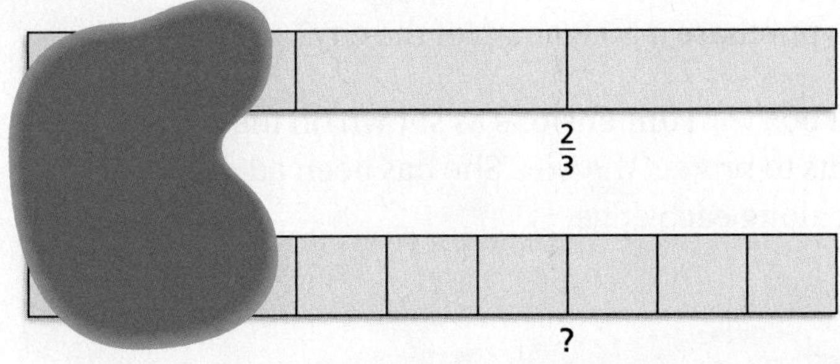

23.

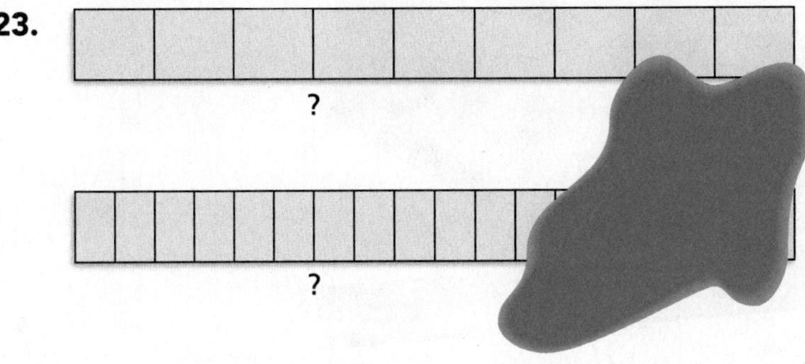

For Exercises 24–27, find numbers that will make each sentence true. If there is more than one solution, show at least two solutions.

24. $\frac{4}{9} = \frac{\blacksquare}{\blacksquare}$

25. $\frac{\blacksquare}{\blacksquare} = \frac{3}{5}$

26. $\frac{\blacksquare}{3} = \frac{8}{\blacksquare}$

27. $\frac{5}{\blacksquare} = \frac{\blacksquare}{18}$

Extensions

28. If you shop in Chicago, Illinois, the state sales tax is $9\frac{1}{4}\%$. What is your total cost when you purchase a $5.00 map of the city?

29. Lynette owns a beautiful box with dimensions as shown on the diagram below. She wants to protect the box. She has been advised to put a strip of molding along each edge.

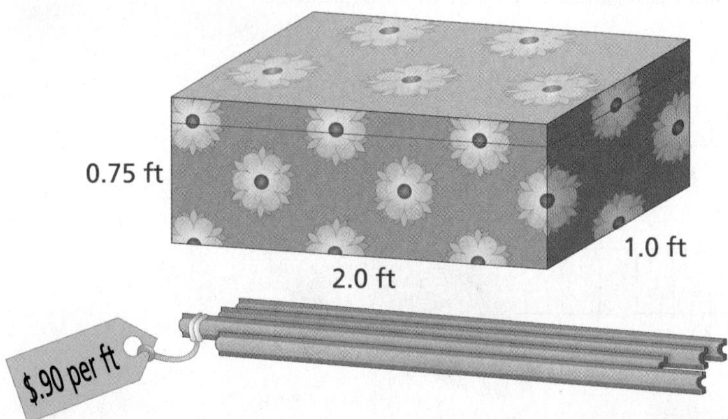

a. Lynette decides she needs four of each of the 0.75-foot lengths. Is she correct?

b. How much molding does Lynette need in all?

c. Molding costs $.90 a foot. How much is her bill without tax?

d. Suppose the sales tax is 4%. How much will her final bill be?

30. Carrie buys a pair of jeans from the stack below. The local sales tax is $2\frac{1}{2}\%$ and the state sales tax is 5%.

a. What is the amount of each tax?

b. What is the total cost of the jeans?

For Exercises 31 and 32, copy the given number line (including all the labeled marks). Mark each number line at 1. Write each fraction, including 1, as a decimal and as a percent.

31. 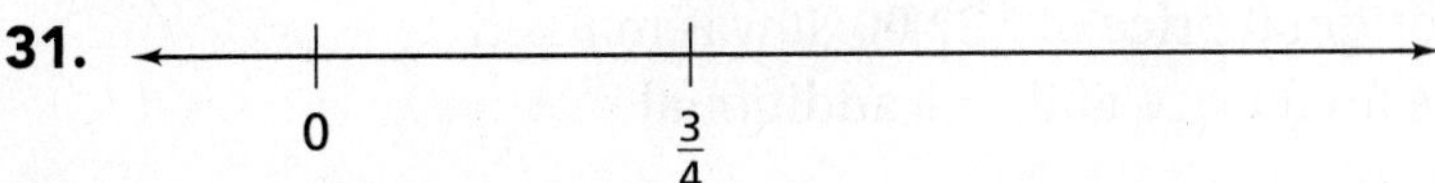

32. 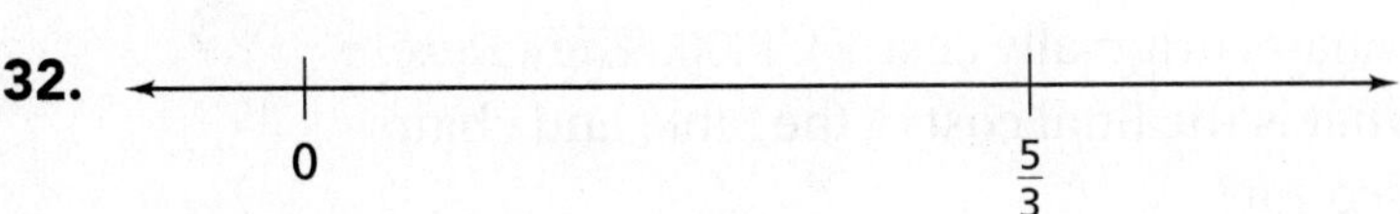

For Exercises 33–36, find numbers that will make each sentence true.

33. $\frac{1}{3} = \frac{\blacksquare}{9} = \frac{\blacksquare}{6}$

34. $\frac{\blacksquare}{18} = \frac{8}{12} = \frac{4}{\blacksquare}$

35. $\frac{3}{\blacksquare} = \frac{12}{\blacksquare} = \frac{9}{\blacksquare}$

36. $\frac{\blacksquare}{3} = \frac{\blacksquare}{21} = \frac{\blacksquare}{6}$

37. In Exercises 33–36 above, which sentences have more than one possible answer? Explain.

38. Copy the percent bar below. Mark it carefully to show the location of 100%.

0% 120%

39. Write a percent problem that involves discounts on food, cars, books, clothes, or other items. Then solve your problem.

40. Each year the Mannel Department Store has a big end-of-summer sale. At the sale, they give customers an additional 25% off on all marked-down merchandise.

a. A beach towel had an original price of $22.00. It was marked down 10%. What is the final price after the additional 25% discount?

b. A patio table and four chairs originally cost $350.00. They were marked down 50%. What is the final cost of the table and chairs with the additional discount?

41. A box of macaroni and cheese says that it makes 25% more than the regular box. If a regular box makes three cups of macaroni and cheese, how many cups will this box make?

42. The Consumer Price Index (CPI) gives a number that attempts to measure the average cost of certain basic items at a particular time. The percent that this index increases each year is known as the *rate of inflation*.

a. Suppose the CPI had a value of 225.3 exactly one year ago, and the current value of this index is 231.16, a rise of 5.86 points. What was the rate of inflation over the past year?

b. If the value of the index rises in the coming year by the same amount, 5.86 points up from 231.16 points, will the rate of inflation be the same for the coming year as for the past year? Explain.

Mathematical Reflections 4

In this Investigation, you solved problems that involved finding percents of numbers. You computed discounts, sale prices, tips, and sales tax. The following questions will help you summarize what you have learned.

Think about these questions. Discuss your ideas with other students and your teacher. Then write a summary of your findings in your notebook.

1. **a. How** do you find the tax on a purchase and calculate the final bill? Give an example, then write and solve a number sentence to illustrate your strategy.

   b. How do you find the price of a discounted item if you know the percent of the discount? Give an example, then write and solve a number sentence to illustrate your strategy.

   c. How do you find the cost of a purchase if you know the percent and the amount of the tax on the purchase? Give an example, then write and solve a number sentence to illustrate your answer.

   d. How can you find the percent one number is of another? For example, what percent of 35 is 7? Write and solve a number sentence to illustrate your answer.

   e. How are all the number sentences in parts (a)–(d) the same?

2. **How** do you recognize when addition, subtraction, multiplication, and/or division of decimals is required to solve a problem?

Common Core Mathematical Practices

As you worked on the Problems in this Investigation, you used prior knowledge to make sense of them. You also applied Mathematical Practices to solve the Problems. Think back over your work, the ways you thought about the Problems, and how you used Mathematical Practices.

Hector described his thoughts in the following way:

In Problem 4.4, we had to think of questions that would go with either percent bars or mathematical sentences.

I liked how a percent bar could model many different problems. For example, the bar below could model a question about a \$24 increase being the same as a 15% increase. You can work out the original price and the increased price from this.

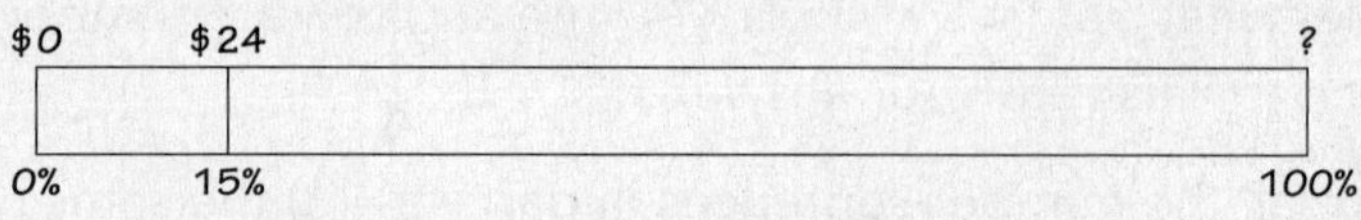

Or it could be about a tip. But who would ever leave a \$24 tip?!

Common Core Standards for Mathematical Practice

MP4 Model with mathematics

- What other Mathematical Practices can you identify in Hector's reasoning?
- Describe a Mathematical Practice that you and your classmates used to solve a different Problem in this Investigation.

Unit Project

Ordering From a Catalog

Families frequently buy things from catalogs. Have you ever been the family member to fill out the form? This project gives you a chance to show what you have learned about decimals and percents as you dream about things that you would love to order from a catalog.

Part 1: Placing an Order

Choose a catalog and fill out the order form your teacher gives you. Be sure that you correctly compute the taxes and shipping costs for your items. You need to find the shipping costs in the catalog you choose. You also need to find the tax on merchandise in your state.

Complete the Order

- Find three different items you would like to order from a catalog. Each item must cost at least \$10. Tape or glue a picture and description of each item to the order form, or draw a picture of the item and write out its description. Include the price with the picture.
- Fill out the rest of the order form as if you were ordering your three items from the C. M. Project catalog. Record all the work you do to calculate the amounts for shipping and tax.

1. **a.** Choose one of the items you ordered. List the item with a brief description and give its price.

b. What would this item cost if it were on sale for 25% off? Explain your reasoning.

c. What would the item cost if it were on sale for $\frac{1}{3}$ off? Explain.

2. Suppose another catalog has the first item on your order form listed for \$5 less than the price you have listed. A third catalog has your item marked down 20%. If shipping charges and tax are the same, which is the better deal? Explain.

Part 2: Spending Birthday Money

3. Wayan got $125 for his twelfth birthday. He is going to order three items. Wayan's state has a tax rate of 6%. The shipping costs are 9% of the cost before tax.

   a. Find the most the three items can cost, before tax and shipping, so that Wayan has enough money to order the items. Show your work and explain your reasoning.

   b. Find three items in your catalog that use as much of Wayan's birthday money as possible. Remember to calculate the sales tax and shipping charges.

Looking Back

The Problems in this Unit helped you to develop strategies for operating with decimals and percents. You then used those operations to solve problems. You learned how to:

- use algorithms to add, subtract, multiply, and divide with decimals,
- decide when using each operation on decimals is appropriate,
- estimate solutions for problems involving decimal operations,
- compute with percents to calculate taxes, tips, and discounts when shopping.

Use Your Understanding: Decimals and Percents

Use your knowledge of decimals and percents to solve the following problems.

For Exercises 1–4:

- **Write a number sentence to represent the problem.**
- **Estimate the answer and explain how you estimated.**
- **Use an algorithm to calculate an exact answer.**

1. Watermelon sells for \$.25 per pound at a local store. Rodrigo buys a piece that weighs 7.8 pounds. What is the price of the piece of watermelon?

2. a. Fairview Middle School wants to buy flooring for their cafeteria. A vendor offers to sell the flooring for \$9,538. The cafeteria has an area of 313.75 m^2. What is the cost per square meter of the flooring?

b. The vendor decides to give the school a 15% discount on the flooring. How much does the school pay for the flooring? How much of a discount does the school receive?

3. On a trip, the Brackman family stops three times to buy gas. The diagram shows how much gas the Brackmans buy at each stop.

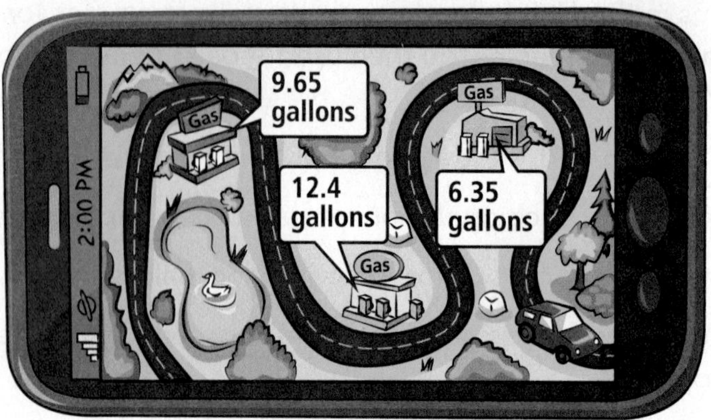

a. How much gasoline did the Brackmans buy on the trip?

b. The car's gas tank holds 16 gallons. After the Brackmans bought 9.65 gallons of gas, the gas tank was full. How much gas was in the tank before they bought 9.65 gallons of gas?

c. At the end of the trip, the Brackman family had driven 902 miles and used 32.8 gallons of gas. On average, how many miles did the Brackmans drive per gallon of gas? How many gallons of gas did they use for each mile they drove?

4. A local landscaper charges a flat fee of $30 for any delivery. Mr. Ortiz orders mulch for his yard. The mulch costs $150.

a. What percent of the cost of the mulch is the delivery charge?

b. What percent of the total cost of the order (mulch plus delivery) is the delivery charge?

Explain Your Reasoning

When you use mathematical calculations to solve a problem or make a decision, it is important to be able to justify each step in your reasoning.

5. Describe an algorithm for each operation on decimals: addition, subtraction, multiplication, and division.

6. For each of the following calculations, estimate the result. Then, use a standard algorithm to find the exact result. Be sure to explain how you estimated. Show your work for your calculations.

a. $23.405 + 17.23$

b. $23.405 - 17.23$

c. 3.51×1.2

d. $38.76 \div 8.5$

English / Spanish Glossary

D

describe Academic Vocabulary To explain or tell in detail. A written description can contain facts and other information needed to communicate your answer. A diagram or a graph may also be included.

related terms *explain, tell, present*

sample Describe the difference between a terminating decimal and a repeating decimal.

A repeating decimal repeats a number or a set of numbers over and over again; for example, $\frac{1}{3}$ is $0.\overline{3}$. (The 3 repeats.) A terminating decimal is a decimal that does not repeat a number or set of numbers; for example, $\frac{2}{5}$ is 0.4.

describir Vocabulario académico Explicar o decir con detalle. Una descripción escrita puede contener datos y otra información necesaria para comunicar tu respuesta. También se puede incluir un diagrama o una gráfica.

términos relacionados *explicar, decir, presentar*

ejemplo Describe la diferencia entre un decimal finito y un decimal periódico.

Un decimal periódico repite un número o un conjunto de números una y otra vez; por ejemplo, $\frac{1}{3}$ es $0.\overline{3}$. (El 3 repite.) Un decimal finito es un número decimal que no repite un número o conjunto de números; por ejemplo, $\frac{2}{5}$ es 0.4.

dividend The name for the number into which you are dividing in a division problem. For example, 26.5 is the dividend in the problem $26.5 \div 4$.

dividendo El nombre del número que divides en un problema de división. Por ejemplo, 26.5 es el dividendo en el problema $26.5 \div 4$.

divisor The name for the number by which you are dividing in a division problem. For example, 4 is the divisor in the problem $26.5 \div 4$.

divisor El nombre del número por el que divides en un problema de división. Por ejemplo, 4 es el divisor en el problema $26.5 \div 4$.

E

estimate Academic Vocabulary
To find an approximate answer that is relatively close to an exact amount.

related terms *approximate, guess*

sample Jonathan takes \$10 with him to lunch. He orders a chicken sandwich for \$1.99, a side salad for \$1.79, a yogurt for \$1.29, and a soda for \$.99. Estimate the total cost for Jonathan's lunch and the amount of change he should receive from \$10.

I used benchmarks to make my estimate. The sandwich is close to \$2, the salad is close to \$1.75, the yogurt is close to \$1.25, and the soda is close to \$1.

\$2 \$1.75 \$1.25 \$1

0 1 2 3 4 5 6 7 8

The total cost of the lunch is about \$6. Since 10 – 6 = 4, he should receive about \$4 in change.

hacer una estimación Vocabulario académico Hallar una respuesta aproximada que esté relativamente cerca de una cantidad exacta.

términos relacionados *aproximar, suponer*

ejemplo Jonathan tiene \$10 dólares para su almuerzo. Pide un sándwich de pollo que cuesta \$1.99, una ensalada, \$1.79, un yogur, \$1.29 y una gaseosa, \$.99. Estima el costo total del almuerzo de Jonathan y la cantidad de cambio que debe recibir de \$10.

Usé puntos de referencia para hacer mi estimación. El costo del sándwich está cerca de \$2, el de la ensalada de \$1.75, el del yogur de \$1.25 y el de la gaseosa de \$1.

\$2 \$1.75 \$1.25 \$1

0 1 2 3 4 5 6 7 8

El costo total del almuerzo es de aproximadamente \$6.00. Puesto que 10 – 6 = 4, él debe recibir aproximadamente \$4 de cambio.

expanded form The form of an expression made up of sums or differences of terms rather than products of factors. Expanded form of a decimal number shows the place value of each digit. For example, the expanded form of 324.05 is $3(100) + 2(10) + 4(1) + 5\left(\frac{1}{100}\right)$.

forma desarrollada La forma de una expresión compuesta de sumas o diferencias de términos, en vez de productos de factores. La forma desarrollada de un número decimal muestra el valor de posición de cada dígito. Por ejemplo, la forma desarrollada de 324.05 es $3(100) + 2(10) + 4(1) + 5\left(\frac{1}{100}\right)$.

explain Academic Vocabulary
To give facts and details that make an idea easier to understand. Explaining can involve a written summary supported by a diagram, chart, table, or a combination of these.

Related terms *describe, show, justify, tell, present*

sample Using a 6% sales tax, explain how to find the total cost of a pack of tennis balls priced at $10.

> To find the sales tax, change 6% to 0.06. Then multiply the price of the tennis balls by 0.06. 10 × 0.06 = 0.60. Add this to the cost of the tennis balls.
> 10 + 0.60 = 10.60. The total cost is $10.60.

explicar Vocabulario académico
Proporcionar datos y detalles que hagan que una idea sea más fácil de comprender. Explicar puede incluir un resumen escrito apoyado por un diagrama, una gráfica, una tabla o una combinación de estos.

términos relacionados *describir, mostrar, justificar, decir, presentar*

ejemplo Usando un impuesto sobre la venta del 6%, explica cómo hallar el costo total de un paquete de pelotas de tenis que vale $10.

> Para hallar el impuesto sobre ventas, cambio 6% a 0.06. Luego, multiplico el precio de las pelotas de tenis por 0.06. 10 × 0.06 = 0.60. Sumo esto al costo de las pelotas de tenis.
> 10 + 0.60 = 10.60. El costo total es de $10.60.

P

percent "Out of 100." A percent is a fraction in which the denominator is 100. When we write 68%, we mean 68 out of 100, $\frac{68}{100}$, or 0.68. We write the percent sign (%) after a number to indicate percent. The shaded part of this square is 68%.

porcentaje "De 100". Un porcentaje es una fracción en la que el denominador es 100. Cuando escribimos 68%, queremos decir 68 de 100, $\frac{68}{100}$, ó 0.68. Para indicar un porcentaje, escribimos el signo correspondiente (%) después del número. La parte coloreada de este cuadrado es el 68%.

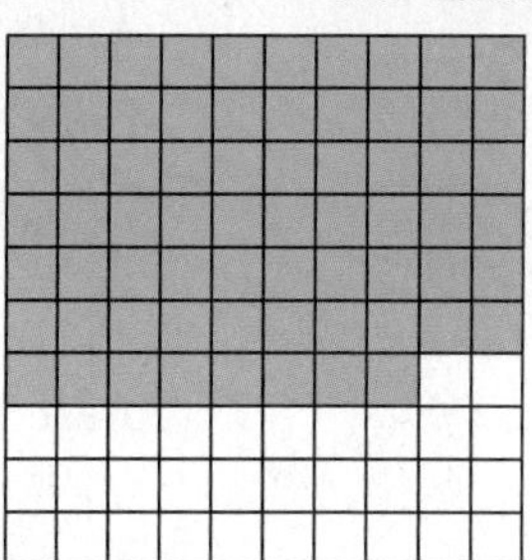

Q

quotient The name for the answer to a division problem. For example, 6.625 is the quotient in the number sentence $26.5 \div 4 = 6.625$.

cociente El nombre de la respuesta a un problema de división. Por ejemplo, 6.625 es el cociente en la oración numérica $26.5 \div 4 = 6.625$.

R

ratio A comparison of two quantities expressed with a phrase such as "the ratio of 3 to 5" which means "3 for every 5." Such ratio comparisons are often written as common fractions and in the special notation 3 : 5.

$\frac{3}{5}$ 3 to 5 3 : 5

razón Una comparación de dos cantidades que se expresa con frases como "la razón de 3 a 5", que significa "3 de cada 5". Con frecuencia, estas comparaciones se escriben como fracciones comunes y con la notación especial 3 : 5.

$\frac{3}{5}$ 3 a 5 3 : 5

repeating decimal A decimal with a pattern of a fixed number of digits that repeats forever, such as 0.3333333. . . and 0.73737373. . . . Repeating decimals are rational numbers.

decimal periódico Un número decimal con un patrón de un número fijo de dígitos que se repite infinitamente, como 0.3333333. . . y 0.73737373. . . . Los decimales periódicos son números racionales.

T

terminating decimal A decimal that ends, or terminates, such as 0.5 or 0.125. Terminating decimals are rational numbers.

decimal finito Un número decimal que se acaba o termina, como 0.5 ó 0.125. Los decimales finitos son números racionales.

U

unit rate A unit rate is a rate in which one of the numbers (usually written as the denominator) is 1, or 1 of a quantity. For example, 3.1 miles per hour $\left(\frac{3.1 \text{ miles}}{1 \text{ hour}}\right)$ is a unit rate that compares the number of miles walked to the number of hours walked. This can also be expressed as 1 mile per 0.32 hours or 0.32 hours per mile.

tasa por unidad Una tasa por unidad es una tasa en la que un de números (normalmente escrito como el denominador) es 1, ó 1 de una cantidad. Por ejemplo, 3.1 millas por hora $\left(\frac{3.1 \text{ millas}}{1 \text{ hora}}\right)$ es una tasa por unidad que compara el número de millas caminadas con el número de horas caminadas. Esto también se puede expresar como 1 milla por 0.32 horas o como 0.32 horas por milla.

use Academic Vocabulary
To draw upon given information to help you determine something else.

related terms *utilize, employ*

sample Consider the following fractions and their decimal representations.

$\frac{1}{9} = 0.1111111\ldots$

$\frac{2}{9} = 0.2222222\ldots$

$\frac{3}{9} = 0.3333333\ldots$

Use the pattern you see to write decimal representations of $\frac{7}{9}$ and $\frac{8}{9}$.

> When the denominator is 9, the digit in the numerator repeats in the decimal representation. Therefore,
>
> $\frac{7}{9} = 0.7777777777\ldots$ and
>
> $\frac{8}{9} = 0.8888888888\ldots.$

usar Vocabulario académico Recurrir a una información dada como ayuda para determinar algo más.

términos relacionados *utilizar, emplear*

ejemplo Considera las siguientes fracciones y sus representaciones decimales.

$\frac{1}{9} = 0.1111111\ldots$

$\frac{2}{9} = 0.2222222\ldots$

$\frac{3}{9} = 0.3333333\ldots$

Usa el patrón que ves para escribir representaciones decimales de $\frac{7}{9}$ y $\frac{8}{9}$.

> Cuando el denomindador es 9, el dígito en el numerador se repite en la representación decimal. Por lo tanto,
>
> $\frac{7}{9} = 0.7777777777\ldots$ y
>
> $\frac{8}{9} = 0.8888888888\ldots.$

Index

Acknowledgments

Cover Design
Three Communication Design, Chicago

Photographs
Photo locators denoted as follows: Top (T), Center (C), Bottom (B), Left (L), Right (R), Background (Bkgd)

002 (TR) Matthew Mawson/Alamy, (BR) Humannet/Shutterstock;
003 Mark J. Terrill/AP Images; **015** Matthew Mawson/Alamy
033 Ocean/Corbis; **035** only4denn/Fotolia; **088** Humannet/Shutterstock.

CONNECTED MATHEMATICS® 3

Focus on Algebra

Lappan, Phillips, Fey, Friel

Variables and Patterns

Focus on Algebra

3 Relating Variables With Equations 65

4 Expressions, Equations, and Inequalities 89

Looking Ahead

At different times of the year, the number of hours of daylight changes each day. **How** does the number of daylight hours change with the passage of time in a year? **Why** does this happen?

How much should a bike tour company charge each customer in order to make a profit?

The group admission price for Wild World Amusement park is \$50, plus \$10 per person. **What** equation relates the price to the number of people in the group?

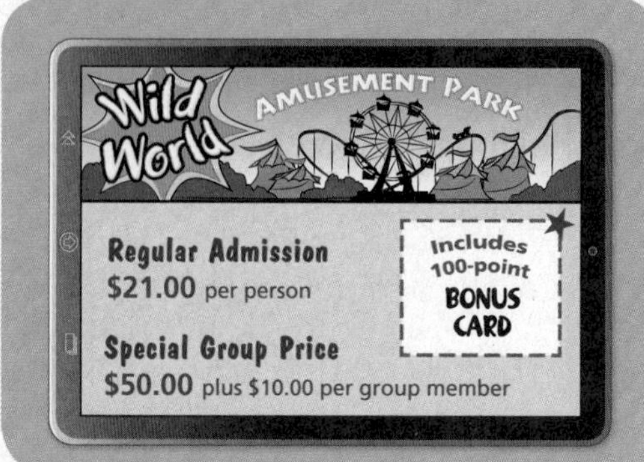

Some things never seem to change. The sun always rises in the east and sets in the west. The United States holds a presidential election every four years. Labor Day always falls on the first Monday of September.

Many other things are always changing. Temperatures rise and fall within a day and from season to season. Store sales change in response to rising and falling prices and shopper demand. Audiences for television shows and movies change as viewers' interests change. The speeds of bikes on streets and roads change in response to variations in traffic, terrain, and weather.

In mathematics, science, and business, quantities that change are called *variables*. Many problems require predicting how changes in the values of one variable are related to changes in the values of another. To help you solve such problems, you can represent the relationships between variables using word descriptions, tables, graphs, and equations. The mathematical ideas and skills used to solve such problems come from the branch of mathematics called *algebra*. This Unit introduces some of the basic tools of algebra.

Mathematical Highlights

Variables and Patterns

In *Variables and Patterns,* you will study some basic ideas of algebra and learn some ways to use those ideas to solve problems and make decisions.

The Investigations in this Unit will help you learn how to

- Recognize situations in which variables are related in predictable ways
- Describe patterns of change in words, data tables, graphs, and equations
- Use data tables, graphs, equations, and inequalities to solve problems

As you work on the problems in this Unit, ask yourself questions about problem situations that involve related quantitative variables:

What are the variables in the problem?

Which variables depend on or change in relation to others?

How can I use a table, graph, equation, or inequality to represent and analyze a relationship between variables?

Common Core State Standards

Mathematical Practices and Habits of Mind

In the *Connected Mathematics* curriculum you will develop an understanding of important mathematical ideas by solving problems and reflecting on the mathematics involved. Every day, you will use "habits of mind" to make sense of problems and apply what you learn to new situations. Some of these habits are described by the *Common Core State Standards for Mathematical Practices* (MP).

MP1 Make sense of problems and persevere in solving them.

When using mathematics to solve a problem, it helps to think carefully about

- data and other facts you are given and what additional information you need to solve the problem;
- strategies you have used to solve similar problems and whether you could solve a related simpler problem first;
- how you could express the problem with equations, diagrams, or graphs;
- whether your answer makes sense.

MP2 Reason abstractly and quantitatively.

When you are asked to solve a problem, it often helps to

- focus first on the key mathematical ideas;
- check that your answer makes sense in the problem setting;
- use what you know about the problem setting to guide your mathematical reasoning.

MP3 Construct viable arguments and critique the reasoning of others.

When you are asked to explain why a conjecture is correct, you can

- show some examples that fit the claim and explain why they fit;
- show how a new result follows logically from known facts and principles.

When you believe a mathematical claim is incorrect, you can

- show one or more counterexamples—cases that don't fit the claim;
- find steps in the argument that do not follow logically from prior claims.

MP4 Model with mathematics.

When you are asked to solve problems, it often helps to

- think carefully about the numbers or geometric shapes that are the most important factors in the problem, then ask yourself how those factors are related to each other;
- express data and relationships in the problem with tables, graphs, diagrams, or equations, and check your result to see if it makes sense.

MP5 Use appropriate tools strategically.

When working on mathematical questions, you should always

- decide which tools are most helpful for solving the problem and why;
- try a different tool when you get stuck.

MP6 Attend to precision.

In every mathematical exploration or problem-solving task, it is important to

- think carefully about the required accuracy of results; is a number estimate or geometric sketch good enough, or is a precise value or drawing needed?
- report your discoveries with clear and correct mathematical language that can be understood by those to whom you are speaking or writing.

MP7 Look for and make use of structure.

In mathematical explorations and problem solving, it is often helpful to

- look for patterns that show how data points, numbers, or geometric shapes are related to each other;
- use patterns to make predictions.

MP8 Look for and express regularity in repeated reasoning.

When results of a repeated calculation show a pattern, it helps to

- express that pattern as a general rule that can be used in similar cases;
- look for shortcuts that will make the calculation simpler in other cases.

You will use all of the Mathematical Practices in this Unit. Sometimes, when you look at a Problem, it is obvious which practice is most helpful. At other times, you will decide on a practice to use during class explorations and discussions. After completing each Problem, ask yourself:

- What mathematics have I learned by solving this Problem?
- What Mathematical Practices were helpful in learning this mathematics?

Variables, Tables, and Graphs

The bicycle was invented in 1791. Today, people around the world use bicycles for daily transportation and recreation. Many spend their vacations taking organized bicycle tours.

For example, the RAGBRAI, which stands for Register's Annual Great Bicycle Ride Across Iowa, is a weeklong cycling tour across the state of Iowa. Cyclists start by dipping their back bicycle wheels into the Missouri River along Iowa's western border. They end by dipping their front wheels into the Mississippi River on Iowa's eastern border.

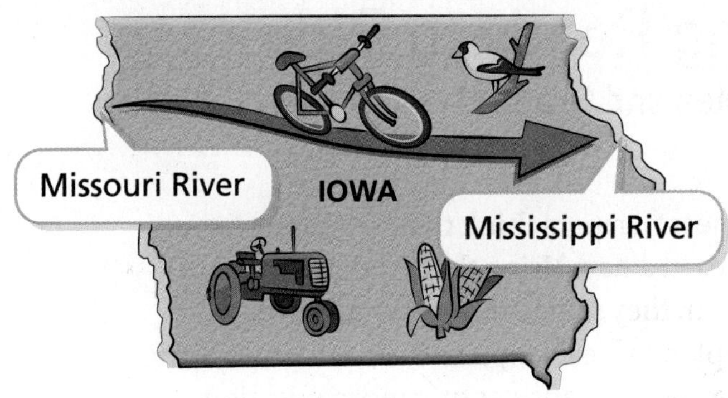

Common Core State Standards

6.RP.A.3a Make tables of equivalent ratios relating quantities with whole-number measurements, find missing values in the tables, and plot the pairs of values on the coordinate plane. Use tables to compare ratios.

6.RP.A.3b Solve unit rate problems including those involving unit pricing and constant speed.

6.EE.C.9 Use variables to represent two quantities in a real-world problem that change in relationship to one another; write an equation to express one quantity, thought of as the dependent variable, in terms of the other quantity, thought of as the independent variable. Analyze the relationship between the dependent and independent variables using graphs and tables, and relate these to the equation.

Also 6.NS.C.6c, 6.NS.C.8

Sidney, Celia, Liz, Malcolm, and Theo heard about the RAGBRAI. The five college students decide to operate bicycle tours as a summer business. They choose a route along the ocean from Atlantic City, New Jersey, to Colonial Williamsburg, Virginia. The students name their new business Ocean Bike Tours.

1.1 Getting Ready to Ride

Data Tables and Graphs

The Ocean Bike Tours business partners think their customers could ride between 60 and 90 miles in a day. Using that guideline, a map, and campground information, they plan a three-day tour route. The business partners also plan for rest stops and visits to interesting places. To finalize plans, they need to answer one more question:

- How are the cyclists' speed and distance likely to change throughout a day?

An answer to that question could only come from a test ride. Because this is difficult to do in school, you can get some ideas by doing a jumping jack experiment. This experiment will test your own physical fitness.

In this experiment, there are two quantities involved, the number of jumping jacks and time. The number of jumping jacks changes over time.

Suppose you did jumping jacks as fast as possible for a 2-minute test period.

- How many jumping jacks do you think you could complete in 2 minutes?
- How do you think your jumping jack rate would change over the 2-minute test?

Problem 1.1

A Do the jumping jack fitness test with help from a timer, a counter, and a recorder. Enter the total number of jumping jacks after every 10 seconds in a data table:

Jumping Jack Experiment

Time (seconds)	0	10	20	30	40	50	60	70	...
Total Number of Jumping Jacks									

B Record your data on a copy of the coordinate grid shown below.

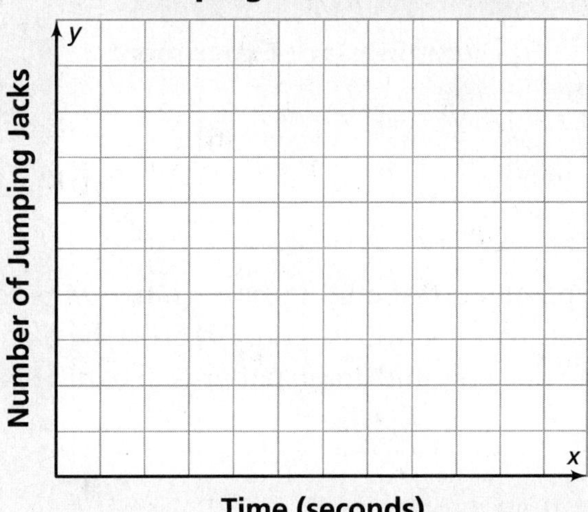

continued on the next page >

Problem 1.1 continued

C How did the jumping jack rate (number per second) change over time?

1. How is the change over time shown in the data table?
2. How is the change over time shown in the graph?

D Use your jumping jack data. What can you say about the cyclists' speed during the Ocean Bike Tours ride?

E One group said, "Our jumper did 8 jumping jacks for every 10 seconds."

1. **a.** Copy and complete the table to show results if a student jumped at a steady pace matching that ratio over 60 seconds.

Jumping Jack Experiment

Time (seconds)	0	10	15	20	■	30	■	40	■	50	■	60
Total Number of Jumping Jacks	■	8	12	■	20	■	28	■	36	■	44	■

b. Plot the points corresponding to the (*time, jumping jack total*) pairs in the table on a coordinate grid. Describe the pattern you see.

2. **a.** Another group's jumper did 4 jumping jacks for every 6 seconds. Copy and complete the table to show results if a student jumped at a steady pace matching that ratio over 30 seconds.

Jumping Jack Experiment

Time (seconds)	0	6	9	12	■	■	30
Total Number of Jumping Jacks	■	4	■	■	10	12	■

b. Plot the points corresponding to the (*time, jumping jack total*) pairs in the table on a coordinate grid. Describe the pattern you see. Compare the table and graph patterns in parts (1) and (2).

ACE Homework starts on page 20.

1.2 From Atlantic City to Lewes

Time, Rate, and Distance

In the jumping jack experiment, the number of jumping jacks and time are variables. A **variable** is a quantity that may take on different values. One way in which values of real-life variables may change is with the passage of time. You saw this in the jumping jack experiment. The number of jumping jacks changes based on the elapsed time.

The jumping jack experiment gives some ideas about what cyclists might expect on a daylong trip. To be more confident, the Ocean Bike Tours business partners decide to test their bike tour route.

The cyclists begin their bike tour in Atlantic City, New Jersey, and ride south to Cape May.

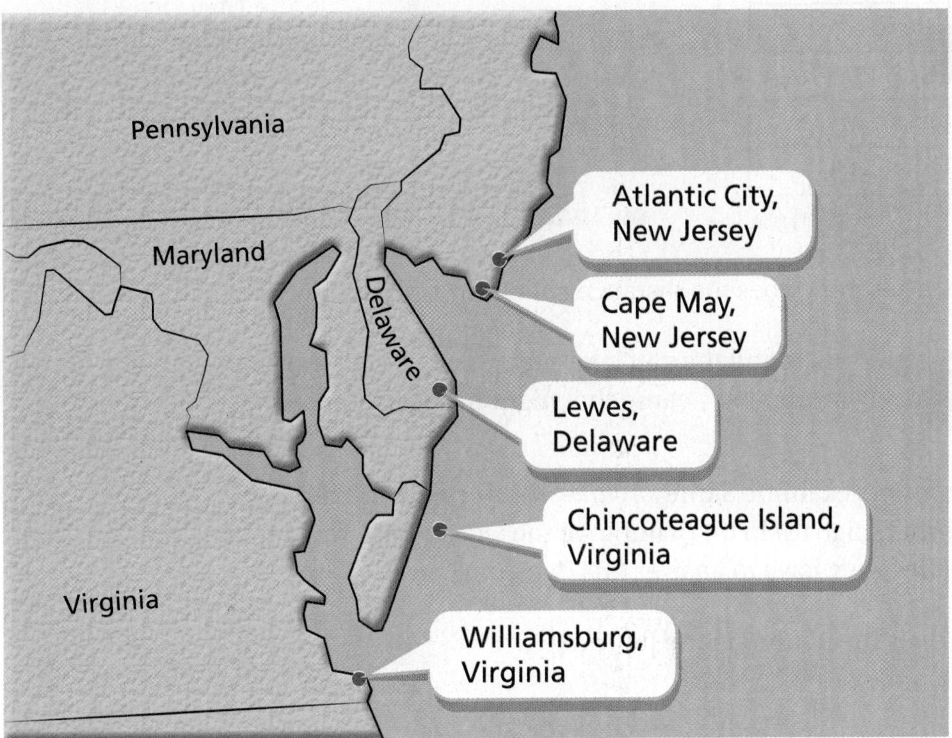

Sidney follows the cyclists in a van with a trailer for camping gear and bicycles. Every half-hour, he records in a table the distances the cyclists have traveled from Atlantic City.

Atlantic City to Cape May

Time (h)	Distance (mi)
0	0
0.5	8
1.0	15
1.5	19
2.0	25
2.5	27
3.0	34
3.5	31
4.0	38
4.5	40
5.0	45

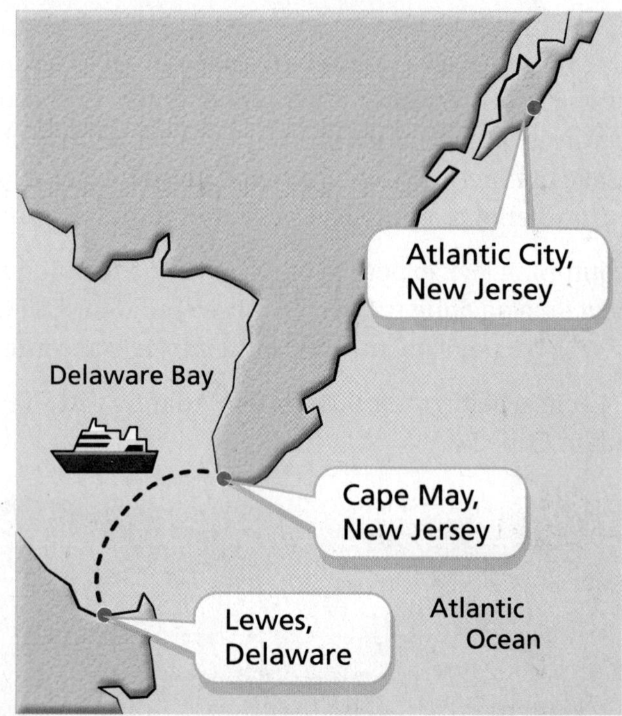

- As time increases, how does the distance change?

From Cape May, the cyclists and the van take a ferry across Delaware Bay to Lewes (LOO-is), Delaware. They camp that night in a state park along the ocean.

The business partners examine Sidney's (*time, distance*) data. They hope to find patterns that might help them improve the Ocean Bike Tours route and schedule. First, they have to answer this question:

- What story does the pattern in the table tell?

Problem 1.2

A **1.** Plot the (*time, distance*) data pairs on a coordinate grid.

2. What interesting patterns do you see in the (*time, distance*) data?

3. Explain how the patterns are shown in the table.

4. Explain how the patterns are shown on the graph.

B **1.** At what times in the trip were the cyclists traveling fastest? At what times were they traveling slowest?

2. Explain how your answer is shown in the table.

3. Explain how your answer is shown by the pattern of points on the graph.

C Connecting the points on a graph can help you see patterns more clearly. It also helps you consider what is happening in the intervals between the points. Different ways of connecting the given data points tell different stories about what happens between the points.

Consider the data (4.5, 40) and (5.0, 45) from the first day of the Ocean Bike Tours trip. Here are five different ways to connect the graph points on the plot of (*time, distance*).

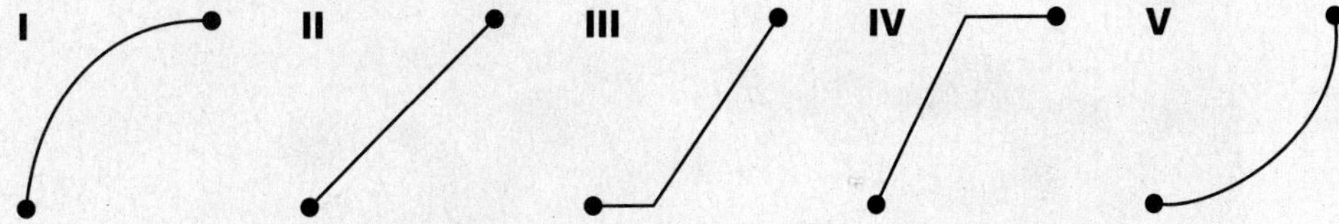

Match the given connecting paths to these travel stories.

1. Celia rode slowly at first and gradually increased her speed.

2. Theo rode quickly and reached the Cape May ferry dock early.

3. Malcolm had to fix a flat tire, so he started after the others.

4. Tony and Sarah started off fast. They soon felt tired and slowed down.

5. Liz pedaled at a steady pace throughout this part of the trip.

D What are the advantages and disadvantages of tables or graphs to represent a pattern of change?

ACE Homework starts on page 20.

1.3 From Lewes to Chincoteague Island

Stories, Tables, and Graphs

On the second day of the bike tour test run, the team leaves Lewes, Delaware, and rides through Ocean City, Maryland. The team stops on Chincoteague (SHING kuh teeg) Island, Virginia. Chincoteague Island is famous for its annual pony auction. Here, the team camps for the night.

Did You Know?

Assateague (A suh teeg) Island is home to herds of wild ponies. The island has a harsh environment of ocean beaches, sand dunes, and marshes. To survive, these sturdy ponies eat salt marsh grasses, seaweed, and even poison ivy.

To keep the population of ponies under control, an auction is held every summer. During the famous "Pony Swim," the ponies for sale swim across a quarter mile of water to Chincoteague Island.

Problem 1.3

Malcolm and Liz drove the tour van on the way from Lewes to Chincoteague. They forgot to record time and distance data. Fortunately, they wrote some notes about the trip.

TripJournal **All Entries** June 7

Entry 1: We started at 8:00 A.M. and rode against a strong wind until our midmorning break.

Entry 2: About midmorning, the wind shifted to our backs.

Entry 3: Around noon, we stopped for BBQ lunch and rested for about an hour. By this time we had traveled about halfway to Chinoteague.

Entry 4: Around 2:00 P.M., we stopped for a brief swim in the ocean.

Entry 5: At about 4:00 P.M., all of the riders were tired. There were no bike lanes. So we packed the bikes in the trailer and rode in the van to our campsite in Chincoteague. We took 9 hours to complete today's 80-mile trip.

Edit

A Make a table of (*time, distance*) values to match the story told in Malcolm and Liz's notes.

B Sketch a coordinate graph that shows the information in the table. Does it make sense to connect the points on the graph? Explain your reasoning.

C Explain how the entries in your table and graph illustrate the trip notes.

D Which representation of the data (*table, graph,* or *written notes*) best shows the pattern of change in distance over time? Explain.

ACE Homework starts on page 20.

1.4 From Chincoteague to Colonial Williamsburg

Average Speed

Malcolm noticed that, on Day 1, the cyclists sometimes went very fast or very slow in any given hour. He also noticed that the cyclists covered 45 miles in 5 hours.

Atlantic City to Cape May

Time (h)	0	0.5	1.0	1.5	2.0	2.5	3.0	3.5	4.0	4.5	5.0
Distance (mi)	0	8	15	19	25	27	34	31	38	40	45

- Malcolm claims that, on average, the cyclists covered 9 miles per hour. Is he correct?
- Did the cyclists actually cover 9 miles per hour in any one hour on Day 1? Explain.

The **average speed** per day is the rate in miles per hour for that day. Malcolm was curious to know what the average speed for Day 3 would be.

On the third day of the bike tour test run, the team travels from its campsite on Chincoteague Island to Williamsburg, Virginia. Here, they visit the restored colonial capital city.

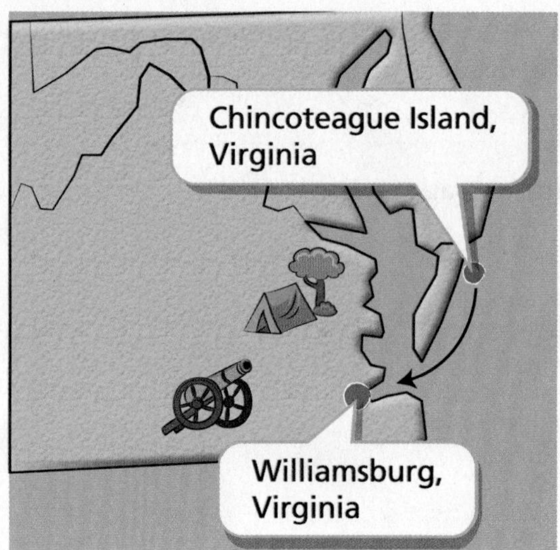

Did You Know?

Williamsburg was the political, cultural, and educational center of Virginia from 1699 to 1780. Williamsburg was the largest, most populous, and most influential of the American colonies.

Near the end of the Revolutionary War, the capital of Virginia was moved to Richmond. For nearly 150 years afterward, Williamsburg was a quiet town.

Then, in 1926, a movement began to restore and preserve the city's historic buildings. Today, Williamsburg is a very popular tourist destination.

Malcolm drove and Sarah rode in the tour van on the way from Chincoteague to Williamsburg. They made a graph showing the cyclists' progress each hour.

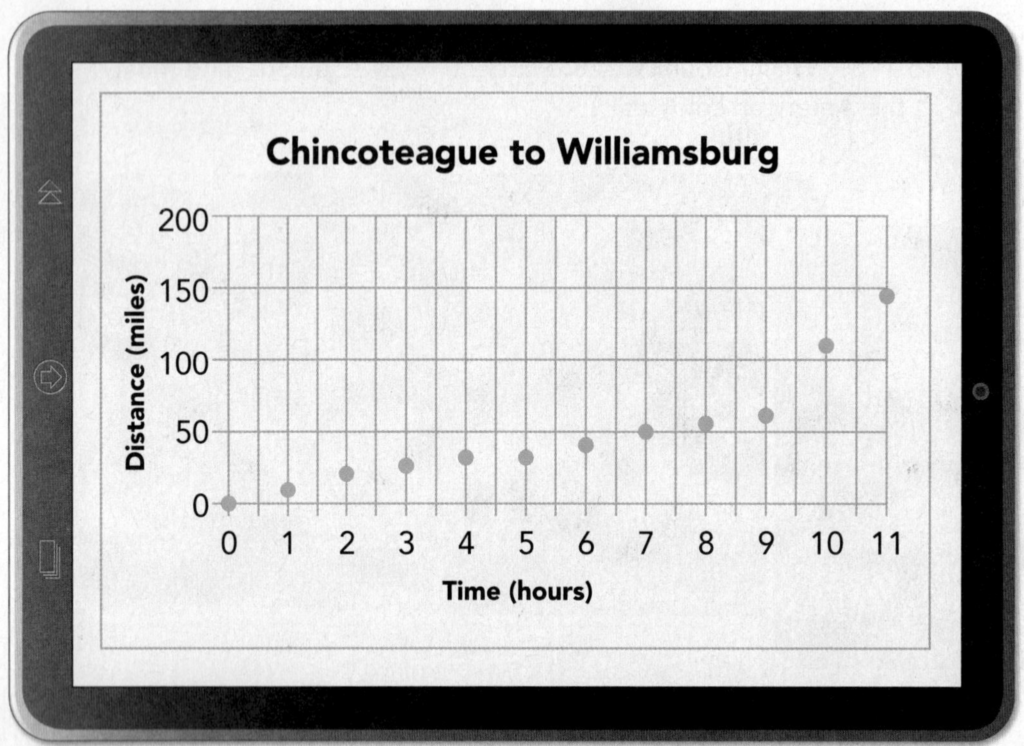

- Describe some interesting patterns that you see in the graph.

Problem 1.4

A Make a table of the (*time, distance*) value pairs shown in the graph.

1. What does the point with coordinates (3, 25) tell about the cyclists' progress?
2. Which points on the graph have coordinates (9, 60) and (10, 110)? What do those coordinates tell about the cyclists' time, distance, and speed on Day 3?
3. What was the cyclists' average speed in miles per hour for the trip? How can you find this from the graph? From the table?

B The team has to cross the Chesapeake Bay Bridge and Tunnel. Then, they travel on an interstate highway from Norfolk to Williamsburg. So, the team bikes for only the first part of the trip.

1. Based on the graph and your table, when did the team put its bikes on the trailer and begin riding in the van?
2. What was the team's average speed for trip time completed on bikes?
3. What was the team's average speed for trip time completed in the van?
4. How are differences in travel speed shown in the graph?

C A very strong cyclist makes the trip from Chincoteague to Williamsburg in 8 hours pedaling at a constant speed.

1. At what speed did the cyclist travel?
2. Describe the graph of (*time, distance*) data for the trip.

ACE Homework starts on page 20.

Applications | Connections | Extensions

Applications

1. A convenience store has been keeping track of its popcorn sales. The table below shows the total number of bags sold beginning at 6:00 A.M. on a particular day.

Popcorn Sales

Time	Total Bags Sold
6:00 A.M.	0
7:00 A.M.	3
8:00 A.M.	15
9:00 A.M.	20
10:00 A.M.	26
11:00 A.M.	30
noon	45
1:00 P.M.	58
2:00 P.M.	58
3:00 P.M.	62
4:00 P.M.	74
5:00 P.M.	83
6:00 P.M.	88
7:00 P.M.	92

a. Make a coordinate graph of these data. Explain your choice of labels and scales on each axis.

b. Describe the pattern of change in the number of bags of popcorn sold during the day.

c. During which hour did the store sell the most popcorn? During which hour did it sell the least popcorn?

2. When Ming and Jamil studied growth in the population of their city, they found these data:

Population of Okemos

Year	1970	1980	1990	1995	2000	2005	2010
Population (1000's)	20	25	30	35	40	45	50

a. Ming made the graph below.

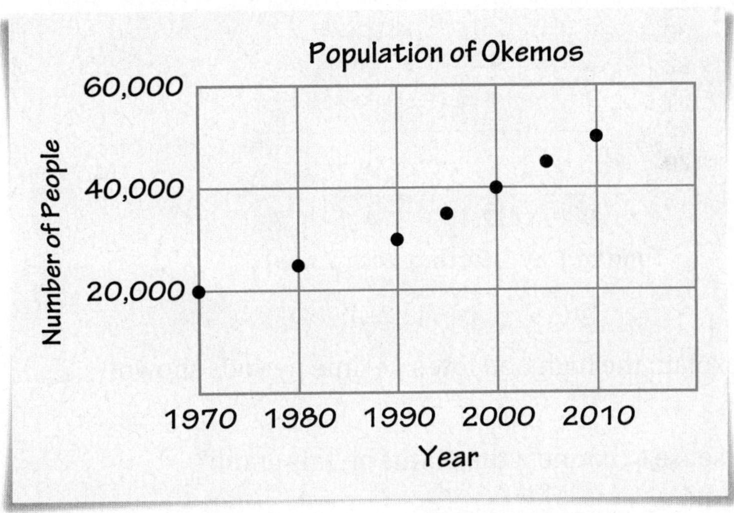

She said, "The graph shows population growing faster in the period from 1995 to 2010 than earlier." Is Ming's claim accurate? Why or why not?

b. Jamil made a different graph. It is shown below.

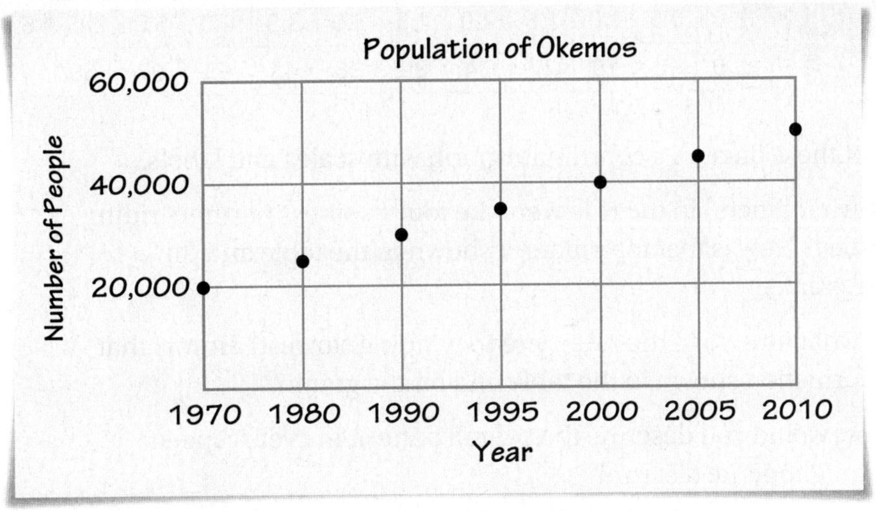

Jamil said, "The graph shows population growing at a steady rate." Is his claim accurate? Why or why not?

3. The graph below shows the numbers of cans of juice purchased each hour from a school's vending machines in one day. On the x-axis of the graph, 7 means the time from 7:00 to 8:00, and so on.

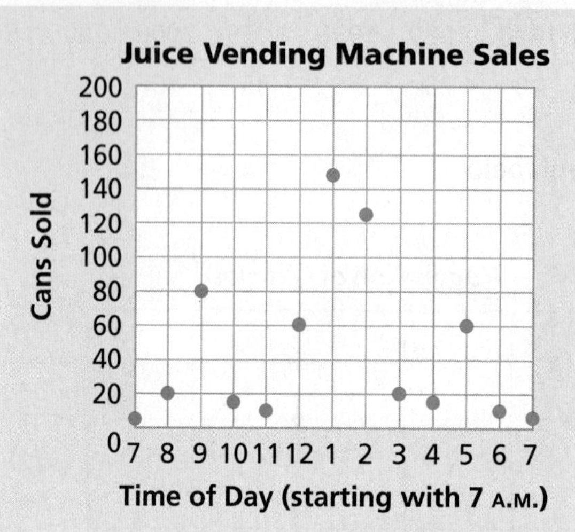

a. What might explain the high and low sale time periods shown by the graph?

b. Does it make sense to connect the points on this graph? Why or why not?

4. Before deciding that bike tour customers could ride 60–90 miles each day, the Ocean Bike Tours partners went on a test ride. The (*time, distance*) data for their ride are shown in the table below.

Ocean Bike Tours Test Ride

Time (h)	0	0.5	1.0	1.5	2.0	2.5	3.0	3.5	4.0	5.0	5.5	6.0
Distance (mi)	0	10	19	27	34	39	36	43	53	62	66	72

a. Plot these data on a coordinate graph with scales and labels.

b. At what time(s) in the ride were the four business partners riding fastest? How is that information shown in the table and on the graph?

c. At what time(s) in the ride were they riding slowest? How is that information shown in the table and on the graph?

d. How would you describe the overall pattern in cyclist speed throughout the test run?

e. What might explain the dip in the distance data between 2.5 and 3.5 hours?

5. Students have a test to see how many sit-ups they can complete in 10 minutes. Andrea and Ken plot their results. Their graphs are shown below.

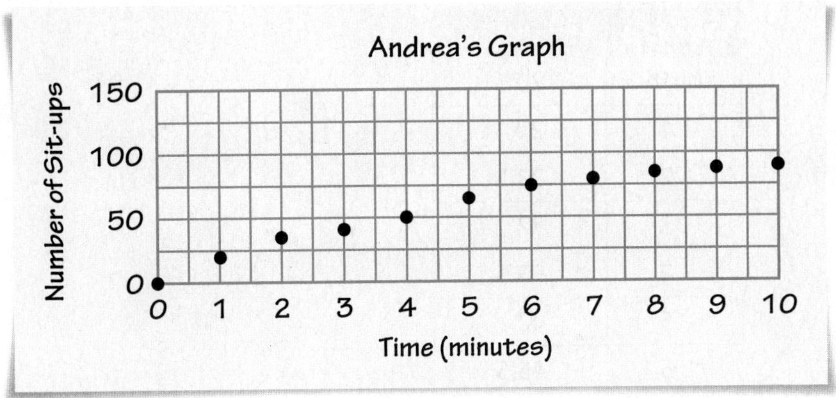

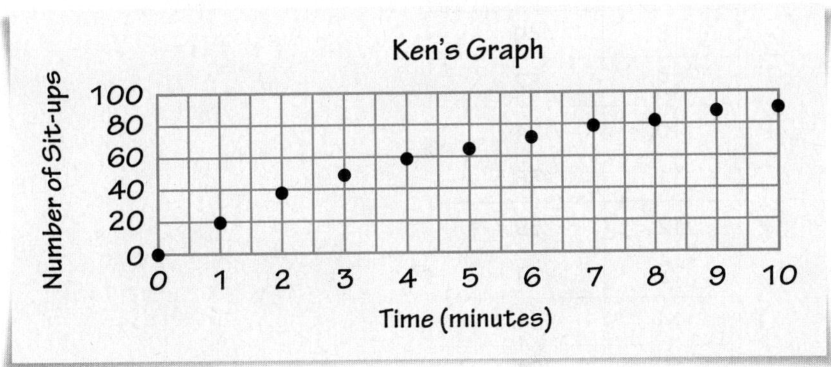

a. Ken claims that he did better because the points on his graph are higher than the points on Andrea's graph. Is Ken correct? Explain.

b. In what ways do the results of the sit-up test show a pattern of endurance in physical activity that is similar to the results of the test ride by the Ocean Bike Tours partners?

c. Which person had the greatest average number of sit-ups per minute?

d. Compare Ken's pace in the first two minutes to his pace in the last two minutes.

6. Katrina's parents kept a record of her growth in height from birth until her 18th birthday. Their data is shown in the table below.

Katrina's Height

Age (yr)	Height (in.)
birth	20
1	29
2	33.5
3	37
4	39.5
5	42
6	45.5
7	47
8	49
9	52
10	54
11	56.5
12	59
13	61
14	64
15	64
16	64
17	64.5
18	64.5

a. Make a coordinate graph of Katrina's height data.

b. During which time interval(s) did Katrina have her greatest "growth spurt"?

c. During which time interval(s) did Katrina's height change the least?

d. Would it make sense to connect the points on the graph? Why or why not?

e. Is it easier to use the table or the graph to answer parts (b) and (c)? Explain.

7. Below is a chart of the water depth in a harbor during a typical 24-hour day. The water level rises and falls with the tides.

Effect of the Tide on Water Depth

Hours Since Midnight	0	1	2	3	4	5	6	7	8
Depth (m)	10.1	10.6	11.5	13.2	14.5	15.5	16.2	15.4	14.6

Hours Since Midnight	9	10	11	12	13	14	15	16
Depth (m)	12.9	11.4	10.3	10.0	10.4	11.4	13.1	14.5

Hours Since Midnight	17	18	19	20	21	22	23	24
Depth (m)	15.4	16.0	15.6	14.3	13.0	11.6	10.7	10.2

a. At what time is the water the deepest? Find the depth at that time.

b. At what time is the water the shallowest? Find the depth at that time.

c. During what time interval does the depth change most rapidly?

d. Make a coordinate graph of the data. Describe the overall pattern you see.

e. How did you choose scales for the x-axis and y-axis of your graph? Do you think everyone in your class used the same scales? Explain.

8. Three students made graphs of the population of a town called Huntsville. The break in the *y*-axis in Graphs A and C indicates that there are values missing between 0 and 8.

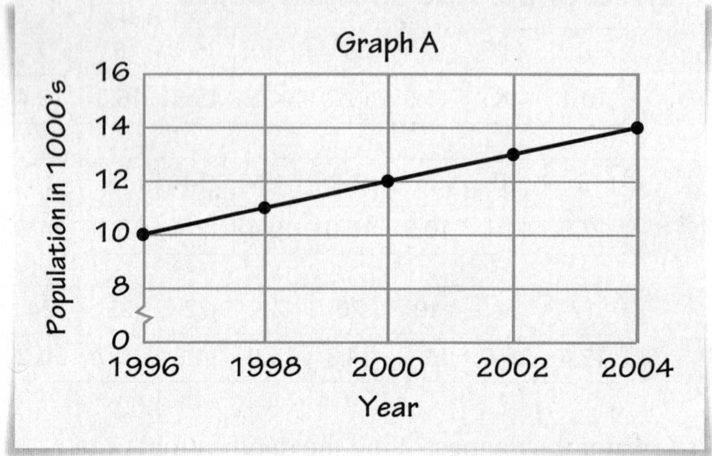

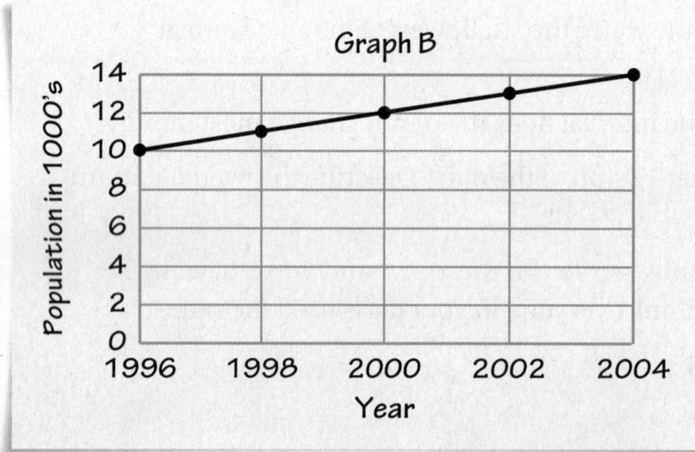

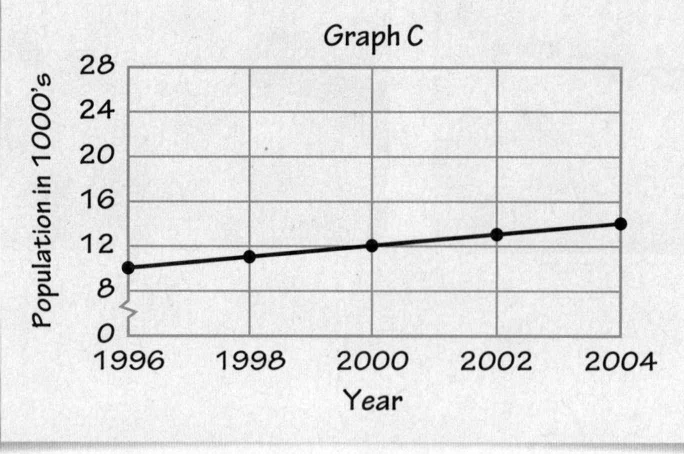

a. Describe the relationship between time and population as shown in each of the graphs.

b. Is it possible that all three graphs correctly represent the population growth in Huntsville? Explain.

9. Here is a graph of temperature data collected on the Ocean Bike Tours test trip from Atlantic City to Lewes.

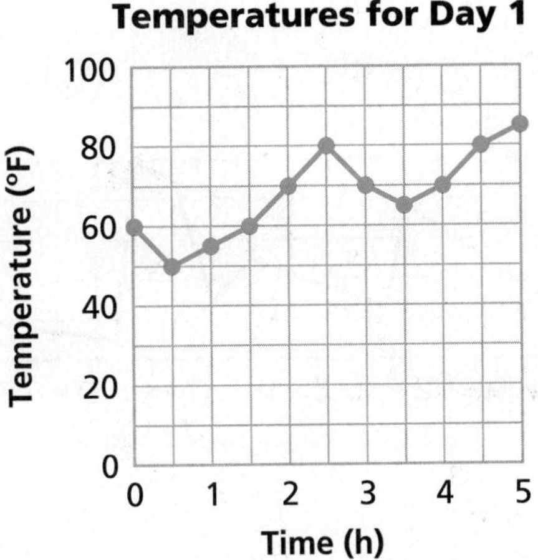

a. Make a table of (*time, temperature*) data from this graph.

b. What is the difference between the day's lowest and highest temperatures?

c. During which time interval(s) did the temperature rise the fastest? During which time interval did it fall the fastest?

d. Do you prefer using the table or the graph to answer questions like those in parts (b) and (c)? Explain your reasoning.

e. What information is shown by the lines connecting the points?

10. Make a table and a graph of (*time, temperature*) data that fit the following information about a day on the road with the Ocean Bike Tours cyclists:

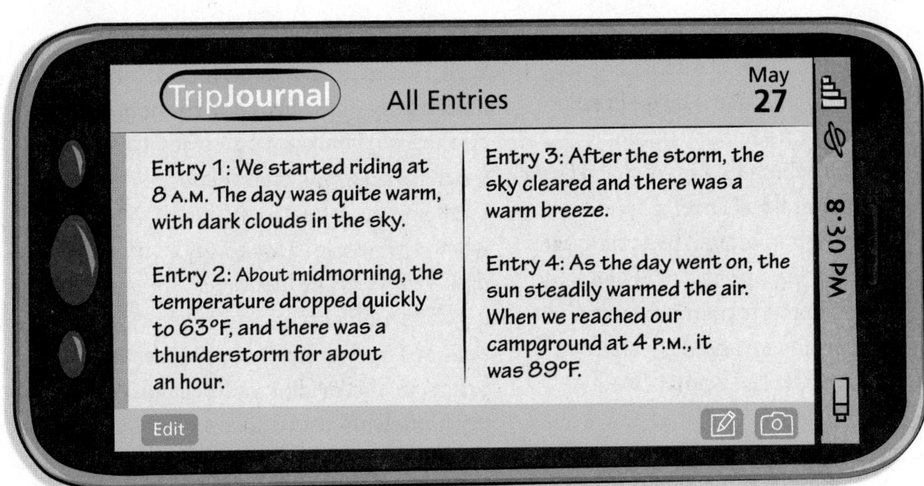

11. Amanda made the graphs below to show how her level of hunger and her happiness changed over the course of a day. She forgot to label the graphs.

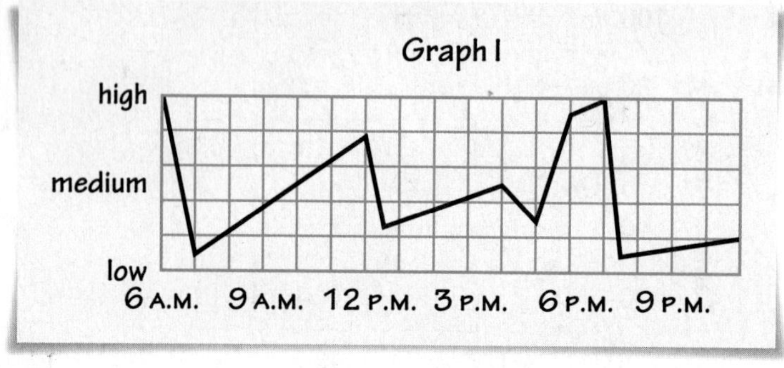

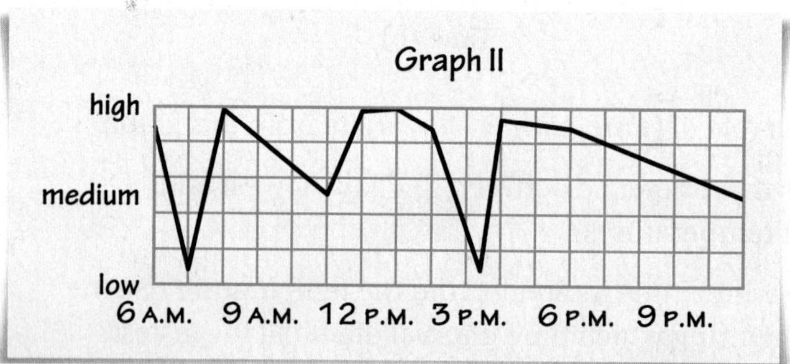

Use the following descriptions to determine which graph shows Amanda's hunger pattern and which graph shows Amanda's happiness. Explain.

AMANDA My Everyday Life Search

Home | Past Projects | Future Projects | Contact | About Me

My Hunger

Hmmm.... I woke up really hungry and ate a large breakfast. I was hungry again by lunch, which began at 11:45. After school, I had a snack before basketball practice, but I had a big appetite by the time I got home for dinner. I was full after dinner and didn't eat much before I went to bed.

My Happiness

Well, I woke up in a good mood, but got mad at my older brother for hogging the bathroom. I talked to the guy I like on the morning bus. My classes were good, but I got bored by lunch. At lunch, I had fun with my friends. I loved my computer class right after lunch, but the rest of my afternoon classes were boring. After school, I had an awesome basketball practice. After dinner, I still had to do my homework and chores.

12. Celia uses (*time, distance*) data from one part of the bike tour test run to draw the following graph relating time and speed. Celia forgot to include scales on the axes of the graph.

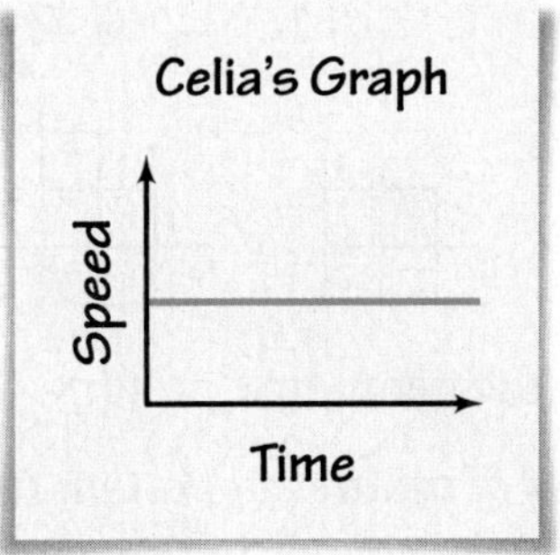

a. What does this graph show?

b. Is the graph most likely a picture of speed for a cyclist, the tour van, or the wind over a part of one day's trip? Explain your reasoning about each possibility.

13. The following table shows (*time, distance*) data from the bike tour group's van ride home from Williamsburg to Atlantic City.

Williamsburg to Atlantic City Van Ride

Time (h)	0	1	2	3	4	5	6	7	8
Distance (mi)	0	50	110	150	200	220	280	315	345

a. What was their average speed for the whole trip?

b. What was their average speed for the first four hours of the trip?

c. What was their average speed for the second four hours of the trip?

d. Suppose that for the first four hours of the trip the van had traveled at a steady rate equal to the average speed calculated in part (b). For the second four hours of the trip, suppose the van traveled at a steady rate equal to the average speed calculated in part (c).

1. Sketch the (*time, distance*) graph that would result from this pattern of driving.
2. Sketch the (*time, speed*) graph that would result from this pattern of driving.

Connections

14. Consider the pattern below.

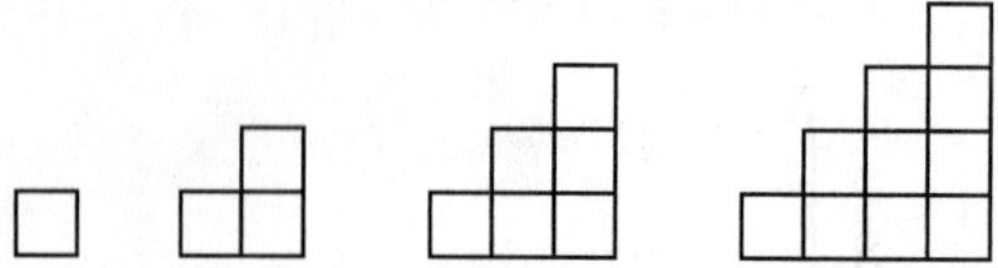

a. Draw the next shape in the geometric pattern.

b. Make a table of (*number of squares in bottom row, total number of squares*) data for the first ten shapes in the pattern.

c. Describe the pattern of increase in total number of squares as length of the bottom row increases.

15. Make a table to show how the total number of cubes in these pyramids changes as the width of the base changes from 3 to 5 to 7. Then use the pattern in those numbers to predict the number of cubes for pyramids with base width of 9, 11, 13, and 15.

For Exercises 16–18, order the given numbers from least to greatest. Then, for each ordered list, describe a pattern relating each number to the next number.

16. 1.75, 0.25, 0.5, 1.5, 2.0, 0.75, 1.25, 1.00

17. $\frac{3}{8}$, 1, $\frac{1}{4}$, $\frac{7}{8}$, $\frac{3}{4}$, $\frac{1}{2}$, $\frac{1}{8}$, $\frac{5}{8}$

18. $\frac{4}{3}$, $\frac{1}{3}$, $\frac{1}{6}$, $\frac{4}{6}$, $\frac{8}{3}$, $\frac{32}{6}$

19. The partners in Ocean Bike Tours want to compare their plans with other bicycle tour companies. The bike tour they are planning takes three days, and they wonder if this might be too short. Malcolm called 18 different companies and asked, "How many days is your most popular bike trip?" Here are the answers he received:

a. Make a line plot of the data.

b. Based on part (a), should Ocean Bike Tours change the length of the three-day trip? Explain.

20. The graph below shows the results of a survey of people over age 25 who had completed different levels of education. The graph shows the average salary for people with each level of education.

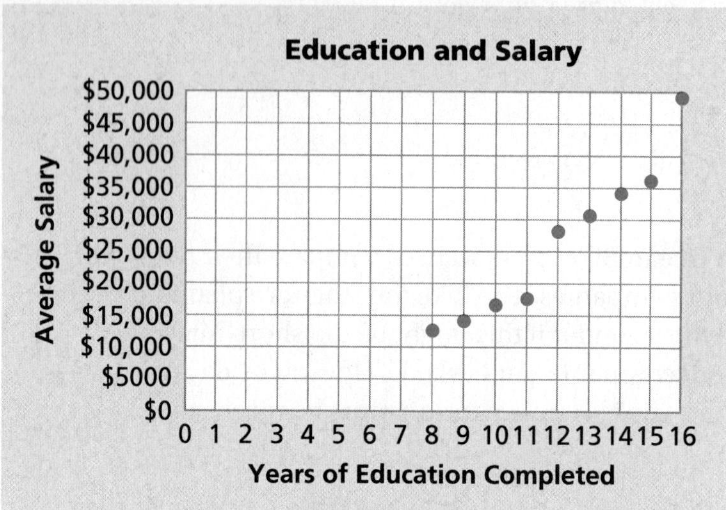

a. Make a table that shows the information in the graph.

b. After how many years of education do salaries take a big jump? Why do you think this happens?

c. Do you find it easier to answer part (b) by looking at the graph or at your table? Explain.

21. Think of something in your life that varies with time. Make a graph to show the pattern of change.

Extensions

22. The number of hours of daylight in a day changes throughout the year. We say that the days are "shorter" in winter and "longer" in summer. The table shows the number of daylight hours in Chicago, Illinois, on a typical day during each month of the year (January is Month 1, and so on).

Daylight Hours

Month	Number of Hours
1	10.0
2	10.2
3	11.7
4	13.1
5	14.3
6	15.0
7	14.5
8	13.8
9	12.5
10	11.0
11	10.5
12	10.0

a. Describe any relationships you see between the two variables.

b. On a grid, sketch a coordinate graph of the data. Put months on the x-axis and daylight hours on the y-axis. What patterns do you see?

c. The seasons in the Southern Hemisphere are the opposite of the seasons in the Northern Hemisphere. When it is summer in North America, it is winter in Australia. Chicago is about the same distance north of the equator as Melbourne, Australia, is south of the equator. Sketch a graph showing the relationship you would expect to find between the month and the hours of daylight in Melbourne.

d. Put the (*month, daylight*) values from your graph in part (c) into a table.

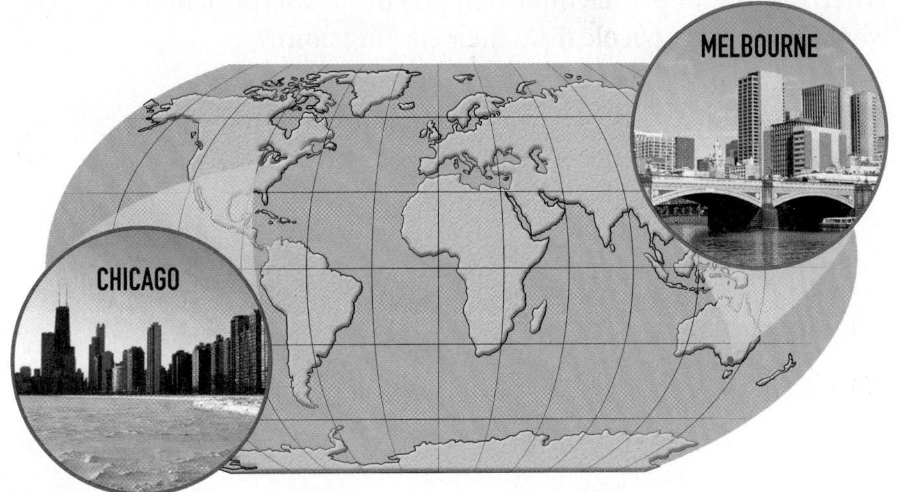

23. **a.** A school club sells sweatshirts to raise money. Which, if any, of the graphs below describes the relationship you would expect between the price charged for each sweatshirt and the profit? Explain your choice, or draw a new graph that you think better describes this relationship.

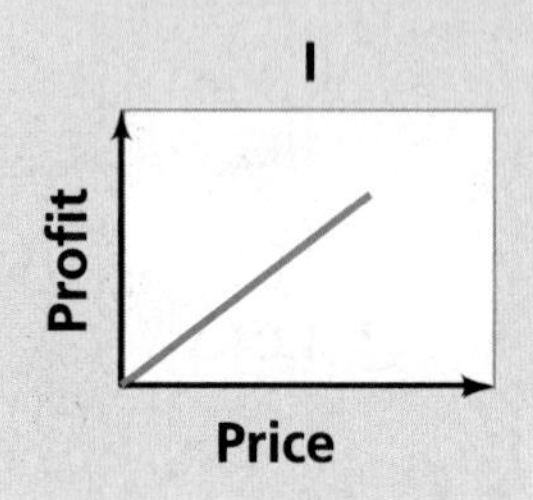

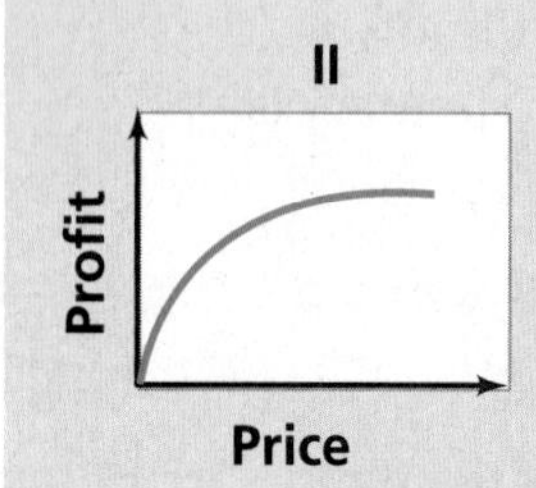

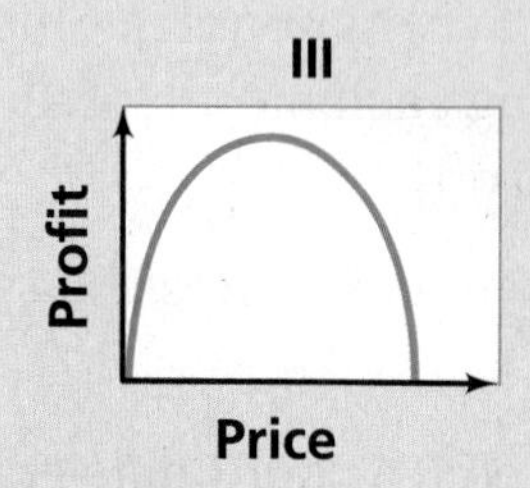

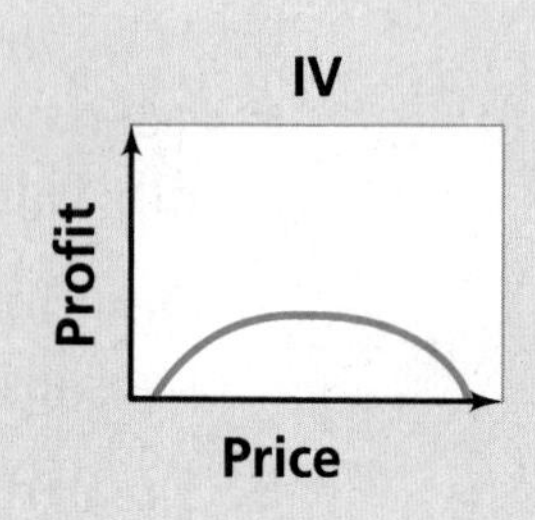

b. What variables might affect the club's profits?

24. Chelsea and Nicole can paddle a canoe at a steady rate of 5 miles per hour in calm water.

a. On Saturday, they paddle for 3 hours on a calm lake. Sketch a graph of their speed over the 3-hour period.

b. On Sunday, they go canoeing on a river with a 2-mile-per-hour current. They paddle with the current for 1 hour. Then, they turn around and paddle against the current for 2 hours. Sketch a graph of their speed over this 3-hour period.

c. When the 3-hour paddle indicated in part (b) was over, how far were Chelsea and Nicole from their starting point?

25. In parts (a)–(e) below, how does the value of one variable change as the value of the other changes? Estimate pairs of values that show the pattern of change you would expect. Record your estimates in a table with at least five data points.

Sample: hours of television you watch in a week and your school grade-point average

Answer: As television time increases, I expect my grade-point average to decrease. See the table below.

TV Time (hours per week)	0	5	10	15	20
Grade Point Average	3.5	3.25	3.0	2.75	2.5

a. distance from school to your home and time it takes to walk home

b. price of popcorn at a theater and number of bags sold

c. speed of an airplane and time it takes the plane to complete a 500-mile trip

d. monthly cell phone bill and number of text messages sent

e. cost of a long-distance telephone call and length of the call in minutes

26. Some students did a jumping jack experiment. They reported data on the student who could do the most jumping jacks in a certain amount of time.

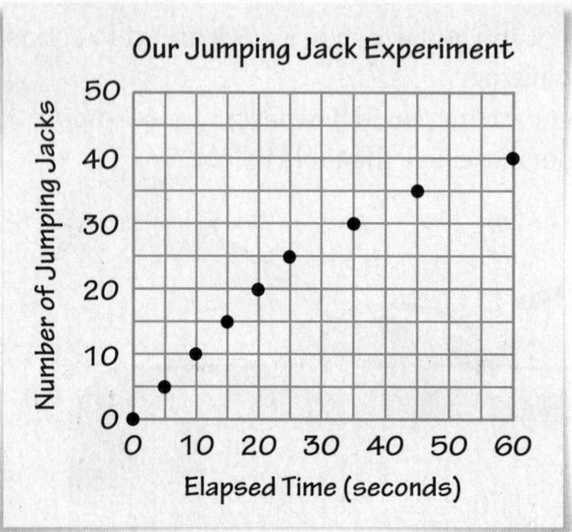

a. According to the graph, how many jumping jacks did the jumper make by the end of 10 seconds? By the end of 20 seconds? By the end of 60 seconds?

b. Give the elapsed time and number of jumping jacks for two other points on the graph.

c. What estimate would make sense for the number of jumping jacks in 30 seconds? The number in 40 seconds? The number in 50 seconds?

d. What does the overall pattern in the graph show about the rate at which the test jumper completed jumping jacks?

e. Suppose you connected the first and last data points with a straight line. Would this line show the overall pattern? Explain.

Mathematical Reflections 1

The Problems in this Investigation helped you to think about variables and patterns relating values of variables. In particular, they helped you develop understanding and skill in the use of data tables and graphs in order to study quantities or variables that change over time.

This Investigation challenged you to use those mathematical tools to find important patterns in the relationships between distance, time, and speed of moving objects.

Think about these questions. Discuss your ideas with other students and your teacher. Then write a summary of your findings in your notebook.

1. You can show patterns of change over time with tables, graphs, and written reports.
   a. **What** are the advantages and disadvantages of showing patterns with tables?
   b. **What** are the advantages and disadvantages of showing patterns with graphs?
   c. **What** are the advantages and disadvantages of showing patterns with written reports?
2. a. **How** do you see patterns in the speed of a moving object by studying (*time, distance*) data in tables?
   b. **How** do you see patterns in the speed of a moving object by studying (*time, distance*) data in coordinate graphs?

Common Core Mathematical Practices

As you worked on the Problems in this Investigation, you used prior knowledge to make sense of them. You also applied Mathematical Practices to solve the Problems. Think back over your work, the ways you thought about the Problems, and how you used Mathematical Practices.

Hector described his thoughts in the following way:

Our group made a table and a graph of our jumping jack experiment. We evaluated the data.

We noticed something about two adjacent table entries. The difference between those entries, divided by 10, tells the number of jumping jacks per second.

However, on our graph, greater rates are shown by bigger jumps upward from one data point to the next.

Common Core Standards for Mathematical Practice

MP4 Model with mathematics.

- What other Mathematical Practices can you identify in Hector's reasoning?
- Describe a Mathematical Practice that you and your classmates used to solve a different Problem in this Investigation.

Analyzing Relationships Among Variables

The test run by the Ocean Bike Tours partners raised many questions.

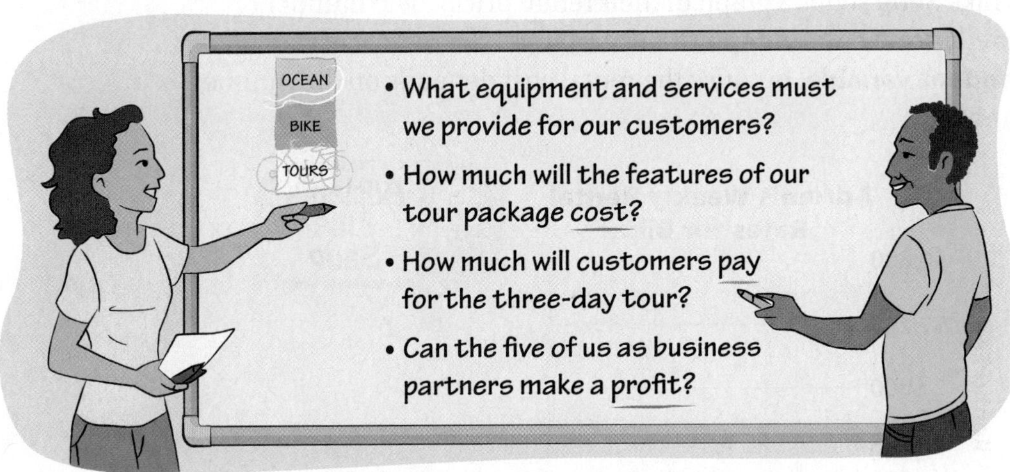

To make their choices, the five partners decided to do some research. In this Investigation you will use tables, graphs, and words to analyze information from their research and advise the tour business partners.

Common Core State Standards

6.NS.C.6b Understand signs of numbers in ordered pairs as indicating locations in quadrants of the coordinate plane; recognize that when two ordered pairs differ only by signs, the locations of the points are related by reflections across one or both axes.

6.NS.C.6c Find and position integers and other rational numbers on a horizontal or vertical number line diagram; find and position pairs of integers and other rational numbers on a coordinate plane.

6.NS.C.8 Solve real-world and mathematical problems by graphing points in all four quadrants of the coordinate plane. Include use of coordinates . . . to find distances between points with the same first coordinate or the same second coordinate.

6.EE.B.6 Use variables to represent numbers and write expressions when solving a real-world or mathematical problem; understand that a variable can represent an unknown number, or, depending on the purpose at hand, any number in a specified set.

Also 6.NS.C.6, 6.EE.C.9

2.1 Renting Bicycles
Independent and Dependent Variables

The tour operators decide to rent bicycles for their customers. They get information from two bike shops. Rocky's Cycle Center sends a table of rental fees for bikes.

Bike Rental at Rocky's

Number of Bikes	5	10	15	20	25	30	35	40	45	50
Rental Cost ($)	400	535	655	770	875	975	1,070	1,140	1,180	1,200

Adrian's Bike Shop sends a graph of their rental prices. The number of bikes rented is called the **independent variable**. The rental cost is called the **dependent variable**, because the rental cost depends on the number of bikes rented.

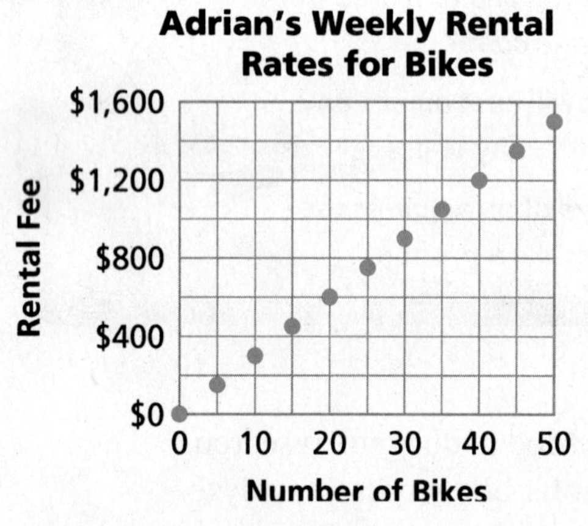

Graphs usually have the independent variable on the x-axis and the dependent variable on the y-axis.

The Ocean Bike Tour partners need to choose a bike rental shop. Suppose that they ask for your advice.

- Which shop would you recommend?
- How would you justify your choice?

Problem 2.1

Use entries in the table and the graph to answer the following comparison questions.

A What are the costs of renting from Rocky and Adrian if the tour needs 20 bikes? 40 bikes? 32 bikes?

B About how many bikes can be rented from Rocky or Adrian in the following cases?

1. A group has $900 to spend.
2. A group has $400 to spend.

C You want to see how rental cost is related to number of bikes.

1. What pattern do you see in the table from Rocky's Cycle Center?
2. What pattern do you see in the graph from Adrian's Bike Shop?

D How can you predict rental costs for numbers of bikes that are not shown by entries in the table or points on the graph?

E What information about bike rental costs was easier to get from the table and what from the graph?

F Which data format is most useful?

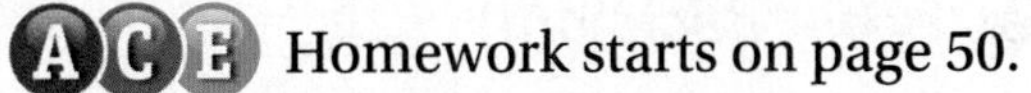

ACE Homework starts on page 50.

2.2 Finding Customers
Linear and Nonlinear Patterns

The tour operators have planned a route and chosen a bike rental shop. The next task is to figure out a price to charge for the tour. They want the price low enough to attract customers. They also want it high enough to have **income** that is greater than their expenses. That way their business makes a **profit.**

The partners conduct a survey to help set the price. They ask people who have taken other bicycle tours what they would pay for the planned bike tour.

Prices That Customers Would Pay

Tour Price	$100	$150	$200	$250	$300	$350	$400	$450	$500
Number of Customers	40	35	30	25	20	15	10	5	0

Look carefully at the data relating price and number of customers.

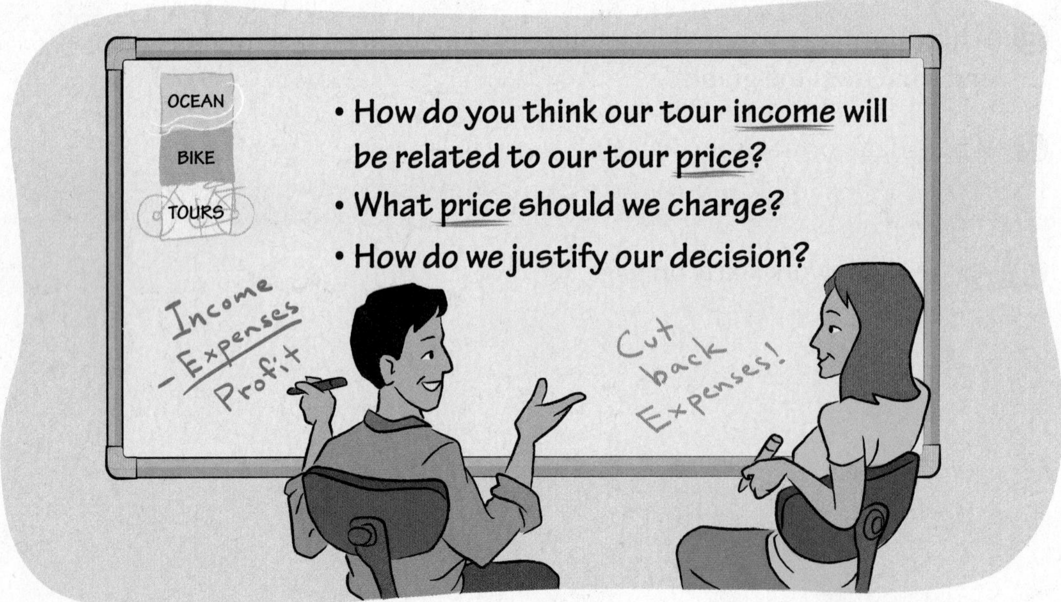

Problem 2.2

The following questions can help you choose a tour price.

A **1.** Make a graph of the data relating price and number of customers. Which is the independent variable? Which is the dependent variable? Explain how you know.

2. How does the number of customers change as the price increases?

3. How is the change in number of customers shown in the table? How is the change shown by the graph?

4. How would you estimate the number of customers for a price of $175? For a price of $325?

B **1.** The partners need to know what income to expect from the tour. They extend the (*price, customers*) table as shown below. Copy and complete the table to find how income would be related to price and number of customers.

Predicting Tour Income

Tour Price	$100	$150	$200	$250	$300	$350	$400	$450	$500
Number of Customers	40	35	30	25	20	15	10	5	0
Tour Income	$4,000	■	■	■	■	■	■	■	■

2. Make a graph of the (*price, income*) data.

3. Describe the pattern relating tour income to tour price. Use a sentence that begins, "As tour price increases, tour income . . . ." Explain why that pattern does or does not make sense.

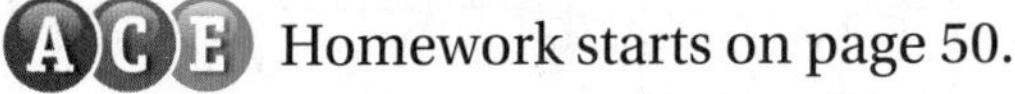
ACE Homework starts on page 50.

2.3 Predicting Profits

Four-Quadrant Graphing

The survey conducted by Ocean Bike Tours showed that income depends on the tour price. The partners want to see if they can make any profit from their business. As well as income, they have to consider the costs of operating the tour. Their research shows that bike rental, camping fees, and food will cost $150 per customer.

The partners want to make a profit. They need to figure out how profit depends on the tour price.

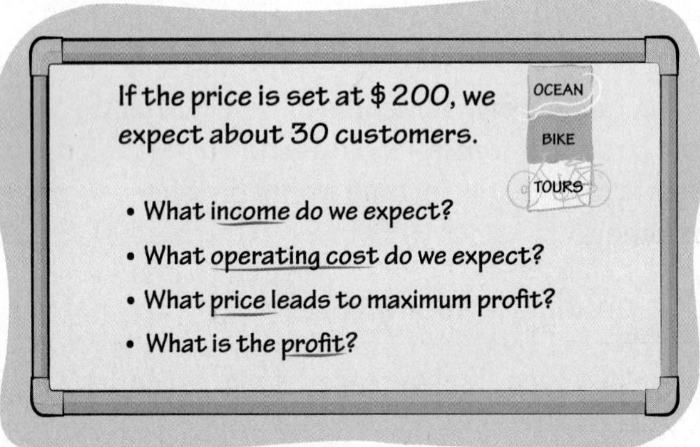

Problem 2.3

A **1.** The table below shows the relationship between profit and price. Copy and complete the table.

Predicted Tour Profit

Tour Price	$100	$150	$200	$250	$300	$350	$400	$450	$500
Number of Customers	40	35	30	25	20	15	10	5	0
Tour Income ($)	4,000	■	■	■	■	■	■	■	■
Operating Cost ($)	6,000	■	■	■	■	■	■	■	■
Tour Profit or Loss ($)	−2,000	■	■	■	■	■	■	■	■

Problem 2.3 continued

2. Celia and Malcolm want a picture of profit prospects for the tour business. They need to graph the (*price, profit*) data. Some of the data are negative numbers. Those numbers represent possible losses for the tour operation.

   The key to graphing data that are negative numbers is to extend the *x*- and *y*-axis number lines. Both the *x*- and *y*-axes can be extended in the negative direction. This gives a grid like the one shown below. Use the grid to sketch a graph for the (*price, profit*) data points from the table in part (1).

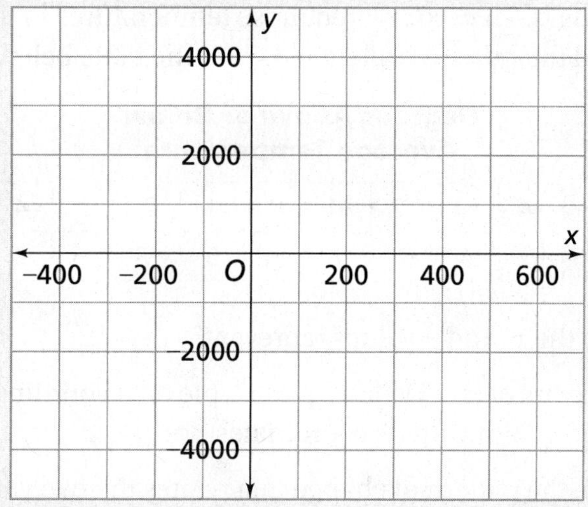

3. a. Describe the pattern in the table in part (1) and the graph in part (2).

   b. Explain why the pattern occurs.

   c. Think about the analysis of profit predictions. What tour price would you suggest? Explain your reasoning.

continued on the next page >

Problem 2.3 continued

B In January, the partners thought about offering a winter bike tour. They looked at the forecast for the next four days. They wrote down the number of degrees above or below each day's average temperature.

Degrees Above or Below Average Temperature

x	0	1	2	3	4
y	−1	5	−3	−5	2

They did not see any pattern, so they checked the temperatures for the previous five days. They compared those temperatures to the average. They recorded their data for all nine days in the table below.

Degrees Above or Below Average Temperature

x	−4	−3	−2	−1	0	1	2	3	4
y	−2	4	−3	1	−1	5	−3	−5	2

1. What do the x- and y-values represent?
2. Plot the pairs of (x, y) values in the table on a coordinate grid. Label each point with its coordinates.
3. Describe the pattern of change that relates the two variables.

C 1. Suppose that you are standing at the point with coordinates (3, 4). Tell how you would move on the grid lines to reach the points below.

a. (−3, 4) **b.** (−3, −4) **c.** (3, −4)

d. (1.5, −2) **e.** (−1.5, 2) **f.** (−2.5, −3.5)

2. How far would you have to move on the grid lines to travel between each pair of points?

a. (3, 4) to (−3, 4) **b.** (3, 4) to (3, −4) **c.** (3, 4) to (−3, −4)

D 1. Jakayla was looking at the points (3, 4), (−3, 4), (−3, −4), and (3, −4). She said that the locations of the points with different signs are mirror images of each other. Does Jakayla's conjecture make sense? Explain.

2. Mitch says this is like a reflection. Does Mitch's comment make sense?

ACE Homework starts on page 50.

2.4 What's the Story?
Interpreting Graphs

Information about variables is often given by coordinate graphs. So, it is important to be good at reading the "story" in a graph. Here are some questions to ask when you look at a graph.

- What are the variables?
- Do the values of one variable seem to depend on the values of the other?
- What does the shape of the graph say about the relationship between the variables?

For example, the number of cars in your school's parking lot changes as time passes during a typical school day. Graph 1 and Graph 2 show two possibilities for the way the number of parked cars might change over time.

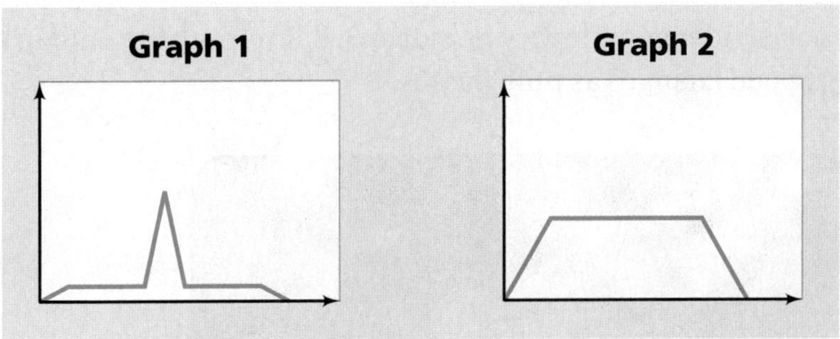

- Describe the story each graph tells about the school parking lot.
- Which graph shows the pattern you expect?
- How could you label the graph you chose so that someone else would know what it represents?

Problem 2.4

Questions A–H describe pairs of related variables.
For each pair, do the following.

- Decide what the variables are.
- Decide which variable is the dependent variable and which is the independent variable.
- Think about what a graph or table of these data would look like.
- Find the graph at the end of the Problem that tells the story of how the variables are related. If no graph fits the relationship as you understand it, sketch a graph of your own.
- Explain what the graph tells about the relationship of the variables.
- Give the graph a title.

A The number of students who go on a school trip is related to the price of the trip for each student.

B When a skateboard rider goes down one side of a half-pipe ramp and up the other side, her speed changes as time passes.

C The water level changes over time when someone fills a tub, takes a bath, and empties the tub.

D The waiting time for a popular ride at an amusement park is related to the number of people in the park.

Problem 2.4 continued

E The daily profit or loss of an amusement park depends on the number of paying customers.

F The number of hours of daylight changes over time as the seasons change.

G The daily profit or loss of an outdoor skating rink depends on the daytime high temperature.

H Weekly attendance at a popular movie changes as time passes from the date the movie first appears in theaters.

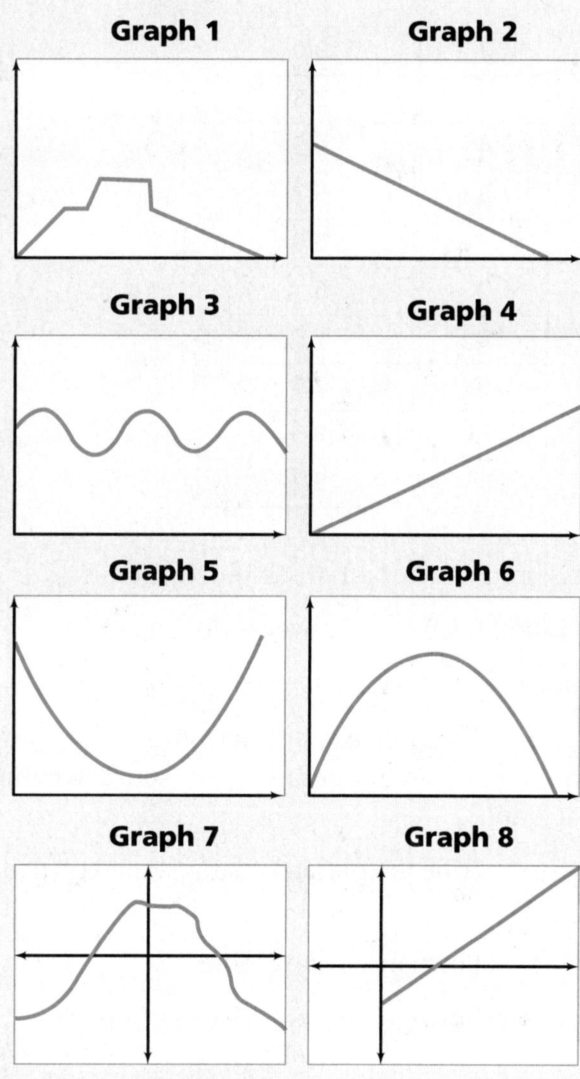

ACE Homework starts on page 50.

Applications

1. The following table shows typical weights for young tiger cubs from birth to 11 weeks. Use the data to answer parts (a)–(g).

Typical Weights for Tiger Cubs

Age (weeks)	Expected Body Weight (kg)
birth	1.3
1	2.3
2	3.0
3	3.8
4	4.5
5	5.2
6	6.0
7	6.7
8	7.5
9	7.6
10	8.9
11	9.7

   a. What weight is predicted for a 1-week-old tiger cub?

   b. What weight is predicted for a 10-week-old tiger cub?

   c. At what age do tiger cubs typically weigh 7 kilograms?

   d. Plot the (*age, weight*) data on a coordinate grid with appropriate scales. Explain why it does or does not make sense to connect the points on that graph.

   e. How would you describe the pattern relating tiger cub age and weight?

   f. How is the pattern shown in the data table?

   g. How is the pattern shown in the coordinate graph?

2. Desi is planning a go-kart party. Kartland gives him a table of group rates. Thunder Alley gives him a graph. The table and graph are shown below.

Kartland Price Packages

Number of Laps Raced	10	20	30	40	50	60
Cost	$25	$45	$65	$85	$105	$125

Thunder Alley Group Rates

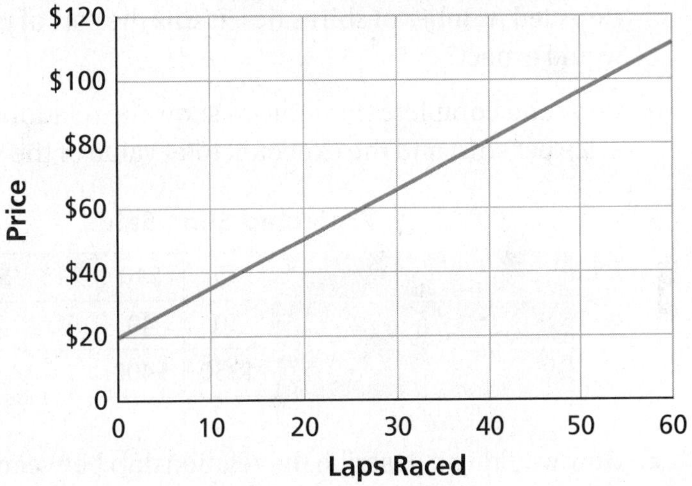

a. Find the cost at both locations for 50 laps.

b. Find the cost at both locations for 20 laps.

c. Find the cost at both locations for 35 laps.

d. Look for patterns in the relationships between number of laps and cost at Thunder Alley. How is the pattern shown in the table?

e. Look for patterns in the relationships between number of laps and cost at Kartland. How is the pattern shown in the graph?

f. Which location seems to offer the better deal?

3. The following table shows the fees charged for campsites at one of the campgrounds on the Ocean Bike Tours route.

Campground Fees

Number of Campsites	1	2	3	4	5	6	7	8
Total Fee	$12.50	$25.00	$37.50	$50.00	$62.50	$75.00	$87.50	$100.00

a. Make a coordinate graph of the data.

b. Does it make sense to connect the points on the graph? Explain.

c. Using the table, describe the pattern of change in the total campground fee as the number of campsites increases.

d. How is the pattern you described in part (c) shown in your graph?

4. Some class officers want to sell T-shirts to raise funds for a class trip. They ask the students in their class how much they would pay for a shirt and recorded the data in a table.

Projected Shirt Sales

Price per Shirt	$5	$10	$15	$20	$25
Number of Shirt Sales	50	40	30	20	10

a. Describe the relationship between the price per shirt and the expected number of shirt sales. Is this the sort of pattern you would expect?

b. Copy and complete this table to show the relationship between price per shirt and the expected total value of the shirt sales.

Projected Shirt Sales

Price per Shirt	$5	$10	$15	$20	$25
Number of Shirt Sales	50	40	30	20	10
Value of Shirt Sales	$250	$400	■	■	■

c. How would you describe the relationship between price per shirt and expected total value of shirt sales? Is this the sort of pattern you would expect?

d. Make coordinate graphs of the data like the ones started below.

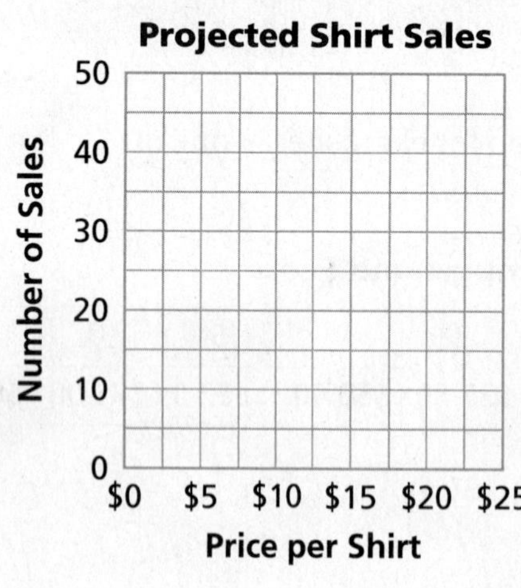

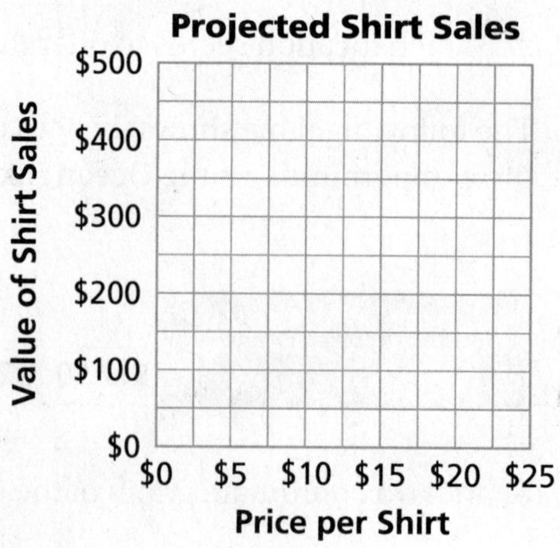

e. Explain how your answers to parts (a) and (c) are shown in the graphs.

5. A camping-supply store rents camping gear for $25 per person for a week.

   a. Make a table of the total rental charges for 0, 5, 10, . . . , 40 campers.

   b. Make a coordinate graph using the data in your table.

   c. Compare the pattern in your table and graph with patterns you found in the campground fee data in Exercise 3. Describe the similarities and differences between the two sets of data.

6. The bike tour partners need to rent a truck to transport camping gear, clothes, and bicycle repair equipment. They check prices at two truck-rental companies.

   a. East Coast Trucks charges $4 for each mile driven. Make a table of the charges for 0, 100, 200, . . . , 800 miles.

   b. Philadelphia Truck Rental charges $40 per day and an additional $3.00 for each mile driven. Make a table of the charges for renting a truck for five days and driving it 0, 100, 200, . . . , 800 miles.

   c. On one coordinate graph, plot the charges for both rental companies. Use different colors to mark points representing the two companies' plans.

   d. Based on your work in parts (a)–(c), which company offers the better deal? Explain.

7. The table below shows fees for using a campsite at a state park for 1 day up to the park limit of 10 days.

Campsite Fees

Days of Use	1	2	3	4	5	6	7	8	9	10
Total Fee	$20	$30	$40	$50	$60	$70	$75	$80	$85	$90

   a. Make a coordinate graph representing data in the table.

   b. Does it make sense to connect the points on your graph? Explain.

   c. Describe the pattern relating the variables *days of use* and *campsite fee.*

8. The graph at the right shows the relationship between daily profit and outdoor temperature at an indoor water park on ten days at various times of the year.

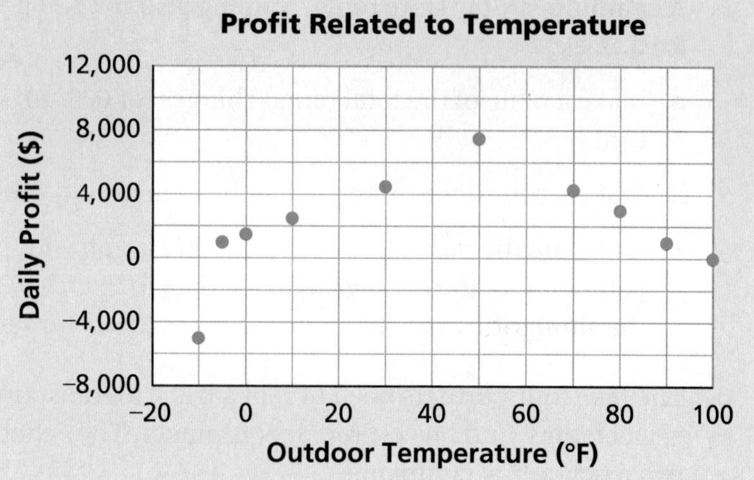

   a. Complete a table showing the data values represented.

   b. Describe the pattern relating profit to outdoor temperature. Explain how the pattern is shown by the points of the graph.

9. Coordinate graphs with four quadrants can also be used for locating places on a map. The four boxes in the table below show where in the four quadrants the *x*- and *y*-values will be positive and negative.

(–, +)	(+, +)
(–, –)	(+, –)

Use the table and the map grid to give coordinates locating each labeled site. Write the coordinates as (x, y).

   a. City Hall
   b. hospital
   c. stadium
   d. police station
   e. fire station
   f. middle school
   g. high school
   h. shopping mall

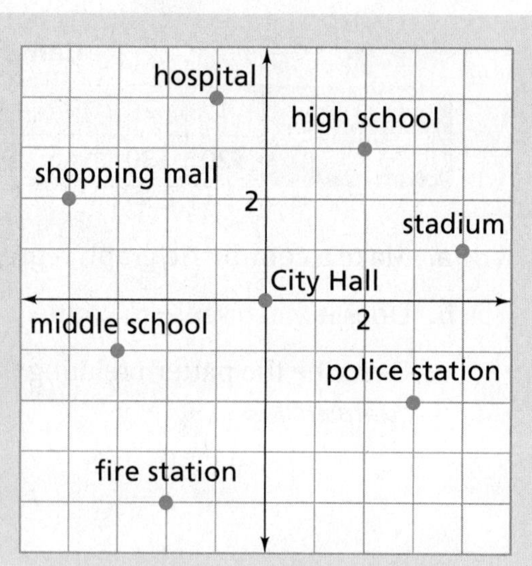

Suppose a motion detector tracks the time and the distance traveled as you walk 40 feet in 8 seconds. The results are shown in the graphs below. Use them to answer Exercises 10–11.

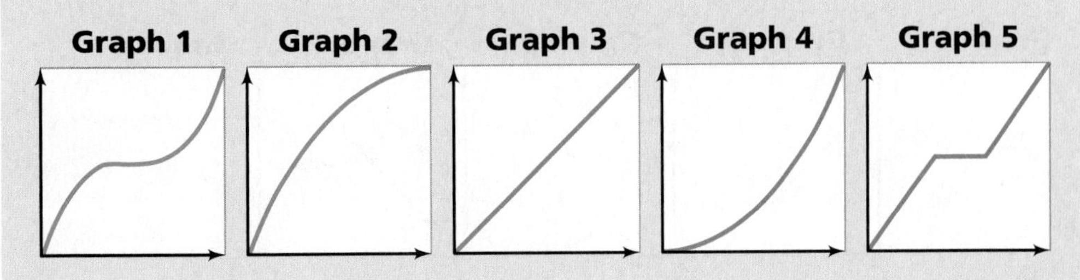

10. Match one of the (*time, distance*) graphs above with the story that describes each walk.

a. You walk at a steady pace of 5 feet per second.

b. You walk slowly at first, and then steadily increase your walking speed.

c. You walk rapidly at first, pause for several seconds, and then walk at an increasing rate for the rest of the trip.

d. You walk at a steady rate for 3 seconds, pause for 2 seconds, and then walk at a steady rate for the rest of the trip.

e. You walk rapidly at first, but gradually slow down as you reach the end of the walk.

11. For each walk in the graphs above, complete a (*time, distance*) table like the one begun below. Use numbers that will match the pattern shown in the graph.

Time (seconds)	1	2	3	4	5	6	7	8
Distance (feet)	■	■	■	■	■	■	■	40

12. The graphs below show five patterns for the daily sales of a new video game as time passed after its release. Match each (*time, sales*) graph with the "story" it tells.

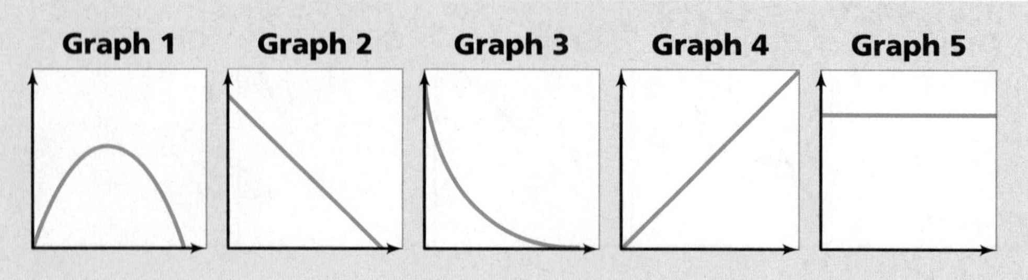

a. The daily sales declined at a steady rate.

b. The daily sales did not change.

c. The daily sales rose rapidly, then leveled off, and then declined rapidly.

d. The daily sales rose at a steady rate.

e. The daily sales dropped rapidly at first and then at a slower rate.

13. Multiple Choice Jamie is going to Washington, D.C., to march in a parade with his school band. He plans to set aside $25 at the end of each month to use for the trip. Choose the graph that shows how Jamie's savings will grow as time passes.

A.

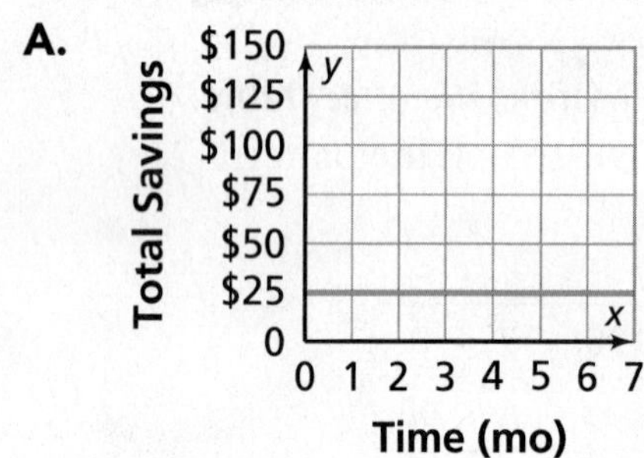

B.

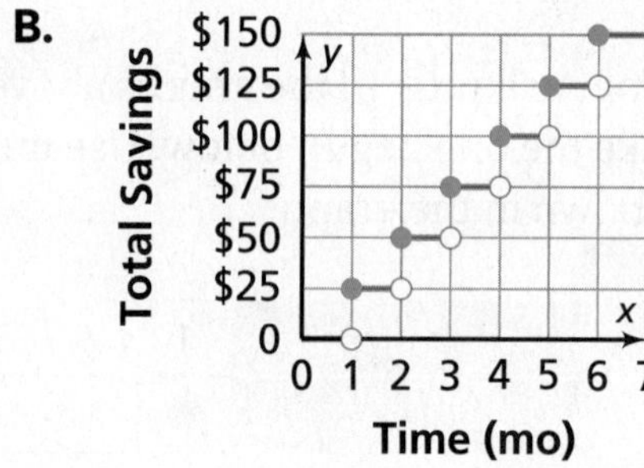

C.

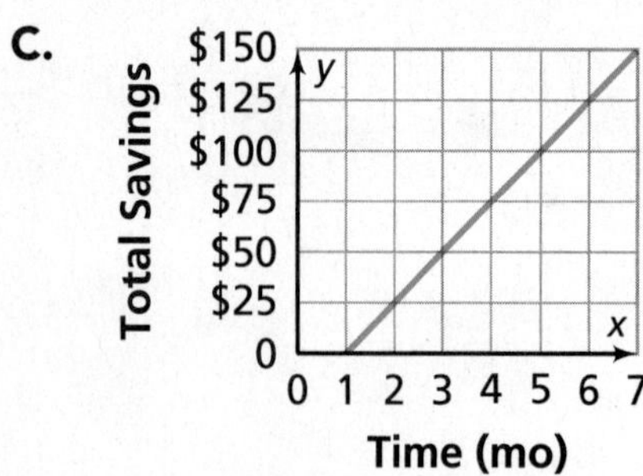

D. None of these is correct.

14. The graph below shows how the temperature changed during an all-day hike by students in the Terrapin Middle School science club.

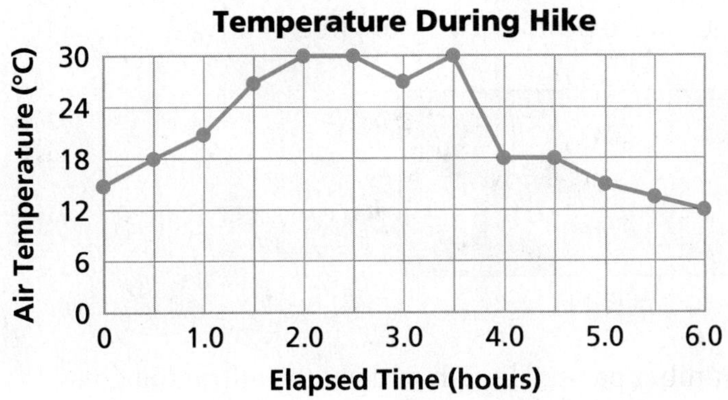

a. What was the maximum temperature and when did it occur?

b. When was the temperature rising most rapidly?

c. When was the temperature falling most rapidly?

d. When was the temperature about 24°C?

e. The hikers encountered a thunderstorm with rain. When do you think this happened?

Jacy works at a department store on the weekends. The graph at the right shows parking costs at the garage Jacy uses.

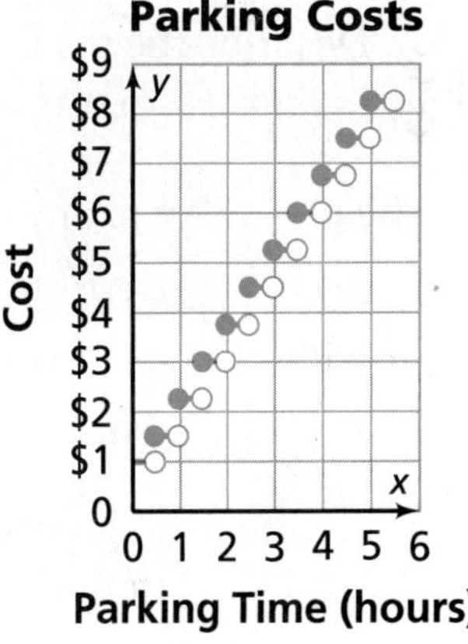

15. Multiple Choice How much will Jacy spend to park for less than half an hour?

F. $0.50

G. $0.75

H. $1.00

J. $1.50

16. Multiple Choice How much will Jacy spend to park for 4 hours and 15 minutes?

A. $6.00

B. $6.50

C. $6.75

D. $7.00

Connections

17. The area of a rectangle is the product of its length and its width.

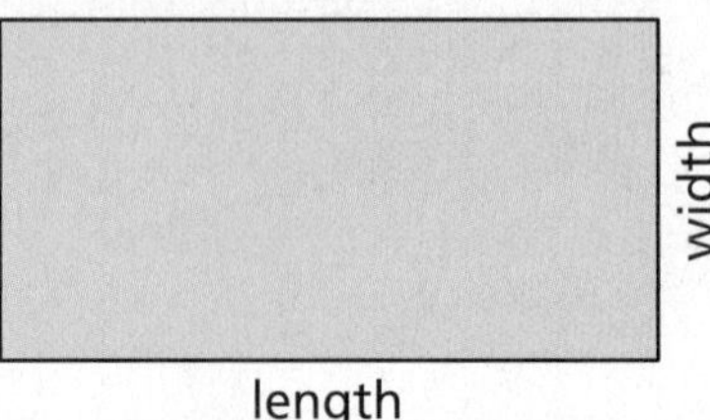

a. Find all whole-number pairs of length and width values that give an area of 24 square meters. Copy and extend the table here to record the pairs.

Rectangles With Area 24 m^2

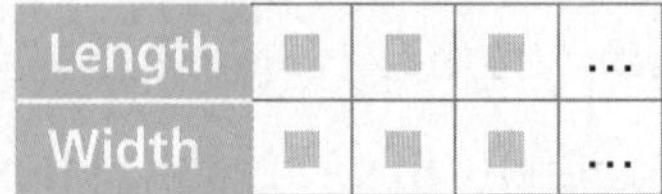

Length	■	■	■	...
Width	■	■	■	...

b. Make a coordinate graph of the (*length, width*) data from part (a).

c. Connect the points on your graph if it makes sense to do so. Explain your decision.

d. Describe the relationship between length and width for rectangles of area 24 square meters.

18. The perimeter of any rectangle is the sum of its side lengths.

a. Make a table of all possible whole-number pairs of length and width values for a rectangle with a perimeter of 18 meters.

b. Make a coordinate graph of the (*length, width*) data from part (a).

c. Connect the points on your graph if it makes sense to do so. Explain your decision.

d. Describe the relationship between length and width for rectangles of perimeter 18 meters. Explain how that relationship is shown in the table and graph.

19. The table below shows the winning countries and the winning times for the women's Olympic 400-meter dash since 1964.

Women's Olympic 400-meter Dash

Year	Country	Time (seconds)
1964	Australia	52.01
1968	France	52.03
1972	East Germany	51.08
1976	Poland	49.29
1980	East Germany	48.88
1984	United States	48.83
1988	Union of Soviet Socialist Republics	48.65
1992	France	48.83
1996	France	48.25
2000	Australia	49.11
2004	Bahamas	49.41
2008	United Kingdom	49.62
2012	United States	49.55

a. Make a coordinate graph of the (*year, time*) information. Choose a scale that allows you to see the differences between the winning times.

b. What patterns do you see in the table and graph? Do the winning times seem to be rising or falling? In which year was the best time earned?

20. Here are the box-office earnings for a movie during each of the first eight weeks following its release.

Box Office Earnings

Weeks in Theaters	1	2	3	4	5	6	7	8
Weekly Earnings ($ millions)	16	22	18	12	7	4	3	1

a. Make a coordinate graph showing the data from the table.

b. Explain how the weekly earnings changed as time passed. How is this pattern of change shown in the table and the graph? Why might this change have occurred?

c. What were the total earnings of the movie in the eight weeks?

d. Make a coordinate graph showing the total earnings after each week.

e. Explain how the movie's total earnings changed over time. How is this pattern of change shown in the table and the graph? Why might this change have occurred?

21. Two students were thinking about the relationship between price and number of T-shirt sales in a school fundraiser. They had different ideas about independent and dependent variables.

> Shaun argued that changing the price would change the number sold, so price is the independent variable.
>
> Victoria argued that the goal for number sold would dictate the price to be charged, so number of sales is the independent variable.

What do you think of these two ideas? Does it always matter which variable is considered independent and which dependent?

Extensions

22. Students plan to hold a car wash to raise money. The students ask some adults how much they would pay for a car wash. The table below shows the results of the research.

Price Customers Would Pay for a Car Wash

Car Wash Price	$4	$6	$8	$10	$12	$14
Number of Customers	120	105	90	75	60	45

a. Make a coordinate graph of the (*price, customers*) data. Connect the points if it makes sense to do so.

b. Describe the pattern relating the price to the number of customers. Explain how the table and the graph show the pattern.

c. Based on the pattern, what number of customers would you predict if the price were $16? If the price were $20? If the price were $2?

d. Copy and complete the following table relating car wash price to projected income.

Projected Car Wash Income

Car Wash Price	$4	$6	$8	$10	$12	$14
Number of Customers	120	105	90	75	60	45
Projected Income	■	■	■	■	■	■

e. Make a coordinate graph of the (*price, income*) data.

f. Explain why it makes sense to consider price the independent variable and income the dependent variable.

g. Does it make sense to connect the points on the coordinate graph data plot? Why or why not?

h. Describe the way projected car wash income changes as the price increases. Explain how this pattern is shown in the graph.

i. Suppose the students must pay $1.50 per car for water and cleaning supplies. How can you use this factor to find the profit from the car wash for various prices?

23. Use what you know about decimals to find coordinates of five points that lie on the line segment between the labeled points on each of these graphs:

a.

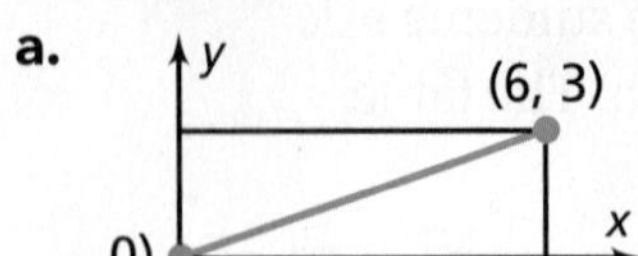

b.

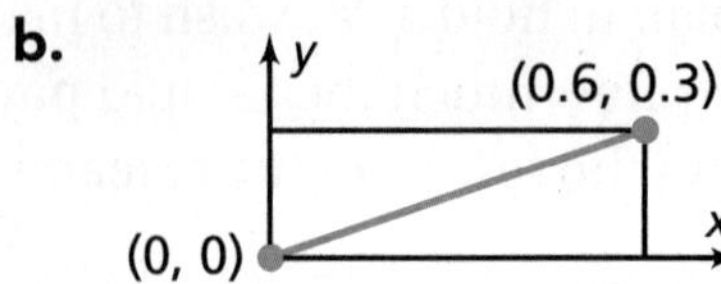

24. Each of the graphs below shows a relationship between independent (x-axis) and dependent (y-axis) variables. However, the scales on the coordinate axes are not the same for all the graphs.

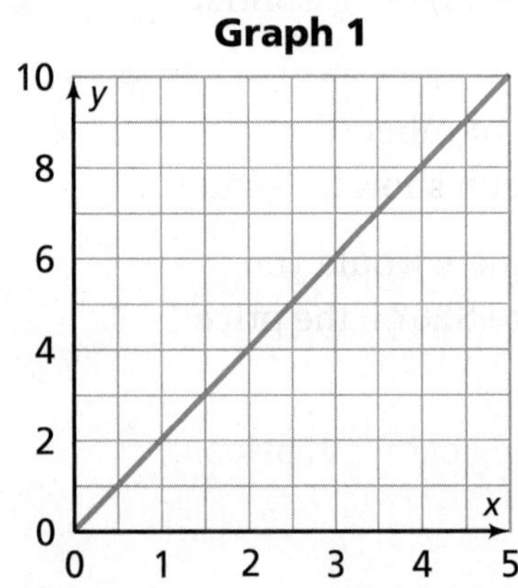

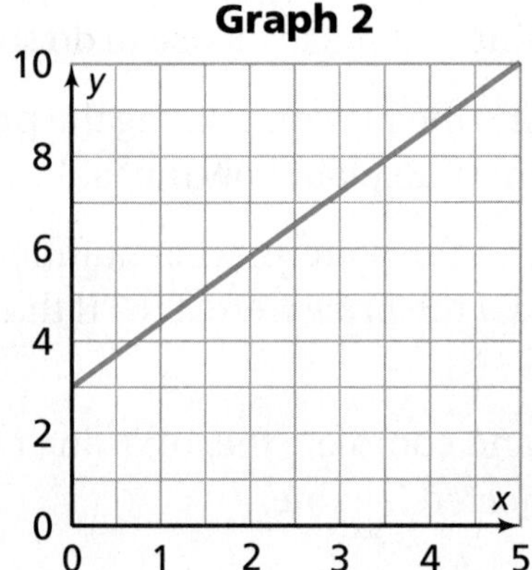

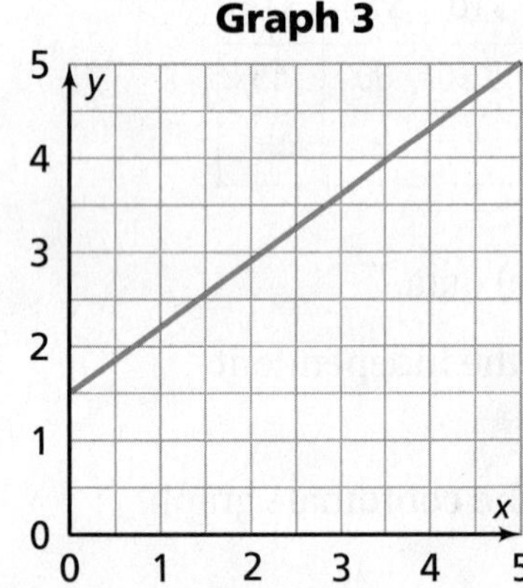

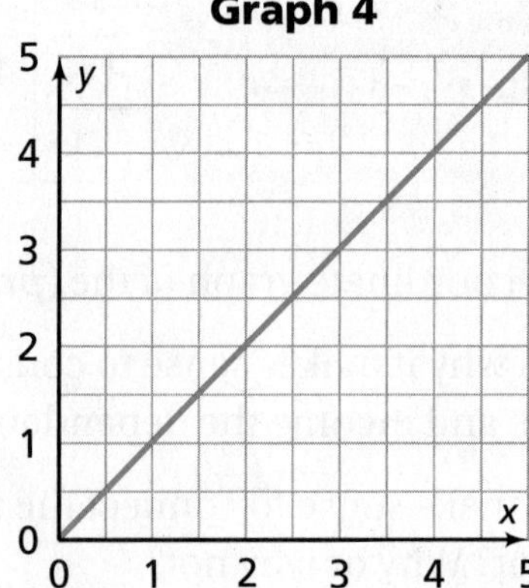

a. For each graph complete this statement: The graph shows that y increases by ▒ for every increase of 1 in x.

b. Which graph shows the dependent variable increasing most rapidly as the independent variable increases?

c. Which graph shows the dependent variable increasing most slowly as the independent variable increases?

Mathematical Reflections 2

In this Investigation, you looked at patterns relating the values of variables. You also thought about the ways that those patterns are shown in tables of values and coordinate graphs. The following questions will help you to summarize what you have learned.

Think about these questions. Discuss your ideas with other students and your teacher. Then write a summary of your findings in your notebook.

1. The word *variable* is used often to describe conditions in science and business.

   a. Explain what the word *variable* means when it is used in situations like those you studied in this Investigation.

   b. When are the words *independent* and *dependent* used to describe related variables? How are they used?

2. Suppose the values of a dependent variable increase as the values of a related independent variable increase. **How** is the relationship of the variables shown in each of the following?

   a. a table of values for the two variables

   b. a graph of values for the two variables

3. Suppose the values of a dependent variable decrease as the values of a related independent variable increase. **How** is the relationship of the variables shown in each of the following?

   a. a table of values for the two variables

   b. a graph of values for the two variables

Common Core Mathematical Practices

As you worked on the Problems in this Investigation, you used prior knowledge to make sense of the Problems. You also applied Mathematical Practices to solve the Problems. Think back over your work, the ways you thought about the Problems, and how you used Mathematical Practices.

Jayden described his thoughts in the following way:

We looked at two bicycle shops in Problem 2.1. We noticed that, for both shops, the rental cost increases as the number of bikes increases.

The cost for renting from Rocky starts higher. Beyond a certain point, Rocky's cost increases more slowly than the cost for renting from Adrian.

Another group noticed that Adrian charges a flat rate of $30 per bike. Rocky's charge per bike decreases as the number of bikes increases.

Then Mike, in a third group, graphed the costs for renting from Rocky. He noticed that the pattern resembles the pattern for jumping jacks. The points rise rapidly at first, but then the rate of increase gets smaller.

Common Core Standards for Mathematical Practice

MP8 Look for and express regularity in repeated reasoning.

- What other Mathematical Practices can you identify in Jayden's reasoning?
- Describe a Mathematical Practice that you and your classmates used to solve a different Problem in this Investigation.

Relating Variables With Equations

In the first two Investigations of this Unit, you used tables and graphs to study relationships between variables. It is helpful to express those relationships with rules. Those rules tell how to calculate the value of the dependent variable given the value of the independent variable.

In many cases, you can write the rules as algebraic equations or formulas. Working on the Problems of this Investigation will help you develop that skill.

Representations of Relationships
Problem Context

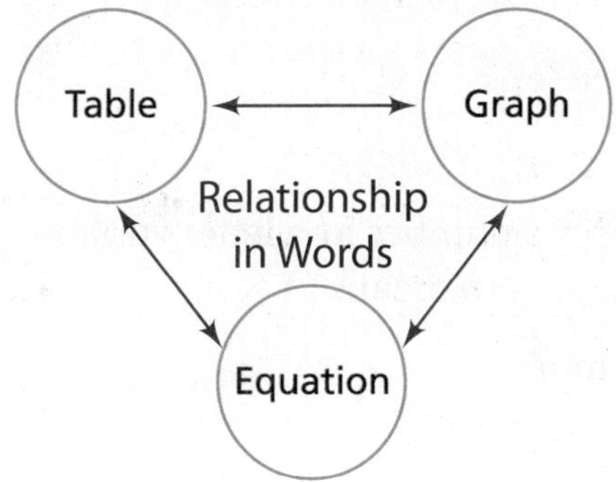

Common Core State Standards

6.EE.A.2 Write, read, and evaluate expressions in which letters stand for numbers.

6.EE.A.2c Evaluate expressions at specific values of their variables. Include expressions that arise from formulas used in real-world problems. Perform arithmetic operations, including those involving whole-number exponents, in the conventional order when there are no parentheses to specify a particular order (Order of Operations).

6.EE.B.7 Solve real-world and mathematical problems by writing and solving equations of the form $x + p = q$ and $px = q$ for cases in which p, q and x are all nonnegative rational numbers.

6.EE.C.9 Use variables to represent two quantities in a real-world problem that change in relationship to one another; write an equation to express one quantity, thought of as the dependent variable, in terms of the other quantity, thought of as the independent variable. Analyze the relationship between the dependent and independent variables using graphs and tables, and relate these to the equation.

Also 6.RP.A.2, 6.RP.A.3, 6.RP.A.3a, 6.RP.A.3b, 6.RP.A.3d, 6.EE.A.1, 6.EE.A.2a, 6.EE.A.3, 6.EE.A.4, 6.EE.B.6

3.1 Visit to Wild World

Equations With One Operation

On the last day of the Ocean Bike Tours trip, the riders will be near Wild World Amusement Park. They want to plan a stop there.

- What variables would affect the cost of the amusement park trip?
- How would those variables affect the cost?

Malcolm finds out that it costs $21 per person to visit Wild World. Liz suggests that they make a table or graph relating admission price to the number of people. However, Malcolm says there is a simple rule for calculating the cost:

The cost in dollars is equal to 21 times the number of people.

He wrote the rule as the statement:

$$\textit{cost} = 21 \times \textit{number of people}$$

Liz shortens Malcolm's statement by using single letters to stand for the variables. She uses c to stand for the cost and n to stand for the number of people:

$$c = 21 \times n$$

Note on Notation When you multiply a number by a letter variable, you can leave out the multiplication sign. So, $21n$ means $21 \times n$.

You can shorten the statement even more:

$$c = 21n$$

So, $21n$ is an **expression** for the total cost C. You obtain the total cost by multiplying 21, the cost per person, by n, the number of people. The fact that C and $21n$ are equal gives the **equation** $C = 21n$. Here, the number 21 is called the **coefficient** of the variable n.

The equation $c = 21n$ involves one calculation. You multiply the number of customers n by the cost per customer, $21. Many common equations involve one calculation.

Problem 3.1

A Theo wants to attract customers for the bike tour. He suggests a discount of $50 off the regular price for early registration.

1. What is the discounted price if the regular tour price is is $400? $500? $650?
2. Write an equation that represents the relationship of discounted price *D* to regular tour price *P*.

B When the Ocean Bike Tours partners set a price for customers, they need to find the 6% sales tax.

1. What is the sales tax if the tour price is $400? $500? $650?
2. Write an equation that represents the relationship of the amount of sales tax *T* to tour price *P*.

C Suppose a professional cyclist sustained a speed of about 20 miles per hour over a long race.

1. About how far would the cyclist travel in 2 hours? 3 hours? 3.5 hours?
2. At a speed of 20 miles per hour, how is the distance traveled *d* related to the time *t* (in hours)? Write an equation to represent the relationship.
3. Explain what information the coefficient of *t* represents.

D The trip from Williamsburg, Virginia, to Atlantic City, New Jersey, is about 350 miles.

1. How long will the trip take if the average speed of the van is 40 miles per hour? 50 miles per hour? 60 miles per hour?
2. Write an equation that shows how total trip time *t* depends on average driving speed *s*.

ACE Homework starts on page 76.

3.2 Moving, Texting, and Measuring

Using Rates and Rate Tables

There are many relationships between variables that you can write as algebraic equations. One simple type is especially important.

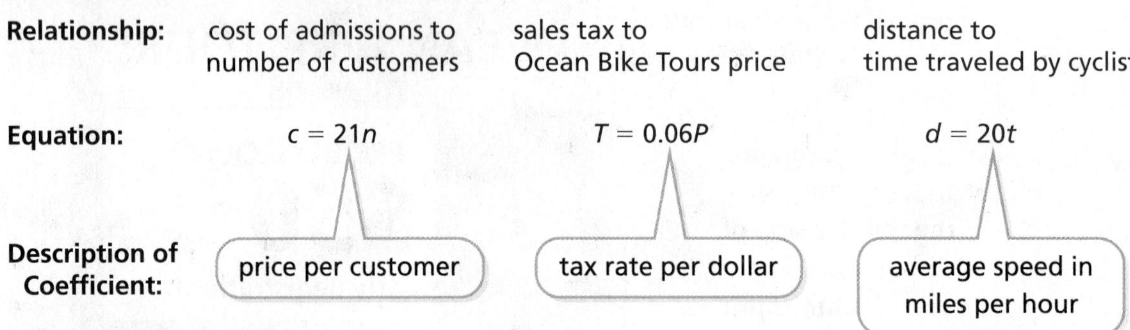

Relationships with rules in the form $y = mx$ occur often. It is important to understand the patterns in tables and graphs that those relationships produce. It is also useful to understand the special information provided in each case by m—the coefficient of x.

In these equations, the coefficient tells the **rate of change** in the dependent variable as the independent variable increases steadily.

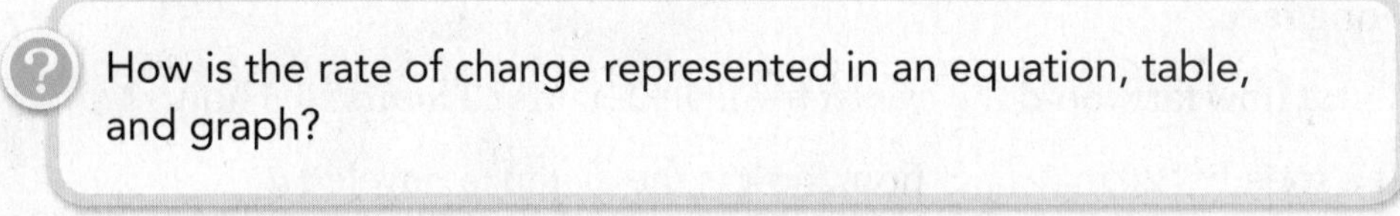

The questions in this Problem will develop your understanding and skill in working with rates in many different situations.

Problem 3.2

A When the bike tour is over, the riders will put their bikes and gear into vans and head back to Atlantic City.

1. Copy and complete the rate table to show how distance depends on time for different average speeds.

Distance Traveled at Different Average Speeds

Time (h)	Distance for Speed of 50 mi/h	Distance for Speed of 55 mi/h	Distance for Speed of 60 mi/h
0	0	■	■
1	50	■	■
2	100	■	■
3	■	■	■
4	■	■	■

2. Write an equation to show how distance d and time t are related for travel at each speed.
   - **a.** 50 miles per hour
   - **b.** 55 miles per hour
   - **c.** 60 miles per hour
3. Graph the (*time, distance*) data for all three speeds on the same coordinate grid. Use a different color for each speed.
4. For each of the three average speeds:
   - **a.** Look for patterns relating distance and time in the table and graph. Explain how the pattern shows up in the table and graph.
   - **b.** Theo observed that the coefficient of the independent variable in each equation is the average speed or unit rate. Is he correct? Explain.
5. **a.** Explain how you can use the table, graph, or equation to find the distance when $t = 6$ hours.
   - **b.** How can you use the table, graph, or equation to find the time when the distance is 275 miles? Explain.

continued on the next page >

Problem 3.2 continued

B A smartphone plan charges $.03 per text message.

1. a. Make a table of monthly charges for 0; 500; 1,000; 1,500; 2,000; and 2,500 text messages.

   b. Use the table. What is the cost for 1,000 messages? For 1,725 messages?

   c. Use the table. How many text messages were sent in a month if the charge for the messages is $75? $60? $18?

2. a. How is the monthly charge B for text messages related to the number of text messages n? Write an equation that represents the monthly charge for n messages.

   b. Use the equation you wrote in part (a) to find the cost for 1,250 text messages in one month.

3. a. Sketch a graph of the relationship between text message charges and number of messages.

   b. Explain how you could use the graph to answer the questions in parts (1b), (1c), and (2b).

C The metric and English system units for measuring length are related. The rule is that 1 inch is equal to about 2.5 centimeters.

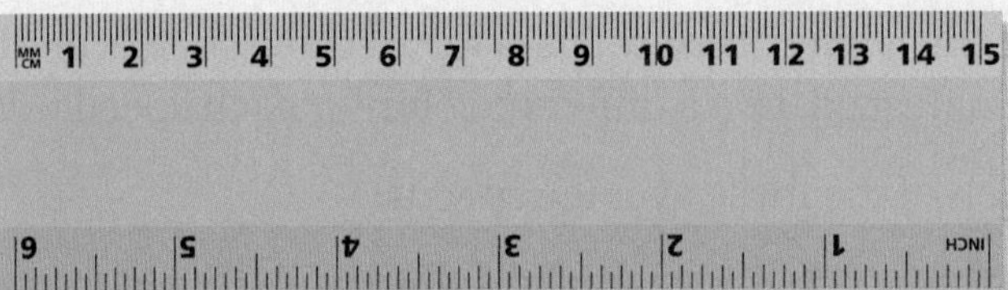

1. What is the length in centimeters of a line segment that has measure 5 inches? 12 inches? 7.5 inches?
2. How can you calculate the length in centimeters C of an object that you have measured in inches I? Write an equation to represent this calculation. Use the equation to find the number of centimeters that corresponds to 12 inches.
3. What is the approximate length in inches of a line segment that has measure 10 centimeters? 30 centimeters? 100 centimeters?
4. Sketch a graph of the relationship between length in centimeters and length in inches in part (2). Explain how you could use the graph to answer the questions in parts (1) and (3).

Problem 3.2 continued

D The equations you wrote in Questions A–C all have the form $y = mx$.

1. For each equation below, make a table of (x, y) values. Use whole-number values of x from 0 to 6. Then use your table to make a graph.

   a. $y = 2x$ **b.** $y = 0.5x$ **c.** $y = 1.5x$ **d.** $y = x$

2. Explain the connection between the number m and the pattern in the table of values and graph of $y = mx$.

3. **a.** Explain how you can find the value of y using a table, graph, or equation if $x = 2$.

   b. Explain how you can find the value of x using a table, graph or equation if $y = 6$.

4. Write a story to represent each equation in part (1).

E What similarities and differences do you find in the equations, tables, and graphs for the relationships in Questions A–D?

Homework starts on page 76.

3.3 Group Discounts and a Bonus Card

Equations With Two Operations

Each equation you wrote in Problems 3.1 and 3.2 involved only one operation (+, −, ×, ÷). Some equations involve two or more arithmetic operations. To write such equations, you can reason just as you do with one-operation equations:

- Identify the variables.
- Work out some specific numeric examples. Examine them carefully. Then, look for patterns in the calculations used.
- Write a rule in words to describe the general pattern in the calculations.
- Convert your rule to an equation with letter variables and symbols.
- Think about whether your equation makes sense. Test it for a few values to see if it works.

Problem 3.3

Liz and Theo want to visit Wild World with their friends. Theo checks if the park offers special prices for groups larger than 3 people. He finds this information on the park's Web site:

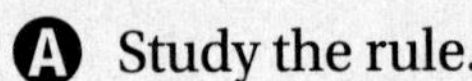

A Study the rule.

1. **a.** Make a table to show the admission price for groups of size 4, 8, 12, 16, 20, 24, 28, 32, 36, and 40 people. Then sketch a graph of the data.

   b. Describe the pattern of change that shows up in the table and graph.

2. **a.** Describe in words how you can calculate the admission price for a group with any number of people.

   b. Write an equation relating admission price p to group size n.

   c. How is this pattern of change in prices for group admissions similar to the pattern of change for the equations in Problem 3.2? How is it different?

3. **a.** Describe how you can use the table, graph, or equation to find the cost for 18 people.

   b. Describe how you can use the table or graph to find the number of people in the group if the total charge is $350 or $390.

Problem 3.3 continued

B Admission to Wild World includes a bonus card with 100 points that can be spent on rides. Rides cost 6 points each.

1. Copy and complete the table below to show a customer's bonus card balance after various numbers of rides.

Bonus Card Balance

Number of Rides	0	1	2	3	5	7	10	15
Points on Card	100	■	■	■	■	■	■	■

2. Explain how you can calculate the number of points left after any number of rides.
3. Write an equation showing the relationship between points left on the bonus card and number of rides taken.
4. How does cost per ride appear in the equation? How does the number of bonus points at the start appear in the equation?
5. Sketch a graph of the relationship between points left and number of rides for up to 20 rides. Describe the relationship between the variables.

C Liz wonders whether they should rent a cart to carry their backpacks. The equation $c = 20 + 5h$ shows the cost in dollars c of renting a cart for h hours.

1. What information does each number and variable in the expression $20 + 5h$ represent?
2. Use the equation to make a table showing the cost of renting a cart for 0, 1, 2, 3, 4, 5, and 6 hours. Then make a graph of the data.
3. Explain how the cost per hour shows up in the table, graph, and equation.
4. Explain how the 20 in the equation is represented in the table and in the graph.
5. Which of the following points satisfy the relationship represented by the equation? (0, 4), (0, 20), (7, 55) Explain your reasoning.

ACE Homework starts on page 76.

3.4 Getting the Calculation Right

Expressions and Order of Operations

The equation $p = 50 + 10n$ represents the relationship between the Wild World admission price p in dollars and the number of people n in a group. The right side of the equation $50 + 10n$ is an algebraic expression. It represents the value of the dependent variable, p. It involves two operations, addition and multiplication.

The critical question is, 'Which operation comes first?'

Theo wants to find the admission price for an Ocean Bike Tours group with 17 members. He first works from left to right:

$$50 + 10 \times 17$$
$$= 60 \times 17$$
$$= 1{,}020$$

He gets a number that seems too large.

Then Theo enters the same expression on his calculator and gets:

$$50 + 10*17 = 220$$

He is puzzled by the difference in results. Then Theo remembers that there are rules for evaluating expressions.

- Which is the correct answer? Why?

Here are the rules known as the Order of Operations:

1. Work within parentheses.
2. Write numbers written with exponents in standard form.
3. Do all multiplication and division in order from left to right.
4. Do all addition and subtraction in order from left to right.

Use the Order of Operations with $7 + (6 \times 4 - 9) \div 3$.

$$7 + (6 \times 4 - 9) \div 3 = 7 + (24 - 9) \div 3$$
$$= 7 + (15) \div 3$$
$$= 7 + 5$$
$$= 12$$

Problem 3.4

Practice the Order of Operations rules on these examples.

A The group admission price at Wild World is given by the equation $p = 50 + 10n$. Find the prices for groups with 5, 11, and 23 members.

B The equation $b = 100 - 6r$ gives the number of points left on a Wild World bonus card after r rides. Find the numbers of points left after 3, 7, and 14 rides.

C Celia makes plans for the van ride home to Atlantic City from Williamsburg. She plans for a 2-hour stop in Baltimore, Maryland. To predict trip time t from average driving speed s, she writes the equation

$$t = 2 + \frac{350}{s}$$

Find the predicted trip times for average driving speeds of 45, 55, and 65 miles per hour.

D Sidney writes two equations: $I = 350n$ and $E = 150n + 1000$. The equations relate income I and operating expenses E to number of customers.

Sidney writes the equation $P = 350n - (150n + 1000)$ to show how tour profit P depends on the number of customers n. Use the rule to find profits P for 8, 12, 20, and 30 customers.

E The Ocean Bike Tours partners have an Atlantic City workshop in the shape of a cube. The formula for the surface area of a cube is $A = 6s^2$. The formula for the volume of a cube is $V = s^3$.

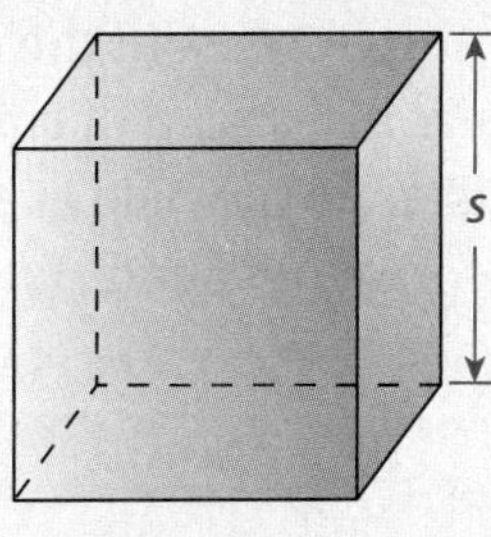

Area = $6s^2$
Volume = s^3

1. If each edge of the cubical workshop is 4.25 meters long, what is the total surface area of the floor, walls, and ceiling?
2. What is the volume of the workshop?

ACE Homework starts on page 76.

Applications | Connections | Extensions

Applications

1. a. Natasha charges $12 per hour for babysitting in her neighborhood. What equation relates her pay for a job to the number of hours she works?

   b. A gasoline service station offers 20 cents off the regular price per gallon every Tuesday. What equation relates the discounted price to the regular price on that day?

   c. Write an equation to show how the perimeter of a square is related to the length of a side of the square.

   d. A middle school wants to have its students see a movie at a local theater. The total cost of the theater and movie rental is $1,500. What equation shows how the cost per student depends on the number of students who attend?

2. Celia writes the equation $d = 8t$ to represent the distance in miles d that riders could travel in t hours at a speed of 8 miles per hour. Make a table that shows the distance traveled every half hour, up to 5 hours, if riders travel at this constant speed.

3. A girls' basketball team is playing in the Texas state championship game. They are going 560 miles from El Paso to San Antonio. Their bus travels at an average speed of 60 miles per hour.

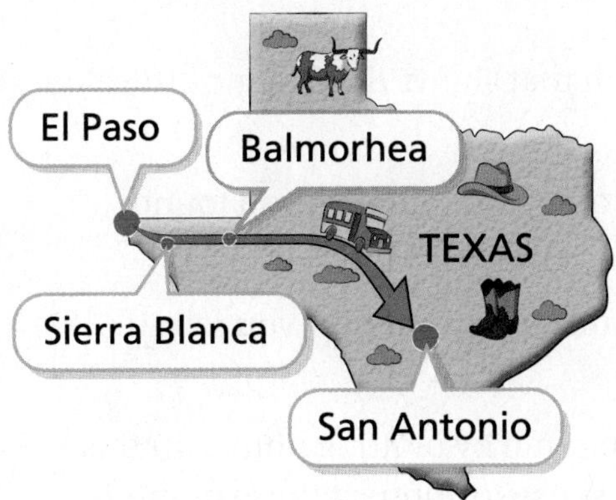

a. Suppose the bus travels at an almost steady speed throughout the trip. Make a table and a graph of time and distance data for the bus.

b. Estimate the distance the bus travels in 2 hours, $2\frac{3}{4}$ hours, $3\frac{1}{2}$ hours, and 7.25 hours.

c. Describe in words and with an equation a rule you could use to calculate the distance traveled for any given time on this trip.

d. The bus route passes through Sierra Blanca, which is 90 miles from El Paso. About how long does it take the bus to get to Sierra Blanca?

e. The bus route also passes through Balmorhea, which is $\frac{1}{3}$ of the way from El Paso to San Antonio. About how long does it take the bus to get to Balmorhea?

f. How long does it take the bus to complete its 560-mile trip to San Antonio?

g. Explain in words and with an equation how time t for the 560-mile trip depends on average speed s.

h. Use the rule from part (g) to calculate trip time if the average bus speed is 50 miles per hour, 45 miles per hour, and 70 miles per hour.

4. The equation $d = 70t$ represents the distance in miles covered after traveling at 70 miles per hour for t hours.

a. Make a table that shows the distance traveled every half hour from 0 hours to 4 hours.

b. Sketch a coordinate graph that shows the distance traveled between 0 and 4 hours.

c. What is d when $t = 2.5$ hours? Explain how you found your answer.

d. What is t when $d = 210$ miles? Explain how you found your answer.

e. You probably made your graph by plotting points. In this situation, would it make sense to connect these points?

5. The table shows the relationship between the number of riders on a bike tour and the daily cost of providing box lunches.

Bike Tour Box Lunch Costs

Number of Riders	1	2	3	4	5	6	7	8	9
Lunch Cost	$4.25	$8.50	$12.75	$17.00	$21.25	$25.50	$29.75	$34.00	$38.25

a. Explain in words and with an equation how lunch cost L depends on the number of riders n.

b. Use your equation to find the lunch cost for 25 riders.

c. How many riders could eat lunch for $89.25? Explain how you found your answer.

For Exercises 6–8, use the equation to complete the table.

6. $y = 4x + 3$

x	1	2	5	10	20	■
y	■	■	■	■	■	203

7. $m = 100 - k$

k	1	2	5	10	20	■
m	■	■	■	■	■	50

8. $d = 3.5t$

t	1	2	5	10	20	■
d	■	■	■	■	■	140

9. Sean plans to buy a new tablet for $315. The store offers him an interest-free payment plan that allows him to pay in monthly installments of $25.

a. How much will Sean still owe after one payment? After two payments? After three payments?

b. Explain in words how the amount owed depends on the number of payments made. Then write an equation for calculating the amount owed a for any number of payments n.

c. Use your equation to make a table and graph showing the relationship between n and a.

d. As n increases by 1, how does a change? How is this change shown in the table? How is it shown on the graph?

e. How many payments will Sean have to make in all? How is this shown in the table? How is it shown on the graph?

For Exercises 10–13, express each rule with an equation. Use single letters to stand for the variables. Identify what each letter represents.

10. The area of a rectangle is its length multiplied by its width.

11. The number of hot dogs needed for a picnic is two for each student.

12. The amount of material needed to make curtains is 4 square yards per window.

13. Taxi fare is \$2.00 plus \$1.10 per mile.

14. The sales tax in a state is 8%. Write an equation for the amount of tax t on an item that costs d dollars.

15. Potatoes sell for \$.25 per pound at the produce market. Write an equation for the cost c of p pounds of potatoes.

16. A cellphone family plan costs \$49 per month plus \$.05 per text. Write an equation for the monthly bill b when t texts are sent.

For Exercises 17–19, describe the relationship between the variables in words and with an equation.

17.

x	0	1	2	5	10	20
y	0	4	8	20	40	80

18.

s	0	1	2	3	6	12
t	50	49	48	47	44	38

19.

n	0	1	2	3	4	5
z	1	6	11	16	21	26

20. Multiple Choice Which equation describes the relationship in the table?

n	0	1	2	3	4	5	6
C	10	20	30	40	50	60	70

A. $C = 10n$

B. $C = 10 + n$

C. $C = 10$

D. $C = 10 + 10n$

21. Use the Order of Operations to evaluate each algebraic expression when $n = 5$ and when $n = 10$.

a. $3n - 12$

b. $45 - 3n$

c. $7(4n + 2) - 8$

d. $3(n - 4)^2 + 9$

Connections

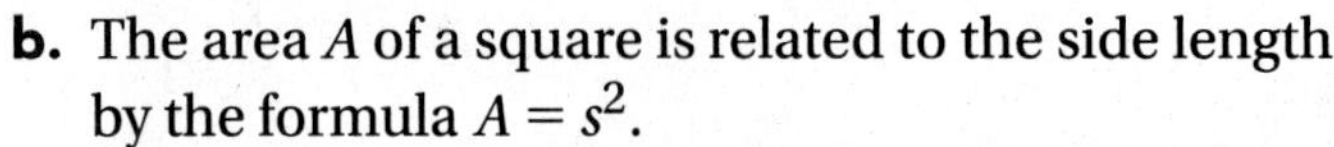

22. **a.** The perimeter P of a square is related to the side length s by the formula $P = 4s$.

Make a table showing how the perimeter of a square increases as the side length increases from 1 to 6 in 1-unit steps. Describe the pattern of change.

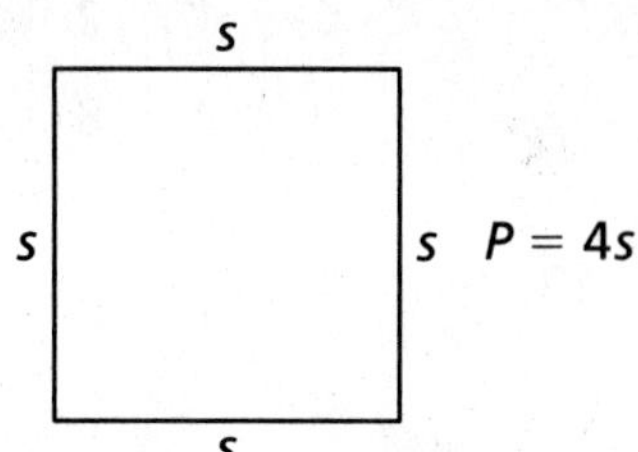

b. The area A of a square is related to the side length by the formula $A = s^2$.

Add a row to the table in part (a) to show how the area of the square increases as the side length increases. Describe the pattern of change.

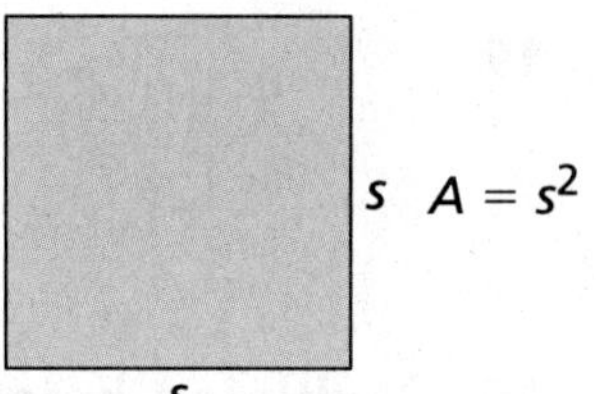

For Exercises 23–25, find the indicated value or values.

23. the tenth odd number (1 is the first odd number, 3 is the second odd number, and so on.)

24. the area of a triangle with a base of 10 centimeters and a height of 15 centimeters

25. $3^3 \times 5^2 \times 7$

For Exercises 26–30, write a formula for the given quantity.

26. the area A of a rectangle with length l and width w

27. the area A of a parallelogram with base b and height h

28. the perimeter P of a rectangle with base b and height h

29. the nth odd number, O (1 is the first odd number, 3 is the second odd number, and so on.)

30. the area A of a triangle with base b and height h

For Exercises 31 and 32, copy and complete the table of values for the given equation.

31. a. $y = x + \frac{1}{2}$

x	$\frac{1}{5}$	$\frac{1}{4}$	$\frac{1}{3}$	$\frac{2}{5}$	$\frac{1}{2}$	$\frac{2}{3}$	$\frac{3}{4}$	5
y	■	■	■	■	■	■	■	■

b. $y = x - \frac{1}{2}$

x	$\frac{1}{2}$	$\frac{2}{3}$	$\frac{3}{4}$	1	$1\frac{1}{2}$	2	3	4
y	■	■	■	■	■	■	■	■

32. a. $y = \frac{1}{2}x$

x	$\frac{1}{5}$	$\frac{1}{4}$	$\frac{1}{3}$	$\frac{2}{5}$	$\frac{1}{2}$	$\frac{2}{3}$	$\frac{3}{4}$	5
y	■	■	■	■	■	■	■	■

b. $y = \frac{1}{2} \div x$

x	$\frac{1}{5}$	$\frac{1}{4}$	$\frac{1}{3}$	$\frac{2}{5}$	$\frac{1}{2}$	$\frac{2}{3}$	$\frac{3}{4}$	5
y	■	■	■	■	■	■	■	■

For Exercises 33–35, describe in words the relationship between *x* and *y*.

33.

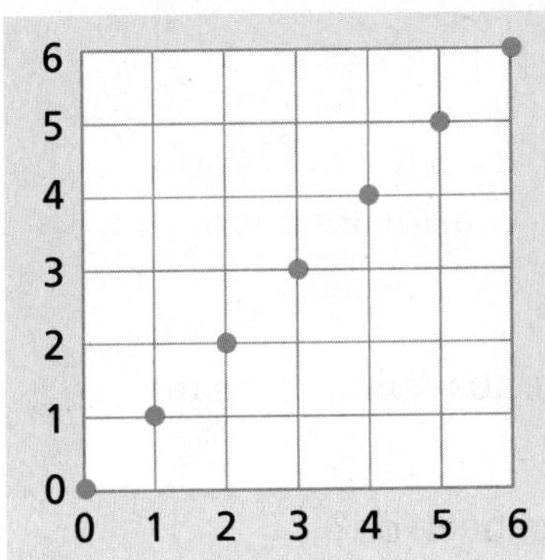

34.

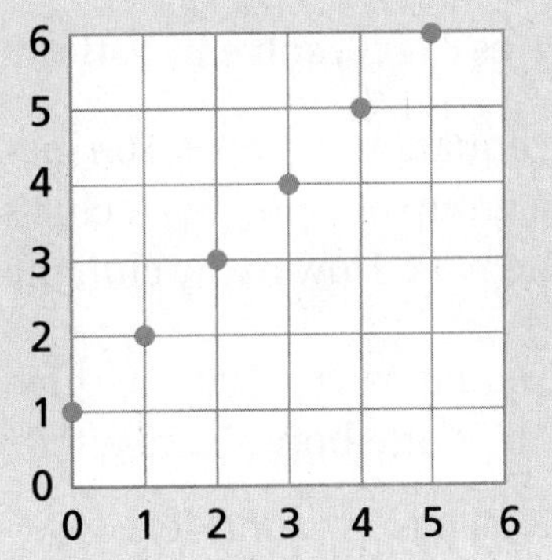

35.

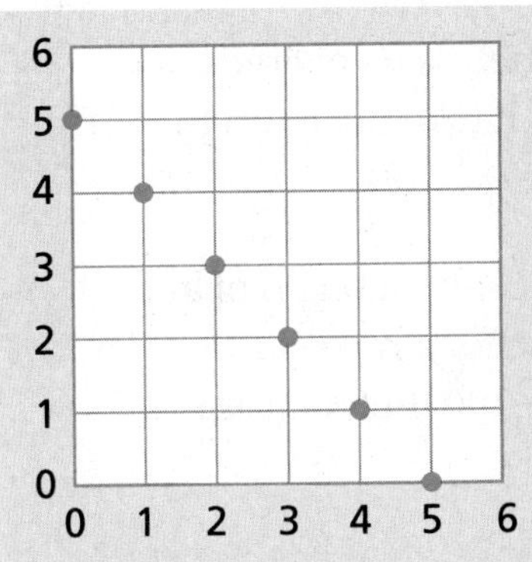

Extensions

36. You can calculate the average speed of a car trip if you know the distance and time traveled.

a. Copy and complete the table below.

Car Trips

Distance (mi)	Time (h)	Average Speed (mi/h)
145	2	■
110	2	■
165	2.5	■
300	5.25	■
446	6.75	■
528	8	■

b. Write a formula for calculating the average speed s for any given distance d and time t.

For Exercises 37–40, solve by estimating and checking.

37. The equation $p = 50 + 10n$ gives the admission price p to Wild World for a group of n people. A club's budget has \$500 set aside for a visit to the park. How many club members can go?

38. The equation $b = 100 - 6r$ gives the number of bonus points b left on a Wild World bonus card after r rides.

a. Rosi has 34 points left. How many rides has she been on?

b. Dwight has 16 points left. How many rides has he been on?

39. The equation $d = 2.5t$ describes the distance in meters d covered by a canoe-racing team in t seconds. How long does it take the team to go 125 meters? 400 meters?

40. The equation $d = 400 - 2.5t$ describes the distance in meters d of a canoe-racing team from the finish line t seconds after a race starts. When is the team 175 meters from the finish line? 100 meters from the finish line?

41. Armen builds models from rods. When he builds bridges, he makes the sides using patterns of triangles like the ones below. The total number of rods depends on the number of rods along the bottom.

Rods along bottom = 3

Total number of rods = 11

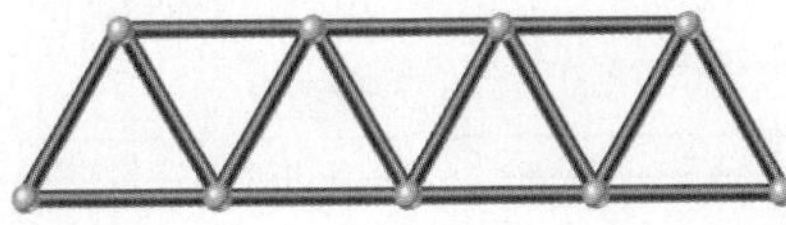

Rods along bottom = 4

Total number of rods = 15

a. Copy and complete the table.

Rod Bridges

Rods Along the Bottom	1	2	3	4	5	6	7	8	9	10
Total Number of Rods	3	7	11	■	■	■	■	■	■	■

b. Write an equation relating the total number of rods t to the number of rods along the bottom b. Explain how the formula you write relates to the way Armen puts the rods together.

c. For the design below, make a table and write an equation relating the total number of rods t to the number of rods along the bottom b.

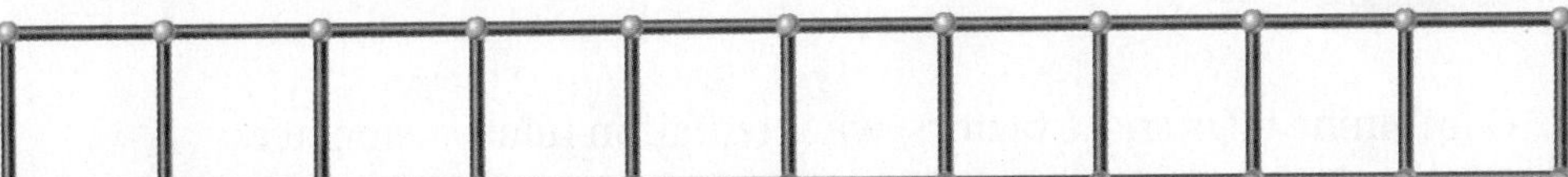

42. The Ocean Bike Tours partners decided to include a visit to Wild World Amusement Park as part of the tour. These are the cost and income factors:

a. Combining all of these factors, what equation relates expected tour profit P to the number of customers n who take the trip?

b. For what number of customers will a tour group produce profit greater than $500?

Mathematical Reflections 3

In this Investigation, you wrote algebraic equations to express relationships between variables. You analyzed the relationships using tables and graphs. You also related the tables and graphs to the equations you wrote. The following questions will help you summarize what you have learned.

Think about these questions. Discuss your ideas with other students and your teacher. Then write a summary of your findings in your notebook.

1. **What** strategies help in finding equations to express relationships?

2. For relationships given by equations in the form $y = mx$:

a. **How** does the value of y change as the value of x increases?

b. **How** is the pattern of change shown in a table, graph, and equation of the function?

3. **a.** In this Unit, you have represented relationships between variables with tables, graphs, and equations. **List** some advantages and disadvantages of each of these representations.

b. If the value of one variable in a relationship is known, **describe** how you can use a table, graph, or equation to find a value of the other variable.

Common Core Mathematical Practices

As you worked on the Problems in this Investigation, you used prior knowledge to make sense of them. You also applied Mathematical Practices to solve the Problems. Think back over your work, the ways you thought about the Problems, and how you used Mathematical Practices.

Tori described her thoughts in the following way:

We looked for patterns among the graphs and equations in Problem 3.1.

We noticed something about the graphs for the equations of the form $y = mx$. They all contained the point $(1, m)$. Kelly said that m is also the unit rate.

Common Core Standards for Mathematical Practice

MP8 Look for and express regularity in repeated reasoning.

- What other Mathematical Practices can you identify in Tori's reasoning?
- Describe a Mathematical Practice that you and your classmates used to solve a different Problem in this Investigation.

Expressions, Equations, and Inequalities

Working on Investigation 3 developed your skill in writing expressions for relationships between independent and dependent variables. The Problems of this Investigation deal with three more questions about such relationships between variables:

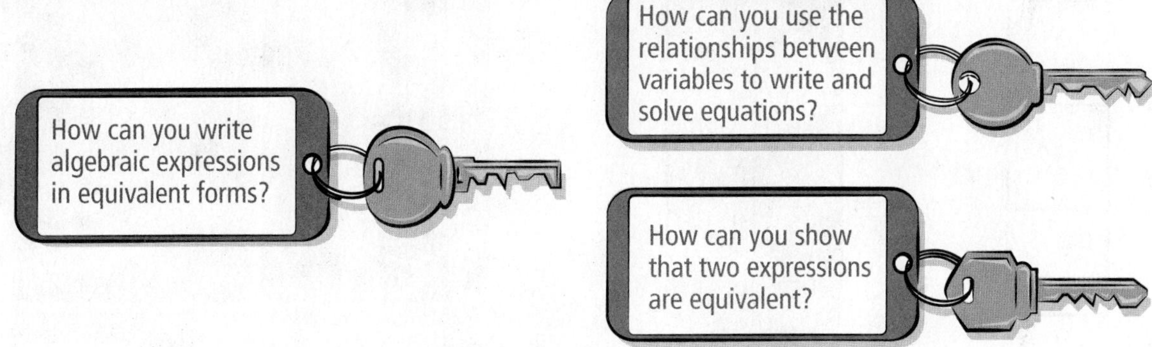

Answers to these questions are key ideas of algebra.

Common Core State Standards

6.EE.A.3 Apply the properties of operations to generate equivalent expressions.

6.EE.B.5 Understand solving an equation or inequality as a process of answering a question: which values from a specified set, if any, make the equation or inequality true? Use substitution to determine whether a given number in a specified set makes an equation or inequality true.

6.EE.B.7 Solve real-world and mathematical problems by writing and solving equations of the form $x + p = q$ and $px = q$ for cases in which p, q and x are all nonnegative rational numbers.

6.EE.B.8 Write an inequality of the form $x > c$ or $x < c$ to represent a constraint or condition in a real-world or mathematical problem. Recognize that inequalities of the form $x > c$ or $x < c$ have infinitely many solutions; represent solutions of such inequalities on number line diagrams.

Also 6.RP.A.3a, 6.RP.A.3b, 6.EE.A.2, 6.EE.A.2a, 6.EE.A.2b, 6.EE.A.2c, 6.EE.A.4, 6.EE.B.6, 6.EE.C.9

4.1 Taking the Plunge
Equivalent Expressions I

One of the most popular rides at Wild World is the Sky Dive. Riders are lifted in a car 250 feet in the air. When the car is released, it falls back to the ground. It reaches a speed near 50 miles per hour.

The riders' seats are around a tower that looks like a stack of cubes made from steel pieces. Each face of the Sky Dive tower looks like a ladder of squares.

Ladder

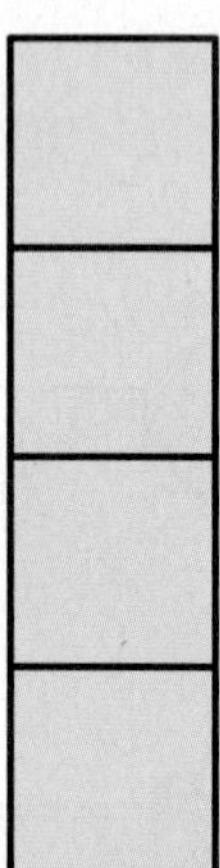

Tower

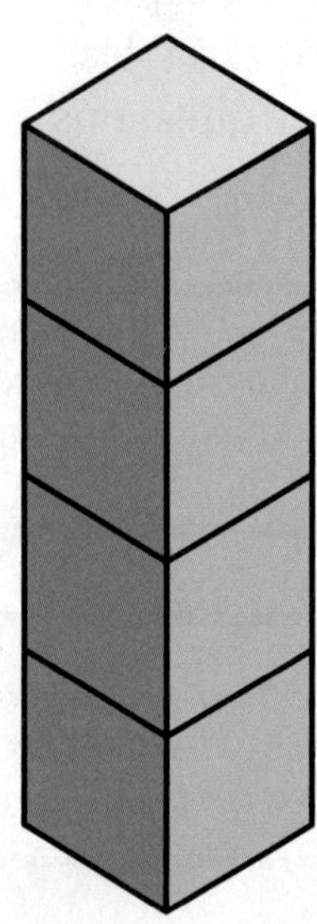

- How many steel pieces do you need to build each of these figures?

Suppose that you were building the tower for a similar ride.

- How many steel pieces would you need to make a ladder of n squares?
- How many steel pieces would you need to make a tower of n cubes?

As you work on these questions, it might help to make some model ladders using toothpicks.

Problem 4.1

A **1.** Look at the ladder of squares. What numbers would go in the second row of this table?

Number of Squares	1	2	3	4	5	10	20
Number of Pieces	4	■	■	■	■	■	■

2. Write an equation that shows how to find the number of pieces P needed to make a ladder of n squares.

B **1.** Look at the tower of cubes. What numbers would go in the second row of a table that counts steel pieces needed to make a tower of n cubes?

Number of Cubes	1	2	3	4	5	10	20
Number of Pieces	12	■	■	■	■	■	■

2. Write an equation that shows how to find the number of steel pieces in a tower of n cubes.

ACE Homework starts on page 100.

4.2 More Than One Way to Say It

Equivalent Expressions II

A group of students worked on the ladder problem. Four of them came up with equations relating the number of steel pieces P to the number of squares n.

Tabitha: $P = n + n + n + 1$	Chaska: $P = 1 + 3n$
Latrell: $P = 4n$	Eva: $P = 4 + 3(n - 1)$

Recall that groups of mathematical symbols such as $n + n + n + 1$, $1 + 3n$, $4n$, and $4 + 3(n - 1)$ are called *algebraic expressions.* Each expression represents the value of the dependent variable P. When two expressions give the same results for every value of the variable, they are called **equivalent expressions.**

 Which expressions for P are equivalent? Explain why.

Problem 4.2

A

1. What thinking might have led the students to their ideas?
2. Do the four equations predict the same numbers of steel pieces for ladders of any height n? Test your ideas by comparing values of P when $n = 1$, 5, 10, and 20.
3. Which of the expressions for the number of steel pieces in a ladder of n squares are equivalent? Explain why.
4. Are any of the expressions equivalent to your own from Problem 4.1? How can you be sure?

B

1. Think about building a tower of cubes. Write two more expressions that are equivalent to the expression you wrote in part (2) of Question B in Problem 4.1. Explain why they are equivalent.

2. Pick two equivalent expressions from part (1). Use them to generate a table and graph for each. Compare the tables and graphs.

ACE Homework starts on page 100.

4.3 Putting It All Together

Equivalent Expressions III

In an expression such as $1 + 3n$, the 1 and the $3n$ are called **terms** of the expression. In the expression $4 + 3(n - 1)$ there are 2 terms, 4 and $3(n - 1)$. Note that the expression $(n - 1)$ is both a factor of the term $3(n - 1)$ and a difference of two terms. The 3 is the **coefficient** of n in the expression $1 + 3n$.

The Distributive Property helps to show that two expressions are equivalent. It states that for any numbers a, b, and c the following is true:

$$a(b + c) = ab + ac$$

This means that:

- A number can be expressed both as a product and as a sum.
- The area of a rectangle can be found in two different ways.

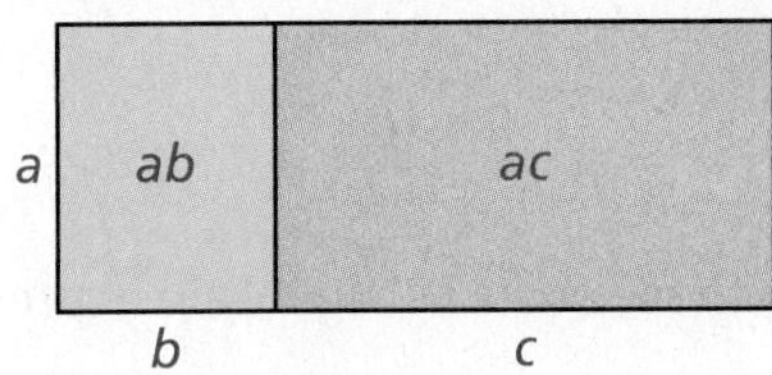

The expression $a(b + c)$ is in *factored form.*

The expression $a(b) + a(c)$ is in *expanded form.*

The expressions $a(b + c)$ and $ab + ac$ are *equivalent expressions.*

- Use the Distributive Property to write an equivalent expression for $5x + 6x$.
- How does this help write an equivalent expression for $n + n + n + 1$?

With their plans almost complete, the Ocean Bike Tours partners have made a list of tour operating costs.

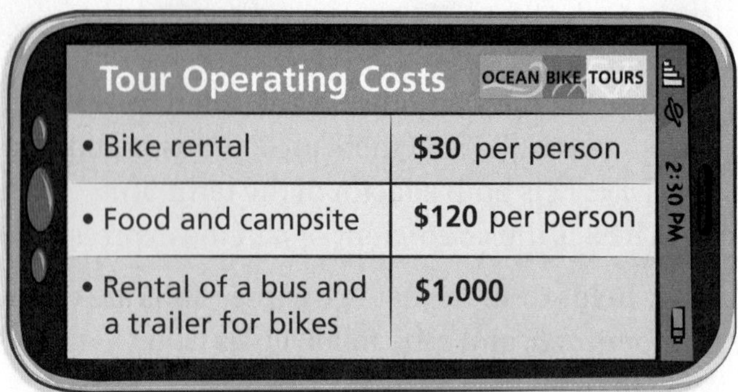

Tour Operating Costs	OCEAN BIKE TOURS
• Bike rental	$30 per person
• Food and campsite	$120 per person
• Rental of a bus and a trailer for bikes	$1,000

- What equation can represent the total costs?
- Is there more than one possible equation? Explain.

Problem 4.3

The next step in planning is to write these costs as algebraic expressions.

A What equations show how the three cost variables depend on the number of riders n?

1. bike rental $B = \blacksquare$
2. food and campsite fees $F = \blacksquare$
3. rental of the bus and trailer $R = \blacksquare$

B Three of the business partners write equations that relate total tour cost C to the number of riders n:

Celia's equation: $C = 30n + 120n + 1000$

Theo's equation: $C = 150n + 1000$

Liz's equation: $C = 1150n$

1. **a.** Are any or all of these equations correct? If so, are they equivalent? Explain why.

   b. For the equations that are correct, explain what information each term and coefficient represents in the equation.

Problem 4.3 continued

2. Compare the equations. Use Order of Operations guidelines to complete the table below of sample (n, C) values. What does the table suggest about which expressions for C are equivalent?

Operating Cost Related to Number of Customers

Number of Customers n	5	10	15	20	25
$C = 30n + 120n + 1000$	■	■	■	■	■
$C = 150n + 1000$	■	■	■	■	■
$C = 1150n$	■	■	■	■	■

3. What results would you expect if you were to graph the three equations below?

$$C = 30n + 120n + 1000$$

$$C = 150n + 1000$$

$$C = 1150n$$

Check your ideas by graphing.

4. Use properties of operations such as the Distributive Property to show which expressions for cost are equivalent.

C 1. For each expression below, list the terms and the coefficient in each term.

a. $5x + x + 6$ **b.** $10q - 2q$

2. Use the properties of operations to write an equivalent expression for each expression above.

3. Show that $1 + 3n = 4 + 3(n - 1)$.

D Sidney points out that all three partners left out the cost of the Wild World Amusement Park trip. The cost for that part of the tour is $W = 50 + 10n$. How does this cost factor change each correct equation?

ACE Homework starts on page 100.

4.4 Finding the Unknown Value

Solving Equations

The Ocean Bike Tours partners decide to charge \$350 per rider. This leads them to an equation giving tour income I for n riders: $I = 350n$. You can use the equation to find the income for 10 riders.

$$I = 350n$$

$$I = 350 \times 10$$

$$I = 3{,}500$$

Suppose you are asked to find the number of riders needed to reach a tour income goal of \$4,200. In earlier work you used tables and graphs to estimate answers. You can also use the equation: $4{,}200 = 350n$.

Solving the equation means finding values of n that makes the equation $4{,}200 = 350n$ a true statement. Any values of n that work are called **solutions of the equation.**

One way to solve equations is to think about the fact families that relate arithmetic operations. Examples:

$5 + 7 = 12$
$5 = 12 - 7$

Both equations describe true relationships between 5, 7, and 12.

$5(7) = 35$
$5 = 35 \div 7$

Both equations describe true relationships between 5, 7, and 35.

- How are fact families helpful to solve equations such as $c = 350n$?

When you find the solution of an equation, it is always a good idea to check your work.

Is $n = 12$ a solution for $4{,}200 = 35n$?

Substitute 12 for n: $4{,}200 = 35(12)$.

Is this a true statement?

Multiplying 35 by 12 equals 4,200.

Yes, 12 is the solution.

Problem 4.4

A Single admissions at Wild World Amusement Park cost \$21. If the park sells n single admissions in one day, its income is $I = 21n$.

1. Write an equation to answer this question: How many single admissions were sold on a day the park had income of \$9,450 from single admissions?
2. Solve the equation. Explain how you found your answer.
3. How can you check your answer?

B On the Ocean Bike Tours test run, Sidney stopped the van at a gas station. The station advertised 25 cents off per gallon on Tuesdays.

1. Write an equation for the Tuesday discount price d. Use p as the price on other days.
2. Use the equation to find the price on days other than Tuesday if the discount price is \$2.79.

C Ocean Bike Tours wants to provide bandanas for each person. The cost of the bandanas is \$95.50 for the design plus \$1 per bandana.

1. Write an equation that represents this relationship.
2. Use the equation to find the cost for 50 bandanas.
3. Use the equation to find the number bandanas if the total cost is \$116.50.

In Questions A–C you wrote and solved equations that match questions about the bike tour. Knowing about the problem situation often helps in writing and solving equations. But the methods you use in those cases can be applied to other equations without stories to help your reasoning.

D Use ideas you've learned about solving equations to solve the equations below. Show your calculations. Check each solution in the equation.

1. $x + 22.5 = 49.25$
2. $37.2 = n - 12$
3. $55t = 176$

ACE Homework starts on page 100.

4.5 It's Not Always Equal

Solving Inequalities

In each part of Problem 4.4 you wrote and solved an equation about Ocean Bike Tours. For example, you wrote the equation $21I = C$. Then you were told that income was $9,450. You solved the equation $21I = 9{,}450$ to find the number of riders. The solution was $I = 450$.

Suppose you were asked a related question: How many single-admission sales will bring income of more than $9,450?

To answer this question, you need to solve the inequality $21I > 9{,}450$. That is, you need to find values of the variable I that make the given inequality true. This task is very similar to what you did when comparing rental plans offered by the two bike shops in Problem 2.1.

If $21I = 9{,}450$, then $I = 450$. So, any number $I > 450$ is a solution to the inequality $21I > 9{,}450$. A graph of these solutions on a number line is:

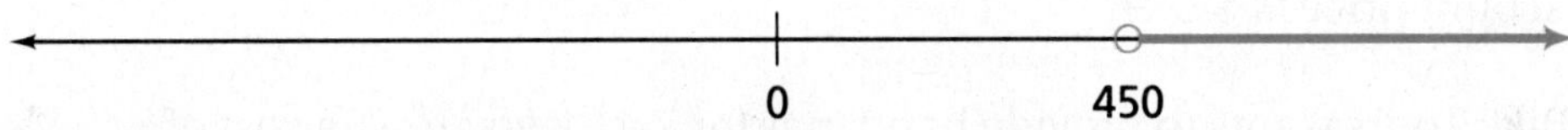

- What are five possible solutions for I?
- What are five more possible solutions for I?
- How many possible solutions does this inequality have?

In general, the solution to a simple inequality can be written in the form $x > c$ or $x < c$. Those solutions can be graphed on a number line. Below are two examples.

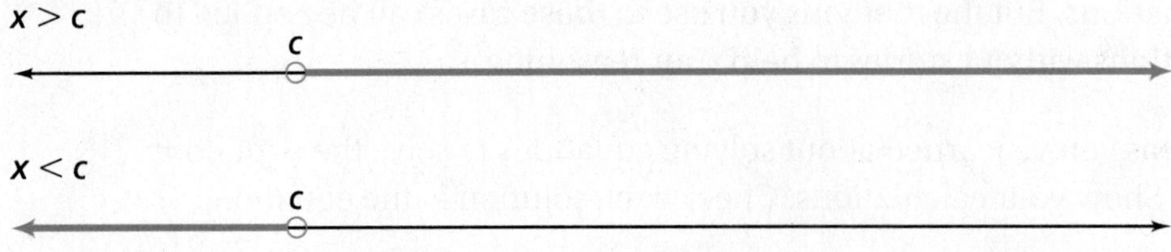

- What does the thicker part of each number line tell you about solutions to the inequality?

Problem 4.5

Use what you know about variables, expressions, and equations to write and solve inequalities that match Questions A–C. In each case, do the following.

- Write an inequality that helps to answer the question.
- Give at least 3 specific number solutions to the inequality. Then explain why they work.
- Describe all possible solutions.

A The bungee jump at Wild World charges \$35. How many jumpers are needed for the jump to earn income of more than \$1,050 in a day?

B A gas station sign says regular unleaded gasoline costs \$4 per gallon. How much gas can Mike buy if he has \$17.50 in his pocket?

C Ocean Bike Tours wants to provide bandanas for each customer. The costs are \$95.50 for the design plus \$1 per bandana. How many bandanas can they buy if they want the cost to be less than \$400?

D Use ideas about solving equations and inequalities from Questions A, B, and C to solve the inequalities below.

1. $84 < 14m$
2. $55t > 176$
3. $x + 22.5 < 49.25$
4. $37.2 > n - 12$

E Draw number lines to graph the solutions to all inequalities in Question D.

F
1. Make up a problem that can be represented by the equation $y = 50 + 4x$.
2. Which of these points lie on the graph of the equation? (8, 92), (15, 110)
3. Use a point that lies on the graph to make up a question that the point can answer.
4. Use a point that lies on the graph to write an inequality that the point satisfies.

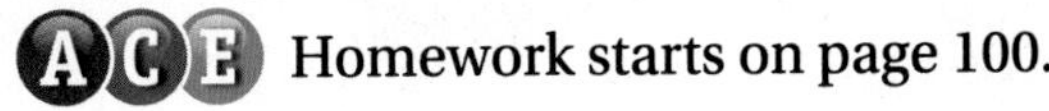

Homework starts on page 100.

Applications

For Exercises 1–3, use the toothpick patterns created by Scott, Ahna, and Lloyd.

1. Scott's Pattern

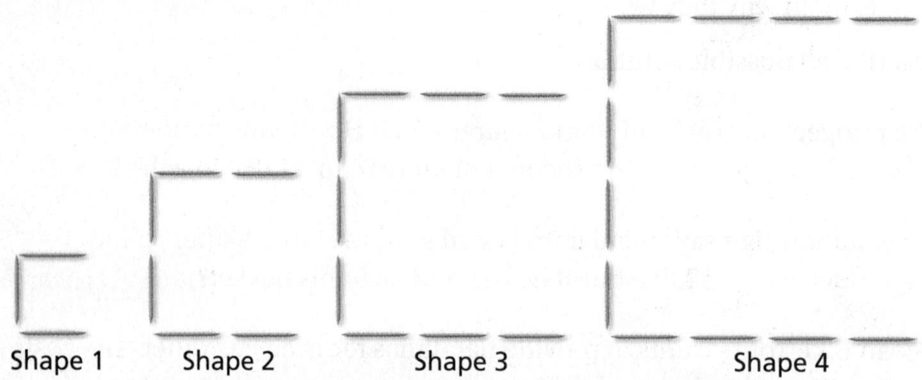

a. Look at the table comparing the shape number to the number of toothpicks. What numbers go in the second row?

Shape Number	4	5	6	7	8	10	20
Number of Toothpicks	12	■	■	■	■	■	■

b. What equation shows how to find the number of toothpicks needed for shape number n?

c. Is there a different equation you could write for part (b)?

2. Ahna's Pattern

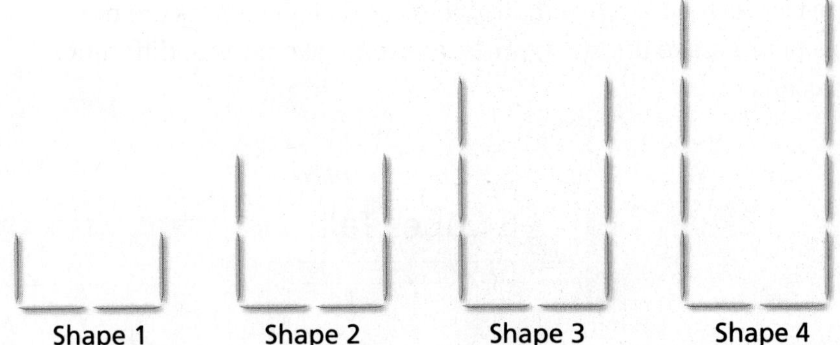

a. What numbers go in the second row of the table comparing the shape number to the number of toothpicks?

Shape Number	4	5	6	7	8	10	20
Number of Toothpicks	10	■	■	■	■	■	■

b. What equation shows how to find the number of toothpicks needed for shape number n?

c. How are Ahna and Scott's Patterns similar or different?

3. Lloyd's Pattern

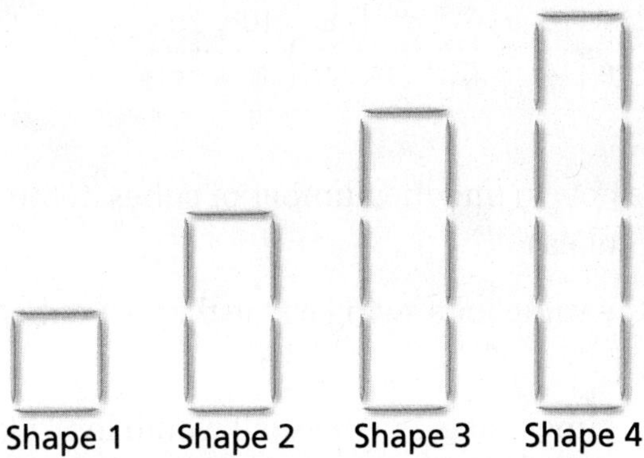

a. What numbers go in the second row of a table comparing the shape number to the number of toothpicks?

Shape Number	4	5	6	7	8	10	20
Number of Toothpicks	10	■	■	■	■	■	■

b. What equation shows the number of toothpicks needed for shape number n?

c. How is the relationship between Lloyd and Ahna's Patterns similar or different?

4. Wild World is designing a giant swing using a structure built in much the same way as the Sky Dive in Problem 4.1. The designers are not sure how tall to make the swing. Here are some sketches of different swing designs.

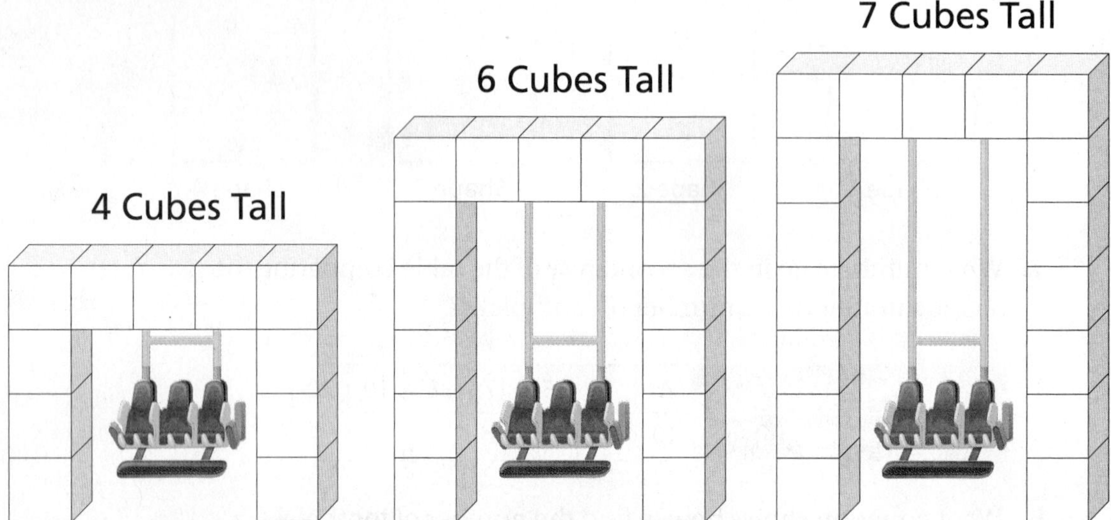

a. What numbers would go in the second row of a table that compares the height to the total number of cubes?

Height (squares)	4	5	6	7	8	10	20
Number of Cubes	11	■	■	■	■	■	■

b. What equation shows how to find the number of cubes in the swing frame that is n cubes tall?

c. Could you calculate the value for a swing frame that is 1 cube tall? Explain.

d. Explain what a swing frame that is 50 cubes tall would look like. In what ways would it look similar to and different from the swing frames shown above? How could you use this description to calculate the total number of cubes in it?

5. Mitch, Lewis, and Corky were discussing equations that they wrote for Exercise 4. They called the height T and the number of cubes c.

Mitch's thinking: The top of the swing frame has 5 cubes, and then there are $T - 1$ cubes underneath it. The total number of cubes needed is $c = 5 + (T - 1) + (T - 1)$.

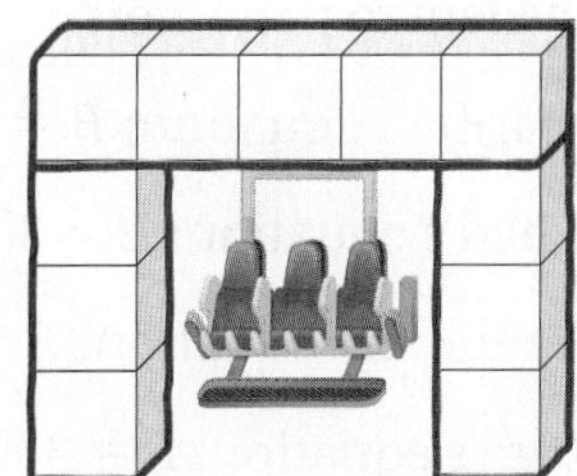

Lewis's thinking: When I see the drawing, I think of two upside-down L shapes with a middle piece. My equation for the number of cubes is $c = 2(T + 1) + 1$.

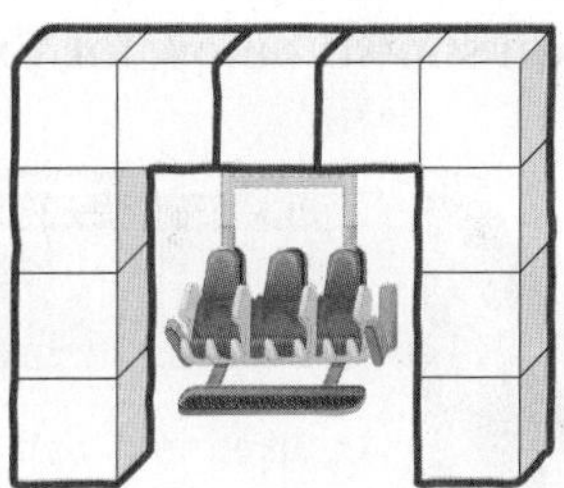

Corky's thinking: On the left side I see a single tower, and the right side is a tower with three extra cubes. My equation is $c = T + (T + 3)$.

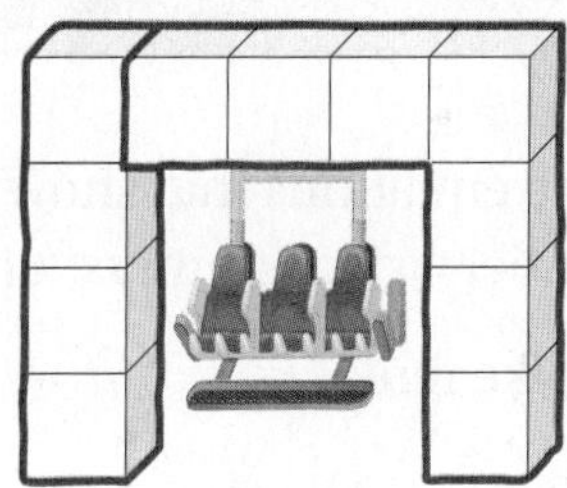

a. Create a table for the three equations.

b. Which of the expressions are equivalent? Explain.

c. Write a new expression that is equivalent to the ones that are equivalent in part (b).

6. Students created some interesting expressions for Problem 4.2. They were not sure if these were equivalent to Chaska's, Tabitha's, and Eva's equations. Determine if each of the equations below is equivalent to the others.

a. Martha's equation: $B = 2n + 2 + (n - 1)$

b. Chad's equation: $B = 3(n + 1) - 2$

c. Jeremiah's equation: $B = 4n - (n - 1)$

d. Lara's equation: $B = 3 + 1n$

The Ocean Bike Tours partners decided to offer a two-day trip from Philadelphia, Pennsylvania, to Atlantic City, New Jersey, and back. They did some research and found these costs for the trip. Use the information shown below for Exercises 7–8.

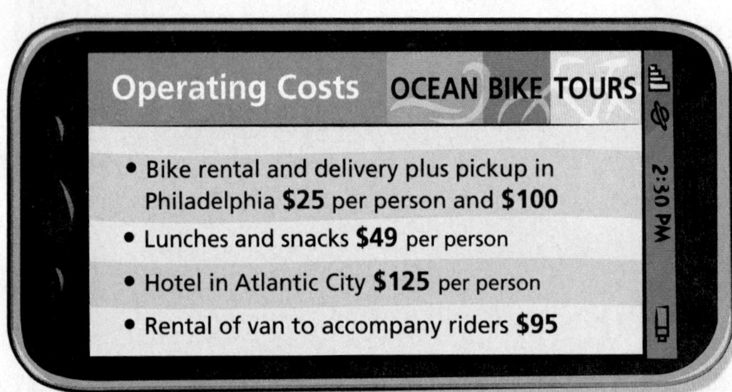

7. Write equations that show how these cost variables depend on the number n of customers for the two-day tours.

a. bike rental B

b. lunch and snacks L

c. hotel rooms H

d. rental of the tour support van V

8. a. Write a rule that shows how total operating cost C depends on the number n of riders. The rule should show how each cost variable adds to the total.

b. Write another rule for total operating cost C. This rule should be as simple as possible for calculating the total cost.

c. Give evidence showing that your two expressions for total cost are equivalent.

The organizers of a youth soccer league want to give each player a special T-shirt and hat. The costs are shown here.

YOUTH SOCCER LEAGUE

ORDER FORM

T-shirts	
1	**$75.00** design
Quantity ☐	**$7.50** per shirt
Hats	
1	**$50.00** design
Quantity ☐	**$10.00** per hat

9. Show how the cost for each of the variables below depends on the number n of players in the tournament.

a. T-shirts T

b. hats H

10. **a.** Write an equation that shows how total cost C for providing T-shirts and hats depends on the number of tournament players n. The equation should show how each separate cost variable adds to the total.

b. Write a second equation for C. The second equation should be as simple as possible.

c. Give evidence to show that your two expressions for total cost are equivalent.

11. You are given the expression $350n - 30n + 350 - (50 + 10n)$.

a. What are the terms in the expression?

b. What numbers are coefficients in the expression?

c. Explain how the words *term* and *coefficient* are used in talking about the algebraic expression.

12. The owner of a horse farm has 500 yards of fencing to enclose a rectangular pasture. One side of the pasture must be 150 yards long. Write and solve an equation that tells the length of the other side.

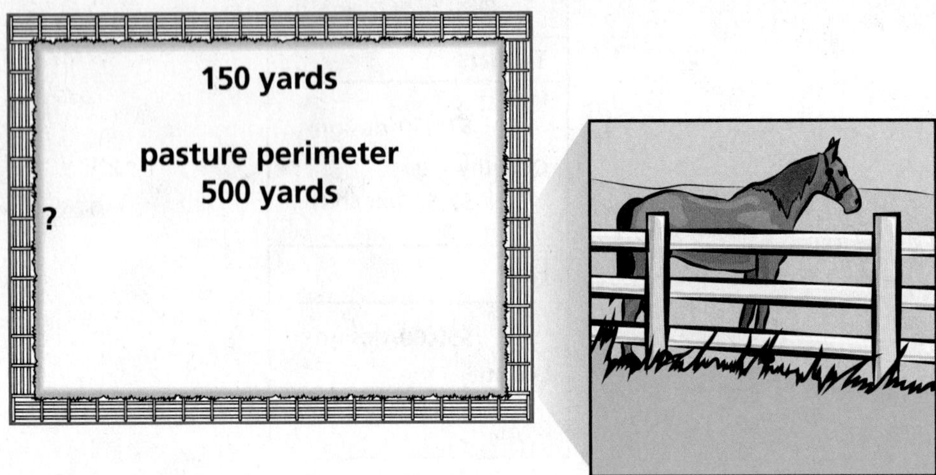

A baseball team wanted to rent a small bus for travel to a tournament. Superior Bus charges $2.95 per mile driven. Coast Transport charges $300 plus $2 per mile. Use these data for Exercises 13–16.

13. For each company, show how rental cost *C* depends on number of miles driven *m*.

14. The rental for a bus from Superior Bus was $590.

- Write and solve an equation to find the distance driven.
- Check your solution by substituting its value for the variable *m* in the equation.
- Explain how you found the solution.

15. The rental for a bus from Coast Transport was $600.

- Write and solve an equation to find the distance driven.
- Check your solution by substituting its value for the variable *m* in the equation.
- Explain how you found the solution.

16. The team wanted to know which bus company's offer was a better value. Use the table and graph below to answer their questions.

Miles	Superior Bus	Coast Transport
100	295	500
200	590	700
300	885	900
400	1180	1100
500	1475	1300

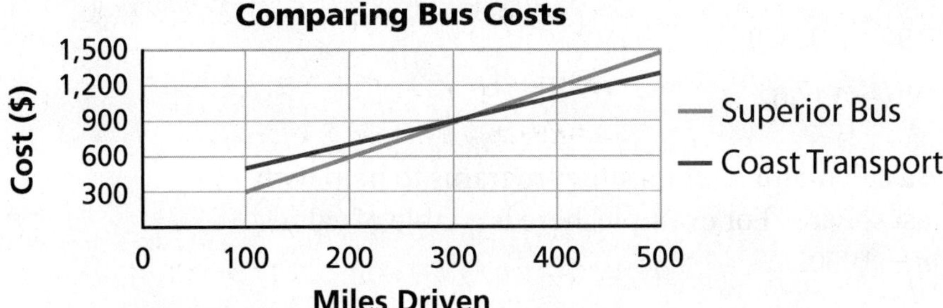

There are several ways to estimate solutions for equations.

The simplest method is often called **guess and check**. It involves three basic steps.

- Make a guess about the solution.
- Check to see if that guess solves the equation.
- If it does not, revise your guess and check again in the equation.

a. The two rental companies charge the same amount for one distance. Write an equation to find that distance. Then solve the equation by guess and check. (The table and graph will help.)

b. For what numbers of miles will the charge by Superior Bus be less than that by Coast Transport?

c. For what numbers of miles will the charge by Coast Transport be less than that by Superior Buses?

The Ocean Bike Tours partners decided to charge $350 per rider. This led them to a relationship giving tour profit as $P = 190n - 1{,}050$. For 20 riders the profit will be $190(20) - 1{,}050 = 2{,}750$.

The partners want to find the number of riders needed to reach a profit of $3,700. They have to solve $3{,}700 = 190n - 1{,}050$. That means finding a value of n that makes $3{,}700 = 190n - 1{,}050$ a true statement.

Use the information below for Exercises 17–20.

17. Use the guess and check method to solve these equations. In each case write a sentence explaining what the solution tells about profit for Ocean Bike Tours.

a. $3{,}700 = 190n - 1{,}050$.

b. $550 = 190n - 1{,}050$

18. You can use a calculator or computer programs to help with guess and test solving. For example, here is a table of values for $P = 190n - 1050$.

Profit Related to Number of Customers

Number of Customers	5	10	15	20	25	30
Profit ($)	−100	850	1,800	2,750	3,700	4,650

a. What do the entries in the table tell about solutions for the equation $1{,}230 = 190n - 1{,}050$?

b. Use the table and the guess and check strategy to solve the equation.

c. Use a table to help in solving these equations. In each case, write a sentence explaining what the solution tells about profit for Ocean Bike Tours.

i. $2{,}560 = 190n - 1{,}050$ **ii.** $5{,}030 = 190n - 1{,}050$

19. Another version of the guess and test strategy uses graphs for the profit relationship.

a. Study the graph below to estimate the value of n that is a solution for the equation $2{,}000 = 190n - 1{,}050$. Then check to see if your estimate is correct (or close to correct).

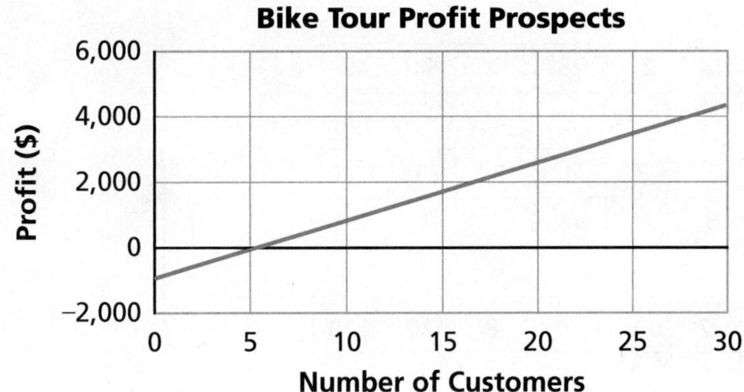

b. Use graphing to solve these equations. In each case, sketch a graph and label points with coordinates that show the solution.

i. $45 = 5x + 10$

ii. $60 = 100 - 2.5x$

20. The Ocean Bike Tours partners expect their profit P to depend on the number n of riders according to the relation $P = 190n - 1{,}050$.

a. Use the relation to write an equation for the number of riders needed to give a profit of $2,180. Then solve the equation.

b. What arithmetic operations give the solution?

Connections

For Exercises 21–24, use the pattern in each table to find the missing entries. Then write an equation relating the two variables.

21.

a	0	1	2	3	■	8	20	100
b	0	7	14	21	28	■	■	■

22.

x	0	1	2	3	4	8	20	100
y	6	7	8	9	■	■	■	■

23.

m	0	1	2	3	4	8	20	100
n	1	3	5	7	■	■	■	■

24.

r	0	1	2	3	4	6	10	20
s	0	1	4	9	16	■	■	■

25. a. The table below shows the relationship between the number of cubes and number of squares in the tower. Use the information in Problem 4.1 to fill in the second row of the table.

Relationship of Cubes to Squares in a Tower

Number of Cubes in the Tower	1	2	3	4	5	6	10
Number of Squares in the Tower	■	■	■	18	■	■	■

b. What equation shows how to find the total number of squares *s* given the number of cubes *c*?

26. Determine if the pairs of expressions below are equivalent. Explain how you know.

a. $4n + 12$ and $4(n + 3)$

b. $m + m + 3m$ and $3m + 2$

c. $p + p$ and $p + 7$

d. $5r + 5 - (r - 1)$ and $4r + 4$

e. $3(2t + 2)$ and $(t + 1)6$

For Exercises 27–30 use what you know about equivalent expressions to write an expression equivalent to the one given.

27. $5n$

28. $2n + 2$

29. $4n - 4$

30. $3n + 2n + n$

The diagrams in Exercises 31–34 show rectangles divided into smaller rectangles. Use the Distributive Property to write two equivalent expressions for the area of each large rectangle.

31.

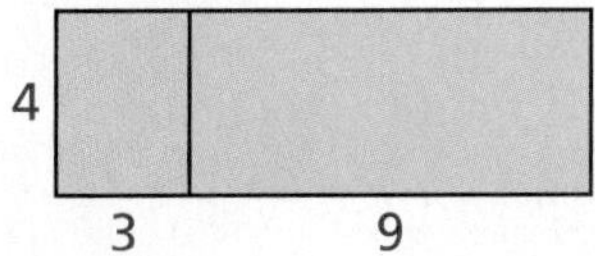

32.

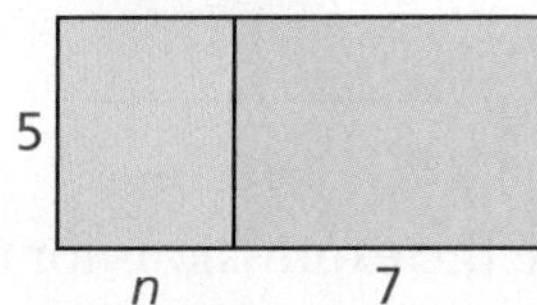

33.

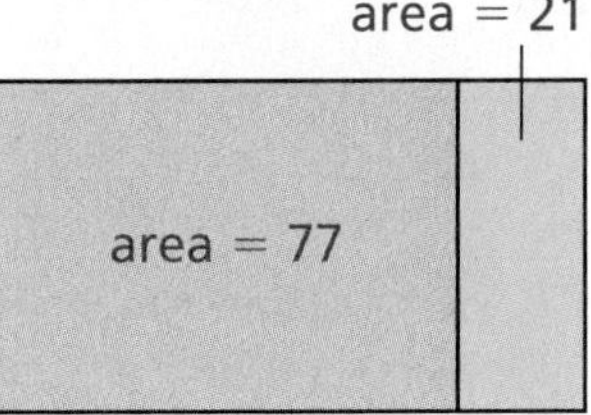

34.

area = $8n$ area = 40

For Exercises 35–38, draw a figure to match each description. Then use the Distributive Property to write each area as a product and as a sum.

35. a 4-by-$(7 + 5)$ rectangle

36. an n-by-$(3 + 12)$ rectangle

37. a 3-by-$(2 + 4 + 2)$ rectangle

38. an n-by-$(n + 5)$ rectangle

39. Use the Distributive Property to write two equivalent expressions for the area of each figure below.

a.

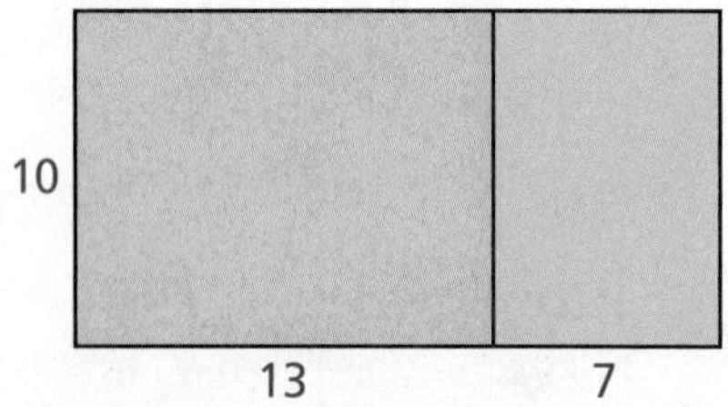

10

13 7

b.

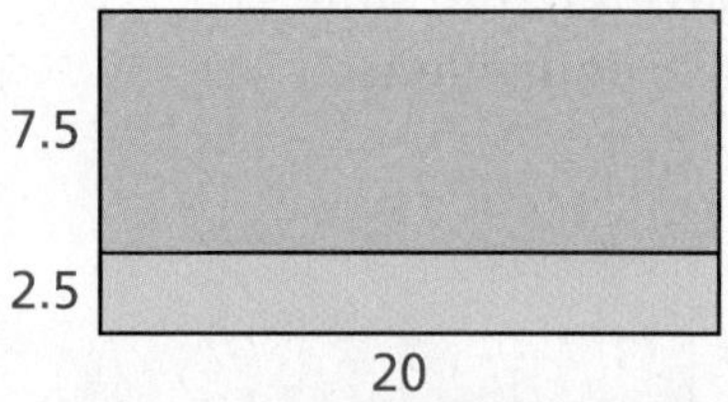

7.5

2.5

20

c. Compare the expressions for the two figures.

For Exercises 40–47, write $<$, $>$, or $=$ to make each statement true.

40. $2.4 \blacksquare 2.8$

41. $\frac{5}{3} \blacksquare 1.666\ldots$

42. $1.43 \blacksquare 1.296$

43. $\frac{9}{2} \blacksquare 4.500$

44. $5.62 \blacksquare 5.602$

45. $0.32 \blacksquare 0.032$

46. $3\frac{1}{4} \blacksquare 3\frac{1}{8}$

47. $\frac{343}{7} \blacksquare \frac{343}{5}$

For Exercises 48–51, identify the coefficients. Then, determine how many terms are in each expression.

48. $4n + 5n + 3$

49. $6n + 4 + n + n$

50. $2n + 3 + 2n + 3$

51. $5(n + 3)$

52. Most states add a sales tax to the cost of nonfood purchases. Let p stand for the price of a purchase, t stand for the sales tax, and c for the total cost.

a. What equation relates c, p, and t?

For parts (b)–(d), suppose a state has a sales tax of 8%.

b. What equation relates t and p?

c. What equation relates c and p?

d. Use the Distributive Property to write the equation relating c and p in a simpler equivalent form.

In Exercises 53–56, solve the given equations. Check your answers. Explain how you could find each solution with one or two arithmetic operations.

53. $x + 13.5 = 19$

54. $23 = x - 7$

55. $45x = 405$

56. $8x - 11 = 37$

57. Each equation below is a member of a fact family. Write other members of the fact families.

a. $8 + 7 = 15$

b. $7 \times 3 = 21$

c. $23 - 11 = 12$

d. $12 \div 4 = 3$

58. Show how fact families can be used to solve these equations.

a. $x + 7 = 15$

b. $7y = 21$

c. $w - 11 = 12$

d. $n \div 4 = 3$.

59. You are given the equation $y = 24 + 3x$.

a. Create a problem that can be represented by the equation.

b. Which of the points (60, 12) and (17, 75) lies on the graph of the equation?

c. Use the point that lies on the graph to make up a question that can be answered with the point.

60. You are given the equation $y = 120 + 4.5x$.

a. Create a problem that can be represented by the equation.

b. Which of these two points lies on the graph of the equation, (15, 180) or (8, 156)?

c. Use the point that lies on the graph to write an inequality that can be answered with the point.

In questions 61–64, solve each given inequality for *x*. Draw a number line graph of each solution.

61. $x + 13.5 < 19$

62. $23 > x - 7$

63. $45x < 405$

64. $8x > 48$

Extensions

65. In planning for a dance, the student government came up with these figures for income and costs.

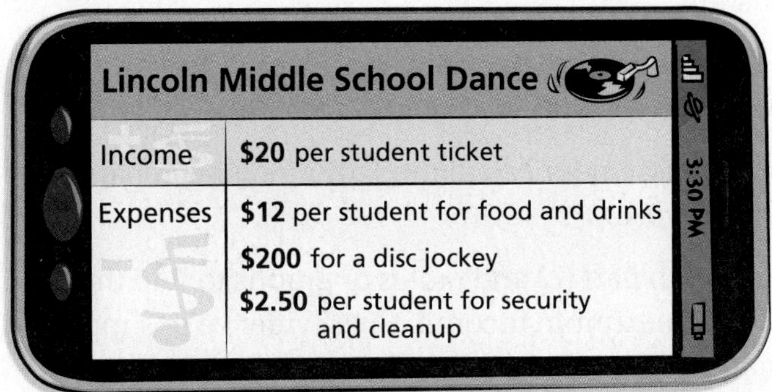

a. Write an equation that relates income I to the number of tickets sold for the dance n.

b. Write an equation that relates food and drink costs F to the number of tickets sold for the dance n.

c. Write an equation that relates the disc jockey fee D to the number of tickets sold for the dance n.

d. Write an equation that relates security and cleanup staff cost S to the number of tickets sold for the dance n.

e. Jamal and Sophie came up with two expressions for the relationship between profit P and number n of tickets sold.

Jamal's Rule: $P = 20n - (12n + 200 + 2.5n)$

Sophie's Rule: $P = 20n - 12n - 200 - 2.50n$

Are these equations correct models for the relationship between profit and number of customers? How do you know?

f. What simpler expression can be used to calculate profit for any number of tickets sold? Explain how you know that your answer is correct.

66. While planning their tour, the Ocean Bike Tours partners came up with an equation relating the number n of riders to the price p of the tour. The equation was $n = 50 - 0.10p$.

a. How does the number of riders change as the price per rider increases? How is that pattern shown in a table and a graph of the relationship?

b. Explain how the relationship between tour income I and tour price p can be expressed with the equation $I = (50 - 0.10p)p$.

c. Show how the expression for calculating tour income in part (b) is equivalent to $50p - 0.10p^2$.

d. Use the expression in part (c) and tables or graphs to find the tour price that will give maximum income. Give evidence to support your conclusion.

67. To get publicity for their Ocean Bike Tours business, the partners held a 30-mile bike race.

- They gave riders under age 14 a half-hour head start.
- The leading young riders rode at a steady speed of 12 miles per hour for the first half hour. Then, they rode 10 miles per hour for the rest of the race.
- When the older riders started, the leading older riders went at a steady speed of 15 miles per hour.

a. Write an equation that gives the distance d covered by the leading under-14 rider in t hours.

b. Write an equation that gives the distance d covered by the leading older riders in t hours after the under-14 riders start.

c. Use the equations from parts (a) and (b) to make a table and a graph comparing the progress of the two groups of riders.

d. Write an equation for the time when the leading older riders catch up to the leading under-14 riders. Then solve it.

e. Will the older riders catch up to the younger riders before the end of the 30-mile race? Explain how your answer is shown in the table and in the graph.

68. The managers of Wild World Amusement Park had an idea for changing the bonus card offered to park customers. Instead of giving 100 bonus points and charging 6 points per ride, they would give 150 bonus points and charge 12 points per ride. They thought that the card offering 150 bonus points would seem like a better deal.

a. Which plan would actually offer the most rides?

b. Write and solve an equation that finds the number of rides for which the two cards would leave the same number of points.

c. For what numbers of rides would holders of the 150-point card have a greater number of points left?

69. A principal wants to send her top science students on a field trip to the state science center. The trip costs $250 for a bus and driver, plus $17.50 per student for food and admission.

a. What is the cost of sending 30 students? 60 students?

b. What equation shows how the total trip cost C depends on the number of students s who go on the trip?

c. Write and solve an inequality that answers this question:

How many students can go on the trip if the budget allows a maximum cost of $1,000?

Mathematical Reflections

The Problems in this Investigation asked you to develop understanding and skill in writing equivalent algebraic expressions and solving equations. The following questions will help you summarize what you have learned.

Think about these questions. Discuss your ideas with other students and your teacher. Then write a summary of your findings in your notebook.

1. **What** does it mean to say that two expressions are equivalent? **How** can you test the equivalence of two expressions?
2. **What** does it mean to solve an equation. **What** strategies are available for solving equations?
3. **What** does it mean to solve an inequality? **What** will graphs of such solutions look like for inequalities in the form $ax > b$ and $a + x < b$? (Assume a and b are both positive numbers.)
4. **Describe** how expressions, equations, inequalities, and representations are used in this Unit. **How** are they related?

Common Core Mathematical Practices

As you worked on the Problems in this Investigation, you used prior knowledge to make sense of them. You also applied Mathematical Practices to solve the Problems. Think back over your work, the ways you thought about the Problems, and how you used Mathematical Practices.

Elena described her thoughts in the following way:

In our group, we came up with several different ways to write the number of pieces needed to make the towers in Problem 4.1.

Sally noticed that the first frame needs four pieces. Each frame after that only needs three more pieces. So, she wrote the expression $4 + 3(n - 1)$.

Mitch made a table for the first 10 frames. He noticed a pattern relating the two variables in the table. The number of pieces is 3 times the frame number plus 1. So, he wrote $3n + 1$.

We think that these two expressions are equivalent because the reasoning behind each made sense. We also substituted values for n into each expression and got the same value every time.

Common Core Standards for Mathematical Practice

MP3 Construct viable arguments and critique the reasoning of others.

- What other Mathematical Practices can you identify in Elena's reasoning?
- Describe a Mathematical Practice that you and your classmates used to solve a different Problem in this Investigation.

Looking Back

In this Unit, you studied some basic ideas of algebra. You learned ways to use those ideas to solve problems about variables and the patterns relating variables. In particular, you studied the following topics:

- Recognizing situations in which changes in variables are related in patterns
- Describing patterns of change shown in tables and graphs of data
- Constructing tables and graphs to display relationships between variables
- Using algebraic symbols to write equations relating variables
- Using tables, graphs, and equations to solve problems

Test Your Understanding and Skill

In the following Exercises, you will test your understanding of algebraic ideas and your skill in using algebraic techniques. You will consider how algebra is involved in shipping packages.

1. A shipping company offers two-day shipping of any package weighing as much as 2 pounds for \$5 plus \$0.01 per mile.

   a. Copy and complete the table.

Two-Day Shipping Costs

Distance (mi)	100	200	300	400	500	1,000	1,500	2,000
Shipping Cost	■	■	■	■	■	■	■	■

   b. Describe the pattern by which the shipping cost increases as the shipping distance increases.

   c. Make a graph showing shipping charges for distances from 0 to 2,000 miles. Use appropriate labels and scales on the axes.

   d. Write an equation relating distance d in miles and shipping cost c in dollars.

   e. Use a graphing calculator and the equation from part (d) to check the graph you made in part (c).

   f. Use the table, graph, or equation to find the cost to ship a 1-pound package 450 miles.

   g. Use the table, graph, or equation to figure out how far you can ship a 2-pound package for \$35.

   h. Write an inequality that describes the number of miles you can send a package for less than \$15. Show the solution on a number line.

Look back at your work and answer the following questions.

2. What are the independent and dependent variables? How do you know?

3. How did you develop the equation relating distance and cost?

4. How did you choose scales for axes in the graph of the cost equation?

5. How could the relations in parts (f) and (g) be expressed as equations relating variables d and c?

6. How could the equations in Exercise 5 be solved by using the table or the graph? By reasoning with the symbolic forms alone?

English / Spanish Glossary

A

average speed The number of miles per hour averaged over an entire trip. For instance, if you travel 140 miles in 2 hours, then the average speed is 70 miles per hour.

velocidad media El promedio del número de millas por hora durante un recorrido completo. Por ejemplo, si se recorren 140 millas en 2 horas, entonces la velocidad media es de 70 millas por hora.

C

change To become different. For example, temperatures rise and fall, prices increase and decrease, and so on. In mathematics, quantities that change are called *variables*.

cambiar Variar, volverse diferente. Por ejemplo, las temperaturas suben y bajan, los precios aumentan y se reducen, y así sucesivamente. En Matemáticas, las cantidades que cambian se llaman *variables*.

coefficient The numerical factor in any term of an expression.

coeficiente El factor numérico en cualquier término de una expresión.

compare Academic Vocabulary
To tell or show how two things are alike and different.

related terms *analyze, relate*

sample Two river rafting companies offer tours. The Rocky River Company charges \$150 per group. Bailey's Rafting charges \$37.50 per person. Compare these offers, and explain for which situations each offer is a better deal.

Each choice would cost the same for 4 people since 4 x \$37.50 = \$150. If a group has fewer than 4 people, Bailey's is the better deal. If there are more than 4 people, Rocky River is the better deal.

I can also use a table to find a solution.

People	1	2	3	4	5
Rocky River	\$150	\$150	\$150	\$150	\$150
Bailey's	\$37.50	\$75	\$112.50	\$150	\$187.50

The cost is the same for 4 people.

comparar Vocabulario académico
Decir o mostrar en qué se parecen y en qué se diferencian dos cosas.

términos relacionados *analizar, relacionar*

ejemplo Dos compañías de canotaje ofrecen excursiones. La Rocky River Company cobra \$150 por grupo. La Bailey's Rafting cobra \$37.50 por persona. Compara las dos ofertas y explica en qué situaciones una oferta es mejor que la otra.

Cada opción costaría lo mismo por 4 personas, ya que 4 x \$37.50 = \$150. Si el grupo tuviera menos de 4 personas, Bailey's es la mejor opción. Si tuviera más de 4 personas, Rocky River sería la mejor opción.

También puedo usar una tabla para hallar la solución.

Personas	1	2	3	4	5
Rocky River	\$150	\$150	\$150	\$150	\$150
Bailey's	\$37.50	\$75	\$112.50	\$150	\$187.50

El costo es el mismo por 4 personas.

coordinate graph A graphical representation of pairs of related numerical values that shows the relationship between two variables. It relates the independent variable (shown on the *x*-axis) and the dependent variable (shown on the *y*-axis).

gráfica de coordenadas Una representación gráfica de pares de valores numéricos relacionados que muestra la relación que existe entre dos variables. Dicha representación relaciona la variable independiente (que se muestra en el eje de las *x*) y la variable dependiente (que se muestra en el eje de las *y*).

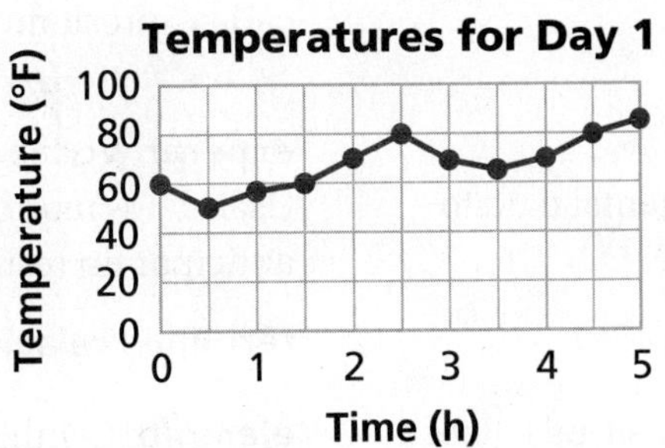

coordinate pair An ordered pair of numbers used to locate a point on a coordinate grid. The first number in a coordinate pair is the value for the *x*-coordinate, and the second number is the value for the *y*-coordinate. A coordinate pair for the graph shown above is (0, 60).

par de coordenadas Un par ordenado de números que se usa para localizar un punto en una gráfica de coordenadas. El primer número del par de coordenadas es el valor de la coordenada *x* y el segundo número es el valor de la coordenada *y*. Un par de coordenadas de la gráfica que se muestra arriba es (0, 60).

D

dependent variable One of the two variables in a relationship. Its value depends upon or is determined by the other variable, called the *independent variable*. For example, the cost of trail mix (dependent variable) depends on how much you buy (independent variable).

variable dependiente Una de las dos variables de una relación. Su valor depende o está determinado por el valor de la otra variable llamada *variable independiente*. Por ejemplo, el costo de una mezcla de nueces y frutas secas (variable dependiente) depende de la cantidad de mezcla que compras (variable independiente).

E

equation A rule containing variables that represents a mathematical relationship. An example is the formula for finding the area of a circle, $A = \pi r^2$.

ecuación Una regla que contiene variables que representa una relación matemática. Un ejemplo de ello es la fórmula para hallar el área de un círculo, $A = \pi r^2$.

equivalent expressions Expressions that represent the same quantity when the same number is substituted for the variable in each expression.

expresiones equivalentes Expresiones que representan la misma cantidad cuando el mismo número se sustituye por la variable en cada expresión.

expect Academic Vocabulary
To use theoretical or experimental data to anticipate a certain outcome.

related terms *anticipate, predict*

sample Cynthia counted her sit-ups. Based on her data, how many sit-ups would you expect her to do in 40 seconds? Would you expect this pattern to continue indefinitely?

Seconds	10	20	30
Number of Sit Ups	6	12	18

Cynthia's sit-ups increased by 6 every 10 seconds. Since 40 seconds is 10 more seconds than 30, I expect her to do 18 + 6 = 24 sit-ups.
I can also make a graph to represent this.

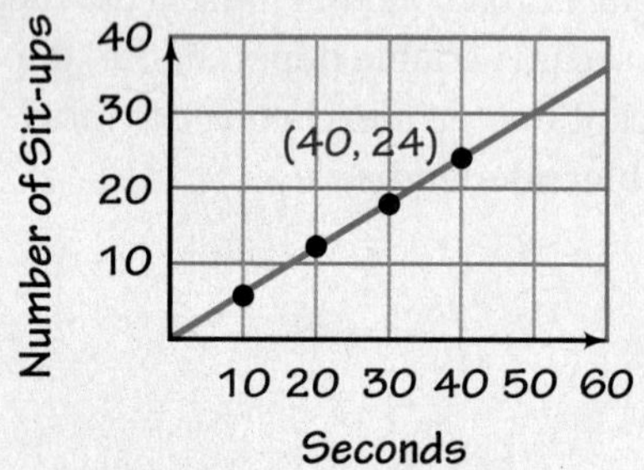

The graph shows 24 sit-ups at 40 seconds. I would not expect this pattern to continue because Cynthia will get tired and probably do fewer sit-ups.

esperar Vocabulario académico
Usar datos teóricos o experimentales para anticipar un resultado determinado.

términos relacionados *anticipar, predecir*

ejemplo Cynthia contó sus abdominales. Según sus datos, ¿cuántos abdominales esperas que haga en 40 segundos? ¿Esperas que este patrón continúe indefinidamente?

Segundos	10	20	30
N° de abdominales	6	12	18

Los abdominales que hace Cynthia aumentaron en 6 cada 10 segundos. Ya que 40 segundos son 10 segundos más que 30, espero que ella haga 18 + 6 = 24 abdominales.
También puedo hacer una gráfica para representar estos datos.

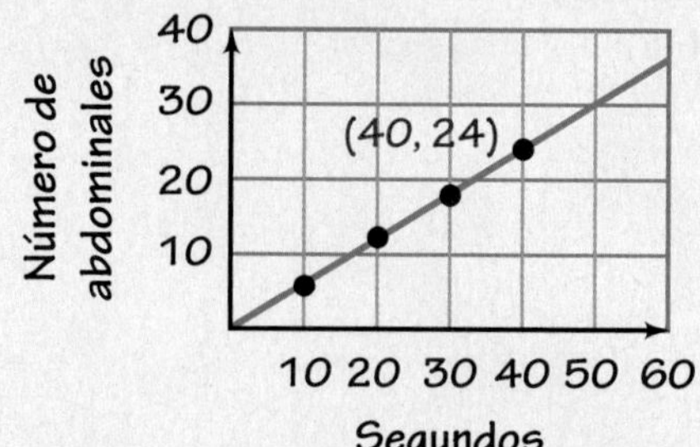

La gráfica muestra 24 abdominales en 40 segundos. No espero que este patrón continúe porque Cynthia se cansará y probablemente hará menos abdominales.

expression A mathematical phrase containing numbers, variables, and operation symbols.

expresión Una frase matemática que contiene números, variables y símbolos de operaciones.

G

guess and check A method of solving an equation that begins with a guess. The first guess is checked against the equation and corrected until an exact solution is reached.

suponer y comprobar Un método para resolver una ecuación que comienza con una suposición. La primera suposición se comprueba contra la ecuación y se corrige hasta que se llega a una solución exacta.

I

income The amount of money taken in.

ingresos La cantidad de dinero que se gana.

independent variable One of the two variables in a relationship. Its value determines the value of the other variable, called the *dependent variable.* If you organize a bike tour, for example, the number of people who register to go (independent variable) determines the cost for renting bikes (dependent variable).

variable independiente Una de las dos variables relacionadas. Su valor determina el de la otra variable, llamada variable dependiente. Por ejemplo, si organizas un recorrido en bicicleta, el número de personas inscritas (variable independiente) determina el costo del alquiler de las bicicletas (variable dependiente).

O

order of operations

A set of agreements or conventions for carrying out calculations with one or more operations, parentheses, or exponents.

1. Work within **parentheses**.
2. Write numbers written with **exponents** in standard form.
3. Do all **multiplication and division** in order from left to right.
4. Do all **addition and subtraction** in order from left to right.

orden de las operaciones Un conjunto de acuerdos o convenciones para llevar a cabo cálculos con más de una operación, paréntesis o exponentes.

1. Resolver lo que está entre **paréntesis**.
2. Escribir los números con **exponentes** en forma estándar.
3. **Multiplicar y dividir** en orden de izquierda a derecha.
4. **Sumar y dividir** en orden de izquierda a derecha.

P

pattern A change that occurs in a predictable way. For example, the squares on a checkerboard form a pattern in which the colors of the squares alternate between red and black. The sequence of square numbers: 1, 4, 9, 16, . . . forms a pattern in which the numbers increase by the next odd number. That is, 4 is 3 more than 1, 9 is 5 more than 4, 16 is 7 more than 9, and so on.

patrón Un cambio que ocurre de manera predecible. Por ejemplo, los cuadrados del tablero de damas forman un patrón en el que los colores de los cuadrados se alternan entre el rojo y el negro. La secuencia de cuadrados de números: 1, 4, 9, 16, . . . forma un patrón en el que los números aumentan según la cifra del siguiente número impar. Es decir, 4 es 3 más que 1, 9 es 5 más que 4, 16 es 7 más que 9, y así sucesivamente.

profit The amount by which income is greater than expenses.

ganancias La cantidad en la cual los ingresos son mayores que los gastos.

R

rate of change The amount of change in the dependent variable produced by a given change in the independent variable.

tasa de cambio La cantidad de cambio en la variable dependiente producida por un cambio dado en la variable independiente.

relationship An association between two or more variables. If one of the variables changes, the other variable may also change, and the change may be predictable.

relación Una asociación entre dos o más variables. Si una de las variables cambia, la otra variable también puede cambiar y dicho cambio puede ser predecible.

represent Academic Vocabulary
To stand for or take the place of something else. Symbols, equations, charts, and tables are often used to represent particular situations.

related terms *symbolize, stand for*

sample The Snowy Heights resort rents snowboards for \$12 plus \$3 for each hour. Write an equation to represent this situation. Explain what the variables and numbers in your equation represent.

My equation is $c = 12 + 3h$. The c represents the total cost. The 12 represents the initial charge for renting the snowboard. The h represents the number of hours rented, and the 3 represents the hourly charge.

representar Vocabulario académico
Significar o tomar el lugar de algo más. Los símbolos, las ecuaciones, las gráficas y las tablas a menudo se usan para representar situaciones particulares.

términos relacionados *simbolizar, significar*

ejemplo El centro de esquí Snowy Heights alquila tablas de snowboard por \$12 más \$3 por hora. Escribe una ecuación que represente esta situación. Explica lo que representan las variables y los números de tu ecuación.

Mi ecuación es $c = 12 + 3h$. La c representa el costo total. El 12 representa el cobro inicial por alquilar una tabla de *snowboard*. La h representa el número de horas de alquiler y el 3 representa el costo por hora.

rule A summary of a predictable relationship that tells how to find the value of a variable. A rule may be given in words or as an equation. For example, this rule relates time, rate, and distance: distance is equal to rate times time, or $d = rt$.

regla Un resumen de una relación predecible que indica cómo hallar el valor de una variable. Una regla se puede dar en palabras o como una ecuación. Por ejemplo, la siguiente regla relaciona tiempo, velocidad y distancia: la distancia es igual al producto de la velocidad y el tiempo, o sea $d = rt$.

S

scale A labeling scheme used on each of the axes on a coordinate grid.

escala Un esquema de rotulación que se usa en cada uno de los ejes de una gráfica de coordenadas.

solution of an equation The value or values of the variables that make an equation true.

solución de una ecuación El valor o valores de las variables que hacen que una ecuación sea verdadera.

solving an equation Finding the value or values of the variables that make an equation true.

resolver una ecuación Hallar el valor o valores de las variables que hacen que una ecuación sea verdadera.

T

table A list of values for two or more variables that shows the relationship between them. Tables often represent data made from observations, from experiments, or from a series of arithmetic operations. A table may show a pattern of change between two variables that can be used to predict values not in the table.

tabla Una lista de valores para dos o más variables que muestra la relación que existe entre ellas. Frecuentemente, las tablas representan datos provenientes de observaciones, experimentos o de una serie de operaciones aritméticas. Una tabla puede mostrar un patrón de cambio entre dos variables que se puede usar para predecir valores que no están en la tabla.

term A number, a variable, or the product of a number and a variable.

término Un número, una variable o el producto de un número y una variable.

V

variable A quantity that can change. Letters are often used as symbols to represent variables in rules or equations that describe patterns.

variable Una cantidad que puede cambiar. Suelen usarse letras como símbolos para representar las variables en las reglas o ecuaciones que describen patrones.

X

_x_-axis The number line that is horizontal on a coordinate grid.

eje de las _x_ La recta numérica horizontal en una gráfica de coordenadas.

Y

_y_-axis The number line that is vertical on a coordinate grid.

eje de las _y_ La recta numérica vertical en una gráfica de coordenadas.

Index

Acknowledgments

Text

050 Tiger Missing Link Foundation

"*Typical Weights for Tiger Cubs*" from TIGERLINK.ORG. Used by permission.

Photographs

Photo locators denoted as follows: Top (T), Center (C), Bottom (B), Left (L), Right (R), Background (Bkgd)

002 David Maenza/Superstock; **003** Andre Jenny/Alamy; **014** Scott Neville/AP Images; **017** (TL) Michele & Tom Grimm/Alamy, (TR) InterFoto/Travel/Alamy; **019** SuperStock/Glow Images; **025** (BL, BR) GIPhotoStock/Science Source; **033** (BL) David Maenza/Superstock, (CR) Dallas and John Heaton/Free Agents Limited/Corbis; **048** Tony Donaldson/Icon SMI Tony Donaldson/Icon SMI Icon Sports Photos/Newscom; **090** Shirley Kilpatrick/Alamy.

CONNECTED MATHEMATICS® 3

Statistics and Data Analysis

Lappan, Phillips, Fey, Friel

Data About Us

Statistics and Data Analysis

Looking Ahead

What is the greatest number of pets owned by the students in your class? How can you find out?

How much do the sugar contents of different kinds of cereals vary?

How can you determine which of two basketball teams has taller players? Older players?

Charlestown Spartans

Player	Age	Height (cm)
#37	23	185
#29	27	173
#56	19	204
#39	35	202
#28	32	190
#16	33	209
#25	30	189

Part of a biologist's job is to collect data on organisms, such as coral. They do this to understand the organism and its role in the world. Not all coral is the same, so biologists study many corals in order to learn more about the species as a whole.

In a similar way, the United States government gathers information about its citizens. They do this to learn more about the population as a whole. Collecting data from every household in the United States is a huge task. So, many surveys involve gathering information from much smaller groups of people.

People often make statements about the results of surveys. It is important to understand these statements. For example, what does it mean when reports say that the average middle-school student watches three hours of television on a weekday and has four people in his or her family?

In *Data About Us*, you will learn to collect and analyze data. You will also learn to use your results to describe people and their characteristics.

Mathematical Highlights

Data About Us

In *Data About Us,* you will learn different ways to collect, organize, display, and analyze data.

In this Unit you will learn to:

- Use the process of data investigation by posing questions, collecting and analyzing data, and interpreting the data to answer questions
- Organize and represent data using tables, dot plots, line plots, bar graphs, histograms, and box-and-whisker plots
- Describe the overall shape of a distribution and identify whether or not it is symmetrical around a central value
- Compute the mean, median, and mode of a data distribution, and use these measures to indicate what is typical for the distribution
- Describe the variability of a distribution by identifying clusters and gaps, and by calculating the range, Interquartile Range (IQR), and Mean Absolute Deviation (MAD)
- Identify which statistical measures of center and spread should be used to describe a particular distribution of data
- Distinguish between categorical data and numerical data, and identify which graphs and statistics may be used to represent each type of data
- Compare two or more distributions of data, including using measures of center and spread to make comparisons

When you encounter a new problem, it is a good idea to ask yourself questions. In this Unit, you might ask questions such as:

What question is being investigated to collect these data?

How might I organize the data?

What statistical measures will help describe the distribution of data?

What will these statistical measures tell me about the distribution of the data?

How can I use graphs and statistics to report an answer to my original question?

Common Core State Standards

Mathematical Practices and Habits of Mind

In the *Connected Mathematics* curriculum you will develop an understanding of important mathematical ideas by solving problems and reflecting on the mathematics involved. Every day, you will use "habits of mind" to make sense of problems and apply what you learn to new situations. Some of these habits are described by the *Common Core State Standards for Mathematical Practices* (MP).

MP1 Make sense of problems and persevere in solving them.

When using mathematics to solve a problem, it helps to think carefully about

- data and other facts you are given and what additional information you need to solve the problem;
- strategies you have used to solve similar problems and whether you could solve a related simpler problem first;
- how you could express the problem with equations, diagrams, or graphs;
- whether your answer makes sense.

MP2 Reason abstractly and quantitatively.

When you are asked to solve a problem, it often helps to

- focus first on the key mathematical ideas;
- check that your answer makes sense in the problem setting;
- use what you know about the problem setting to guide your mathematical reasoning.

MP3 Construct viable arguments and critique the reasoning of others.

When you are asked to explain why a conjecture is correct, you can

- show some examples that fit the claim and explain why they fit;
- show how a new result follows logically from known facts and principles.

When you believe a mathematical claim is incorrect, you can

- show one or more counterexamples—cases that don't fit the claim;
- find steps in the argument that do not follow logically from prior claims.

MP4 Model with mathematics.

When you are asked to solve problems, it often helps to

- think carefully about the numbers or geometric shapes that are the most important factors in the problem, then ask yourself how those factors are related to each other;
- express data and relationships in the problem with tables, graphs, diagrams, or equations, and check your result to see if it makes sense.

MP5 Use appropriate tools strategically.

When working on mathematical questions, you should always

- decide which tools are most helpful for solving the problem and why;
- try a different tool when you get stuck.

MP6 Attend to precision.

In every mathematical exploration or problem-solving task, it is important to

- think carefully about the required accuracy of results; is a number estimate or geometric sketch good enough, or is a precise value or drawing needed?
- report your discoveries with clear and correct mathematical language that can be understood by those to whom you are speaking or writing.

MP7 Look for and make use of structure.

In mathematical explorations and problem solving, it is often helpful to

- look for patterns that show how data points, numbers, or geometric shapes are related to each other;
- use patterns to make predictions.

MP8 Look for and express regularity in repeated reasoning.

When results of a repeated calculation show a pattern, it helps to

- express that pattern as a general rule that can be used in similar cases;
- look for shortcuts that will make the calculation simpler in other cases.

You will use all of the Mathematical Practices in this Unit. Sometimes, when you look at a Problem, it is obvious which practice is most helpful. At other times, you will decide on a practice to use during class explorations and discussions. After completing each Problem, ask yourself:

- What mathematics have I learned by solving this Problem?
- What Mathematical Practices were helpful in learning this mathematics?

Unit Project

Is Anyone Typical?

What are the characteristics of a typical middle-school student? Does a typical middle-school student really exist? As you proceed through this Unit, you will identify some "typical" facts about your classmates, such as:

- The typical number of letters in a student's full name
- The typical number of people in a student's household
- The typical height of a student

After you have completed the Investigations in *Data About Us,* you will carry out a statistical investigation to answer the question,

"What are some of the characteristics of a typical middle-school student?"

These characteristics may include:

- Physical characteristics (such as age, height, or eye color)
- Family and home characteristics (such as number of siblings or number of computers)
- Behaviors (such as hobbies or number of hours spent watching television)
- Preferences, opinions, or attitudes (such as favorite musical group or choice for class president)

As you work through this Unit, make and refine your plans for your project. Keep in mind that a statistical investigation involves posing questions, collecting data, analyzing data, and interpreting the results of the analysis. As you work through each Investigation, think about how you might use what you are learning to complete your project.

What's in a Name? Organizing, Representing, and Describing Data

People are naturally curious about themselves and others. As you work on this Unit, make notes on how you would describe the "typical" middle-school student. At the end of the Unit, you will use what you have learned to conduct a statistical investigation.

Statistical problem solving involves using data to answer questions. The Problems in each Investigation will help you to think about the steps in a statistical investigation. This involves

- asking a question,
- collecting data,
- analyzing the data,
- interpreting the results and writing a report to answer the question asked.

You have already used bar graphs, line plots, and tables to organize and compare data. In *Data About Us,* you will use other tools and representations.

Common Core State Standards

6.SP.A.2 Understand that a set of data collected to answer a statistical question has a distribution that can be described by its center, spread, and overall shape.

6.SP.B.4 Display numerical data in plots on a number line, including dot plots...

6.SP.B.5a Summarize numerical data sets in relation to their context, such as by reporting the number of observations.

Also 6.SP.A.1, 6.SP.A.3, 6.SP.B.5c

1.1 How Many Letters Are in a Name?

Names are filled with tradition. *Onomatologists* study names to discover clues about family ancestors or where people settled around the world. One characteristic that you might not think about is the *length* of a person's name.

There are times when name length matters. Computers may truncate, or shorten, a long name on a library card or an e-mail address. Likewise, only a limited number of letters may fit on a friendship bracelet.

In Problem 1.1, a middle-school class is studying various countries in Asia, as shown in the map below. The class is pen pals with a class in China.

The table on the next page shows the names of the 30 students in each class. Next to the names are the **data** values or *observations* for name length—the total number of letters in the first and last names of each student.

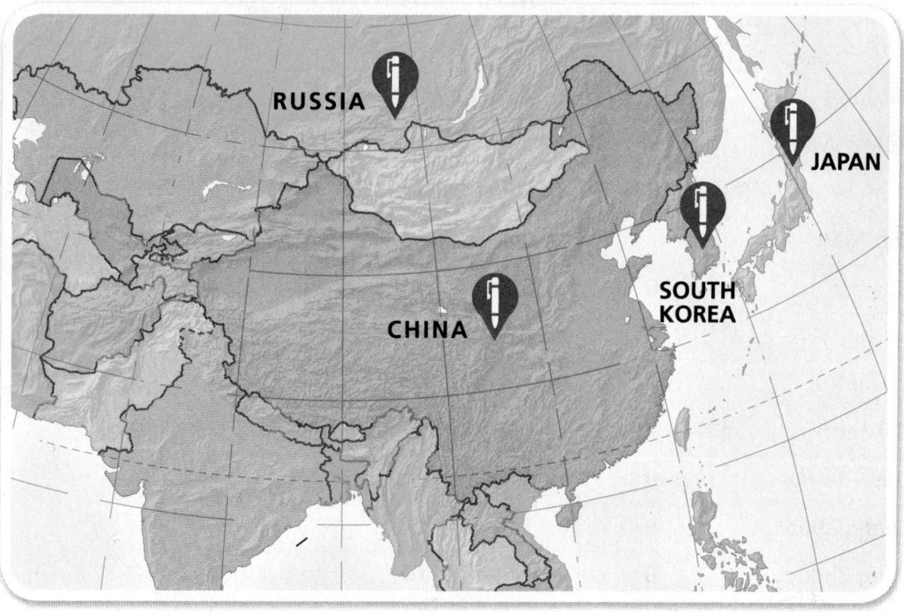

Name Lengths Table 1

Chinese Students	Number of Letters	U.S. Students	Number of Letters
Hua Gao	6	Carson Alexander	15
Liu Gao	6	Avery Anderson	13
Xiang Guo	8	Makayla Bell	11
Zhang Guo	8	Hunter Bennett	13
Li Han	5	Jacob Campbell	13
Yu Han	5	Alexandria Clark	15
Miao He	6	Antonio Cook	11
Yu Hu	4	Kaitlyn Cooper	13
Kong Huang	9	Takisha Davis	12
Ping Li	6	Rebecca Diaz	11
Li Liang	7	Sofia Garcia	11
Chen Lin	7	Arlo Gonzales	12
Yanlin Liu	9	Elijah Hall	10
Dan Luo	6	Kaori Hashimoto	14
Lin Ma	5	Dalton Hayes	11
Lin Song	7	Noah Henderson	13
Chi Sun	6	Haley Jenkins	12
Bai Tang	7	Jack Kelly	9
Dewei Wang	9	Bryce Moore	10
Zhou Wu	6	Lillian Richardson	17
Yun Xiao	7	Liam Rogers	10
Hua Xie	6	Savannah Russell	15
Le Xu	4	Kyle Simmons	11
Xiang Xu	7	Adam Smith	9
Chi Yang	7	Marissa Thomas	13
Qiao Zhang	9	Danielle Thompson	16
Zheng Zhao	9	Esperanza Torres	15
Yang Zheng	9	Ethan Ward	9
Chung Zhou	9	Mackenzie Wilson	15
Wu Zhu	5	Nathaniel Young	14

- An **attribute** is a characteristic or feature about a person or object. What attribute is being investigated here?
- How are the data values for the 60 observations determined?
- What graphs might you make to organize and compare this information?
- Compare the name lengths of the U.S. students to the name lengths of the Chinese students. What do you notice?

In this Problem, you will represent data with tables and graphs in order to examine their **distribution**—the shape of the data set as a whole.

Problem 1.1

A A **frequency table** shows the number of times each value in a data set occurs. It arranges observations in order from least to greatest with their corresponding frequencies.

The frequency table shows some of the data about the Chinese class. The lengths of the first seven names (Hua Gao through Miao He) are recorded using tally marks.

Lengths of Chinese Names (From Name Lengths Table 1)

Number of Letters	Tally	Frequency
1		0
2		0
3		0
4		■
5	‖	■
6	‖‖	■
7		■
8	‖	■
9		■

continued on the next page >

Problem 1.1 continued

1. a. Some name lengths do not occur, such as a name one letter long. How does the table show this?

   b. On a copy of the table, complete the entries for the Chinese class.

2. For the U.S. class data, make a frequency table like the one on the previous page.

3. Compare the two frequency tables of class data.

   a. What are the shortest and longest Chinese names?

   b. What are the shortest and longest U.S. names?

B A **line plot** is a graph that shows data values on a number line using *X*s or other marks.

1. Make two line plots, one for each class. Use the same *scale* on both line plots.

2. Describe how the frequency tables helped you make the line plots.

C Use the line plots you made in Question B. Look at the shapes of the distributions of the data sets.

1. How would you describe the *shape* of the distribution? Are there any places where the data values **cluster,** or group together? Are there any **gaps,** or places where there are no data values?

2. Write two questions about the Chinese and U.S. classes that you can answer from your graphs.

3. Write three statements to compare the name lengths of the U.S. students and the Chinese students.

4. Describe how the line plots helped you compare the name lengths for the two classes.

D 1. Identify a typical name length or name lengths for the Chinese class. Explain your reasoning.

2. Identify a typical name length or name lengths for the U.S. class. Explain your reasoning.

ACE Homework starts on page 19.

1.2 Describing Name Lengths
What Are the Shape, Mode, and Range?

Problem 1.1 asked you to describe a typical name length or name lengths for the U.S. class and for the Chinese class. One way to describe what is *typical* is to identify the data value that occurs most frequently. This is the **mode** of the data set. A data set may have more than one mode. Look back at the graphs you made in Problem 1.1.

- What is the mode of the U.S. class data? The Chinese class data?

In any data set, data values vary from a **minimum value** to a **maximum value.** The difference of the maximum data value and the minimum data value is the **range** of the data.

- What is the range of the U.S. class data? The Chinese class data?

Did You Know?

There are almost 7,000 spoken languages in the world today. Languages change as people of different cultures interact with each other. Some languages have identical or similar alphabets, such as English and Spanish. Other languages, such as Arabic and Japanese, use systems of characters that look quite different from the alphabet that we use in the United States.

The U.S. middle-school class now receives a 20-name list of pen pals from a class in Japan.

Name Lengths Table 2

Japanese Students	Number of Letters
Ai Kiyomizu	10
Daiki Kobayashi	14
Tsubasa Tanaka	13
Eric Katou	9
Kana Hayashi	11
Miyuu Shimizu	12
Ken Satou	8
Manami Ikeda	11
Hina Mori	8
Ryo Takahashi	12
Taka Yamamoto	12
Takumi Itou	10
Haruto Nakamura	14
Tomo Sasaki	10
Youta Kichida	12
Yuki Ine	7
Kiro Suzuki	10
Yumi Matsumoto	13
Yumi Yamasaki	12
Yusuke Yoshida	13

How do the Japanese name lengths compare to the U.S. name lengths?

In this Problem, you will use *dot plots* to represent the frequency of data. **Dot plots** and line plots are the same types of graphs. Instead of Xs, dot plots use filled-in circles, or dots.

Problem 1.2

A The students in the U.S. class start making a dot plot to show the distribution of the Japanese name-length data. They record the data values for the first 12 names in the list on the dot plot below.

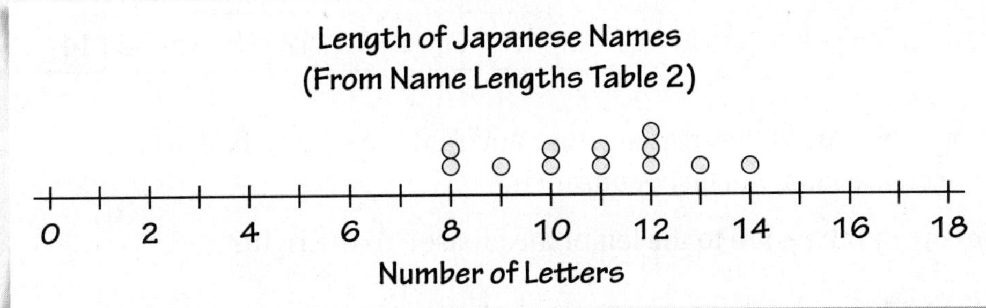

1. On a copy of the dot plot, insert the data for the last eight names (Haruto Nakamura to Yusuke Yoshida).
2. Look at the shape of the distribution.
   a. Are there *clusters* of data? Explain your reasoning.
   b. Are there gaps in the distribution? Explain.

B
1. What is the *mode* of this distribution?
2. Is the mode a good description of the typical name length of the Japanese students? Why or why not?

C
1. What is the *range* of the data?
2. Use the range of each data set to compare the lengths of U.S., Chinese, and Japanese names.

ACE Homework starts on page 19.

1.3 Describing Name Lengths
What Is the Median?

Another way to describe what is typical is to mark the midpoint, or the **median**, of a data set. To identify the median, begin by making an *ordered list* of the data values.

Use a strip of 20 squares from a sheet of grid paper to organize the Japanese pen-pal data from Problem 1.2. Write the name lengths in order from least to greatest on the grid paper, as shown below.

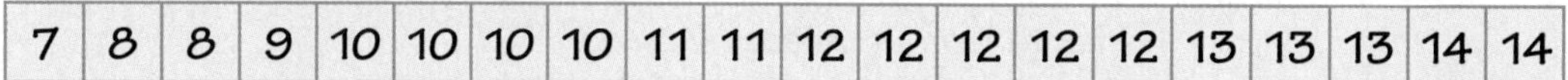

7	8	8	9	10	10	10	10	11	11	12	12	12	12	12	13	13	13	14	14

- If you put the ends of the strip together and fold the strip in half, where does the crease fall in the list of numbers?
- How many numbers are to the left of the crease? To the right?

The median is always located at the "half-way" point in a set of ordered data. Since there are 20 data values, the *position* of the median is at the crease that falls between the 10th and 11th data values. The *value* of the median is determined using the actual values of the 10th and 11th data values.

- What is the median of the data set?

A **summary statistic** is one number calculated from all the data values in a distribution. It summarizes something important about the distribution. The median is a summary statistic. The range and the mode are also summary statistics.

- What can you say about the lengths of the Japanese students' names when you know the median?

Problem 1.3

A The sticky notes below display the name-length data for the Japanese students. The red line shows the *position* of the median, the midpoint of the 20 observations. The *value* of the median is $11\frac{1}{2}$ letters, determined by the 10th and 11th data values of "11" and "12" letters.

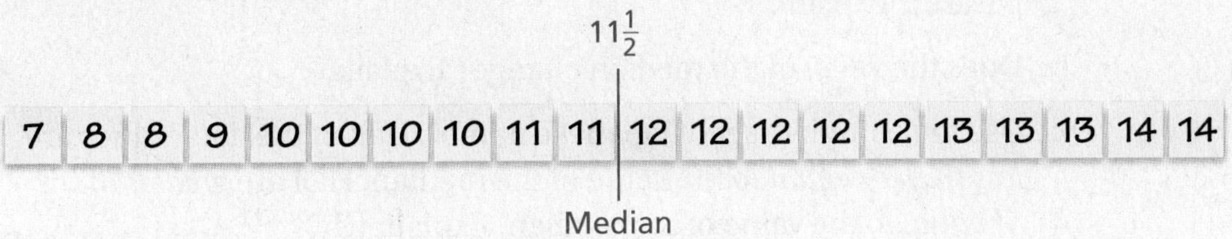

1. The Japanese teacher sent over two more names, Arisa Hasimoto and Yui Inoue. How many observations are there now? What is the *position* of the median? What is the *value* of the median? Explain.

2. One more name, Hina Abe, is added. How many observations are there now? What is the *position* of the median? What is the *value* of the median? Explain.

continued on the next page >

Problem 1.3 continued

3. The names Aya Yamaguchi, Ayumi Rin, Eri Matsumoto, Haruka Kimura, Kazu Ohayashi, Kazuki Yamada, and Sayake Saitou are added to the list. There are now 30 names from the Japanese class.
   - **a.** Does the position of the median change from its location in part (2)? Explain.
   - **b.** Does the value of the median change? Explain.
   - **c.** Use the complete set of Japanese names. Half of the data values are *less than or equal to* the value of the median. Half are *greater than or equal to* the value of the median. Explain why.

B Compare the Japanese data to the Chinese and U.S. data from Problem 1.1.

1. Identify the value of the median and the range for each of the three data sets.
2. Use these statistics to write at least three statements comparing the three name-length distributions.

C

1. What is the position of the median in a distribution that has 9 data values? 19 data values? 999 data values?
2. What is the position of the median in a distribution that has 10 data values? 20 data values? 1,000 data values?
3. Describe how to locate the position of the median and find the value of the median when
   - **a.** there is an odd number of data values.
   - **b.** there is an even number of data values.

ACE Homework starts on page 19.

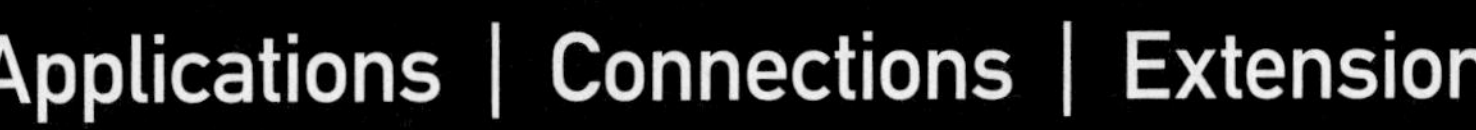

Applications

For Exercises 1–4, use the table below.

Name Lengths Table 3

Korean Pen Pals	Number of Letters	Korean Pen Pals	Number of Letters
Kim Ae-Cha	8	Hwang Il	7
Lee Chin-Hae	10	Song Ja	6
Park Chin	8	Ahn Jae-Hwa	9
Choi Chung-Cha	12	You Jung	7
Jung Chung-Hee	12	Hong Kang-Dae	11
Kang Bae	7	Kim Hyo-Sonn	10
Cho Dong-Yul	10	Yi Mai-Chin	9
Yoon Eun-Kyung	12	Pak Mi-Ok	7
Chang Hei-Ran	11	Kim Mun-Hee	9
Lim Hak-Kun	9	Yun Myung	8
Han Hei	6	Sin Myung-Hee	11
Shin Hwan	8	Gwon Myung-Ok	11
Suh Eun-Kyung	11	Hong Sang-Ook	11
Kwon Hyun	8	Jeong Shin	9
Son Hyun-Ae	9	Bak Soo	6

1. Make a frequency table and a dot plot for the Korean class data.

2. What are the shortest and longest Korean names?

3. How would you describe the shape of the distribution of Korean data?

4. Identify a typical name length or name lengths for the Korean class data. Explain your reasoning.

5. Recall the name length tables from Problems 1.1 and 1.2 and the names from Exercises 1–4. Below are four dot plots representing each set of names. There are no titles to show which graph represents which set of data.

   a. Write a correct title for each graph, such as *Graph A: Name Lengths From* ? . Explain your reasoning.

   b. Write four statements that compare the name lengths from the different classes.

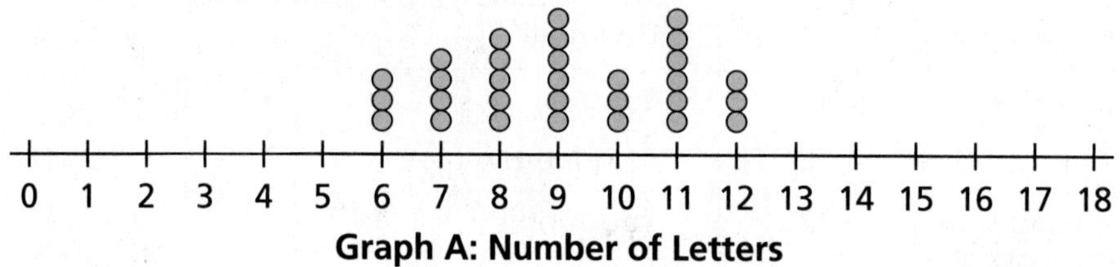

Graph A: Number of Letters

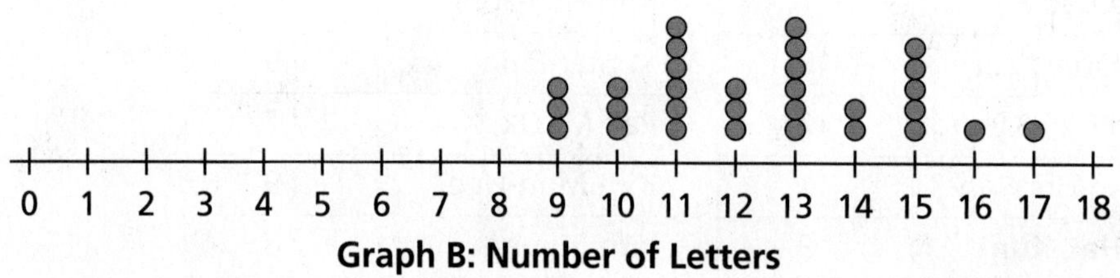

Graph B: Number of Letters

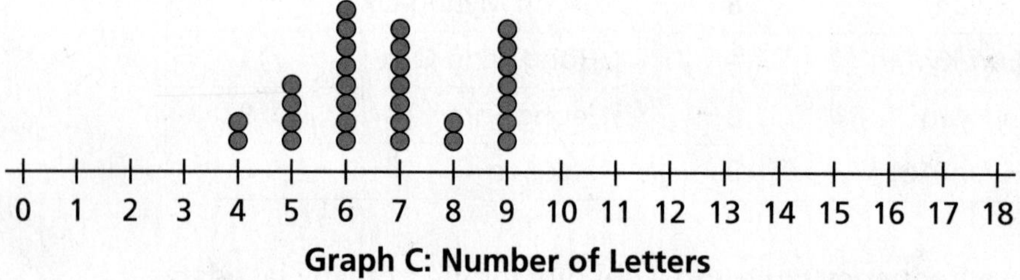

Graph C: Number of Letters

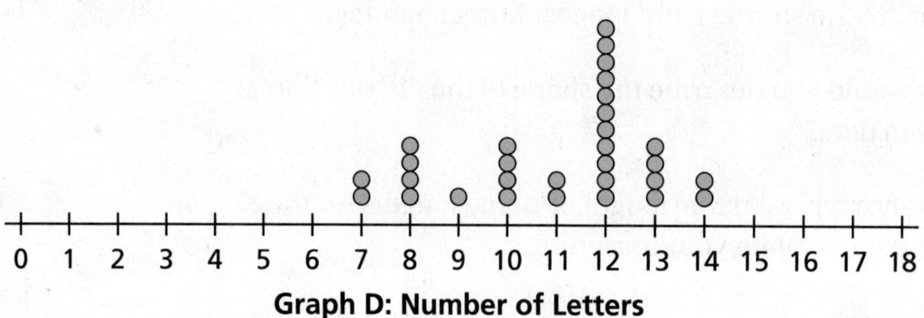

Graph D: Number of Letters

c. Jasmine says that the graphs show a lot of empty space. She thinks the graphs work better if they look like the dot plots below. How are these graphs different from the dot plots displayed in part (b)? Do you agree with Jasmine? Explain your reasoning.

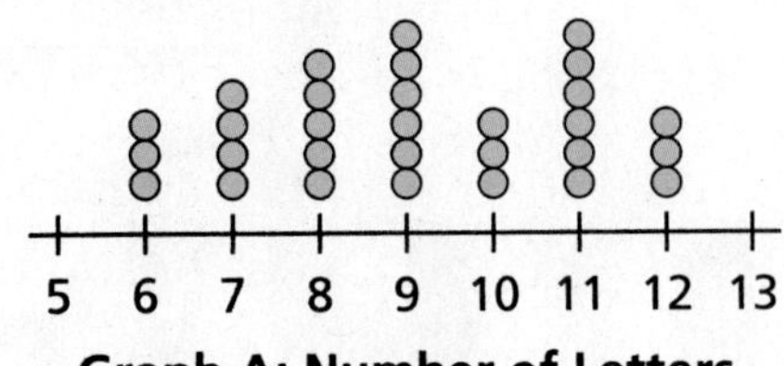

Graph A: Number of Letters

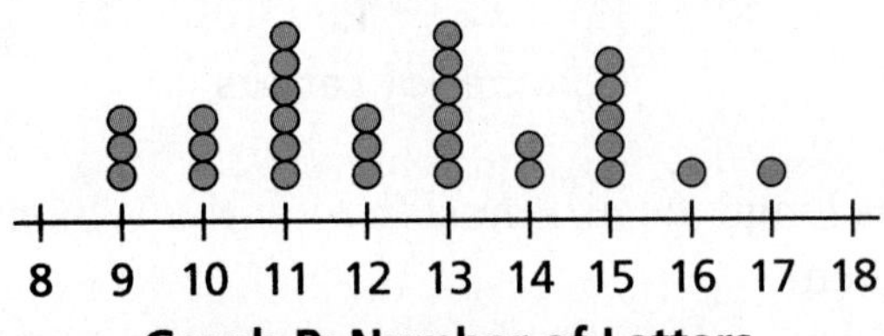

Graph B: Number of Letters

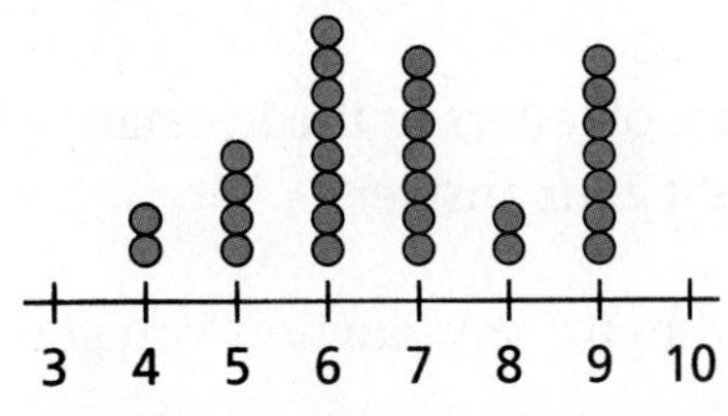

Graph C: Number of Letters

6 7 8 9 10 11 12 13 14 15

Graph D: Number of Letters

The U.S. class is also pen pals with a Russian class. For Exercises 6–9, use the bar graph below.

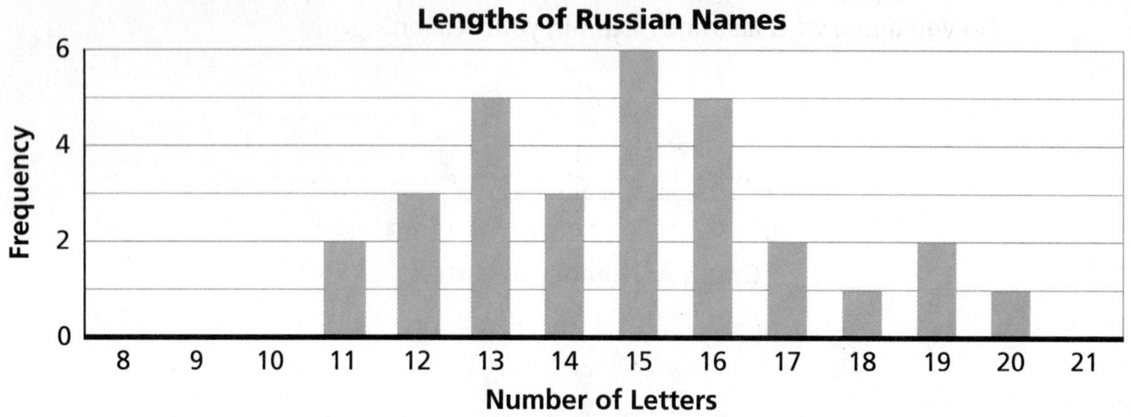

6. Which value for name length occurs most frequently? What is this summary statistic called?

7. How many Russian students are in this data set? Explain how you got your answer.

8. What is the range of number of letters in the Russian pen pals' names? Explain how you got your answer.

9. What is the median name length? Explain how you got your answer.

10. Alicia has a pet rat that is 1 year old. She wonders if her rat is old compared to other rats. At the pet store, she finds out that the median lifespan of a rat is 2.5 years.

a. What does the median tell Alicia about the lifespan of a rat?

b. What other information would help her predict her rat's lifespan?

Rat Facts

- Rats are gentle and friendly. They bond with their owners and are fun to play with.
- Rats are noctural. They are most active at night.
- Average Lifespan is 2.5 years.
- Rats may be lactose intolerant; be careful in giving them cheese!
- A rat's front teeth could grow up to 5 or 6 inches each year, but they are worn down by gnawing.

Make a line plot for a set of data that fits each description.

11. 24 names that vary in length from 8 letters to 20 letters

12. 7 names with a median length of 14 letters

13. 13 names with a range of 9 letters and a median length of 13 letters

14. 16 names with a median length of $14\frac{1}{2}$ letters and that vary in length from 11 letters to 20 letters

Connections

15. Below is a bar graph that shows the number and type of pet owned by a class of middle-school students.

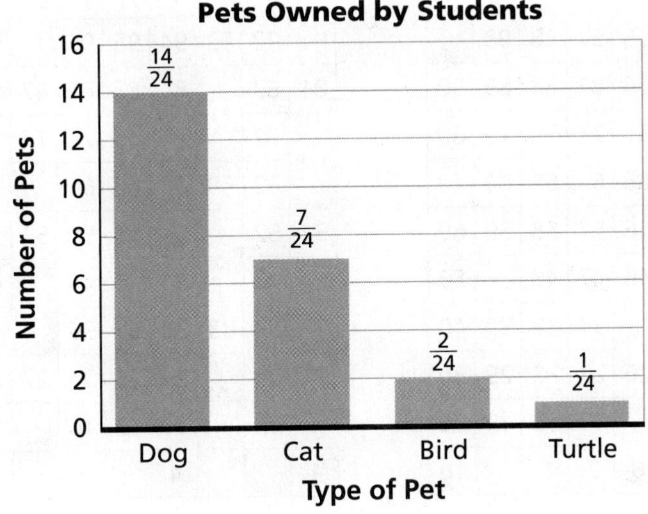

a. The fraction $\frac{14}{24}$ shows the *relative frequency* of pet dogs. What does the numerator tell you? What does the denominator tell you?

b. Can you use the fractions on the bars to determine the number of students surveyed? Explain why or why not.

16. Each grid is numbered 1 to 100. Find the rule that describes the white numbers.

a.

91	92	93	94	95	96	97	98	99	100
81	82	83	84	85	86	87	88	89	90
71	72	73	74	75	76	77	78	79	80
61	62	63	64	65	66	67	68	69	70
51	52	53	54	55	56	57	58	59	60
41	42	43	44	45	46	47	48	49	50
31	32	33	34	35	36	37	38	39	40
21	22	23	24	25	26	27	28	29	30
11	12	13	14	15	16	17	18	19	20
1	2	3	4	5	6	7	8	9	10

b.

91	92	93	94	95	96	97	98	99	100
81	82	83	84	85	86	87	88	89	90
71	72	73	74	75	76	77	78	79	80
61	62	63	64	65	66	67	68	69	70
51	52	53	54	55	56	57	58	59	60
41	42	43	44	45	46	47	48	49	50
31	32	33	34	35	36	37	38	39	40
21	22	23	24	25	26	27	28	29	30
11	12	13	14	15	16	17	18	19	20
1	2	3	4	5	6	7	8	9	10

c.

91	92	93	94	95	96	97	98	99	100
81	82	83	84	85	86	87	88	89	90
71	72	73	74	75	76	77	78	79	80
61	62	63	64	65	66	67	68	69	70
51	52	53	54	55	56	57	58	59	60
41	42	43	44	45	46	47	48	49	50
31	32	33	34	35	36	37	38	39	40
21	22	23	24	25	26	27	28	29	30
11	12	13	14	15	16	17	18	19	20
1	2	3	4	5	6	7	8	9	10

d.

91	92	93	94	95	96	97	98	99	100
81	82	83	84	85	86	87	88	89	90
71	72	73	74	75	76	77	78	79	80
61	62	63	64	65	66	67	68	69	70
51	52	53	54	55	56	57	58	59	60
41	42	43	44	45	46	47	48	49	50
31	32	33	34	35	36	37	38	39	40
21	22	23	24	25	26	27	28	29	30
11	12	13	14	15	16	17	18	19	20
1	2	3	4	5	6	7	8	9	10

17. Make a coordinate grid like the one below. Along the x-axis, write the numbers 1 to 30. Do the same for the y-axis. For each number on the x-axis, plot its factors above it.

The graph below gives part of the answer, showing the factors for numbers 1 through 6.

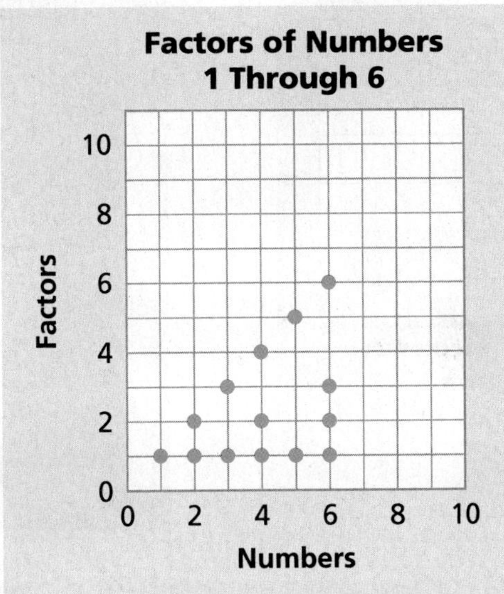

a. Which numbers have only two factors? What is common about the factors they have?

b. What numbers are even numbers? How can you use their factors to help you answer this question?

c. Make observations about the factors of a number.

i. What is the greatest factor of any number?

ii. What is the least factor of any number?

iii. What is the second-greatest factor of any number? How do these factors relate to the greatest factor of any number?

iv. Make your own observations about the factors of a number.

18. Each graph in parts (a)–(c) is misleading. For each, answer the following:

- What information is the graph seeking to provide?
- What is wrong with how the information is displayed?

a.

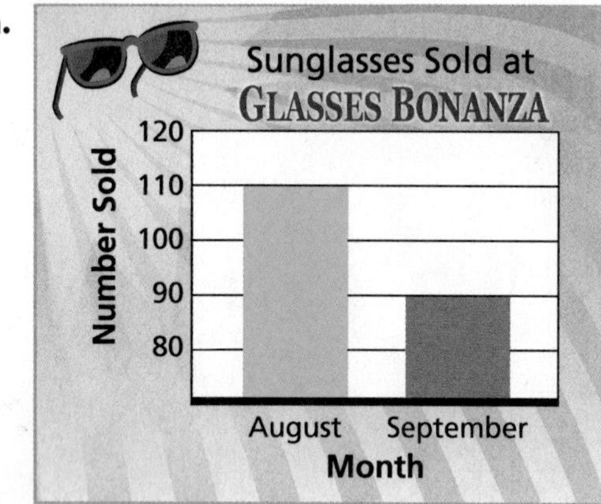

b.

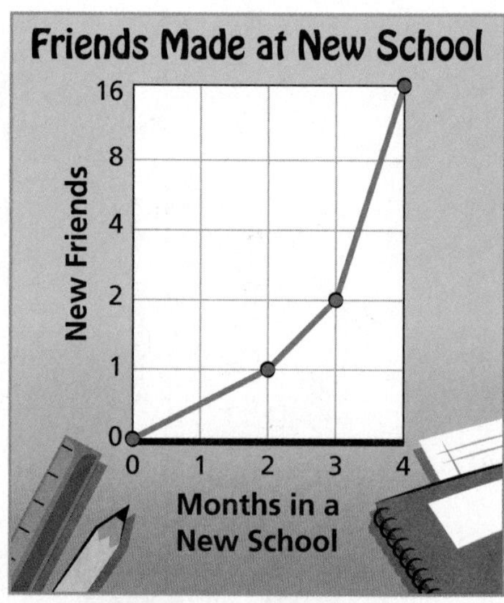

c.

19. The graph below shows the heights of two brothers, Trevor and Trey, over time.

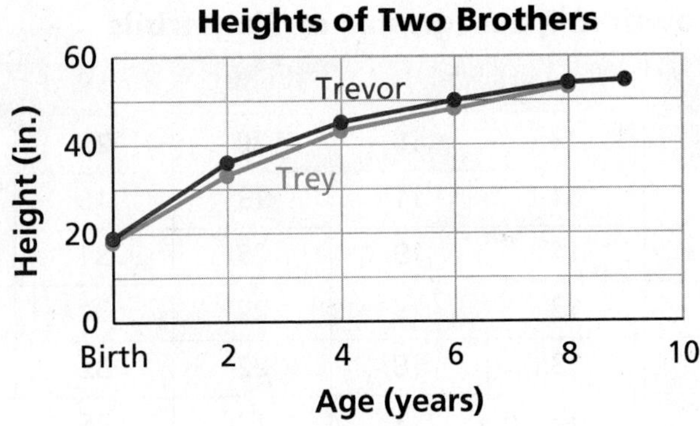

a. Write two statements about Trevor's height using the data displayed on the graph.

b. Write two statements about Trey's height using the data displayed on the graph.

c. Write two statements comparing the brothers' heights using the data.

d. Suzanne wrote the statement below. Do you agree with her reasoning? Explain.

> Suzanne:
>
> I know that Trevor is taller than Trey because the line showing his height is above the line showing Trey's height. I also know that Trevor is growing faster than his brother Trey.

20. The table below shows data collected about some gerbil babies and their growth over time.

Growth in Mass (grams) of Six Gerbils

Name	Age in Days					
	11	13	18	20	25	27
Fuzz Ball	10	11	11	13	16	19
Scooter	12	14	19	28	31	36
Sleepy	11	13	13	22	34	38
Racer	12	13	18	22	32	35
Cuddles	10	12	13	17	25	27
Curious	11	12	12	15	19	22

a. Make a graph showing a line for each gerbil's mass on the same coordinate grid. Think carefully about how you label and scale the *y*-axis (mass) and the *x*-axis (age in days). Label each line to indicate which gerbil it represents.

b. Write four statements comparing the growth rates of the six gerbils.

c. Suppose someone asks, "About how much do gerbils grow in the first month after they are born?" How would you answer? Explain.

For Exercises 21–23, use the bar graphs below. The graphs show information about a class of middle-school students.

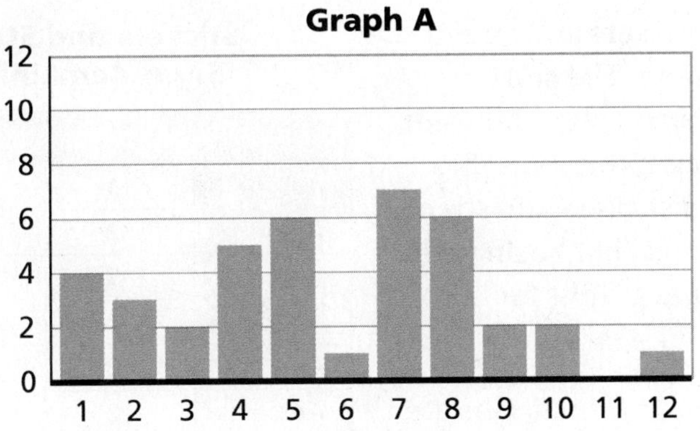

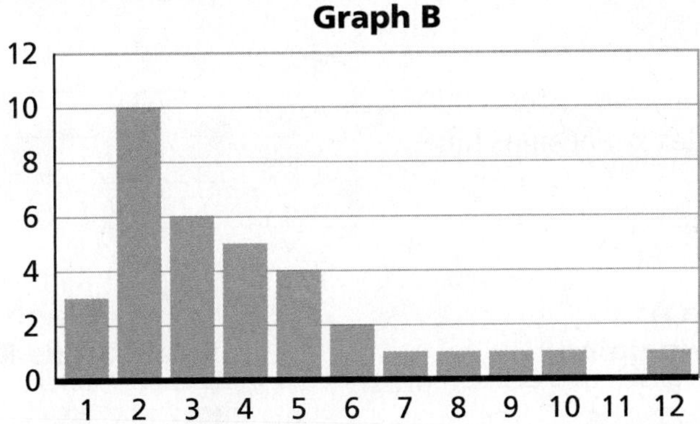

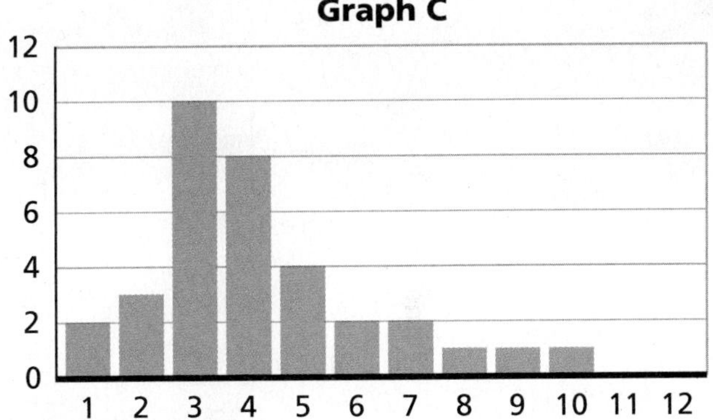

21. Which graph might show the number of children in the students' families? Explain.

22. Which graph might show the birth months of the students? Explain.

Note: Months are often written using numbers instead of names. For example, 1 means January, 2 means February, etc.

23. Which graph might show the number of toppings students like on their pizzas? Explain.

Extensions

A greeting card store sells stickers and street signs with first names on them. The store ordered 12 stickers and 12 street signs for each name. The table and the four bar graphs that follow show the numbers of stickers and street signs remaining for the names that begin with the letter A. Use the table and graphs for Exercises 24–30.

Stickers and Street Signs Remaining

Name	Stickers	Street Signs
Aaron	1	9
Adam	2	7
Alex	7	4
Allison	2	3
Amanda	0	11
Amber	2	3
Amy	3	3
Andrea	2	4
Andrew	8	6
Andy	3	5
Angel	8	4
Ava	10	7

24. Use Graph A. How many Alex stickers are left? How many Alex stickers have been sold? Explain.

25. Use Graph B. How many Alex street signs are left? How many Alex street signs have been sold? Explain.

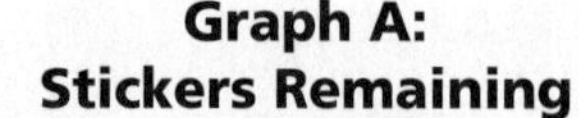

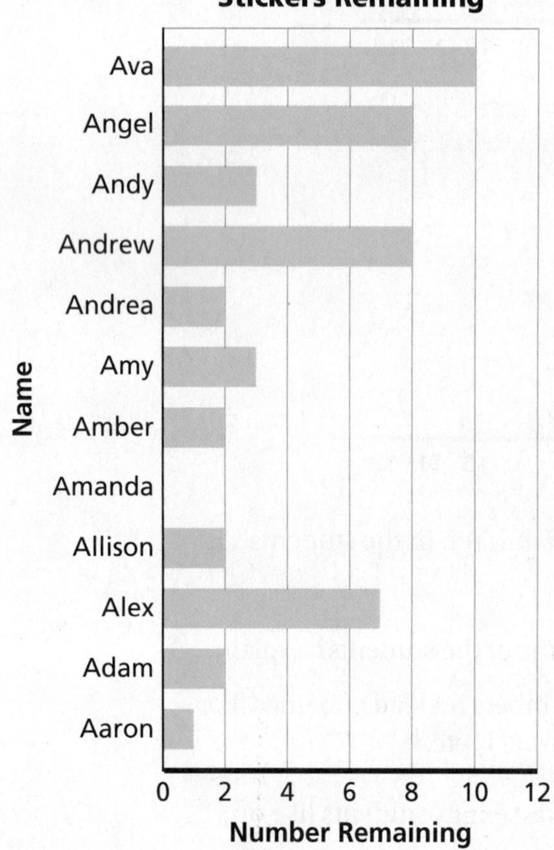

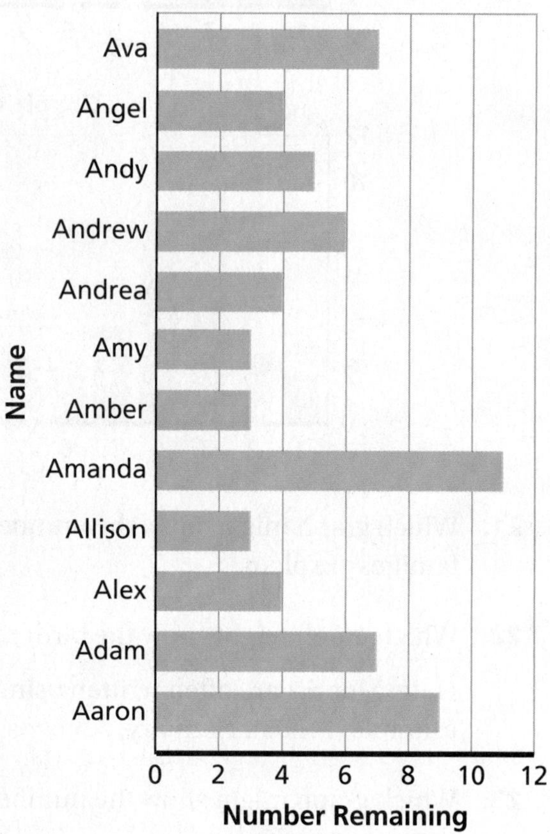

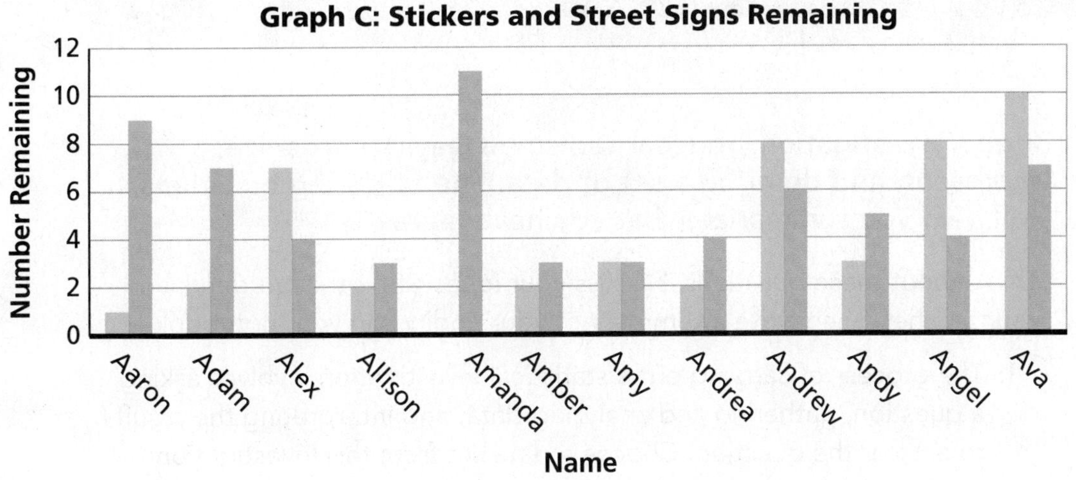

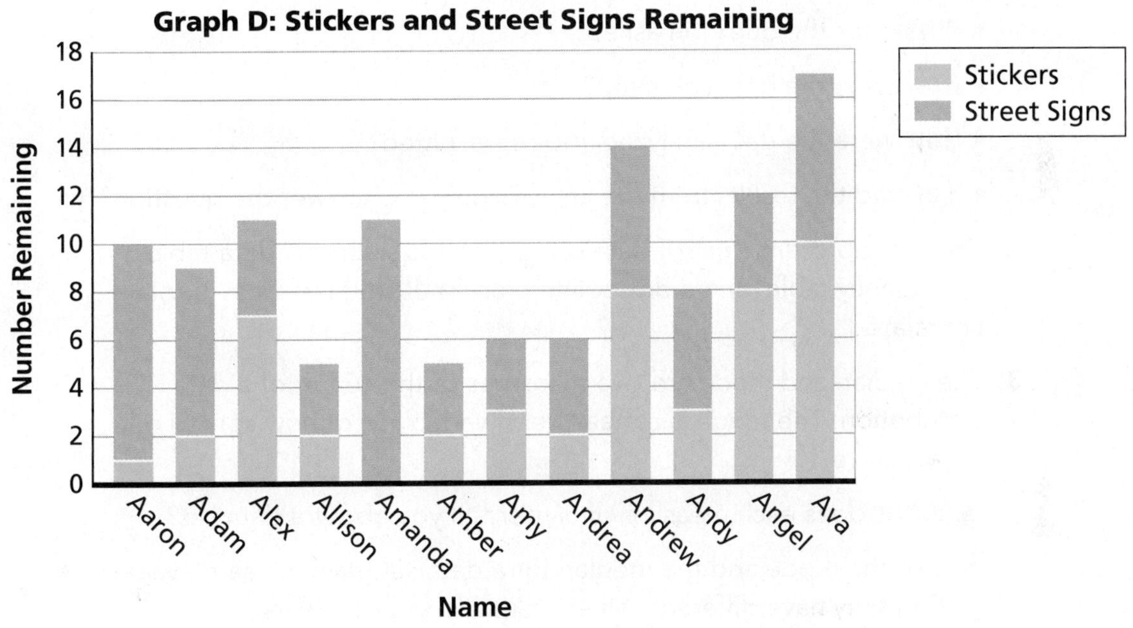

26. For names beginning with A, which are more popular, the stickers or the street signs? Explain your answer.

27. If each sticker costs $1.50, how much money has the store collected from selling name stickers that begin with the letter A?

28. For which name has the store sold the most stickers? The least?

29. Graph C is a *double bar graph*. Use this graph to determine the name(s) for which the number of street signs sold and the number of sticker packages sold are the same.

30. Graph D is a *stacked bar graph*. Use this graph to determine whether some names are more popular than others. Justify your answer.

Mathematical Reflections 1

In this Investigation, you learned some ways to organize, represent, and describe a set of data. The following questions will help you summarize what you have learned.

Think about these questions. Discuss your ideas with other students and your teacher. Then write a summary of your findings in your notebook.

1. The process of carrying out a statistical investigation involves asking a question, gathering and analyzing data, and interpreting the results to answer the question. Choose a data set from this Investigation. Use the data set to answer each question below.
   - **What** was the question asked?
   - **How** were the data collected?
   - **How** were the data analyzed and represented?
   - **How** did the results from the analysis help you answer the question?
2. You can represent a set of data using displays such as a data table, a frequency table, and a dot or line plot. **Explain** how these displays are related.
3. The median and mode are two measures of the center of a data distribution. The range is a measure of variability, or how spread out the data are.
   a. **What** does each measure of center tell you about a data set?
   b. Can the mode and the median for a data set have the same value? Can they have different values? **Explain** your answers.
   c. **How** does the range tell you how much the data vary?
   d. Suppose we add a new data value to a set of data. Does this new value affect the mode? The median? The range? **Explain**.
4. **What** strategies can you use to make comparisons among data sets?

Unit Project

Think about the survey you will be developing.

How might you collect and display the data you gather?

Common Core Mathematical Practices

As you worked on the Problems in this Investigation, you used prior knowledge to make sense of them. You also applied Mathematical Practices to solve the Problems. Think back over your work, the ways you thought about the Problems, and how you used Mathematical Practices.

Nick described his thoughts in the following way:

In Problem 1.1, we used tables and dot plots to show the different sets of data about name lengths. We talked about why we would call each of these data sets a "distribution."

Seeing how the data were distributed across the name lengths, and then noticing things like clusters, gaps, and shape in general, gave us an idea about typical name lengths for each group of students.

When we used the graphs, we made sure to have the same scale on each graph. That made it easier to compare the name lengths of the students from the different countries.

Common Core Standards for Mathematical Practice

MP4 Model with mathematics

- What other Mathematical Practices can you identify in Nick's reasoning?
- Describe a Mathematical Practice that you and your classmates used to solve a different Problem in this Investigation.

Who's in Your Household? Using the Mean

The United States Census is carried out every ten years. Among other statistics, the Census provides useful information about household size. The Census uses the term *household* to mean all the people who live in a "housing unit" (such as a house, an apartment, or a mobile home).

When you work with a set of numbers, a single statistic is often calculated to represent the "typical" value to describe the center of a distribution. In Investigation 1, you used median and mode. Another *measure of center* is the **mean.** It is the most commonly used measure of center for numerical data. The mean of a set of data is often called the *average*.

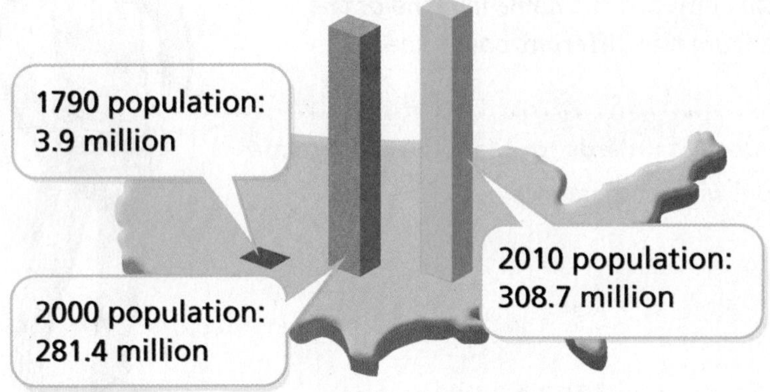

Common Core State Standards

6.SP.A.3 Recognize that a measure of center for a numerical data set summarizes all of its values with a single number . . .

6.SP.B.5b Summarize numerical data sets in relation to their context, such as by describing the nature of the attribute under investigation, including how it was measured and its units of measurement.

6.SP.B.5d Summarize numerical data sets in relation to their context, such as by relating the choice of measures of center . . . to the shape of the data distribution and the context in which the data were gathered.

Also **6.NS.C.6, 6.NS.C.7, 6.SP.A.1, 6.SP.A.2, 6.SP.B.4, 6.SP.B.5a, 6.SP.B.5c**

2.1 What's a Mean Household Size?

Six students in a middle-school class use the United States Census guidelines to find the number of people in their households. Each student made a stack of cubes to show the number of people in his or her household. The stacks show that the six households vary in size.

- What is the attribute being investigated?
- How can you use the cube stacks to find the median of the data? The mode?

One way to find the *mean,* or average, household size is to make all the stacks the same height by moving cubes. The evened-out stacks tell you how many people there would be per household if all households were the same size.

- How can you use the cube stacks to find the mean household size for these six students?

You can also use a table to show the data.

Household Size Table 1

Name	Number of People
Ollie	2
Yarnell	3
Gary	3
Ruth	4
Pablo	6
Brenda	6

- How else might you represent this data set?
- Which representation tells you how many people are in all six households?

In this Problem, you will look at the mean of a data set and how it is calculated.

Problem 2.1

A You can use an **ordered-value bar graph** to find the mean of a data set. An ordered-value bar graph and a dot plot are shown below. Both display the number of people in the six households found in Household Size Table 1. You already found the mean, four people, by evening out the cube stacks.

Household Size 1

6
6
4
3
3
2

0 1 2 3 4 5 6 7

Number of People

Household Size 1

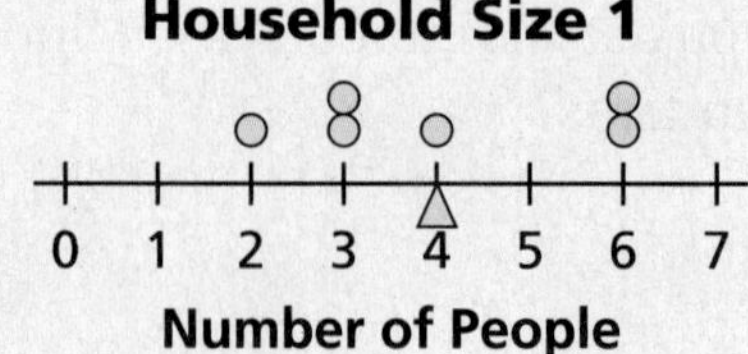

Number of People

1. Explain how the ordered-value bar graph and dot plot are related.

Problem 2.1 continued

2. Brenda used the ordered-value bar graph at the right to identify the mean. Her first steps are shown. On a copy of the graph, complete Brenda's steps.

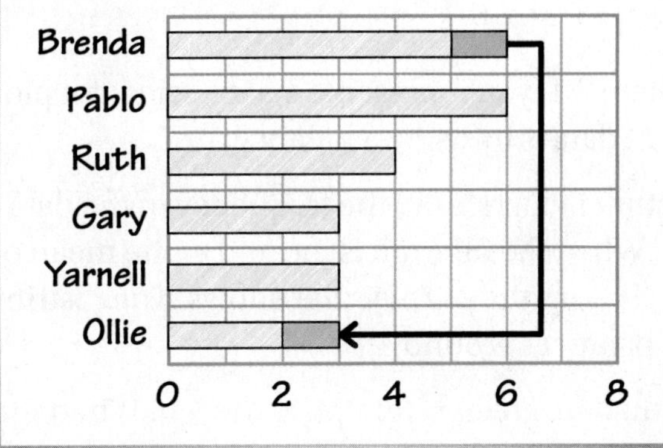

3. Ollie says that, after evening out the bars, the graph looks like six households with four people each. How might you have predicted the mean? Explain.

B Another group of students made the table below for a different set of data.

1. Make an ordered-value bar graph and a dot plot to display the data.
2. Find the mean of the data. Explain how you found it.
3. How does the mean of this data set compare to the mean of the data in Question A?
4. How does identifying the mean on an ordered-value bar graph help you find the mean on a dot plot? Explain.

Household Size Table 2

Name	Number of People
Reggie	6
Tara	4
Brendan	3
Felix	4
Hector	3
Tonisha	4

5. Does knowing the mean help you answer the question, "What is the typical household size?" Explain.

ACE Homework starts on page 48.

2.2 Comparing Distributions With the Same Mean

In Problem 2.1, you represented data using dot plots. Another way to represent data is by using a balance.

The picture below shows the frequency of the data from Household Size Table 1. When the fulcrum is located at the mean of the distribution, the ruler is level, as the purple ruler shows. The distribution in Household Size Table 1 balances around 4.

Notice that the green ruler tips to the left. When the fulcrum is not located at the mean of the distribution, the ruler is not level.

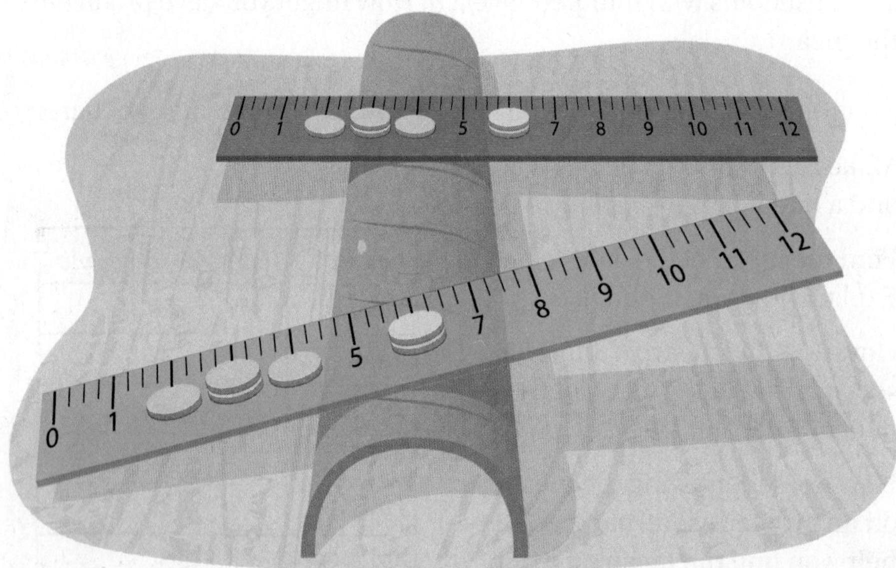

- How does the picture help explain why the mean is often called the *balance point* of a distribution?
- What information do you need to calculate the mean of a data set?

Problem 2.2

A Household Size Table 1 and Household Size Table 2 in Problem 2.1 each show six households with a mean of four people.

1. Make up a different data set of six households that has a mean of four people per household.
2. Make an ordered-value bar graph and a line or dot plot to represent your set of data.
3. Describe how to use your bar graph to verify the mean is four people.
4. Explain how you can find the following on your graphs:
   a. each person's household size
   b. the total number of households
   c. the total number of people in the combined households
   d. How can you use the information in parts (a)–(c) to find the mean?

B A group of seven students has a mean of three people per household.

1. Make up a data set that fits this description.
2. Make an ordered-value bar graph and a line or dot plot to represent your set of data.
3. Describe how to use your bar graph to verify the mean is three people.
4. Suppose you found another data set with seven households and a mean of three people per household, but with a greater range. How would this change the appearance of your line or dot plot?
5. Explain how you can find the following on your graphs:
   a. each person's household size
   b. the total number of households
   c. the total number of people in the combined households
   d. How can you use the information in parts (a)–(c) to find the mean?

continued on the next page >

Problem 2.2 continued

C A group of six students has a mean of $3\frac{1}{2}$ people.

1. Make up a data set that fits this description.
2. Make an ordered-value bar graph and a line or dot plot to represent your set of data.
3. How can the mean be $3\frac{1}{2}$ people when "half" a person does not exist?

D The dot plot below shows the household sizes for a group of eight students.

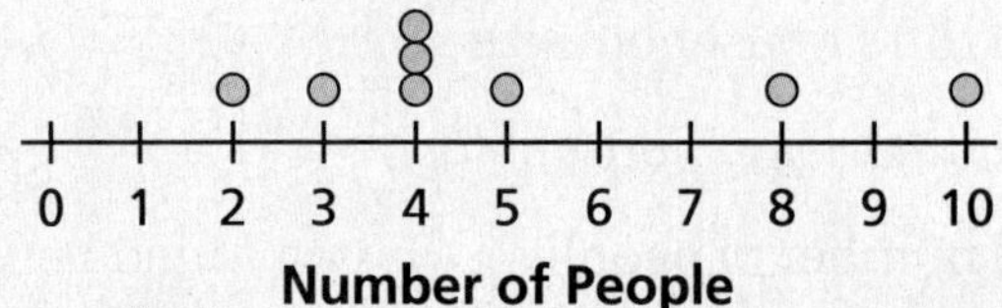

1. Identify the median, mode, and range of the distribution.
2. Think about viewing the distribution on a balance. Make an estimate or guess about where the mean is located.
3. Identify the mean of the distribution. How does this compare with your estimate or guess? Explain.
4. **a.** Compare the three measures of center—mean, median, and mode. How are they the same or different? Explain.

   b. Is it possible to have the three measures of center of a distribution all be the same? All be different? Explain.

   c. Which measure would you choose to describe the typical household size for the eight households? Explain.

E Look back at the work you did in Questions A–D and in Problem 2.1. Describe a method to compute the mean in any situation.

ACE Homework starts on page 48.

2.3 Making Choices
Mean or Median?

When you gather data about the typical middle-school student, you may want to inquire about what interests students have. In Problem 2.3, you will use data about skateboard prices to investigate when to use the mean or median to describe what is "typical."

Problem 2.3

The table below shows prices of skateboards at four different stores.

Retail Table 1: Prices of Skateboards (dollars)

Store A	Store B	Store C	Store D
60	13	40	179
40	40	20	160
13	45	60	149
45	60	35	149
20	50	50	149
30	30	30	145
35	15	13	149
60	35	45	100
50	15	40	179
70	70	50	145
50	50	60	149
50	70	70	149
60	50	70	149
50	10	50	149
35	120	90	145
15	90	120	150
70	120	120	149
120		200	149

continued on the next page >

Problem 2.3 *continued*

A The dot plots below show the data from Stores B and C.

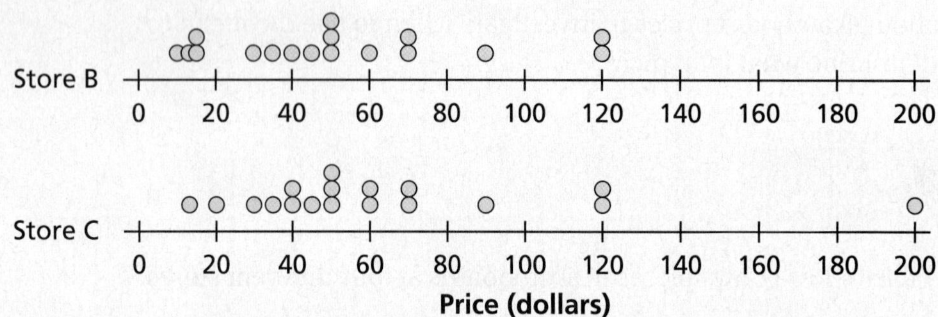

1. Compute the median and mean of the data from the two stores.
2. For each store,
   - Describe how the measures of center and dot plots are related.
   - Describe how the distribution of the data influences the location of the mean and the median.

B Use the information in Retail Table 1.

1. Make a line plot showing the data from Store A.
2. Compute the mean and the median of Store A's prices.
3. Store A decides to stock some higher-priced skateboards. Using a different color, include these data values one at a time on your line plot. After you include each value, find the new mean and the new median of the data. Complete a copy of the table below.

Store A's New Stock

New Stock Price	New Mean	New Median
$200	■	■
$180	■	■
$180	■	■
$160	■	■
$170	■	■
$140	■	■

Problem 2.3 *continued*

4. Suppose the price of the last skateboard were $200, not $140. What would happen to the mean? To the median?

5. When do additional data values influence the mean of the distribution? Influence the median?

6. Which measure of center would you use to answer the question "What is the typical price of skateboards at Store A when all the higher-priced skateboards are included?" Explain your reasoning.

C Each dot plot below shows combined data for two stores from Retail Table 1. For one set of combined data, the mean is $107.11 and the median is $132.50. For the other set of combined data, the mean is $50.17 and the median is $50.00.

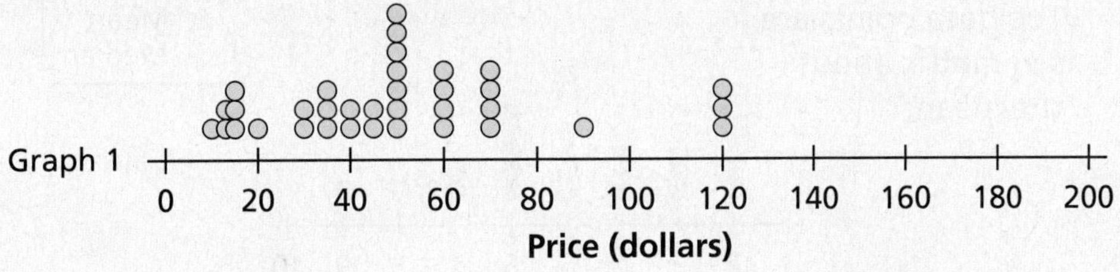

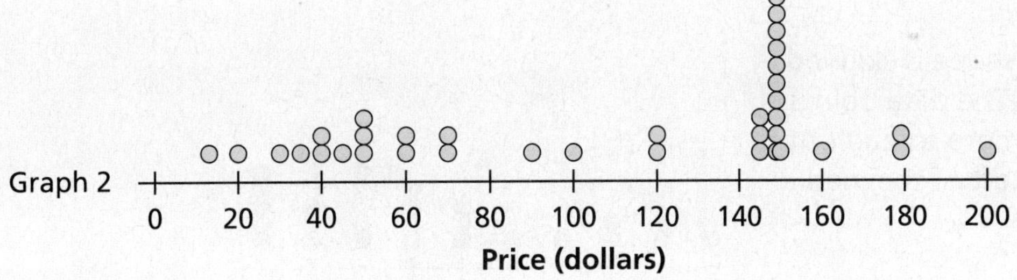

1. Write a complete title for each dot plot by identifying the two sets of data it shows. For example, *Graph 1: Skateboard Prices From Stores* __?__ *and* __?__. Explain your reasoning.

2. For one graph, the mean and median are almost the same. For the other, the mean and median are different. Explain how the distribution of the data influences the location of the mean or the median.

D In a blog, Dr. Statistics says that "the median is a resistant measure of center, and the mean is *not* a resistant measure of center." Explain the meaning of this statement using your results from Questions A–C.

continued on the next page >

Problem 2.3 continued

E A distribution's shape can help you see trends in the data. The shape is **symmetric** if the data are spread out evenly around a center value. The shape is right- or left-**skewed** if the points cluster at one end of the graph.

Three groups of middle-school students were asked: "Using a scale of 1 to 10 (with 10 being the best), how would you rate skateboarding as a sport?" The dot plots below show the responses.

1. Find the mean and median marked on each dot plot. Describe how the measures are influenced, or not, by the shape of the distribution.
2. Describe how the students in each group feel about skateboarding. Which measure of center would you use to answer the question: "What is the students' typical rating?" Explain.

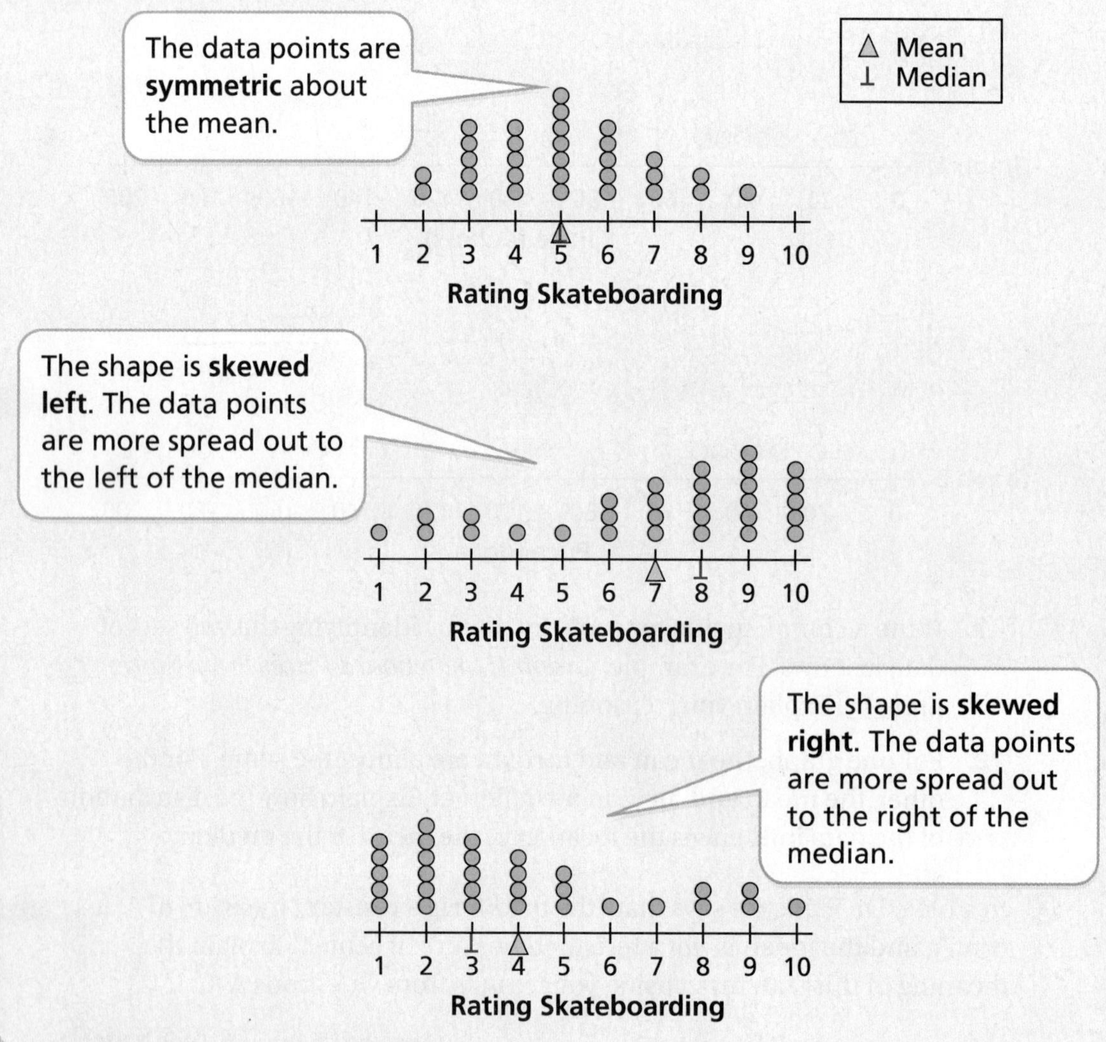

ACE Homework starts on page 48.

2.4 Who Else Is in Your Household?

Categorical and Numerical Data

Some statistical questions have answers that are words or categories. For example, "What is your favorite sport?" has answers that are words. Other questions have answers that are numbers. For example, "How many inches tall are you?" has answers that are numbers.

Categorical data can be grouped into categories, such as "favorite sport." They are usually not numbers. Suppose you asked people how they got to school or what kinds of pets they had. Their answers would be categorical data.

Numerical data are counts or measures. Suppose you asked people how tall they were or how many pets they had. Their responses would be numerical data.

- Which questions below have words or categories as answers? Which have numbers as answers?

One middle-school class gathered data about their pets by tallying students' responses to these questions:

- How many pets do you have?
- What is your favorite kind of pet?

The students made tables to show the tallies, or frequencies. Then they made bar graphs to show the data distributions.

Number of Pets

Number	0	1	2	3	4	5	6	7	8	9	10	11	12	13	14	15	16	17	18	19	20	21
Frequency	2	2	5	4	1	2	3	0	1	1	0	0	1	0	1	0	0	1	0	1	0	1

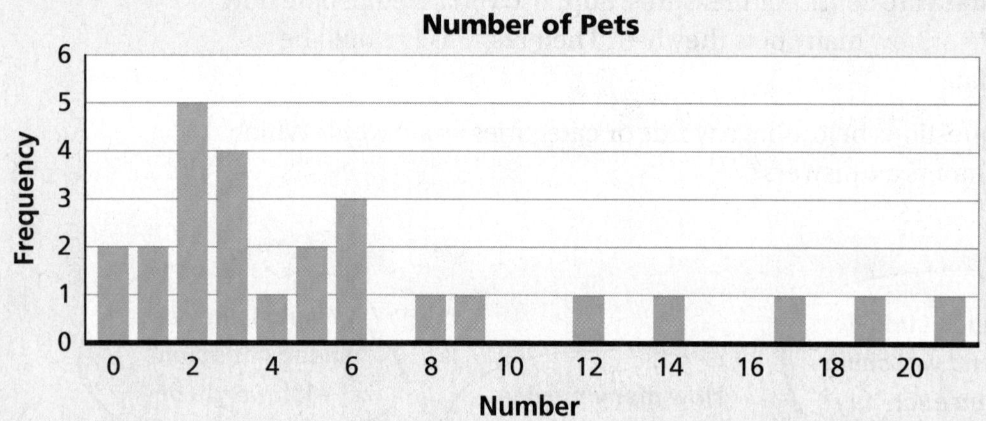

Favorite Pet

Pet	Frequency
cat	4
dog	7
fish	2
bird	2
horse	3
goat	1
cow	2
rabbit	3
duck	1
pig	1

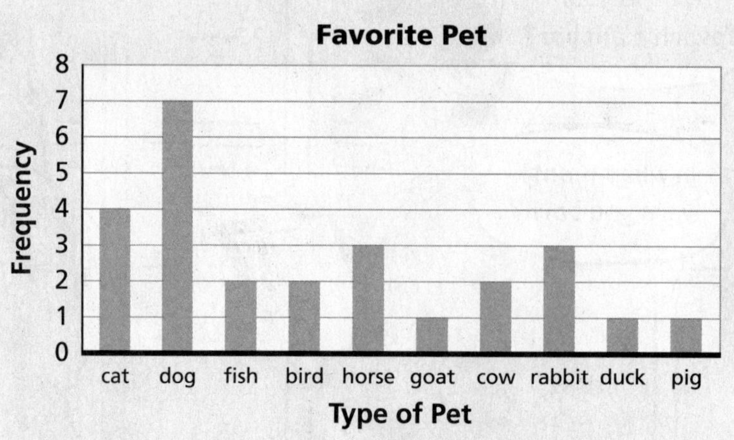

Problem 2.4

Decide whether Questions A through E can be answered by using data from the graphs and tables. If so, give the answer and explain how you got it. If not, explain why not.

A Which graph shows categorical data? Numerical data?

B
1. What is the total number of pets the students have?
2. What is the greatest number of pets a student has?

C
1. How many students are in the class?
2. How many students chose a cat as their favorite kind of pet?
3. How many cats do students have as pets?

D
1. What is the mode of the favorite kind of pet? The mean?
2. What is the median number of pets students have? The range?

E
1. Tomas is a student in this class. How many pets does he have?
2. Do the girls in the class have more pets than the boys?

F Using the distribution of the data, how would you describe the number of pets owned by this class? What would you say were the favorite kinds of pets? Use measures of center and other tools to help you describe the results of the survey.

ACE Homework starts on page 48.

Did you know?

Goldfish are trainable. With coaching, goldfish can learn to swim through hoops and tunnels, push a tiny ball into a net, and pull a lever for food.

Applications

For Exercises 1–3, use the line plot below.

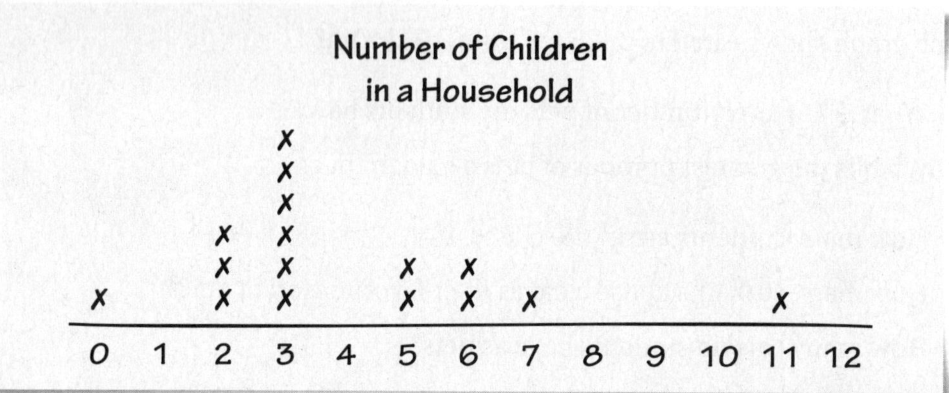

1. **a.** What is the median number of children in the 16 households? Explain how to find the median. What does the median tell you?

b. Do any of the 16 households have the median number of children? Explain why this is possible.

2. **a.** What is the mean number of children per household for the 16 households? Explain how to find the mean. What does the mean tell you?

b. Do any of the 16 households have the mean number of children? Explain why this is possible.

3. Use either the mean or the median to answer this question: "What is the typical household size for the data?" Explain your reasoning.

For Exercises 4–7, the mean number of people per household in eight households is six people.

4. **Multiple Choice** What is the total number of people in the eight households?

   A. 16 B. 64 C. 14 D. 48

5. Make a line plot showing one possible arrangement of the numbers of people in the eight households.

6. Make a line plot showing a different possible arrangement of the numbers of people in the eight households.

7. Are the medians the same for the two distributions you made? Is it possible to have two distributions that have the same means, but not the same medians? Explain your reasoning.

8. A set of nine households has a mean of $3\frac{1}{3}$ people per household. Make a line plot showing a data set that fits this description.

9. A set of nine households has a mean of five people per household. The largest household in the group has ten people. Make a line plot showing a data set that fits this description.

For Exercises 10–16, tell whether the answers to the question are numerical or categorical data.

10. What is your height in centimeters?

11. What is your favorite musical group?

12. In which month were you born?

13. What would you like to do when you graduate from high school?

14. Use your foot as a unit of measure. How many of your “feet” tall are you?

15. What kind(s) of transportation do you use to get to school?

16. On average, how much time do you spend doing homework each day?

Connections

17. During Mr. Wilson's study hall, students spent the following amounts of time on their homework:

$\frac{3}{4}$ hour $\frac{1}{2}$ hour $1\frac{1}{4}$ hours $\frac{3}{4}$ hour $\frac{1}{2}$ hour

a. What is the mean time Mr. Wilson's students spent on homework?

b. Multiple Choice What is the median time the students spent on homework?

F. $\frac{1}{2}$ hour **G.** $\frac{3}{4}$ hour

H. 1 hour **J.** $1\frac{1}{4}$ hours

18. A soccer league wants to find the average amount of water its players drink per game. There are 18 players on a team. During one game, the two teams drank a total of 1,152 ounces of water.

a. How much water did each player drink per game if each player drank the same amount of water?

b. Does this value represent the mean or the median? Explain.

19. Sabrina, Diego, and Marcus entered a Dance-a-thon that ran from 9 A.M. to 7 P.M. The times that each student danced are shown at the right.

a. Write the number of hours each student spent dancing as a mixed number.

b. Look at the data from part (a). Without doing any computations, do you think the mean time spent dancing is the same as, less than, or greater than the median? Explain.

Dance-a-thon SCHEDULE

STUDENT	TIME
Sabrina	9:15 A.M. to 1:00 P.M.
Diego	1:00 P.M. to 4:45 P.M.
Marcus	4:45 P.M. to 7:00 P.M.

20. Jon has a pet rabbit that is 5 years old. He wonders if his rabbit is old compared to other rabbits. At the pet store, he finds out that the mean life span for a rabbit is 7 years.

a. What does the mean tell Jon about the life span for a rabbit?

b. What additional information would help Jon to predict the life span of his rabbit?

21. A store carries nine different brands of granola bars. What are possible prices for each of the nine brands of granola bars if the mean price is \$1.33? Explain how you determined values for each of the nine brands. You may use pictures to help you.

For Exercises 22–25, a recent survey of 25 students in a middle-school class yielded the data in the table below.

Mean Time Spent on Leisure Activities by Students in One Class

Activity	Time (minutes per day)
Watching videos	39
Listening to music	44
Using the computer	21

22. Did each student watch videos for 39 minutes per day? Explain.

23. Jill decides to round 39 minutes to 40 minutes. Then she estimates that the students spend about $\frac{2}{3}$ of an hour watching videos. What percent of an hour is $\frac{2}{3}$?

24. Estimate what part of an hour the students spend listening to music. Write your answer as a fraction and as a decimal.

25. The students spend about 20 minutes per day using a computer. How many hours do they spend using a computer in 1 week (7 days)? Write your answer as a fraction and as a decimal.

26. Three candidates are running for the mayor of Slugville. Each has determined the typical income of residents of Slugville, and they use that information for campaign sound bites.

Some of the candidates are confused about "average." Slugville has only 16 residents. Their weekly incomes are $0, $0, $0, $0, $0, $0, $0, $0, $200, $200, $200, $200, $200, $200, $200, and $30,600.

a. Explain what measure of center each of the candidates used as an "average" income for the town. Check their computations.

b. Does anyone in Slugville have the mean income? Explain.

c. Does anyone in Slugville have an income that equals the median? Explain.

d. Does anyone in Slugville have an income that equals the mode? Explain.

e. When you decide to use a measure of center—mode, median, or mean—you must choose which measure best helps you tell the story of the data. What do you consider to be the typical income for a resident of Slugville? Explain your choice of measure.

f. Suppose four more people moved to Slugville. Each has a weekly income of $200. How would the mean, median, and mode change?

27. A recent survey asked 25 middle-school students how many movies they see in one month. The table and line plot below show the data.

Movies Watched in One Month

Student	Number	Student	Number	Student	Number
Wes	2	Susan	4	Julian	2
Tomi	15	Gil	3	Alana	4
Ling	13	Enrique	2	Tyrone	1
Su Chin	1	Lonnie	3	Rebecca	4
Michael	9	Ken	10	Anton	11
Mara	30	Kristina	15	Jun	8
Alan	20	Mario	12	Raymond	8
Jo	1	Henry	5	Anjelica	17
Tanisha	25				

Movies Watched in One Month

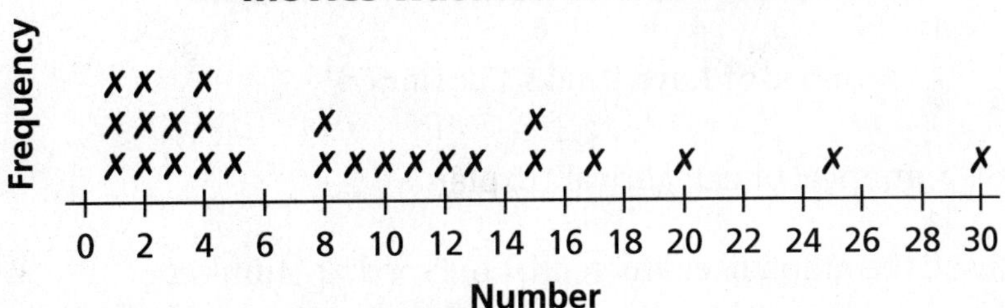

a. Identify one section of the line plot where about half the data values are grouped and a different section where about one quarter of the data is grouped.

b. What is the range of the data? Explain how you found it.

c. Find the mean number of movies watched by the students. Explain.

d. What do the range and mean tell you about the typical number of movies watched for this group of students?

e. Find the median number of movies watched. Are the mean and the median the same? Why do you think this is so?

For Exercises 28–32, use the graph below. The graph shows the number of juice drinks 100 middle-school students consumed in one day.

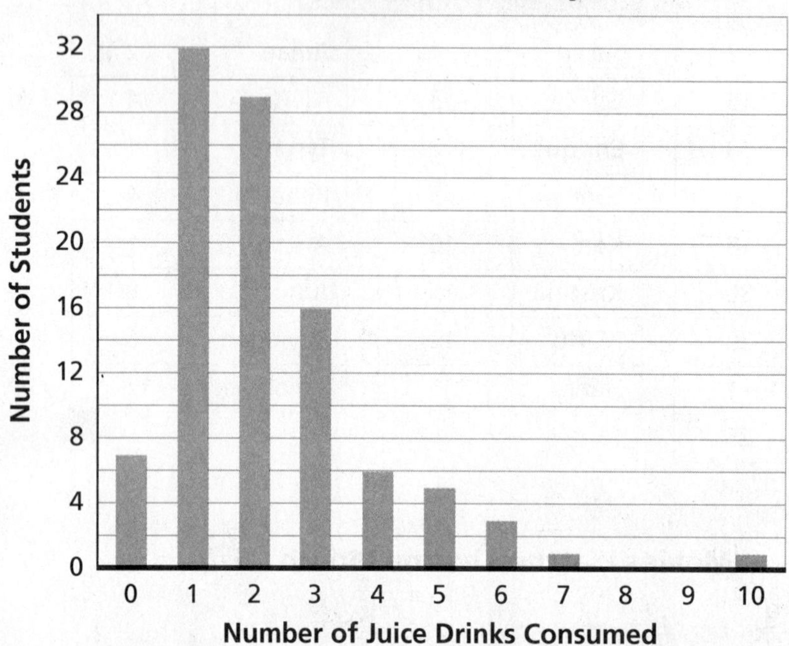

28. Are the data numerical or categorical? Explain.

29. A student used the graph to estimate that the median number of juice drinks students consume in a day is 5. Is this estimate correct? Explain your answer.

30. Another student estimates that the median number of juice drinks is 1. Is this estimate correct? Explain your answer.

31. What is the total number of juice drinks these 100 students consume in one day? How did you determine your answer?

32. Suppose the survey had asked, "What juice drinks do you like?"

a. List three possible responses.

b. Are the data numerical or categorical? Explain.

c. Describe how to make a bar graph showing the distribution of the data collected in answer to this question. How would you label the horizontal axis? The vertical axis? How would you title the graph? What would each bar on the graph show?

Extensions

For Exercises 33 and 34, use the newspaper headlines.

33. Do you think that each headline refers to a mean, a median, or something else? Explain.

34. About how many hours per day does the average sixth grader spend watching television or using the Internet if he or she spends 1,170 hours of screen time in a year?

For Exercises 35–37, use the table at the right.

35. Make a bar graph to display the data. Think about how you will set up and label the horizontal and vertical axes with the correct scales.

36. Use the information in your graph to write a paragraph about the pets these students own. How do these results compare to the results from the class data used in Problem 2.4?

37. Estimate how many students were surveyed. Explain your reasoning.

Types of Pets Students Own

Pet	Frequency
bird	61
cat	184
dog	180
fish	303
gerbil	17
guinea pig	12
hamster	32
horse	28
rabbit	2
snake	9
turtle	13
Total	**841**

Mathematical Reflections

In this Investigation, you explored a measure of center called the mean. It is important to understand how the mean, or average, is related to the mode and the median. The following questions will help you summarize what you learned.

Think about these questions. Discuss your ideas with other students and your teacher. Then write a summary of your findings in your notebook.

1. **Describe** a method for calculating the mean of a set of data. Explain why your method works.
2. You have used three measures of center—mode, median, and mean—to describe distributions.
   a. **Why** do you suppose they are called "measures of center"?
   b. **What** does each tell you about a set of data?
   c. **How** do you decide which measure of center to use when describing a distribution?
   d. **Why** might you want to include both the range and a measure of center when reporting a statistical summary?
3. a. One student says you can only use the mode to describe categorical data, but you can use the mode, median, and mean to describe numerical data. Is the student correct? Explain.
   b. Can you find the range for categorical data? Explain.

Unit Project

Think about the survey you will be developing to gather information about middle-school students.

How might the new ideas you have learned in this Investigation be useful when you are designing a statistical analysis?

Common Core Mathematical Practices

As you worked on the Problems in this Investigation, you used prior knowledge to make sense of them. You also applied your Mathematical Practices to solve the Problems. Think back over your work, the ways you thought about the Problems, and how you used Mathematical Practices.

Sophie described her thoughts in the following way:

If a set of seven numbers has a mean of 11, then the sum of the numbers is going to equal 77—no matter what.

For example, the set of numbers 5, 9, 9, 9, 12, 15, and 18 has a mean of 11 and a sum of 77. Another set of numbers, 4, 5, 6, 10, 10, 11, and 31, has a mean of 11. That set of numbers also has a sum of 77.

I can just replace each of the original seven numbers with the number 11, just like evening out the cube stacks. And when I add 11 seven times, the sum is 77.

Common Core Standards for Mathematical Practice

MP7 Look for and make use of structure

- What other Mathematical Practices can you identify in Sophie's reasoning?
- Describe a Mathematical Practice that you and your classmates used to solve a different Problem in this Investigation.

What's Your Favorite...? Measuring Variability

A statistical investigation begins by asking a question. Decisions about what data to collect are based on the question.

When people collect answers to a question, the data may be similar, such as the number of raisins found in each of 30 different half-ounce boxes of raisins. More often, however, the data vary, such as the pulse rates of 30 different people after each person rides a roller coaster.

When you are interested in learning about a person, you may ask a question that begins "What is your favorite . . .?" For example, you might ask "What is your favorite cereal?"

Common Core State Standards

6.SP.A.1 Recognize a statistical question as one that anticipates variability in the data related to the question and accounts for it in the answers.

6.SP.A.3 Recognize that a measure of center for a numerical data set summarizes all of its values with a single number, while a measure of variation describes how its values vary with a single number.

Also 6.RP.A.3, 6.RP.A.3a, 6.NS.C.6, 6.NS.C.7, 6.SP.A.2, 6.SP.B.4, 6.SP.B.5c, 6.SP.B.5d

The graph below shows the results of an online survey of 4,500 people. Each person took the survey once.

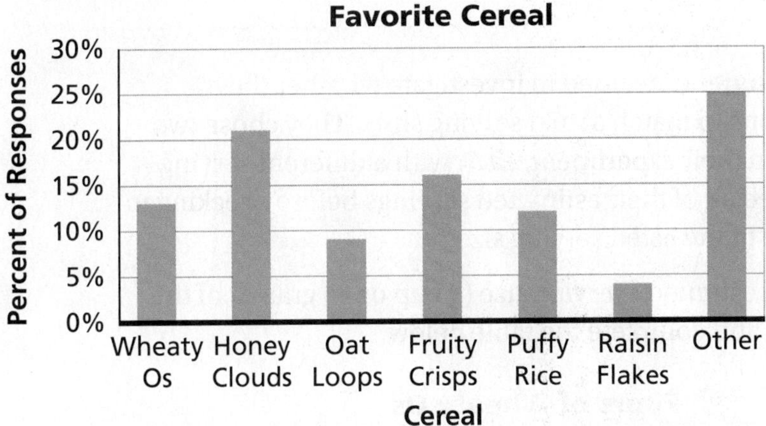

- What do you know about cereal choices from this survey?

You can investigate other information related to cereal. For example, a recent report claims that children "overpour" their cereal, meaning they pour portions that are larger than a single serving size. This is a problem because many cereals have high sugar contents.

- Do you think that children overpour by the same amount for all cereals? Explain.

Understanding and explaining variability in data is the essence of statistical problem solving. **Variability** in numerical data indicates how spread out a distribution of data is. One way to compare data distributions is to describe which data set is *more variable* (spread out) or *less variable* (clustered together). In this Investigation, you will learn some other ways to describe how data vary.

3.1 Estimating Cereal Serving Sizes
Determining the IQR

Twelve middle-school students decided to investigate whether they could pour cereal portions to match actual serving sizes. They chose two different cereals to use in their experiment, each with a different serving size. The students poured all of their estimated servings before checking to see how close they were to the listed serving sizes.

Each student poured an estimated serving size ($\frac{3}{4}$ cup or 28 grams) of the cereal Wheaty Os. Copy and complete the table below.

Pours of Wheaty Os

Grams Poured	52	29	32	59	43	24	28	23	20	30	37	27
Serving Size	1.86	1.04	1.14	■	■	0.86	■	0.82	0.71	1.07	■	0.96

- How could you compute the data values in the serving-size row?

The dot plot below shows the distribution of the serving-size data. The data values you calculated to complete the table are already included.

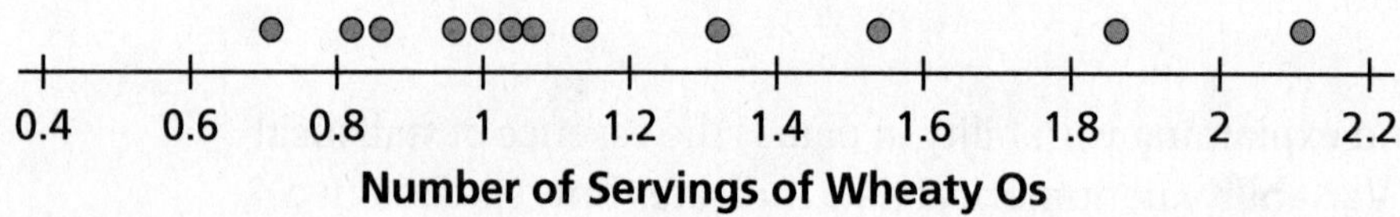

- Which measure of center—mean, median, or mode—might you use to describe a typical serving size poured by the students?
- How well do you think students estimated the serving size when they poured Wheaty Os?

You have already learned how to find the median of a data set. In Problem 3.1, you will work with values called **quartiles**—the three points that divide an ordered set of data into four equal groups, with each group containing one-fourth of the data values.

Problem 3.1

A The students agreed that being "about right" means pouring a serving size that is in the middle 50% of the data distribution. The students arranged the twelve Wheaty Os data values in order from least to greatest on sticky notes.

0.71	0.82	0.86	0.96	1.00	1.04	1.07	1.14	1.32	1.54	1.86	2.11

1. What is the median?
2. Identify the **lower quartile** (Q1). Its *position* is located midway between the serving sizes 0.86 and 0.96. Find the *value* of the lower quartile.
3. Identify the **upper quartile** (Q3). Its *position* is located midway between the serving sizes 1.32 and 1.54. Find the *value* of the upper quartile.
4. How are the positions of Q1 and Q3 related to the position of the median (sometimes called Q2)?
5. The serving size estimates between Q1 and Q3 are in the middle 50% of the data. Do you agree that serving size estimates in the middle 50% are "about right"? Explain.
6. The **interquartile range (IQR)** is the difference Q3 – Q1. The IQR measures the *spread* of the middle 50% of the data. What is the IQR for the Wheaty Os data?

continued on the next page >

Problem 3.1 continued

B The students also poured estimated servings ($1\frac{1}{4}$ cup or 33 grams) of Raisin Flakes.

1. On a copy of the table below, write the serving sizes of the data they gathered.

Pours of Raisin Flakes

Grams Poured	44	33	31	24	42	31	28	24	15	36	30	41
Serving Size	1.33	1.00	■	■	■	0.94	■	■	■	1.09	■	■

2. Make a line plot or a dot plot to show the frequency of the distribution of data values. Use the same number-line labels as the Wheaty Os dot plot at the beginning of Investigation 3.
3. Arrange the data in order from least to greatest. What is the median?
4. Find Q1 and Q3. Use these to identify the middle 50% of the data.
5. Describe the estimated servings that are in the middle 50% of the distribution. Do you agree that the estimated servings in the middle 50% are "about right"? Explain.
6. Calculate the IQR of the estimated servings of Raisin Flakes. Explain how you found this number.

C Use the interquartile ranges of the Wheaty Os and Raisin Flakes data.

1. For which cereal are the data more spread out? Explain.
2. Is IQR a good measure of whether students consistently underpour or overpour cereal servings? Explain.
3. How would you describe a typical serving of Wheaty Os as poured by the students? Of Raisin Flakes?

Problem 3.1 continued

D Recall that the range of a data set is a measure of variability (or spread).

1. Compute the range of the Wheaty Os data. Compute the range of the Raisin Flakes data.
2. What do the ranges tell you about how the poured servings vary? Explain.
3. Compare the ranges and the IQRs of each data set. How are they alike? How are they different?

E Each student wrote a report comparing the two data sets. Two students, Seamus and Deanna, gave the answers below. Do you agree with Seamus or with Deanna? Explain your reasoning.

> **Seamus**
>
> For servings of Raisin Flakes, both the range (0.88 g) and the IQR (0.375 g) are less than the range (1.4 g) and IQR (0.52 g) of Wheaty Os.
>
> About one third of the students overpoured the servings of Raisin Flakes (33 g), but almost two thirds of the students overpoured the servings of Wheaty Os (38 g). Students seem more accurate at estimating servings of Raisin Flakes.

> **Deanna**
>
> The median serving size poured for the Raisin Flakes data is 0.94 of a serving. The median serving size poured for the Wheaty Os data is 1.055 of a serving. Students seem to overpour Wheaty Os and underpour Raisin Flakes.

Homework starts on page 72.

3.2 Connecting Cereal Shelf Location and Sugar Content

Describing Variability Using the IQR

Cereal boxes have nutritional information on the side panel. Sugar content is reported in grams per serving.

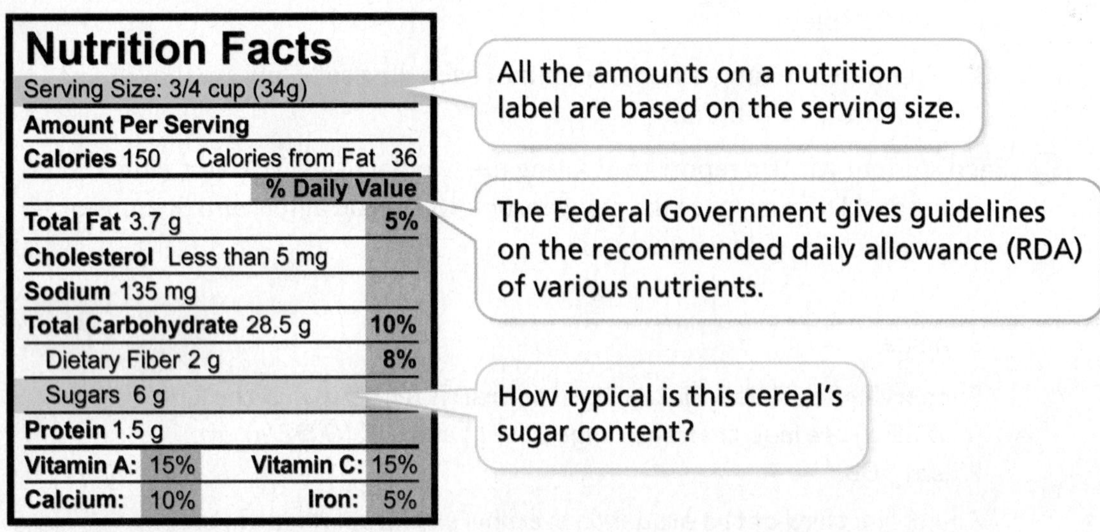

The dot plot below shows the distribution of grams of sugar per serving for 70 cereals. The median is 7.5 grams of sugar, or about 2 teaspoons of sugar, per serving. The red marker (⊥) indicates the median.

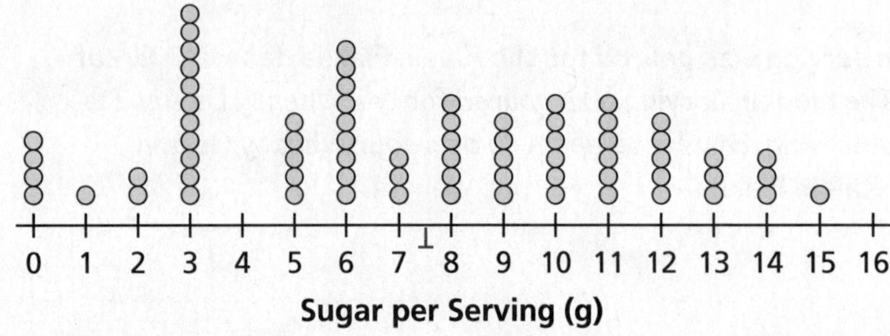

- What surprises you about the data set or its distribution? Explain.
- What questions do you have as you look at the distribution?

You have used two measures of variability: range and interquartile range (IQR). In Problem 3.2, you will use the IQR to describe variability in grams of sugar for different groups of cereals.

Problem 3.2

A Use the dot plot on the previous page showing the distribution of sugar in cereals.

1. Are there intervals where the data cluster? What does this tell you about the data?
2. The table below shows some of the data. On a copy of the dot plot from the previous page, locate each data point.

Distribution of Sugar in Several Cereals

Cereals From Data Set	Sugar (grams)	Shelf Location
Bran-ful	5	Bottom
Crispy Bran	6	Top
Wheaty Os	1	Top
Fruity Crisps	13	Middle
Sugary Flakes	11	Top
Frosted Bites	7	Middle
Healthy Nuggets	3	Bottom
Honey Oats	6	Middle
Honey Wheaty Os	10	Top
Raisin Flakes	14	Middle

continued on the next page >

Problem 3.2 continued

B The dot plots below show data for the 70 cereals organized by supermarket shelf location.

Sugar in Top-Shelf Cereals

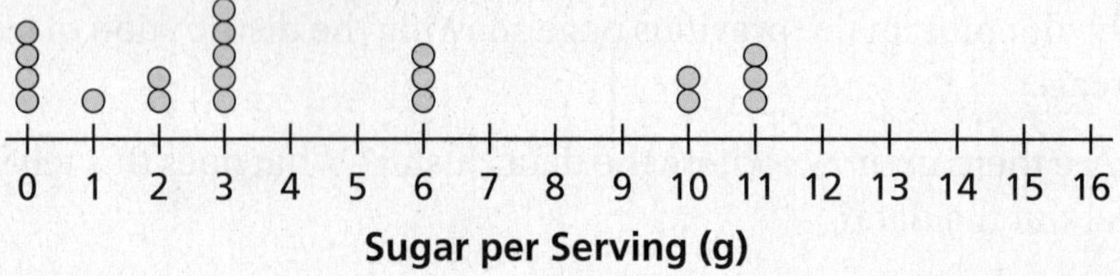

Sugar in Middle-Shelf Cereals

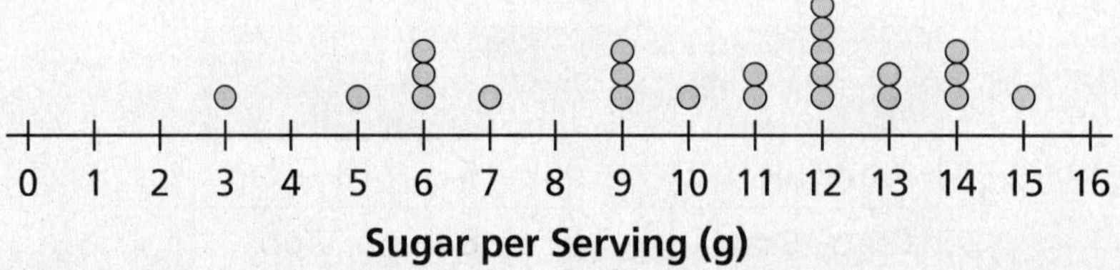

Sugar in Bottom-Shelf Cereals

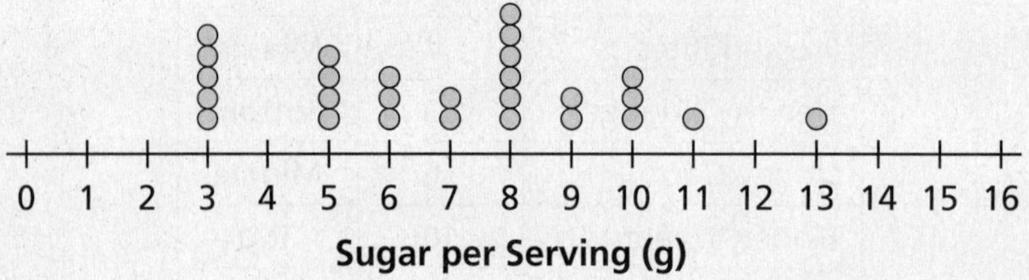

1. Is there any pattern to how sugary a cereal is and its shelf location? Find ways to describe and compare the three distributions of data.

2. a. Find the IQR for each distribution.

   b. Which of the three distributions has the greatest variability in grams of sugar per serving? The least variability?

Problem 3.2 continued

3. Write a report comparing the cereals located on each of the shelves. Your report should
   - use a measure of center to describe the typical number of grams of sugar in the cereals on each shelf.
   - use a measure of spread to describe the variability in the number of grams of sugar in the cereals on each shelf.
   - compare the distributions of grams of sugar in the cereals on each of the three shelves by using the measures of center and spread above.
   - point out anything unusual or interesting.

 Homework starts on page 72.

3.3 Is It Worth the Wait?

Determining and Describing Variability Using the MAD

In your lifetime, you spend a lot of time waiting. Sometimes it feels like you could stand in line forever. For example, you may wait a long time for your favorite ride at an amusement park.

During the summer, one estimate of average wait time at an amusement park is 60 minutes. The most popular rides can accommodate 1,500 people per hour. Lines form when more people arrive than the rides can fit. Amusement parks are designed to minimize wait times, but variability in the number of people who choose a particular ride can result in lines.

Sally and her family spent the day at an amusement park. At the end of the day, Sally noticed the sign below.

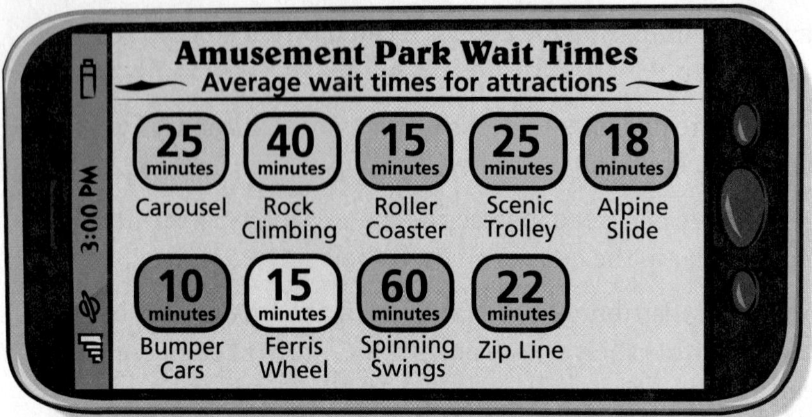

- Which ride has the shortest average wait time? The longest?
- Sally waited in line longer than 25 minutes for the Scenic Trolley ride. How could this have happened?

In Investigation 2, you learned that it is possible for a data set to include values that are quite different from the mean. In Problem 3.3, you will find a way to describe *how much* data values vary from an average.

Problem 3.3

A Since Sally waited in line longer than the average wait time, she wondered how much wait times vary.

The dot plot below shows a distribution of ten wait times for the Scenic Trolley ride.

Scenic Trolley Wait Times

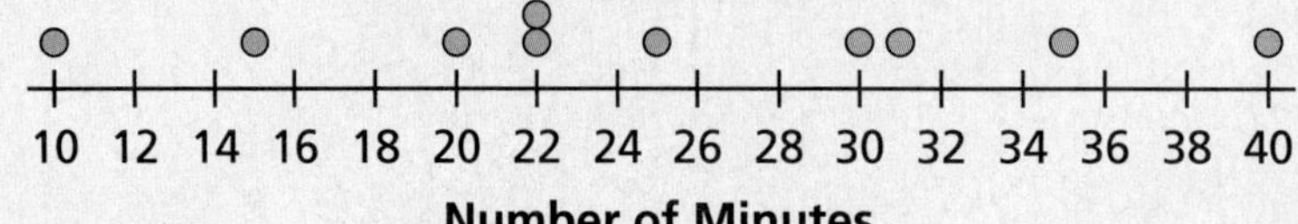

Number of Minutes

1. Sally says that the mean wait time is 25 minutes, just like the sign claimed. Do you agree? Explain.

Problem 3.3 continued

2. Sally wonders how typical a wait time of 25 minutes is. She says "I can find how much, on average, the data values vary from the mean time of 25 minutes." She uses the graph below to find the distance each data value is from the mean.

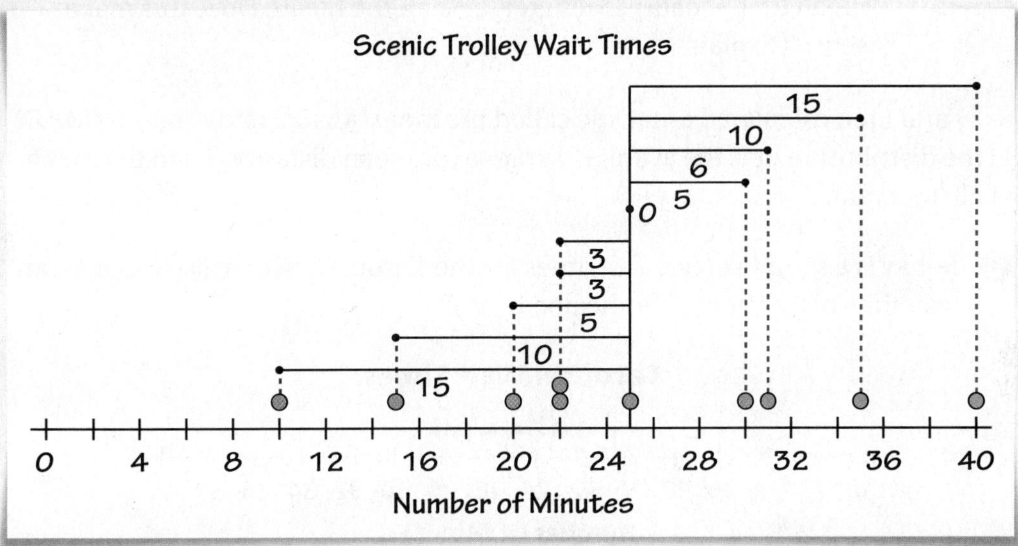

Fred says "That's a good idea, but I used an ordered-value bar graph to show the same idea."

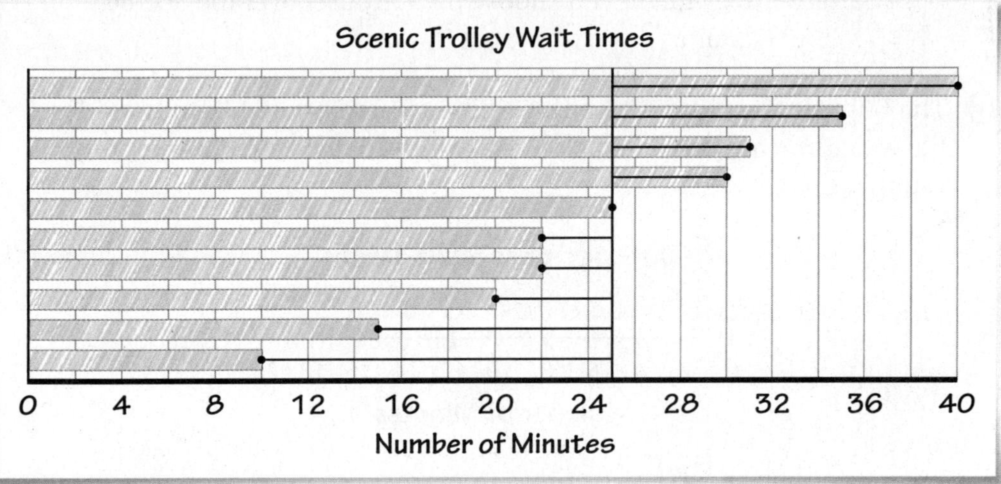

a. Describe how you can use each graph to find how much, on average, the data values vary from the mean time of 25 minutes.

continued on the next page >

Problem 3.3 continued

b. What does this information tell you about how long you might have to wait in line to ride the Scenic Trolley?

c. Sally noticed that the sum of the distances to the mean for the data values less than the mean equaled the sum of the distances to the mean for the data values greater than the mean. Does this make sense? Explain.

Sally and Fred calculated a statistic called the **mean absolute deviation (MAD)** of the distribution. It is the average distance (or mean distance) from the mean of all data values.

B Below is a sample of ten wait times for the Carousel, which also has a mean wait time of 25 minutes (indicated by △).

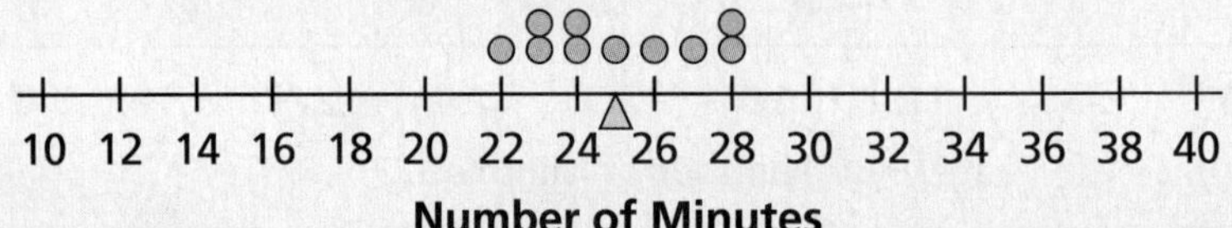

1. Find the mean absolute deviation (MAD) for this distribution.
2. Compare the MAD for the Scenic Trolley with the MAD for the Carousel. Why might you choose the Carousel over the Scenic Trolley? Explain.

C The Bumper Cars have a mean wait time of 10 minutes. Like other rides, the wait times are variable. Below is a sample of ten wait times for the Bumper Cars.

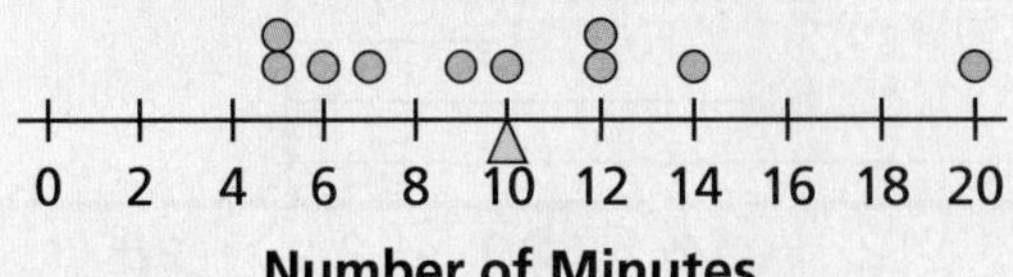

1. What is the MAD for the Bumper Cars data?
2. Compare the mean wait time of the Scenic Trolley and of the Bumper Cars. What do you notice? Then compare the MADs of both rides. What do you notice? Explain.

Problem 3.3 continued

D Use these two signs for amusement park rides. Suppose you have to leave the park in 30 minutes. You want one last ride. Each ride lasts 3 minutes. Which ride would you choose? Explain.

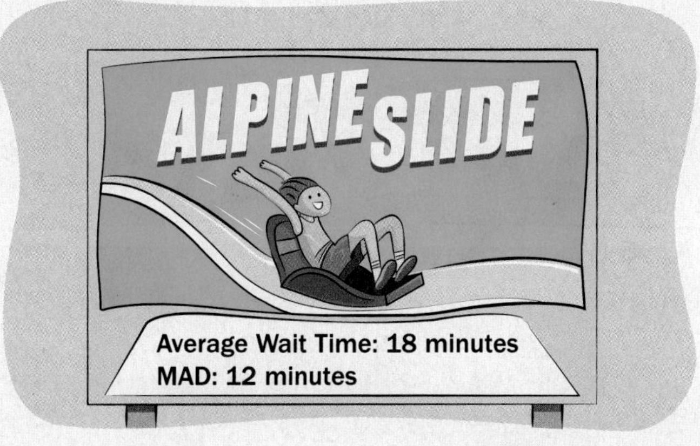

ACE Homework starts on page 72.

Applications

Servers at the Mugwump Diner receive tips for excellent service.

1. a. On Monday, four servers earned the tips below. Find the range of the tips.

b. The four servers shared their tips equally. How much money did each server get? Explain.

c. Yanna was busy clearing a table when the tips were shared. Yanna also received $16.10 in tips. Suppose Yanna's tips were included with the other tips, and the total was shared equally among the five servers. Without doing any computations, will the four servers receive less than, the same as, or more than they did before Yanna's tips were included? Explain.

2. On Tuesday, all five servers shared their tips equally. Each received $16.45. Does this mean someone originally received $16.45 in tips? Explain.

3. a. On Wednesday, Yanna received $13.40 in tips. When tips were shared equally among the five servers, each received $15.25. How could this have happened? Explain.

b. Based on the information in part (a), what can you say about the variability of the tip data on Wednesday? Explain your reasoning.

4. Recall the name-length data from Investigation 1. You explored name lengths from several different countries. The dot plots below show four distributions of data. Each dot plot shows the median (⊥).

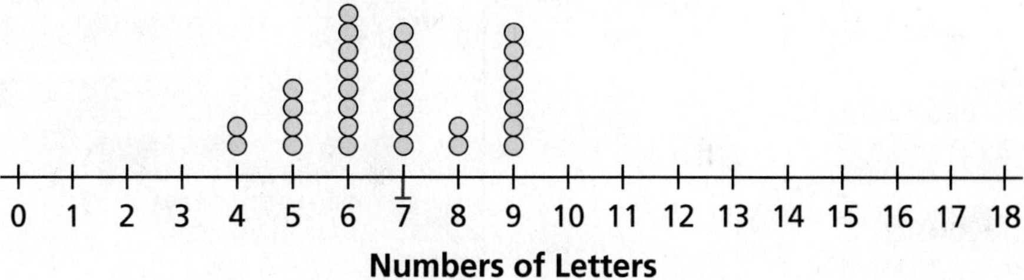

Japanese Pen-Pal Names

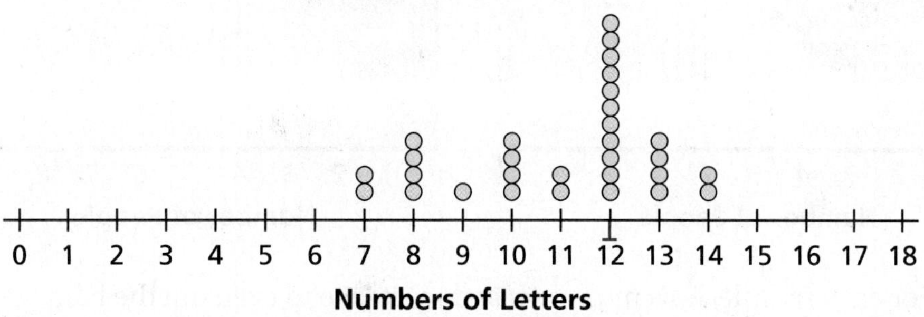

Korean Pen-Pal Names

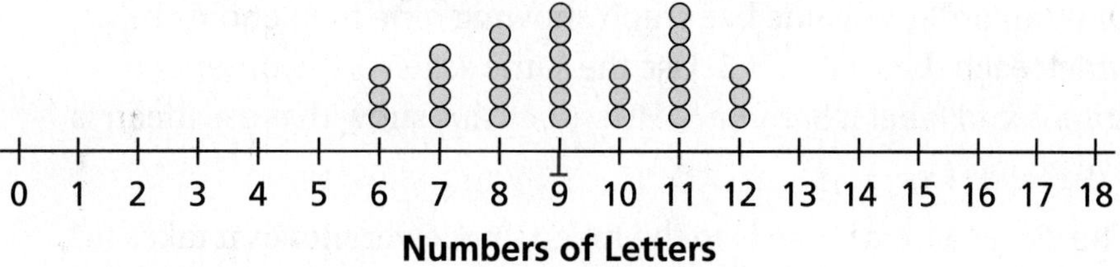

U.S. Student Names

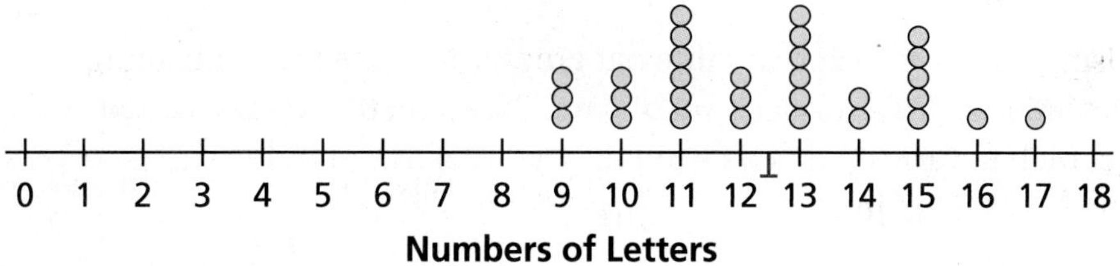

a. What is the interquartile range (IQR) of each distribution? Explain how you found each IQR.

b. Using the IQRs, for which distribution is the middle 50% the least spread out? The most spread out? Explain.

5. Below are two ordered-value bar graphs (Sample 1 and Sample 2), each showing nine households with a mean of five people per household.

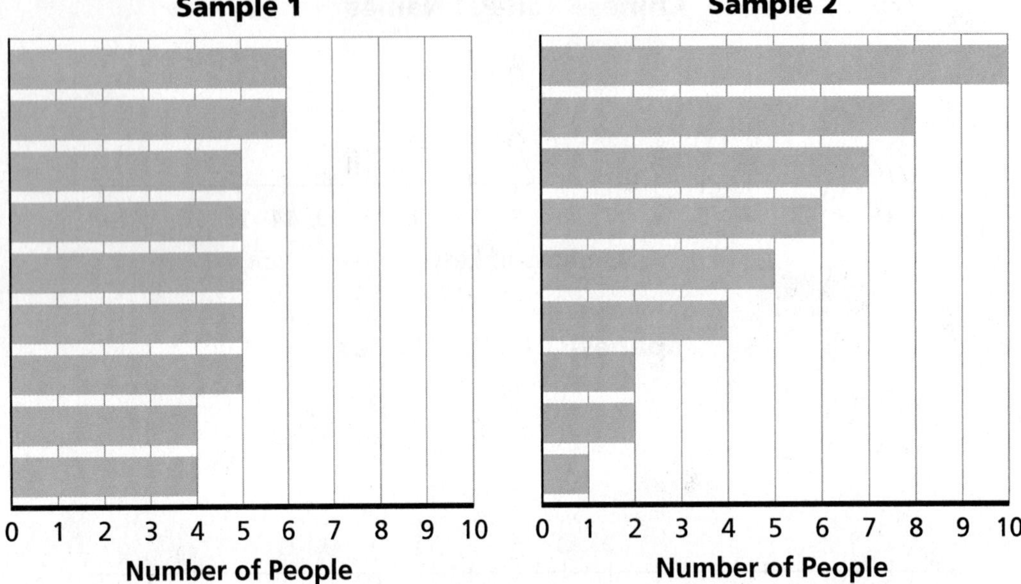

a. For each sample, how many *moves* does it take to even out the bars so that the mean is 5? A "move" is the movement of one person from one household to another household.

b. Draw an ordered-value bar graph showing nine households in which each data value is 5. Use the same scale as the other two graphs and label it Sample 3. How does this show that the mean is five people?

c. The closer a data value is to the mean, the fewer moves it takes to even out the data. In which graph (Sample 1, 2, or 3) are the data closest to the mean (vary the least)? Farthest from the mean (vary the most)? Explain.

d. Using the three ordered-value bar graphs, find the mean absolute deviation (MAD) for each set of data. Based on the MADs, which set of data varies the most from the mean of five people? Varies the least? Explain.

6. Jeff and Elaine are studying for their final exam. The grading spreadsheet below shows their practice-test scores. Each test has a top score of 100.

File Edit Tool View Chart Class Help

Algebra 1 Practice Tests | Algebra 1 Homework

Class	Name	Student Number	Test 1	Test 2	Test 3	Test 4	Test 5	Test 6	Test 7	Test 8	Test Average
001	Jeff	# 18	75	80	75	80	75	80	85	90	
001	Elaine	# 24	60	70	80	70	80	90	100	90	

Low Score | High Score

a. Make a line plot of each person's practice tests scores.

b. What are the median and IQR of each distribution?

c. What are the mean and MAD of each distribution?

d. On the day of the exam, who is more likely to receive a score of 80, Jeff or Elaine? Explain your reasoning.

7. The dot plots below show the distributions of ten wait times at two rides.

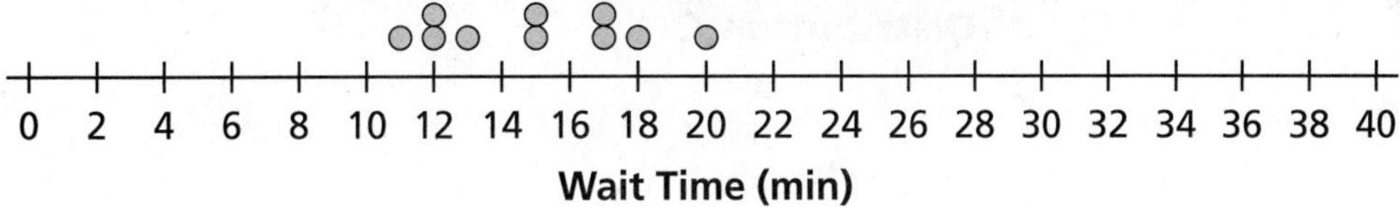

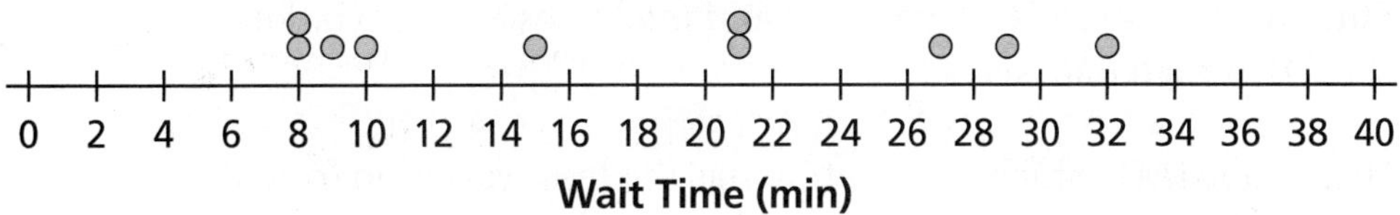

a. Find the mean of each data set.

b. Compute the MAD of each data set.

c. Compare the MADs. In which distribution do the data vary more from the mean? Explain.

d. i. Make your own data set of ten wait times. Draw a dot plot.

ii. Compute the MAD.

iii. Compare the three distributions. In which distribution do the data vary more from the mean? Explain your thinking.

For Exercises 8–10, use the line plots below.

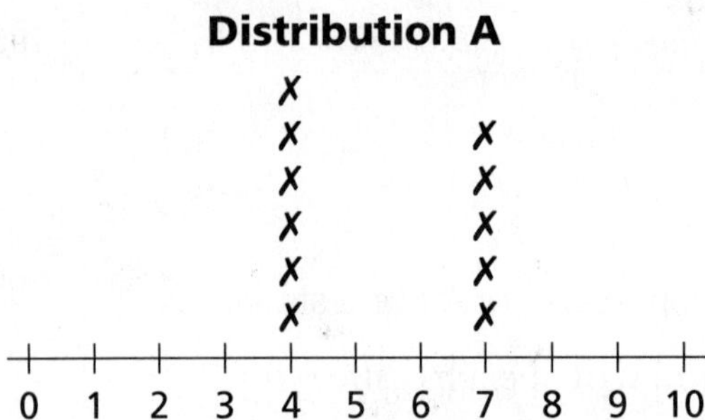

Distribution B

0 1 2 3 4 5 6 7 8 9 10

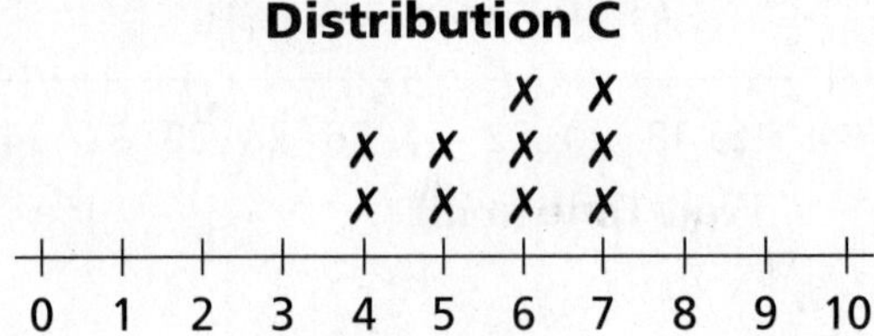

8. Find the interquartile range (IQR) and mean absolute deviation (MAD) of each data set.

9. Using the MAD, which distribution has the least variation from the mean? The most?

10. Using the IQR, which distribution has the greatest spread in the middle 50% of data? The least?

11. The frequency table below shows the number of pets owned by students in three different sixth-grade classes.

Pet Ownership

Number of Pets	Class 1	Class 2	Class 3
0	5	4	2
1	3	1	2
2	5	5	5
3	2	3	4
4	0	3	1
5	0	1	2
6	1	2	3
7	0	0	0
8	0	0	1
9	0	0	1
10	0	0	0
11	0	1	0
12	0	0	1
13	1	0	0
14	1	0	1
15	0	0	0
16	0	0	0
17	0	0	1
18	0	0	0
19	0	0	1
20	0	0	0
21	0	0	1
22	0	0	0
23	1	0	0
24	1	0	0

a. Draw a line plot or dot plot of each data set. Use the same scale on each graph so you can easily compare the distributions.

b. Compute the median and IQR for each distribution. Write at least three statements to compare the classes using the median and IQR.

c. Below are the means and MADs for each data set. Write at least three statements to compare the classes using the means and MADs.

Pet Ownership Statistics

Number of Pets	Class 1	Class 2	Class 3
Mean	5	2.67	6
MAD	3.6	1.74	4.46

Connections

For Exercises 12 and 13, use the bar graph below.

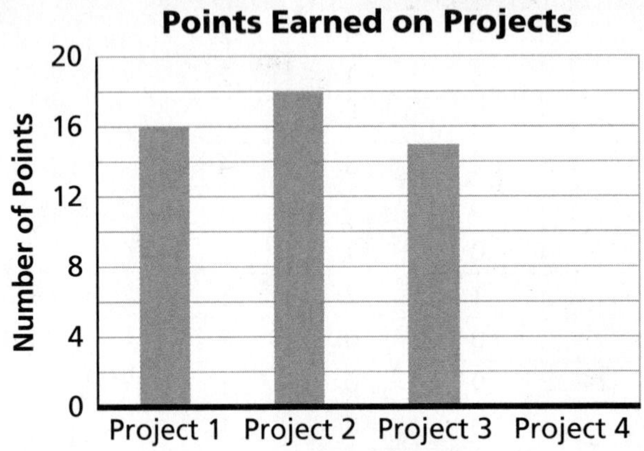

12. **a.** Malaika's mean score is 17 points. How many points did Malaika receive on Project 4? Explain.

b. What is the range of Malaika's scores on the four projects? What does this tell you about the variation in her scores?

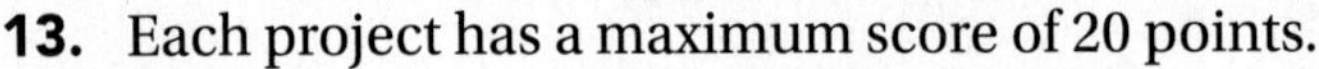

13. Each project has a maximum score of 20 points.

a. What would Malaika's mean score be if she had a total of 80 points for the four projects? A total of 60 points?

b. Give four possible project scores that would result in each mean score in part (a).

c. What is the range of the scores for each of your sets of four project scores? What does this tell you about how spread out or variable the scores are?

d. Are these ranges more spread out, or variable, than the range of Malaika's set of scores? Explain.

For Exercises 14–16, use the tables below.

Caffeine Content of Selected Soda Drinks

Name	Caffeine in 8 Ounces (mg)
Soda A	38
Soda B	37
Soda C	27
Soda D	27
Soda E	26
Soda F	24
Soda G	21
Soda H	15
Soda J	23

Caffeine Content of Selected Other Drinks

Name	Caffeine in 8 Ounces (mg)
Energy Drink A	77
Energy Drink B	70
Energy Drink C	25
Energy Drink D	21
Iced Tea A	19
Iced Tea B	10
Coffee Drink	83
Hot Cocoa	2
Juice Drink	33

14. **a.** Find the mean and median amounts of caffeine in the soda drinks.

b. Find the mean and median amounts of caffeine in the other drinks.

c. Using parts (a) and (b), is it possible to say which type of drink—sodas or other drinks—has greater variability in caffeine content? Explain.

d. Write three statements comparing the amounts of caffeine in sodas and other drinks.

15. Indicate whether each statement is true or false.

a. Soda B has more caffeine than Soda F or Soda D.

b. Energy Drink C has about three times as much caffeine per serving as Energy Drink A.

c. 75% of all the drinks have 25 mg or less of caffeine per serving.

16. In Exercise 14, you found the means and medians of the sodas and the other drinks. Two MADs and two IQRs are listed below.

MAD = 5.16 mg IQR = 10 mg	MAD = 25.93 mg IQR = 59 mg

a. Which statistics describe the variability of caffeine content in the sodas? Explain your reasoning.

b. Which statistics describe the variability of caffeine content in the other drinks? Explain.

For Exercises 17 and 18, use the dot plots below.

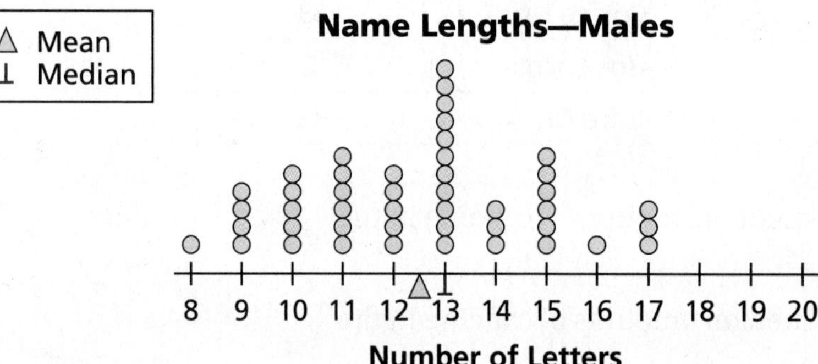

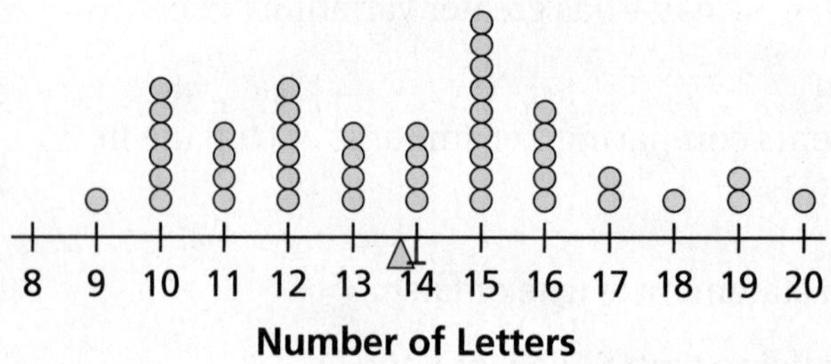

17. Compare the two sets of data. Which group has longer names? Explain.

18. Look at the distribution for females. Suppose that the data for four names with 18 or more letters changed. These students now have name lengths of ten or fewer letters.

a. Draw a dot plot showing this change.

b. Will the change affect the median name length for females? Explain.

c. Will the change affect the mean name length for females? Explain.

19. Multiple Choice John's test scores were 100, 84, 88, 96, and 96. His teacher told him that his final grade is 96. Which measure of center did his teacher use to report John's final grade?

A. Mean
B. Median
C. Mode
D. Range

20. Multiple Choice Sal's Packages on the Go mails 6 packages with a mean weight of 7.1 pounds. Suppose the mean weight of five of these packages is 6.3 pounds. What is the weight of the sixth package?

F. 4.26 lb
G. 6.7 lb
H. 10.3 lb
J. 11.1 lb

21. Multiple Choice Which of the following is true about the IQR?

A. It describes the variability of the middle 50% of the data values.

B. It describes, on average, the distance of each data value from the mean.

C. It uses the minimum and maximum data value in its computation.

D. It is a statistic that is affected by extremely high values or extremely low values.

22. A gymnast receives the six scores below.

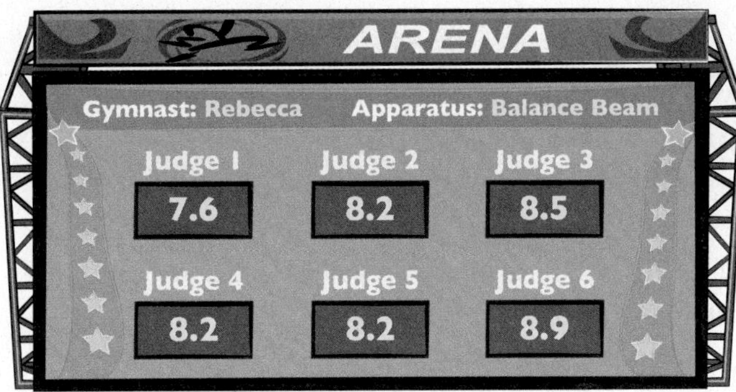

a. What is her mean score?

b. What happens to the mean when you multiply each data value by 2? By $\frac{2}{3}$? By 0.2?

c. Why does the mean change in each situation?

For Exercises 23–25, use the data below.

- Four pop songs have durations of 162, 151, 174, and 149 seconds.
- Four folk songs have durations of 121, 149, 165, and 184 seconds.

23. Multiple Choice What is the MAD of the folk songs' durations?

F. 18 seconds **G.** 19 seconds **H.** 18.25 seconds **J.** 19.75 seconds

24. Multiple Choice What is the MAD of the pop songs' durations?

A. 2 seconds **B.** 5 seconds **C.** 6 seconds **D.** 9 seconds

25. Multiple Choice Which of the following statements is true?

F. The variability in folk songs' durations is about half that of pop songs.

G. The variability in folk songs' durations is about twice that of pop songs.

H. The variability in folk songs' durations is about three times that of pop songs.

J. The variability in folk songs' durations is about four times that of pop songs.

Extensions

26. Mark has an easy way to find his mean test score: "Each math test is worth 100 points. Suppose I get 60 on my first test and 90 on my second. My average would be 75, because half of 60 is 30, half of 90 is 45, and 30 + 45 is 75. Now suppose I had three test scores: 60, 90, and 84. My average would be 78, because one third of 60 is 20, one third of 90 is 30, one third of 84 is 28, and 20 + 30 + 28 = 78."

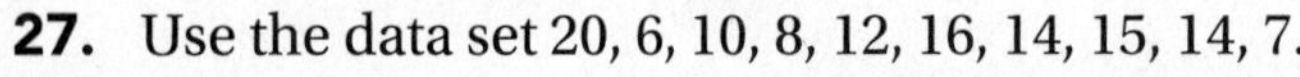

Does Mark's method always work? Explain.

27. Use the data set 20, 6, 10, 8, 12, 16, 14, 15, 14, 7.

a. Find the mean, mode, and median. Then find the IQR and MAD.

b. Add 3 to each data value in the set. Now determine the mean, mode, median, IQR, and MAD. What happened? Explain.

c. Multiply each data value in the set by 2. Now determine the mean, mode, median, IQR, and MAD. What happened? Explain.

Mathematical Reflections 3

In this Investigation, you explored how data vary and how summary statistics can be used to describe variability. The following questions will help you summarize what you learned.

Think about your answers to these questions. Discuss your ideas with other students and your teacher. Then, write a summary of your findings in your notebook.

1. **Explain** and illustrate the following words.

   a. Range

   b. Interquartile range

   c. Mean absolute deviation

2. a. **Describe** how you can use the range to compare how two data distributions vary.

   b. **Describe** how you can use the IQR to compare how two data distributions vary.

   c. **Describe** how you can use the MAD to compare how two data distributions vary.

Unit Project

Think about the survey you will be developing to gather information about middle-school students.

Will measures of variability, such as IQR and MAD, help you report observations about your data?

Common Core Mathematical Practices

As you worked on the Problems in this Investigation, you used prior knowledge to make sense of them. You also applied your Mathematical Practices to solve the Problems. Think back over your work, the ways you thought about the Problems, and how you used Mathematical Practices.

Shawna described her thoughts in the following way:

I figured out how to compare the IQR and the MAD. The IQR is related to the median. First, I find the median. Then, I find the midpoint of the data that are less than the median and the midpoint of the data that are greater than the median. The IQR is the difference of those two midpoints.

The MAD is related to the mean. First, I find the mean. Then I find the distance each data value is from the mean. To get an average deviation, I add up all the distances and divide the sum by the number of data values.

What this means is that the greater the IQR, the more the data vary from the median. The same goes for the MAD: The greater the MAD, the more the data vary from the mean.

Common Core Standards for Mathematical Practice

MP7 Look for and make use of structure

- What other Mathematical Practices can you identify in Shawna's reasoning?
- Describe a Mathematical Practice that you and your classmates used to solve a different Problem in this Investigation.

What Numbers Describe Us? Using Graphs to Group Data

People use numbers to describe a variety of attributes, or characteristics, of people, places, and things. These attributes include:

- activities, such as the amount of time it takes a student to get to school
- performances, such as the number of consecutive times a person can jump rope
- physical characteristics, such as a person's height

In this Investigation, you will examine graphs to identify patterns and trends in large sets of data. Grouping data before graphing makes the data easier to analyze. Your analysis can help you draw conclusions about the attribute being studied.

Common Core State Standards

6.SP.B.4 Display numerical data in plots on a number line, including dot plots, histograms, and box plots.

6.SP.B.5a Summarize numerical data sets in relation to their context, such as by reporting the number of observations.

6.SP.B.5c Summarize numerical data sets in relation to their context, such as by giving quantitative measures of center (median and/or mean) and variability (interquartile range and/or mean absolute deviation), as well as describing any overall pattern and any striking deviations from the overall pattern with reference to the context in which the data were gathered.

6.SP.B.5d Summarize numerical data sets in relation to their context, such as by relating the choice of measures of center and variability to the shape of the data distribution and the context in which the data were gathered.

Also 6.NS.C.6, 6.NS.C.7, 6.SP.A.1, 6.SP.A.2, 6.SP.A.3

4.1 Traveling to School

Histograms

A middle-school class studied the times that students woke up in the morning. They found that two students woke up almost an hour earlier than the others. The class wondered how much time it took each student to travel to school in the morning. The table below shows the data they collected.

- Based on the data, what three questions do you think the class asked?
- How might the class have collected the data?
- What information would a line plot of the data give you? A bar graph?

Students' Travel Times to School

Student	Travel Time (minutes)	Distance (miles)	Mode of Travel
LS	5	0.50	bus
CD	5	0.25	walking
ME	5	0.50	bus
EL	6	1.00	car
KR	8	0.25	walking
NS	8	1.25	car
NW	10	0.50	walking
RC	10	1.25	bus
JO	10	3.00	car
ER	10	1.00	bus
TH	11	1.50	bus
DD	15	2.00	bus
SE	15	0.75	car
AE	15	1.00	bus
CL	15	1.00	bus
HCP	15	1.50	bus
JW	15	1.50	bus
SW	15	2.00	car
CW	15	2.25	bus
KG	15	1.75	bus

Student	Travel Time (minutes)	Distance (miles)	Mode of Travel
DW	17	2.50	bus
MN	17	4.50	bus
AP	19	2.25	bus
MP	20	1.50	bus
AT	20	2.75	bus
JW	20	0.50	walking
JB	20	2.50	bus
MB	20	2.00	bus
CF	20	1.75	bus
RP	21	1.50	bus
LM	22	2.00	bus
QN	25	1.50	bus
AP	25	1.25	bus
CC	30	2.00	bus
BA	30	3.00	bus
BB	30	4.75	bus
FH	35	2.50	bus
KLD	35	0.75	bus
AB	50	4.00	bus
DB	60	4.50	bus

You can draw a histogram to display the data in the table. A **histogram** is a graph that organizes numerical data into *intervals*.

Step 1: Draw a dot plot or make a frequency table to display the data.

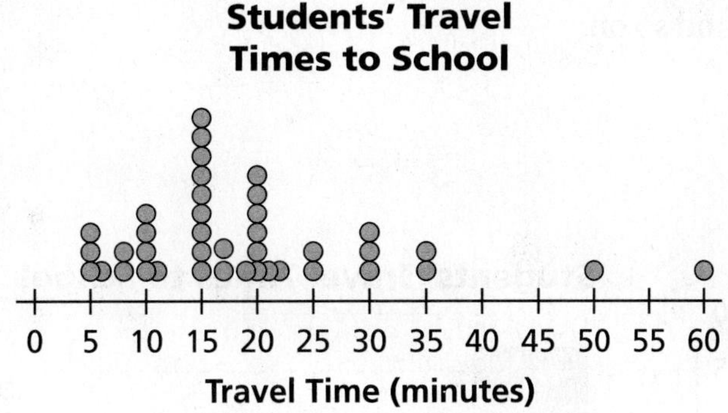

The data on student travel times vary from 5 minutes to 60 minutes.

- Why is the number line on the dot plot labeled every 5 minutes instead of every minute?
- How can you identify the data values of the dot plot when the number line is labeled every 5 minutes?

Step 2: Determine the frequency of the data values that fall into each interval, or group of consecutive numbers.

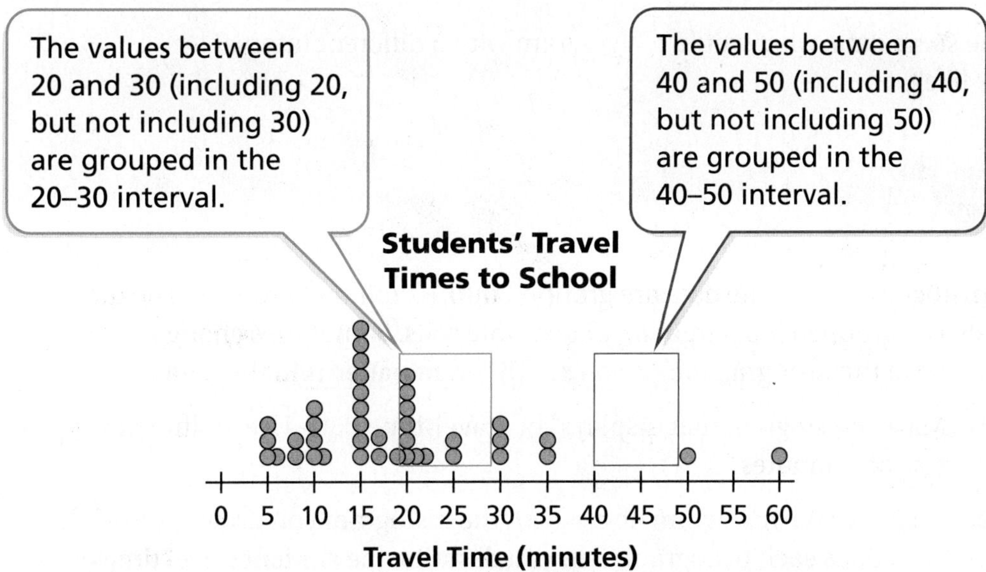

The height of each bar of the histogram represents the number of data values within a specified **interval,** or group of consecutive numbers.

Step 3: Draw the histogram. The histogram below has an interval size of 10 minutes.

Note: In the histogram below, data values of 10 minutes are graphed in the interval 10–20 minutes, data values of 20 minutes are graphed in the interval 20–30 minutes, and so on.

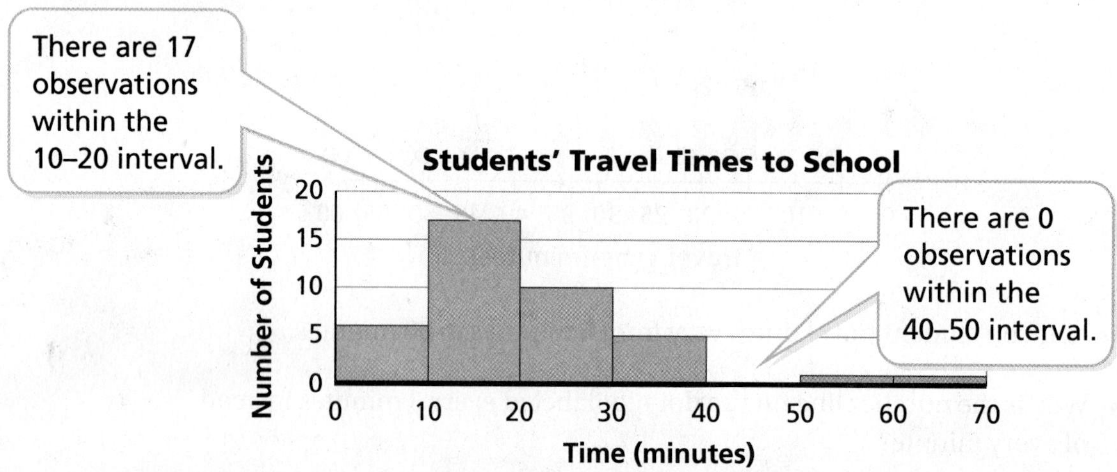

- How is a histogram like a bar graph? How is it different?
- How can you use a dot plot or a frequency table to help you make a histogram?
- What does *interval size* mean?
- Using the same data, what would a histogram with a different interval size look like?

Problem 4.1

In the histogram above, the data are grouped into 10-minute intervals. The data could also be grouped into larger or smaller intervals. Sometimes changing the interval size of the histogram helps you see different patterns in the data.

A **1.** Make a histogram that displays the travel-time data. Use an interval size of 5 minutes.

2. Compare the histogram above with the histogram you drew in part (1). How does each histogram help you describe the student travel times?

B Which students most likely wake up the latest in the morning? Explain.

C Which students most likely wake up the earliest? Explain.

Problem 4.1 continued

D **1.** For the data on travel time, find the mode, the median, the mean, and the range. Explain how you found these statistics.

2. In what interval does the mode fall? The median? The mean?

E Which statistic, the mean or the median, would you choose to report when describing the average time it takes a student to travel to school? Explain.

ACE Homework starts on page 98.

4.2 Jumping Rope
Box-and-Whisker Plots

A **box-and-whisker plot,** or *box plot,* uses five statistical measures: the minimum data value, the lower quartile, the median, the upper quartile, and the maximum data value. These values separate a set of data into four groups with the same number of data values in each group.

The example below shows how these five statistics form a box plot.

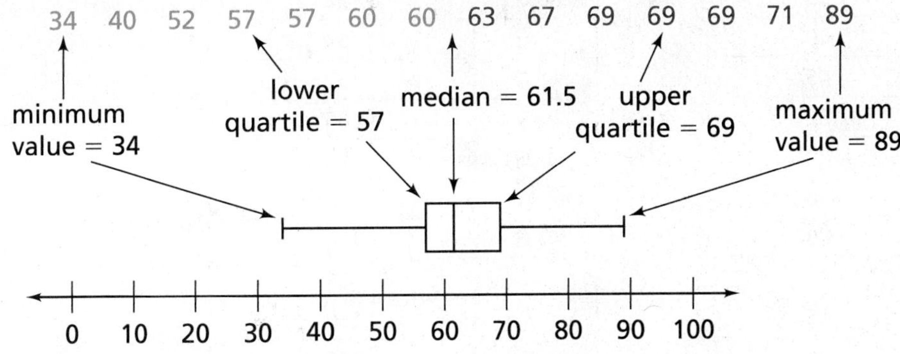

Two middle-school classes competed in a jumping-rope contest. The tables below show the data from each class.

Number of Consecutive Jumps, Mrs. R's Class

Gender	Number of Jumps
B	1
B	1
B	5
B	7
B	7
B	7
B	8
B	11
B	11
B	16
B	20
G	20
G	23
B	26
G	30
B	33
B	35
B	36
G	37
B	39
B	40
G	45
B	62
G	80
G	88
G	89
G	91
G	93
G	96
B	125

Number of Consecutive Jumps, Mr. K's Class

Gender	Number of Jumps
B	1
B	2
B	5
B	7
B	8
B	8
G	14
B	17
B	17
G	27
B	27
B	28
B	30
G	30
B	39
B	42
G	45
B	47
B	50
G	52
G	54
G	57
B	65
G	73
G	102
G	104
G	151
G	160
B	160
G	300

- Mr. K's class claims it is better at jumping rope than Mrs. R's class. What evidence might Mr. K's class be using?

The dot plots below show the distributions of the data from the tables.

- How are the dot plots similar? How are they different?

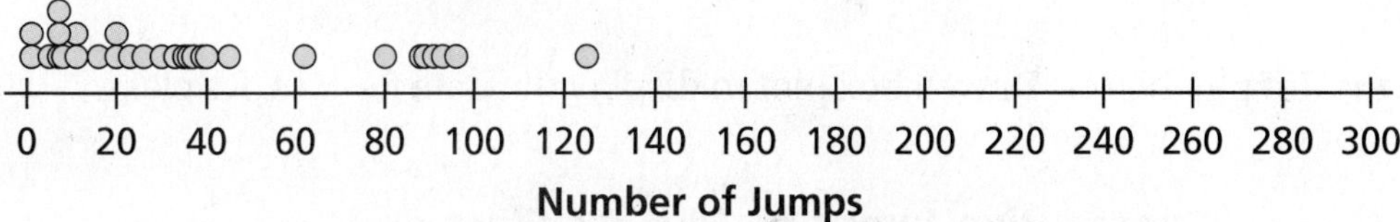

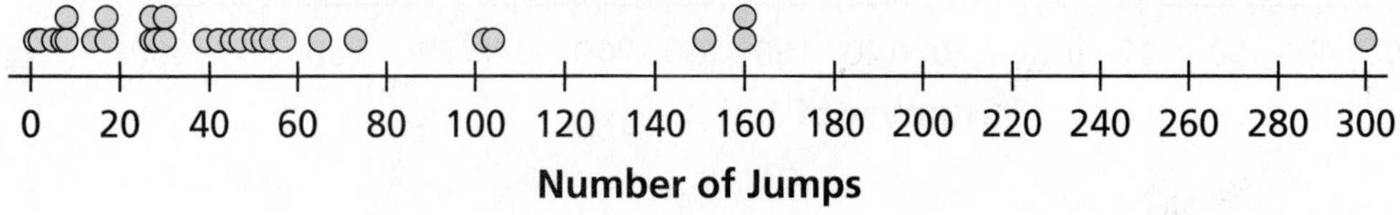

The minimum value (1), the lower quartile (17), the median (40.5), the upper quartile (65), and the maximum value (300) are shown on the dot plot below.

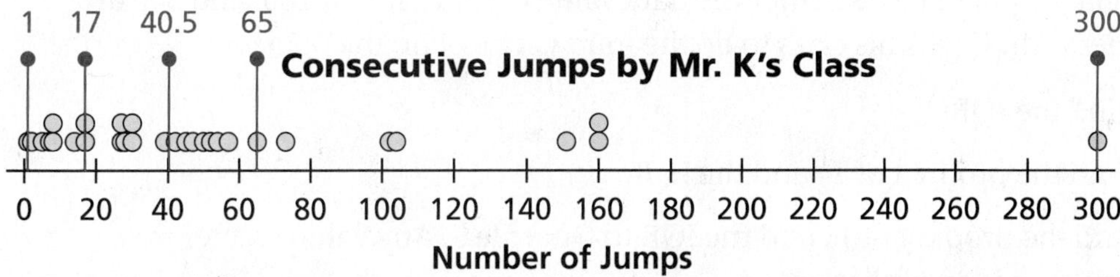

This box plot shows the same distribution of data as the dot plot above.

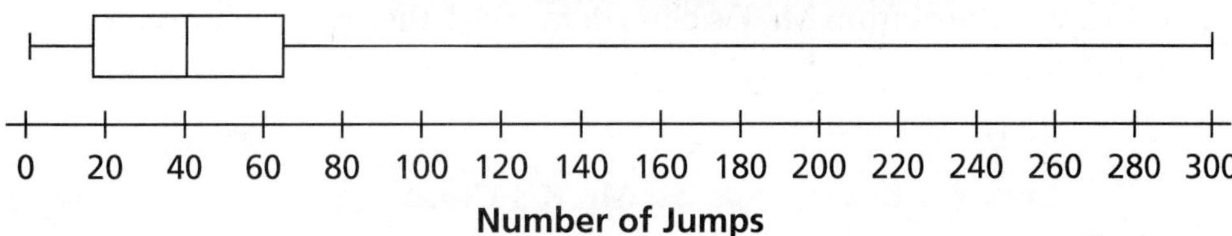

An **outlier** is an unusually high or low data value in a distribution. It could indicate that a value was recorded incorrectly. It could also indicate that the data value is unusual and is important to study.

- What values might be outliers in the data set for Mr. K's class?
- Look at the box-and-whisker plot. What is the typical number of jumps for a student in Mr. K's class? Explain your reasoning.
- Use what you know about box plots. Explain how box plots group a data distribution into quartiles, or four equal parts.

Problem 4.2

In this Problem, you will use box plots to compare data from the two classes.

A Use the dot plot below. Draw a box plot to display the data for Mrs. R's class.

Consecutive Jumps by Mrs. R's Class

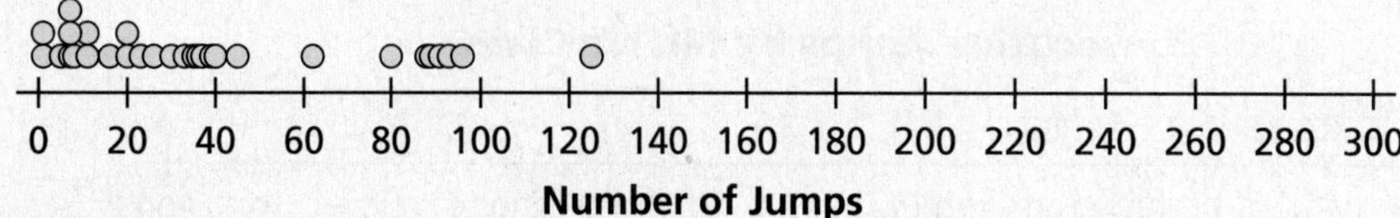

B Which class performed better in the jump-rope activity? Use information from the dot plots, box plots, and tables to explain your reasoning.

C Mr. K's class notices unusually high values in its class data. The students in the class want to test whether the data values 102, 104, 151, 160, and 300 are outliers. Mr. K tells his class to do the following test on the data:

- Find the IQR.
- Find the product of $1\frac{1}{2}$ and the IQR.
- Add the product of $1\frac{1}{2}$ and the IQR to Quartile 3. Any value greater than this sum is an outlier.
- Subtract the product of $1\frac{1}{2}$ and the IQR from Quartile 1. Any value less than this sum is an outlier.

1. Locate any outliers from Mr. K's class data. Mark them on a copy of the box plot below.

Consecutive Jumps by Mr. K's Class

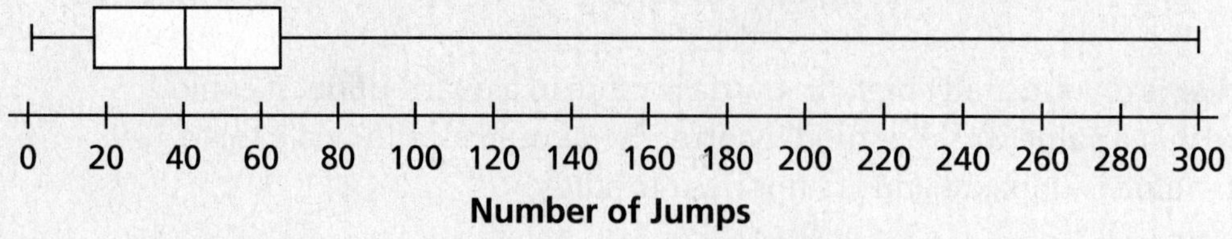

2. Does Mrs. R's class data include outliers? Explain your reasoning. If Mrs. R's class data contains outliers, redraw your box plot to show which data values are outliers.

Problem 4.2 continued

D 1. Calculate the mean of Mr. K's class data. Then calculate the mean and the median for Mr. K's class data without the outliers.

2. Do the outliers in Mr. K's class data have more of an effect on the median or on the mean? Explain.

3. Consider what you know about the outliers in the data. Does this change your answer to Question B? Explain.

E In Investigation 2, you used the words *symmetric* and *skewed* to describe the shapes of distributions. These descriptions can also be applied to distributions represented by box plots.

Below are three box plots. They show symmetric and skewed distributions.

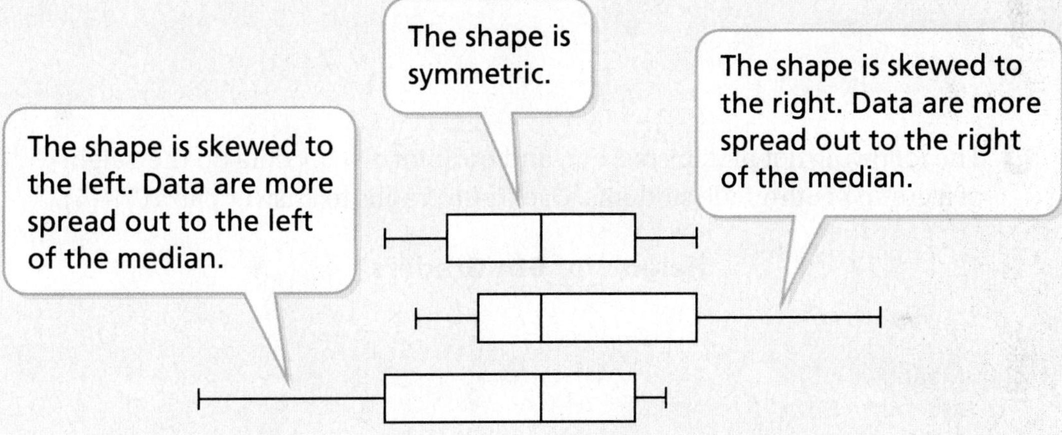

1. How does the location of the median in a box plot provide information about its shape?
2. How would you describe the shape of Mr. K's class data?
3. How would you describe the shape of Mrs. R's class data?
4. How does the shape of each distribution help you compare the two classes?

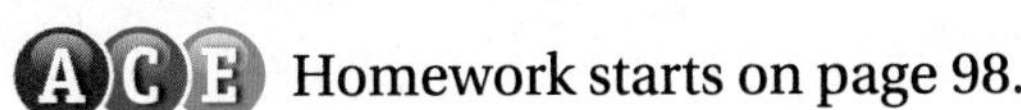
Homework starts on page 98.

4.3 How Much Taller Is a 6th Grader Than a 2nd Grader?

Taking Variability Into Consideration

You can use various physical measures, such as height, to describe people. In this Problem, you will compare the heights of 6th-grade students and the heights of 2nd-grade students.

It is important to identify which graphs are most useful for answering different questions. You have used several types of graphs in this Unit: dot plots, line plots, histograms, and box plots. While answering the questions in this Problem, think about which graphs are most helpful.

- How much taller is a 6th grader than a 2nd grader?

Problem 4.3

A The following dot plot, histogram, and box plot display data on the heights of a group of 6th-grade students. Use these graphs to answer parts (1)–(5).

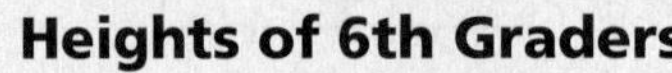

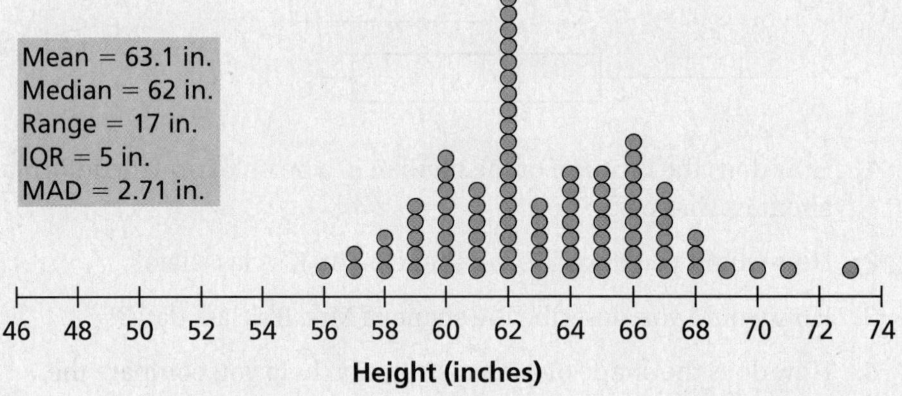

Problem 4.3 *continued*

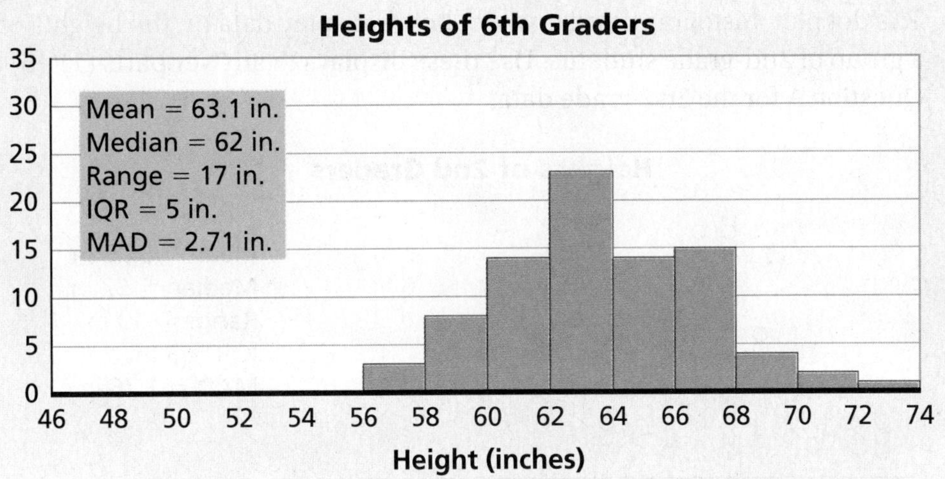

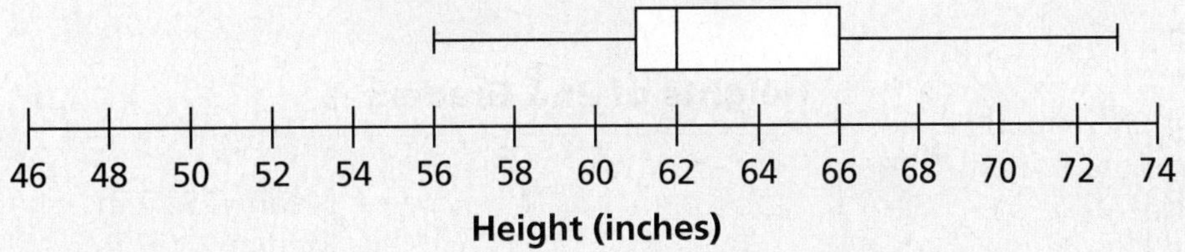

1. Use one or more of the graphs to find the number of students in the group. Explain your reasoning.
2. What do you notice about the data values and their distribution? Explain which graph is most useful when describing the distribution.
3. Describe any clusters or gaps in the distribution. Explain which graph is most useful for identifying clusters or gaps.
4. Describe the spread of the distribution. Which data values occur frequently? Which data values occur infrequently? How close together are the data values? Explain which graph is most useful when describing how the data vary.
5. Describe how the dot plot, histogram, and box plot displaying the data are alike. Describe how they are different.

continued on the next page >

Problem 4.3 continued

B The dot plot, histogram, and box plot below display data on the heights of a group of 2nd-grade students. Use these displays to answer parts (1)–(5) of Question A for the 2nd-grade data.

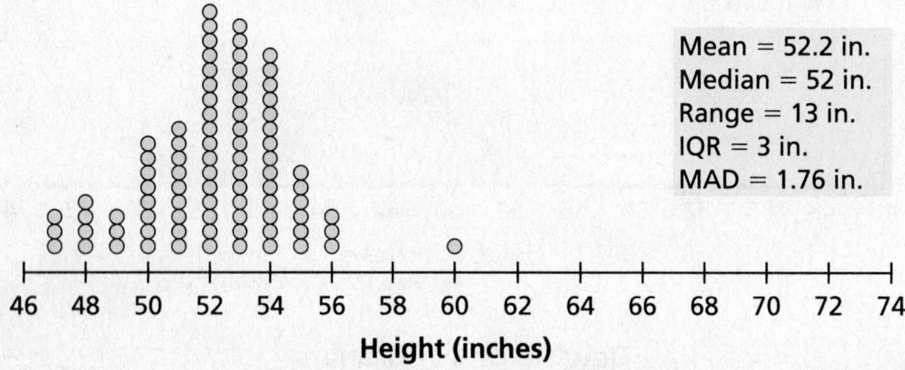

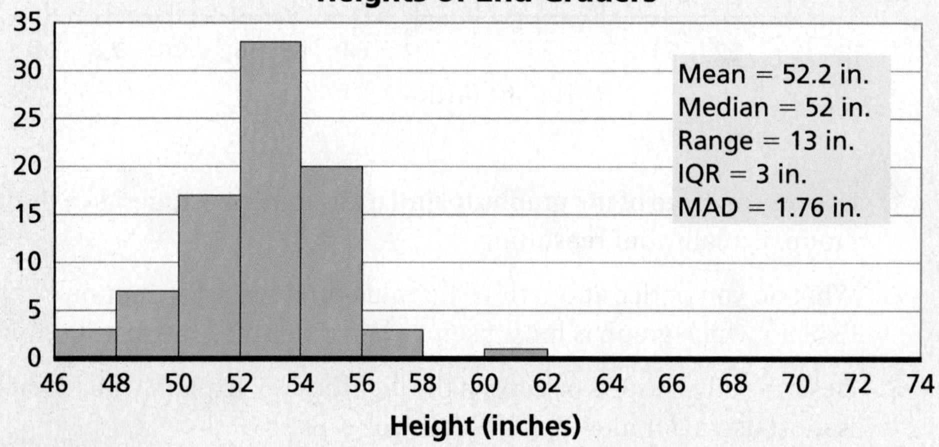

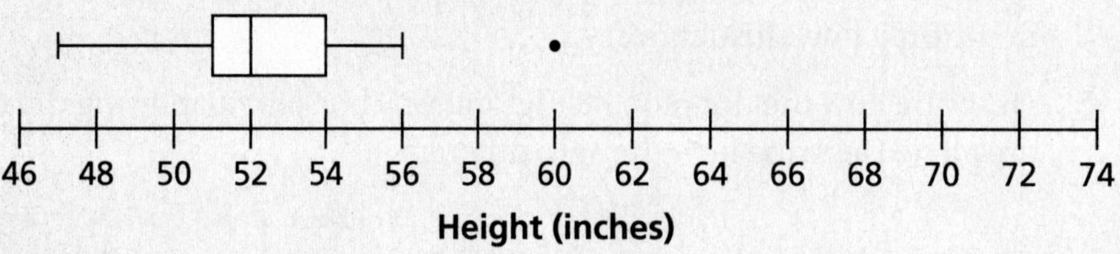

Problem 4.3 continued

C Compare the graphs of the 6th-grade students to the graphs of the 2nd-grade students. For parts (1)–(4), consider the question below.

How much taller is a 6th-grade student than a 2nd-grade student?

1. Use the dot plots, means, and medians of both sets of data to answer the question. Explain your reasoning.
2. Use the histograms, means, and medians of both sets of data to answer the question. Explain your reasoning.
3. Use the box plots and medians of both sets of data to answer the question. Explain your reasoning.
4. Suppose you were writing a report to answer the question above. Which type of graphs would you choose to display? Explain.

D Use the range, IQR, and MAD for the 6th-grade and the 2nd-grade distributions. Is one distribution more spread out than the other? Explain.

E Suppose you were asked to write a report answering the question below. How would you collect data to answer the question? How would you display the data? What measures would you report?

How much taller is an 8th-grade student than a 6th-grade student?

ACE Homework starts on page 98.

Did You Know?

Growth patterns in humans change over time. While people's heights change significantly through their late teens or early twenties, their heads grow much more slowly after early childhood.

Head and Body Growth Over Time

The length of a **baby's** head is one quarter of its total height. | **Age 2** | **Age 6** | **Age 12** | The length of an **adult's** head is one seventh of its total height.

Applications

For Exercises 1–4, use the dot plot and histograms below. The graphs show the number of minutes it takes a class of students to travel to school.

Student Travel Times

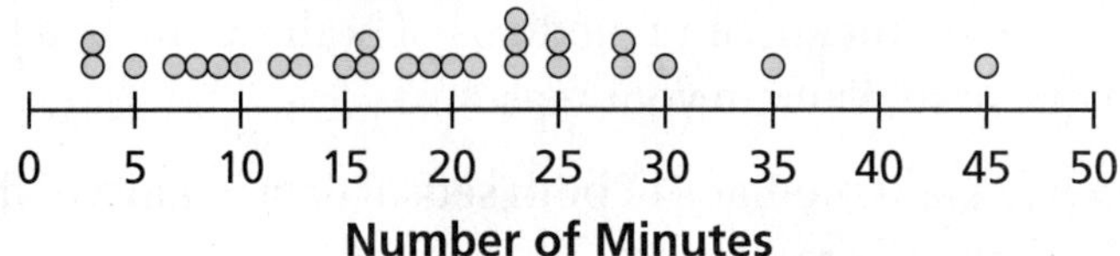

Student Travel Times

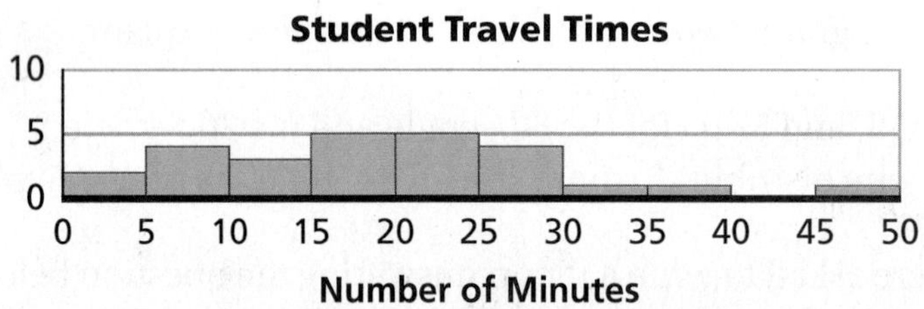

Student Travel Times

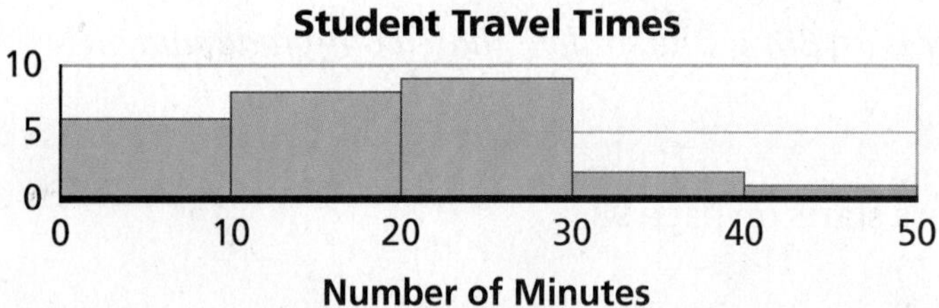

1. How many students spend exactly 10 minutes traveling to school?

2. Which histogram can you use to determine how many students spent at least 15 minutes traveling to school? Explain your reasoning.

3. How many students are in the class? Explain how you can use one of the histograms to find your answer.

4. What is the median time it takes the students to travel to school? Explain your reasoning.

For Exercises 5–9, use the graphs below. The graphs compare the percent of real juice found in different juice drinks.

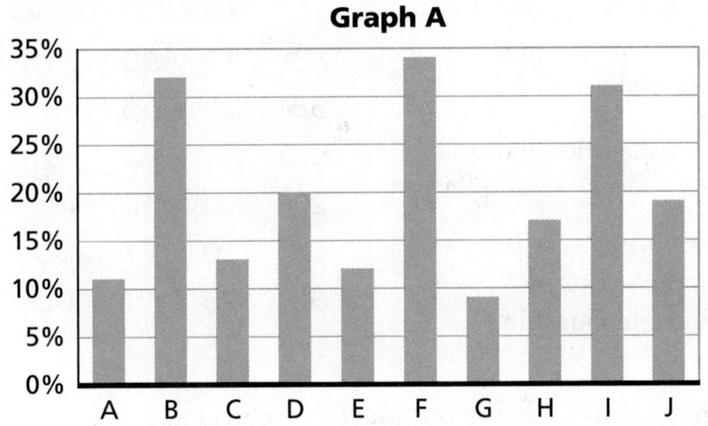

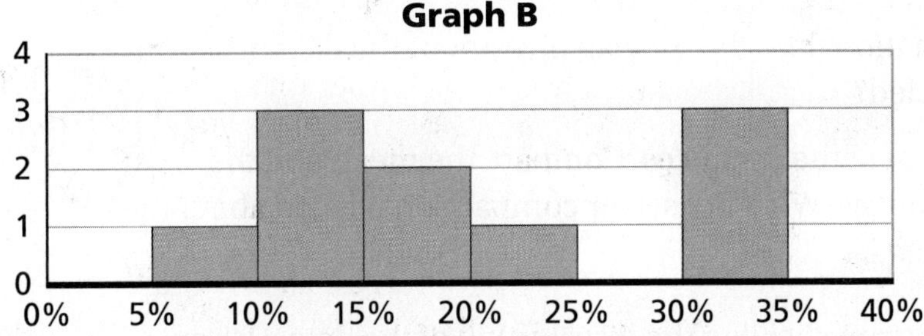

5. **a.** Which juice drink(s) has the greatest percent of real juice? The least percent of real juice? Which graph did you use to find your answer? Explain why you chose that graph.

b. For each juice you named in part (a), what percent of real juice does the drink contain? Which graph did you use? Explain.

6. **a.** Which graph can you use to find the percent of real juice found in a typical juice drink? Explain your reasoning.

b. What is the typical percent of real juice? Explain your reasoning.

7. What title and axis labels would be appropriate for Graph A? For Graph B?

8. If you were given only Graph A, would you have enough information to draw Graph B? Explain your reasoning.

9. If you were given only Graph B, would you have enough information to draw Graph A? Explain your reasoning.

For Exercises 10–12, use the information below.

Jimena likes to hike in the hills. She drives to a new place almost every weekend. The distances Jimena traveled each weekend for the past 30 weekends are listed at the right.

Weekend Travel

33	10	95	71	4
38	196	85	19	4
209	101	63	10	4
27	128	32	11	213
95	10	77	200	27
62	73	11	100	16

10. **a.** Draw a box-and-whisker plot to display the data.

b. Why is the left-hand whisker of the box plot (between of the box plot the minimum value and Quartile 1) so short?

c. Why is the right-hand whisker of the box plot (between Quartile 3 and the maximum value) so long?

d. What information does the median give about the distances Jimena traveled?

e. Find the mean of the distances. Compare the mean and the median distances. What does your comparison tell you about the distribution?

11. **a.** Draw a histogram showing the distribution of the data. Use an interval size of 20 miles.

b. How many weekends did Jimena drive at least 20 miles but less than 40 miles? Explain how you can use the histogram to find your answer.

c. How many weekends did Jimena drive 100 miles or more? Explain how you can use the histogram to find your answer.

d. Use the median you found in Exercise 10. In what interval of the histogram does the median fall? How is this possible?

12. Consider the box plot you made in Exercise 10 and the histogram you made in Exercise 11.

a. Compare the shape of the histogram to the shape of the box plot.

b. How does the height of the first bar in the histogram relate to the length of the left-hand whisker in the box plot?

c. How does the histogram help you understand the length of the right-hand whisker in the box plot?

For Exercises 13 and 14, use the jump-rope data from Problem 4.2.

13. Draw two box plots to compare one gender in Mrs. R's class to the same gender in Mr. K's class. For example, make box plots to compare either the girls from the two classes or the boys from the two classes. Did the girls (or boys) in one class do better than the girls (or boys) in the other class? Explain your reasoning.

14. Make a box plot for all the girls in Mrs. R's class and Mr. K's classes combined. Make a box plot for all the boys in Mrs. R's and Mr. K's classes combined. Compare the box plots. Who did better, the boys or the girls? Explain your reasoning.

15. Multiple Choice Which value is NOT needed to construct a box plot?

A. upper quartile

B. minimum value

C. median

D. mean

16. Tim and Kadisha used the box plots below.

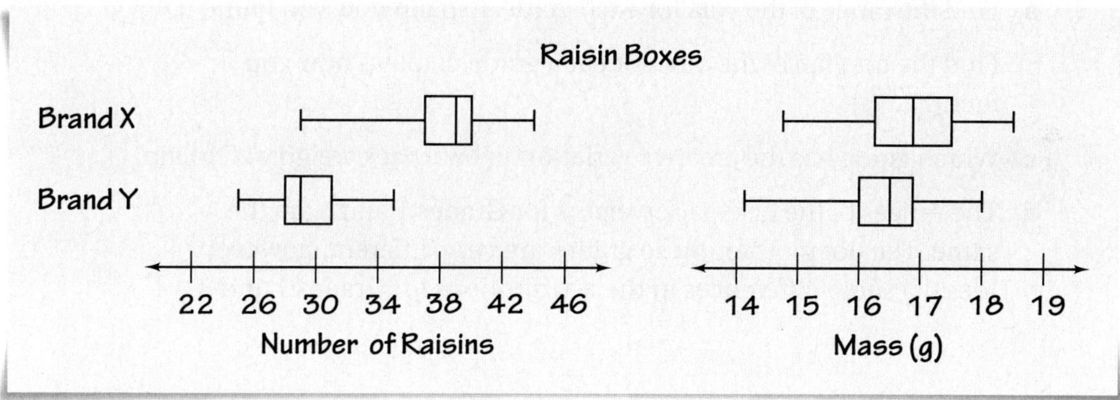

Tim says that Brand X raisins are a better deal than Brand Y raisins because Brand X has more raisins in each box. Kadisha says that since each box has a mass of about 16 or 17 grams, the brands give you the same amount for your money. Do you agree with Tim or with Kadisha? Explain.

For Exercises 17–19, use the dot plots below. The dot plots show the weights of backpacks for students in Grades 1, 3, 5, and 7.

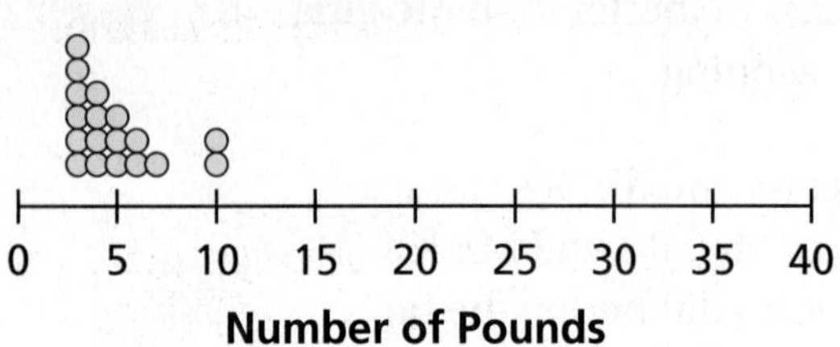

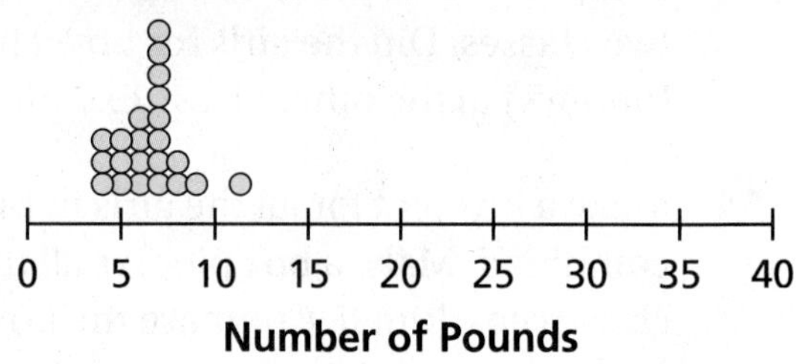

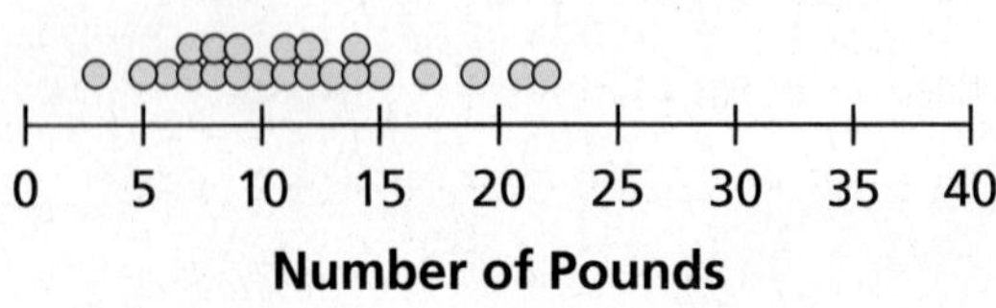

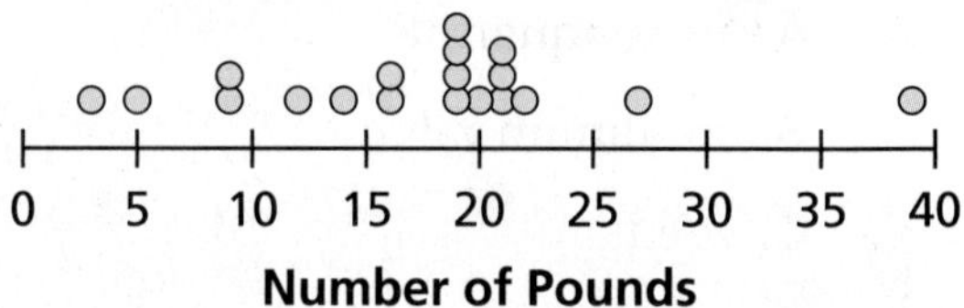

17. Use the dot plots above.

a. Find the range of the data for each grade. Explain how you found it.

b. Find the median of the data for each grade. Explain how you found it.

c. Which grade has the greatest variation in backpack weights? Explain.

d. The ranges of the backpack weights for Grades 1 and 3 are the same. The dot plots for these grades are very different, however. Identify some differences in the distributions for Grades 1 and 3

18. The box plots show the data from the dot plots on the previous page.

A. 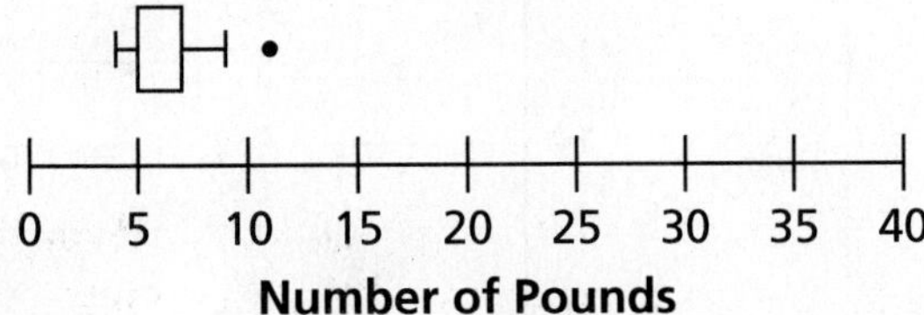

B. 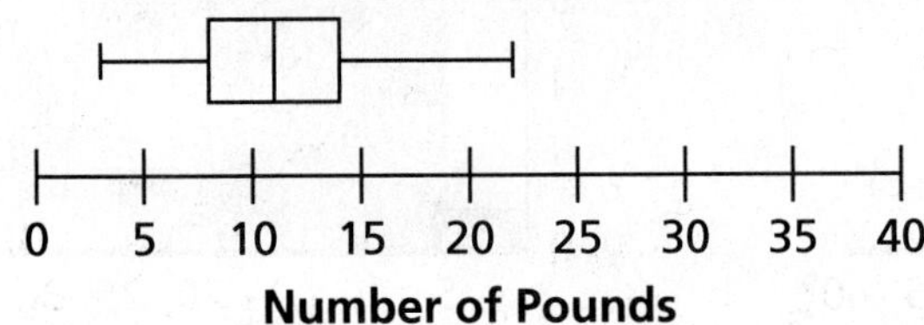

C. 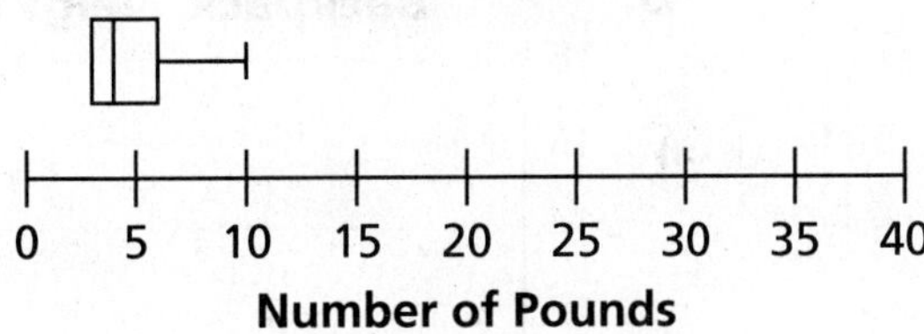

D. 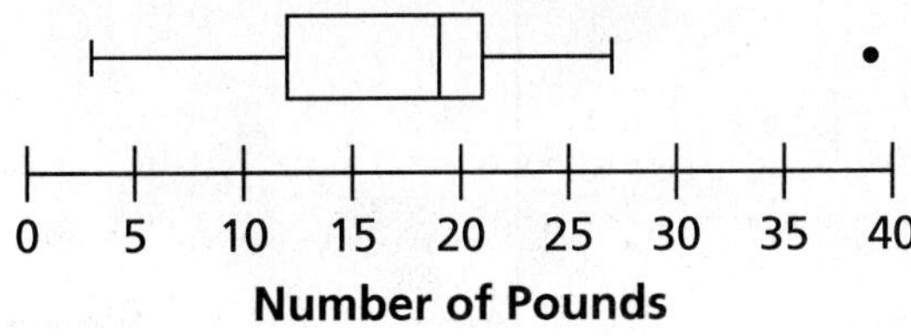

a. Which box plot shows the Grade 1 distribution? Explain.

b. Which box plot shows the Grade 3 distribution? Explain.

c. Which box plot shows the Grade 5 distribution? Explain.

d. Which box plot show the Grade 7 distribution? Explain.

e. Describe the shape of each distribution. Tell whether each is symmetric or skewed. Explain your reasoning.

19. The histograms below display the same data sets as the dot plots and box plots on the previous pages.

A.

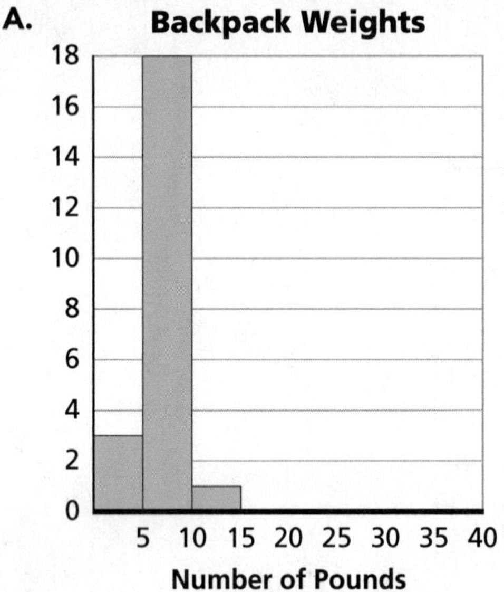

B.

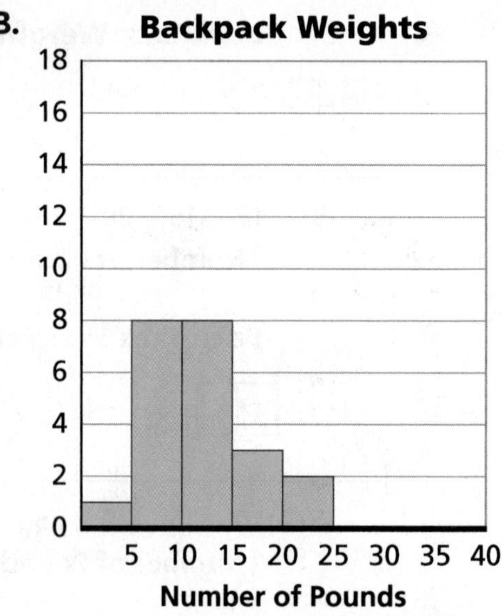

C.

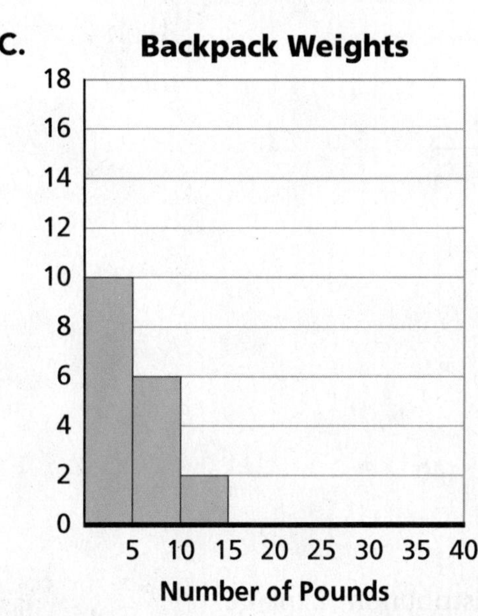

D.

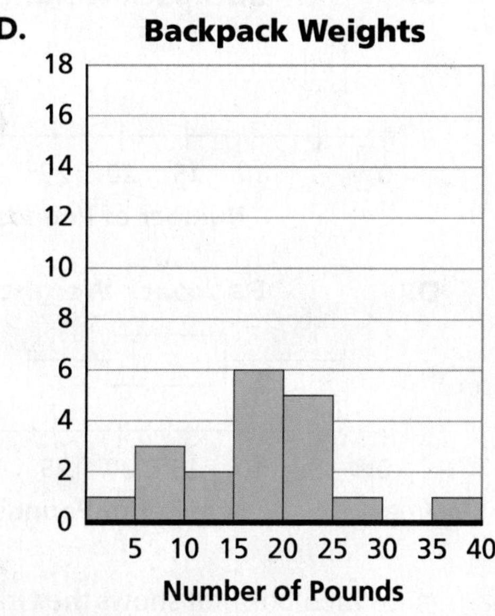

a. Which histogram shows the Grade 1 distribution? Explain.

b. Which histogram shows the Grade 3 distribution? Explain.

c. Which histogram shows the Grade 5 distribution? Explain.

d. Which histogram show the Grade 7 distribution? Explain.

e. Describe the shape of each distribution. Tell whether each is symmetric or skewed. Explain your reasoning.

For Exercises 20–23, use the box plots below. Each box plot shows the distribution of heights of 30 students at a particular grade level.

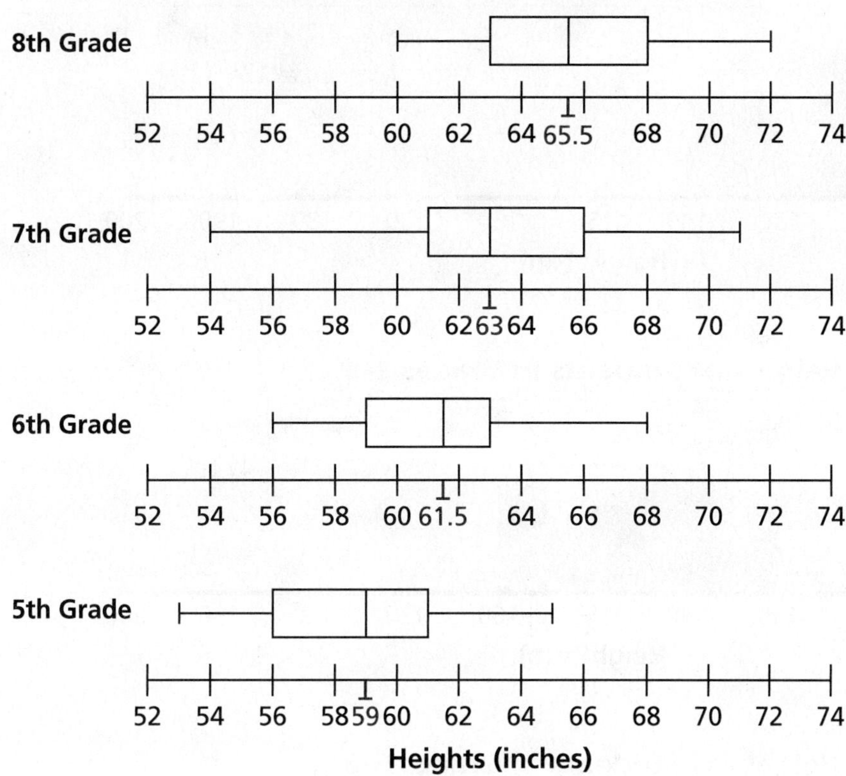

20. How much taller is an 8th grader than a 7th grader? Explain your reasoning.

21. On average, how much do students grow from Grade 5 to Grade 8? Explain.

22. Describe the shape of the Grade 6 distribution. Is it symmetric or skewed? Explain.

23. Describe the shape of the Grade 8 distribution. Is it symmetric or skewed? Explain.

For Exercises 24–26, use the histograms below. Each histogram shows the heights of 30 students in several grades.

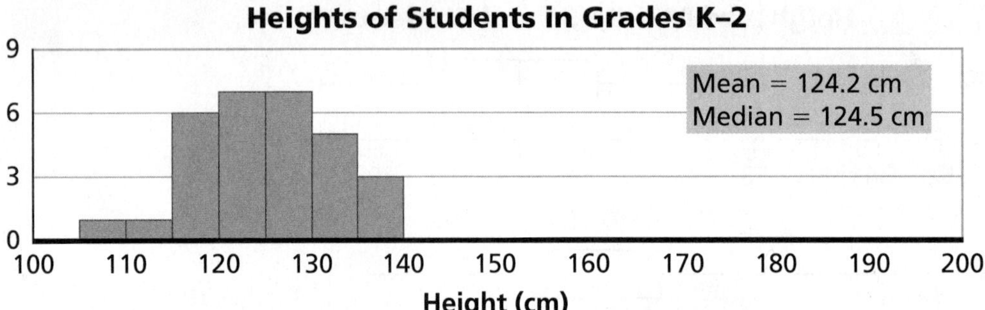

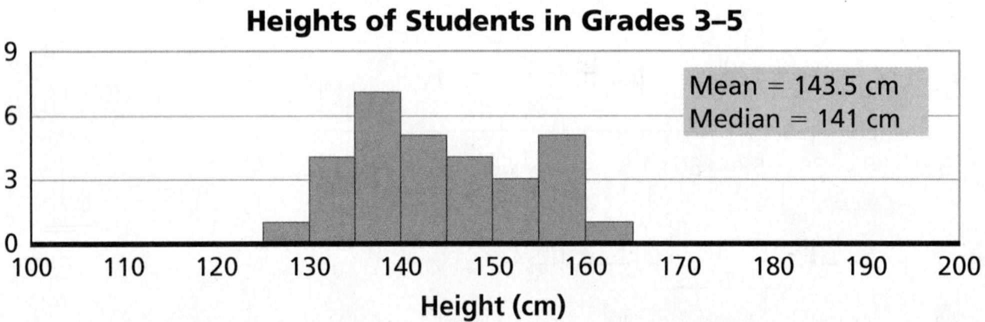

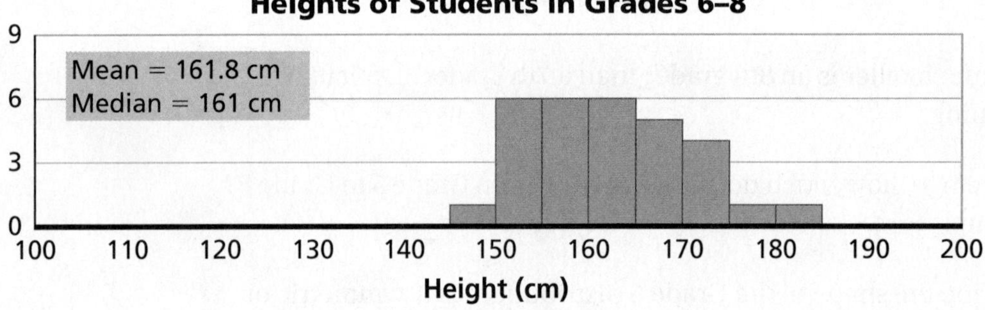

24. On average, how much taller is a student in Grades 6–8 than a student in Grades K–2? Explain.

25. On average, how much taller is a student in Grades 6–8 than a student in Grades 3–5? Explain.

26. How is the shape of the histogram for Grades 3–5 different from the other histograms? Why might this be so?

Connections

27. Suppose the sum of the values in a data set is 250, and the mean is 25.

a. Write a data set that fits this description.

b. Do you think other students in your class wrote the same data set you did? Explain.

c. What is the median of your data set? Does the median of a data set have to be close in value to the mean? Explain.

28. Each of the students in a seventh-grade class chose a number from 1 to 10 at random. The table below shows the results.

Number Chosen	Percent Who Chose the Number
1	1%
2	5%
3	12%
4	11%
5	10%
6	12%
7	30%
8	9%
9	7%
10	3%

a. Draw a bar graph of the data.

b. According to the data, is each number from 1 to 10 equally likely to be chosen?

c. What is the mode of the data?

d. Nine students chose the number 5. How many students are in Grade 7? Explain.

29. Moesha's mean score for six algebra quizzes is 79.5. She has misplaced a quiz. Her scores on the other quizzes are 82, 71, 83, 91, and 78. What is her missing score?

30. The tablet below shows data for the ages and heights of two 2012–2013 professional basketball teams.

Charlestown Spartans

Player	Age	Height (cm)
#37	23	185
#29	27	173
#56	19	204
#39	35	202
#28	32	190
#16	33	209
#25	30	189
#42	26	205
#34	27	193
#27	31	203
#41	24	198
#30	29	198
#18	26	205

Springfield Yellows

Player	Age	Height (cm)
#37	24	210
#54	23	203
#26	20	198
#16	22	207
#25	26	209
#34	23	194
#18	21	183
#24	24	203
#29	22	189
#45	23	203
#35	26	195
#31	30	185

Team Rosters

a. Compare the ages of the two teams. Use statistics and graphs to support your answer.

b. Compare the heights of the two teams. Use statistics and graphs to support your answer.

c. Based on the data for these two teams, what age is a typical professional basketball player? What height is a typical professional basketball player? Do you think your generalizations are accurate? Why or why not?

Extensions

31. Alejandro and Katya are researching baseball facts. They find out that the durations of baseball games vary from game to game. The graph below shows the data Alejandro and Katya collected about the duration of baseball games.

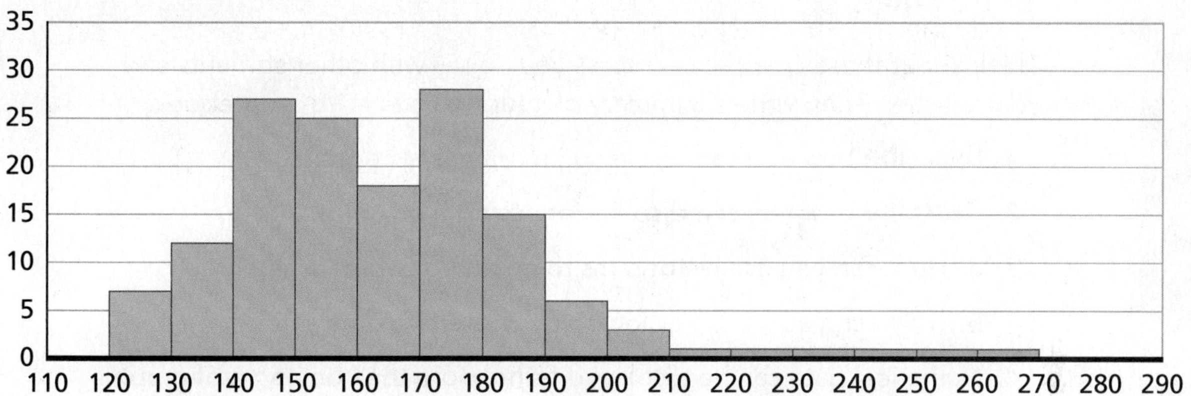

a. What title and axis labels would be appropriate for this graph?

b. Describe the shape of the graph. What does the shape tell you about the length of a typical baseball game?

c. How many games are represented in the graph?

d. Estimate the lower quartile, the median, and the upper quartile of the data distribution. What do these statistics tell you about the length of a typical baseball game?

32. Each box-and-whisker plot below has a median of 4. For each plot, provide a possible data set that would result in the distribution.

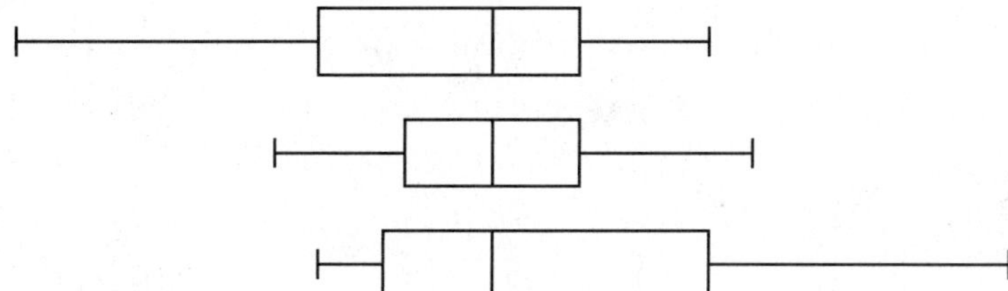

Mathematical Reflections

In this Investigation, you drew box plots and histograms to organize data into groups or intervals. You also used histograms and box plots to analyze and compare data distributions. The following questions will help you to summarize what you have learned.

Think about these questions. Discuss your ideas with other students and your teacher. Then write a summary of your findings in your notebook.

1. **Describe** how you can display data using a histogram.
2. **Describe** how you can display data using a box plot.
3. a. **How** can you use histograms to compare two data sets?

   b. **How** can you use box plots to compare two data sets?
4. Numerical data can be displayed using more than one type of graph. **How** do you decide when to use a dot plot, line plot, bar graph, histogram, or box plot?

Unit Project

Think about the survey you will be developing to gather information about middle school students.

Which type of graph will best display the data you collect?

Common Core Mathematical Practices

As you worked on the Problems in this Investigation, you used prior knowledge to make sense of them. You also applied Mathematical Practices to solve the Problems. Think back over your work, the ways you thought about the Problems, and how you used Mathematical Practices.

Ken described his thoughts in the following way:

During Problem 4.3, and the rest of this Investigation, we realized that histograms and box plots group data. You don't see individual data values in those types of graphs. Histograms group data in intervals that you choose. Box plots group data into quartiles. Quartiles group the data into four equal parts.

It is easy to use graphs that show individual data values when the data values are not spread out and there aren't too many. When the values are spread out, or when there are a lot of data values, it's easier to use graphs that group data.

Common Core Standards for Mathematical Practice

MP4 Model with mathematics

- What other Mathematical Practices can you identify in Ken's reasoning?
- Describe a Mathematical Practice that you and your classmates used to solve a different Problem in this Investigation.

Unit Project

Is Anyone Typical?

Use what you learned in this Unit to conduct a statistical investigation. Answer the question,

"What are some characteristics of a typical middle-school student?"

Complete your data collection, analysis, and interpretation. Then make a poster, write a report, or find another way to display your results. Your statistical investigation should consist of four parts.

Part 1: Asking Questions

Decide what information to gather. You should gather numerical data and categorical data. Your data may include physical characteristics, family characteristics, behaviors, and preferences or opinions.

Then, write clear and appropriate questions for your survey. Each person taking the survey should understand the questions. You may provide answer choices for some questions. For example, instead of asking, "What is your favorite movie?" you may ask, "Which of the following movies do you like the best?" and list several choices.

Part 2: Collecting Data

You can collect data from your class or from a larger group of students. Decide how to distribute and collect the survey.

Part 3: Analyzing the Data

Organize, display, and analyze your data. Think about the types of displays and the measures of center and variability that are most appropriate for each set of data.

Part 4: Interpreting the Results

Use the results of your analysis to describe some characteristics of the typical middle-school student. Is there a student that fits all the "typical" characteristics you found? Explain.

Looking Back

The Problems in this Unit helped you understand the process of statistical investigation. You learned how to:

- Distinguish between categorical data and numerical data
- Organize and represent data with tables, dot plots, line plots, frequency bar graphs, ordered-value bar graphs, histograms, and box-and-whisker plots
- Calculate and interpret measures of center and measures of spread
- Compare two or more distributions of data

Use Your Understanding: Data and Statistics

You can gather and analyze data in statistical investigations to help you make sense of the world around you. Follow these steps when you need to conduct an investigation.

- Pose questions.
- Collect data.
- Analyze data.
- Interpret the results.

For Exercises 1–4, use the information below.

Pet Ownership Survey Results

- *Over 70 million households in the United States own a pet.*
- *About 6 out of 10 households in the United States own at least one pet.*
- *About two-fifths of pet owners have multiple pets.*

1. What questions might have been asked in this survey?
2. Which questions from part (1) collected categorical data? Numerical data? Explain your reasoning.

3. What kinds of people may have responded to the survey?

4. Who might be interested in these results?

Explain Your Reasoning

5. Tyler decided to survey his classmates. He posed two questions:

What is your favorite kind of pet?

How many pets do you have?

Each classmate responded to the questions using student response systems. The answers appeared on the board.

Pet Survey

2	3	3	17	cat	horse	cow	rabbit
5	9	5	0	dog	dog	cat	cat
6	2	6	1	cat	duck	rabbit	bird
1	5	14	6	cow	dog	dog	horse
8	3	2	2	bird	goat	fish	pig
1	2	3		dog	dog	rabbit	
0	4	21		horse	fish	dog	

a. Which data set goes with which question? Explain your reasoning.

b. Which data set includes categorical data?

c. Which data set includes numerical data?

d. Make a frequency table for each set of data.

6. Which types of graphs can be used to display categorical data? Explain your reasoning.

7. Which types of graphs can be used to display numerical data? Explain your reasoning.

For Exercises 8–11, use the information below.

A local candle-shop owner wonders which of his products lasts the longest. The owner does an experiment. He records the number of minutes that each candle burns. He completes 15 trials for each type of candle.

Candle-Burning Durations (minutes)

Trial	Brilliant Candle	Firelight Candle	Shimmering Candle
1	60	66	68
2	49	68	65
3	58	56	44
4	57	59	59
5	61	61	51
6	53	64	58
7	57	53	61
8	60	51	63
9	61	60	49
10	62	50	56
11	58	64	59
12	56	60	62
13	61	58	64
14	59	51	57
15	58	49	54

8. For each type of candle, find the median candle-burning time. Find the IQR. Explain how you found the median and IQR.

9. For each type of candle, find the mean candle-burning time. Find the MAD. Explain how you found the mean and MAD.

10. The dot plots, histograms, and box plots below show data on two of the candles. For each graph, identify the candle.

Dot Plot A

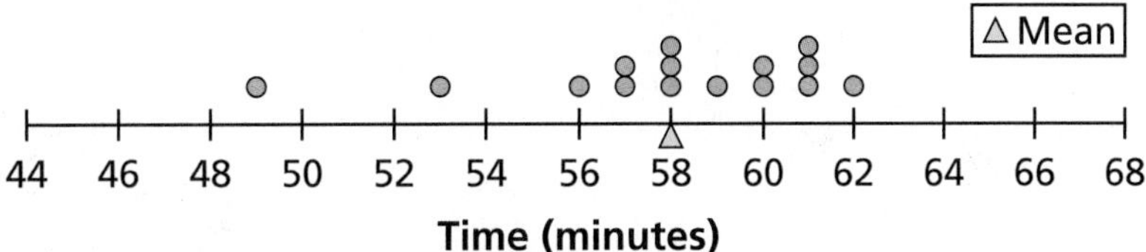

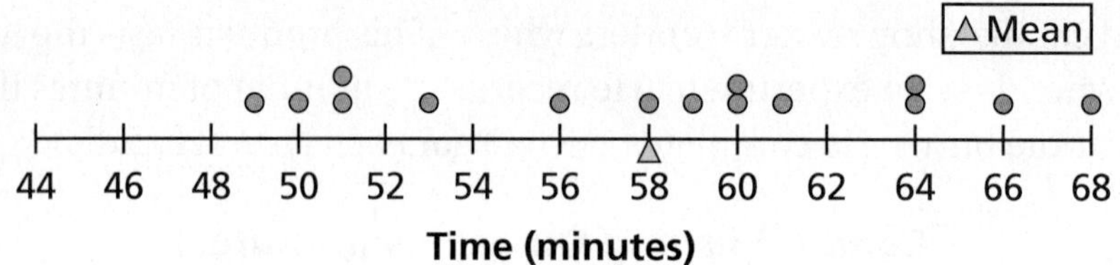

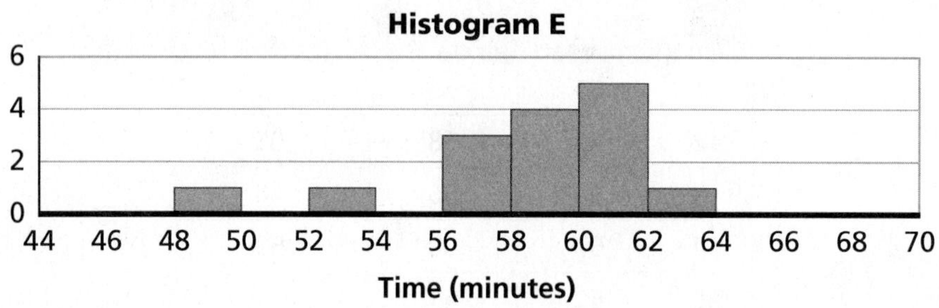

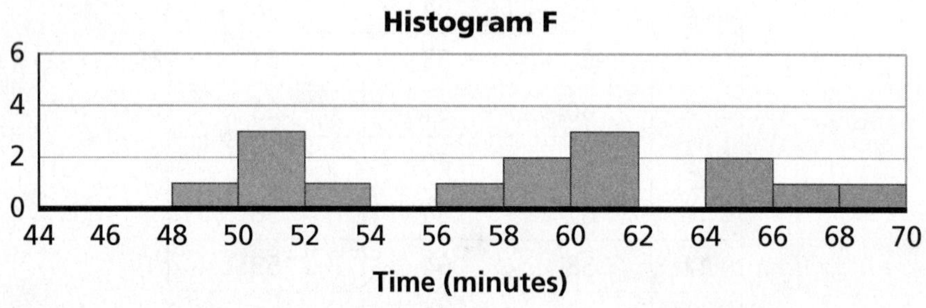

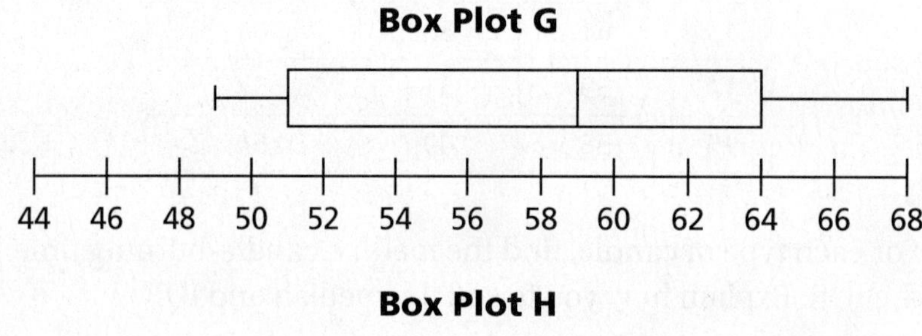

Box Plot H

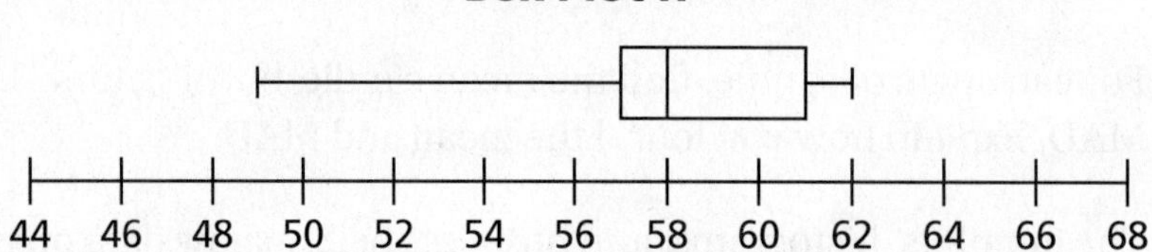

11. Use your answers for Exercises 8–10. Which candle burns for the longest amount of time? The shortest amount of time? Explain.

English / Spanish Glossary

A

analyze Academic Vocabulary
To think about and understand facts and details about a given set of information. Analyzing can involve providing a written summary supported by factual information, a diagram, chart, table, or a combination of these.

related terms *examine, evaluate, determine, observe, investigate*

sample Analyze the following data to find the mean and the mode.

Getting to School

Student	Krista	Mike	Lupe	Kareem
Time (min)	10	15	20	10

analizar Vocabulario académico
Pensar para comprender datos y detalles sobre un conjunto determinado de información dada. Analizar puede incluir un resumen escrito apoyado por información real, un diagrama, una gráfica, una tabla o una combinación de estos.

términos relacionados *examinar, evaluar, determinar, observar, investigar*

ejemplo Analiza los siguientes datos para hallar la media y la moda.

Tiempo para ir a la escuela

Estudiante	Krista	Mike	Lupe	Kareem
Tiempo (minutos)	10	15	20	10

attribute An attribute is a characteristic or feature that is being investigated.

atributo Un atributo es una característica o cualidad que está siendo investigada.

B

box-and-whisker plot, or box plot A display that shows the distribution of values in a data set separated into four equal-size groups. A box plot is constructed from a five-number summary of the data.

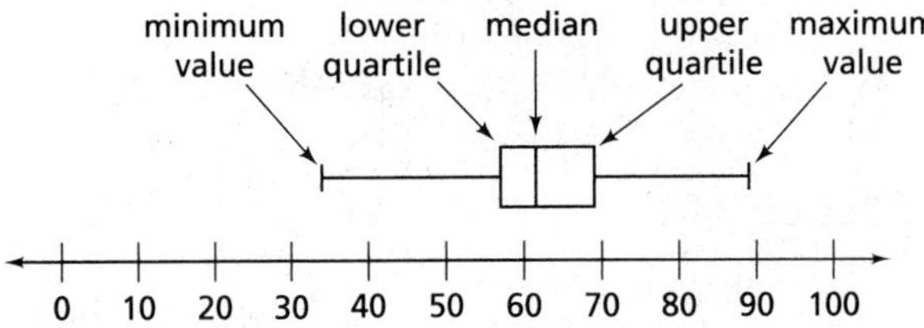

gráfica de caja y bigotes o diagrama de caja Una representación que muestra la distribución de los valores de un conjunto de datos separados en cuatro grupos de igual tamaño. Un diagrama de caja se construye con un resumen de cinco números de los datos.

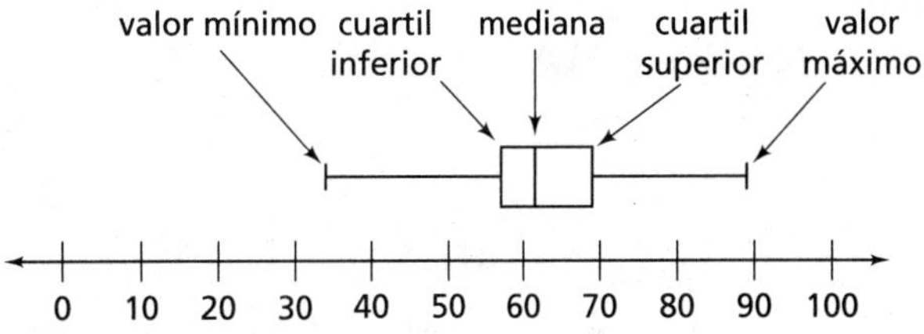

C

categorical data Non-numerical data sets are categorical. For example, the responses to "What month were you born?" are categorical data. Frequency counts can be made of the values for a given category. The table below shows examples of categories and their possible values.

Category	Possible Values
Month people are born	January, February, March
Favorite color to wear	magenta, blue, yellow
Kinds of pets people have	cats, dogs, fish, horses

datos categóricos Los conjuntos de datos no numéricos son categóricos. Por ejemplo, las respuestas a "¿En qué mes naciste? " son datos categóricos. Los conteos de frecuencia se pueden hacer a partir de los valores de una categoría dada. La siguiente tabla muestra ejemplos de categorías y sus posibles valores.

Categoría	Valores posibles
Mes de nacimiento de las personas	enero, febrero, marzo
Color preferido para vestir	magenta, azul, amarillo
Tipos de mascotas que tienen las personas	gatos, perros, peces, caballos

cluster A group of numerical data values that are close to one another.

For example, consider the data set 2, 2, 2, 2, 3, 3, 7, 7, 8, 9, 10, 11. There is a *cluster* of data values at 2 (or from 2 to 3) and a *gap* between data values 3 and 7.

grupo Un grupo de valores de datos numéricos que están cercanos unos a otros

Por ejemplo, considera el conjunto de datos 2, 2, 2, 2, 3, 3, 7, 7, 8, 9, 10, 11. Hay un *grupo* de valores de datos en 2 (o de 2 a 3) y una *brecha* entre los valores de datos 3 y 7.

D

data Values such as counts, ratings, measurements, or opinions that are gathered to answer questions. The table below shows data for mean temperatures in three cities.

Daily Mean Temperatures

City	Mean Temperature (°F)
Mobile, AL	67.5
Boston, MA	51.3
Spokane, WA	47.3

datos Valores como los conteos, las calificaciones, las mediciones o las opiniones que se recopilan para responder a las preguntas. Los datos de la siguiente tabla muestran las temperaturas medias en tres ciudades.

Temperaturas medias diarias

Ciudad	Temperatura media (°F)
Mobile, AL	67.5
Boston, MA	51.3
Spokane, WA	47.3

distribution The entire set of collected data values, organized to show their frequency of occurrence. A distribution can be described using summary statistics and/or by referring to its shape.

distribución Todo el conjunto de valores de datos recopilados, organizados para mostrar su frecuencia de incidencia. Una distribución se puede describir usando la estadística sumaria y/o haciendo referencia a su forma.

E

explain Academic Vocabulary
To give facts and details that make an idea easier to understand. Explaining can involve a written summary supported by a diagram, chart, table, or a combination of these.

related terms *analyze, clarify, describe, justify, tell*

sample Explain how to determine the mean and the mode of the data set 10, 15, 20, 10.

The mean is $\frac{10+15+20+10}{4} = 13.75$.

The mode of this data is 10 because 10 is the value that occurs most often.

explicar Vocabulario académico
Proporcionar datos y detalles que hagan que una idea sea más fácil de comprender. Explicar puede incluir un resumen escrito apoyado por un diagrama, una gráfica, una tabla o una combinación de estos.

términos relacionados *analizar, aclarar, describir, justificar, decir*

ejemplo Explica cómo determinar la media y la moda del conjunto de datos 10, 15, 20, 10.

La media es $\frac{10+15+20+10}{4} = 13.75$.

La moda de estos datos es 10 porque 10 es el valor que ocurre con mayor frecuencia.

F

frequency table A table that lists all data values, and uses tally marks or some other device to show the number of times each data value occurs.

tabla de frecuencias Una tabla que enumera todos los valores de datos y usa marcas de conteo o algún otro recurso para mostrar el número de veces que se produce cada valor de datos.

Lengths of Chinese Names
(From Name Lengths Table 1)

Number of Letters	Tally	Frequency
1		0
2		0
3		0
4		■
5	||	■
6	|||	■
7		■
8	||	■
9		■

English/Spanish Glossary

G

gap A value or several consecutive values, between the minimum and maximum observed data values, where no data value occurred.

For example, consider the data set 2, 2, 2, 2, 3, 3, 7, 7, 8, 9, 10, 11. There is a *cluster* of data values at 2 (or from 2 to 3) and a *gap* between data values 3 and 7.

brecha Un valor o varios valores consecutivos, entre los valores de datos mínimo y máximo observados, donde no se produjo ningún valor de datos.

Por ejemplo, considera el conjunto de datos 2, 2, 2, 2, 3, 3, 7, 7, 8, 9, 10, 11. Hay un *grupo* de valores de datos en 2 (o de 2 a 3) y una *brecha* entre los valores de datos 3 y 7.

H

histogram A display that shows the distribution of numeric data. The range of data values, divided into intervals, is displayed on the horizontal axis. The vertical axis shows frequency in numbers or in percents. The height of the bar over each interval indicates the count or percent of data values in that interval.

The histogram below shows quality ratings for certain brands of peanut butter. The height of the bar over the interval from 20 to 30 is 4. This indicates that four brands of peanut butter have quality ratings greater than or equal to 20 and less than 30.

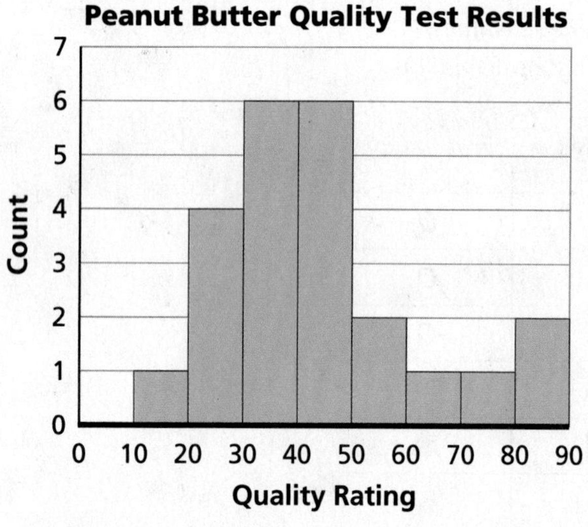

histograma Una representación que muestra la distribución de datos numéricos. El rango de valores de datos, dividido en intervalos, se representa en el eje horizontal. El eje vertical muestra la frecuencia en números o en porcentajes. La altura de la barra sobre cada intervalo indica el conteo o porcentaje de valores de datos en ese intervalo.

El siguiente histograma representa la calificación de la calidad de ciertas marcas de mantequilla de maní. La altura de la barra sobre el intervalo de 20 a 30 es 4. Esto indica que cuatro marcas de mantequilla de maní tienen una calificación mayor que o igual a 20 y menor que 30.

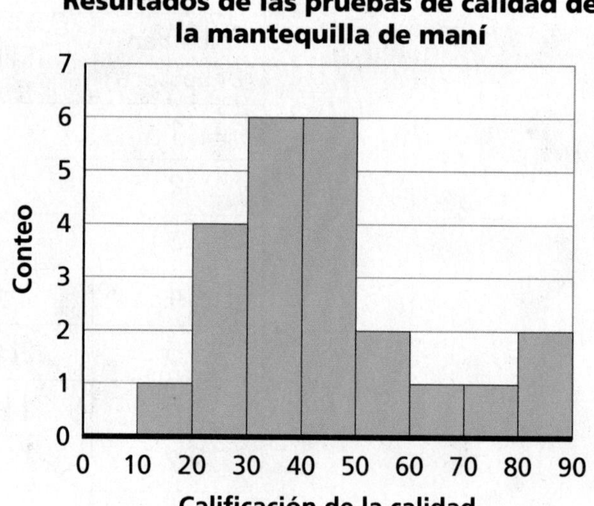

I

interquartile range (IQR) The difference of the values of the upper quartile (Q3) and the lower quartile (Q1).

rango entre cuartiles (REC) La diferencia de los valores del cuartil superior (C3) y el cuartil inferior (C1).

In the box-and-whisker plot below, the upper quartile is 69, and the lower quartile is 58. The IQR is the difference 69–58, or 11.

En el siguiente diagrama de caja y bigotes, el cuartil superior es 69 y el cuartil inferior es 58. El REC es la diferencia de 69 a 58, u 11.

IQR = 69 − 58 = 11

REC = 69 − 58 = 11

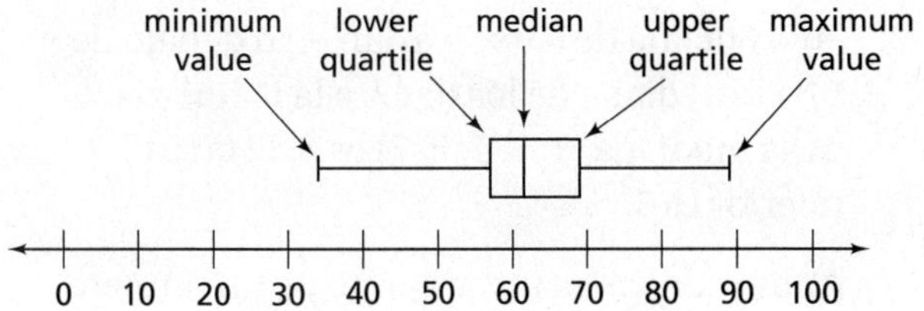

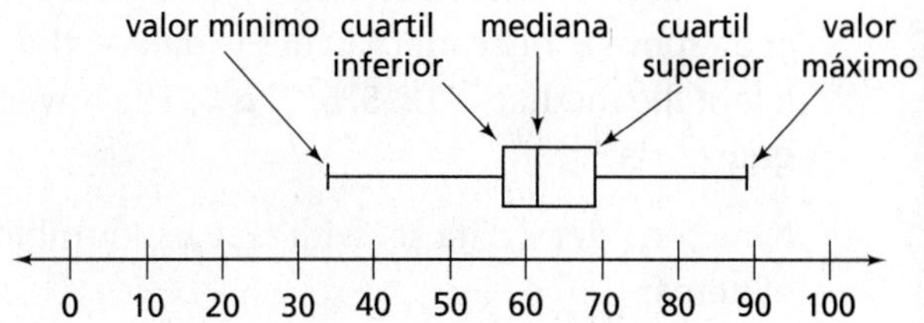

interval A continuous group of numbers. For example, a survey might collect data about people's ages. The responses could be grouped into intervals, such as 5–9, 9–12, and 12–16.

intervalo Un grupo continuo de números. Por ejemplo, una encuesta puede recopilar datos sobre las edades de las personas. Las respuestas se pueden agrupar en intervalos, como 5 a 9, 9 a 12 y 12 a 16.

The interval 5–9 would include all ages 5 and older but not quite 9. If your ninth birthday were tomorrow, your data would fall into the interval 5–9.

El intervalo de 5 a 9 incluiría todas las edades de 5 y mayores de cinco, pero no exactamente 9. Si tu noveno cumpleaños fuera mañana, tus datos se encontrarían en el intervalo de 5 a 9.

L

line plot A way to organize data along a number line where the ✗s (or other symbols) above a number represent how often each value is mentioned. A line plot made with dots is sometimes referred to as a dot plot.

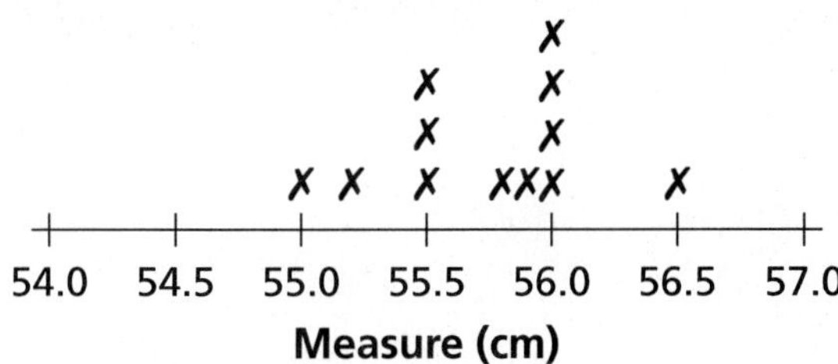

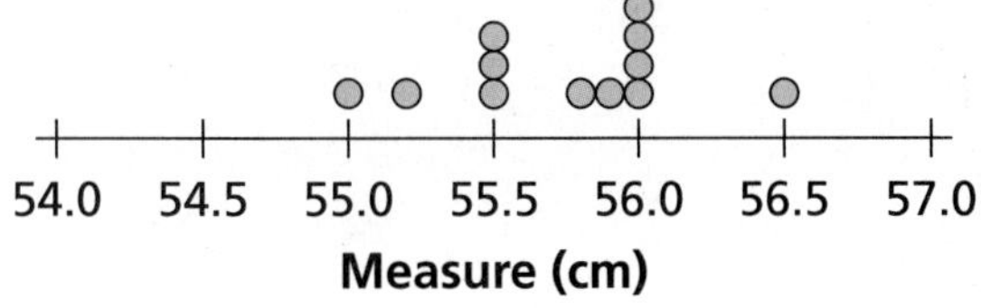

diagrama de puntos Una manera de organizar los datos a lo largo de una recta numérica donde las ✗ (u otros símbolos) colocadas encima de un número representan la frecuencia con que se menciona cada valor. Un diagrama de puntos hecho con puntos algunas veces se conoce como gráfica de puntos.

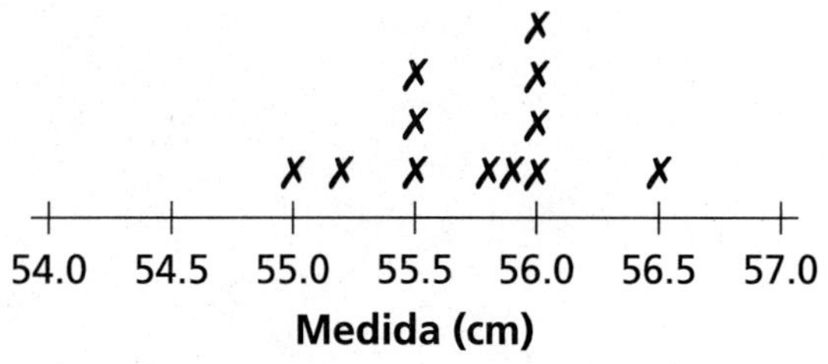

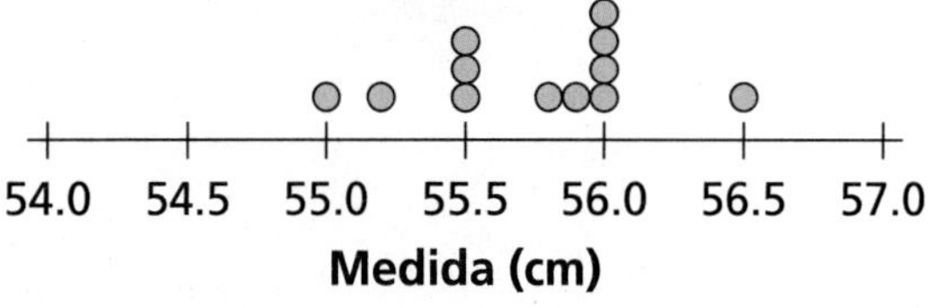

lower quartile The median of the data to the left of the median (assuming the data are listed from least value to greatest value).

For example, consider a data set with an odd number of items:

1, 2, 5, 6, 7, 8, 8, 10, 12, 15, 20

There are 11 items. The median of the data set is 8. (Six values are at or below 8 and six are at or above 8.) The median of the data to the left of the median (1, 2, 5, 6, 7) is 5. The lower quartile is 5.

Now consider a data set with an even number of items:

2, 3, 4, 5, 6, 6, 8, 8

There are eight items. The median of the data set is 5.5, the average of 5 and 6. The data items to the left of the median are 2, 3, 4, and 5. The median of these values is 3.5. The lower quartile is 3.5.

cuartil inferior La mediana de los datos a la izquierda de la mediana (asumiendo que los datos indicados van de menor a mayor).

Por ejemplo, considera un conjunto de un número impar de datos:

1, 2, 5, 6, 7, 8, 8, 10, 12, 15, 20

Hay 11 valores de datos. La mediana del conjunto de datos es 8. (Seis valores están en o encima de 8 y seis están en o debajo de 8). La mediana de los datos a la izquierda de la mediana (1, 2, 5, 6, 7) es 5. El cuartil inferior es 5.

Ahora considera un conjunto de un número par de datos:

2, 3, 4, 5, 6, 6, 8, 8

Hay ocho valores de datos. La mediana del conjunto de datos es 5.5, el promedio de 5 y 6. Los valores de datos a la izquierda de la mediana son 2, 3, 4 y 5. La mediana de estos valores es 3.5. El cuartil inferior es 3.5.

M

maximum value The data item with the greatest value in a data set. In the data set 2, 2, 2, 2, 3, 3, 7, 7, 8, 9, 10, 11, the maximum value is 11.

valor máximo El dato con el mayor valor en un conjunto de datos. En el conjunto de datos 2, 2, 2, 2, 3, 3, 7, 7, 8, 9, 10, 11, el valor máximo es 11.

mean The value found when all the data are combined and then redistributed evenly. For example, the total number of siblings for the data in the line plot below is 56. If all 19 students had the same number of siblings, they would each have about 3 siblings. Differences from the mean "balance out" so that the sum of differences below and above the mean equal 0. The mean of a set of data is the sum of the values divided by the number of values in the set.

Number of Siblings Students Have

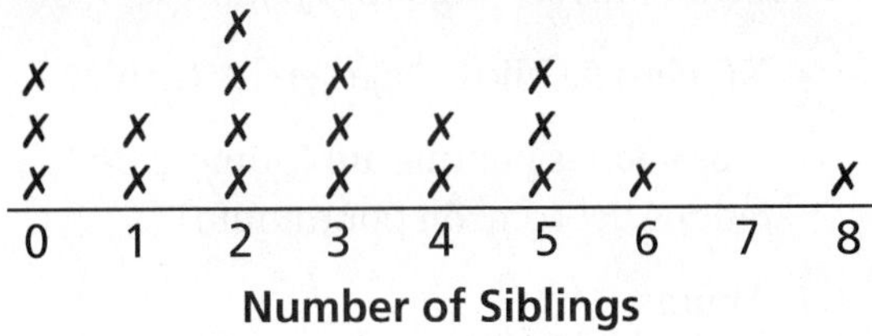

media El valor que se halla cuando todos los datos se combinan y luego se redistribuyen de manera uniforme. Por ejemplo, el número total de hermanos y hermanas en los datos del siguiente diagrama es 56. Si los 19 estudiantes tuvieran la misma cantidad de hermanos y hermanas, cada uno tendría aproximadamente 3 hermanos o hermanas. Las diferencias de la media se "equilibran" de manera que la suma de las diferencias por encima y por debajo de la media sea igual a 0. La media de un conjunto de datos es la suma de los valores dividida por el número de valores en el conjunto.

Número de hermanos y hermanas que tienen los estudiantes

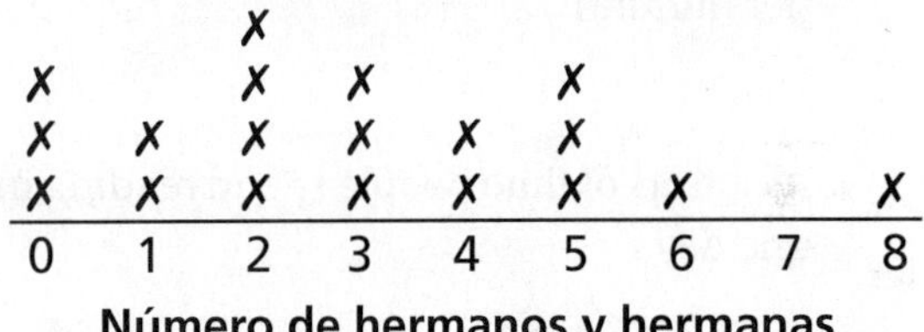

mean absolute deviation (MAD) The average distance of all of the data values in a data set from the mean of the distribution.

desviación absoluta media (DAM) La distancia media de todos los valores de datos en un conjunto de datos a partir de la media de la distribución.

median The number that marks the midpoint of an ordered set of data. At least half of the values lie at or above the median, and at least half lie at or below the median. For the sibling data (0, 0, 0, 1, 1, 2, 2, 2, 2, 3, 3, 3, 4, 4, 5, 5, 5, 6, 8), the median of the distribution of siblings is 3 because the tenth (middle) value in the ordered set of 19 values is 3.

When a distribution contains an even number of data values, the median is computed by finding the average of the two middle data values in an ordered list of the data values. For example, the median of 1, 3, 7, 8, 25, and 30 is 7.5 because the data values 7 and 8 are third and fourth in the list of six data values.

mediana El número que marca el punto medio de un conjunto ordenado de datos. Por lo menos la mitad de los datos se encuentran en o encima de la mediana y por lo menos la mitad se encuentran en o debajo de la mediana. Para los datos de los hermanos y hermanas (0, 0, 0, 1, 1, 2, 2, 2, 2, 3, 3, 3, 4, 4, 5, 5, 5, 6, 8), la mediana de la distribución de hermanos y hermanas es 3 porque el décimo valor (el del medio) en el conjunto ordenado de 19 valores es 3.

Cuando una distribución contiene un número par de valores de datos, la mediana se calcula hallando el promedio de los dos valores de datos del medio en una lista ordenada de los valores de datos. Por ejemplo, la mediana de 1, 3, 7, 8, 25 y 30 es 7.5, porque los valores de datos 7 y 8 son tercero y cuarto en la lista de seis valores de datos.

minimum value The data item with the least value in a data set. In the data set 2, 2, 2, 2, 3, 3, 7, 7, 8, 9, 10, 11, the minimum value is 2.

valor mínimo El dato con el menor valor en un conjunto de datos. En el conjunto de datos 2, 2, 2, 2, 3, 3, 7, 7, 8, 9, 10, 11, el valor mínimo es 2.

mode The value that appears most frequently in a set of data. In the data set 2, 2, 2, 2, 3, 3, 7, 7, 8, 9, 10, 11, the mode is 2.

moda El valor que aparece con mayor frecuencia en un conjunto de datos. En el conjunto de datos 2, 2, 2, 2, 3, 3, 7, 7, 8, 9, 10, 11, la moda es 2.

N

numerical data Values that are numbers such as counts, measurements, and ratings. Here are some examples.

- Number of children in families
- Pulse rates (number of heart beats per minute)
- Heights
- Amounts of time people spend reading in one day
- Ratings such as: on a scale of 1 to 5 with 1 as "low interest," how would you rate your interest in participating in the school's field day?

datos numéricos Valores que son números como conteos, mediciones y calificaciones. Los siguientes son algunos ejemplos.

- Número de hijos e hijas en las familias
- Pulsaciones por minuto (número de latidos del corazón por minuto)
- Alturas
- Cantidades de tiempo que las personas pasan leyendo en un día
- Calificaciones como: en una escala de1 a 5, en la que 1 representa "poco interés", ¿cómo calificarías tu interés por participar en el día de maniobras de tu escuela?

O

ordered-value bar graph A bar graph in which the bars are arranged by increasing (or decreasing) order of length.

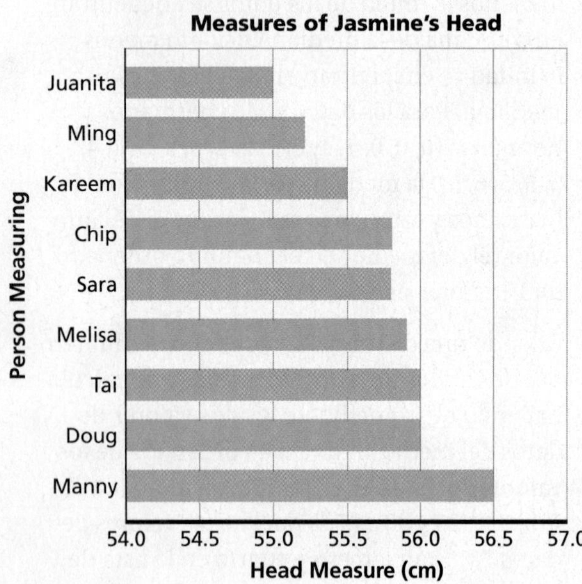

gráfica de barras de valores ordenados Una gráfica de barras en la que las barras están ordenadas en orden de longitud creciente (o decreciente).

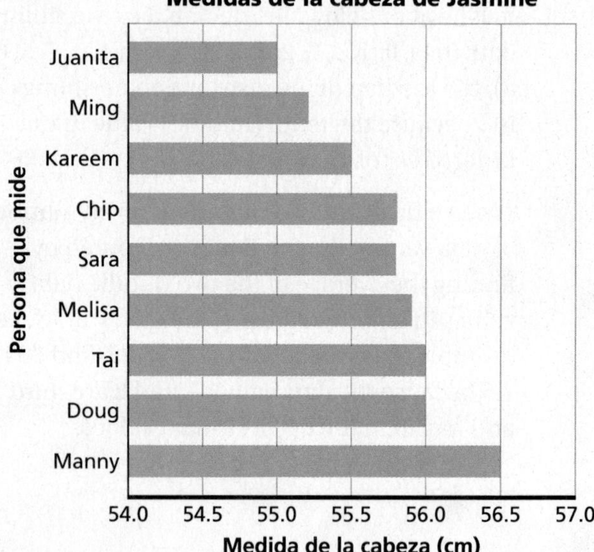

outlier A value that lies far from the "center" of a distribution and is not like other values. *Outlier* is a relative term, but it indicates a data point that is much higher or much lower than the values that could be normally expected for the distribution.

To identify an outlier in a distribution represented by a boxplot, measure the distance between Q3 and any suspected outliers at the top of the range of data values; if this distance is more than 1.5 × IQR, then the data value is an outlier. Likewise, if the distance between any data value at the low end of the range of values and Q1 is more than 1.5 × IQR, then the data value is an outlier.

valor extremo Un valor que se encuentra lejos del "centro" de una distribución y no es como los demás valores. El *valor extremo* es un término relativo, pero indica un dato que es mucho más alto o mucho más bajo que los valores que se podrían esperar normalmente para la distribución.

Para identificar un valor extremo en una distribución representada por un diagrama de caja, se mide la distancia entre C3 y cualquier valor que se sospeche es extremo en la parte superior del rango de los valores de datos; si esta distancia es mayor que 1.5 × REC, entonces el valor de datos es un valor extremo. Del mismo modo, si la distancia entre cualquier valor de datos en la parte inferior del rango de valores y C1 es mayor que 1.5 × REC, entonces el valor de datos es un valor extremo.

P

predict Academic Vocabulary
To make an educated guess based on the analysis of real data.

related terms *estimate, survey, analyze, observe*

sample Dan knows that the mean life span of his type of tropical fish is 2 years. What other information could help Dan predict how long his fish will live?

If Dan also knew the median life span he would have more information to predict how long his fish will live. The mean could be skewed because of one or more outliers.

predecir Vocabulario académico
Hacer una suposición basada en el análisis de datos reales.

términos relacionados *estimar, encuestar, analizar, observar*

ejemplo Dan sabe que la media de vida de su tipo de pez tropical es de 2 años. ¿Qué otra información podría ayudar a Dan a predecir cuánto vivirá su pez?

Si Dan también supiera la mediana de vida, tendría más información para predecir cuánto vivirá su pez. La media podría estar sesgada debido a uno o más valores extremos.

Q

quartile One of three points that divide a data set into four equal groups. The second quartile, Q2, is the median of the data set. The first quartile, Q1, is the median of the lower half of the data set. The third quartile, Q3, is the median of the upper half of the data set.

cuartil Uno de los tres puntos que dividen un conjunto de datos en cuatro grupos iguales. El segundo cuartil, C2, es la mediana del conjunto de datos. El primer cuartil, C1, es la mediana de la mitad inferior del conjunto de datos. El tercer cuartil, C3, es la mediana de la mitad superior del conjunto de datos.

R

range The difference of the maximum value and the minimum value in a distribution. If you know the range of the data is 12 grams of sugar per serving, you know that the difference between the minimum and maximum values is 12 grams. For example, in the distribution 2, 2, 2, 2, 3, 3, 7, 7, 8, 9, 10, 11, the range of the data set is 9, because $11 - 2 = 9$.

rango La diferencia del valor máximo y el valor mínimo en una distribución. Si se sabe que el rango de los datos es 12 gramos de azúcar por porción, entonces se sabe que la diferencia entre el valor mínimo y el máximo es 12 gramos. Por ejemplo, en la distribución 2, 2, 2, 2, 3, 3, 7, 7, 8, 9, 10, 11, el rango del conjunto de datos es 9, porque $11 - 2 = 9$.

---

represent Academic Vocabulary
To stand for or take the place of something else. Symbols, equations, charts, and tables are often used to represent particular situations.

related terms *symbolize, stand for*

sample Jerry surveyed his classmates about the number of pets they have. He recorded his data in a table. Represent the results of Jerry's survey in a bar graph.

How Many Pets?

Number of Pets	Number of Students
0 pets	10
1 pet	11
2 or more pets	8

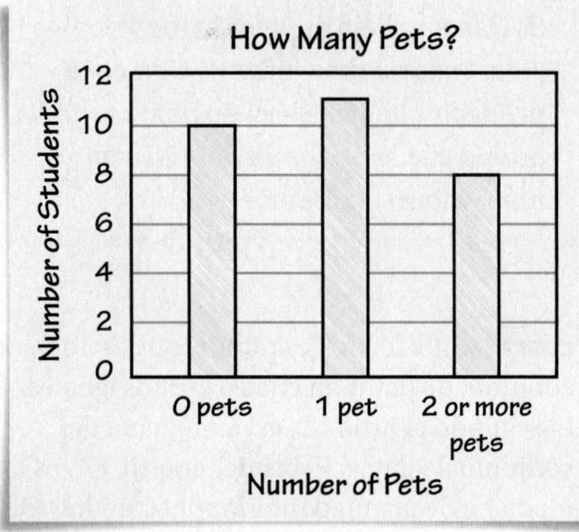

representar Vocabulario académico
Significar o tomar el lugar de algo más. Los símbolos, las ecuaciones, las gráficas y las tablas a menudo se usan para representar situaciones particulares.

términos relacionados *simbolizar, significar*

ejemplo Jerry hizo una encuesta entre sus compañeros de clase sobre el número de mascotas que tienen. Anotó sus datos en una tabla. Representa los resultados de la encuesta de Jerry en una gráfica de barras.

¿Cuántas mascotas?

Número de mascotas	Número de estudiantes
0 mascotas	10
1 mascota	11
2 o más mascotas	8

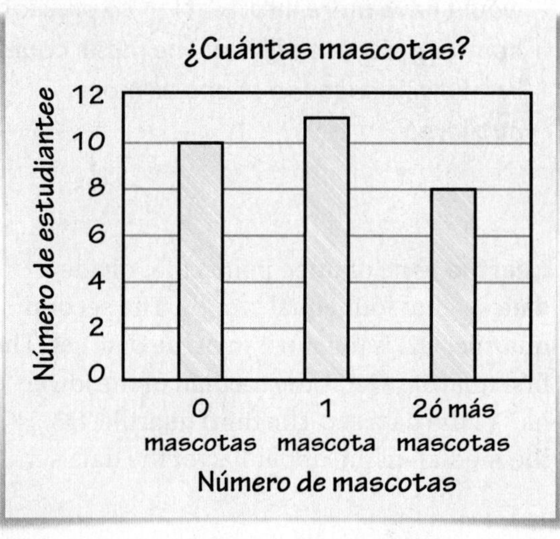

S

scale The size of the units on an axis of a graph or number line. For instance, each mark on the vertical axis might represent 10 units.

escala El tamaño de las unidades en un eje de una gráfica o recta numérica. Por ejemplo, cada marca en el eje vertical puede representar 10 unidades.

shape of a distribution The shape of a distribution can be described by identifying clusters and gaps, and by noting whether the distribution is symmetric or skewed.

forma de una distribución La forma de una distribución se puede describir al identificar grupos y brechas, y al observar si la distribución es simétrica o asimétrica.

skewed distribution Any distribution that is not symmetrical about the mean.

distribución asimétrica Cualquier distribución que no es simétrica alrededor de la media.

summary statistic A single number that conveys basic, but important, information about a distribution. Examples of summary statistics include the mean, median, mode, range, MAD, and IQR.

estadística sumaria Un solo número que transmite información básica, pero importante, sobre una distribución. Los ejemplos de la estadística sumaria incluyen la media, la mediana, la moda, el rango, la DAM y el REC.

symmetric distribution A distribution in which the mean and median are the same or almost the same, and in which the values above and below the mean form an approximate mirror image.

distribución simétrica Una distribución en la que la media y la mediana son iguales o casi iguales y en la que los valores por encima y por debajo de la media forman una imagen reflejada aproximada.

T

table A tool for organizing information in rows and columns. Tables let you list categories or values and then tally the occurrences.

Favorite Colors

Color	Number of Students
Red	6
White	15
Blue	9

tabla Una herramienta para organizar información en filas y columnas. Las tablas permiten que se hagan listas de categorías o de valores y luego se cuenten las incidencias.

Colores favoritos

Color	Número de estudiantes
Rojo	6
Blanco	15
Azul	9

U

upper quartile The median of the data to the right of the median (assuming the data are listed from least value to greatest value).

For example, consider a data set with an odd number of items:

1, 2, 5, 6, 7, 8, 8, 10, 12, 15, 20

There are 11 items. The median of the data set is 8. (Six values are at or below 8 and six are at or above 8.) The median of the data to the right of the median (8, 10, 12, 15, and 20) is 12. The upper quartile is 12.

Now consider a data set with an even number of items:

2, 3, 4, 5, 6, 6, 8, 8

There are eight items. The median of the data set is 5.5, the average of 5 and 6. The data items to the right of the median are 6, 6, 8, and 8. The median of these values is 7, the average of 6 and 8. The upper quartile is 7.

cuartil superior La mediana de los datos a la derecha de la mediana (asumiendo que los datos indicados van de menor a mayor).

Por ejemplo, considera un conjunto de un número impar de datos:

1, 2, 5, 6, 7, 8, 8, 10, 12, 15, 20

Hay 11 valores de datos. La mediana del conjunto de datos es 8. (Seis valores están en o encima de 8 y seis están en o debajo de 8). La mediana de los datos a la derecha de la mediana (8, 10, 12, 15 y 20) es 12. El cuartil superior es 12.

Ahora considera un conjunto de un número par de datos:

2, 3, 4, 5, 6, 6, 8, 8

Hay ocho valores de datos. La mediana del conjunto de datos es 5.5, el promedio de 5 y 6. Los valores de datos a la derecha de la mediana son 6, 6, 8 y 8. La mediana de estos valores es 7, el promedio de 6 y 8. El cuartil superior es 7.

V

variability An indication of how widely spread or closely clustered the data values are. Range, minimum and maximum values, and clusters in the distribution give some indication of variability. The variability of a distribution can also be measured by its IQR or MAD.

variabilidad Indicación de cuán dispersos o agrupados están los valores de datos. El rango, los valores mínimo y máximo, y los grupos en la distribución dan cierta indicación de variabilidad. La variabilidad de una distribución también se puede medir por su REC o por su DAM.

Index

Acknowledgments

Cover Design

Three Communication Design, Chicago

Text

113 American Pet Products Association
Data from "*2011–2012 National Pet Owners Survey*" from the American Pet Products Association (APPA).

Photographs

Photo locators denoted as follows: Top (T), Center (C), Bottom (B), Left (L), Right (R), Background (Bkgd)

002 Solent News/Splash News/Newscom; **003** WaterFrame/Alamy; **013** (CL) Plusphoto/AmanaimagesRF/Getty Images, (CR) iStockPhoto/Thinkstock, (BC) Jeayesy/Fotolia, **022** Lculig/Shutterstock; **047** Solent News/Splash News/Newscom.